Crime and Justice in the Netherlands

Crime and Justice in the Netherlands

Edited by Michael Tonry and Catrien Bijleveld

Crime and Justice
A Review of Research
Edited by Michael Tonry

VOLUME 35

The University of Chicago Press, Chicago and London

The University of Chicago Press, Chicago 60637
The University of Chicago Press, Ltd., London

© 2007 by The University of Chicago
All rights reserved. Published 2007
Printed in the United States of America

ISSN: 0192-3234

ISBN: 978-0-226-80873-4 (cloth)
ISBN: 978-0-226-80874-1 (paper)

LCN: 80-642217

Library of Congress Cataloging-in-Publication Data

Crime and justice in the Netherlands / edited by Michael Tonry and Catrien Bijleveld.
    p. cm.—(Crime and justice ; v. 35)
    Includes bibliographical references and index.
    ISBN 0-226-80873-4 (hardcover : alk. paper)—ISBN 0-226-80874-2 (pbk. : alk. paper)
    1. Crime—Netherlands. 2. Criminal justice, Administration of—Netherlands.
I. Tonry, Michael H. II. Bijleveld, Catrien C. J. H.
HV7008.5.C73 2007
364.9492—dc22   2006032114

The paper used in this publication meets the minimum requirements of American National Standard for Information Sciences—Permanence of Paper for Printed Library Materials, ANSI Z39.48-1984. ∞

Contents

Preface

This is the thirty-fifth volume of *Crime and Justice*, the fourteenth thematic volume, and the first in a subset of thematic volumes on criminal justice research and policy in individual countries and regions. The aim is to look and learn across national boundaries, to see what appears distinctive to outsiders and what familiar. This volume looks at the Netherlands and the next one at Scandinavia. What comes after that will have to be seen.

This volume, and the subseries of which it is the initiator, could not have been developed ten or twenty years ago. One reason is that criminology and criminal justice are young specialties in which research and teaching have only recently burgeoned. A second is that the world is becoming a smaller place, with what are increasingly recognized to be common problems, and with common interests in learning about causes and consequences and solutions. A third is that, for good and ill, English has become the international language of scholarship; ambitious scholars outside the English-speaking countries feel obliged to speak and often to write in English. A final reason is that the first three considerations make the very idea of distinctive national social science literatures obsolete and parochial. Serious scholars and scholarship can no longer credibly ignore what happens elsewhere. This has long been true of the physical and biological sciences and to a lesser extent of the humanities; the social sciences are at the end of the queue but are catching up.

We have developed this volume in its own right and as a pilot, to test the idea of an ongoing series of English-language volumes of refereed, state-of-the-art review essays on research subjects relating to crime and criminal justice systems in particular places. A glimmer of a possibility in the backs of our minds is the establishment of an ongoing publication series like *Crime and Justice* but whose primary focus is European, as that of the original *Crime and Justice*, despite its internationalist aspirations, inevitably has been North American.

Publication of a short series of volumes on countries and regions is a first step. It affords opportunity to test in Europe traditions and processes that we know work in North America. It enables us to convene people who know one another and one another's work in planning meetings and conferences to discuss drafts. It enables us to limit the scope of essays to work published in or about one place, although often in more than one language. And it enables us to publish volumes that provide relatively comprehensive overviews of current knowledge and policy in particular places that, for language reasons, are not readily available to outsiders.

A *Crime and Justice in Europe* series will need to be more ambitious. Planners and conference participants will be from many countries, and writers will have to cover a subject on the basis of research across Europe. The initial, more narrowly focused volumes, however, will provide a foundation on which to build. Scholars from a number of countries will become familiar with *Crime and Justice* processes and expectations, and essays published in the country and region volumes will provide prototypes of what is needed.

This volume was developed like every other *Crime and Justice* thematic volume. A one-day planning meeting at Oud Poelgeest castle, Oegstgeest, the Netherlands, was convened to identify possible topics and lists of qualified writers. Papers were commissioned and outlines of their contents were negotiated. A second conference attended by the writers, and a dozen other scholars and researchers from the Netherlands and elsewhere, was convened to discuss the first drafts and issues they raised. On the basis of those discussions and written reports from paid referees, decisions were made to solicit revised drafts from most of the writers. In due course those revised drafts were received, edited, source- and cite-checked, and published. This volume is the result.

This volume follows the model set out in the preface to the first volume of *Crime and Justice*: "Essays will be of several types. The staple will be a summary by a leading scholar of the state of the art on a defined topic, together with his views on the policy and research implications of that knowledge. Others will be more speculative and idiosyncratic, and will report on analytical, conceptual or empirical developments, or consider promising but novel lines of inquiry" (p. viii).

One of our aims was to commission state-of-the-art reviews of subjects in which the research traditions and literatures are especially strong in the Netherlands. The essays by Gottfried Engbersen, Joanne van der Leun, and Jan de Boom (immigration and crime), Gerben Bruinsma (urban crime), Edward Kleemans (organized crime), Henk van de Bunt and Wim Huisman (organizational crime), Catrien Bijleveld (sex offenses and offenders), and Frank Weerman (juvenile crime) are of this type. We also sought to commission essays that are more conceptual and idiosyncratic. Essays by Ybo Buruma (Dutch tolerance), David Downes and René van Swaaningen (Dutch penal policy), and Josine Junger-Tas and Marianne Junger (Dutch criminology) are of this type. The final essay by Rolf Loeber and Wim Slot provides a comprehensive, multidisciplinary look at the causes, prevalence, prevention, and treatment of serious and violent youth crime in the Netherlands.

A volume like this inevitably reflects the efforts of many people. The authors (at least seemingly) cheerfully endured a lengthy process of initial drafts, readers' reports, editorial comment letters, more drafts, and source and cite checks, and all this before the essays were delivered to Chicago for thoroughly professional style and copyediting. The initial planning meeting was attended by Bert Berghuis, Gerben Bruinsma, Henk van de Bunt, Ybo Buruma, Josine Junger-Tas, Rolf Loeber, Jan Nijboer, Sonja Snacken, and René van Swaaningen. A second, larger meeting to discuss initial drafts was attended by the authors and Bert Berghuis, Annelies Daalder, Anthony Doob, Arie van der Hurk, Jan de Keijser, Max Kommer, Peter van Koppen, Erwin Muller, Jan Nijboer, David J. Smith, and Franklin E. Zimring. Referees provided written, usually detailed comments and suggestions. Su Smallen and Adepeju Solarin handled sources, citations, and artwork; prepared manuscripts for delivery to the publisher; and coordinated the circulation of edited copy and proofs. Ariena van Poppel organized and managed the two conferences and all the related logistics and kept the two of us on track. Victor van der Geest helped out with graphics. We are enormously grateful to them all.

Finally, last but certainly not least, we are grateful to the several sponsors who provided the financial support that made the venture doable: Frans Leeuw, director of the Research and Documentation

Centre of the Netherlands Ministry of Justice; Gerben Bruinsma, director of the Netherlands Institute for the Study of Crime and Law Enforcement; Alex Johnson, dean of the University of Minnesota Law School; and Alec Broers, vice-chancellor of the University of Cambridge.

Michael Tonry
Catrien Bijleveld
Leiden, February 2007

Michael Tonry and Catrien Bijleveld

Crime, Criminal Justice, and Criminology in the Netherlands

The Netherlands is particularly appropriate as the subject of the first *Crime and Justice* volume to focus on a single European country or region. Its criminal justice policies have long been well known, its social policies and problems receive widespread international attention, and it has among the longest and strongest research traditions in criminology in Europe.

For nearly fifty years after World War II, the Netherlands was commonly portrayed as having the most liberal and humane criminal justice system among Western countries (e.g., Downes 1988). In the early twenty-first century it is sometimes viewed as having one of Europe's most severe criminal justice systems, perhaps following that of England and Wales (Downes 2007). By the end of 2006, many judges and lawyers were complaining that the criminal law system had become overheated, with criminalization of behavior increasing and procedural rights of defendants decreasing (Ippel and Heeger 2006).

During most of the postwar period, the Netherlands exemplified (at least to outsiders) generous social welfare policies, sensible criminal justice policies, and tolerant social attitudes. Drug policies were generally seen as pragmatic and lenient, as were abortion laws.

Social policies relating to ethnic minority groups seemed to be working. Immigrants from Indonesia after its independence were assimilated

Errors of analysis or fact in this introduction are alas our own, but we are grateful to the following people who kindly read an earlier draft and helped us avoid some errors and tried to save us from others: Gerben Bruinsma, Ybo Buruma, Henk van de Bunt, David Downes, Edward Kleemans, Godfried Engbersen, René van Swaaningen, and Frank Weerman.

1

almost without notice. Subsequent waves of immigrants came from former Dutch colonies in South America and the Caribbean, and especially from Turkey and Morocco, as guest workers and their families. Most recently, sizable numbers of asylum seekers and their families came to live in the Netherlands. For the most part, Dutch policies supported maintenance of immigrants' cultural traditions and did not pressure them to assimilate.

By the end of the twentieth century, and early in the twenty-first, changes were becoming evident. Welfare provision had become less generous, criminal justice policies hardened, and policies concerning immigrants and refugees became stricter. Right-wing political parties and anti-immigrant politicians exemplified widespread feelings that Dutch multiculturalism had failed (Buruma, in this volume; Engbersen, van der Leun, and de Boom, in this volume).

The Netherlands has long been internationally prominent in criminology and criminal justice research. The Ministry of Justice Research and Documentation Centre (the WODC, its acronym in Dutch) is among the best-known government research agencies in Europe and among the most internationalist. The International Crime Victims Survey (e.g., van Kesteren, Mayhew, and Nieuwbeerta 2001), the International Self-Report Delinquency Study (e.g., Junger-Tas, Haen Marshall, and Ribeaud 2003), and the *European Sourcebook of Crime and Criminal Justice Statistics* (e.g., Aebi et al. 2006) have all at various times found their homes there. Widespread English fluency has meant that Dutch research is well known elsewhere. The Netherlands Institute for the Study of Crime and Law Enforcement (NSCR, another Dutch acronym), jointly supported by the National Organization for Scientific Research, the Ministry of Justice, and Leiden University, is one of Europe's few independent, stably funded research institutes specializing in mid- and long-term fundamental research on crime and the justice system. Dutch scholars were prominent in the creation in 2000 of the European Society of Criminology and in its subsequent development.

The essays in this volume discuss the development of Dutch criminal justice policies and research and provide comprehensive overviews of research areas in which Dutch research is especially strong and Dutch researchers are especially prolific. In this essay we provide a backdrop to what follows. Sections I–III provide thumbnail sketches of the country, its population, and its criminal justice system. The Netherlands is

densely populated, particularly in the West. Big-city populations, especially among the young, are increasingly non-Dutch. The economy
is strong, unemployment rates are low, and income inequality is relatively modest (but growing). As in most of western Europe, criminal
justice officials are neither elected nor politically selected, and most are
career civil servants.

Section IV sketches crime and punishment trends. Dutch crime
trends do not stand out in a European context. Dutch incarceration
trends do. Crime trends—broadly rising from the 1970s through the
1990s and stabilizing or falling since then (for property offenses, falling, for sure; the evidence is less clear concerning violence)—parallel
those of most western European countries (e.g., Bijleveld and Smit
2005; Aebi et al. 2006). However, they stand out concerning imprisonment: incarceration rates per 100,000 have increased continuously
since the early 1970s, when they were the lowest in Europe. The three-
decade rate of increase is by a wide margin the largest in Europe,
rivaling that of the United States during the same period (though from
a much lower starting point).

Section V, necessarily impressionistic and idiosyncratic, is our effort
to generalize about criminological and criminal justice research in the
Netherlands. Research on organized crime, organizational crime, juvenile delinquency, some kinds of violent offending, and ethnicity and
crime is especially rich. Research on criminal justice system operations—police, prosecutors, courts, probation, and prisons—and on
women and crime, costs of crime, and cost- and treatment-effectiveness
is comparatively meager. The strategic implications for research priorities and funding are straightforward.

I. The Netherlands[1]

The Netherlands, small and densely populated, has historically been
perceived as a tolerant and at times permissive country. The Dutch
have long been known for their practicality and their trading spirit.
They have for as long been and still are commonly characterized as
down-to-earth, frugal, and unostentatious. Wim Kok often bicycled to

---

[1] Unless otherwise indicated, demographic, economic, social, and other statistical data
used in this and the following section were obtained from the Netherlands' Central Bureau
of Statistics (http://www.cbs.nl).

work in The Hague and to visit the queen when he was prime minister, as did Piet Hein Donner when he was minister of justice.

Many a dissident writer printed his books in the Netherlands beginning in the late Middle Ages (e.g., Bayle, Erasmus, Luther, Spinoza). Waves of migrants and refugees fleeing persecution settled there, notably including Sephardic Jews in the sixteenth and seventeenth centuries, French Huguenots in the seventeenth and eighteenth centuries, and many former residents (mainly of mixed descent) from the former Dutch East Indies. The Puritans who settled Massachusetts Bay Colony, the first permanent English-speaking settlement in America, sheltered in Leiden for a decade to escape persecution in England before leaving for America.

Many liberal social policies remain. Dutch drug policy is famous for its pragmatism and permissiveness and for its irreconcilable elements (users may legally buy small amounts of soft drugs in designated shops, but there are no legal markets in which shop owners may buy their supplies) (Leuw 1991). Same-sex partners may marry and adopt children. Prostitution is legalized. So is euthanasia under certain circumstances. Private possession of firearms is prohibited.

The Netherlands is a constitutional monarchy and a parliamentary democracy. The queen, aside from symbolic constitutional functions, plays mainly a ceremonial role. The lower house (Tweede Kamer), which plays the central role, has 150 seats, and the upper (Eerste Kamer) has 75.

The Netherlands has long been ruled by coalition governments. Starting in 1994, a coalition of Christian-democratic, liberal-conservative, and liberal-democratic parties made up the governing coalition. Following an election in 2002 held shortly after the murder of the flamboyant populist and anti-immigrant politician Pim Fortuyn, the Dutch government moved distinctly to the right. A coalition of religious, conservative and liberal democratic parties took office, and policy on a number of high-visibility subjects—support for the U.S.-led war in Iraq, treatment of immigrants, criminal justice—shifted. The subsequent murder of filmmaker and provocateur Theo van Gogh, who made a practice of insulting unassimilated Muslims, produced still harsher attitudes toward immigrants and heightened doubts about the wisdom and effects of Holland's traditional multicultural approach toward assimilation.

Demographic characteristics resemble those of other affluent European countries. The population is aging fast. Life expectancy in 2001 was 75.8 for males and 80.7 for females. About one in three marriages ends in divorce. About one in four children is born out of wedlock, and one in six lives in a single-parent household. All children aged five to fifteen receive full-time education. About 22 percent of the population between fifteen and sixty-four is in or has received higher education; this figure has been increasing in recent years. The unemployment rate is low, as is inflation. Most households have one or more cars. There are more bicycles than people. Many people use them (or mopeds) for transportation since the country is flat, towns are congested, and distances are short.

The Netherlands is an advanced social welfare state: those without jobs are entitled to income and other support. Levels of financial support have recently decreased, and eligibility rules have tightened, but no legal resident in the Netherlands need go hungry or without a place to live. Families with children receive child benefits. Medical care for legal residents is provided under state-supervised insurance schemes, and health insurance subsidies are provided to people with incomes below designated levels.

The relaxed and tolerant atmosphere of earlier times has changed in recent years. Pim Fortuyn was murdered by an animal rights activist and Theo van Gogh by a jihadist of Moroccan origin. Antiterrorism laws have been enacted. Closed-circuit television is in operation in many places. The Somali-born liberal-conservative parliamentarian Ayaan Hirsi Ali and the extreme right-wing politician Geert Wilders have been threatened because of their radical views (Buruma 2006).

II. The People

The Netherlands is rapidly becoming a multiethnic, multicultural country. Only 9.2 percent of the population in 1972 were of non–ethnic Dutch origin; 1.2 percent were of non-Western origin. By 2006, people who were foreign-born or had at least one foreign-born parent made up 19.3 percent of the population; more than half, 10.5 percent, were of non-Western origin. Citizens of Dutch ethnic or other Western descent are generally wealthier, better educated, better employed, healthier, and less involved in violent and property crimes than non-Western minority residents (particularly younger ones).

There are big differences, however, between and within minority ethnic groups.

Large cities have concentrations of lower-income minorities and indigenous Dutch, but there are no residential areas equivalent to the urban ghettos of the United States or the *banlieus* of Paris. Dutch people generally dislike racial and ethnic categories and labels, perhaps because of the persecution of Dutch Jews by German occupiers during World War II: 70 percent of Jewish inhabitants were deported and killed, including 90 percent of those in Amsterdam. Perhaps for this reason, records of individuals' racial characteristics are not maintained. In official statistics, residents are identified as non–ethnic Dutch when at least one parent was born outside the Netherlands.

The composition of the Dutch population has never before changed as rapidly as in the past four decades. After the relatively easy integration of people from the former Dutch East Indies after Indonesia became independent in 1949, retroactively formalized as from 1945, labor migrants mainly from Turkey and Morocco made up the next big wave of immigrants. Their stays were initially envisioned as temporary, but most settled. Their families came later, and their descendants make up a growing part of the population.

Almost all Turkish and Moroccan migrants are Muslims. Turkish migrants came mainly from rural areas in central and eastern Turkey. Many are ethnic Kurds. The Moroccans mainly came from the poor rural area called the Rif. Most are Berbers, not ethnic Arabs, and speak Tamazight, a Berber language, as a first language and Arabic as a second.

Postindependence migrants from the former colony of Dutch Guyana (now Surinam) came to the Netherlands in large numbers around 1975, just before Surinam became independent. Its inhabitants were given the choice to remain in Surinam or to settle in the Netherlands. Most Surinamese speak Dutch. Their ethnic makeup is diverse and includes descendants of people brought as laborers to Surinam from the Indian subcontinent, Africa, Java, and China.

The Netherlands Antilles remain part of the kingdom of the Netherlands. Travel is not unrestricted, but many (mostly young male) Antilleans have settled in the Netherlands, more or less permanently. They often do not speak Dutch, but Papiamento.

More recent migrant groups, mostly asylum seekers (prominently from Iraq, China, Iran, Afghanistan, and Somalia), have augmented the nonindigenous population. Many who obtain a residence permit subsequently seek and obtain approval for migration by relatives for family reunification or formation.

Many nonindigenous Dutch migrants, particularly from the former Dutch East Indies, have successfully integrated, but this is less true for many of the more recent migrants. Many non-Western immigrants live in the big towns (about a third each of the populations of Amsterdam and Rotterdam in 2002 were of non-Western descent). A sizable fraction occupies the country's lower socioeconomic strata. Those with refugee status and families of Moroccan origin are especially likely to be found there.

The employment rate for non-Western migrants is worse than for indigenous Dutch: 73 percent of indigenous Dutch were employed in 2003, compared with 56 percent of nonindigenous Dutch and 51 percent of non-Western residents. The data for unemployment benefits are similar: 13 percent of indigenous Dutch are in some kind of unemployment scheme compared with 16 percent of Western migrants and 25 percent of non-Western migrants. Among asylum migrants the unemployment rate was 23–40 percent for males and 38–70 percent for females (Bijl et al. 2005). Children from ethnic minority families finish school less often and with lower degrees than children from ethnically Dutch families, and the gap is not decreasing significantly; girls overall do better than boys (Bijl et al. 2005).

Members of some ethnic minority groups are overrepresented in Dutch crime statistics. Of all registered suspects in 2002, 62.5 percent were ethnically Dutch and 37.5 percent were from other groups. Overall, 1.6 percent of male ethnic Dutch residents were identified in police data systems as a suspect; among non–ethnic Dutch males, 4.2 percent were. Among ethnic Dutch and other females, the corresponding figures are 0.3 percent and 0.8 percent (Blom et al. 2005). The overrepresentation is higher for juveniles: first-generation Antillean and Moroccan juveniles' representation in police statistics is three times that of Dutch juveniles, according to Blom et al. In Dutch prisons, 74 percent of detainees have Dutch nationality; however, 50 percent were born outside the Netherlands (Dienst Justitiële Inrichtingen [DJI]: http://www.dji.nl/main.asp?pid = 40&sectorid = 2&catid = 3, 2005).

III. The Criminal Justice System[2]

Dutch police, prosecutors, and judges have wide discretionary powers. During the closing decades of the twentieth century, the powers of the police and the prosecution grew substantially. Their authority to dispose of cases without referring them to the courts expanded substantially. The judiciary has wide discretionary powers in sentencing. Legislation establishes maximum sentences for particular crimes, and there are no minimums.

A. Police

The police are divided into twenty-five regional forces. Each falls under the administrative authority of the mayor of the largest city in the region. The public prosecutor, however, is responsible for overseeing police investigations. A small national force handles specific tasks (e.g., motorway policing, central criminal investigations, international contacts, international and war crimes). There is also a military police force with several "civil" tasks, most notably border control and Amsterdam's Schiphol Airport. Special agencies handle regulatory offenses such as tax and social security fraud.

Suspects are processed first through the police system. When the police decide that a suspect has committed a crime, the case in principle should be transferred to the public prosecutor. In some cases, especially for juveniles who have committed minor offenses, the police may send the suspect home with a warning or a small fine and no prosecution ensues. Since 1987, the police have had authority to handle less serious offenses committed by juveniles by means of a HALT disposition, which is usually a kind of community service. For driving offenses, shoplifting, and other lesser property crimes, police can dispose of cases on the condition that the suspect pays a fine; this is in effect a lower-level version of the prosecutorial transactions described in the next subsection. In other situations, the case is referred to the public prosecutor's office.

B. Prosecution

The prosecutor's role is central. The prosecution is responsible for overseeing the investigation and decides whether to prosecute or to drop the case. The prosecution is authorized to deal with less serious

---

[2] Junger-Tas (2004) and Tak (2001, 2003) respectively provide comprehensive overviews of the Dutch juvenile and (adult) criminal justice systems.

cases without referring them to the courts by means of "transactions" (agreements that the suspect will accept a penalty that might have been imposed had the case gone to trial) or other conditions for dismissal of the case. The offender can refuse the offer (if so, the case will go to court). One advantage for the offender is that agreement to a transaction will not result in a criminal record that will show up in a background check. Only a judge has authority to find a suspect guilty. This means that there is no institutionalized "plea bargain," although the transaction resembles one functionally.

Public prosecutors in the Netherlands, though appointed directly by the minister of justice and the Crown, fall under a central office (the Board of Procurators General, the *Parket-Generaal*) led by three to five chief prosecutors. Prosecutors, unlike judges, are not appointed for life.

C. Courts

Judges are appointed for life by the minister of justice and the Crown. Juries are not involved in the trial of cases, and lay judges are almost absent. This is different from most surrounding countries, where juries or lay judges without specialized academic training, or both, play important roles trying cases and deciding punishments.

The courts of first instance consist of one judge (*politierechter*) for less severe offenses (with authority to impose custodial sentences up to six months) or three judges for the more serious cases (*meervoudige kamer*). Appellate courts generally consist of three judges.

Most investigation is done by the police in the pretrial stage. Findings are reported in the case file. Most of the time, no interrogation of witnesses and experts takes place at the trial. Judges base their decisions primarily on interrogations of suspects and written dossiers (Malsch and Nijboer 1999). Interpreters are provided during trials and interrogation to defendants who do not speak Dutch.

The media have access to criminal trials, but use of cameras is limited. Media coverage is generally limited to imposition of the sentence or the start of a prosecution. Compared with media in other countries, the Dutch media are relatively restrained in reporting about criminal trials.

D. Punishment

Sanctions range from fines and community service to treatment measures (*leerstraf*) to imprisonment. All can be imposed conditionally as well as unconditionally. Sanctions can be *punishments*, which must be proportionate to the offense, or *measures* (such as treatment), which serve a more rehabilitative goal and need not be proportionate.

Especially for violent and sexual crimes, entrustment orders (*terbeschikkingstelling*, commonly called TBS) may be given, often in combination with a prison sentence. An entrustment order can be imposed for crimes carrying a statutory maximum sentence of four years or more imprisonment, if the offender cannot be held fully responsible for his or her behavior, and if hospital care is deemed necessary to protect other people, the general public, or property. The order lasts two years but may be extended. The average time spent on an entrustment order is more than six years. Some on whom treatment is imposed may spend the rest of their lives in confinement if treatment is unsuccessful and their chances of recidivism remain high (Leuw 1999).

Determinate custodial sentences vary between one day and twenty years. Life sentences are seldom imposed (though their use has increased in recent years). Sentence length depends on the severity of the offense, whether the offender is a recidivist, and other case-specific circumstances. Prisoners are entitled to release after serving a specified percentage of their sentences. There is no system of discretionary parole release.

All prisons are operated by the state. They are small, the largest having a capacity of fewer than 400 cells. The total regular capacity for adults (nonjuveniles, non-TBS) by the end of 2005 was 15,601 cells (DJI 2007). Besides adult institutions, there are institutions for young offenders, psychiatric institutions for offenders, and places for detained illegal aliens who are subjects of civil administrative law proceedings. Three-quarters of prisoners are in short-stay facilities that house pretrial detainees and persons serving short terms.

An inmate's quality of life in a Dutch prison is high, compared with prisons elsewhere, at least in a material sense. Detainees can have a television and video in their cell (at their own expense), and sports activities are available. Prisoners serving long sentences may be granted unsupervised visits.

In other respects, the regimes are strict and have recently become stricter. Sentenced prisoners can be required to participate in prison labor. Contacts with the outside world are strictly regulated. Because of the rapid growth of the prison population, sharing of cells has been allowed since 2003.

IV. Crime and Punishment Trends[3]

Among European countries, the Netherlands stands out in the growth over three decades of its imprisonment rate and its prison capacity and population. Otherwise—in crime and victimization rates and trends, changes in sanctioning policies and practices, and evolution of systems of official data—it is in the mainstream. There is, however, some confusion about imprisonment rates, and for some offenses there is some uncertainty about crime rate trends.

A. Imprisonment Rates

The broad patterns are clear. The imprisonment rate grew steeply and continuously for three decades from being the lowest in western Europe to being one of the highest. In contrast to the United States and England, other countries that experienced steeply rising imprisonment rates over extended periods through 2006, the increase occurred without enactment of dramatically harsher sentencing laws and without crime control becoming a preoccupying partisan political issue.

Figure 1 shows the imprisonment rate per 100,000 population aged fifteen to sixty-five for the period 1960–2005, including remand and sentenced adult prisoners, juveniles detained under a criminal law order, and TBS detainees. Represented in this way, the rate approximately halved between 1960 and the early 1970s and then quadrupled, approaching 160 per 100,000 in 2005. Calculating imprisonment rates this way adjusts demographically for the size of the population realistically at risk of being in prison, but it is not generally the basis for international comparisons.

International comparisons generally use imprisonment rates per 100,000 national population, but this can be misleading depending on what subpopulations are included (e.g., adults only or including juveniles, whether illegal aliens, whether residents of psychiatric institutions for offenders). Figure 2 shows the Dutch imprisonment rate per 100,000 general population and calculated to include the same categories of confined persons as in figure 1.

Dutch imprisonment rates are sometimes said to have increased six-fold since 1973–74, but that is wrong and appears to result from comparing recent rates based on the population aged fifteen to sixty-five

[3] Bijleveld and Smit (2004, 2005) provide detailed analyses of crime and punishment trends in 1980–99.

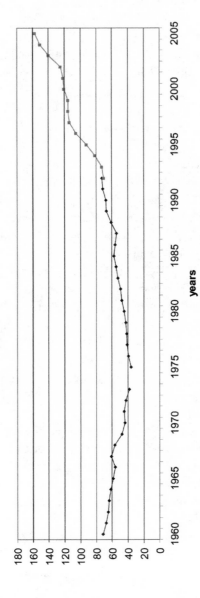

FIG. 1.—Netherlands imprisonment rates per 100,000 population aged fifteen to sixty-five, 1960–2005. Sources: 1960–92: van Ruller and Beijers (1995); 1990–2005: http://www.wodc.nl/images/6.01_tcml1-135961.pdf. Series 1960–92: average incarcerated population, including TBS, juveniles detained under a criminal law order, and patients in penitentiary hospitals. Series 1992–2005: average incarcerated population, including TBS and juveniles detained under a criminal law order; 1992–99: number of aliens detained under civil law order estimated as 10 percent of the total and deducted from totals published.

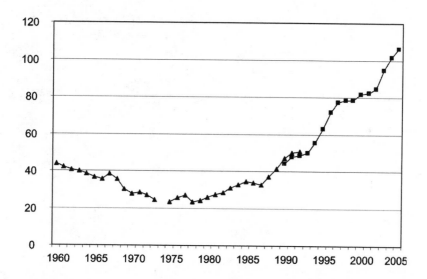

FIG. 2.—Netherlands imprisonment rates per 100,000 population, 1960–2005. Sources: 1960–92: van Ruller and Beijers (1995); 1990–2005: http://www.wodc.nl/images/ 6.01_tcm11-135961.pdf. Series 1960–92: average incarcerated population, including TBS, juveniles detained under a criminal law order, and patients in penitentiary hospitals. Series 1992–2005: average incarcerated population, including TBS and juveniles detained under a criminal law order; 1992–99: number of aliens detained under civil law order estimated as 10 percent of the total and deducted from totals published.

(150–160 per 100,000) with the 1973–74 rate based on the total population (mid-20s per 100,000).

Notwithstanding those qualifications, however, and whichever method is used to calculate rates, Dutch use of imprisonment has increased substantially and rapidly by European standards. Table 1, based on Council of Europe data, shows imprisonment rates for selected European countries in 2004.[4] Among ten E.U. countries (out of fifteen) for which data were available and Switzerland, only England and Wales and Spain had higher imprisonment rates than the Netherlands; the Dutch rates were nearly double those in Scandinavia and a third higher than in France, Germany, and Italy.

Table 2 shows imprisonment rates from the Council of Europe for

[4] The data shown in tables 1 and 2 are as reported to the Council of Europe by national governments. The Dutch data, consistent over time, include categories of confined persons (e.g., young persons confined under civil law orders) not included in our figs. 1 and 2.

TABLE 1

Imprisonment Rates, Selected European Countries,
September 1, 2004

Country	Population (2004)	Number of Prisoners (2004)	Per 100,000 (9/1/2004)
Denmark	5,397,600	3,762	69.7
England and Wales	53,046,300	74,488	140.4
Finland	5,219,700	3,446	66
France	62,177,000	56,271	90.5
Germany	82,531,700	79,676	96.5
Italy	57,888,200	56,090	96.9
Netherlands	16,258,000	20,075	123.5
Norway	4,577,500	2,975	65
Spain	42,197,900	59,224	140.3
Sweden	8,975,700	7,332	81.7
Switzerland	7,364,100	6,021	81.8

SOURCE.—Council of Europe (2005), table 1.

the same eleven countries in 1977, 1990, 1999, and 2004 and percent-age changes from each prior year through 2004. In each period the cumulative Dutch increase is substantially higher than any other. Over the entire twenty-seven years the Dutch imprisonment rate grew 375 percent. Spain was next highest at 119 percent.

An interesting question is why imprisonment rates rose so rapidly and for so long, especially in the absence of dramatic policy changes—such as three-strikes and mandatory minimum sentence laws in England and the United States—meant to increase prison use dramatically. Crime rates increased substantially in the 1970s, 1980s, and 1990s, and it is not unreasonable to suppose that led to increased imprisonment. In practice, however, comparative research shows that there is no necessary relation between crime and imprisonment rates (Tonry 2007). Parts of the explanation for the Dutch pattern are known. A first, and the most mechanical, is that periodic expansions in prison capacity have to some extent driven the size of the prison population. Until 2003, the Netherlands observed a policy of one prisoner to a cell. When space was unavailable, both remand and sentenced prisoners were placed on waiting lists for admission; when the wait became too long, many were spared prison altogether. In 1995, remand prisoners were sent home on more than 5,000 occasions because of a lack of space (Verhagen 2005, fig. 39).

TABLE 2

Imprisonment Rates per 100,000 Population, Selected Countries,
1977, 1990, 1999, and 2004

Country	1977	1990	1999	2004	Change 1999–2004 (%)	Change 1990–2004 (%)	Change 1977–2004 (%)
Denmark	62	65	67	69.7	4.0	7.2	12.4
England and Wales	81	93	122	140.4	15.1	51	73.3
Finland	115	65	50.5	66	30.7	−1.5	−42.3
France	62	82	88.5	90.5	2.23	10.34	46
Germany	83*	78*	98.3	96.5	−1.8	23.7	16.3
Italy	56	57	9.3	96.9	8.5	70	73
Netherlands	27	44	84	123.5	47	180.68	357.41
Norway	49	57	58.5	65	11.1	14	32.65
Spain	64	NA	114	140.3	23.1	NA	119.2
Sweden	51	58	61.9	81.7	32	40.9	60.2
Switzerland	55	NA	88.5	81.8	−7.6	NA	48.7

SOURCE.—2004: Council of Europe (2005), table 1; 1999: Council of Europe (2001), table 1; 1990: Council of Europe (1992), table 1; 1977: Kaiser (1984), p. 184.
* West Germany only.

In the 1970s, after a round of prison closings, capacity was very low, and exceptionally low rates in the mid-twenties were the result. The comparatively level imprisonment rates shown in figures 1 and 2 in the 1990s occurred at a period of insufficient capacity, and the subsequent rise coincides with a substantial expansion in capacity. The expansion after 2003 results in part from abrogation of the one-prisoner, one-cell policy.

A second explanation is a general turn toward greater severity that manifested itself throughout the justice system. More suspects were held in pretrial detention, and the fraction of pretrial detainees in the total prison population significantly increased. The actors and agencies that make up the criminal justice system over time sent increasingly larger percentages of convicted offenders to prison and (for many offenses) for longer times. Between 1985 and 1995, the percentages of registered crimes resulting in unsuspended prison sentences increased substantially for violent (16–21 percent), drug (22–34 percent), and property crimes (13–18 percent) (Tak 2001, table 4.9). The average prison sentence increased from 59 days in 1970 to 96 in 1980, 152 in 1990, and 197 in 1995 (table 4.11). Between 1980 and 1999, both conviction and imprisonment probabilities increased for assaulters and robbers, as did the odds of receiving a prison sentence and average days of imprisonment if convicted (Bijleveld and Smit 2004, tables 4–6).

Data on increasing prison capacity and severer punishment practices give some indication of what is happening, but not why. A growing comparative and cross-national literature explores determinants of changing penal policies, focusing on such things as changing crime rates, public attitudes and anxieties, and criminal justice policies; deeper changes in social and economic conditions; and evolving cultural norms and sensibilities (Boutellier [2005] has written of these changes in the Dutch context).

The history of penal policy in the Netherlands remains to be written, and perforce it will explore such subjects. It is clear that something fundamental has changed (Downes and van Swaaningen, in this volume). Van Ruller and Beijers (1995) analyzed Dutch incarceration data, broadly defined to include adult prisons, juvenile facilities, and mental institutions, from 1837 to 1992. Their data suggest that something dramatic happened in the 1970s (see fig. 3). We have added comparable data through 2005. Aggregate imprisonment rates fell steeply and almost continuously from 1837 to 1975 and then changed direction. The increase since then has not been continuous but would have been had imprisonment rates not been distorted by changes in capacity, waiting lists, and the one-prisoner, one-cell rule.

Van Ruller and Beijers describe a number of factors that may have influenced the post-1975 rise. One is the combination of limited capacity, the one to a cell policy, and waiting lists. A second is an increase in the number of serious offenses. A third is harsher sentencing practices. A fourth is more vigorous enforcement of hard-drug laws. A fifth is a combination of the Netherlands' role as a transit hub combined with open borders and easy international mobility, which necessitates locking up suspects for fear that they may otherwise leave the country. A sixth and seventh are two "psychological" considerations: that judges have perceived the Dutch mild penal climate to be out of synch with those of surrounding countries, and that the climate had changed from one of compassion for the perpetrator to one of compassion for the victim, resulting in harsher attitudes toward crime and criminals.

B. Crime Rates

Rates of recorded crime broadly rose in most Western countries during the 1970s and 1980s, reaching peaks at some point in the early

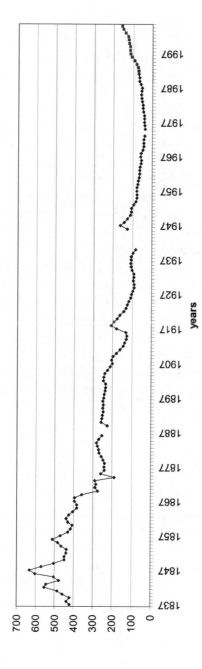

FIG. 3.—Average daily population in institutions, per year and per 100,000 population aged fifteen to sixty-four, including prisons, jails (since 1846), juvenile institutions (since 1883), and mental institutions (since 1929). Sources: 1837–1992: van Ruller and Beijers (1995); 1992–2005: http://www.wodc.nl/ images/6.01_tcm11-135961.pdf. Series 1837–1992: average incarcerated population, including TBS, juveniles detained under a criminal law order, beggars institutionalized under a criminal law order, and patients in penitentiary hospitals. Series 1992–2005: average incarcerated population, including TBS and juveniles detained under a criminal law order; 1992–99: number of aliens detained under civil law order estimated as 10 percent of the total and deducted from totals published.

to mid-1990s and declining or stabilizing thereafter. Changes in reporting and recording took place in all countries during that period, and some countries changed their criminal codes to redefine offenses in ways that make comparison of crime rates over time even more difficult. Homicide, because of its seriousness and the possibility of validating police data with health system data, and automobile theft, because insurers typically will not cover a claim unless the loss was reported to the police, are generally believed to be the most accurate official crime data. Assaults and sexual offenses are generally believed to be the offenses least accurately measured by official data because there have been substantial and repeated changes in social attitudes and official policies toward both in recent decades that conduce to higher recording and reporting rates. In general, people have become less tolerant of violence and unwanted sexual contacts and more likely to report them to the police. The police in turn have become more likely to record them as crimes.

Identifying trends in the incidence of serious crimes in the Netherlands is more difficult than in some other countries because of the nature of some definitions of offenses in Dutch criminal law. For some of the offenses about which citizens are most concerned, the existing definitions make trend statistics difficult to compile or interpret. There is, for example, no separate article for burglaries; they make up about a fifth of the entries under article 311 ("qualified theft"). There is likewise no separate offense of motor vehicle thefts; they are classified sometimes as general theft (art. 310), sometimes under 311, and sometimes under other articles. Dutch victimization surveys and the International Crime Victimization Survey (ICVS) in which the Netherlands participates have working definitions for some of these offenses, but those definitions have changed over time and are difficult to relate to the criminal code definitions (Bijleveld and Smit 2004, p. 164).

It is likely that crime trends in the Netherlands in recent decades followed those in other Western countries, but that is less clear from official records than is true elsewhere. Figure 4 shows police data on recorded aggregate property and violent crime rates per 100,000 population aged twelve to seventy-nine years for the years 1960–2004. The property crime rate rose steadily from 1960 to 1985, reaching a plateau that lasted through the early 1990s, followed by a sizable fall, an increase to a point lower than the prior peak, and another fall. The violent crime rate increased throughout the entire period.

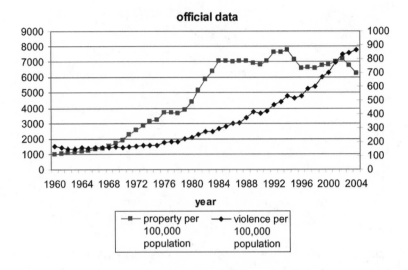

FIG. 4.—Property and violent crime rates per 100,000 population aged twelve to seventy-nine years, Netherlands, 1960–2004. Sources: CBS Statline, WODC (http://www.wodc.nl/Cijfers/CriminaliteitenRechtshandhaving/), tables 4.2, 4.3.

It is difficult to know how much of the apparent increases, especially for violence, is real and how much is the artifactual effect of reporting and recording changes. Much of the increase in violence rates is almost certainly the product of changes in police recording practices. During the period 1980–99, the probability that an assault was reported to the police increased slightly, but the probability that the reported incident was recorded as an assault by the police increased threefold (from 19.4 percent in 1980 to 58.1 percent in 1999). For robbery the recording increase is less (from 5.8 percent in 1980 to 14 percent in 1999) (Bijleveld and Smit 2004, tables A3, A4), but still a 150 percent increase. Assaults and threats are the most frequent violent crimes, and their numbers drive the total violent crime rate. Trends in recorded violent crime accordingly probably overstate the increase in violence.

The story for property crimes is much the same. Although levels of citizen reporting of burglary and motor vehicle theft did not change much between 1980 and 1999, police recording practices did. For burglary, the probability of police recording of reported offenses nearly doubled from 22.3 percent in 1980 to 42.1 percent in 1999. For motor vehicle theft, the recording rate rose from 23.9 percent of reported

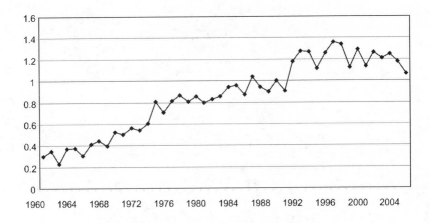

FIG. 5.—Homicides per 100,000 inhabitants, 1960–2004. Source: Nieuwbeerta and Deerenberg (2005).

offenses to 58.1 percent (Bijleveld and Smit 2004, figs. 2a, 2b). Although theft is the most numerous of property crimes, burglary and motor vehicle thefts also are common. The substantial increases in recording rates for those offenses, especially in the 1990s, when property crime rates were falling, suggest that the falls were real.

In principle, homicide should provide a leading indicator of violence trends, assuming that the number of homicides is probabilistically related to the number of violent incidents. Reasons why this assumption might be incorrect include changes in the circumstances in which deaths occur (e.g., an increase in the fraction of homicides occurring in organized crime contexts, changes in weapon lethality such as shifts from knives to guns or from lower- to higher-caliber guns) and changes in the effectiveness of medical responses to violence.

Homicide is less likely than other crimes to be susceptible to large changes in reporting and recording. If homicide is viewed as the tip of the iceberg of violent offending, research on homicide levels suggests that violence increased from 1960 through the early 1990s, after which it stabilized and most recently may have begun to decline. This can be seen in figure 5, which shows homicide rates per 100,000 population from 1960 to 2004. From 1965 to 1990, yearly homicide rates increased nearly threefold, to 1.2 per 100,000, and have remained fairly stable since, hovering around a little over 200 per year. Nieuwbeerta and

Deerenberg (2005) show that the rise took place mainly in the three largest cities (Rotterdam, Amsterdam, and The Hague) and among young and adult males. Firearms were involved in an increasing fraction of deaths over this period.

The homicide data thus show a marked rise since 1960, although not as strong as the rise in police-recorded violent offenses. Plausible hypotheses, however, can be offered that part of the rise is explained by the increasing prevalence of firearms (an assault with a gun is more likely to result in death than are other assaults) and that part is explained by an increasing proportion of homicides related to otherwise criminal activities.

Whatever the reasons for the rise, the levels reached in the 1990s and sustained since then are typical of western European countries. Most have homicide rates between 1.0 and 1.5 per 100,000 population (Aebi et al. 2006, tables 1.2.1.4, 1.1.2.5).

From official records, then, it appears that both property and violent crime increased in the 1970s and 1980s, though considerably less than official data suggest, and that property crime rates began to fall in the 1990s. It is more difficult to generalize about recent violence trends. However, under the assumption that homicide is a leading indicator of violence generally, the stabilization of homicide rates in the early 1990s and the subsequent slight decline suggest that the true incidence of violence in society has not been increasing for more than a decade. Wittebrood and Nieuwbeerta (2006), using victimization data, showed for the period 1980–2004 for a number of smaller categories of offenses that most of the rise in recorded crime could be explained by increased reporting and recording, and only a small proportion by rising crime levels as such.

C. Victimization Surveys

Data generated by victim surveys, the other source of data on crime over time, agree with the official data on property crime but disagree about violence (in contrast to the police data, also showing a decline). Figure 6 provides aggregate data on victimization rates per 100,000 for violent and property crimes from 1980 through 2006. Reported victimization levels are fairly stable, decreasing from 16,000 to 14,000 incidents per 100,000 population per year. It shows that reported victimization by property crime declined in the late 1990s. For violent crime,

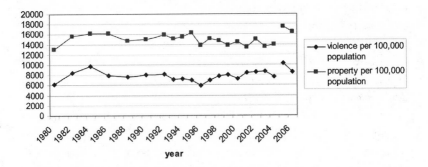

FIG. 6.—Victimization violent and property offenses, Netherlands, 1980–2006. Source: WODC and CBS victim surveys.

it indicates a drop in the mid-1980s followed by another drop in the mid-1990s to a stable lower level.

Most writers in the Netherlands contend that the victim surveys give better information and that the rising crime levels indicated by the official data reflect increased administrative efficiency and, for violent offending, increased labeling of behavior by victims and officials. There clearly have been changes in reporting behavior and recording practices. The overriding difficulty is not knowing how much those changes have affected apparent crime levels and trends

While an argument can be made that victimization data are more reliable indicators of trends because they are not distorted by officials' recording decisions and because often they are based on large samples, other considerations make them less persuasive. They do not measure one of the most serious crimes, homicide, and do not report data for another, rape (the former for obvious reasons and the latter because rape is too rare an event to obtain credible estimates from victim surveys); what they do measure is heavily biased toward less serious crimes. There are also questions about their representativeness; response rates for Dutch national victimization surveys hover around 50 percent and have gone down steadily over the years. Since the hardest-to-locate respondents (poor, mobile, living socially disorganized lives) are the likeliest to be high-rate offenders and victims, nonrepresentativeness is a nontrivial problem. Figure 6 is derived from data from several surveys: the WODC victim survey (1973–80), three different subsequent Statistics Netherlands victim surveys (1981–2004), and the latest VeiligsheidsMonitor Rijk victim survey (2005 and 2006). The last was not synchronized with its predecessors.

However, the ICVS does confirm that victimization in the Netherlands has declined since 1989, when that survey was first administered. Table 3 shows levels of reported victimization per 100,000 residents for burglary, thefts of and from cars, and theft of personal property (the sample sizes are too small to generate useful estimates about violent crimes) for eight western European countries for the years 1988, 1991, 1995, and 1999, including many of those whose imprisonment rates are included in tables 1 and 2. The two patterns that stand out for the Netherlands are that reported victimization rates are in the mainstream and, as in almost every other European country, peaked in the 1990s and have since fallen. These two patterns are confirmed by findings from the latest wave of ICVS data collection in 2004 (van Dijk 2006; van Dijk et al. 2007, chap. 2). Aggregate victimization rates in every western European country participating in the 2004 wave had fallen substantially from high points in the 1990s.

This brief overview of crime, victimization, and punishment trends in the Netherlands shows several things: Dutch imprisonment rates have risen much faster and more steeply than those in other European countries, and Dutch rates are now at or near the top in Europe; official and victimization data indicate that property crime rates have fallen and violent crime rates have stabilized.

V. Implications for Research

The Netherlands has a rich tradition in criminology and criminal justice research, and thriving (and rapidly growing) research and teaching communities (van Swaaningen 2006; Junger-Tas and Junger, in this volume). Its crime control and punishment policies have consistently attracted attention from outsiders because of the liberality of its longstanding policies on drugs and prostitution and because of its gradual, long-term shift away from having one of the most restrained punishment systems in Europe.

Dutch research is reasonably ample and impressively vibrant in a number of subjects, notably including organizational and white-collar crime (e.g., van de Bunt and Huisman, in this volume), organized crime (Kleemans, in this volume), juvenile delinquency (Weerman, in this volume), juvenile justice (Junger-Tas 2004), and immigration and crime

TABLE 3

Victimization per 100,000 Inhabitants, 1988, 1991, 1995, and 1999: Selected Offenses and Countries

Country	1988	1991	1995	1999
		Burglary		
Belgium	2,800	2,600	. . .	2,400
England	2,200	3,200	3,400	3,400
Finland	600	600	800	500
France	3,300	. . .	2,900	1,000
Mean	2,800	2,800	2,500	2,300
Netherlands	**2,600**	**2,400**	**3,300**	**2,300**
Scotland	2,300	. . .	1,600	1,500
Sweden	. . .	1,500	1,500	2,300
Switzerland	1,100	. . .	1,600	1,200
		Car-Related Crime		
Belgium	1,650	1,590	. . .	1,540
England	2,220	3,640	3,690	3,010
Finland	1,100	1,350	1,110	1,340
France	2,060	. . .	2,640	2,180
Mean	2,050	2,330	2,280	2,020
Netherlands	**2,340**	**2,860**	**2,540**	**2,350**
Scotland	2,520	. . .	3,120	2,640
Sweden	. . .	1,390	1,690	1,960
Switzerland	880	. . .	1,530	890
		Theft, Personal Property		
Belgium	4,300	4,000	. . .	4,800
England	4,000	5,000	5,500	5,700
Finland	5,000	3,900	3,600	3,900
France	4,200	. . .	4,800	3,100
Mean	4,900	6,100	5,800	5,500
Netherlands	**5,200**	**4,900**	**9,000**	**6,000**
Scotland	2,800	. . .	5,500	5,000
Sweden	. . .	5,400	5,800	7,200
Switzerland	5,700	. . .	6,800	5,400
		Contact Crimes		
Belgium	2,900	2,100	. . .	3,500
England	2,100	4,100	5,900	8,900
Finland	2,900	6,600	5,600	5,100
France	2,200	. . .	4,100	4,000
Mean	3,800	4,800	4,800	4,800
Netherlands	**4,400**	**3,800**	**3,500**	**4,000**
Scotland	2,800	. . .	4,500	6,300
Sweden	. . .	3,200	4,800	4,900
Switzerland	1,800	. . .	3,600	3,300

SOURCE.—Nieuwbeerta (2002), pp. 51–52.

(Engbersen, van der Leun, and de Boom, in this volume). Work in these areas matches that anywhere else in the world in vigor, sophistication, and imagination.

On a second set of subjects, the literatures and research communities are not yet large but are promising and will justify sustained investment over time in strategic programs of research and in the career development of subject matter specialists. Examples include urbanization and crime (e.g., Bruinsma, in this volume), sex offenses and offenders (e.g., Bijleveld, in this volume), violent and serious offending (e.g., Loeber and Slot, in this volume), and crime and human development (e.g., Blokland and Nieuwbeerta 2006).

On some other subjects, however, notwithstanding the existence of important individual studies, the corpus of research is comparatively meager and the number of involved researchers is small. Examples include gender and crime, costs of crime, cost-benefit and effectiveness studies, and treatment effectiveness.

There are, however, two major general areas in which Dutch research is conspicuously underdeveloped. The first is the operation of the criminal justice system. There is an astonishing lack of investment in baseline empirical studies of the operations of the police, prosecutors, courts, prisons, and community penalty systems and in the effectiveness of policy changes and experiments. In a country that has been increasing its use of imprisonment steadily for thirty years, it is remarkable that little important research on the operation of prisons and the effects of imprisonment has been carried out in recent decades. It is similarly remarkable in a country in which the public prosecutor occupies a considerably more powerful and influential role than prosecutors in most other countries that prosecutors receive so little research scrutiny. Similar observations could be offered about Dutch police, judges, and community corrections. There have been individual publications of note (e.g., van Koppen 2003; van Koppen and Schalken 2004), but none of these literatures are large.

Prison research can be used to illustrate the current lack of research and (therefore) knowledge about critically important subjects. Despite the example of extensive literatures in the English-speaking countries and Scandinavia on life inside prisons, on inmate and staff subcultures, on how they have changed over time, and on how they relate to prison management and to prisoners' postrelease behavior, there is no modern Dutch research. Despite the example of large international literatures on how prisoners adapt to and cope with prison life and on the prison's effects on their mental and physical health, there is no modern research. There is not a rigorous evaluative literature on the effects of recent changes in prison regime (e.g., greater austerity, multiple celling, longer sentences) on prison management, prisoner well-being, or prisoners' postrelease behavior. Fundamental baseline facts are not known: for example, concerning the lifetime probability of imprisonment for men and women and for members of different ethnic groups. There are no cost-benefit or cost-effectiveness literatures on the use of imprisonment compared with other sanctions or compared with other social policies for dealing with crime (comparing, e.g., the cost-effectiveness of investments in prisons with investments in developmental and other forms of crime prevention). There is no published research on the collateral consequences of a prison sentence (or any other sanction) on prisoners' subsequent employment, earnings, physical and mental health, or family functioning or on the lives of prisoners' partners and children.

Similar paragraphs could be written about the police, prosecution, judicial, and community penalty systems. Greatly expanded programs of research on these subjects are important not only from rationalistic and humanitarian perspectives. Governments make better choices when their decisions are based on credible information. Precious little credible, research-based information is available on criminal justice system operations or on the effects of recent policy changes.

Historical studies of crime and justice system operations are a second area in need of reinvigoration. René van Swaaningen (2006) recently showed that historical scholarship on the subjects flowered in the 1990s but has since gone into hibernation. Historical research, for which the Netherlands' well-kept archives make it especially well suited, should be revived. Important work was carried out earlier by Faber (1983), van Egmond (1993), and van Ruller and Beijers (1995), but little important work has recently been published. Exceptions are Pieter Spierenburg's ongoing research, Croes and Tammes' (2004) landmark study of the persecution of the Jews in World War II, and Fijnault's (2007) history of Dutch police. Van Ruller and Beijers in their statistical analyses showed that overall confinement rates fell steadily for a century and a half and in 1975 changed direction. Explaining why that happened is but one among many worthy missions for Dutch historians.

A specific modern historical subject that is starkly underresearched is the evolution of criminal justice policy in the Netherlands since World War II. The unprecedented rise in American imprisonment rates and changes in American criminal justice policies since 1973 have provoked a sizable literature that documents those developments, attempts to measure their effects, and tries to explain why what happened happened (e.g., Garland 2001; Tonry 2004a; Simon 2007). The stark rise in imprisonment and the harshening of English policies since 1993 have provoked similar literatures (e.g., Garland 2001; Ryan 2003; Tonry 2004b; Jones and Newburn 2006). The toughening of criminal justice practices in the Netherlands has been going on for as long as the American toughening, and much longer than the English. Neither of those countries, however, was ever regarded as an exemplar of enlightened criminal justice policies. How and why the Netherlands moved from exemplifying liberal to exemplifying repressive criminal justice policies is a story that has not yet fully been told.

REFERENCES

Aebi, Marcelo F., et al. 2006. *The European Sourcebook of Crime and Criminal Justice Statistics—2006*. The Hague: Boom Juridische uitgevers.

Bijl, R. V., A. Zorlu, A. S. van Rijn, R. P. W. Jennissen, and M. Blom. 2005. *Integratiekaart 2005. De maatschappelijke integratie van migranten in de tijd gevolgd: Trend- en cohortanalyses* [Integration map 2005. The societal integration of migrants followed over time: Trend- and cohort analyses]. The Hague: WODC.

Bijleveld, Catrien. In this volume. "Sex Offenders and Sex Offending."

Bijleveld, Catrien, and Paul Smit. 2004. "Netherlands." In *Cross-National Studies in Crime and Justice*, edited by David P. Farrington, Patrick A Langan, and Michael Tonry. Washington, DC: U.S. Department of Justice, Bureau of Justice Statistics.

———. 2005. "Crime and Punishment in the Netherlands, 1980–1999." In *Crime and Punishment in Western Countries, 1980–1999*, edited by Michael Tonry and David P. Farrington. Vol. 33 of *Crime and Justice: A Review of Research*, edited by Michael Tonry. Chicago: University of Chicago Press.

Blokland, Arjan, and Paul Nieuwbeerta, eds. 2006. *Developmental and Life Course Studies in Delinquency and Crime: A Review of Contemporary Dutch Research*. The Hague: Boom Legal Publishers.

Blom, M., J. Oudhof, R. V. Bijl, and B. F. M. Bakker. 2005. *Verdacht van criminaliteit: Allochtonen en autochtonen nader bekeken* [Suspected of an offense: Indigenous and nonindigenous Dutch scrutinized]. The Hague: WODC.

Boutellier, Hans. 2005. *The Safety Utopia: Contemporary Discontent and Desire as to Crime and Punishment*. Dordrecht: Kluwer Academic.

Bruinsma, Gerben J. N. In this volume. "Urbanization and Urban Crime: Dutch Geographical and Environmental Research."

Buruma, Ian. 2006. *Murder in Amsterdam: The Death of Theo van Gogh and the Limits of Tolerance*. London: Penguin.

Buruma, Ybo. In this volume. "Dutch Tolerance: On Drugs, Prostitution, and Euthanasia."

Council of Europe. 1992. *Council of Europe Annual Penal Statistics: 1990 Enquiry*. Strasbourg: Council of Europe.

———. 2001. *Council of Europe Annual Penal Statistics: 1999 Enquiry*. Strasbourg: Council of Europe.

———. 2005. *Council of Europe Annual Penal Statistics: Survey 2004*. Strasbourg: Council of Europe.

Croes, Marnix, and Peter Tammes. 2004. *"Gif laten wij niet voortbestaan": Een onderzoek naar de overlevingskansen van joden in de Nederlandse gemeenten, 1940–1945* [Poison shall not live on: A study of the survival chances of Jews in Dutch municipalities, 1940–1945]. Amsterdam: Aksant.

Downes, David. 1988. *Contrasts in Tolerance: Post-war Penal Policies in the Netherlands and England and Wales*. Oxford: Clarendon.

———. 2007. "Visions of Penal Control in the Netherlands." In *Crime and Justice: A Review of Research*, vol. 36, edited by Michael Tonry. Chicago: University of Chicago Press.

Downes, David, and René van Swaaningen. In this volume. "The Road to Dystopia? Changes in the Penal Climate of the Netherlands."

Engbersen, Godfried, Joanne van der Leun, and Jan de Boom. In this volume. "The Fragmentation of Migration and Crime in the Netherlands."

Faber, Sjoerd. 1983. *Strafrechtspleging en criminaliteit de Amsterdam, 1680–1811* [Criminal justice and crime in Amsterdam, 1680–1811]. Arnhem: Gouda Quint.

Fijnault, Cyrille. 2007. *De geschiedenis van der Nederlandse politie* [The history of the Dutch police]. The Hague: Boom Juridische uitgevers.

Garland, David. 2001. *The Culture of Control*. Chicago: University of Chicago Press.

Ippel, Pieter, and Susanne Heeger. 2006. *Sprekend de rechtbank* [Court voices]. Utrecht: University of Utrecht.

Jones, Trevor, and Tim Newburn. 2006. *Policy Transfer and Criminal Justice*. Milton Keynes, UK: Open University Press.

Junger-Tas, Josine. 2004. "Youth Justice in the Netherlands." In *Youth Crime and Youth Justice: Comparative and Cross-National Perspectives*, edited by Michael Tonry and Anthony N. Doob. Vol. 31 of *Crime and Justice: A Review of Research*, edited by Michael Tonry. Chicago: University of Chicago Press.

Junger-Tas, Josine, Ineke Haen Marshall, and Denis Ribeaud. 2003. *Delinquency in International Perspective—the International Self-Reported Delinquency Study*. Monsey, NY: Criminal Justice Press.

Junger-Tas, Josine, and Marianne Junger. In this volume. "The Dutch Criminological Enterprise."

Kaiser, Günther. 1984. *Prison Systems and Correctional Laws: Europe, the United States, and Japan*. New York: Transnational Publishers.

Kleemans, Edward R. In this volume. "Organized Crime, Transit Crime, and Racketeering."

Leuw, Ed. 1991. "Drugs and Drug Policy in the Netherlands." In *Crime and Justice: A Review of Research*, vol. 14, edited by Michael Tonry. Chicago: University of Chicago Press.

———. 1999. *Recidive na de tbs: Patronen, trends en processen en de inschatting van gevaar* [Recidivism after TBS: Patterns, trends, and processes and risk assessment]. The Hague: WODC.

Loeber, Rolf, and Wim Slot. In this volume. "Serious and Violent Juvenile Delinquency: An Update."

Malsch, Marijke, and Hans Nijboer, eds. 1999. *Complex Cases: Perspectives on the Netherlands Criminal Justice System*. Amsterdam: Thela Thesis.

Nieuwbeerta, Paul. 2002. *Crime Victimization in Comparative Perspective: Results from the International Crime Victims Survey, 1989–2000*. The Hague: Boom Juridische uitgevers.

Nieuwbeerta, Paul, and Ingeborg Deerenberg. 2005. "Moord en doodslag in Nederland, 1911–2002" [Homicide in the Netherlands, 1911–2002]. *Bevolkingstrends* 53:56–63.

Ryan, Mick. 2003. *Penal Policy and Political Culture in England and Wales*. Winchester, UK: Waterside.

Simon, Jonathan. 2007. *Governing through Crime*. New York: Oxford University Press.

Tak, Peter J. 2001. "Sentencing and Punishment in the Netherlands." In *Sentencing and Sanctions in Western Countries*, edited by Michael Tonry and Richard S. Frase. New York: Oxford University Press.

———. 2003. *The Dutch Criminal Justice System: Organization and Operation*. The Hague: WODC.

Tonry, Michael. 2004*a*. *Thinking about Crime: Sense and Sensibility in American Penal Culture*. New York: Oxford University Press.

———. 2004*b*. *Punishment and Politics: Evidence and Emulation in the Making of English Crime Control Policy*. Cullompton, Devon, UK: Willan.

———, ed. 2007. *Crime, Punishment, and Politics in Comparative Perspective*. Chicago: University of Chicago Press.

van de Bunt, Henk, and Wim Huisman. In this volume. "Organizational Crime in the Netherlands."

van Dijk, Jan. 2006. "What Goes Up, Must Come Down: Explaining Falling Crime Rates." *Criminology in Europe* 5:1, 17–18.

van Dijk, Jan, Robert Manchin, John van Kesteren, and Gegerly Hideg. 2007. *The Burden of Crime in the EU*. Tilburg, Netherlands: Intervict.

van Egmond, Florike. 1993. *Organized Crime in the Netherlands, 1650–1800*. Cambridge: Polity.

van Kesteren, John, Pat Mayhew, and Paul Nieuwbeerta. 2001. *Criminal Vic-

timisation in Seventeen Industrialised Countries: Key Findings from the 2000 International Crime Victims Survey. The Hague: WODC.

van Koppen, Peter J. 2003. *De Schiedammer parkmoord: Een rechtspsychologische reconstructie* [The Schiedam park murder: A legal-psychological reconstruction]. Nijmegen: Ars Aequi Libri.

van Koppen, Peter J., and T. M. Schalken. 2004. "Rechterlijke denkpatronen als valkuilen: Over zes grote zaken en der zelver bewijs" [Judges' ways of thinking as pitfalls: Six large cases and their proof]. In *Het Maatschappelijk oordeel van de strafrechter* [The social judgment of the criminal judge], edited by Jan de Keijser and Henk Elffers. The Hague: Boom Juridische uitgevers.

van Ruller, Sibo, and Guillaume Beijers. 1995. "De gevangenisstatistiek in het licht van de geschiedenis" [Prison statistics in historical perspective]. *Justitiële Verkenningen* 21:35–52.

van Swaaningen, René. 2006. "Criminology in the Netherlands." *European Journal of Criminology* 3(4):463–501.

Verhagen, Jos L. M. 2005. *Waar vrijheid ophoudt en weer kan beginnen* [Where freedom ends and can restart]. The Hague: Dienst Justitiële Inrichtingen.

Weerman, Frank M. In this volume. "Juvenile Offending."

Wittebrood, Karin, and Paul Nieuwbeerta. 2006. "Een kwart eeuw stijging in geregistreerde criminaliteit: Vooral meer registratie, nauwelijks meer criminaliteit" [A quarter century of rising registered crime: Mainly more registration, hardly more crime]. *Tijdschrift voor Criminologie* 48:227–42.

David Downes and René van Swaaningen

The Road to Dystopia? Changes in the Penal Climate of the Netherlands

ABSTRACT

Postwar developments in Dutch penal policy encompass one period of sustained reduction in the scale of imprisonment (1947–74), producing the most humane penal system in Europe, followed by a second (1975 to date) in which that trend reversed, producing an imprisonment rate that exceeds the European average, with adverse consequences for the character of prison regimes. The causes of the initial period are not self-evident, taking place while crime was rising, and based on a philosophy of minimizing the resort to custody. Key elements of that approach continued from 1975 to the mid-1980s, during a period of sharply rising crime rates. The period of sustained recarceration after 1985, and its prolongation, into the 1990s and beyond, entailed a sweeping reconfiguration of penal policy. Managerial, instrumental, and incapacitative measures took precedence over previous goals of resocialization and restorative justice.

The Netherlands has long been a symbol of hope for penal reform. Over two centuries ago, John Howard wrote that "prisons in the United Provinces are so quiet and most of them so clean, that a visitor can hardly believe he is in a gaol" (1784, p. 44) The story since then has been harsher than that conjured by Howard (see Franke [1995] for the fullest account). As late as 1947, Dutch prisoners were subject to solitary confinement and could be forced to wear cardboard masks in association periods.

Since then, a new era of "emancipation of prisoners" (to use Franke's term) was ushered in by the 1947 Fick report (Ministerie van Justitie

David Downes is professor emeritus of social policy at the London School of Economics. René van Swaaningen is professor of international and comparative criminology, Erasmus University, Rotterdam.

31

1947). For three to four decades afterward, Dutch penal policy became a byword for humane prison conditions and sparing use of custody. These changes were brought about by the judiciary embracing a philosophy that took seriously the often abused cliche of using prison "as a last resort"; by a pragmatic adaptation of existing practices such as waiver of prosecution, waiting lists for prison places, use of pardons, and generous home leave that served as "shields" against penal expansion and prison overcrowding (Rutherford 1986); by a political culture and media that respected professional expertise; and by a series of measures, such as generous visiting times and "conjugal visits," that reduced the "depth" as well as the length of imprisonment (Downes 1988).

During the 1980s, however, in the context of a steep rise in the crime rate, that era began to give way to a radically reformulated approach to criminal justice in general and penal policy in particular. The "shields" were dismantled or evaporated. Prisons ceased to be an outpost of a civilizing welfare mission and became a bastion of social defense. The transition is far from complete, and it would be unwise simply to extrapolate punitive trends into the indefinite future. As late as 1986 in the Netherlands, for example, prisoners were given the right to vote. What is at stake is how far the grounds on which the new, more disciplinary and punitively expansionist era rests will be consolidated in the future or reined back to recover the ideals of the earlier postwar era. These issues have a relevance far wider than the Netherlands, but the Dutch case is freighted with an intense symbolism that lends it unusual prominence.

In his seminal history of the penal present, *The Culture of Control: Crime and Social Order in Contemporary Society,* David Garland (2001) analyzes how the period of "penal welfarism," in which the belief in the "improvement" of the delinquent took a central position, from the mid-1970s on was gradually replaced by a far bleaker and more punitive "culture of control" in which the expressive character of punishment and the protection of the public took center stage. Changes in the emotional tone of crime policy, the return of the victim, and an emerging populism in the media and in politics are key indices of this change. Ultimately, however, it is the changing political economy of late modern capitalism that has driven so profound a transformation in the criminal justice sphere. As a result, the penal trends thus set in motion are unlikely to be halted, let alone reversed, in the foreseeable future.

This thesis has stimulated intense interest and dispute. For example, in her trenchant critique of Garland's book, Lucia Zedner (2002, p. 342) takes issue with his "grimly pessimistic" and "determinedly dystopic" analysis of the "rise of the criminal justice state." While the United States may be fairly reckoned to have achieved a state of penal dystopia in the 1990s, with mass imprisonment passing the 2 million mark and 150,000 prisoners—not far off twice the number in U.K. prisons as a whole—held under conditions of "super maximum security," American exceptionalism should not be generalized globally even as a tendency. In particular, Europe is not America, and the "stronger, and more enduring, traditions of European social democracy (and indeed British welfare liberalism)" (p. 365) provide some ground for penal optimism. Among other major countries responding differently to the problem of crime in late modernity, she singles out Canada, Norway, the Netherlands, and Japan as suggesting a "very different picture of continuing penal optimism and parsimony in the use of punishment" (p. 353). While acknowledging the force of Zedner's argument, we are—regretfully—no longer so convinced that the Netherlands can stand as an unalloyed example of either penal optimism or continuing parsimony. Moreover, in recounting the shift from the Netherlands as a *relative* penological utopia (if utopias can ever be relative) to a society seemingly locked into continuous penal expansionism, we find Garland's analysis all too relevant to an explanation and understanding of what has occurred.

This essay has three sections. The first discusses the period 1945–85. During the first thirty years, the use of imprisonment declined to the lowest level in Europe, twenty to twenty-five per 100,000 during the early 1970s. Though that level may in part reflect decisions to close prisons, observance of a policy of one prisoner per cell, and the consequential development of waiting lists for prison admission, that is but a very small part of the story.[1] Larger parts concern the general lib-

---

[1] The waiting list system for places in prisons was estimated by Downes (1988, p. 52) to equate with an extra 15 percent of the prison population in 1980; i.e., eliminating that system would have raised the 1980 prison population from about thirty per 100,000 to 34.5. The waiting list system, in which less serious categories of offenders were not detained before trial, was mainly used in the early 1990s—with a peak of 5,316 people who should have been remanded in custody sent away in 1994 (Reijntjes and van Ekelenburg 2005, pp. 550–52). If we take average time served into account, that is about 16.5 percent of the prison population of that year. It was far less developed in 1973, and

eralization of Dutch social policy and the influence of academics and policy makers who believed in minimalist and humane prison policies. During the final decade of this period, 1975–85, the harbingers of change can be seen in government policy documents and in the beliefs of influential figures.

Section II discusses the period 1985 to the present, which in retrospect can be seen as one continuous shift away from more humane earlier policies. Among the precipitants, besides rising crime rates and harshening public attitudes, were the influence of key policy makers, shifts in Dutch political culture, and the emergence of managerial, actuarial, zero-tolerance, and incapacitative policies that for long appeared to distinguish Dutch penal policies from those of England and America.

In Section III, we observe that the forces that Garland suggest produced contemporary penal policies in England and the United States appear to have done the same thing in the Netherlands.

I. From "Tolerance" to Disillusionment, 1945–85

There were two major achievements of what we may as well term Dutch exceptionalism. First, over a period of two decades, from the early 1950s until the mid-1970s, the prison population was gradually reduced to the extremely low point of eighteen per 100,000 of the adult population by 1973. Even though this trend was then reversed, it remained the lowest in Europe, at thirty-five to forty per 100,000 (depending on whether or not those in closed mental institutions for their offenses are included) until the late 1980s (fig. 1). Second, the opportunity thus created for radical change to prison regimes was seized by penal policy makers, administrators, and reformers, who transformed the character of imprisonment from a largely cell-bound, austere system, which retained many of the features of the nineteenth-century silent system, to one based on the "principle of resocialization," association, education, and a system of prisoners' rights that observers rated the finest in Europe (see, e.g., Vagg 1994). This period of decarceration gave the Netherlands the unique and at times unwanted burden of symbolizing the hopes of penal reformers around the globe.

Both achievements in tandem constituted a unique social experi-

---

the notional extra population would then have been that much lower. Its growth in the 1980s increasingly became a factor in the case for accelerated penal expansion.

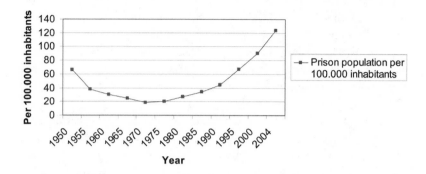

FIG. 1.—Prison population per 100,000 inhabitants in the Netherlands, 1950–2005. Source: Council of Europe, *Penological Information Bulletin* (various annual volumes), partly as quoted in Rutherford (1986, p. 122).

ment, albeit one whose significance is now being thrown into doubt and even somewhat devalued as naive and overly idealistic. It stood in sharp contrast to experience not only in Britain and the United States but also in most comparable countries, Scandinavia and Japan excepted. From the mid-1950s until the mid-1970s, Dutch decarceration exceeded that in the Nordic countries and was accomplished in the context of a rising, not a falling, crime rate, as in Japan. How can the causes and character of this largely silent revolution be accounted for?

It may well be the case that the circumstances and context within which so distinctively reductionist a trend was accomplished were unusually favorable and are now things of the past—though any such argument would be hard-pressed to account for the persistence of policies favoring low rates of imprisonment in Scandinavia and Japan. The Netherlands was not *that* unique. In the postwar period, however, once the years of immediate austerity passed, the Netherlands did arguably enjoy some two decades of rapidly growing prosperity and an efflorescence of freedom that, following the Nazi occupation and the hardships of postwar reconstruction, resembled a virtual second Golden Age.

By contrast with the celebrated "embarrassment of riches" of the seventeenth century (Schama 1987), this was not so much a period of high artistic achievement as a period of national buoyancy and self-confidence rooted in social cohesion, economic growth, cultural freedoms, and political stability: a particularly benign case of what Eric Hobsbawm termed the "Golden Age" that lasted from the end of

World War II until the oil price crises of 1973 (Hobsbawm 1994, pt. 2). The Netherlands had industrialized and modernized relatively late and did so on the basis of a pillarized structure, *verzuiling*, which integrated the Protestant, Catholic, and secular communities and ideologies through a system of interelite bargaining that provided for a century the basis for a distinctively Dutch "politics of accommodation" (Goudsblom 1967; Lijphart 1968; Bax 1990).

On that foundation, the Netherlands enjoyed three postwar decades of economic prosperity, full employment, cultural efflorescence, and international idealism. The Dutch were again to the fore in decolonization, the building of the Common Market and the European "economic miracle," active support for the United Nations, and sundry good causes. Large numbers of immigrants from the former Dutch colony Indonesia were in general successfully integrated into Dutch society in this period. Standards of living rose steadily, doubling between 1949 (the point at which the prewar peak was reattained) and 1970 (Bax 1990, p. 187). A rebuilt Rotterdam became the major entrepot for western Europe and The Hague a nucleus for international law.

It was, however, Amsterdam that gained a worldwide reputation in the 1960s as a crucible of tolerance and cultural experimentation, the limits of which were tested, but not ultimately breached, by new forms of adaptation to marijuana use, youthful dissent, and student rebellion. Marijuana use was gradually decriminalized via the licensing of certain venues and coffee shops as sites for its legitimate use and possession in small amounts. A necessary anomaly for this policy to succeed was virtually to decriminalize its supply to those so licensed. This approach was later extended to other cities. Youthful dissent took such novel forms of "direct action" as the "white bikes" scheme created by the *provos*—a name taken with pride from their condemnation as "provocateurs"—which were intended as freely available forms of transport for anyone to ride.[2] Other forms of dissent, such as "happenings," squatting, and demonstrations against, most notably, the monarchy, led to confrontations with the police, tear gas, and outbreaks of street violence. These and later forms of student dissent were smaller-scale versions of the more substantial upsurges of student revolt in France and the United States and were dealt with by the Dutch authorities in

---

[2] See the British journal of anarchist ideas, *Anarchy* (no. 66), for generally admiring reports on these nonviolent forms of challenge to convention.

characteristic fashion: the elaboration of committees to effect compromise solutions to grievances. While Lijphart's (1968) contention that such developments spelled the end of the "politics of accommodation" seems overdrawn, the 1960s are generally held to constitute the start of the decline of "pillarization" in the Netherlands (see also Bax 1990), but more for its growing incompatibility with modernization than as a result of youthful deviance, which was a symptom rather than a cause of deeper changes.

In Bax's view, modernization is causally related to both pillarization in the late nineteenth century and depillarization in the late twentieth century. How and why is this so, especially since most comparable societies achieved modernity without undergoing this process? His analysis links the phenomenon with the very origins of Dutch nation-building in resistance and rebellion against the Spanish occupation of the Low Countries in the sixteenth century, in which opposition to Catholicism played a crucial role. Seven autonomous provinces united against Spain and, later, encirclement by hostile powers such as England and France, by evolving a federation based on "segmented pluralism," a form of political government that stressed negotiation, compromise, and backstage committees. This system survived in key respects the centralizing tendencies of Napoleonic rule.

In the second half of the nineteenth century, the Catholic Church, which had long been tolerated unofficially, regained official acceptance as a political force. The Catholic community became a distinct "pillar" alongside that of the Protestant denominations.

In making the transition from a successful trading and colonial power to an industrial economy, the Netherlands required improvements in education and other spheres that were accomplished only on a denominational, pillarized basis. Along with the secular and radical pillars that emerged on the basis of liberal and trade union movements at this period, the pillarized structure was both sufficiently stable and flexible to provide the basis for the "politics of accommodation" that lasted until the 1960s and, in modified form, beyond.

It was in the 1960s, however, that modernization accelerated beyond the point at which it remained compatible with the traditional structure. Secularization weakened the hold of denominational communities over substantial minorities of their members. Social and geographical mobility brought them into greater interaction with those of other pillarized communities. The denominational character of schools, the media, and welfare agencies, all of which were state-subsidized, became more standardized. Individualism flourished in the context of greater affluence. The backstage, opaque processes of interelite bargaining became open to challenge, especially by the rising generation.

Government formation became subject to pressure group, single-issue, and new party challenges. Coalitions took longer to form and were less stable. However, though the heyday of the "politics of accommodation" was over by the late 1960s, its influence waned only gradually, and its spirit even now remains influential in the political culture of the Netherlands.

None of this explains in itself how and why Dutch criminal justice and penal policy evolved as it did in the postwar period. But it is important to convey the dominant perspective, which ultimately made sense of so striking a departure from the comparative norm. The Netherlands is a society whose prosperity is based on the application of inventiveness, industriousness, and intelligence in a country largely bereft of natural resources, one-third of which has been reclaimed from the sea, and which—especially in the postcolonial era—must now support a population of some 16 million people by their own enterprise and productiveness.

Dutch "tolerance" was born of the liberal humanism that generated the rationality, scientific method, and flow of ideas that underlay this achievement. A cast of mind and sensibility somewhat similar to that theorized by Norbert Elias[3] as central to the growth of civilization was arguably embraced by Dutch elites in the three postwar decades. The Netherlands adopted a form of liberal social democracy, with a generous welfare state assuring comprehensive social insurance over the life span. Deviance and control, including prisons, became aspects of a civilizing mission, in which the social sciences and welfare services would combine to reduce the resort to crime, minimize recourse to punitive sanctions, and extend the principle of resocialization to those who nevertheless continued to offend (Franke 1995). Dutch penal policy from the Fick report of 1947 until the mid-1980s was arguably the

---

[3] It was Elias's contention in his two-volume magnum opus *The Civilising Process* (1978, 1982) that the Western transition from the medieval to the modern world entailed a transformation of the "psychical process of civilization," whereby greater self-restraint and self-control came to be increasingly inculcated. Garland links this with "the extension of sympathy . . . to the offender, a development which has gradually ameliorated the lot of the offender and lessened the intensity of the punishment brought to bear" (1990, p. 236).

best example of what David Garland termed "penal-welfarism" (Garland 1985).

At the same time, even at its height, Dutch tolerance was never a simple acceptance of crime and deviant behavior, a form of "anything goes" amorality. It was framed by an insistence that the basic "rules of the game" were accepted by those who tested or breached the limits of the law. At bottom, members of Dutch society are prepared for a ruthless response to those who challenge its fundamental tenets: the acceptance of the need to negotiate with the possibility of rational outcomes. Thus, for example, the hijacking of a train in the late 1970s by Moluccan protestors, who held the Dutch government to a claim they could not possibly honor—a free Moluccan state, independent from Indonesia—led to the fatal shooting of several hostage takers (Schmid and de Graaf 1982). During the 1980s, a decisive shift in Dutch elite opinion occurred in which prison came to be seen not so much as an aspect of the civilizing mission but as a key defense against those who threatened the very integrity of Dutch society.

A. The Period of Decarceration, 1945–74

A number of immediate factors were crucial to the policy of reduced but more humane imprisonment. First, the war and its aftermath gave penal reformers an exceptional experience and opportunity to effect long-germinated change. According to Franke (1995, pp. 245–46), "After the war, prison experts were immediately struck with an almost revolutionary urge to reform. This had much to do with 'their own suffering in prison' of many members of the underground." The Fick Committee of 1947 recommended sweeping changes that led to the 1953 Penitentiary Principles Act, which substituted resocialization for retribution as the key principle governing prison regimes, entailing a host of changes from austere isolation to communal association. While the precise links between the people allegedly so involved in reform and the actual changes that eventuated, and what led Dutch internees, as distinct from those in other occupied countries, to effect such powerful momentum for reform, remain unclear, there can be no doubt about the purposive pursuit of new directions in penal reform.

A second development, unique to the Netherlands, was the pivotal role in penal reform played by a diverse group of criminal lawyers, criminologists, and psychiatrists known as the "Utrecht School," which "set the standards for the penal climate in the decades to follow" (de

Haan 1990, p. 69; also see Junger-Tas and Junger, in this volume). Although the group varied in their views on the precise role of psychiatry in rehabilitation, they shared a deep aversion to imprisonment, especially long-term confinement, which they regarded as intellectually and morally corrosive.

The single most influential book of the Utrecht School was Rijksen's 1958 study of its damaging effects as documented by prisoners themselves, which influenced a critical mass of the judiciary. It reinforced the impact of the writings and practical example of the leading exponents of reductionist penal philosophy, Willem Pompe, Pieter Baan, and Ger Kempe, whose "advocacy of rehabilitative measures . . . went far beyond that of any comparable group in Britain. . . . The fact that by 1955 a third of all 'prisoners' serving over a year, and a third of the average daily population in liberty-depriving institutions, were in TBR [psychiatric treatment] indicates the extent to which judges in The Netherlands were prepared to invest considerable faith in these measures" (Downes 1988, p. 88). Their widespread and lasting influence can be attributed to their work at all levels of the criminal justice and penal process, their acceptance of the need for *some* punishment, their lack of a radical political agenda, and their broad working philosophy based on the principle of resocialization. This hinged on their belief that prisoners must be credited with the capacity to respond creatively to the praxis of dialogue and encounter, a principle that also appealed greatly to social workers and probation officers.

Their high point of influence was probably in the mid-1950s, when the heads of the prison, probation, and mental health systems joined with psychiatrists at the Psychiatric Observation Clinic in Utrecht to discuss cases, sometimes with the prisoners concerned (Downes 1988, pp. 90–95). Though their influence waned during the late 1960s, the "new" Utrecht School, led by Antonie Peters and Constantijn Kelk, whose members stressed the primacy of due process and prisoners' rights, retained their anticustodial emphases.

Third, adherence to both a minimum and a humane use of custody necessitated several pragmatic measures to match prison capacity to the numbers confined. The waiver of prosecution, "self-reporting" to be admitted, home leave, and interruptions to sentence, along with parole and pardons, amounted to a set of "shields" against overcrowding and penal expansion (Rutherford 1986). By the late 1960s, the reductionist trend had been set out in policy terms by the senior prosecutors, leading to the closure of prisons despite a rising crime rate. Though, with hindsight, the prison closures in1972 seem more a result of an error in planning penal capacity than a testimony to yet more reductionism, the policy was not reversed but served as a stimulus to the liberal adaptations to the system referred to above.

In the policy plan for the prison system (*Beleidsvraagstukken Gevangeniswezen*) of 1977, the closure of some smaller penitentiary institutions was, for example, criticized not because the reduction of the prison system would have been undesirable, but because it would have contributed to longer travel times for visits to imprisoned relatives. It was also argued that the level of security of the remaining, larger prisons would be "unnecessary" for a large number of inmates. Prisoners got more personal freedom with respect to receiving visitors (with and without supervision), sending and receiving letters, wearing one's own clothes, making formal complaints, and furloughs (Verhagen 1999, pp. 10–11).

These moves were made possible, into the 1980s, by such nonjudicial shields as the mass media, which deferred to expert opinion, and the signal absence of a "politics of law and order." Though prison numbers resumed their rise, after the strikingly low figure of 2,200 had been attained in 1973, the shields proved effective in restraining the growth in numbers so that, even by the late 1980s, the Dutch prison population rate remained the lowest in Europe (see fig. 2). By then, however, the penal climate had entered a decisive period of change.

Fourth, the political climate was unusually favorable to such developments for at least three decades after 1945. Full employment, rising prosperity, and an uncommonly generous welfare state were the basis for a social and political stability that avoided the class, ethnic, and religious conflicts endemic in other advanced societies such as Britain and the United States. The so-called pillars of Dutch society—the Protestant, Catholic, and secular communities—cooperated in relative harmony, thanks to the interelite bargaining process famously termed the "politics of accommodation" by Lijphart (1968). The liberal penal policy favored by the broad Left was integrated into the progressive politics of the day by pragmatic accommodations with the Right over contested terrain.

As argued above, the evolution of the politics of accommodation had generated the conditions for successful modernization in the late nineteenth and first seven decades of the twentieth centuries (Bax 1990).

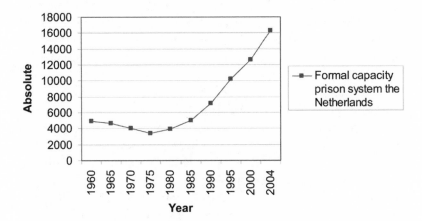

FIG. 2.—Formal capacity prison system, the Netherlands, 1960–2004 (TBS, deportation centers, and police cells excluded). Source: WODC and Dienst Justitiële Inrichtingen (DJI).

However, the means to modernization in the Netherlands eventually became the victim of its own success. With rapid economic growth came social, cultural, and demographic changes that the pillarized structure could not contain.

Fifth, the precondition for two decades of decarceration was a crime rate that did not rise at all until the 1960s and, until the 1970s, rose less sharply than in Britain. Social cohesion was sustained on a pillarized basis sufficiently well for the early growth of immigration, economic change, generational conflict, and mass tourism to be absorbed without undue strain. The crime rate doubled from its low 1950 base of roughly 1,000 per 100,000 to some 2,000 by 1970. By that stage, in Britain, it had trebled.

However, the volume of crime was to more than double again in the 1970s (see fig. 3), and as the decade wore on, signs of a weakening of the postwar liberal social democratic consensus began to appear, particularly around immigration and drug control. In the Netherlands, as well as in Britain and the United States, the stage was set for an embryonic "culture of control" (Garland 2001) to challenge the liberal consensus.

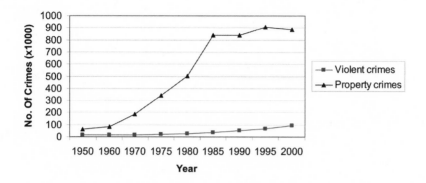

FIG. 3.—Registered property and violent crime in the Netherlands, 1950–2000. Source: CBS Statline.

B. The Onset of Disillusion, 1975–85

This ten-year period was to prove a decisive phase of transition from a liberal penal climate favoring decarceration to a more managerial penal climate oriented toward the expansion of imprisonment. Whatever its causes, the rise in crime was a decisive factor in the overthrow of the older liberal elites' philosophy of punishment, largely because it enabled its challengers to contest their legitimacy as experts in crime control and upholders of social order. By 1985, the crime rate had risen yet more steeply, from some 4,500 per 100,000 population to just under 7,000 offenses in 1980 in the space of five years.

Thereafter, it began to level out, with fluctuating trends upward or downward in all but a few offense categories such as street and armed robbery, which continued to rise substantially (fig. 4).

In the 1990s, the crime rate as a whole largely stabilized, but the prison climate continued to harden and the prison population to rise regardless of changing crime trends. According to Bert Berghuis (1994, p. 310), the main reason was that unsuspended prison sentences were imposed in cases that earlier would have been dismissed or sentenced with a suspended sanction, and in many cases longer sentences were passed for the same kind of offenses (see also fig. 5).

What seems to have occurred in the Netherlands during 1978–85 is an experience parallel to that of England in the post-1989 period and the United States in the post-1965 era: a sharp and sustained rise in the crime rate, involving some highly visible crimes that came to be

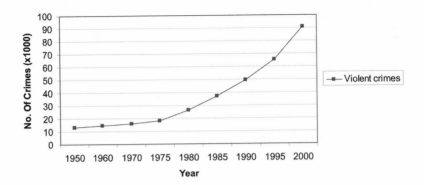

FIG. 4.—Registered violent crime in the Netherlands, 1950-2000. Source: CBS Statline

loaded with an intense and expressive symbolism redolent of social collapse. Against what is presented as a "heart of darkness" narrative by the mass media and salient politicians, harsher punishment was reinvented as the only feasible means of social defense.

Once in place, this culture of control has so far proved—at least in the late modern era—invulnerable to alternative paradigms. It has a self-confirming character that is prophetic, in the Popperian sense: it cannot be falsified. If crime rates continue to rise, clearly more punitive

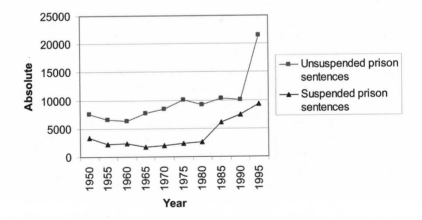

FIG. 5.—(Un)suspended prison sentences in the Netherlands, 1950–95. Source: CBS Statline.

measures are called for. If they stabilize, more punitive measures are needed to reduce crime. If they fall, then clearly the tougher measures are working.

The irony is that, of the three countries, the Netherlands seemed most intellectually resistant to, even culturally inoculated against, such a reversal of the penal climate that had held sway since 1945. How and why, then, did even this beacon of penal hope become dimmed?[4] For it remains the case that other societies, particularly Scandinavia, but also Canada and Germany, have experienced steady postwar rises in crime rates without undergoing so profound a shift to a more punitive mind-set.

The postwar liberal consensus had begun to be shaken in part by reason of its own success. The Netherlands acted as a magnet for both immigrants from former colonies and migrant labor from a swathe of developing countries. In the late 1960s, Dutch companies actively re-cruited unskilled labor, particularly in Turkey and Morocco. Language barriers were to prove an exclusionary factor for both workers and their children to a disproportionate extent, despite Dutch acceptance of their rights to citizenship and welfare. In anticipation of the independence of Surinam in 1975, ever increasing numbers of this Dutch colony's mostly unskilled, lower-class population came to the Netherlands hop-ing for a better future, just after the oil crisis and just after the politics of family reunification had brought the families of the guest workers from Turkey and Morocco to the Netherlands. They often ended up unemployed, living in their own "ghettos" mainly in Amsterdam and Rotterdam, and many ended up as problematic heroin users.

There were other reasons for social cohesion to come under strain. Cultural freedoms and a risqué ambience—Amsterdam was gaining al-lure as the red-light district of western Europe—facilitated the com-mercial exploitation of mass tourism. Rapid social and economic changes began to prise apart some traditional informal bases of social control. Enough anomic strain was generated to fuel a steepening rise in the crime rate from the mid-1970s on, with drug-related crime com-ing to symbolize newly emergent problems, which began to test the penal consensus to destruction.

Ironically, it was not the decriminalization of cannabis that fed the rise in crime but the criminalization of heroin addiction, one field in

---

[4] "A Beacon of Tolerance Dimmed"—without a question mark—is the title of the chapter on the Netherlands in Cavadino and Dignan (2006, pp. 113–28).

which the Dutch proved less liberal than the British, whose policy of prescribing heroin to registered addicts arguably curtailed the rise of drug-related crime until the early 1980s, several years after it had been largely replaced in the treatment centers by methadone.

To Andrew Rutherford (1996, p. 60), "by the end of the 1970s it was clear that the new shape of criminal policy had sharply departed from the tolerant attitudes of the previous generation. Most notably, beginning in 1975, prison numbers began to steadily rise and by the mid-1980s it was clear that the transformation of Dutch criminal policy was one of profound dimension." We differ somewhat on the periodization of change, while agreeing about the general direction. In the late 1970s, experts—and the key proponents of elite views—had certainly begun to divide over the appropriate set of responses to rising crime, basically a clash between those who favored more social reform and decriminalization, those who wanted to "hold the line," and those who argued for distinctly tougher measures.

By the early 1980s, these differences of view began to harden and became polarized throughout the decade. A good indicator of the upcoming change was the far less ambitious way the principle of resocialization got redefined in the 1982 report *Task and Future of the Dutch Prison System* (Tweede Kamer 1982). From a general dedication to prepare every prisoner for his return into society, it was now interpreted as an attempt to limit the damage from detention by humane execution of the penalty. This modest, but probably more realistic, goal turned out to be the overture for a further decline of resocialization as a leading penitentiary principle.

However, the transition was neither as sudden nor as smooth as Rutherford suggests. The defenders of the reductionist line were no pushovers. Senior administrators such as Hans Tulkens, head of the Prison Service from 1975 to 1984, penologists such as Constantijn Kelk and Antonie Peters, and more critical reformist voices in the Coornhert League for Penal Reform (van Swaaningen 1997, pp. 155–63) mounted a stubborn rearguard action that persists in some respects to this day and has arguably helped to restrain the rise in the prison population to the European average (while that in England has risen well above it). Had the crime rate leveled out in the late 1970s, instead of rising at an even faster rate of growth of some 10 percent a year from 1978 to 1983, they would not have been so readily outvoiced. The bureaucratic maneuverings in that period, eloquently criticized both at the time and later, were aimed at keeping the prison population within established bounds. But the Dutch flair for pragmatic innovation in the interests of reductionist "humane paternalism" (Kelk 1995, p. 2) increasingly came under fire as undermining the system's efficiency and credibility.

In this context, the career of Dato Steenhuis has commanded some attention as a transformative influence in Dutch penal culture (Rutherford 1996, pp. 59–76). Steenhuis had studied law and gained his doctorate for a dissertation that concluded that fines should replace imprisonment as the standard penalty for drunken driving, since area variations in custodial sentencing made no difference to its incidence. Published in 1977, when Steenhuis joined the Research and Documentation Centre (WODC) of the Ministry of Justice, it reinforced the logic of postwar penal policy.

Promoted to direct the WODC only two years later, Steenhuis stayed for three years, writing papers that revealed a marked disquiet about the character of penal policy, viewing it as inefficient, poorly coordinated, and badly in need of reorganization. His most influential paper was a two-part article that appeared in 1984 and depicted the criminal justice system by analogy as a badly run company that had lost sight of its key goal: the "maintenance of the penal legal order" (quoted in Rutherford 1996, p. 62).

Steenhuis's principal statement of this approach in the authoritative journal *Delikt en Delinkwent* in 1984 stressed the need for the criminal justice system to go beyond the administration of justice to reinforce the conformity of the law-abiding majority by increased efficiency and coordination at every stage of the criminal justice process (Steenhuis 1984, 1986). His appointment as the director of national training programs for public prosecutors signaled a swing toward the "instrumentalization" of the system.

Steenhuis was an influential voice in the *Society and Crime* report (Ministerie van Justitie 1985), generally taken to be the decisive point of change in Dutch criminal justice policy. The report originated in the parliamentary motion of October 1984 for a policy plan "motivated by a growing concern among the population over the increase in crime, by the fear of a loss of confidence on the part of the public in government and its role as a protector of private and public interests, and by the fear of a further erosion in the citizen's conception of standards and in social control" (Commissie Roethof 1984, p. 1) Moreover, "the gap between the number of infringements of standards embodied in the criminal law and the number of real responses to them by the criminal justice authorities has become unacceptably wide" (p. 1). With such a brief, the report's authors had little choice but to devise ways of closing that gap.

The main purpose of the report was ostensibly to restore the credibility of the justice system by a series of measures meant to achieve better coordination and crime prevention. Its major recommendation was a policy of bifurcation, the combination of lenient (but more extensively used) penalties for minor offenses with harsher penalties for the most serious. Another concern was, however, to defend the system and, in particular, the sparing use of imprisonment by explaining the rise in crime as a consequence of social and economic changes rather than more narrowly conceived flaws in the criminal policy realm.

Here the mark of Jan van Dijk, Steenhuis's successor as head of the WODC, is notably visible. Van Dijk's creative application of insights from routine activity and attachment theories to the decline of social control in the Netherlands turned out to be a policy theory that appealed to a wide range of politicians (Brants 1986). However, in putting forward the perfectly respectable sociological thesis that depillarization was a key cause of declining social control, and thus of burgeoning problems of crime, the report unwittingly roused public and political anxieties about the loss of social cohesion. To be told that the very foundations of society are collapsing is not only far from reassuring: it is distinctly alarming.

At this point, ironically just as the crime rate overall was leveling out—having risen by 50 percent between 1980 and 1985, it rose only by 0.5 percent between 1985 and 1990—Steenhuis stepped up his rhetoric to depict a society in moral free fall. In 1986, he told a Council of Europe research seminar that "the walls of the criminal justice system-building, once a stable rock in a society morally in decay, are tottering" (Rutherford 1996, p. 70).

Seminars are, of course, held in private, their papers read by few apart from professionals in the field. However, though more restrained in public pronouncement, the tenor of such views was presumably a leitmotif in Steenhuis's training of the key cadre in the rising generation of public prosecutors, statements to the media, and discussions with parliamentary committees. A difficult situation, on the point of some improvement, was being defined as a full-on state of social and moral collapse.

Had Steenhuis been a lone voice, despite his seniority, his views would have been of little lasting account. But he spoke for a growing part of the professional and corporate elites that constitute the inner circle of policy makers in Dutch society, as elsewhere. Moreover, other developments synchronized adversely with such pronouncements to consolidate the changes now firmly under way. There was, in the actual and foreseeable future, no turning back.

In the 1990s, the managerial discourse initiated by Steenhuis would become very dominant indeed. There is no institution in the whole criminal justice system that could escape the new rationale of flexibility, market orientation, and output measurement. Insights from business administration came to replace the sociological theories that had earlier informed crime policies. Because many of these reforms mainly resulted in too many, too expensive managers who knew too little of the content of what they were supposed to manage, and far less money for people who have to do the actual work, all those reorganizations of the actors in the "penal chain," as Steenhuis called it, probably made the criminal justice system less rather than more efficient. First, the penal chain is no stronger than its weakest link. Second, many of the new "responsibilized" partners in the fight against crime are supposed to collaborate, but there is little evidence that they actually do. Third, it is an error to believe that all the actors in the penal chain would really know from each other what they are actually doing (van de Bunt and van Swaaningen 2005).

The probation service is a clear victim and has lost track of its way in the managerial revolution in criminal justice. According to a blueprint for a reorganization of 1993, the service should be transformed into a "flexible, result-oriented and entrepreneurial organisation, which can, by means of a wide delegation of powers, and by profiling and prioritising its activities, quickly capitalise the demands of the market" (quoted in van Swaaningen 2000, p. 100).

With all these managerial clichés, one forgets to ask where the "demand of the market" with respect to probation comes from, who the market's superintendent is, or who indeed the clients are. Its later development from a social work organization dedicated to resocialization to an executive field organization that predominantly monitors noncustodial sanctions has led to its virtual demise. Owing to a rationale in which that which cannot be measured is no longer justified, resources are withdrawn from at least two of the most classic tasks of the probation service: providing aid to prisoners and aftercare.

II. From Disillusion to Dystopia? 1985–2005

In 1985, the Dutch prison population of some thirty per 100,000 remained the lowest in Europe by quite a substantial margin, and even by 1990 it had climbed to a rate of only forty-five. By 2005, the rate of about 120 had surpassed the western European average but remained at around 80 percent of the rate for England and Wales and well under a fifth of that of the United States. Invocation of the term "dystopia" may seem more than a little absurd in this comparative perspective.

In this section, we explain our reasoning and our use of the term dystopia as a reference to trajectory and trend rather than an accomplished state. It is not simply that the Netherlands has quintupled or even sextupled its prison population from a very low baseline. It is more a matter of the speed and volatility with which this trend has persisted, and the political and policy grounds on which it has been based. This section explores several significant shifts that have been effected in the realm of criminal justice and penal policy: a far more emotive politics of law and order; a growing fear of ethnic minority, drug-related, and organized crime; a much more extensive use of longer sentences; prioritization of managerial instrumentalism rather than a broad welfare orientation throughout the system; and the growth of more disciplinary, specialist, and incapacitative regimes in the prisons. To some extent, these changes can be understood as responses to changing crime patterns: while the crime rate as a whole virtually "plateaued" in the post-1985 period, crimes of violence continued to rise; and several hostage-taking incidents in 1991–92 in prisons shook the accepted wisdom that treating prisoners humanely would be reciprocated. But it is all too easy for pendulums to swing too far in policy reaction, normalizing what should be regarded as exceptional and institutionalizing crisis management. Thus, while dystopia may yet be far off, even in the Netherlands it can be said to be in view.

A. The Preconditions for Sustained Recarceration, 1985–90

Until the 1990s, having a high imprisonment rate was seen as something deeply problematic in the Netherlands, both for economic reasons and as a civilized society. Even in 1997, when the Netherlands had a Liberal Democrat minister of justice (Winnie Sorgdrager), a report from the Ministry of Justice's research center, WODC, that seeks to analyze and explain the rising imprisonment rates between 1985 and 1995 starts by arguing that we should seek to stop the "unrestrained expansion" of the prison system over that period of time (Grapendaal, Groen, and van der Heide 1997, p. 6). The authors explicitly argue for reductionist strategies that counter the most important causes of the increase. According to the researchers, neither legal changes, an increased willingness to report delinquency to the police, nor the expansion of the capacity of the police and the prosecution service could be held responsible for the increase in sentencing. Basically, they blame it on a more punitive attitude within the prosecution service, the judiciary, the legislature, the police, and the prison service (p. 59). This more punitive attitude is seen as a cause for the higher sentences for similar offenses and is in its turn influenced by the more serious character of crime in the Netherlands. Up to 1985, the rise in crime was quantitative; after 1985, it was qualitative.

This summary of crime trends by Bert Berghuis, then head of the Statistics Branch of the Ministry of Justice in 1994, goes far to explain the continued rise in the use of imprisonment even when the crime rate in general had leveled out (Berghuis 1994). In other words, until 1985 the crimes that increased the most had been mainly unsettling but largely nuisance-value crimes, such as domestic burglary, shoplifting, theft from cars and of bicycles, and vandalism. After 1985, these offenses were reined in by the policies of "norm reinforcement" recommended by the 1984 Roethof Committee and further developed by the 1985 *Society and Crime* report. For example, a Department of Crime Prevention was created, unconditional waivers of court proceedings were to be cut by 50 percent, and ticket inspection on public transport was to be far more rigorously enforced.

After 1985, the increase in crime was more keenly experienced in drug trafficking, armed robbery, and complex frauds. However, though some serious offenses conformed to this pattern, others did not (see Downes 1998, p. 152, table 1). For example, rape offenses rose by only 9 percent in 1985–90 compared with 52 percent in 1980–85. The rate of increase of other serious offenses, such as robbery, also slowed. Part of the increase of robbery had been due to the recategorization of bag snatching, which in some cases in 1977 had been termed aggravated theft but by 1989 was in all cases defined as robbery (Freeling 1993). Moreover, Margret Egelkamp (2002) found that the police in 1996 sent minor incidents of violence, especially when they were intensively discussed in the media, to the prosecutor's office, whereas they would have dismissed similar cases in 1986. She also found that bodily harm was far more easily considered to be proved in 1996 than in 1986. For these reasons she speaks of an "inflation" of the term violence in the Netherlands and concludes that a similar thing had not occurred in neighboring Germany. The combination of net widening, "up-tariffing," and the linking of crime, often spuriously, to illegal immigration was a recipe for fueling the fear of crime and an embryonic moral panic (Cohen 1972).

Other developments fed the view that "qualitative" rises in more serious crime were taking place. The trade in illicit drugs and services was seen as producing a Mecca effect for organized crime and foreign drug users and tourists. As the major entrepot for Europe, the Netherlands was inevitably a conduit for illegal and legal goods. Though the murder rate remained comparatively low, it had grown, especially in Amsterdam, in ways that could be linked with drug-related violence over territory and market share. The media in the 1980s had abandoned their traditionally circumspect mode of crime reportage and now engaged in "reality television," enabling viewers to be on-the-spot during police raids and arrests and at the scene of violent crimes.

In 1989, the first International Crime Victims Survey took place (van Dijk, Mayhew, and Killias 1990) and showed the Netherlands to have the highest crime rate of the fourteen countries involved, including the United States. The report was strategically presented at a press conference preceding the 1990 conference of the Netherlands Society of Criminology. "Although this study was criticised heavily by criminologists for its method, limitations and conclusions, the effect on public opinion was very strong. Every newspaper brought the news on the front page, and on radio and television a lot of programs had the survey as an issue for weeks. Politicians and professionals used the international survey in their own interests" (Berghuis and Franke 1992, p. 192). A second, wider survey in 1992 found the country less crime-prone than several others, England included, but the damage to national self-confidence, and to trust in liberal expertise, had been done. The traditional reductionist agenda of penal professionals, though still defended by Grapendaal, Groen, and van der Heide in 1997, was now widely seen as a sign that they were out of touch with reality.

The politics of law and order was tilted in a more punitive direction by a changing moral climate. "No left-wing politician can afford to be seen to be soft on law and order," said one criminologist in an interview in 1994, acknowledging a trend begun several years earlier (Downes 1998, p. 153). A flurry of administrative changes to the criminal justice system, which centered on the growing power of the Public Prosecution Service to coordinate and direct policy overall, set in train police reorganization that for a time left the detection of major crimes in disarray. Cases of police corruption multiplied. Interagency conflicts, formerly kept behind closed doors, now surfaced in public.

In this context, rising concern about the scale of immigration, both legal and illegal, and its links with crime, grew apace. The Muslim minority from Morocco in particular was viewed as excessively involved in street crime. A senior judge stated in an interview that he had "given up on" hopes that the younger generation of Moroccans could ever be integrated into Dutch society, whatever welfare measures were introduced (Downes 1998, p. 150). So bleak a view from so pivotal a figure symbolized a new disillusionment about the scope for ameliorative social policies to curtail social conflicts from what he termed "the huge and growing gulf between rich and poor. The Netherlands has tried very hard with social policies but it doesn't help the underclass group" (p. 153). Addressing the Muslim community as a new pillar did not work, given that the pillarized structure of the Netherlands had already weakened. Moreover, that most Muslim spiritual leaders, for example from Morocco, came for just a couple of years and knew very little of Dutch society was not helpful for the integration of the Muslim community.

Such sentiments set the scene for the *Law in Motion* report of 1990, which went far beyond the *Society and Crime* report of 1985 in condemning "modern trends in criminology" (Ministerie van Justitie 1990, p. 15) for allegedly encouraging euphemisms about criminality and abolitionist views about the criminal law. The report "dictated a change in the whole philosophy of criminal policy" (Fionda 1995, p. 120). It replaced a humane paternalism with a managerial instrumentalism, aimed at restoring credibility to the system of criminal justice, "a state of affairs which the report asserts rather than demonstrates as in crisis" (Downes 1998, p. 155). The report embodied the approach of Steenhuis rather than the earlier compromise attempt to "hold the line" of van Dijk, main author of the 1985 report. By now, however, it was van Dijk who wrote the report that combined the new managerialist approach with the harder and more moralistic views of the minister of justice, Ernst Hirsch Ballin. And, having ruled out both resocialization and social policies as the principal means of tackling the causes of crime, the report reinforced the shift to imprisonment as the ultimate mainstay of the social order:

> Evidence that the general public in the Netherlands consider the level of crime to be unacceptably high is provided by an opinion survey conducted by . . . the Ministry of Justice in March 1989. This shows that eighty five percent of Dutch nationals aged eighteen and over believed that crime was "a very serious problem" in the Netherlands. None of the other social problems such as environmental pollution, health care, unemployment and transport was regarded as being of such gravity. . . . The replacement in the Netherlands of a society divided along denominational lines by a modern consumer-oriented welfare state radically altered the position of the law. Owing to the disappearance of the social ties between individuals and to the expansion of the functions of the State, the need for measures to make, enforce and apply the law increased sharply. (Ministerie van Justitie 1990, pp. 25–26, 30).

Data on sentencing trends in the period 1983–93 bear out this view. Berghuis's summation of the trend does not capture the net increase in sentencing severity after controlling for the increase in qualitative offenses. The proportionate contribution to total custodial time served by increases in the *length* of sentence, as distinct from the volume of recorded offenses and the proportion imprisoned, varies between offenses in ways that do not match the quantitative/qualitative contrast: nil for hard drugs; 17 percent for offenses against life, that is, serious violence, including murder; 29 percent for robbery; 80 percent for burglary; and 96 percent for rape (see table 1). That these are not across-the-board increases also indicates, however, that the resistance of the Dutch judiciary to more punitive measures had by no means been abandoned.

TABLE 1

Sentencing for Serious Offenses in the Netherlands, 1983 and 1993

Offense	Total Cases (Excluding Technical Waivers)	% Prison	Mean Sentence Duration (Months)	% Policy Waivers	Total Custody Months
Hard drugs:					
1983	4,059	32	13	55	16,885
1993	7,719	29	12	35	26,862
Versus life:					
1983	568	44	27	41	6,750
1993	1,029	54	34	9	18,904
Burglary:					
1983	14,586	21	3	49	9,189
1993	12,654	24	6	16	18,221
Rape:					
1983	351	54	10	21	1,895
1993	357	56	20	12	3,998
Robbery:					
1983	1,494	48	10	27	7,171
1993	3,086	55	15	6	25,460

SOURCE.—1983: Downes (1988, 1998); 1993: Ministerie van Justitie (1994a), tables 6, 9, 10, 16, 17. Figures recalculated to yield percentages net of technical waivers. Note: First published, with column heads misaligned, in Downes (1998, p. 158).

B. The "Multicultural Drama" and the Shift toward Zero Tolerance

With the report *Law in Motion* a distinctly more moralistic tone was added to the managerial discourse introduced five years before. Dutch policy documents traditionally described crime in a rather neutral manner, but from now on it was condemned explicitly. The ideal of a neutral, rational state that commanded respect in the 1960s was losing support, and politicians started to demand a moral entrepreneurial role for the state (van Swaaningen 1997, pp. 177–81). Playing the "tough on crime" card gradually became a key issue in electoral campaigns.

By 2002 every political party, from the Far Right to the Radical Left, had an elaborate paragraph on crime and insecurity in its electoral program. Moreover, these paragraphs were similar in their orientation: more punitive responses, more prevention, and early intervention, within the limits of due process (Brants 2002).

The number of parliamentary debates on crime and insecurity rose from fifteen in 1995 to almost sixty in 2003, a fourfold increase in less than a decade (Keijzers 2005, p. 90). Thus, from the late 1990s on, there is some support for the "governance through crime" thesis in the Netherlands (Tonry 2001, p. 524; van Swaaningen 2005).

This development, in which crime and insecurity are central themes in the political debate, was accompanied by the shift from a rather general disbelief in the effectiveness of prison sentences to a renewed belief in prison as the obvious, sound reaction to crime. "Prison works," albeit mainly as a symbol of collective condemnation and not so much because of its actual effects (van Ruller 1993). Similarly, community safety also gains another dimension. In most local plans for community safety, safety was no longer linked to positive ideals, such as a social policy guaranteeing everyone full participation in society, as a result of which a number of social causes (e.g., marginalization and exclusion) are ignored. Not seldom, it was nearly exclusively interpreted as taking action against those who threaten the citizen's *feelings* of security. Apart from people who really menace or rob, here it was also a question of beggars, streetwalkers, and "addicts avoiding treatment": in short, all those whom the law-abiding citizen considered an "antisocial" irritant (van Swaaningen 2005).

After terrorism, the political debate on crime largely focused on mischief in the public domain. Little distinction was made between crime and nuisance, and politicians had unwarrantedly high expectations of "strong intervention." Not only were general nuisances, incivilities, and disorder treated as crime, but also the limits between policing and intelligence gathering in relation to acts of war were blurring—especially with respect to the "war on [Muslim] terrorism."

In contrast to Garland (2001), who discerns a process in which crime is "defined up" and "defined down," depending on the political context, in the Netherlands a process of defining crime down unevenly took place in the 1980s (notably with respect to petty criminality), but the 1990s and 2000s witnessed a continual tendency to define crime up. Examples in the public domain are the criminalization of begging, alcohol or cannabis consumption, gatherings of groups of homeless or youths in certain urban areas, public urination, and insubordination to police officers.

"Governance through crime" can be understood only if we pay attention to the contemporary process by which crime was increasingly situated among "other people," that is, people who are not like "us." Through this process, punitive responses become far more acceptable than if one sees an offender as a person basically like oneself.

Because ethnic minorities are the most victim-prone of such "othering," we need to pay attention to the changed attitude toward immigrants in the Netherlands. By the turn of the millennium, the multicultural ideal was seen to have resulted in a multicultural melodrama, in which most ethnic minorities were not integrated into Dutch society at all, undermine social cohesion and social control even further, and "just cause trouble."[5] In this context, the public debate on crime control was often defined in terms of the white Dutch against them, the foreigners who make Dutch lives increasingly unpleasant. Crime was implicitly portrayed as a problem outside of Dutch society rather than as a problem rooted in social and economic relations, as was hitherto the common vision. Many journalists—and particularly columnists—took issue with the supposedly soft approach of the past, on which many contemporary problems were blamed.

Three events contributed to a social climate of fear and rancor: the attack on the Twin Towers in New York in 2001, the murder of the right-wing populist political leader Pim Fortuyn by a radical environmentalist in 2002, and the murder of film director Theo van Gogh—who had made a film about the allegedly misogynous nature of Islam—by a Dutch-Moroccan Muslim fundamentalist in 2004.[6] The subsequent fear and moral panic resulted in an "Islamophobia" that varied from attempts by schools to exclude girls with headscarves, a proposal for a "stop to immigration" in Rotterdam, cultural pleas to punish differently immigrant youths who commit misdemeanors, a number of—rather shadowy—terrorist processes, arsons in churches, mosques, and Islamic schools, ever stiffer regulations for asylum seekers and other immigrants, and new antiterrorist legislation that allowed far-reaching infringements of civil rights.

Until the 1990s, it was not done to address social problems along ethnic lines. This taboo gradually disappeared, and since then newspaper articles about street nuisances, juvenile gangs, and terrorism seldom lack a reference to the cultural background of offenders. Criminological analyses of a criminal justice system that was biased against

[5] This term was originally launched by the journalist Paul Scheffer in an article in *NRC Handelsblad* (2000), but it soon became the new political buzzword.

[6] Van Gogh often took a very polemic position in the debate on Islam and multiculturalism. As a filmmaker, he was, however, more subtle and nuanced. His last film, written by the Somali member of the Dutch Parliament, Ayaan Hirsi Ali (an apostate, who went into hiding after the assassination of van Gogh), showed a battered wife with Koran texts written on her body.

ethnic minorities were less in evidence after 1990, and large numbers
of studies began to demonstrate a far larger involvement of various
ethnic minority groups in crime, even when corrected for demographic
and socioeconomic differences (de Haan 1997; Junger-Tas 1997; Bovenkerk 2003; Tweede Kamer 2004; Engbersen, van der Leun, and de
Boom, in this volume).[7]

In public debate, high crime rates had long been linked to the large
number of immigrants, but it took politicians until the late 1990s to
agree with "public opinion" that immigrants were responsible for the
majority of street offenses because they never wanted to adapt to Dutch
society. The 1997 report *Criminality and the Integration of Ethnic Minorities* included proposals for a broad range of measures (from educational support for immigrant "problem families" to specific detention
regimes for immigrant youths) designed to stem the overrepresentation
in crime of certain groups of young immigrants (Ministeries van Justitie and BZK 1997).

A parliamentary inquiry was started in 2003 on the question whether
Dutch integration policy had failed. The conclusions presented in the
2004 report *Building Bridges*, that integration had "been wholly or partially successful," came under severe fire in Parliament as naive even
before the parliamentarians could have known the content of the report
(Tweede Kamer 2004).

Experts on migration issues argued, however, that there was no obvious link between lack of integration in Dutch society and crime-
proneness. Many ethnic minority youths who committed crimes were,
on the contrary, all too integrated, in the sense that they knew exactly
how Dutch society works, but simply felt unaccepted and unrespected
(e.g., de Haan and Bovenkerk 1995).

That the percentage of foreign-born detainees in Dutch prisons has
remained stable at around 50 percent for the last two decades was
seldom mentioned in this respect (see fig. 6; cf. van Swaaningen and
de Jonge 1995). It is, however, a very high number that does not tell
very much about the ethnic mix of the prison population. The overwhelming "color" of the detainees is dark, although this is not reflected

---

[7] The most elaborate survey of these developments is probably given in the final report
"Building Bridges" (*Bruggen bouwen*) of the parliamentary committee on the integration
of ethnic minorities into Dutch society (Tweede Kamer 2004). The whole report—in
Dutch—and a thirty-one-page summary in English are available online at http://
www.tweedekamer.nl/organisatie/voorlichting/commissies/eindrapport_integratiebeleid
.jsp.

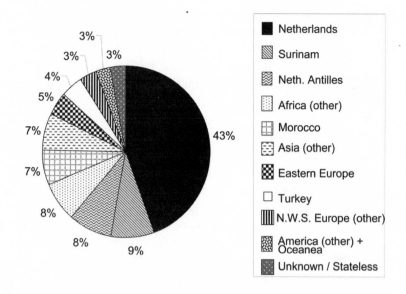

FIG. 6.—Country of birth of detainees in the Dutch prison system. Source: DJI, 2004

in statistics since people are registered only on the basis of their country of birth. The composition has slightly changed; there are more
eastern European and African prisoners, and of the traditional migrant
groups the number of Antilleans has strongly risen, the number of
Surinamese remains high, and those of Moroccans and Turks are
slightly decreasing—if only because higher percentages of them are
now Dutch-born.

The most significant change in all likelihood is that in the 1980s
this overrepresentation would have been explained as the result of a
selective criminal justice system in concert with the underprivileged
position of many migrant groups. Today, however, it is more readily
accepted that it is a true reflection of a real overrepresentation in criminal behavior by these groups. It is hard to say which of these two is
correct. The limited research shows that it is probably both, but also
that the possibility of a racial bias of the criminal justice system and
counterevidence—of lower crime rates of certain ethnic minorities in
a certain era—are omitted in many studies. Moreover, the whole issue
is so blurred by misunderstood ideas on causality, false comparisons,
and generalizations that it is very hard to give an exact picture (de
Haan and Bovenkerk 1993).

C. Acting Out and Actuarial Justice, 1990–2005

In the twentieth century there was no real conservative tradition in Dutch politics. The political turnover provoked by Pim Fortuyn resulted in neoconservative pleas for a strong, interventionist state that contested neoliberal ideas on governance of the 1990s. The enormous increase of the prison system is an important symbol of this new vigor. In 2004, 123.5 people per 100,000 inhabitants were detained.[8] With figures such as thirty-three in 1987 and eighteen in 1973, the Netherlands has had the highest increase in the number of detainees in western Europe (see fig. 1). Longer sentences on the whole, extra punishment for systematic offenders, an intensified "war on drugs," more incidents of serious violence, broader use of the qualification "serious violent crime," and the incarceration of street people who cannot pay fines given for being a nuisance in the public domain are the main causes of this steep rise.

Another important factor is that, with the principle of one prisoner to a cell having been abandoned, the number of prisoners is no longer limited by the formal capacity of a facility (van Ruller and Beijers 1995; uit Beijerse and van Swaaningen 2004). All problems are simply defined as a capacity shortage, and there is little talk of too much sanctioning—that is, a typical strategy of denial, to put it in Garland's terms (2001, pp. 131–35). It is a doubly dangerous denial, as abandoning a principle of such long standing, having quadrupled prison capacity to respect it, opens up the possibility of doubling the prison population at a stroke. That the one to a cell principle was arguably the most important shield against undue expansion of imprisonment, and the fear of losing its relatively humane character, explains the stubborn resistance of prison governors and staff to its attenuation, a resistance that has now evidently been overwhelmed.

"Acting out" against crime and insecurity accompanied the "adaptive strategies" of crime management of the 1980s (cf. Garland 2001, pp. 113–27). The glue between these two strategies is provided by a third kind of discourse: that of actuarialism and its new penology (Feeley and Simon 1992). The old penology is rooted in a concern for individuals and preoccupied with such concepts as guilt, responsibility, and

---

[8] If we exclude people detained in forensic psychiatric TBS clinics, youth prisons, and deportation centers, the number is 99.8 detainees per 100,000 inhabitants. See http://www.coe.int/T/E/Legal_affairs/Legal_co-operation/Prisons_and_alternatives/Bulletin/Bulletin.asp#TopOfPage and http://www.dji.nl/main.asp?pid=40.

obligation, as well as diagnoses, intervention, and treatment of the individual offender. In the new penology, crime is seen as a normal phenomenon, and the key problem is how to manage it efficiently. The answer to this question is risk calculation concerned with techniques for identifying, classifying, and managing groups sorted by levels of dangerousness. A key document that embodies the actuarial rationale of the present penal policy is the "Trajectory Modernisation Application of Sanctions." The revealing title of the report that accompanies this trajectory is "Better, Different and Cheaper" (Wartna, Baas, and Beenakkers 2004). Applying "what works" criteria to the Dutch situation, the document investigates the international literature on the effectiveness of various sanctions, the possibility of cheaper alternatives, and the effects of a more austere prison regime. The authors are careful in their conclusions on the effectiveness of various sanctions. We can say something meaningful in this respect only if we are specific about the different circumstances and the questions of why, for whom, and how. On the latter two issues, the authors offer support to the government's policy (with respect to creating more special regimes) as well as critical points (with respect to budget cuts for prison labor and social activities).

There has also been a shift in the "depth of imprisonment" (Downes 1988, pp. 163–88). The 1994 report *Effective Detention* (Ministerie van Justitie 1994*b*) introduced a policy that, in addition to a respect for human dignity, had as its starting point a definite emphasis on security and efficiency. It was thought that a wide-ranging and undefined offer of activities and facilities for resocialization was no longer suitable for a prison population that, supposedly, consisted more and more of problem groups such as dangerous escapees, psychologically disturbed offenders, addicts, long-term prisoners, and detainees posing control risks. Verhagen (1999, pp. 17–18) argues that this changed prison population has been the overture for the introduction of all kinds of "special regimes." We doubt whether this was the only, or even the most important, reason. The political desire to stress the expressive character of punishment and the need to keep the budget for the prison system under control in a period of unprecedented expansion seem at least equally important.

A "standard regime" was introduced, highly structured in form without any "welfare frills." Work forms its central tenet beside a number of legally guaranteed activities such as outside time, visits, recreation, and sport. Only suitably motivated prisoners would be accorded basic educational opportunities as an impetus for a workplace. This standard regime was defined as austere but dignified. Two-thirds of unsentenced detainees and half of those already sentenced take part in this standard regime (uit Beijerse and van Swaaningen 2004).

Separate sections have been created for the previously mentioned "problem groups." These have also increased in number since 1994, as has the number of acronyms they are identified with. For addicts there is the VBA, or Addicts Supervision Section. In this section addicts who wish to kick their habit follow a special supervisory program of six months' duration and are systematically subjected to stringent drug usage tests. For detainees who present control problems because of their aggressive behavior, there is the LAA, or National Isolation Section. For psychologically disturbed prisoners, an ever-increasing group because of a lack of facilities in forensic psychiatric TBS clinics, there is the IBA or individual supervisory section. Here relatively intensive therapeutic supervision is undertaken and an environment created with the fewest possible stimuli. There is also the BZA, or special care section, for people with special needs, and the JOVO or department for young adults, youths in the eighteen to twenty-four-year age group. A special place is reserved for the EBI, a maximum security institution, for potential escapees. The EBI has been criticized, and the Dutch government has been admonished about it by the European Committee for the Prevention of Torture and Inhuman or Degrading Treatment and Punishment and the European Court for Human Rights (case of *Van der Ven v. the Netherlands*, application no. 50901/99; case of *Lorsé v. the Netherlands*, application no. 52750/99).

An additional regime has been added since 1994, which since 1996 has been applied broadly to temporary detainees, people with short sentences, and those who have not paid their fines. This austere regime was a result of the debate in the mid-1990s about security problems in the large cities. It was meant for the large group, typically drug users committing small-property crimes who, because of "cell shortages," were turned away. With the construction of cheaper, more austere cells, this group could be kept off the streets. Despite a 1998 evaluation, which indicated that there were few savings and that those savings did not compensate for the loss of detention conditions, the more austere regime has been bedded down in the Penitentiary Principles Act (discussed in Bosch [1999]). Some 1,000 austere cells are in use in custodial institutions.

The latest development is the introduction in 2006 of the "New Institution." This is a prison in which prisoners are electronically monitored twenty-four hours per day, fewer staff are required, and less room per inmate because the space is used in a more efficient way: prisoners are not in their cells during the day and cells are occupied by more than one person.

D. Incapacitation and the Protection of Society

The maximum security prison EBI was the forerunner of a trend that has become apparent over the last few years with the creation of regimes and measures for specific groups. The introduction in 2001 of the regulation SOV (Penal Detention of Addicts) is the first since the introduction of the hospital order TBR in 1928, the creation of a detention measure aimed at a specific group (uit Beijerse 2002). The development of this measure is not related solely to the protection of society, but also to the nature of the target group and its inherent problems. It is, in other words, oriented toward social defense, selective incapacitation, and actuarial justice.

With the introduction of the SOV measure, such practices as a certain measure of "voluntary choice" and the opportunity to be heard by a magistrate disappeared (uit Beijerse 1999). It is no longer a question of a request by the addict himself or herself, and it is not the magistrate who determines the provisional detention, but the judge in court who determines whether the legal measure is imposed. Even drug addicts who do not want to kick their habits can have this measure imposed on them.

That raised the question of how effective the measure would be. Its nature contains negative elements for the suspect. The time spent in detention is not reduced by time spent in pretrial detention, and the judge can also add an additional sentence; the application of the measure does not have to have any relationship to the seriousness of the offense. These features have attracted critical reviews from judicial circles. This measure is based as much on the principle of "tackling a societal nuisance" as on tackling the addiction problem; as such, that purpose is said by some not to justify incarceration (Bleichrodt 1995; Mevis 1996).

The SOV measure in the first instance was introduced only in four institutions, and an evaluation of the experience had not been completed when this was written. During the last, open phase of the project there was a distinct lack of the required municipal support and assistance. However, some time before the first SOV participants were released, and therefore also well before the experiment's evaluation (van 't Land et al. 2005), the government announced its intention to introduce a legal proposal for the introduction of the measure in order to be able to incarcerate habitual offenders (*Inrichting voor Stelselmatige Daders* or ISD). In this "stripped down" SOV measure, the aim of resocialization is pushed firmly into the background. The main aim seems to be fighting social nuisances (Elzinga and Gaarthuis 2004). The ISD Act of 2004 allows extra punishment to be inflicted because someone is a systematic offender—regardless of the seriousness of the offense. In a first calculation of the costs and benefits of this new measure, Blokland, Bijleveld, and Nieuwbeerta (2003) concluded that if one aims at a kind of Dutch approach to "three strikes and you're out," the workload of judges and magistrates will be reduced considerably (by about 30 percent), but the number of required cells will have to increase some seven times, up to 700 detainees per 100,000 inhabitants.

The speed with which this law was steered through Parliament is matched by the speed with which the Emergency Law Drug Couriers was adopted. The law was introduced into Parliament on January 25, 2002, and a little more than a month later it appeared in the *Law Gazette*. The background was the debate surrounding the large number of drug capsule swallowers and body packers arrested at Amsterdam's Schiphol Airport. In order to retain its credibility with the public and to give a signal to that effect vis-à-vis drug couriers—a frequently used term with politicians these days—it was decided to detain these people at all times. With this new law, which excludes this group from the guarantees set by the Penitentiary Principles Act, it has become possible to construct quite rapidly new detention centers—which as far as construction and regime are concerned do not have to meet as many requirements as traditional prisons. Its regime consists of an extremely short day program and offers even fewer opportunities for outside time and work than the already austere regimes in prisons. Detainees, whether sentenced or not, are kept together, and staff are acquired from employment agencies.

An evaluation painted a very negative picture of the detention center, the expertise of the staff, and the perception of the detention itself

(Maalsté et al. 2002). The number of capsule swallowers and body packers is quite small in comparison with other drug couriers, and mixing serious and not-so-serious cases in the same barracks has led to feelings of insecurity by the staff and by the detainees.

The new law did nothing to stem the flood of capsule swallowers and body packers, and so many were arrested that their numbers were putting pressure on other prisons. In spite of these concerns, the law was extended for another two years in 2003. The justice minister acknowledged that the law had not had any effect, but that he needed it to get some understanding of the influx. A good half year later, however, he admitted that it did nothing to stop the influx and that he would review his policy with regard to tackling the drug courier problem.

In 2005 the emergency law was withdrawn, and capsule swallowers and body packers caught with less than three kilos are sent back, as of old, to their country of origin—with the stamp "undesired alien" in their passport. Physically, the emergency penitentiary provisions have, however, remained in place; they have even been integrated into the normal prison system. In this way, the emergency law that allowed the use of these cheap and austere cells for a special purpose led to a permanent loss in quality of the regular prison system (Boone 2005).

III. From Where to Where?

From an exemplary penal-welfare approach from the 1950s to the 1970s, the penal climate in the Netherlands, especially since the early 1990s, has been marked by a very different approach. The penal system is mainly informed by managerial (leading to budget cuts), moral (leading to higher penalties), and actuarial (leading to selective incapacitation) notions. The process of decarceration through 1973 was followed by a relatively slow increase of prison capacity through 1987 and an enormous expansion since then. The principal goal of penalties has shifted from resocialization to incapacitation. These changes coincided with the decline of the welfare state in the 1980s, the emergence of a neoliberal entrepreneurial model of government at a distance in the 1990s, and the emergence of neoconservative ideas of a severe, interventionist state in the new millennium.

Over the last decade, the regime in prisons and custodial institutions has also made prison conditions for most detainees significantly more harsh as a result of policies driven by efficiency and security. The introduction of special regimes had an actuarial and managerial rationale. An urban backlash has resulted from the enormous emphasis being placed on street nuisances and the related policy of getting rid of beggars, addicts avoiding treatment, and prostitutes. The selective incapacitation of people creating these nuisances had an effect on prison institutions: all those plucked off the streets who can neither pay a fine nor be permanently removed from the Netherlands finally end up there.

To some extent, the huge expansion of prisons can be viewed as an inevitable result of the increasing seriousness of crime in the Netherlands, but that development stabilized some fifteen years ago. The increased austerity of prisons can be explained as a necessary means of keeping prison expenditure within limits. If we leave such technical explanations aside and interpret those developments rather as a sign of increased punitiveness, Dutch exceptionalism as a relative penal utopia no longer exists. Despite all the differences in time, size, and intensity, the Netherlands is following much the same lines as David Garland (2001) analyzes in his *Culture of Control* for the United States and England. If we follow Garland's analysis and consider punishment to be a cultural agent, the current message is that the Dutch have purged themselves of the misplaced leniency of the past and are no longer afraid to punish. Hans Boutellier (2004) has argued that the new penal policy implies a new civilizing imperative—protecting society—that replaces the old one—taking good care of the underprivileged and outcasts. There is of course nothing very new about that approach, which, in many ways, is a return to the ideas of the late nineteenth century "Modern" school of "social defense" (see, e.g., Peters 1986; van Swaaningen 1997, pp. 29–44).

When we determine that the driving force behind the expansion, the more austere approach, and the many special regimes is the result of "control problems," "political signals," and a simple "tit for tat" stance, while legal principles and questions of the regimes are dismissed lightly, we must conclude that a social and political hardening contribute considerably to a far tougher penal climate in the Netherlands. Whether we are on the road to dystopia may be a matter of political appreciation, but if we adopt Lucia Zedner's qualifications of the culture of control as "grimly pessimistic" and "determinedly dystopic," we must unfortunately subscribe to that view of the Dutch predicament.

REFERENCES

Bax, Erik H. 1990. *Modernization and Cleavage in Dutch Society: A Study of Long Term Economic and Social Change.* Groningen: University of Groningen.

Beijerse, Jolande uit. 1999. "Eindelijk aandacht voor recidiverende drugsverslaafden?; het breekbare ideaal van de SOV." *Sancties* 1999:217–26.

———. 2002. "De SOV-maatregel in uitvoering in de Rotterdamse stadsgevangenis." *Sancties* 2002:330–39.

Beijerse, Jolande uit, and René van Swaaningen. 2004. "Gevangen in Nederland." *Panopticon* 25:172–86.

Berghuis, Bert. 1994. "Punitiviteitsfeiten." In *Hoe punitief is Nederland?* edited by Martin Moerings. Arnhem: Gouda Quint.

Berghuis, Bert, and Herman Franke. 1992. "Dutch Tolerance under Pressure." *Tijdschrift voor Criminologie* 34(3):189–97.

Bleichrodt, F. W. 1995. "Eerherstel voor de Rijkswerkinrichting?" *Sancties* 1995: 313–17.

Blokland, Arjan, Catrien Bijleveld, and Paul Nieuwbeerta. 2003. "Kosten en baten van de invoering van three strikes and you're in Nederland; een scenariostudie." *Tijdschrift voor Criminologie* 45(2):178–92.

Boone, Miranda. 2005. "Noodwet drugskoeriers." In *Detentie: Gevangen in Nederland,* edited by E. R. Muller and P. C. Vegter. Alphen a/d Rijn: Kluwer.

Bosch, A. G. 1999. "Het sober regime." *Sancties* 1999:146–54.

Boutellier, Hans. 2004. "Beschavingspretenties van straf en herstel." In *Straf en herstel: Ethische reflecties over sanctiedoeleinden,* edited by Bas van Stokkom. The Hague: BJU.

Bovenkerk, Frank. 2003. "Taboe in de criminologie." *Proces* 82(5):242–51.

Brants, Chrisje. 2002. "Criminologie en politiek: Een ongemakkelijke LAT-relatie." *Tijdschrift voor Criminologie* 44(1):2–24.

Brants, Kees. 1986. "Criminaliteit, politiek en criminele politiek; de Haagse receptie van een nieuwe heilsleer." *Tijdschrift voor Criminologie* 28(5/6): 219–35.

Cavadino, Michael, and James Dignan. 2006. *Penal Systems: A Comparative Approach.* London: Sage.

Cohen, Stanley. 1972. *Folk Devils and Moral Panics: The Creation of Mods and Rockers.* London: MacGibbon and Kee.

Commissie Roethof. 1984. *Interimrapport van de commissie kleine criminaliteit.* The Hague: Staatsuitgeverij.

de Haan, Willem. 1990. *The Politics of Redress: Crime, Punishment and Penal Abolition.* London: Unwin Hyman.

———. 1997. "Minorities and Crime in the Netherlands." In *Minorities and Crime: Diversity and Similarity across Europe and the United States,* edited by Ineke Haen Marshall. London: Sage.

de Haan, Willem, and Frank Bovenkerk. 1993. "Moedwil en misverstand: Overschatting en overschatting van allochtone criminaliteit in Nederland." *Tijdschrift voor Criminologie* 35(3):277–300.

———. 1995. "Sociale integratie en criminaliteit." In *Sferen van integratie:*

Naar een gedifferentieerd allochtonenbeleid, edited by Godfried Engbersen and René Gabriëls. Meppel: Boom.

Downes, David. 1988. *Contrasts in Tolerance: Post-war Penal Policy in the Netherlands and England and Wales.* Oxford: Clarendon.

———. 1998. "The Buckling of the Shields: Dutch Penal Policy 1985–1995." In *Comparing Prison Systems*, edited by R. Weiss and N. South. Amsterdam: Gordon and Breach.

Egelkamp, Margarethe M. 2002. "Inflation von Gewalt? Strafrechtliche und kriminologische analysen von qualifikationsentscheidungen in den Niederlanden und Deutschland." PhD dissertation, University of Groningen, Department of Criminal Law and Criminology.

Elias, Norbert. 1978, 1982. *The Civilizing Process.* Vol. 1: *The History of Manners.* Vol. 2: *State Formation and Civilization.* Oxford: Blackwell. (Originally published 1939.)

Elzinga, H. K., and R. S. T. Gaarthuis. 2004. "Beveiliging tegen gevaar dat overlast heet." *Sancties* 2004:35–49.

Engbersen, Godfried, Joanne van der Leun, and Jan de Boom. In this volume. "The Fragmentation of Migration and Crime in the Netherlands."

Feeley, Malcolm M., and Jonathan Simon. 1992. "The New Penology." *Criminology* 30(4):452–74.

Fionda, Julia. 1995. *Public Prosecutors and Discretion: A Comparative Study.* Oxford: Clarendon.

Franke, Herman. 1995. *The Emancipation of Prisoners: A Socio-historical Analysis of the Dutch Prison Experience.* Edinburgh: Edinburgh University Press.

Freeling, Wouter. 1993. "De straf op tasjesroof; hoe het strafklimaat strenger werd." *Proces* 72(5):76–82.

Garland, David. 1985. *Punishment and Welfare: A History of Penal Strategies.* Aldershot, U.K.: Gower.

———. 1990. *Punishment and Modern Society.* Oxford: Clarendon.

———. 2001. *The Culture of Control: Crime and Social Order in Contemporary Society.* Oxford: Oxford University Press.

Goudsblom, Johan. 1967. *Dutch Society.* New York: Random House.

Grapendaal, M., P. P. Groen, and W. van der Heide. 1997. *Duur en volume. Ontwikkeling van de onvoorwaardelijke vrijheidsstraf tussen 1985 en 1995: Feiten en verklaringen.* Series Onderzoek en beleid, no. 163. The Hague: Ministry of Justice, Research and Documentation Centre.

Hobsbawm, Eric. 1994. *Age of Extremes: The Short Twentieth Century, 1914–1991.* London: Michael Joseph.

Howard, John. 1784. *The State of the Prison in England and Wales: With Preliminary Observations and an Account of Some Foreign Prisons and Hospitals.* 3rd. ed., rev. Warrington, U.K.: Eyres.

Junger-Tas, Josine. 1997. "Ethnic Minorities and Criminal Justice in the Netherlands." In *Ethnicity, Crime, and Immigration: Comparative and Cross-National Perspectives*, edited by Michael Tonry. Chicago: University of Chicago Press.

Junger-Tas, Josine, and Marianne Junger. In this volume. "The Dutch Criminological Enterprise."

Keijzers, Arjan P. H. 2005. "Nederland: Vrij veilig. De opkomst van het thema veiligheid in de Nederlandse samenleving." Master's thesis, Erasmus University Rotterdam, Department of Sociology.

Kelk, Constantijn. 1995. "Criminal Justice in the Netherlands." In *Criminal Justice in Europe: A Comparative Study*, edited by C. Harding et al. Oxford: Clarendon.

Lijphart, Arend. 1968. *The Politics of Accommodation: Pluralism and Democracy in the Netherlands*. Berkeley: University of California Press.

Maalsté, Nicole, Ingeborg Janssen, Esther van Fessum, and Arnt Mein. 2002. *Noodvoorziening drugskoeriers: Tussenrapportage van de evaluatie van de Tijdelijke wet noodcapaciteit drugskoeriers*. The Hague: E S and E.

Mevis, Paul A. M. 1996. "Vrijheidsbeneming ter bestrijding van overlast; inderdaad uniek drugsbeleid." *Sancties* 1996:208–16.

Ministerie van Justitie. 1947. *Report of the Committee for the Further Development of the Prison System*. The Hague: Ministry of Justice. (Dutch original: *Rapport van de Commissee voor de Verdere Uitbouw van het Gevangeniswezen*.) The Hague: Staatsuitgeverij.

———. 1985. *Society and Crime: A Policy Plan for the Future*. The Hague: Ministry of Justice. (Dutch original: *Samenleving en criminaliteit: Een beleidsplan voor de komende jaren*.) The Hague: Tweede Kamer, vergaderjaar 1984–85, 18 995, nos. 1, 2.

———. 1990. *Law in Motion: A Policy Plan for Justice in the Years Ahead*. The Hague: Ministry of Justice. (Dutch original: *Recht in beweging: Een beleidsplan voor de komende jaren*.) The Hague: Tweede Kamer, vergaderjaar 1990–91, 21 829, no. 1.

———. 1994a. *Prosecution and Trial of Indictable Offenses in the Kingdom of the Netherlands*. The Hague: Ministerie van Justitie.

———. 1994b. *Werkzame detentie: Beleidsnota voor het gevangeniswezen*. The Hague: Tweede Kamer, vergaderjaar 1993–94, nos. 10, 11.

Ministeries van Justitie and BZK. 1997. *Criminaliteit in relatie tot de integratie van etnische minderheden*. The Hague: Tweede Kamer, vergaderjaar 2001–2, 28 282, nos. 1, 2.

Peters, Antonie A. G. 1986. "Main Currents in Criminal Law Theory." In *Criminal Law in Action*, edited by Jan van Dijk, Charles Haffmans, Frits Rüter, Julian Schutte, and Simon Stolwijk. Arnhem: Gouda Quint.

Reijntjes, Jan M., and Dick H. van Ekelenburg. 2005. "Heenzendingen." In *Detentie: Gevangen in Nederland*, edited by E. R. Muller and P. C. Vegter. Alphen a/d Rijn: Kluwer.

Rijksen, Rijk. 1958. *Meningen van gedetineerden over de strafrechtspleging*. Assen: Van Gorcum.

Rutherford, Andrew. 1986. *Prisons and the Process of Justice*. Oxford: Oxford University Press.

———. 1996. *Transforming Criminal Policy*. Winchester, U.K.: Waterside.

Schama, Simon. 1987. *The Embarrassment of Riches: An Interpretation of Dutch Culture in the Golden Age*. London: Collins.

Scheffer, Paul. 2000. "Het multiculturele drama." *NRC Handelsblad* (January 29).

Schmid, Alex P., and Janny de Graaf. 1982. *Violence as Communication: Insurgent Terrorism and the Western News.* London: Sage.

Steenhuis, Dato W. 1977. *General Deterrence and Drunken Driving.* The Hague: Ministry of Justice, Research and Documentation Centre.

————. 1984. "Strafrechtelijk optreden; een stapje terug en een sprong voorwaarts." *Delikt en Delinkwent* 14(1):395–414; 14(2):497–512.

————. 1986. "Coherence and Coordination in the Administration of Justice." In *Criminal Law in Perspective: An Overview of Current Issues in Western Societies,* edited by Jan van Dijk and Charles Haffmans. Arnhem: Gouda Quint.

Tonry, Michael. 2001. "Symbol, Substance and Severity in Western Penal Policies." *Punishment and Society* 3(4):517–36.

Tweede Kamer. 1982. *Taak en toekomst van het Nederlands gevangeniswezen.* The Hague: Tweede Kamer, vergaderjaar 1981–82, 17 539, nos. 1, 2.

————. 2004. *Bruggen bouwen: Eindrapport van de tijdelijke commissie onderzoek integratiebeleid.* The Hague: Tweede Kamer vergaderjaar 2003–4, 28 689, nos. 8, 9.

Vagg, Jon. 1994. *Prison Systems: A Comparative Study on Accountability in England, France, Germany, and the Netherlands.* Oxford: Oxford University Press.

van de Bunt, Henk, and René van Swaaningen. 2005. "Privatisering van de veiligheidszorg." In *Privatisering van veiligheid,* edited by Laurens W. Winkel, Jacques J. M. Jansen, Heiko O. Kerkmeester, Ruud J. P. Kottenhage, and Vincent Mul. The Hague: BJU.

van Dijk, Jan J. M., Pat Mayhew, and Martin Killias. 1990. *Experiences of Crime across the World: Key Findings of the 1989 International Crime Survey.* Deventer: Kluwer.

van Ruller, Sibo. 1993. "Het irrationele van strafrechtelijke sancties." *Tijdschrift voor Criminologie* 35(4):336–50.

van Ruller, Sibo, and Guillaume Beijers. 1995. "Trends in detentie; twee eeuwen gevangenisstatistiek." *Justitiële Verkenningen* 21(6):35–52.

van Swaaningen, René. 1997. *Critical Criminology—Visions from Europe.* London: Sage.

————. 2000. "Back to the 'Iron Cage': The Example of the Dutch Probation Service." In *Criminal Policy in Transition,* edited by Penny Green and Andrew Rutherford. Oxford: Hart.

————. 2005. "Public Safety and the Management of Fear." *Theoretical Criminology* 9(2):289–305.

van Swaaningen, René, and Gerard de Jonge. 1995. "The Dutch Prison System and Penal Policy in the 1990s; from Humanitarian Paternalism to Penal Business Management." In *Western European Penal Systems: A Critical Anatomy,* edited by Mick Ryan, Joe Sim, and Vincenzo Ruggiero. London: Sage.

van 't Land, Hedda, Karel van Duivenbooden, Annicka van der Plas, and Judith Wolf. 2005. *Opgevangen onder dwang: Procesevaluatie strafrechtelijke opvang verslaafden.* Utrecht: Trimbos Institute.

Verhagen, J. J. L. M. 1999. "Het Nederlandse gevangeniswezen: Uitgebreid en ingschikt." *Justitiële Verkenningen* 25(1):9–24.

Wartna, B. S. J., N. J. Baas, and E. M. Beenakkers. 2004. *Beter, anders en goedkoper: Een literatuurverkenning ten behoeve van het traject modernisering sanctietoepassing*. The Hague: Ministry of Justice, Research and Documentation Center.

Zedner, Lucia. 2002. "Dangers and Dystopias in Penal Theories." *Oxford Journal of Legal Studies* 22(2):341–66.

Ybo Buruma

Dutch Tolerance: On Drugs, Prostitution, and Euthanasia

ABSTRACT

Tolerance as a way to defer negative reactions to things that are not morally approved is a core characteristic of Dutch society. Since the 1970s tolerance has had important manifestations in cultural and legal settings. In Dutch criminal justice policy, tolerance not only refers generally to leniency regarding (petty) crime but also means that government in some circumstances does not prosecute specified infractions of statutory law. This tradition made possible distinctive Dutch ways of handling problems such as drugs, prostitution, and euthanasia. Dutch tolerance makes it possible to differentiate between dangerous and less dangerous forms of questionable behavior and to focus less on moral judgments. Tolerance has not impeded efforts against organized crime, nor has it much influenced levels of drug abuse or medical end-of-life decisions. Dutch policies in some of these fields are more effective than those in other Western countries. Rising criticism of legal tolerance coincides with a decline of cultural tolerance in general. Some blame official tolerance for recent ethnic difficulties involving the rapidly growing Muslim minority.

Tolerance has long been a characteristic of Dutch culture, but recently something seems to have changed. Obituaries on Dutch tolerance could be read after the provocative Dutch filmmaker Theo van Gogh, distant relative of the painter, was slaughtered by a Muslim fanatic on November 2, 2004. After shooting van Gogh from his bicycle, the killer shot him again and then took a bread knife and tried to saw off his head. Finally, with another knife, he pinned a letter to van Gogh's chest. It was to Ayaan Hirsi Ali, a Dutch member of Parliament of Somali descent, who was raised as a Muslim and who wrote the script

Ybo Buruma is dean of the Faculty of Law and chair in criminal law at Radboud University Nijmegen and honorary justice of the Court of Appeals in Arnhem.

for the movie *Submission* in which Koranic verses were written on the bodies of naked women. The killer called Hirsi Ali a soldier of evil. Van Gogh directed the movie, which was meant to speak out against the oppression of women in Muslim culture. The movie and the murder are often discussed as a sequence of events that shows that Dutch tolerance has gone adrift. I do not think it has. Those events are also a horrific example of changing sensibilities in a postmodern society encountering its multicultural boundaries.

The Dutch are not unique in this respect. The troubles of early 2006 after a Danish journal published cartoons considered offensive by many Muslims can be understood in much the same way.

However, the van Gogh murder reveals difficulties in the concept of tolerance itself. Sometimes it is used almost affectionately: tolerance as a prerequisite to freedom and peaceful coexistence. In other contexts, tolerance seems something negative: a prerequisite to blasphemy and the free use of drugs, prostitution, and euthanasia. Different conceptions of the word "tolerance" in different contexts make it hard to use the concept as a basis for empirical study—especially because these different conceptions are intertwined. However, without the notion of tolerance, we cannot understand Dutch culture in general and more specifically Dutch legal culture in particular. Moreover, as I show in this essay, the legal use of tolerance has proved quite effective in setting and implementing policies toward such highly disputed subjects as drugs, prostitution, and euthanasia.

A general definition of tolerance is "a legal way of deferring negative reactions to things we don't approve of" (Schuyt 2001, p. 142). This definition is the outcome of an evolution in the history of ideas on tolerance. Tolerance in the Netherlands has an age-old ring of pragmatic acceptance. It is this pragmatic quality that may be most important from a cultural perspective. However, pragmatic acceptance seems to be under attack when the word is used in the context of "zero tolerance" policing. Not only the phrase but also the practice of penalizing nuisances and prosecuting minor offenses reached the Netherlands by the end of the twentieth century.

I pursue this highly interesting issue, but it will not be a central part of this essay. My main object is to show the consequences of tolerance as a legal category—as a specifically Dutch technique that helps to explain the remarkable Dutch ways of dealing with such morally sensitive issues.

The essay is organized as follows. Section I is a brief historical overview of general cultural meanings of tolerance. I elaborate on two conceptions. First, acceptance (or toleration) of difference in religious matters was where it began. Then it evolved into a more general need to set aside religious (and later on, more generally, cultural) differences to pursue common interests. This first conception of tolerance can be looked at as providing the foundation for the second, the acceptance of moral ambiguity and dissensus.

Section II discusses two more conceptions of tolerance. In relation to crime, tolerance is used in a third sense, as a euphemism for general leniency regarding incivilities and petty crime. Moreover in certain fields, a fourth sense of tolerance took on a connotation of governmental indifference and apathy regarding illegalities. In Dutch administrative and criminal law, tolerance also begot a very specific connotation.

In Section III tolerance is dealt with as a legal concept of its own that means that in specific circumstances government may not respond with sanctions to certain infractions. Thus tolerance came to be, fifth, a pragmatic tool in problem solving and more generally a strategy to minimize negative consequences from too-strict enforcement of legal rules. In the end, a sixth sense of tolerance became part of a "policy of tolerance," a sophisticated complex of regulations (on their faces contrary to statutory law) in administrative and criminal law. These ideas are discussed with as few legal technicalities as possible, but they cannot be left out altogether because they are critical to understanding Dutch law in action.

In Section IV, I discuss the typically Dutch way of "deferring negative reactions to things many don't approve of" with regard to drugs, prostitution, and euthanasia. In Section V conclusions are drawn concerning how tolerance works in the Netherlands. In light of recent developments regarding ethnic and Muslim minorities, these conclusions warrant reflection. Recent, sophisticated ways of thinking about tolerance might seem useless in the area in which it all started, religious tolerance. One could say that most of the six different conceptions of tolerance are losing their power. But, especially among policing and justice professionals, the policy of regulated tolerance is still looked on as a viable, healthy way to deal with ever-increasing demands of politics.

I. Historical Background

From the very beginning, tolerance as a cultural concept was relevant to how officials were supposed to relate to morally ambivalent questions. In the sixteenth and seventeenth centuries, tolerance meant that those in power accepted the existence of religious views that were not compatible with official doctrine. It all started with the Eighty Years War (1568–1648) between the Netherlands and Spain and the Thirty Years War (1618–48) in central Europe. These were international wars of religion between Catholics and Protestants (Toulmin 1990; Barzun 2001, pp. 239–305). The Calvinists won in the Netherlands, but the majority was not overwhelming; freedom from the Spanish oppressor was seen by many in the Netherlands as a common good. In two subsequent generations, the Netherlands became an empire stretching from Dutch Manhattan to the Malaysian Peninsula (Shorto 2005), an empire of successful traders who were embarrassed by their riches (Schama 1987).

Sir William Temple, a British diplomat in Holland—the major province of the Netherlands—wrote as follows in 1672: "No man can here complain of pressure on his conscience, of being forced to any public profession of his faith, of being restrained from his own manner of worship in his house" (Schuyt 2001, p. 115). Spanish and Portuguese Jews and French Protestant Huguenots were tolerated. John Locke (1632–1704) not only wrote his Letter on Toleration in close collaboration with a Dutch friend, but also spent his exile in the Netherlands.

The life of Dutch philosopher Baruch de Spinoza (1632–77) illustrates the experiences of Portuguese Jews finding refuge in the Netherlands. After the conquest of Granada in 1492, Queen Isabella breeched her promises of toleration of the Jews under the influence of the Grand Inquisitor, Tomás de Torquemada. In the following century, many—including the Spinoza family—fled to Portugal or France. Later the Spinozas were drawn to the tiny rebel state on the North Sea that could claim military and economic success against the Spaniards.

Baruch was at first completely immersed in the Sephardic surroundings of his family in Amsterdam. But he came to meet a group of Mennonite (Baptist) businessmen and other free thinkers (in Holland "Baptist" had and has the connotation of "free thinker") (de Vries 1991; Israel 2001). They were highly influenced by earlier Dutch intellectuals such as Erasmus of Rotterdam (1469–1536), the writer of *In Praise of Folly*, and Dirk Coornhert (1522–90), the inventor of the *rasphuis*, a new kind of prison system. Spinoza became one of the most important figures of seventeenth-century rationalism. These ideas were not tolerated in his own religious community and he was excommunicated, but in Holland one could live outside one's own "natural" group. By grinding lenses, he supported himself and moved to a small village near Leiden.

Pierre Bayle (1647–1706) might be seen as the exemplary French Huguenot. In his policies toward the Protestants, the Sun King, Louis XIV, had passed from passive discrimination through petty harassment to violent persecution. In 1685 the king revoked the edict on toleration, and nearly a million of France's most worthy citizens were forced to convert to Catholicism or to flee amid a veritable reign of terror (Davies 1996, pp. 620–21). Bayle, one of those who fled, was a pioneer in disinterested, critical history who probed the troubled and troubling boundary between reason and faith. Of course, that was not always easy. When Bayle lectured on comets and criticized the customary view of these extraterrestrial phenomena as signs of the wrath of God, angry vicars succeeded in persuading the Rotterdam magistrates to withhold his stipend (Schama 1987, chap. III, sec. 1). Even in Holland, tolerance was not then a matter of course.

Not only was the Netherlands a safe haven for Jews and Protestants, but there were no outbreaks of witch hunting. In the Netherlands no one was tortured, burned, or prosecuted for witchcraft after 1600. The Netherlands was an exception, although one should not exaggerate the extent of the witch crazes in the period. Nonetheless, especially in Scotland, Germany, and France, horrible things took place. And not only there. In 1669 in Protestant Sweden, after one witchcraft trial, seventy-two women and fifteen children were killed and 128 younger children were flogged. In 1679 in the Archbishopric of Salzburg, France, ninety-seven people were decapitated, hanged, or burned because they were said to have caused cattle plague by necromancy (Baschwitz 1948, pp. 14–15; Levack 1995). The Salem witch trials of 1692 in Puritan Massachusetts are well known.

The sensible and humane situation in the Netherlands is better understood by focusing on the role of Dutch town magistrates than on the role of intellectuals. It was profitable to be sensible. We might honor the private vices that were public benefits of the seventeenth-century magistrates of Oudewater. This town had obtained the privilege of a witch's stool. The mayor sold certificates under seal to many foreigners who asked to be weighed on this stool, because everyone knew that witches do not weigh a pound (Baschwitz 1948, p. 346). Those who weighed more were officially exonerated from witchcraft with a written certificate. The magistrates did not allow much influence to fanatics. From the late sixteenth century, the burgher elites in the cities preferred a strict division between church and state. Because they did not want to diminish their own powers by according too strong a position to the Calvinist vicars, the magistrates unofficially accepted the existence of Roman Catholic churchgoing as long as Catholics paid a special tax ("recognition money"). They also accepted other religious minorities such as Jews.

Tolerance not only has to do with highbrow things such as freedom of conscience or with the profits of the rich, but also is about living in the vicinity of others who are not loved at first sight. A huge number of immigrants entered the Netherlands, especially after the late sixteenth century, some as refugees, others looking for work in agriculture or on board ships of the East Indian Company and the West Indian Company. Of course, this did not always work out perfectly. Some cities were markedly less tolerant toward Jews than others; for example, even in tolerant Amsterdam, their position was not completely equal to that of *goyim*. And there definitely was intolerance of homosexuality in the eighteenth century.

Nonetheless, tolerance was forced on people who were living together. Much of the land is below sea level. It had to be reclaimed from the sea by hardworking people from all religions. They had to work together—even if they considered one another heretics or heathens. Even in the twenty-first century, the Dutch use the term "the polder system" to describe a political culture premised on the need to set aside sectional differences to address common problems. A similar tolerance existed on board Dutch ships on which about 4,000 men each year went to the East Indies in the seventeenth century and 7,000 in the eighteenth century (van Gelder 2003, p. 174). Especially in the eighteenth century, most came from other countries. If shipmates did not tolerate one another, they would all drown together. The intellectual elite may have displayed its tolerance differently than ordinary people, but Dutch tolerance is sure to be highly influenced by ordinary people's wish to deal with danger rationally by suspending moral judgments.

This basic outline of the historical importance of tolerance in the

Netherlands might easily be expanded. But for present purposes, it may suffice to remember that what started as a concept having primarily to do with religion widened into a concept with a more general meaning of political tolerance. This resulted from a slow change that took place from conflicts about "true religion" in the seventeenth century into conflicts about religious autonomy of different congregations in the eighteenth and nineteenth centuries.

Around 1700 the Dutch political system was complicated, and many thought it unworkable. There was a fairly coherent and efficient system of local government and local or provincial jurisdiction ("the Republic of the Seven United Provinces"). Until 1747, there was no chief of state because the regents—the rich burghers—did not want to broaden the powers of the Orange dynasty. Dutch intellectuals were proud of their constitution. Although its loose federal structure precluded effective internal and foreign policies, its built-in checks and balances ensured that absolute power and arbitrariness were never tolerated over extended periods.

The patricians had to reckon with public opinion (Mijnhardt 1992, p. 201). This kept the Netherlands an area of "mixed religion." Calvinism had become the dominant religion, but the Calvinist world was internally divided. Moreover, there were other Protestant groups, and Catholicism persisted to such a degree that the number of Catholics never fell below one-third of the population (H. Daalder 1966, 1981). In the eighteenth and nineteenth centuries, both the power balance and the intellectual debate were generally to the disadvantage of the more extreme Calvinists. The persisting local character of elite politics, a pamphlet tradition, and differentiation of religious groups helped sustain recognition of the importance of tolerance.

These developments ultimately led to the Dutch politics of accommodation of the twentieth century (Lijphardt 1968; H. Daalder 1974). This is characterized by a societal compartmentalization based on ideology or religion (*verzuiling*), stabilized by pragmatic political bargaining by the elites of each of the subcultural networks. For instance, in the beginning of the twentieth century there were a Catholic political party, a Dutch Reformed party, a liberal party, a social democratic party, and many other smaller parties. However, there were also Catholic, Dutch Reformed, liberal, and social democratic newspapers. Schools, hospitals, trade unions, and sport clubs were also organized on the basis of these four major subcultural communities or "pillars" as the Dutch called them. The most important party members, editors, and directors of schools and hospitals were leaders of these communities. While the leaders of the four pillars did business with one another, ordinary Roman Catholics might never meet a Dutch Reformed person. The leaders of the denominational groups and definable secular groups taught their supporters that the views and values of others would have to be respected. "We have a right to have a separate Dutch Reformed university with some governmental support if we allow the Catholics to do the same." Tolerance was seen as a basic value for a society based on the coexistence of many different religious views. It was a necessity for a political system that was based not on two parties, but on religiously influenced spectrums of parties that had to forge coalitions in order to achieve a majority.

However, in the course of the last thirty years the importance of the religious differences has diminished as a result of an astonishing level of secularization. While in 1970, 39 percent of the Dutch were not church members, in 1980 this was about 50 percent; in 1991, 57 percent; and in 1999, 63 percent. Of the religious minority, 41 percent visit a church at least every fortnight; the rest go less (Becker and de Wit 2000, pp. 13–14). Although the separate identities survived into the twenty-first century, the times of compartmentalization are over. The sports coach is no longer inevitably a member of the same church as the schoolteacher and the trade union leader.

Without its religious background, tolerance had to take on a new, general meaning of acceptance of social and cultural differences in a pluralist society. A shift toward postmodern values that emphasize human autonomy and diversity instead of the hierarchy and conformity that are central to modernity had taken place (Inglehart 1997, pp. 27–33, 88). A competing development was the influx of North African and Turkish workers with their Islamic religion. According to the Dutch Central Bureau of Statistics, in 1971 there were 54,300 Muslims in the Netherlands; in 1979, 200,000; in 1988, 400,000; in 1994, 600,000; in 2000, 800,000; and in 2004, 944,000. Dutch society has had difficulty dealing with fundamental differences between these new inhabitants (*allochtonen*), who generally find it hard to accept postmodern values, and the majority of the population that is highly influenced by the postmodern way of thinking.

The concept of tolerance in a general cultural sense has changed from acceptance (or toleration) of difference in religious matters into a need to set religious and cultural differences aside to pursue common interests. Against this background, tolerance for thoughts and acts of which one disapproves can be understood. Although it is not necessary that disapproved things be criminalized, in modern-day speech, tolerance is often related to petty crime. I discuss this in the next section.

II. The So-Called Tolerance of Crime

In the previous section I offered an outline of tolerance as a cultural trait in Dutch society. I described a cultural phenomenon, not a legal one. Before I turn to the latter, I show how dissatisfaction with leniency in criminal matters has influenced how the Dutch talk about tolerance today. "Tolerance" is sometimes looked at in this regard as a euphemism for leniency regarding incivilities and petty crimes.

Of course, one should not overstate Dutch leniency. Presumably in the eyes of the American public Dutch laws and policies on gun control and on hate speech are incredibly severe: There is zero tolerance for those behaviors: we give fines for toy guns that could be mistaken for real ones.

However, on some subjects, tolerance came to mean governmental indifference and apathy regarding the upholding of certain rules.

At least as seen from elsewhere, the Netherlands was for much of the second half of the twentieth century one of the most liberal and nonmoralistic of Western countries in relation to crime (Downes 1988). As late as 1980, the imprisonment rate was 23 per 100,000 inhabitants, which was then much less than in West Germany (91), France (66), or England and Wales (86). In 2005, the rates were 127 for the Netherlands, 97 for Germany, 88 for France, and 141 for England and Wales (International Centre for Prison Studies 2006). And Holland is still on the rise. A very tolerant country has rapidly changed into an ordinary one. The number of inmates rose from 6,890 on September 30, 1990, to 16,455 in 2004 (Eggen and van der Heide 2005, table 6.3).

In the 1970s, tolerance definitely had a ring of leniency in criminal matters. If one were caught violating traffic rules, receiving social security (welfare) while having an undisclosed job, or polluting the environment, it was supposed by many to be bad luck. More than two-thirds of the Dutch (72 percent) agreed with the proposition that criminals should not be punished, but that they should be changed. By

TABLE 1
Recorded Crime in the Netherlands (× 1,000)

	Total	Violent Crime	Property Crime	Public Order
1960	132	14.5	84.2	11.6
1965	169	14.3	114.6	14.6
1970	266	15.8	188.2	18.8
1975	453	18.4	343	34.3
1980	706	26.5	500.9	84.8
1985	1,094	37.2	840.7	117.5
1990	1,150.2	49.6	840.4	146.9
1995	1,226.7	65.3	904.9	152.8
2000	1,305.6	90.0	887.8	189.8
2004	1,324.6	114.9	829.1	208.2

SOURCE.—Eggen and van der Heide (2005), tables 4.1–4.4.

the mid-1990s, those wanting to change criminals declined to 49 percent. And this comparative mildness has declined even more concerning sex crimes (van den Brink 2002, p. 43).

Postmaterialist values are waning; the current government has made a major issue of "norms and values" as an alternative to individualism and all kinds of freedoms. This might be explained by an erosion of traditional authority and increasing deviant behavior. In the mid-1990s, a significant part of the population—especially relatively uneducated, lower-class religious people, a group called "threatened citizens"—felt morally insecure (van den Brink 2002, table 10).[1] Crime rates had been soaring since 1960.

Although property crime has been stable or going down, violent crime has been on the rise, as table 1 shows. Moreover, especially after 1990, the population had reason to think that the police were not on top of crime: clearance rates were going down. The absolute numbers of crimes cleared changed from 73,000 (1960) to 109,000 (1970) to 210,000 (1980) to 255,000 (1990) and back down to 191,000 (2000) (Eggen and van der Heide 2005, fig. 1). When Amsterdam police commissioner Jelle Kuiper advocated a "zero-tolerance policy" toward certain "incivilities," he was responding to public discontent (van Swaan-

---

[1] According to van den Brink, 71 percent of threatened citizens feel morally insecure because of population diversity and rapid social change; from the acquiescent this percentage was 25; and from active citizens, it was 4. A sample of 1,786 based on cluster analyses showed 35 percent threatened, 45 percent acquiescent, and 20 percent active citizens.

TABLE 2

Cases Sent by the Police to the Prosecutor's Office

	Total	Violence	Property	Public Order
1985	266,074			
1990	260,844			
1995	257,842	28,931	103,276	22,921
2000	233,324	33,548	71,491	26,841
2002	251,291	38,922	73,717	30,118
2004	273,974	47,648	73,651	35,199

SOURCE.—Eggen and van der Heide (2005), tables 5.1, 5.2.

ingen 1998). A third factor behind the general discontent was that many Dutch citizens felt uncomfortable with the rising numbers of ethnic suspects. Of recorded suspects living in the Netherlands, 37.5 percent are non-Dutch or have non-Dutch parents. Non-Dutch suspects are twice as prevalent among suspects as non-Dutch residents are among all residents; for males, the prevalence is four times as high (Blom et al. 2005, p. 4). Most live in big cities, such as Amsterdam and Rotterdam.

In 1987–2000, recorded crime rose to approximately 10,000 citations per 100,000 inhabitants (Eggen and van der Heide 2005, table 4.10), but the number of cases sent to prosecutors was going down, as table 2 shows. However, as table 3 shows, the number of cases being prosecuted was going up. The police thus handled more cases (in terms of input), but their results were going down (in terms of output). The prosecutor's office had to handle fewer cases until 2000, but it brought more cases before court.

One could explain both phenomena in terms of tolerance in two ways. First, Dutch citizens, by reporting more crimes to the police,

TABLE 3

Cases Sent by the Prosecutor to Trial

	Total	Violence	Property	Public Order
1985	83,512			
1990	82,341			
1995	102,310	13,651	43,531	8,991
2000	111,033	18,188	37,775	12,396
2002	116,810	20,706	38,684	13,114
2004	133,218	25,618	39,089	15,579

SOURCE.—Eggen and van der Heide (2005), table 5.6.

and prosecutors, by prosecuting more cases, were becoming less tolerant of crime. Second, crime in the Netherlands was declining but getting worse, and citizens were understandably less tolerant of more serious crime.

The second possibility does not seem likely because the number of intentional killings has oscillated between 200 and 250 a year since 1992: if violent crime really were getting worse (qualitatively), the number of murders should rise (Leistra and Nieuwbeerta 2003, pp. 22–23). Rape presents a similar picture. Recorded rapes oscillated between 1,500 and 1,800 from 1995 to 2004, although the trend is a little upward (Eggen and van der Heide 2005, table 4.6).

I believe, tentatively, that declining tolerance, rather than qualitative worsening of crime, explains changes in citizen reporting and prosecutorial action. Attempts and threats are increasingly being reported, which is consistent with the declining tolerance of crime. The Dutch are defining their crimes up, as is the judiciary.

Egelkamp (2002, p. 273) compared 1,100 court records with cases from 1986 and 1996. She found that in 1996 assaults without consequences were more commonly classified as assaults than in 1986, assaults were more commonly classified as grievous bodily harm in 1996 than in 1986, and in 1996 all cases in which grievous bodily harm was established were classified as attempted manslaughter. An example of defining deviance up is provided by a recent decision of the Dutch Supreme Court. It upheld a conviction of a seventy-two-year-old man for shaking his fists from his garden in the direction of a woman who was passing by on the sidewalk by bike, shouting at her something like "get the hell out of that sidewalk, lady." He was convicted of threatening, a crime that might bring about grievous bodily harm.[2] In this sense tolerance, meaning acceptance of incivilities, is declining. In the 1980s and 1990s there may have existed a form of tolerance as indifference, even though there were real victims; but more recently a tendency to criminalize any incivility has emerged.

Something snapped around 2000. In May 2000, the center of Enschede, a city of 150,000 inhabitants, was hit by a fireworks disaster. The fireworks company had not observed safety regulations, and the government had tolerated this infraction: twenty-two people died, 947 were injured, and over 4,000 lost their houses. In December of the

---

[2] HR September 14, 2004, *NJ* 2005, 61. HR is the Dutch Supreme Court; *NJ* is the periodical in which the most important decisions are published.

same year, a café, Little Heaven, burned down after directions from
the fire department were ignored: fourteen youngsters died and about
200 were injured, of whom some thirty were maimed for life.

"Tolerance" lost its positive connotation of postmaterialism: it became a symbol of governmental indifference. Many inside and outside
Parliament pleaded for criminal prosecutions of local government in
these cases. Negligence in monitoring fire safety regulations of course
can be distinguished from toleration of minor crimes. But in public
opinion, the different types of *gedogen* (tolerance) merged and represent
indifference to people's fears for their safety. Minor offenses, such as
fighting in a bar, can end up in a deadly accident, and the same goes
for minor infringements of safety regulations. A recent analysis shows
that fear for one's safety is connected with attributions of responsibility,
guilt, and blame. Consequently, "fear of crime" exceeds fear and fear
exceeds crime (van der Veen 2006, p. 320).

These sad incidents had nothing to do with (non)acceptance of incivilities. Criticism of tolerance had to do with frustrated expectations
of safety. But the result was that many blamed too high a level of
tolerance for increasing crime rates and governmental indifference.
Forbearance was scorned: every small mistake should be answered for
immediately: tit for tat. Government had to react to this general feeling. Such a reaction was more complicated than one would think. Tolerance became a legal concept with a meaning of its own.

III. Tolerance as a Legal Concept

Not only is tolerance a historical and cultural phenomenon; it can also
be looked at as an analytical category in the Dutch legal system. In
this specific sense, tolerance refers to policies of nonprosecution of
things forbidden in the Criminal Code or other codes. *Gedogen* is the
current Dutch word. Here I discuss this kind of tolerance from a criminal law perspective, although it is just as important in administrative
law. This form of tolerance is not necessarily the same as "indifference." Nor is it necessarily "turning a blind eye." Ordinarily it means
that administrative or punitive reactions are postponed if the perpetrator agrees to act according to precise instructions. These instructions
might be given in a specific case, but there are also more general instructions. In certain fields—for instance, environmental law—there
exists something called a "tolerance order" (*gedoogbeschikking*), which

means that the local or provincial authorities promise not to punish for a certain period under certain conditions. Such an order is legally binding on the relationship between local authorities and citizens. However, it is not the same as a permit (and if the Public Prosecutor finds out, he is free to prosecute). In other fields it is possible for the authorities to find other slightly less informal forms of tolerance (see, e.g., Engbersen, van der Leun, and de Boom 2007).

A comparable system exists in Dutch criminal procedure. According to Article 167 of the Code of Criminal Procedure (1926), the prosecutor may refrain from prosecution when that is deemed to be in the public interest. This is "the expediency principle." Since 1970, however, this has been reversed: prosecution will take place only if it is in the public interest. No longer was the rule "prosecution, unless . . . ."; the new rule was "prosecution only if . . . ." The basic idea was that the general population should want the prosecution to happen. It might be interesting to note that this "decision" was made in the typical Dutch way: there was no decision. The Public Prosecutor's 1970 annual report stated that this was the correct way to interpret the expediency principle and did not stress that a change had taken place (Jaarverslag Openbaar Ministerie 1970). This change was a direct consequence of the cultural revolution of the 1960s and 1970s. People wanted the police to look the other way if their children smoked pot, protested against failing universities, or bought pornography or contraceptives (which were forbidden in some parts of the Netherlands in the 1950s).

This new interpretation led to so much discretionary authority that the Public Prosecutor General's Office soon issued rules (*beleid*) describing in what cases illegal practices could be allowed and in what cases prosecution had to take place. These rules are sometimes very specific, and for an outsider they are hard to distinguish from ordinary legal rules. Dutch lawyers are accustomed to regulations in administrative law, but in criminal law only to common law or statutes; the policy rules of the Public Prosecutor General's Office are neither.

Here, for illustration, are two examples, and in the following sections there are more. Under a directive on soft drugs of November 2, 2000, prosecution is not allowed against someone who possesses less than thirty grams of marijuana or against a licensed "shop" with a stock of less than 500 grams of hashish or marijuana. Under a directive on tax fraud of December 12, 2000, the prosecutors are not to prosecute if a fraud by an individual is less than 5,500 euros and for a company if it is less than 11,500 euros. If the prosecutor is not allowed to prosecute, the police are not allowed to arrest. But according to the Opium and General Tax laws, it is forbidden to have any amount of weed or to evade any taxes.

From a democratic point of view, this system might seem silly: the law says that something is forbidden, but rules governing law enforcement authorities explicitly state that in some cases they must act as though it is permitted. However, from a pragmatic view, and especially from a rule-of-law perspective, it is clever. In most countries it is a criminal offense to sell drugs, exploit brothels, or commit euthanasia, but the police "look without seeing" in many cases. One can buy drugs in the inner cities of the United States; one can pick up hookers in the prudish United Kingdom; and in Germany euthanasia is unlawful, but the doctors will help one to commit suicide. In these systems, tolerance is something clandestine. The secrecy creates situations in which it may be wise to buy the policeman a couple of glasses to help him look the other way. In the Netherlands, tolerance is no secret: written rules indicate when the official must look the other way.

Since the early 1970s there have been regular—and since 1993 statutorily prescribed—meetings of the chief of police, the most important mayor in a region, and the Public Prosecutor in which decisions about legal tolerance are made ('t Hart 1986). For instance, locations in which addicts may use heroin or crack without being bothered by the police are discussed, and sometimes the city council does not agree. Meanwhile, other applications of tolerance, for instance regarding environmental crime and tax evasion, are also discussed openly. For the population, it sometimes is difficult to understand why a policeman who tolerates a certain crime on his own cannot make promises that bind the prosecutor; nor can anyone else. One time the secretary of state for the environment decided to tolerate a certain environmental crime; when the prosecutor nevertheless prosecuted, the Supreme Court decided that he was not bound by the secretary of state's utterances (HR, December 17, 1985, *NJ* 1986, 591; afterward standard case law). However, if there is an official prosecutorial guideline or a decision of a specific prosecutor, individuals can hold the prosecutor to it (standard case law since HR, May 29, 1978, *NJ* 1978, 358; e.g., HR, February 22, 2000, *NJ* 2000, 557).

IV. Tolerating Morally Ambiguous Behavior

In this section, I discuss Dutch policies on drugs, prostitution, and euthanasia. In all three areas, legal tolerance in the sense described in the last paragraph, as a legal concept of its own, is decisive. Comparing these three topics shows how this kind of tolerance may be the basis for decriminalization. Directives for prosecutors indicate when they must refrain from prosecuting. But in the case of euthanasia, these directions were upgraded to statutory conditions that function as legal justifications for mercy killing. Tolerance sometimes is upgraded from a grey zone of the law in action to an official level of decriminalization.

A. Tolerating Drugs

Most Dutch citizens are not proud of it, but many tourists visit the Netherlands because of the *coffee shops*. The term coffee shop does not connote the hot brown liquid: it is a place where cannabis can be bought freely. Sometimes such a shop is a greasy joint in a back alley; sometimes it is a trendy café with bright lights, huge plants, and tropical music, and one can even buy all kinds of real coffee. Why wouldn't you? A slice of hash-cake can be served on the side.

This does not mean that the selling of drugs is legally permitted. It has been since the 1919 Opium Act. But since the 1970s the Dutch have chosen a drug control system based on accommodation, with relatively weak law enforcement and a strong public health component (Leuw and Haen Marshall 1996; Boekhout van Solingen 2004). This was done by discriminating between soft drugs (cannabis etc.) and hard drugs (cocaine, Ecstasy, etc). At first soft drugs were tolerated in order to prevent their serving as stepping-stones for youngsters who would like to experiment, but it seemed safer if they could do so without being exposed to hard drugs. Since the 1980s, coffee shops have been permitted to operate and to sell marijuana under certain restrictions. And although party life in the 1990s undermined this differentiation a little bit with Ecstasy and GHB, both synthetic hard drugs, the basic idea seemed to work.

On two counts, there were huge problems. It was inconsistent that a user buying small quantities of cannabis in a coffee shop was tolerated but it was illegal for anyone to supply the coffee shop with its merchandise. Moreover, the Netherlands is a small country, and many people from Germany and France hopped over to buy their cannabis. This led to complex disputes in the context of the European Union. Off the record, some officials say the only reason the Dutch policy on drugs was tolerated in the Union was that Dutch representatives always replied that if it was not, they wanted to tighten the laws on guns in Europe; in Holland having toy guns if you are over twelve years old is criminally prosecuted (I'm really not kidding)! Nonetheless, the current government is trying to reduce the number of coffee shops and is not in favor of further liberalization.

As in other Western countries, Dutch authorities were confronted with modern drug use during the 1960s. In the beginning the police would hunt intensively for a few grams of cannabis. However, the youth cultures of hippies and so-called *provos*, youngsters who engaged in "mellow anarchistic" activities to provoke the authorities, such as by giving currants (!) to police officers, creating "happenings," and proposing unorthodox plans, were very active in the traditionally liberal city of Amsterdam and appealed to large segments of the population. Parents, educators, and politicians did not accept the sometimes violent reactions of the police toward their children's provocative public smoking of pot.

Two independent expert working groups were appointed by the government in 1967–68. These were chaired by professors Louk Hulsman, a lawyer known for his critical and abolitionist views on criminal law, and Pieter Baan, psychiatrist and cofounder of the humanist so-called Utrecht School (see Junger-Tas and Junger, in this volume). Most drug use consists of short-term experimentation, said the Baan report. Criminalizing drug users makes it difficult for users to return to socially accepted lifestyles, said Hulsman. Around 1970 a policy of tolerance toward illicit drugs was adopted: there was no fixed moment. But there was no misunderstanding that the 1970 interpretation of the expediency principle (see Sec. III), prosecution only in the public interest, was relevant for drug offenses. In 1973, the left-wing government chaired by Den Uyl took office. Health Minister Irene Vorrink—her son Koos Zwart gave the latest cannabis market prices on public radio—openly declared support for cannabis legalization, and only because of foreign (German and Swedish) pressure did this not happen. However, in the early 1970s, most police reports on offenses under the Opium Act (62–71 percent) concerned possession of cannabis under twenty-five grams. Heroin reached the Netherlands only in 1972 (Blom 1998, vol. I, pp. 82–84).

In the 1976 Opium Act, a distinction was made between soft drugs

TABLE 4

Comparing Drug Abuse in the United
States and the Netherlands (%)

	United States	Netherlands
Opiates	.6	.3
Cocaine	2.5	1.1
Ecstacy	1.3	1.5
Cannabis	11.0	6.1

SOURCE.—United Nations (2004), vol. II, pp.
390–401.

(cannabis) and hard drugs (heroin, cocaine, amphetamines, LSD, and,
later on, Ecstasy). Import and export of hard drugs are punishable with
a maximum sentence of twelve years; selling and manufacturing, eight
years; possession, four years; possession for private use, one year. Im-
portation and exportation of soft drugs and selling go for four years;
commercial growing and possession of more than thirty grams, two
years; and possession and selling up to thirty grams, one month.

By separation of the markets for hard and soft drugs, public health
benefits were aimed for. On the basis of the expediency principle, the
public prosecutors decided that possession of thirty grams (about one
ounce) of cannabis would be tolerated; possession for consumer use of
half a gram of hard drugs is also tolerated. The basic idea is that users
should be treated from a medical point of view and with adequate social
assistance, whereas the criminal justice system should be used only
against criminal entrepreneurs. This multiple and multidimensional
approach was thought to be the best way to have as few problems as
possible of overdoses and addiction.

This basic idea as described in *Crime and Justice* in 1991 still seems
to be correct (Leuw 1991). Moreover, it seems to work. The level of
drug abuse in the Netherlands is relatively low, as can be seen, for
instance, when Dutch and American levels of drug use by people between fifteen and sixty-four are compared (see table 4).

According to the Netherlands National Drug Monitor of the Trimbos Institute, a reputable Dutch scientific institution, in 2001, 17 percent of the population had ever used cannabis and 3 percent had done
so in the previous month. More important than these small differences
is the trend. After steep increases until 1996, only a slight increase in
the use of cannabis was reported between 1997 and 2001 (see table 5).

TABLE 5

Trends in the Use of Cannabis in the Netherlands
(Percentage of Population Aged 12–64)

	1997	2001
Has ever used	15.6	17.0
Male	20.6	21.3
Female	10.8	12.8
Has used in last month	2.5	3.0
Male	3.5	4.3
Female	1.4	1.8
Has used for the first time last year	1.3	1.0
Average age of actual users	28	28

SOURCE.—National Drug Monitor (2003), table 2.1.

The Netherlands does not have significantly higher cannabis use than other European countries. While a significant increase in the annual prevalence of Ecstasy used took place between 1997 and 2001 (from 0.8 to 1.5 percent), the rising tide seems to have stopped in 2002 (United Nations 2004, pp. 148, 193). Heroin is not popular, and the number of opiate addicts in the Netherlands is stable. Dying by overdose is not frequent: seventy-one persons died by heroin overdose in 2003 (CBS 2003, table 7.19; National Drug Monitor 2003, p. 90). The estimated prevalence of problem users of hard drugs (heroin, crack, cocaine, Ecstacy, and amphetamines) is the lowest per thousand inhabitants in western Europe. Concerning recent drug users (i.e., last year), the Netherlands level is average (table 6).

Mere users of cannabis have not much to fear from the police. Using drugs is not prohibited, though possession is; but no one gets busted for possession of small amounts. Prosecution is impossible because of the 2000 directive of the Prosecutors General (see Sec. III).

The general population has accepted the current situation, and many would support decriminalization, especially of soft drugs. Some 40 percent of cannabis is bought by consumers in the so-called coffee shops. At the end of 2002, there were 782 officially tolerated coffee shops, of which 51 percent were located in cities with over 200,000 inhabitants. However, in 78 percent of all Dutch municipalities, coffee shops are not tolerated at all (National Drug Monitor 2003, para. 2.8; United Nations 2004, p. 149). On the basis of the expediency principle, these coffee shops will be left alone if they keep to the following rules: no advertising, no hard drugs, no nuisance, no selling to minors (under

TABLE 6

Recent Drug Use in the Netherlands (Percentage of Population Aged 12–64)

	Hard Drug Problem	Recent Cannabis Use	Recent Cocaine Use	Recent Ecstacy Use
The Netherlands	.26	6	1.1	1.5
Germany	.31	6	.9	.7
France	.43	8	.3	.3
Sweden	.45	1	0	<.05
United Kingdom	.69	11	1.9	2.2
United States	?	10	2	1.5

SOURCE.—National Drug Monitor (2003), tables 2.8A–B, 3.4A–B, 4.5, 5.3A–B.

eighteen), and no large stocks. The shops are allowed to have 500 grams in stock (U.S. retail value about $3,000). Because it is nearly impossible to do business with such a stock, they always have something more outside the back door. The police are in a position to enforce the law. It is a little bit illogical to accept selling by retail and to forbid retailers to build stocks, but nevertheless the system works.

This is not to say that drugs are accepted in the Netherlands. They are not. Although drug crimes are not a large fraction of crimes recorded by the police, they affect the case loads of prosecutors and judges. Most of all they affect prison population figures, because of the relatively long sentences imposed (see table 7).

A separate category of criminals consists of those who do not commit drug offenses in a strict sense but who abuse drugs. One in seven to eight of the slightly more than 230,000 criminal cases dealt with by the Public Prosecutor's Office in 2000 involved a person who used drugs (Meijer et al. 2004, p. 98). This mere 12 percent of criminal defendants is low compared with the 60–70 percent of defendants who tested positive on drugs when arrested in the United States and the United Kingdom (Holloway, Bennett, and Lower 2004).

So the criminal justice system is not slack in fighting drug-related crimes. By the early 1980s, it was clear that Dutch traffickers were organizing rapidly. From then on the fight against organized drug crime became the number one target of law enforcement. Both court cases and custodial sentencing for drug offenders are on the rise, absolutely and compared with the general rise in indictments. Soft drug crimes are not excluded, which is partly the result of a rise in amateur production of marijuana in attics of ordinary houses (table 8).

TABLE 7

Drug Crimes and the Criminal Justice System, 2004

	Absolute	Relative	Per 100,000
Total crime recorded by police	1,324,600	100	9,966
Drugs	15,700	.01	118
Hard drugs	8,500		
Soft drugs	7,200		
Case load Prosecutor's Office	273,974	100	
Drugs	18,451	6.7	
Hard drugs	12,035	4.4	
Soft drugs	6,416	2.3	
Trial by court	133,218		
Drugs	9,266	7	
Hard drugs	6,394	4.8	
Soft drugs	2,872	2.2	
In prison (after conviction)	16,455	100	
Drugs	3,260	19.8	

SOURCE.—Eggen and van der Heide (2005), tables 4.6, 4.7, 5.2, 5.3, 5.6, 6.3.

Of all cases brought before the criminal courts, 7 percent involve an offense against the Opium Act. One in eight of the total of 33,406 (partially) unconditional prison sentences by irrevocable judgment involves an offense against the Opium Act. The cause is the severe punishments for organized criminals.

Dutch law enforcers have actively combated drugs since it became clear that Dutch traffickers are important traffickers and that the Netherlands plays a dominant role in Ecstasy and cannabis production (United Nations 2004, pp. 19, 135). The largest worldwide seizures of Ecstasy are reported from Belgium (25 percent of global seizures) and the Netherlands (24 percent). Seizures in Europe of cocaine are second highest in the Netherlands (exceeded only by Spain), and seizures of heroin are among the highest (after Turkey, Italy, and the United Kingdom). The largest European seizures of cannabis (after Italy) are also in the Netherlands (United Nations 2004, vol. I, p. 172; vol. II, pp. 283, 300).

The major reason for the central Dutch role is that the Netherlands is central as a place of transit and as a destination. Schiphol Airport and Rotterdam harbor are gateways into Europe, including for those who want to distribute drugs. Cocaine smugglers from Colombia often found their way into the Netherlands via the Dutch Antilles or former Dutch Surinam because the locals had relatives in the Netherlands.

TABLE 8

Convictions and Custodial Sentences for Drug Crimes

	Total	Hard Drugs	Soft Drugs	Custodial Sentence (of Total Drugs)
1995	97,208	3,908	698	2,974
2000	105,393	4,421	1,914	3,025
2004	126,174	6,207	2,763	4,562

SOURCE.—Eggen and van der Heide (2005), tables 5.7, 5.16.

Immigrants from Turkey were available to distribute heroin from the East. Immigrants from Morocco did the same with hashish. Research among Colombian cocaine traffickers shows that it is not so much the tolerance of Dutch authorities as the highly developed system of transportation and the relative trustworthiness of Dutch criminal entrepreneurs (!) that make the Netherlands a fine starting point to enter Europe (Zaitch 2002).

The Dutch drug policy picture seemed clear, and almost everyone seemed satisfied with it. Individual users are left alone unless they have health problems. Organized crime is fought with relatively good results. The logistical situation, however, gives the police a mission impossible.

However, some cracks have begun to appear in this sunny picture. Some doubts are arising regarding the relative harmlessness of cannabis. Current Dutch home-grown weed has a very high level of the active substance (tetrahydrocannabinol). And although under-aged people are not allowed to buy in coffee shops, in reality 32 percent of minor users buy their cannabis there, especially in the major cities (National Drug Monitor 2003, table 2.4). Moreover, the current semilegal position of coffee shops has criminal side effects. In some lower-class neighborhoods, weed is grown in attics and criminal entrepreneurs collect the harvest to supply the shops.

Tolerance of hard drugs is more difficult. Some experts favor decriminalization here as well: the board of advisors of the foundation Stichting Drugsbeleid (http://www.drugsbeleid.nl), which promotes this view, include a former health minister, a former advocate general of the Supreme Court, an acting president of a court of appeals, and a former secretary general of the Royal Dutch Medical Association.

However, theirs is a less popular view than decriminalization of soft drugs.

A recent ethnographic study described the difficulties that arose in different parts of Rotterdam (van der Torre 2004). The situation in the beginning of the 1990s was typically defined by tolerance as acceptance: a vicar persuaded the public prosecutor, mayor, and chief of police to tolerate a free zone near the central station, Platform Zero, where about 600 prostitutes, pimps, dealers, illegal cabdrivers, and voyeurs and about 1,000 hard drug addicts did their thing. It was an exceptional situation. Eventually ordinary people became fed up. It was hard for local government to do anything because it had accepted the situation. In the end, the mayor closed the platform down, but without being authorized by the city council. The situation stabilized in 1995.

A completely different story regarding tolerance, in this case negligence, unfolded in the Rotterdam *Millinxbuurt*, creating huge problems in 1998–99. While Platform Zero was for a time thought to be a good idea because it concentrated problems, keeping junkies and prostitutes out of other neighborhoods, the Millinxbuurt was thought to be a place where the problems were not significant. So when things deteriorated, there was no sense of political urgency. Government was unaware of the level and speed at which the drug scene took root. It did not realize that the neighborhood was great for the dealers from a logistical point of view because it did not understand how the drug trade works. And it did not have street-level information on what was happening and did not pay attention to the problems in housing and the lack of social control. Government was not in sync.

This was one of the major issues that made the Rotterdam-based politician Pim Fortuyn popular. He was killed in 2001 by a left-wing activist. He was an interesting politician in view of Dutch tolerance: an openly gay man who revealed explicit pornographic details about his sex life, but was nevertheless very popular with right-wing voters because of his strict ideas on crime, drugs, and illegal immigrants. Tolerance in the sense of acceptance of drug use may be declining, but this does not mean that all tolerance is going down the drain.

Fighting organized drug crime is an important part of Dutch policing, but the general population is not very interested in that. The general population primarily cares about drug use when it affects public order. Because it can be a public nuisance, the Amsterdam city council recently forbade open use of cannabis. There is some feeling that cannabis may not be harmless after all, but many remain in favor of further decriminalization. This is one issue in which a majority of the population, most intellectuals, and police authorities favor official tolerance but in which politics, presumably especially because of outside pressure, does not want to go further than it goes.

B. Tolerating Prostitution

The Amsterdam red-light district is almost as synonymous with Holland as windmills and tulips. The Dutch history of prostitution is quite complex. The Calvinist ministers of the sixteenth to nineteenth centuries looked on it with great displeasure, but the magistrates did not accept their views; even then there were few cities in which it was illegal to exploit a brothel (van Deursen 1999, pp. 118–20). In the Penal Code of 1886, prostitution and exploiting a brothel were not forbidden, though the latter changed in 1911. In the discussions of a U.N. treaty in 1949, however, it was decided that Dutch policy did not favor criminalization of prostitution. Action is taken only in cases of exploitation in which force or deception has been used or advantage has been taken of the dependent situation of the prostitute (Haveman 1998; Noyon et al. 2003, Art. 250a, n. 1). In the second half of the twentieth century, exploitation and profits from prostitution were allowed. The trade union for prostitutes founded in 1985 established official contacts with the government (it was subsidized by the Ministry of Social Affairs after 1987) and with people who "sold windows" in the several red-light districts.

The system seemed to work reasonably well, although it was hard to know with reliable figures what really was going on. According to one estimate, about 20,000 prostitutes work in the Netherlands, of whom about one-fourth are victims of trafficking in human beings and of whom only 920 work as independent entrepreneurs.[3] But these estimates are hard to substantiate.

One study that tried to provide data found that in 1995 the Amsterdam police registered 1,005 women of fifty-six nationalities doing window prostitution and that there were about 700 streetwalkers, plus women working in about seventy-seven clubs and sixty-five escort bureaus or working from home, plus the 500 men and boys in the

[3] Christen Unie Amsterdam, "Prostitutie 'hype' in verkiezingen," press statement, December 16, 2005. The Christen Unie is a rather strict religious Christian party. Its city council member in Amsterdam has been working as a prostitute herself.

business (Fijnaut and Bovenkerk 1995, pp. 89–91). These figures suggest some knowledge regarding the spread of prostitution, but the sex industry is so diverse that it is almost impossible to generate reliable figures.

Nonetheless, that the police tried to register sex workers, basically for public health reasons, is interesting from the perspective of tolerance. Known prostitutes and known brothels were not necessarily prosecuted, and many in the business had sufficient trust in the police that they let themselves be registered.

In 2000, prostitution was legalized and the ban on brothels was lifted. Control and regulation of voluntary prostitution were pursued through introduction of a municipal licensing policy. Voluntary adult prostitution is no longer illegal. One aim was to improve the fight against forced prostitution, for instance, by victims of human trafficking. Another was to improve protections of minors from sexual abuse. That is why facilitating nonvoluntary prostitution and prostitution by minors are still categorized as serious crimes. The new law aims to separate prostitution from its crime-related side effects. And it aims to reduce the level of prostitution by foreigners who lack a valid residence and working permit.[4]

In 2002, most municipal authorities were still in the process of granting licenses, and there were signs of a slight improvement in the situation of prostitutes. A bank can no longer refuse to accept a prostitute as a customer. The police are not allowed to refuse to accept a report on violence by a prostitute because of her job. She is entitled to hygienic working conditions and has a right to unemployment benefits if she is out of work.

Nonetheless, for a majority of business service providers, such as banks and insurance companies, doing business with the prostitution sector is believed to frighten off other clients. The financial risk is greater doing business with the prostitution sector than with pubs and restaurants or fitness clubs (A. Daalder 2004, pp. 32–33).

Especially in the nonregulated sector (streetwalking and the escort service), punishable forms of prostitution by minors and illegal foreigners continue to take place. After the new law took effect, many

[4] Dutch government has decided that people from E.U. member states are not allowed to work as laborers in the sex industry, although it is legally impossible to deny a license to nationals from other E.U. member states who want to start as entrepreneurs in this industry.

illegal foreign prostitutes, who were tolerated as window prostitutes under the old regime, were forced to hit the streets. So-called *tippel zones* in which streetwalkers do their work are being closed. These zones are no longer tolerated. Nor are the so-called living room projects, where street walkers can have some coffee, chat with one another, and use small amounts of drugs. Recent reports suggest that very young women from foreign countries do not dare ask their (legalized) colleagues for advice as in the old days (Schaapman and Assante 2005). Maybe that is why some cities have kept to the old policy of tolerance, this time especially for women without a work permit (Goderie, Spierings, and ter Woerd 2002, p. 109).

Most prosecutions now focus on the trade in human persons as the legal infringement (Art. 250a of the Penal Code).[5] In the Netherlands, there is a National Reporter on trade in human persons. Since 2000 an increase in this kind of crime has taken place. In 2002, fifty-five criminal investigations regarding trade in human persons were concluded, of which 76 percent involved transborder trade in human beings. In that year, 201 cases were recorded by prosecutors in which there was a suspicion of trade in human beings; in 13 percent, there were under-aged victims. In most recorded cases, the suspects were prosecuted (70 percent), and in cases reaching the court, 89 percent were punished with an average sentence of twenty-one months' imprisonment. In about 20 percent of registered cases, some form of sexual violence was charged, and the average punishment was three years (Korvinus 2004, pp. 246–47). To non-Dutch readers, these punishments may not seem severe, but they are about the same as those that the average rapist receives.

Crime has a foreign flavor in this area. Of 201 suspects, only fifty-three were born in the Netherlands (most came from Turkey, Bulgaria, and Albania), forty-seven were women, and twenty-five were minors (Korvinus 2004, tables 7.5, 7.7). Of the victims, about a quarter are under-age. In a recent survey of relief organizations, 315 under-age prostitutes were found, of whom 33.5 percent were Dutch, 28 percent foreign (often Moroccan), and 39 percent recently immigrated. Because of the general lack of certainty regarding figures on prostitution, these figures should be assessed with some care.

---

[5] A new act is under consideration in which not only sexual exploitation but all kinds of exploitation will be looked at as trade in human persons, which implies that it is no longer looked at as a crime of vice but as a crime against personal freedom.

The researchers noted that only one in nine minor prostitutes seemed to work on a voluntary basis, but, of course, so-called pocket money prostitutes are not inclined to look for help at the relief organizations (Venicz and van Wesenbeeck 2004). Under-aged girls are often brought into prostitution by so called "lover boys," who start faking love and end up supplying drugs and using violence. Most adult foreign victims come from central and eastern Europe. Foreign women are pressured not only by force, but also by withholding passports and visas; in cases of Nigerian victims, voodoo is being mentioned (see Lehti and Aromaa 2006).

Lifting the ban on brothels did not achieve what it was meant to. Prostitutes are unhappy because of the taxes they must pay on incomes that are estimated by the tax department but that prostitutes say are much higher than the average prostitute can really earn. Only a small minority have their own business. The most vulnerable, children and victims of human trafficking, are worse off than before. These are unintended effects of what some might too easily call the decriminalization of prostitution. A discussion is under way in Amsterdam in which some seem to opt for a new ban on brothels. The earlier situation of tolerance may have been preferable to a decriminalization that has brought new, hard problems in its wake.

C. Tolerating Euthanasia

In Holland, a physician may legally administer a lethal injection to a terminally ill patient who asks to die. The Act on the Termination of Life on Request and Assisted Suicide (hereafter, the Act on Euthanasia 2001) came into force in 2002; a legal control mechanism was established to make this possible.

This can be understood only against the background of tolerance. The drafters of the Penal Code of 1886 thought that a doctor who observed medical ethics should not be punished. But safeguarding life, not the wishes of an individual patient, was at the core of traditional medical ethics. Both abortion and euthanasia were forbidden: a fundamental value was at stake.

This lasted until 1970 and 1982, respectively, when official commissions were established to investigate possibilities of legalized abortion and euthanasia (Sutorius 1986). Because the commissions were not constituted on the basis of expertise, but to represent various religious and secular groups, everyone knew what would happen, and did happen: the commissions did not offer straightforward advice. But as is customary in the Netherlands, this did not stop the debate. The most important decisions are not made (certainly they were not in those days) by government, let alone by expert groups. It all happened in the grey zones of civil society, where no longer only religious groups but also professional groups take the lead.

Concerning both issues, the prosecutor and the Royal Dutch Medical Association were in the front lines of the discussion. Regarding abortion, the first discussions took place in the 1960s, and in 1971 the Medical Association published guidelines that made enforcement of the ban on abortion in ordinary cases no longer feasible ("Richtlijnen," 1971). The discussion on legalization began with strong feelings, but they slowly faded away. The result was an act that took effect in 1984. It authorized licensing of certain hospitals and clinics to perform abortions. However, an abortion is not allowed if the fetus is supposed to be able to live outside the mother's body—that is, after twenty weeks of pregnancy (that is recalculated on a regular basis). Abortions performed outside the licensed clinics are forbidden.

In this subsection I concentrate on euthanasia, but its history is an echo of the history of dealing with abortion, and that story needs telling. Regarding euthanasia, there was first discussion in 1973–84, then acceptance by the Medical Association and the Supreme Court in 1985–90, followed by promises of tolerance from prosecutors after negotiations with the Medical Association in 1990–2001, and followed then by a change of law. In the beginning it was not completely clear what the relevant issues were because of conceptual difficulties in delineating the meaning of the word euthanasia. Concepts such as active and passive euthanasia were insufficiently precise to inform debate over the boundaries between euthanasia and related phenomena such as pain relief and termination of life-prolonging treatment.

The Central Bureau of Statistics (CBS) differentiates between cases of dying with and without an end-of-life decision (CBS 2003, tables 7.20, 7.22). The former cases can be separated into euthanasia (the administration of drugs with the explicit intention of ending the patient's life on his or her explicit request), assisted suicide, and killing without request. This last category is meant for those patients who are dying but are unable to make the request because of serious bodily impairment (table 9).

G. van der Wal and P. J. van der Maas were the first to collect

TABLE 9

Dying in the Netherlands

	1990	1995	2001
Total amount of dead	128.824	135.675	140.377
Without end-of-life decision	78,513	78,689	79,354
	(61%)	(58%)	(56%)
Nonnatural of which			5,444
			(4%)
Suicide			1,473
Homicide and manslaughter			202
Traffic accidents			996
With end-of-life decision	50,311	56,986	61,024
	(39%)	(42%)	(43%)
Probable hastening of death:			
No (further) treatment	11,956	9,404	10,610
	(9%)	(7%)	(8%)
Intensifying alleviation	19,010	21,589	25,793
	(15%)	(16%)	(18%)
Intentional hastening of death	4,851	3,784	2,055
	(4%)	(3%)	(1.5%)
Intended furthering of death:			
No (further) treatment	11,113	18,038	17,902
	(9%)	(13%)	(13%)
Euthanasia	2,163	3,020	3,444
	(1.7%)	(2.2%)	(2.5%)
Assisted suicide	242	238	283
	(.2%)	(.2%)	(.2%)
Killing without request	976	913	938
	(.8%)	(.7%)	(.7%)

SOURCE.—CBS (2003); van der Wal et al. (2003).

empirical data. They conducted in-depth interviews with over 400 physicians and examined death certificate studies based on all deaths reported in the period August 1 to December 1 in various years. Their findings clarify the importance of conceptual differences, especially given cultural difficulties that many people, including doctors, outside the Netherlands have with blunt phrases such as "furthering death." They might prefer "not prolonging life," but in Dutch culture, this is seen as an irresponsible euphemism.

The death certificate studies showed that in 1995 about 39 percent of all deaths appeared to be preceded by a medical decision that probably or certainly furthered death (2001, 43.8 percent). However, in 18.8 percent (in 2001, 20.1 percent) this meant alleviation of symptoms with a possible life-shortening effect—that is, an action that might in some cases be called indirect euthanasia (or terminal sedation[6]) but in other cases simple medical pain relief. And it meant that 17.9 percent (2001, 20.1) of the cases were nontreatment decisions; this might be called "passive euthanasia." Only in 1.7 percent of cases (1995, 2.1; 2001, 2.6) did the certificates show euthanasia (by administering drugs etc.); 0.2 percent (2001, 0.2) physician-assisted suicide; and 0.8 percent (2001, 0.7) ending of life without the patients' explicit request (van der Wal et al. 2003).

According to the interviews, there was an increase over the years in requests for euthanasia (8,900 to 9,700 and 9,700) and an increase in euthanasia practices from 1.9 to 2.3 and 2.2 percent. The proportion of physicians who said that they would never perform euthanasia fell from 4 percent in 1990 to 3 percent in 1995 and 1 percent in 2001. The increase in the number of physicians who had ever performed euthanasia or assisted in suicide between 1995 and 2001 occurred among family physicians (63–71 percent) and nursing home physicians (21–36 percent) but not clinical specialists (37 percent) (van der Wal et al. 2003). The reason is that euthanasia is mainly performed among patients dying of cancer; the rise in euthanasia was largest among these patients. Family doctors ordinarily care for patients dying at home, and many patients dying of cancer prefer to be there, among relatives and loved ones (Muijsenbergh 2001). The reader should bear in mind that it is still accurate to say that almost no one (there are problems with illegal aliens) is excluded from the Dutch health care system. This means that the preference to die at home is not driven by lack of money.

The real liberalization of euthanasia began in 1972 when Ms. Postma, a Dutch doctor, terminated her mother's life with an injection of morphine. The mother, a widow of seventy-eight, had been in a nursing home since a cerebral hemorrhage had left her paralyzed on one side a few months earlier, and she had asked her daughter several times to end her life. The medical inspector testified in court that the average doctor in the Netherlands no longer considered it necessary to prolong a patient's life endlessly. The court convicted Postma, especially because the mother was not in a terminal phase of her illness.

---

[6] This is drugging someone into unconsciousness, after which he or she does not receive any food or fluids. In about 12 percent of deaths, deep sedation has been used. The basic idea is that the moment of dying is not furthered by the doctor. Terminal sedation is not considered euthanasia.

However, in its reasoning it opened the possibility of accepting euthanasia in slightly different situations. This was the beginning of a long-lasting debate (Rechtbank Leeuwarden, February 21, 1972, *NJ* 1973, 183; see also Griffiths, Bood, and Weyers 1998).

Of course, there were opponents: particularly the strict Calvinist churches and the Roman Catholic Church. But advocates of the liberalization of euthanasia such as the Dutch Association for Voluntary Euthanasia began to organize. Even more important, the Medical Disciplinary Tribunal of Amsterdam ruled in 1978 that a doctor had not done wrong in giving a patient sleep-inducing drugs even though he, and the patient and her kin, knew that she might never awaken because she would not notice if she began to suffocate (confirmed by the Central Medical Disciplinary Tribunal, *Tijdschrift voor Gezondheidsrecht* 1978, no. 52).

The legal breakthrough occurred in 1984, when the Supreme Court vacated a verdict of the Amsterdam Court of Appeals with this explanation: "One would have expected the Court of Appeals to have considered . . . whether, according to responsible medical opinion, subject to the applicable norms of medical ethics, this was, as claimed by the defendant, a situation of necessity" (HR, November 27, 1984, *NJ* 1985, 106; partly translated in Griffiths, Bood, and Weyers [1998, pp. 322–28]). In the same year in which the Medical Association specified the official requirements of careful practice regarding euthanasia, the Supreme Court ruled that a doctor who followed these requirements should be acquitted because of justifiable necessity. During this period, the highest-ranking public prosecutors examined about 120 of 6,324 reported cases in the period 1991–95: twenty-two led to new investigations, and thirteen doctors were prosecuted. More important from the perspective of tolerance, the dismissal of the other cases based on the expediency principle was thought to be acceptable (Noyon et al. 2003 [comment on art. 293, n. 18]).

In 1993 a first change was made in the law on the disposal of corpses, and in 1998 an official procedure was established to report euthanasia and assisted suicide ("Wet op de lijkbezorging," *Staatsblad* 1993, 643; "Directive on Regional Review Boards Euthanasia," *Staatscourant* 1998, no. 101). This procedure set into being a new phenomenon (again the really important move was not made by law but by directive, trumping the statutory law): five regional review boards each consisting of a lawyer, a physician, and a specialist on ethics or religion, all of high distinction, to whom reports should be sent by doctors who performed euthanasia.

With the Act on Euthanasia of 2001, the evolution from incidents allowed by general tolerance to codification concluded. The review boards have received slightly wider powers ("Euthanasiewet," *Staatsblad* 2001, 194). Most of the case law of the Supreme Court was codified, and it generally accepted the ideas of professional doctors. The requirements of scrupulousness—as they had evolved in earlier case law—were laid down in the act:

- the doctor must be persuaded that the request for euthanasia was voluntary and well considered;
- the doctor must be persuaded that there is incurable and unbearable suffering;
- the patient must be informed about the situation and his or her prospects;
- the doctor and the patient must both be persuaded that no other solution was available; at least one other, independent physician must be consulted;
- the actual ending of life or the assistance with suicide must have been executed in a medically meticulous way (by the physician himself or herself).

Afterward, the doctor is required to give notice to the municipal physician and the review board. The numbers of reports by doctors of having engaged in euthanasia have definitely risen, from 486 in 1990, to 1,446 in 1995 and 2,216 in 1999; but a decline set in from 2,054 in 2001 to 1,815 in 2003 (Toetsingscommissies 2003 [http://www .toetsingscommissieseuthanasie.nl]). According to the van der Wal and van der Maas research group, 54 percent of physicians report acts of euthanasia and assisted suicide. There is a difference between the 60–66 percent of the family doctors, 41 percent of doctors in nursing homes, and 33 percent of medical specialists (in hospitals). In 2003 there were 1,558 reports from family doctors, 214 reports from specialists in hospitals, and 43 from doctors in nursing homes (Toetsingscommissies 2003). The recent decline probably has to do with improvements in palliative care and pain alleviation, but maybe has occurred also because the review boards are demanding in asking details about incidents.

Between 1998 and 2002 the regional review boards concluded that seven out of 7,000 cases were unjustifiable; in 2003 the number was eight. These cases were passed on to the Public Prosecutor. In the period 1981–2003, twenty physicians were prosecuted (Toetsingscommissies 2003). In seven cases it was decided that the euthanasia was justified because of necessity, three doctors were found guilty without punishment, and six were convicted and punished with conditional imprisonment between one week and six months. The others were acquitted (Noyon et al. 2003 [comment on art. 293, n. 18]). Not included are cases having nothing to do with euthanasia. In 2004 a nurse was sentenced to life imprisonment for murdering four patients and three attempted homicides.

A problem for the public prosecutors is that it is hard to prosecute a physician for murder if everything was done according to the rules but the doctor did not consult an independent second physician selected from a specified group of specialist doctors (*SCEN-doctors*), but another local physician or did not act meticulously as, for example, by using the wrong medication. In the most recent guidelines for the prosecution, it is not thought to be necessary to prosecute in these two instances ("Aanwijzing vervolgingsbeslissing inzake actieve levensbeëindiging op verzoek," *Nederlandse Staatscourant* [December 23, 2003, no. 48].

It is hard to try to assess the attitude of the Dutch general population on euthanasia. In general, however, consensus has been reached concerning the acceptability of "passive" (abstaining from life-sustaining treatment) and "indirect" euthanasia (causing death as a result of using painkillers in doses likely to shorten life). About active euthanasia there were differences in view between those who speak of murder and those who say that it all has to do with respecting a last will. Christian democratic voters were not inclined to accept legalization (decriminalization), but only a few opponents wielded the pen (Griffith, Bood, and Weyers 1998, p. 96). It was more a question of coalition politics that stood in the way of the new statute than fierce public opposition. The debate took place in the open—on television and in newspapers—but it was a debate between lawyers and doctors.

Some want to go a bit further: for instance, assistance with suicide in cases of nonsomatic suffering was accepted by the Supreme Court in theory, but in practice it was rejected because a realistic alternative was at hand. In the public debate a lively discussion was started when a well-known professor of law, Huub Drion, raised the subject of hand-ing out deadly pills in order to give old people the possibility of committing suicide if they are "done with living." Of the Dutch population, 45 percent were in favor of "Drion's pill," 20 percent were neutral, and 35 percent were against it (van der Wal et al. 2003). And there were also lively debates on the legitimacy of terminating life without a specific request of the patient, for instance in cases of severely defective newborn babies and patients in long-term comas. It is supposed to be a very important thing for doctors to be able to discuss openly with the parents the situation of newborn, severely handicapped children. And then there are demented persons who are not entirely competent during the entire course of decision making. Everyone—including advocates—regarded these as hard cases. These were not taken care of in the 2001 legislation, but the spirit of tolerance facilitates an open debate.

V. Conclusion

Tolerance is a way to sidestep negative reactions to things that are morally not approved. Behind the general concept I have differentiated six conceptions that are interconnected. Tolerance as acceptance (or toleration) of difference in religious matters—as it existed in the seventeenth century—has gradually evolved into acceptance of moral ambiguity in general. In the context of crime, the concept has taken on a ring of leniency regarding incivilities and petty crime. Note the difference. In the cultural context, tolerance means something "big." It means accepting something one really does not like. In the legal context at the end of the twentieth century, it has a watered-down connotation of governmental indifference and apathy regarding illegalities.

However, in the Netherlands a little earlier in the culturally tolerant social climate of the1970s, tolerance was also conceptualized as a legal category. In both administrative and criminal law, tolerance became a legal concept. It meant that in specific circumstances government was not allowed to act with a sanction or to prosecute certain infractions. Thus tolerance came to be a pragmatic tool to minimize negative consequences from too-strict enforcement of the ever-increasing number of legal rules in the welfare society, and it became part of a "policy of tolerance," a sophisticated complex of regulations (that are at face value contrary to statutory law). These different conceptions are intertwined: (the cultural) acceptance of moral ambiguity, (the almost organizational) governmental indifference, and (the legal) regulated leniency have something in common. It is sometimes difficult for the general public or politicians to differentiate among these various conceptions of tolerance.

Understanding tolerance is important in understanding Dutch history. Tolerance enables the Dutch to deal with moral problems if priority is given to the reduction of harm over moral outrage. That is why some might say that tolerance is important for civilization; others might think that it is proof of a lack of stamina and backbone. This type of moral evaluation of tolerance is less interesting than the possibility that pragmatic acceptance might go too far, legitimizing restraint after a period of tolerance. This has happened in recent years, when tolerance often was seen not in cultural terms of forbearance but of governmental leniency and indifference.

We might conclude looking at the six conceptualizations I differentiated before. The importance of tolerance or toleration in religious matters has been lost on the Dutch in the late twentieth century, but its importance is on the rise if we bear in mind the difficulties in our understanding of the Muslim communities—and vice versa—after 9/11 and the terrorist attacks, the van Gogh killing, and recently the Danish cartoon controversy.

The acceptance of moral ambiguity, however, is not yet declining. In the late-night hours, everyone can look at *Playboy*'s in-depth "documentaries" of the pornographic industry, spiced up by ads on telephone sex. But things might change: lessening tolerance regarding gays, threatening behavior regarding Jews by Muslim youngsters, and threatening behavior by white youngsters regarding Muslims may also be illustrative.

Incivilities increasingly are not accepted by the general public and by government. People report more often to the police; the police more readily define incivilities as offenses and are prepared to act against them. And so are prosecutors and judges. The conceptual net is widening. According to the Dutch Supreme Court, one is a victim of rape if subjected to a forced French kiss.

Governmental indifference is no longer accepted. One of the Dutch words for tolerance (*gedogen*) seems to have become taboo. Not only indifference but also leniency is loosening its power.

With regard to the first four conceptions, tolerance seems to be in an endangered state. At the religious and cultural levels, reduced organizational tolerance has brought about harsher policies in policing and justice activities.

However, it is worthwhile to look a little more closely at the last two conceptions and to consider the advantages and the disadvantages of tolerance as a pragmatic tool and as a legal policy instrument. Some further conclusions may be drawn from the policies on drugs, prostitution, and euthanasia.

First, Dutch policies of tolerance make it possible to focus on safety and security instead of on moral differences. The Dutch prefer to talk about difficult problems in terms of harm reduction than to dissimulate about the existence of certain illegalities.

Second, morally tinged problems in the Netherlands are differentiated between dangerous and less dangerous forms of questionable behavior. So a line has been drawn between dangerous hard and less dangerous soft drugs and between vice in general and vice against minors or people in dependent situations. And so euthanasia and all kinds of other forms of end-of-life decisions have been differentiated.

Third, by drawing these lines, the Dutch are not saying that one thing is good and the other is bad. Because discussions can be started, it became possible to postpone a direct negative moral judgment regarding the worst of the differentiated categories. Some acceptance of hard drugs was brought about. It became possible to take care of dependent people in the prostitution business. And even killing without request became an issue for discussion. This must be welcomed. In table 9 I provide numbers of murders and traffic accidents in order to show the scope of the problem of end-of-life decisions. The number of mercy killings without request is more than four times higher than the number of homicides and manslaughters. However, even if rational discussion is welcomed, it is possible to differ on whether the activities of the criminal justice system are sufficient regarding all differentiated cases. Those who do not think so, and people who agree with the current situation, are inclined to discuss this in terms of tolerance.

Fourth, in all the issues discussed in the preceding paragraphs there is a logical development from public discussion in general (sometimes after a certain incident), to discussion among experts and acceptance by the Prosecutor's Office (often in general based on guidelines), to legalization by establishing certain formal requirements. The discussions in the first place would not be possible without the postponement of a moral judgment.

Fifth, official tolerance did not end illegalities in the relevant areas. The Dutch differentiate between tolerance of individual illegalities and nontolerance of organized crime. Tolerance regarding individual offenses legitimizes a focus on "big crime." The huge seizures of drugs and increasing activities against traders in human beings prove that tolerance of individual "offenses" in these areas does not imply tolerance of organized crime at all. However, the difficulties of fighting organized crime are huge because of the good logistics of Dutch airports and seaports.

Sixth, official tolerance has not seemed to influence drug use amounts or euthanasia practices. However, this is difficult to substantiate because of a lack of reliable figures. The first rise in the use of cannabis might be partly due to tolerance. Relatively low levels of abuse compared with those in other countries and the recent decline in euthanasia reports (suggesting a slight decline in euthanasia) might also partly result from the open discussions.

Seventh, official tolerance has negative side effects. The Rotterdam case of tolerance of drugs illustrates that it makes a huge difference whether tolerance has taken the form of acceptance after discussion or the form of indifference. The first seems to lead to the proposed advantages; the second, to enormous discontent. The legalization of prostitution has led to a worsened position of foreign prostitutes who do not possess official documents. And the official way of dealing with euthanasia has not put an end to the unknown number of informal euthanasia practices.

Tolerance is a mixed cultural and legal phenomenon. One negative side effect of the legal technique of tolerance is difficulty in distinguishing between governmental indifference and a governmental policy of tolerance. Policies regarding drugs, prostitution, and euthanasia certainly were part of such a policy of tolerance. But relative indifference regarding (petty) crimes of drugs addicts could easily be looked at as a form of indifference—mistakenly legitimized by the lenient policy regarding drug offenses.

In recent years, public opinion has demanded less leniency, especially—it is not pleasant to acknowledge—regarding suspects from ethnic minority groups. And here the cultural side of the phenomenon is revealed. Tolerance as forbearance of a negative reaction has to do with the acceptance of threatening otherness. In the multicultural melting pot the Netherlands has become in a very short time—

54,000 Muslims in 1971 compared with 944,000 in 2004—this is a highly relevant notion. Again it is important to stress that tolerance as a cultural phenomenon is not the same as indifference, nor is it the same as acceptance of something that cannot be confronted. The Protestants of the seventeenth century were not indifferent about the religions of the Catholics or the Jews. They may have disapproved of these heretics, but they hated it even more if the populace started to kill the heretics.

In recent times the Dutch have had to think about religious tolerance. After the murder of filmmaker Theo van Gogh in November 2004 by a young Muslim fanatic, the climate has gotten worse for the Muslim population. The killer reacted to the extremely aggressive way of speaking of van Gogh, who wrote columns in free dailies. It might be hard to understand that it was tolerated that he called Muslims people who have sex with goats. But the same van Gogh made a film of a love story between a Dutch girl and a Moroccan boy, and worked with petty criminals of ethnic descent to make another movie about their predicament. He insulted Jews, but spokespersons from this community successfully initiated criminal procedures. The Muslim community did not have these kinds of spokespersons. They had a guy who nowadays is called a terrorist.

Theo van Gogh was provocative, as was Pim Fortuyn. They were both exponents of an extremely tolerant culture. In this essay, tolerance has been described as a late-twentieth-century technique of dealing with sensitive questions regarding drugs, prostitution, and euthanasia. Just about the year 2000 we were thrown back from tolerance as a technique to tolerance as a cultural imperative. In our multicultural society we have to learn to deal with differences again: with tolerance as something "big." At the moment we do not really have no-go areas as they do in France, Germany, and the United Kingdom. But that will not last long.

I hope we will remember the lessons of our ancestors: maybe we do not like our neighbors, but we will drown together if we do not try to make the best of it. And so again we will start differentiating between terrorists and "angry Muslims," between freedom of speech and insult and threat. We will start making new policies and new laws. But that seems to be a long way ahead. It is hard to learn to postpone judgment in times of crises.

REFERENCES

Barzun, Jacques. 2001. *From Dawn to Decadence*. New York: Harper Collins.
Baschwitz, K. 1948. *De strijd met den duivel*. Amsterdam: Uitgeverij Andries Blitz.
Becker, J. W., and J. S. de Wit. 2000. *Secularisatie in de jaren negentig*. The Hague: Sociaal en Cultureel Planbureau.
Blom, M., J. Oudhof, R. V. Bijl, and B. F. M. Bakker, eds. 2005. *Verdacht van criminaliteit*. The Hague: Ministry of Justice, Research and Documentation Center, Central Bureau of Statistics, Cahier.
Blom, T. 1998. *Drugs in het recht, recht onder druk*. Arnhem: Gouda Quint.
Boekhout van Solingen, Tim. 2004. *Dealing with Drugs in Europe*. The Hague: BJU Legal Publishers.
CBS (Central Bureau of Statistics). 2003. *Vademecum gezondheidsstatistiek. 2003.* The Hague: CBS.
Daalder, A. L. 2004. *Lifting the Ban on Brothels: Prostitution in 2000–2001*. The Hague: Ministry of Justice, Research and Documentation Center.
Daalder, H. 1966. "The Netherlands: Opposition in a Segmented Society." In *Political Oppositions in Western Democracies*, edited by Robert A. Dahl. New Haven, CT: Yale University Press.
———. 1974. "The Consociational Democracy Theme." *World Politics* 26 (July):602–21.
———. 1981. "Consociationalism, Centre and Periphery in the Netherlands." In *Mobilization, Center-Periphery Structures and Nation Building*, edited by P. Torsvik. Oslo/Bergen: Universitaetsforlaget.
Davies, N. 1996. *Europe, a History*. Oxford: Oxford University Press.
de Vries, Theun. 1991. *Spinoza*. Amsterdam: De Prom.
Downes, David. 1988. *Contrasts in Tolerance: Post-war Penal Policy in the Netherlands and England and Wales*. Oxford: Clarendon.
Egelkamp, M. M. E. 2002. "Inflation von Gewalt?" PhD dissertation, Groningen University, Faculty of Law, Department of Criminology.
Eggen, A. Th. J., and W. van der Heide. 2005. *Criminaliteit en rechtshandhaving 2004*. The Hague: Ministry of Justice, Research and Documentation Center, Central Bureau of Statistics.
Engbersen, Godfried, Joanne van der Leun, and Jan de Boom. 2007. "The Fragmentation of Migration and Crime in the Netherlands." In *Crime and Justice: An Annual Review of Research*, vol. 36, edited by Michael Tonry. Chicago: University of Chicago Press.
Fijnaut, C., and F. Bovenkerk. 1995–96. "Georganiseerde criminaliteit in Nederland." In *Kamerstukken* [Papers of Parliament], 24 072, nr. 20, pp. 89–91.
Goderie, M., F. Spierings, and S. ter Woerd. 2002. *Illegaliteit, onvrijwilligheid en minderjarigheid in de prostitutie een jaar na de opheffing van het bordeelverbod*. Utrecht/The Hague: Verwij-Jonker.
Griffiths, A. Bood, and H. Weyers. 1998. *Euthanasia and Law in the Netherlands*. Amsterdam: Amsterdam University Press.
Haveman, R. 1998. *Voorwaarden voor strafbaarstelling van vrouwenhandel*. Arnheim: Gouda Quint.

Holloway, Katy, Trevor Bennett, and Claire Lower. 2004. "Trends in Drug Use and Offending." Home Office Research Findings no. 219. London: Home Office, Research, Development and Statistics Directorate.

Inglehart, R. 1997. *Modernization and Postmodernization*. Princeton, NJ: Princeton University Press.

International Centre for Prison Studies. 2006. *World Prison Brief*. http://www.kcl.ac.uk.

Israel, J. 2001. *Radical Enlightenment*. Oxford: Oxford University Press.

Jaarverslag Openbaar Ministerie. 1970. *Kamerstukken* [Papers of Parliament] 1971–72, 11 500, chap. VI, nr. 3, annex IV.

Junger-Tas, Josine, and Marianne Junger. In this volume. "The Dutch Criminological Enterprise."

Korvinus, A. G. 2004. *Mensenhandel, derde rapportage van de Nationaal Rapporteur* (July). The Hague: National Reporter.

Lehti, Martti, and Kauko Aromaa. 2006. "Trafficking for Sexual Exploitation." In *Crime and Justice: An Annual Review of Research*, vol. 34, edited by Michael Tonry. Chicago: University of Chicago Press.

Leistra, G., and P. Nieuwbeerta. 2003. *Moord en doodslag in Nederland*. Amsterdam: Prometheus.

Leuw, Ed. 1991. "Drugs and Drug Policy in the Netherlands." In *Crime and Justice: A Review of Research*, vol. 14, edited by Michael Tonry. Chicago: University of Chicago Press.

Leuw, Ed, and I. Haen Marshall, eds. 1996. *Between Prohibition and Legalization: The Dutch Experiment in Drug Policy*. Amsterdam: Kugler.

Levack, Brian. 1995. *The Witch-Hunt in Modern Europe*. London: Longman.

Lijphardt, A. 1968. *The Politics of Accommodation: Pluralism and Democracy in the Netherlands*. Berkeley: University of California Press.

Meijer, R. F., M. Grapendaal, M. M. J. van Ooyen, B. S. J. Wartna, M. Brouwers, and A. A. M Essers. 2004. *Geregistreerde drugscriminaliteit in cijfers*. The Hague: Ministry of Justice, Research and Documentation Center.

Mijnhardt, W. M. 1992. "The Dutch Enlightenment." In *The Dutch Republic in the Eighteenth Century*, edited by M. C. Jacob and W. W. Mijnhardt. Ithaca, NY: Cornell University Press.

Netherlands National Drug Monitor. 2003. *Annual Report 2003*. Utrecht: Trimbos Institute.

Noyon, T. J., G. E. Langemeijer, and J. Remmelink (continued by J. W. Fokkens and A. J. Machielse). 2003. *Het wetboek van strafrecht*. Deventer: Kluwer.

"Richtlijnen ten behoeve van de uitvoering van abortus provocatus." 1971. *Medisch Contact* 26:1025–28.

Schaapman, K., and A. Assante. 2005. "Het onzichtbare zichtbaar gemaakt: Prostitutie in Amsterdam anno 2005." Memo for the Amsterdam City Council 2005/337.

Schama, Simon. 1987. *The Embarrassment of Riches*. New York: Knopf.

Schuyt, Kees. 2001. "Tolerantie en democratie." In *Rekenschap 1650–2000*, edited by D. Fokkema and F. Grijzenhoud. The Hague: SDU.

Shorto, Russell. 2005. *The Island at the Center of the World: The Epic Story of*

Dutch Manhattan and the Forgotten Colony That Shaped America. New York: Vintage Books.

Sutorius, E. Ph. R. 1986. "Abortus en euthanasie." In *Gedenkboek honderd jaar wetboek van strafrecht*, edited by J. P. Balkema et al. Arnhem: Gouda Quint.

't Hart, A. C. 1986. "Criminal Law Policy in the Netherlands." In *Criminal Law in Action*, edited by Jan van Dijk, Charles Haffmans, Frits Rüter, Julian Schutte, and Simon Stolwijk. Arnhem: Gouda Quint.

Toulmin, Stephen. 1990. *Cosmopolis: The Hidden Agenda of Modernity*. New York: Free Press.

United Nations. 2004. *World Drug Report*. Vienna: United Nations. http://www.unodc.org.

van den Brink, G. 2002. *Mondiger of moeilijke*. Wetenschappelijke Raad voor het Regeringsbeleid. The Hague: SDU.

van den Muijsenbergh, Maria. 2001. *Palliatieve zorg door de huisarts*. Nijmegen: Drukkerij SSN.

van der Torre, E. J. 2004. "Rotterdamse drugs scenes: Het kostbare gelijk van de straat." In *Veiligheid*, edited by E. R. Muller. Alphen aan den Rijn: Kluwer.

van der Veen, Gabry. 2006. *Interpreting Fear, Crime, Risk and Unsafety*. The Hague: BJU/Legal Publishers.

van der Wal, G., A. van der Heide, B. D. Onwuteaka-Philipsen, and P. J. van der Maas. 2003. *Medische besluitvorming aan het einde van het leven*. Utrecht: De Tijdstroom.

van der Wal, G., P. J. van der Maas, B. D. Onwuteaka-Philipsen, A. van der Heide, D. Koper, I. Keij-Deerenberg, J. A. C. Rietjens, M. L. Rurup, A. M. Vrakking, J. J. Georges, M. T. Muller, G. van der Wal, and P. J. van der Maas. 2003. "Euthanasia and Other End-of-Life Decisions in the Netherlands in 1990, 1995, and 2001." *Lancet* 362(August 2):395-99. http://image.thelancet.com/extras/03art3297web.pdf.

van Deursen, A. Th. 1999. *Mensen van klein vermogen*. Amsterdam: Ooievaar.

van Gelder, R. 2003. *Naporra's omweg, het leven van een VOC-matroos (1731–1793)*. Amsterdam/Antwerp: Atlas.

van Swaaningen, René. 1998. "Regression to the Mean: Managerialism, Actuarialism and (Zero) Tolerance in the Netherlands." Paper presented at the annual meeting of the American Society of Criminology, Washington DC, November.

Venicz, L., and I. van Wesenbeeck. 2004. *Aard en omvang van (gedwongen) prostitutie onder minderjarige (allochtone) meisj*. Utrecht: Nederlands Instituut voor Sociaal Seksuologisch Onderzoek.

Zaitch, Damián. 2002. *Trafficking Cocaine: Colombian Drug Entrepreneurs in the Netherlands*. The Hague: Kluwer Law.

Josine Junger-Tas and Marianne Junger

The Dutch Criminological Enterprise

ABSTRACT

Dutch criminology was influenced first by France, then by Germany, and, since World War II, by the United States. American influence has been strong in many fields of science, particularly in the social sciences, including criminology. The Netherlands has mainly followed American developments in criminological theory. There have been few original Dutch theoretical contributions. Most criminologists, including those mainly interested in qualitative research, respect generally acknowledged methodological rules, increasingly using proven research techniques and sophisticated statistical analysis. Policy research has become prevalent, with most research oriented to answering policy questions. The reason is that in a country without big private foundations, most funding is government-related.

Perhaps no scientific discipline is so intertwined with the society in which it develops as criminology. The way academic criminology has evolved in the Netherlands shows important influences of the social and economic structure of society, the academic structure, the needs of state and local authorities, and, of course, the media. All play a role and made the discipline as it now is.

It is difficult to say exactly when Dutch criminology started. Dirk Volckertszoon Coornhert (1522–90), who was imprisoned during the Spanish rule over the Netherlands, wrote his famous book *The Discipline of Villains* (*Boeventucht* in Dutch) in 1567 while in prison (Franke 1990*b*). He is considered the intellectual father of the *rasphuis* and *spin-*

Josine Junger-Tas is a professor and fellow in the Willem Pompe Institute, University of Utrecht. Marianne Junger is professor of psychology, University of Amsterdam, and is affiliated with the University of Utrecht.

huis, which developed in the eighteenth century. However, although it is somewhat arbitrary, in this essay we mainly consider twentieth-century trends.

Most people in Europe would say that criminology emerged as a distinctive discipline with the publication in 1876 of Lombroso's *L'uome delinquente*. This publication had considerable influence. Lombroso was one of the first empirical criminologists: he collected a mass of empirical material in order to try to support his theories. Later the Englishman Goring (1913) replicated these studies more rigorously and invalidated Lombroso's hypotheses; but because Lombroso was the first to use empirical methods, he is considered a founding father of criminology.

Three main strands run through this essay. The first one is criminological theory: How did Dutch criminologists view crime, and what theoretical approaches did they use, in the twentieth century? To what extent have theoretical dilemmas been addressed, including whether the essential subject of criminology should be the individual offender or the phenomenon of crime in society; are the causes of crime to be found primarily in the individual or in the social environment; why do people persist in or desist from crime; can crime be eradicated in society or can it be controlled, and if so what social and formal reactions should be taken? Our interest is in the extent to which these questions have been more or less satisfactorily addressed in Dutch criminology.

Has there been an original Dutch contribution to the discussion of theoretical dilemmas being debated at the beginning of the twentieth century? Regretfully, not much theory building has taken place in the Netherlands. Most Dutch criminologists follow the dominant theoretical view that crime is essentially the product of individuals with criminal predispositions, whether because of genetic or innate factors or a failing education process, and accordingly that retribution and deterrence are appropriate policy regimes. The consequence is apparent in the country's increasingly harsh penal policies and rising prison rates, which are supposed to lead to drastic reductions in crime. This does not mean that there has been no interest in theory or that there have been no efforts to test theoretical notions. However, despite some exceptions,[1] theories used in research are of Anglo-Saxon origin.

The second strand is empirical criminology. To what extent must

---

[1] For example, Braithwaite's writings on "reïntegrative shaming" (1989) have had considerable influence, particularly in Flemish Belgium.

theoretical notions and hypotheses be based on empirical evidence: what efforts have been deployed to develop empirical research methods and consistently apply them, in both descriptive and theory-testing research? Here the picture is brighter. From the beginnings of Dutch criminology, scholars showed great interest in fact-finding to support scientific or even political ideas. After World War II social scientists generally welcomed American progress in empirical research methods. This became the main research approach, with recent generations of criminologists acquiring increasingly sophisticated techniques and methods of analysis.

The third strand is policy research. To what extent do criminologists recognize the existence of "applied criminology" and consider it a valid branch of the discipline? Although the volume of applied or policy research has increased considerably over time, questions may be asked about its validity and sometimes about its usefulness; has policy research contributed to scientific progress, and in what ways? Most of the research done in the Netherlands is policy-relevant. This has a lot to do with funding sources, the consequence of which is that the bulk of studies are driven by policy-making questions. Although there have been and continue to be fundamental research and policy studies that contribute to better theoretical insights, more fundamental research is certainly needed.

This essay follows important stages in Dutch criminology. Section I describes the origins of Dutch criminology and Section II one of its major figures, Willem Adriaan Bonger. Although Bonger was a convinced empiricist, his successors promoted a psychiatric and holistic ideology, not based on empirical research, which has had an important influence on penal policy, particularly concerning mentally disturbed offenders. This is the subject of Section III. Section IV describes how critical criminology gained support in the Netherlands in the 1960s. Section V deals with the takeoff of empirical research in the 1970s and 1980s. One consequence was the creation of a governmental research center, the Research and Documentation Centre, located in the Ministry of Justice. Section VI treats the rising importance of this institute, and Section VII considers the problems associated with this type of research. Section VIII looks at recent research trends in the Netherlands, and Section IX discusses the state of Dutch criminology in the early twenty-first century.

All universities in the Netherlands now teach criminology and criminal justice, although most—with the exception of the Free University of Amsterdam—did not traditionally offer a full-fledged master's degree in criminology. They offered a minor attached to law or the social sciences. Recently three universities (Leiden [http://www.law.leidenuniv.nl], Erasmus in Rotterdam [http://www.frg.eur.nl], and the Free University [http://www.vu.nl]) joined together to offer bachelor's and master's degrees. The initiative was highly successful and attracted large numbers of students, which was certainly related to the new focus on criminality and criminal justice that characterizes Dutch society, with many students expecting employment in law enforcement. So now, these—and other—universities offer both bachelor's and master's degrees. Apart from the universities, there are many other educational and research institutes, such as the Center for Police Studies at the University of Twente (IPIT [http://www.utwente.nl; c.d. vandervijver@utwente.nl]) in the east of the country (Enschede) and one at the Free University of Amsterdam (j.naeye@rechten.vu.nl), the Police Academy (npa@lsop.nl) for higher police training, and a higher training institute for judges and prosecutors (SSRservicedesk@ssr.drp.minjus.nl), both located in the east of the country. The last provides postgraduate training for judges, prosecutors, court secretaries, and support staff and continuing education for legal staff. It also provides initial training for young lawyers who plan to become a judge or prosecutor.

There are basically four types of criminological research institutions. First are institutes more or less closely related to the government. The Research and Documentation Centre (WODC [wodc-informatiedesk@minjus.nl]), part of the Ministry of Justice, was launched in 1973 to respond to the ministry's pressing research problems within clear time limits, preferably based on quantitative data. The Netherlands Institute for the Study of Crime and Law Enforcement (NSCR [nscr@nscr.nl]; see Sec. VIII) was set up in the 1980s to do more in-depth research on policy issues. It is funded by the Ministry of Justice and the Netherlands Organization for Scientific Research.

The Social Cultural Planning Bureau (http://www.scp.nl), a departmental institute funded by the Ministry of Health and Social Welfare, which works mostly from secondary sources, is famous for its trend studies on major developments in demographics, the economy, education, health, culture, and crime. Although it started as a service institute for the funding ministry, it works for all government departments, including the Ministry of Justice. The institute increasingly publishes trend studies in English for the European Commission.

Finally, several institutes, originally funded by the Ministry of Health and Social Welfare and conducting research mainly in those fields, have been forced by budget cuts to develop a more commercial approach and to do commissioned research in other governmental fields, including crime and justice.

Second are the university institutes. Most universities have a criminological institute. Because of the troubled financial situations of universities, they depend on funding mainly from third parties. The Netherlands does not have the many foundations that characterize Anglo-Saxon countries, so the most important funding source is the government, particularly the ministries of Justice, Internal Affairs (which is responsible for the Dutch police), Health and Welfare (responsible for youth policies and social services), and Education (responsible for prevention policies in schools). The Netherlands Organization for Scientific Research (NWO [http://www.nwo.nl]) mainly funds PhD students or researchers with a PhD to participate in fundamental research. Its research program includes a number of themes covering nine fields, among which are "cultural heritage," "fundamental life processes," and "innovative technologies." Criminological research is funded under the (sub)themes of "social cohesion" and "cognitions and behavior." A similar organization, Zorgonderzoek Nederland (ZonMw [http://www.zonmw.nl]), focuses on health and welfare research. ZonMw funds studies on aggression, attention deficit/hyperactivity disorder, and, in particular, research on experimental preventive interventions of a psychological nature. Both funding agencies receive their budgets from the state. Screening procedures for funding are careful but time-consuming.

Third are a number of (small) research units related, for example, to the Police Academy, some police departments, and treatment institutions, such as those for juveniles or mentally disordered offenders.

Finally, there are many commercial institutes. Although some are better than others, our experience instructs that their studies are usually conducted hastily and without much theoretical reflection. Their methodology is usually weak, and their outcomes often could be expected without any study at all. Above all, recommendations tend to please those who commissioned the research. Some of these organizations have a standing relationship with a ministry: they generally have a fair idea of the views of the ministry and the public's mood and are masters in framing their results accordingly.

I. The Start of Dutch Criminology—the Early Years

The beginnings of Dutch criminology must be seen in the European context. In the nineteenth and early twentieth centuries Europe led the development of the social and human sciences. For the first time the profound conflict appeared between those who believed that the roots of crime lay in the makeup of the individual and those who considered them to lie in the environment, a conflict that has endured to this day, although a new consensus is slowly being reached. In the Netherlands this conflict was represented by the physician Arnold Aletrino and the social scientist Willem Bonger, but it surfaced more recently in criminologists such as Herman Bianchi and Willem Pompe. For a long time the environmentalists dominated the scene in the Netherlands and elsewhere. In terms of policy impact, both Bonger and Pompe were extremely influential. Bonger actively participated in the Social-Democratic Party, where he could spread his ideas. He was convinced of the importance of the environment both in how children are raised and in how they behave. Pompe's most important legacy is the penitentiary clinics for mentally disturbed offenders that he and his colleagues founded. These clinics still exist, and no one wants to abolish them. Although they were recently denounced by some members of Parliament, following an escape that resulted in a murder by the patient (as the inmates are called), the minister of justice vehemently defended the system, and that was that. So here we note an example of influential theoretical approaches reflected in enduring policy changes.

Lombroso was inspired by Darwin's theory of evolution. He believed that some people were born as criminals, their biological characteristics being based on an atavism, a kind of evolutionary reversion. Lombroso assumed that criminals had smaller brains than conventional people. On this basis he measured a great number of skulls to test his theory, and he encouraged others to do the same. This exhortation was taken up by Aletrino, the Dutch physician and lector at the University of Amsterdam. Aletrino believed that the behavior of criminals was entirely determined by their atavistic characteristics. One should not judge them as responsible human beings because there was no such thing as free will, and since criminals were mentally disturbed, they must be treated (Franke 1990*b*, p. 477). He was influenced by evolutionary ideas and social Darwinism and tried to reform the criminal justice system. For example, he introduced modern ideas about prostitution and homosexuality, which at the time were revolutionary. At the turn of the twentieth century he launched an aggressive attack against the cellular prison system and pleaded for indeterminate sentences in educational reformatories, like those that existed in the United States. Aletrino (1902) compared the skulls of police chiefs, firemen, and physicians with those of murderers, concluding that murderers on average had lower foreheads than the other groups. Although Aletrino did not specify his hypotheses in comparing the two groups and although his data were not collected systematically, his studies were an important step forward, since until then theories were mainly based on speculation and dogmatism (van Dijk, Sagel-Grande, and Toornvliet 2002, pp. 15–17).

At about the same time in Europe, the so-called *moral statistics*, a kind of "moral accounting" about what formed a social problem and required political action (van Kerckvoorde 1995, p. 5), were developing the idea of statistical regularities that can explain crime. Important work was undertaken in several European countries, including France, England, Germany, and Belgium. The Belgian astronomer and mathematician Adolphe Quételet (1796–1874) was one of the founders of scientific crime statistics, relating criminality with sex, age, the nature of the act, education, race, geography, and climate. He introduced the concept of criminal propensity (*penchant au crime*) as "a statistical variable indicating the probability of committing a crime by an average person" (van Kerckvoorde 1995, p. 7).

Among European criminologists there were enormous conflicts between Lombroso's supporters and the French environmentalists. A lot was at stake since the political and practical implications for combating crime are very different if one considers that crime has a biological and genetic origin than if one considers that its principal causes are to be found in the environment. This was a major controversy in the late nineteenth and early twentieth centuries, one that influenced and inspired the first great social scientist and criminologist in the Netherlands, Willem Bonger.

II. The Contribution of Sociology: W. A. Bonger
(1876–1940)

Bonger was born in 1876, the youngest of ten children, three of whom died early. The family was poor, but the situation improved and the three youngest children were allowed to continue their studies, which was unusual for lower-middle-class families. Bonger went to the University of Leiden to study law. While the large majority of students were sons of rich families, Bonger met a number of young men in precarious circumstances like his own. This contributed to their common interest in sociology and what they called "scientific socialism," a combination of scientific positivism and a socialist perspective. Another precipitant of this interest was the poverty, bad housing, alcoholism, and bad health of many factory workers they observed in Leiden.

Bonger throughout his life remained a convinced socialist and was sure that his scientific activities would contribute to changed and improved social conditions in the country. As van Weringh observes (1986, p. 49), "the objective researcher shows how a phenomenon (criminality) is influenced in negative ways, and the socialist states that this is an outrageous situation." Policy considerations were never far from his mind. In 1922 he was appointed the first professor of sociology and criminology at the University of Amsterdam. Bonger's life ended tragically. He committed suicide in 1940. He had always been a strong opponent to the Nazi ideology and had shown his aversion in many publications. To Bonger, the German occupation meant the end of free science.

Bonger was a brilliant and an unrestrained workaholic with little family life. He was intellectually oriented toward France, where research similar to his own developed. His magnum opus was his PhD dissertation (1905), which was written in French: "Criminalité et conditions economiques" (Bonger 1967; van Weringh 1986, pp. 45–54; van Heerikhuizen 1987, pp. 63–147). The study gave him international standing and was published in the United States in 1916 in the Modern Criminal Science series. Later on his books *Race and Crime* and *Introduction to Criminology* were also translated into English.

Bonger's dissertation consisted of two parts. The first is a critical review of the literature of his time on the relationship between crime and economic conditions. This is a historical introduction, which he replicated in his later *Introduction to Criminology* (Bonger 1932, 1954). The second part was Bonger's own study of that relationship. His main theoretical concepts and approach are to be found in his dissertation and changed little during his life.

Much of Bonger's work no longer seems revolutionary. But if one remembers that around 1900 most criminologists were convinced that crime was explained by the innate characteristics of criminals, one realizes how epoch-making his work must have been (van Heerikhuizen 1987, p. 67). Bonger knew well the work of the French Milieu School, the main representatives of whom are Gabriel de Tarde and Jean-Alexandre Lacassagne. De Tarde (1843–1904) was a sociologist, lawyer, and professor of philosophy at the Collège de France in Paris who introduced criminology in France at the turn of the century (1890, 1898). He was opposed to Emile Durkheim and believed that social laws are the outcomes of each individual's actions. He tended to reduce sociology to psychology (1890, 1898). Lacassagne (1843–1924)[2] was a forensic scientist and a criminologist at the University of Lyon.

The main claims of the Milieu School were addressed to the biosociologists. In this respect, Lacassagne proposed a purely sociological approach to criminality (*la sociologie criminelle*) and started to test, correct, and improve the milieu approach and to take account of economic conditions (Lacassagne 1878, 2001). Both ideas were new because little had been written to that time on economic conditions. In addition, there were no empirical data on the ways in which the environment shaped crime.

To demonstrate how the environment and economic conditions shape crime, Bonger used statistics and empirical data to test his theories (Bonger 1967 [1905]). He drew a clear distinction between criminality as an individual act and crime as a phenomenon in society, a distinction that even in our time is not always kept straight by researchers or judicial authorities. He attacked the idea that innate personality traits indicated a tendency toward crime (some now would refer to, say, "a crime gene") and the idea that social phenomena can be reduced to individual tendencies. To Bonger these had to be related to other social phenomena, and that is why he saw criminology as a subdiscipline of sociology.

At that time Bonger did not consider economic conditions very important, particularly when compared to other social factors, particularly increasing secularization. This was considered extremely worrying, and

---

[2] Lacassagne has become famous for his statement *"les sociétés ont les criminels qu'elles méritent"* ("societies have the criminals they deserve").

most scholars were convinced that crime increased as the number of nonreligious persons increased. This was one of the questions Bonger studied, and he was able to refute the hypothesis with statistics showing that the provinces with the highest proportion of nonreligious population had the lowest crime rates. He used this study to show that the important variable was not religion but the circumstances and conditions in which people lived (Bonger 1913, p. 75).

However, the main question Bonger examined in his dissertation is how economic conditions in a capitalist, modern, industrialized society produce crime. Distinguishing among economic crimes, sexual crimes, crimes from revenge or other motives, political crimes, and pathological crimes, Bonger showed that the number of thefts increases when more people fall beneath the subsistence level and that this relationship also holds for a crime such as infanticide. Moreover, he showed the relationships between economic misery and alcoholism and prostitution, and between the dreadful housing conditions of factory workers and sexual crimes such as incest or rape.

At the end of the book the idealist socialist appears, and Bonger predicts a future in which capitalism will be replaced by a system in which the means of production are owned by the community instead of by private persons. We mention this because it shows to what degree Bonger believed that sciences such as sociology and criminology should enlighten policy makers and help them improve social and economic conditions.

Bonger was an empiricist whose principal research method was analysis of statistical data. However, being sensitive to problems of reliability and validity, he also referred to other sources such as biographies and his own observations. Research and progress in statistical tests were not highly advanced when he wrote his dissertation. He regretted that he was unable to conduct surveys and found the crime statistics incomplete since, for example, there were no data on the education, religion, or economic positions of convicted persons. Bonger tried to find correlations between variables such as race, climate, age, sex, illiteracy, income, housing, alcoholism, and crime. Van Heerikhuizen (1987, p. 76) observes a clear parallelism between Bonger's ideas and those of Durkheim in his *Les règles de la méthode sociologique* (1986 [1895]). Both condemn theories that reduce social phenomena to the dispositions of individual persons, and both wanted to relate social phenomena such as crime or suicide to other social factors. To both it was obvious that this led to the need for a new autonomous discipline, sociology.

Bonger was proud to be one of the first to join the Socialist Democratic Labour Party. Although he did not become a major figure in the party, he went to all meetings and had great influence on the party's intellectual life. In 1915 the party leadership asked him to start a scientific monthly, *De Sociologische Gids* (the *Sociological Guide*), of which he became the main editor; he remained so for twenty-three years. The journal was his contribution to the intellectual development of socialism in the Netherlands. In the first issue (January 1916) Bonger stated that the major goal was to strive for "a socialist science." Together with other important figures in the history of socialism he made the journal one of the main intellectual arenas in the country for discussion of questions of economy, sociology, philosophy, and history. His editorship was based on a reformist attitude, and he fiercely opposed all forms of radicalism and extremism, although his passionate temper led him regularly to fulminate against opponents and to call them names. However, twenty-three years is a long time, and ideas change. Bonger's orthodox Marxist position was increasingly criticized as old-fashioned, and in 1938 the party launched a new journal, *Socialism and Democracy*, with new editors. That meant the end of his journalistic party activities (van Heerikhuizen 1987, pp. 168–76).

Bonger established sociology and criminology as empirical sciences in the Netherlands and introduced new and innovative ways of looking at crime. His influence was less than it might have been, for three interrelated reasons. Once he was appointed professor at the Amsterdam University, he did not attempt to develop a research unit that might have expanded and continued his work; most of his time was absorbed by his political work; and he had an emotional nature and was at times difficult to live with (Kempe 1976, pp. 67–68, 73–74).

Paralleling Bonger's activities was the quite different development of sociography, the main figure of which was Sebald Rudolf Steinmetz (1862–1940), who taught political geography at the University of Amsterdam (Steinmetz 1892–94, 1908). Steinmetz was an ethnologist, sociologist, and social geographer and a purely empirical researcher who claimed "the facts nothing but the facts." He published studies on punishment and on suicide (Steinmetz 1893, 1907*a*, 1907*b*). He saw sociography as a subdiscipline of sociology, collecting the necessary data for theoretical generalizations. His students produced many mono-graphs on cities, villages, and regions. However, many of these studies were criticized because they did not state any clear research problem and seemed to collect just any kind of data, as if he believed that in-ductive generalizations would follow automatically from the data.

III. The Psychiatric-Holistic Approach—the Utrecht School

In 1934 Willem Pompe created a research institute in Utrecht. One of its first publications was *Crime and the Religious Community*, written by Gerrit Theodoor Kempe. In the preface, Pompe explained that numbers and facts are dumb and that they have meaning only through analysis, emphasizing that facts without theory have no significance. Inspired by Bonger, Kempe explained differences in criminal involve-ment between the religious communities by their respective places in the socioeconomic system, and he added a historical-sociological anal-ysis to explain how the differences arose (Kempe 1938).

However, Pompe and his colleagues' greatest significance in the "Utrecht School" lies elsewhere. Between 1900 and 1930, their move-ment, "the New Way," had promoted the first children's laws (1901), creating a child protection system, a juvenile justice system, and the conditional sentence (probation). All of this was focused on education and the individualization of sentencing (van Ruller 1988, p. 102).

Willem Pompe (1893–1986) was a lawyer. He was appointed pro-fessor in criminal law in 1923, first in Nijmegen and then in Utrecht (1928), where he remained the rest of his life. He developed an entirely new view on punishment and treatment of (serious) offenders, consid-ering the offender as first and foremost a human being. His publi-cations dealt with Dutch law (1935) but also reflected his thinking on the treatment of offenders (1946).

Kempe was a criminologist, and he later developed a great interest in the probation system. He saw probation as a form of social work and thought that the importance of probation lay in assisting ex-offenders and putting their interests first, not those of the judicial au-thorities.

However, in the 1930s the economic crisis hit the Dutch population hard. Unemployment increased exponentially; social assistance was twice lowered, and many people lived in extreme poverty. One consequence was a doubling of property crimes, which continued until 1937. This went together with a revival of repressive ideas about punishment, which appeared new and promising (van Ruller 1988). The Dutch criminal justice system was at that time influenced by Germany, where the system had been reformed in 1933, making it clear to the population that the state had absolute powers over individual citizens. One theoretical underpinning of these ideas was the book *Kriminal-biologie* published in Germany in 1939 by Franz Exner. Exner proposed a mix between Lombroso's ideas and the totalitarian ideas of the Nazi regime (van Weringh 1986, p. 129). The book had an undeniable, although limited, influence in Holland. However, it emphasized repression, the educational content of criminal justice was rejected, and former approaches were repudiated as too sentimental. An elaborate plan of a Dutch judge, Nico Muller, based on deterrence and on the enforcement of behavioral norms, targeted chronic petty offenders and led to an enormous increase in prison sentences within eight years (Muller 1908).

Of course these ideas had opponents, including Bonger, who criticized Muller's enthusiasm for the German system. Pompe and his colleagues, psychiatrist Pieter Baan and Kempe, were vigorously critical of sending so many offenders to prison, and they particularly criticized the cellular system.

Only after the Second World War, however, did the prison system really change. One reason was that many members of the Dutch elite had been imprisoned and experienced what prison was like. A second reason was the enormous trauma that the German occupation produced on the Dutch population in general and on its criminologists.

This was nowhere more clearly illustrated than by the Utrecht School, where Willem Pompe and particularly Kempe developed new principles for criminology: in 1957, the latter gave a speech "50 Years of Criminology in the Netherlands," for the Psychiatric-Juridical Society, in which he rejected the development of crime prediction with its analytical approach and reductionism of human beings (Kempe 1957). Most of these people, besides being attached to the university, worked in prisons and clinics (such as van Mesdag) or in probation (such as Kempe). They saw their mission as reform of the system, particularly the education of offenders and the cure of mentally disturbed "psychopaths."

The Utrecht School[3] concentrated on penal procedures. It was started by Kempe, Baan, and Pompe and was based on a kind of holistic anthropology inspired by the French philosopher Jean-Paul Sartre's existentialism and the German philosopher Martin Heidegger, both being very influential in Holland after World War II (Kempe 1952). Their ideas imply that man is free, he creates his own life, and he is responsible for his own actions.

The Utrecht criminologists had been appalled by national-socialist ideas, expressed in the reduction of human beings to their race and to passive objects of state power. Their reaction was that all persons, including ordinary criminals and mentally disturbed criminals, are responsible for what they do. As a consequence, their approach was based on recognizing that freedom and responsibility. They rejected theories about born criminals and theories claiming that socioeconomic conditions determined criminality.

The Utrecht School had a holistic view of human beings and was based on an essentially philosophical theory. Their approach was offender-centered: they wanted to "understand the criminal," taking into account the uniqueness of the person, who is free to design his own life and bears responsibility for it. The consequence of this theory was, among other things, a rejection of empirical research: they were convinced that empirical research would not enlighten us about the causes of offending and would not enable us to reduce crime. It is ironic that an institute that initially promoted empirical research later developed a predominantly philosophical view of offenders, trading empiricism for a holistic, treatment-oriented, and psychiatric approach.

However, the importance of the Utrecht School lies above all in its orientation toward (psychiatric) treatment of offenders and its humane approach toward offenders in general and toward mentally ill offenders in particular. Its influence led to the creation of specialist clinics for mentally disturbed offenders, such as the Pompe Clinic in Utrecht (1966), the van der Hoeven Clinic in Nijmegen (1955), the Mesdag Clinic in Groningen (1962), and the Observatory, the Pieter Baan center in Utrecht (1978). They contributed important innovations to the handling and treatment of such offenders. It is no wonder that the school attracted the attention of many foreign specialists and practitioners.

[3] The most important members of the "Utrecht School" and colleagues of Pompe and Kempe were the psychiatrists Pieter Baan, S. van Mesdag, and H. van der Hoeven.

Criminology was a marginal discipline. However, in the 1960s there was a new focus on research in Dutch universities. Herman Bianchi and Kempe were among those taking the initiative for the *Dutch Journal of Criminology*, which was launched in 1959. As Bianchi observed, "In those years there came a new generation of criminologists and I was one of them. . . . We read about all kinds of interesting developments in the US, but also about trends we wanted to combat. Moreover, we were dissatisfied with the *Journal of Penal Law* that was old and respectable but dusty and dull" (Bianchi 1999, pp. 107–8). It was time for something new, with an eye open to international trends.

An overview of forty years of the journal's existence showed in a commemorative issue, not surprisingly, that it has reflected evolving Dutch research trends and creation of new institutions (Rovers 1999). The balance of contributions shifted over time from papers written by people associated with the Utrecht School, to those of the Groningen Institute, followed by those of the WODC and most recently also of the NSCR. Lawyers, psychiatrists, and practitioners were gradually replaced as authors by social scientists, particularly sociologists and psychologists. "Dutch" in the title was eliminated in 1977 in order to invite more contributions from Flemish Belgium. However, in 1980, Flemish criminologists created *Panopticon*, their own journal of criminology and penal law. Other well-known journals include *Justitiële Verkenningen* (*Judicial Explorations*), an informative documentation journal published by the WODC. It took shape in 1956 and mainly, but not exclusively, covers criminal policy issues. *Delikt en Delinkwent*, a journal concentrating mainly on penal policy issues, succeeded the *Journal of Penal Law*. In addition, there are a number of specialized journals, such as ones on the penal process (*Sancties*), probation and resocialization issues (*Proces*), and juvenile delinquency, the juvenile justice process, and child protection (*025; Perspectief*).

IV. Developments in the 1960s—Critical Criminology

One criminologist deserves to be mentioned here because of his fame and influence at a time when the notion that empirical research was an absolute requirement for progress in criminology had not yet gained ground in the Netherlands.[4] This is Herman Bianchi, professor at the Free University of Amsterdam. Bianchi's PhD dissertation (1956, 1961)

---

[4] This did not happen before the 1970s and 1980s.

expressed the view that criminology was an umbrella science, encompassing philosophy, sociology, psychology, psychiatry, law, and maybe more. In this he was close to the Utrecht School. However, on the basis of his religious views, he believed that the definition of crime had to include notions of sin and culpability. Later on he abandoned this approach and criticized the Utrecht School for its lack of social criticism and the absence of fundamental criticism of the criminal justice system (Bianchi 1974*a*, 1974*b*). He believed that their ideology of personal responsibility should have led to a considerably more radical criticism of the criminal justice system.

Bianchi was influenced by the writings of the American Edwin Lemert (1967) and by Lemert's concepts of primary and secondary deviance. Gradually Bianchi lost interest in the question why offenders came to commit their acts, but concentrated exclusively on the process of secondary deviance, the ways in which the criminal justice system stigmatizes offenders and thereby causes reoffending. He believed that criminology had been far too much influenced by medicine, and he strongly opposed the "reductionist" approach of empirical research, including the many efforts at prediction. He later joined the European Group for the Study of Deviance and Social Control, a group that favored a nongovernmental approach to crime problems and opposed the positivist ideal of science, preferring a phenomenological criminology.

By the 1960s most Dutch universities had their own criminology departments, all situated within the faculties of law. Most of the departments and institutes of criminology were critical of government policies in general and the policies of the Ministry of Justice in particular. An important abolitionist group, associated with Bianchi and Loek Hulsman, wanted to eliminate the entire criminal justice system, but their influence declined in the 1980s. Several of the university departments (in the 1960s and the 1970s) showed only limited interest in practical and quantitative research. Their production was not so much theoretical as philosophical and political. They were interested in criminal justice policies (the labeling effect) much more than in crime, which was perceived as a fact of life. Many of their writings discuss the fundamentals of the criminal justice system or questions such as "who defines crime?" Without arguing that these questions are unimportant, they did not generate much empirical research (either quantitative or qualitative; see also van Weringh 1986).

It is striking in retrospect that criminological theorizers in the period of 1950–70 did not feel a need to support their theories by testing them, but instead simply assumed that their theories, inspired by theology or by philosophy, must be valid.

One criminologist who made serious efforts to reintroduce empiricism into Dutch criminology is Willem Nagel, appointed as professor in Leiden in 1956, and whose PhD dissertation, "The Criminality in Oss" (1949), raised considerable interest. Oss, a small town in the south of Holland, had relatively high crime rates, which peaked in the 1930s. A group of students at the University of Groningen, among them Nagel, decided to conduct a study based on criminal justice system records, a survey, and fieldwork. Nagel collected records issued by national and local police and court files for the period 1889–1935. He described various famous murder cases of the late nineteenth century, illustrating social conflicts between rich industrialists in that area and the poor and primitive factory workers coming straight from rural areas. In a later section he described visits he made to seventy-one imprisoned Oss residents. A number never returned to Oss after their releases and led conforming lives in another city. Nagel's work sheds important light on a specific period of Dutch industrialization, but in retrospect his empirical methods were crude. Because of the war and occupation, the study was seriously delayed but was eventually completed in 1949.

One of Nagel's objectives, different from the usual sociographic studies, was to examine the relation of nature to nurture, an objective that he was not able to realize. One of the big factories in Oss relocated to Rotterdam and took 250 workers with it. Nagel observed that, much to his disappointment, these people behaved like ordinary, mostly law-abiding, Rotterdam residents. His conclusion was that the company had taken a positive selection of workers with them, leaving the unreliable, criminal-minded ones behind. Although this conclusion may be mistaken, it illustrates Nagel's interest in empirical research. He saw the removal of a group of workers to another place as an experimental change, which would allow for a study of heritable versus environmental factors in crime causation.

In 1965 Nagel wrote a report for the Ministry of Justice on prediction of criminal behavior (Nagel 1965). The report reviews the literature and considers whether the Netherlands should develop and apply a prediction instrument. This was controversial: the Utrecht School was strongly opposed to this approach, which had come from the United States. Nagel dealt with this criticism in an article in the *Dutch Journal of Penal Law* (1963). He examined four questions: what is the nature and extent of the population; what is required for predictive factors to be accepted; how does one establish such a predictive instrument; and has the method reached a level at which it can be applied in practice? Nagel pleaded for Dutch prediction research. He referred to data collected in 1965 and 1966 by his sister, a school doctor in the small city of Boskoop, on all first and sixth graders in the city and its environs. The data included information on the children's medical conditions, school achievements, and social and personal situations. Ten years later she collected data on the same population, including police-recorded delinquent behavior. Unfortunately, for a number of reasons, including the question of ownership of the data, the study was never completed or published. However, it shows again Nagel's great interest in empirical research, which he believed might have great theoretical and practical consequences. He greatly admired Marvin Wolfgang and his colleagues and was influenced by Wolfgang, Figlio, and Sellin's 1972 book *Delinquency in a Birth Cohort.*

Looking back to this period and considering the three strands, we may note a turning of the tide. Gradually criminologists left the path of a predominantly ideologically motivated criminology that rejected empiricism or considered it of little use and moved toward a more neutral approach of "fact-finding." Nagel was an important figure in this respect.

However, although many criminologists criticized the Dutch criminal justice system, they apparently had little expectation that they might influence penal policy. Most studies by the main criminologists, such as Bianchi (1956, 1961, 1971) and Kempe (1952), were university studies and had a high degree of philosophical (and ideological) abstraction. Only in the 1970s did real changes in Dutch criminology become apparent.

V. The 1970s—the Takeoff of Empirical Research

Many criminologists came to realize that it was necessary to test ideas and hypotheses, however plausible they seemed. It took, however, considerable time for empirical methodology to gain a real foothold. The idea that criminologists might use their knowledge to suggest better ways to operate the system was not popular. Dutch criminology was more or less at a dead end.

However, from the 1960s onward, both education and practice in the social sciences in the Netherlands were heavily influenced by the United States. In the social sciences this meant a heavy emphasis on empirical research and quantitative research methods.

The representative figure was Wouter Buikhuisen, who shook up the criminological landscape and led the discipline into a radically new phase. Buikhuisen was an experimental psychologist who had worked in a multinational business enterprise and entered the scene with a businessman's eye and a keen sense of what he wanted to accomplish. He was the first social scientist since Bonger to be appointed a professor of criminology in the Netherlands (in 1965) and created a productive research institute at Groningen University. He observed that there was little empirical criminological knowledge available in the country and stated that there were lots of claims but no research.

In his inaugural lecture (1966), Buikhuisen argued that the objective of criminology should be to discover the criminogenic, crimino-consolidating, and crimino-curative factors. The best way to develop this type of criminology would be to undertake longitudinal developmental studies. In addition, he had a clear interest in studies of hereditary factors in relation to crime (Buikhuisen 1986). He made it clear that he did not believe that people inherit a disposition for particular crimes but instead inherit properties that might predispose them to criminal behavior.

Buikhuisen was above all an empirical innovator. He did the first self-reported delinquency study of university students (Buikhuisen, Jongman, and Oving 1969), followed by a study of recorded and dark figure crime in an adult population in Groningen (Veendrick 1976). He initiated studies of traffic-related problems, including a series of psychological experiments on traffic safety, among which one showed quite clearly the negative consequences of—even very little—alcohol use on visual alertness. The studies resulted in considerably more restrictive legislation on driving under the influence of alcohol.

Although these studies show Buikhuisen's keen interest in empirical research and methodological innovation, he also believed that criminology had an obligation to deliver evidence and analysis that would inform and potentially improve policy making. One illustration is a PhD dissertation by one of his assistants on variations in sentencing for drunk driving in a court district in the north of the country (Steenhuis 1972).

Dato Steenhuis studied the files of all men convicted of drunken driving in the years 1960–64. In the east of the country, he found that judges imposed considerably more prison sentences and fewer fines or withdrawal of driving licenses than in the west. Steenhuis looked at reconvictions and showed that the severity of a sanction had no effect on reconvictions. He recommended increasing the risk of being caught as a much better approach. Although this is now conventional wisdom among criminologists, it was new at the time and attracted much interest in the media and the political arena. After Buikhuisen left Groningen, the institute maintained its quantitative orientation, although prevailing theory changed. Jongman, Buikhuisen's successor, mainly supported strain theory as it had been developed by Cloward and Ohlin (1960).

There has always been and still is a great interest in questions of cultural deviance, in particular among cultural anthropologists. This approach remains characteristic of the criminological center within the Willem Pompe Institute (Utrecht University), led by Frank Bovenkerk, an anthropologist. Important studies examine the situation of ethnic minorities with respect to crime and the criminal justice system (Bovenkerk and Yesilgöz 1998; Gezik 2002; Bovenkerk, Koven, and Yesilgöz 2003), and there are other related studies (Buiks 1983; Kaufman and Verbraeck 1986; Werdmölder 1986). These researchers mainly use qualitative methods.

But despite a generally stronger attachment to qualitative than to quantitative approaches, some university researchers supported the new empirical orientation, as shown by two thorough prediction studies, one at the Groningen institute (Nijboer 1975) and the other in Nijmegen (Zwanenburg 1977), and by the first large-scale victimization studies, also at Nijmegen University (Fiselier 1978; Dijksterhuis and Nijboer 1990). By that time most Dutch universities had their own criminological departments, all situated within faculties of law. The institute in Nijmegen was headed by Ronnie Dessaur from 1973 to 1988. Dessaur had studied in Leiden and been Nagel's student. Her PhD dissertation pleaded for a more rational and empirical approach to criminology (Dessaur 1971). She was one of the first non-Catholic criminologists appointed at the Catholic University of Nijmegen. Later she shifted her interest to philosophy and also became a famous novelist (Dessaur 1987).[5]

Bianchi worked at the Free University of Amsterdam and Jac. van Weringh at the criminological institute in the University of Amsterdam, called the Bonger Institute (van Weringh 1971, 1978). Van Weringh was also a student of Buikhuisen and published among other works a history of Dutch criminology (1968). However, he was also a writer who was particularly interested in politics[6] (he was a socialist) and in political cartoons (1967). Later he was more active as a journalist than as a criminologist.

In Rotterdam, Loek Hulsman was active both at Erasmus University (University of Rotterdam) and internationally. Hulsman was an abolitionist. He argued that most if not all offenses were conflicts between two or more persons that had to be solved by negotiation and what we would now call mediation (Hulsman 1978). Abolitionists wanted to discard crime, stating that "troubles are real, 'crime' is a myth" (quoted by de Haan 1990, p. 27). In Hulsman's vision, prisons were the worst possible solution to crime and consequently should be abolished. He saw criminal justice as a system that creates social problems rather than solves them (Hulsman 1981; Hulsman and Bernat de Célis 1982). Hulsman was active in the Coornhert Liga, the Dutch League for Penal Reform, an organization characterized by two theoretical orientations: a juridical approach emphasizing prisoners' rights and a behavioral science approach striving for depenalization and decriminalization (de Haan 1990, p. 75). Hulsman spoke fluent English and French and sat on a decriminalization commission in the Council of Europe (European Committee on Crime Problems 1980; van Swaaningen 1991, p. 358). The commission pleaded for nonintervention in cases in which the goals of criminal law are unclear or the costs in terms of personal liberty or human rights are higher than the benefits in penal norm maintenance, a structural socioeconomic approach of "problematic situations," support by authorities for mediation, and consideration of the penal system as an *ultimum refugium* for cases in which negotiation and mediation failed.

---

[5] Dessaur was Jewish. She wrote under the pseudonym Andreas Burnier and became famous by describing her childhood during the German occupation (Burnier 1981 [1965]). She was a lesbian, and homosexuality was a recurring theme in her writings.

[6] Van Weringh was raised as an orthodox Protestant but lost his faith. In 1967 he wrote a well-known book about one of the main orthodox political figures from the nineteenth century, *Het maatschappijbeeld van Abraham Kuyper* (The social vision of Abraham Kuyper).

Hulsman and the abolitionist movement had some influence in the 1980s on maintaining a humane penal system. However, in the 1990s this influence gradually waned and the Ministry of Justice throughout remained relatively unmoved by his arguments.

Looking back to this generation of leading criminologists, one is struck by some characteristics. Most were more than just criminologists: they were all what the French call "intellectuals"; their interests were wide and encompassed philosophy, politics, and literature. Nagel, under the pseudonym of J. B. Charles, and Dessaur became celebrated authors; van Weringh was an influential political commentator; both Bianchi and Dessaur were interested in philosophy and theology; and Hulsman tried to change the penal system in a fundamental way. They were thinkers and theorists rather than empiricists and developed a vision of society and how to improve it rather than just doing research.

In 1973 an earthquake shook Dutch criminology when Buikhuisen left Groningen and went to The Hague to create a research center inside the Ministry of Justice (see the next section). In 1978 Buikhuisen left the ministry and was appointed professor of criminology at the University of Leiden. This professorship created one of the fiercest conflicts and most serious crises ever in Dutch criminology. Buikhuisen had become interested in biosocial characteristics of criminals, in particular of violent offenders. He wanted to conduct research into the interaction of biological personality factors with the environment, first by observing aggressive juveniles and second by taking urine and blood samples from experimental subjects. These last elements caused enormous upheaval at a time when the prevailing paradigm was sociological, focusing exclusively on environmental influences. His research plans were seriously attacked in the (leftist) press (in particular the politically left magazine *Vrij Nederland*), attacks that went on for a very long time and eventually undermined his health and resilience. The Dutch criminological community did nothing to support him and took no public stand for the freedom of science. Finally, the University of Leiden, frightened by the political scandal, withdrew Buikhuisen's research funds, which meant de facto that he could not keep his professorship. He resigned, and that ended his career as a criminologist.[7]

Looking back, one might wonder why Buikhuisen's plans provoked such controversy. It is our feeling that Dutch society was not then

[7] Utterly disgusted with the Dutch criminological community, he completely changed careers and became a successful antiques dealer.

ready to accept research on biosocial subjects. Many people in criminology and political circles belonged to a generation that had lived through the German occupation. For many of them, Buikhuisen's research plans, which few understood, evoked that dark period, and they felt threatened. Had Buikhuisen limited his ambitions to observations only, he might have survived as a criminologist. Instead, he tried to convince Dutch society of his good intentions and the merits of such studies, but he failed. This rejection and exclusion of Buikhuisen from criminological research is one of the blackest pages in the history of Dutch criminology.

VI. A Governmental Research Center

In 1973 the minister of justice, probably inspired by the policy-related research undertaken in Groningen, invited Buikhuisen to come to The Hague as a high-ranking civil servant with the main task of developing a research center that would work exclusively for the minister and the ministry. The universities were not keen on conducting research for the ministry: judicial policies were subjected to severe criticism (Kelk 1983; Brants and Silvis 1987; de Haan 1990), and research for the ministry was often characterized as contaminated work. Researchers prepared to conduct "applied research" were sometimes considered second-rate by their colleagues. The term most used was "governmental criminology" (Bianchi 1974a), that is, research done as a service to policy makers and helping them to improve their policies. This was contrasted with university criminology, which was supposed to be fundamental and of higher quality. Criticism was addressed to justice policies and to those who worked for policy makers. This was particularly the case with the government plan *Society and Crime: A Policy Plan for the Future* (Ministry of Justice 1985), which focused on prevention of petty crime and more severe punishment for more serious crime (Franke 1990b) and was based on social control (Hirschi 1969) and routine activity theories (Cohen and Felson 1979; Felson 1998).

Criticism was also immediate and sharp when the first International Victims Crime Survey (ICVS) was published by the WODC (Bruinsma et al. 1990; van Dijk, Mayhew, and Killias 1990). The criticism, mainly addressed at the methodology and the study's presentation, even reached the leading papers (Franke 1990a, 1990c). The innovative character of the study, which has improved over time, was not recognized until much later.

This attitude should be understood in relation to the universities' privileged situations in the 1960s and 1970s, when they had their own research budgets and were not under pressure to look for outside funding. They could afford condescending attitudes toward pragmatic policy-related research and researchers who did such work. In addition, when universities accepted work from the government, they sometimes delivered results only after (considerable) delay. This was not satisfactory to the authorities who needed policy recommendations based on research that the universities could not or would not deliver. This need was related to the expanding role that public authorities played in social life in general and with respect to the judiciary, the police, the probation service, and the youth protection service (van Dijk 1982). Beginning in the late 1960s, there had been a huge increase in juvenile crime. The Ministry of Justice realized that traditional policies were inadequate and that there was a need for more evidence-based approaches.

A complication at the time was that, as in most of Europe, the majority of professors in criminology were lawyers and were not particularly interested in policy research. Buikhuisen was an exception. So as might be expected, he was interested in the new position and accepted the offer, but not without setting conditions. He wanted a guarantee that, although the subjects to be addressed would be determined by the ministry, the center would be independent in the methodologies it used. Also, all research results should be published, and the staff of the center and not policy makers would decide on the content of the publications. In other words, he wanted openness and transparency. The secretary-general, Gerard Mulder, the highest social servant in the Ministry of Justice, and thus the minister of justice, accepted the conditions and allowed Buikhuisen to take on empirical researchers from the universities of Groningen and Nijmegen.

An important reason why the ministry accepted Buikhuisen's conditions was that to maintain his credibility in Parliament, the minister of justice could not ignore research results from his own research center, even if they challenged his policies. Such interventions would inevitably leak to the press, and he would be unable to invoke research results to justify his policies or convince Parliament of the need to take particular measures.

This does not mean that there never were conflicts or pressures; there always were. For example, in 1984 the director of the WODC was summoned by the secretary-general about a critical 1984 issue of the *Dutch Journal of Criminology* on the Dutch prosecutor system (1984, p. 1). Another example was the ministry's concern about the increasing number of evaluative reports on important sections of the criminal justice system (Spickenheuer 1977; Nuyten-Edelbroek and Slothouwer 1988; Aalberts 1989). This was a new phenomenon. The reports were often followed by critical questions in Parliament and prompted the minister of justice to make changes, which were not always welcome. Although the WODC stood up to criticism, referring to the empirical evidence, almost inevitably most researchers developed a degree of self-restraint in both conclusions and recommendations (see the next section).

Those who started the center were convinced that the social sciences had a mission besides fundamental research and the advance of scientific knowledge, that is, to make a contribution, however small, to achieving a somewhat fairer, more humane, and more rational society. Although some may have considered this rather naive, it has been the leading theme of the center and was based on two postulates (Junger-Tas 1979).

The first is the existence of a broad consensus on the main goals of criminal justice policy, the protection of society and the rule of law and the life and possessions of individual citizens, manifested in penal law and more concretely in the criminal justice system. In the memorandum accompanying the annual budget in 1977 (Ministry of Justice 1977), the minister of justice made these goals explicit, recognizing that they are determined by general values and norms that express the ways people want to organize a society. The essential objective of policy research is to contribute to the realization of these goals, the essential assumption being that the system is sufficiently transparent to be studied (van Dijk 1982).

The second postulate is that assisting policy making by means of research is essential. The goal is a better relationship between the objectives to be reached and the means that are used than past experience and common sense by themselves can provide. This is an expression of what Coleman (1972) has called a "scientific" society, a society that uses scientific methods to change itself. The question here, however, is how valid is this in everyday practice, and what are the real contributions of science to policy making?

The first role of researchers in such a center is to assist civil servants in translating and formulating problems into terms that can be studied. Sometimes the problem at hand is related to a second problem or derives from a much more fundamental issue. Sometimes a quick answer is needed to a complex question, which really requires an in-depth study. One of the most useful roles of a government center is to evaluate new penal measures (Junger-Tas 1993).

For example, Polder and van Vlaardingen (1992) evaluated 106 prevention projects funded by the government in the framework of the policy plan *Society and Crime*; only forty-three had an adequate methodology. One conclusion was that serious crime is considerably more difficult to influence by prevention measures than less serious problems. Second, increasing the probability of a sanction is effective in decreasing crime, so police and the courts should attempt to increase both the likelihood of apprehension and the probability of a sanction. Third, reducing the opportunity to commit an offense is effective,[8] particularly concerning petty (juvenile) crime. Measures that had very little impact on offending included providing information on crime (e.g., informing youngsters about the damaging consequences of vandalism), increasing leisure time activities, using welfare workers in programs for high-risk youths, operating meeting centers for youngsters, and regulating graffiti zones.

Another example is an evaluation of alternative sanctions for juveniles. The general aim was to "promote a more educational and pedagogically oriented juvenile justice system" (van der Laan 1991, p. 2). It was hypothesized that alternative sanctions would lead to changes in behavior and, accordingly, to less recidivism. However, it has been hard to support that assumption (van der Laan 1991; Junger-Tas 1994). According to van der Laan, alternative sanctions are mainly used in place of suspended youth detention or in a combination of a suspended sentence with a fine, rather than as alternatives to more severe penalties (p. 240).

The ideal is to introduce innovations under experimental conditions in order to evaluate them, then to modify the pilots as a consequence of the evaluation, and only then to change the law. This succeeded

---

[8] The governmental plan *Society and Crime* was heavily influenced by both social control theory (Hirschi 1969) and opportunity theory (Felson 1998).

several times, including the introduction of community service in penal policy (Bol and Overwater 1984). As a consequence of the evaluation, the new sanction was modified, and only after this process was completed was the sanction adopted in penal law. However, in other cases policy makers were much too pressed by the political process and would not wait for research results.

Other important examples of policy evaluation are studies on drug users (Grapendaal, Leuw, and Nelen 1995), on Dutch drug policy (Leuw and Haen-Marshall 1994), and on criminal careers (Block and van der Werf 1991). A recent example is the development of a recidivism monitor (Wartna 1999, 2004; van der Heiden-Attema 2000), which is useful not only for policy makers but also for researchers. Efforts have been made to link theory to policy, although this was limited to those theories that were productive in leading to workable solutions. For example, the new policy direction taken in 1985[9] was heavily influenced by social control (Hirschi 1969) and routine activities theories (Cohen and Felson 1979; Felson 1998).

The WODC has contributed to a more realistic understanding of crime and criminals. Slowly it was realized that modern societies have and will continue to have high crime levels, that most crime is petty property crime, and that the criminal justice system cannot control crime on its own but needs the collaboration of the general public.

The criticism by universities gradually disappeared, one reason being that their financial positions grew precarious and they were forced to look for government research funding.[10]

The WODC was particularly active internationally. This may relate to its involvement with the Council of Europe and the United Nations, which stimulated a broad view of crime problems and how to deal with them. Successive directors encouraged international exchanges and invited foreign guests to spend time at the center.[11] The center created several English publications, including summaries of experimental programs for widespread international distribution and the *European Journal of Criminal Policy and Research*.[12] The latter reflected the growing importance of the European Union and the need for individual Eu-

---

[9] Exemplified by the policy plan *Society and Crime* (Ministry of Justice 1985).

[10] This is true for all kinds of research in the social sciences.

[11] For example, Richard and Becky Block (United States) and Martin Killias (Switzerland) were among those visiting the center for some time.

[12] The journal was established in 1992 by the center's director, Josine Junger-Tas, and the director of the documentation department, Hans Boutellier.

ropean countries to consider their problems and policies in a wider context and in a comparative perspective.[13]

Two international surveys were launched that have grown in importance over the years, the objective being to start time series in order to show trends in crime and delinquency. The first is the ICVS, an initiative of Jan J. M. van Dijk. Supported by the Ministry of Justice, several waves of the survey have taken place, enlarging the number of participating countries. Its results have found their place alongside police statistics in many countries and in U.N. statistics (van Dijk, Mayhew, and Killias 1990; Mayhew and van Dijk 1997; van Kesteren, Mayhew, and Nieuwbeerta 2000). The other project is the International Self-Report Delinquency Study, launched by Josine Junger-Tas in 1990. The first study involved young people in thirteen countries (Junger-Tas, Terlouw, and Klein 1994; Junger-Tas, Haen-Marshall, and Ribeaud 2003) and is based on self-reports. A second wave is under way, involving some thirty countries. The studies are of interest in more than one way. They give insights into trends over time in specific forms of crime but also illuminate important policy issues, such as whether and why particular countries differ in their crime problems, to what degree drug use among young people is generally accepted as normal behavior, and to what degree the relationship of single-parent households with delinquency holds internationally. Finally, such studies can test theoretical issues, such as Gottfredson and Hirschi's self-control concept (1990), Hirschi's social control theory (1969), and Sampson's theory of the importance of the neighborhood in crime production (Sampson, Raudenbusch, and Earls 1997).

The center contributed to the recognition of criminology as a science. The creation of the WODC gave an enormous stimulus to empirical research, and in the 1970s and 1980s the center was considered as one of the most important criminology research units in the country and internationally. Moreover, the WODC participated in the creation and launching of the European Society of Criminology in 2000.

The position of the WODC in Dutch criminology is unlikely to change. In 2006 as in the 1980s, the research program results from consultations with policy makers, judges, and prosecutors with the objective of making the execution of penal policies as effective and efficient as possible. One important project is the recidivism monitor,

---

[13] Later these publications were discontinued, but the journal was taken over by Springer Publishers, with Ernesto Savona as editor-in-chief.

which follows the total population of ex-detainees, including juveniles. Another project examines the effectiveness of existing and new sanctions in reducing recidivism of particular target groups. The WODC regularly develops predictions of future prison cell needs, has developed cost-benefit analyses of detention policies, and has developed a scale to estimate recidivism risks of prisoners for the probation service. A review and synthesis will be made of research into genetic and psychobiological aspects of criminal behavior and its link to behavioral and environmental data. However, international research activities are somewhat meager, including—together with the English Home Office and the University of Lausanne—the coordination of the *European Sourcebook*,[14] a comparison of fourteen countries on reconviction rates, and the dissemination of Campbell Collaboration standards on evaluation research and the validity of interventions. The Campbell Collaboration Crime and Justice Group is an international network that prepares and disseminates systematic reviews of high-quality research.

VII. Problems in Governmental Research

For many years, crime control policy in the Netherlands was not politicized, and both policy makers and researchers could work in relative peace. For some fifteen years WODC researchers were involved in formulating policy and developing reasonable solutions to policy problems. Their work was generally well received and sometimes resulted in new policies.[15] However, this changed in the 1990s, when crime was on every politician's agenda. This made the government nervous and led to drastic measures, the consequences of which often were not well considered. This had far-reaching effects.

For example, in the 1970s it was felt that basic police training of patrol officers was inadequate. A large study on training objectives and practices, police practices, and public satisfaction with police services resulted in clear-cut recommendations for change, many of which were followed (Junger-Tas and Holten-Vriesema 1978). Theoretical notions such as routine activities (Cohen and Felson 1979; Felson 1998) and social control theories (Hirschi 1969) were tested in WODC studies

---

[14] The *European Sourcebook* includes police and justice data of Council of Europe member states and is published by the WODC.

[15] For example, this was the case when alternative sanctions and prevention policies were introduced.

(Junger-Tas, Junger, and Sampiemon 1983; Junger-Tas, Junger, and Barendse-Hoornweg 1985) and found their way into important policy documents such as *Society and Crime* (1985), which argued that a general crime prevention policy strengthens the bonds of young people with society and reduces opportunities for crime. This was the start of extensive crime prevention policies, mainly concentrated at the local level.

However, this changed at the end of the 1980s and in the 1990s, making pragmatic, evidence-based solutions more difficult, since they had to fit into the evolving political culture and the situation of the moment. This gave rise to a number of concerns and warnings about the dangers that threaten these types of studies.

A central issue is the relevance of research. There are a number of criteria, such as whether authorities are really interested in solving the studied problem, whether those who commissioned the research have sufficient political power to bring about change, and whether there is financial backing for change (Welters 1978).

The distance between policy makers and researchers is usually too large for research to have much impact on political decision making. WODC researchers used to have regular meetings with the policy departments. The frequency of contacts resulted in more ready acceptance of research findings, even when they were negative, and made an impact on policy decisions possible. The danger of such a procedure, however, is that it increases a tendency among researchers to perceive the management and political problems of the ministry as their own, which can lead to cooptation and a lack of critical distance.

A particular practical problem for the conscientious researcher is the urgent policy problem to which he must respond in a limited time, if not immediately. Such research can only be superficial and has little reliability. However, if solid and serious research reaches policy decision makers when the decision has already been made, it is not very useful. This is one reason why policy makers make use of commercial marketing agencies. Unfortunately these studies are usually conducted in haste, often use weak methodology, produce outcomes that would be expected without research, and formulate recommendations designed to please those who commissioned the research.

However, this does not mean that academic and university researchers do not fall into the same trap. Too often they accept the definition of a problem as it is given by those who fund the study, without critical examination of the validity of that definition. To find funding they must embrace any question à la mode. For example, in the United States we have seen successive developments in research topics that were directly influenced by the agendas of the successive political administrations. This explains the waves of research on incapacitation and career criminals, followed by research on drugs, organized crime, and now, of course, terrorism. Letting funding authorities decide research topics may seriously restrict the scope of research.

A real threat to the scientific integrity of researchers is that the research may provide rationales for policy decisions, for example, when the minister has to meet some requirements of Parliament and promises a study of the issue. In these cases the study may serve to delay difficult political decisions. In some cases the study serves to justify decisions that have already been made. Obviously, such studies have no real influence on policy making.

A further problem concerns recommendations. Although researchers are capable of identifying policy problems, they have considerably more difficulty formulating solutions. Moreover, policy makers may not always appreciate the researchers' recommendations, judging the making of recommendations to be their own prerogative. As a result, recommendations tend to be vague, having two characteristics: the well-known formula that "more research is needed really to analyze the problem" and that recommended policy measures concern ministries or departments other than the one that commissioned the research.

Research is only one element in policy making. Policy makers are justified in deciding differently than the research recommends, for example, on the basis of normative considerations, such as other important political issues that must be solved first, the weighing of eventual political acceptance of recommended measures, their economic feasibility, and financial constraints. In this field, research no longer has much of a role to play, and researchers should understand and accept this.

Does this mean that policy-related research has no influence at all? To say that would be a mistake. If policy makers really want to change procedures or practices, they may wish preliminary research done and may be open to recommendations or alternative solutions presented by researchers on the basis of their studies.

VIII. Recent Trends—University Research

Criminological research in Dutch universities long took place mostly in the law departments. When the 1980s came with their drastic budget cuts, criminology was often one of the first victims because it had a peripheral position in the faculties of law. When budget cuts were imposed, criminology institutes were an easy target. This led to a reduction in criminological research. For example, as a result of budget cuts, the number of chairs in criminology, the number of criminological departments, and the number of researchers in criminology centers decreased considerably. Although professorships did not entirely disappear, many appointments were decreased to only one or two days a week. The criminology institute in Nijmegen was entirely dismantled. Other types of research institutes, commercial or academic (e.g., the NSCR; see below), developed. One consequence of this decline in the different law departments is that other faculties—sociology, psychology, and others—tried to fill the gap. Since 1985, for example, the Erasmus Center for Socio-legal Tax Research has conducted research on tax evasion and social security fraud from a psychological perspective. Its research led to an innovative approach in the measurement of that behavior (Weigel, Hessing, and Elffers 1987; Hessing, Elffers, and Weigel 1988; Elffers 1991) and led to a new explanatory model for tax evasion, which may be used for other deviant behaviors as well. The model specifies a set of variables in the social environment conducive to or constraining tax evasion. One main feature of their approach is the combination and comparison—on an individual level—of self-reported tax evasion behavior, behavioral outcome measures (based on official data), and a behavioral simulation measure. From these studies the authors conclude that the use of self-reported behavior in criminological studies should be discouraged (Webley et al. 1991).

At the Free University of Amsterdam, in the Faculty of Psychology, Frans-Willem Winkel and his colleagues focused on nonverbal communication in police interviews of suspects, witnesses, and victims (Winkel, Koppelaar, and Vrij 1988; Winkel and Vrij 1990; Winkel and Koppelaar 1991). One important finding was that higher arrest rates among cultural minorities relative to their crime rate should be explained by problems in intercultural communication with the police rather than racial biases of police officers.

After a serious dip in the 1980s, criminological research revived at the end of the 1990s. Mainstream Dutch criminology now is empirical and quantitative. The center most representative of this type of criminology is the Netherlands Institute for the Study of Crime and Law Enforcement, with studies—like the WODC's—mainly based on a quantitative approach and sophisticated methodology. However, some institutes, including those in Utrecht and Groningen, maintain a more qualitative, anthropological approach and often shed original light on criminological theory, which is related to their methodology of in-depth qualitative analyses of deviant and criminally active group processes, revealing motivations and behavior that go undiscovered in quantitative studies. For example, a 2002 issue of the *Tijdschrift voor Criminologie* was devoted to group delinquency with ethnographic contributions by Weerman and Kleemans, and van Gemert. They contributed to Eurogang, an international working group on gang research initiated by Malcolm Klein and resulting in a publication on gangs in Europe (Decker and Weerman 2005).

An interesting anthropological paper by Miedema examined the relationship between ethnicity, youth groups, and delinquency. This confirmed quantitative research on the social structure of deprived neighborhoods, showing that this structure does not differentiate between the Dutch youth population and ethnic minorities in terms of criminal activities (Miedema 2002; Junger-Tas et al. 2003). Both groups suffer from deficient socialization, a poor school career, and a great distance from the labor market. Both may be "discriminated" against on the basis of their reputations, dress codes, and ethnic stereotypes, continually reaffirming their marginal status and leading to the formation of groups of similar marginal youths. These are not necessarily monoethnic, as we found in a Rotterdam study of fifteen-year-old juveniles (Junger-Tas et al. 2003).

Interestingly, politicization of criminal justice policy made policy makers want more, not less, research. Most universities were prepared to undertake these projects. An important study was done for a parliamentary commission named after its chairman, Maarten van Traa, the van Traa Commission. The commission was appointed in 1994 to examine police investigation methods and control of those methods. The precipitant was the dissolution of a regional investigation unit because of illegal practices in the investigation of drug criminality. In 1995 the commission asked four academic criminologists to study the nature and extent of organized crime in the Netherlands. The project leader was

Cyrille Fijnaut,[16] a well-known researcher on organized crime and the police (Enquêtecommissie Opsporingsmethoden 1996). One of the main conclusions was that organized crime was not a cancerous tumor in a healthy body, but a social phenomenon that had a symbiotic relationship with notaries, lawyers, and fiscal specialists working in lawful businesses but prepared to assist these criminals.[17] The findings formed a basis for the commission's conclusions and were extensively reported in the media (van de Bunt et al. 1996).

The commission concluded that there was a crisis in police investigative work concerning organized crime, caused by a lack of clear behavioral norms, a malfunctioning police organization, and problematic relations of authority. Criticisms were not addressed only at the police organization but also at the prosecution service, which had insufficient control over police practices. The conclusions had far-reaching consequences in terms of legislation on police investigation practices and their control by the prosecution service, limiting some of these practices and tightening control mechanisms.[18] The work of the research group exemplified the influential role of research when authorities want to get to the bottom of a problem and bring about political change. The work raised active and renewed interest among criminologists in research on criminal organizations and organized crime. This has also been stimulated by Henk van de Bunt, who was director of the WODC in the 1990s, producing a series of important studies (van de Bunt 1992, 2002; Kleemans, van den Berg, and van de Bunt 1998; Vervaele et al. 2001). A number of issues of the leading criminological journal, *Tijdschrift voor Criminologie*, were devoted to the subject (van de Bunt et al. 1996; van de Bunt 2002; van de Bunt and Huisman 2004).

Another important development was the creation of a new research center, based on the belief that more empirical research was needed on "fundamental" issues as opposed to short-term policy issues on which the WODC tends to focus. Buikhuisen, while still active, played a role in the creation of that center. He created a working group to design an interdisciplinary research institute meant to do fundamental research, chaired by the secretary-general of the Ministry of Justice

---

[16] The other members were Henk van de Bunt, Gerben Bruinsma, and Frank Bovenkerk.

[17] The study group found forty-nine cases of such blameworthy involvement.

[18] Under the threat of terrorism, some limitations on that practice have again been abolished.

and including several other scientists. After considerable time and endless negotiations, in 1992 the NSCR was officially established.

In 2006 NSCR has about twenty-five full-time staff. It is funded by the Ministry of Justice and the NWO. The University of Leiden is its host. The first director was a psychologist from the University of Groningen, John Michon, who was an expert on traffic and circulation issues with little affinity for criminology. He was invited to take the post by Buikhuisen, who knew him from his time in Groningen. Although without doubt an intelligent man, he tried to approach the sentencing process with mathematical equations without recognizing the irrational complexities of penal policies and penal procedures. Michon's successor, Gerben Bruinsma, came to the NSCR in 1999. Bruinsma is a criminologist and was first attached to the University of Twente in the east of the country and later to a police research institute, IPIT (1985, 1999). He has been quite successful in attracting young and well-qualified researchers to the center.

The NSCR has organized its work around three general themes. The first, "Mobility and the Spread of Crime," studies the distribution of crime in space and the factors that influence this spatial distribution, in particular the interventions of administrative and judicial authorities. A project in The Hague looks at changes in crime distribution in neighborhoods in relation to environmental characteristics, using police data, victimization data, and social, economic, and physical characteristics (Bernasco and Luykx 2003; Bernasco and Nieuwbeerta 2003; Bernasco, Bruinsma, and Huisman 2004). The project investigates explanations based on social disorganization (Shaw and McKay 1942) and routine activities theories (Cohen and Felson 1979; Felson 1998). Another project tests interface theory and transnational crime and examines illegal art traffic and how this is transformed into legal art that can be sold. The study was executed in the United States and the Netherlands and was coordinated by Nikos Passas of Northeastern University and Henk Elffers of NSCR. Other projects include a study on human trafficking from China and one on crime displacement, the main question being to what degree displacement is a function of changing attitudes, opportunities, and law enforcement.

The second theme is the "Relationship between Citizens and the Criminal Justice System," including study of legitimacy, expressed in the confidence of citizens in the criminal justice system, acceptance of judicial decisions, and willingness of citizens to cooperate with police and justice officials. One study concentrated on the position of the victim in penal proceedings (de Keijser and Malsch 2002), and another compares bias in expert witnessing on psychological aspects of offenders and victims in Australian and Dutch courts (Malsch and Freckelton 2005). Other projects examine the impact of lay judges, the social roles of judges, and crime and law enforcement in the Netherlands (van Koppen 2004).

The third theme is "Life History and Criminal Careers" and (non)judicial interventions. The focus is life history and criminal careers, including the development of young children as a possible predictor and explanation of later criminal behavior. Studies consider personality characteristics of delinquent girls (Bijleveld, Hendriks, and Vinke 2003), sex offenders (Leuw, Bijleveld, and Daalder 2003), and long-time recidivism of sex offenders (Nieuwbeerta, Blokland, and Bijleveld 2003). A particularly important project was based on a large statistical study of Dutch citizens convicted in 1977, whose criminal careers were followed until 2002, supplemented by self-report data (Blokland 2005). Testing prevailing influential theories on criminal development (Gottfredson and Hirschi 1990; Moffitt 1993; Sampson and Laub 1993; Moffitt et al. 2001; Laub and Sampson 2003), Blokland came to quite interesting conclusions. His analyses reject Gottfredson and Hirschi's postulate of criminal propensity, the invariability of the age effect, and the assertion that career change is caused by social selection rather than by changing life circumstances. His data support Sampson and Laub's theory concerning the influence of offending and life circumstances, but in agreement with Moffitt, he found that prior offending had less influence on the small group (1.4 percent) of highly persistent offenders than on "mainstream" offenders. However, there appeared to be a change in types of offending in the group of highly persistent offenders during their criminal careers in that violent crime decreased and (petty) property offending increased. This study is an important contribution to the theoretical debates on the development of criminal careers.

Outside the WODC and NSCR, there have been a number of interesting recent research developments (Bruinsma, van de Bunt, and Haen-Marshall 2001). First, Dutch researchers acted as the main coordinators of the ICVS (van Dijk, Mayhew, and Killias 1990; van Kesteren, Mayhew, and Nieuwbeerta 2000) and the International Self-Report Delinquency Study (ISRD) (Junger-Tas, Terlouw, and Klein

1994; Junger-Tas et al. 2003). The ICVS introduced systematic, world-wide, comparative crime victim surveys. These surveys produce results that could not be obtained with other methods, such as, for example, by collecting official statistics. The objective of both surveys is to find new answers to Crime (with a capital *C*) in the World (with a capital *W*). The objectives are very ambitious. To reach their goals, both have methodological improvements to make (see, e.g., Klein 1994), such as devising standardized instruments that take account of differential cultures and yet have the same meaning in all participating countries.

The ICVS has slowly improved its methodology and has completed four sweeps, the latest in 2004. The survey is organized by the United Nations Interregional Criminal Justice Research Institute and the victimology institute at the University of Tilburg. In 2001 the *Dutch Journal of Criminology* devoted a whole issue to these surveys, including an interesting article testing hypotheses from strain theory, social disintegration theory, and opportunity theory in explaining victimization by theft and violence (van Wilsem 2001, 2004). Comparing victimization data from twenty-seven nations, van Wilsem found a clear relationship between income inequality and victimization by theft and violence. In addition, he found a positive relationship of crime with divorce rates. Furthermore, his data showed that criminal opportunity was positively related to theft but not to violence. A similar trend may be observed for the ISRD, which has initiated a second survey of thirty countries, including the new E.U. member states, and is organized by a group of international scholars.[19]

Second, research into reconvictions continues to develop, inspired in large part by government policy concerns. Both the WODC and the NSCR have presented fascinating material on reconvictions of different categories of offenders, dispelling some myths concerning chronic offenders: showing that they tend to commit property offenses repeatedly, but not violent offenses, and that mentally disturbed offenders reoffend at considerably lower rates than other adult and juvenile offenders (Wartna 2000, 2004, 2005; Leuw, Bijleveld, and Daalder 2003; Blokland 2005).

Finally, a laudable effort has been made to discover underpinnings of human smuggling and human trafficking (Nijboer, Hesseling, and Smit 2001). On the basis of official data from the Immigration Service,

[19] These are Josine Junger-Tas (Netherlands), Ineke Marshall (United States), Martin Killias (Switzerland), Dirk Enzmann (Germany), and Beata Gruszczynska (Poland).

the police, records of asylum-assisting organizations, and interviews with smugglers, smuggled persons, and victims of human trafficking, the authors attempt to paint a better picture of what is happening. Given the political and policy controversies surrounding this question, it is important for criminology to provide as accurate data as possible so as to dispel misimpressions among policy makers and the general public.

IX. Dutch Criminology

We now return to the three strands mentioned in the introduction and offer provisional conclusions: Where does Dutch criminology now stand in terms of empiricism, policy research, and theory building?

First, concerning empirical research, mostly, but not exclusively, quantitative studies have been done on subjects such as the etiology of crime, victimization, fear of crime, situational approaches to crime, program evaluations, criminal justice issues (such as differential treatment of some categories of offenders), and alternative sanctions. Empiricism is firmly rooted. This is also clearly the case concerning policy issues, although there is little critical reflection on official policies.[20]

The second strand concerns the question to what extent policy research has developed. Among the choices in research topics, some characteristics stand out. Most topics examined by the WODC are meant to answer practical policy problems and provide hard data on the crime picture. This concerns such topics as the extension of the biannual self-reported youth delinquency survey, evaluations of pilot projects, problems of law enforcement in coffee shops, and infractions of environmental law. One major innovation is the creation of the recidivism monitor.

Although, or perhaps because, the Netherlands is a small country, Dutch criminology tends to look abroad, in particular to the United States, for its inspiration. So the WODC is following developments in Anglo-Saxon countries to improve the execution of penal policies, such as the development of screening instruments for recidivism predictions, cost-benefit analysis, and many evaluations of policy measures. However, the WODC is a "service" institute on behalf of the minister of justice, and theory building is not a primary concern.

---

[20] These are more often to be found in the (penal) law research institutes, such as in Utrecht and Leiden.

Research done by the NSCR offers considerable variation: there is important research on the geographical distribution of crime, displacement of crime, crime victimization, criminal careers, sex offenders, murderers, and juvenile delinquency, all within the Dutch context and most referring directly to policy concerns. Despite overwhelming U.S. influence in terms of methodology and theory, the bulk of the research seems to be dictated by national policy interests rather than by broader scientific interests. Maybe this is to be expected from a study center financed in large part by the Ministry of Justice, but it means that the choice of research topics seems somewhat constrained and lacking in critical reflection on the Dutch criminal justice system.[21]

Most Dutch criminological research is policy research, answering more or less broad questions on etiology and law enforcement, perhaps because most funding sources are government-related.[22] With respect to the universities, there is more variety in research concerns. For example, the Free University of Amsterdam conducts studies on organizational crime and human trafficking. The Groningen institute's research centers on violence in a European context. In Utrecht the tradition of anthropological research has been maintained and is concentrated on problem groups of ethnic minorities and on organized crime. Unfortunately, however, since most of the university criminological units are embedded in law faculties or legal research institutes, they have few or no research resources. Getting funding is difficult and may explain the difference in scope of the studies university research units can undertake, both in manpower and in size, compared with those of the NSCR or the WODC.

The third strand referred to Dutch contributions to theory. Unfortunately, little original work has been done. Hans Boutellier is one of a very few criminologists reflecting on changes in criminal justice in Western society and the growing influence of morality expressed, among other ways, in the central role of the victim in criminal proceedings (Boutellier 2000). A second study examines conflicting popular desires for individual liberty and risk taking in a society that is expected to guarantee absolute security from unexpected and negative

---

[21] There are exceptions based on collaboration with other foreign partners, such as a study on the public character of the penal process, or one on principles of fair trial in the Netherlands compared with other Anglo-Saxon systems.

[22] There are exceptions: for example, some insurance companies fund research on health-threatening deviant behavior.

(criminal) consequences. According to Boutellier, this is a demand that no state can meet (Boutellier 2002).

Criminology in the Netherlands is not so much "internationally" oriented as "American" oriented. For example, in terms of etiology of crime, a similar discussion is taking place between the "risk factor" criminologists (Loeber, Farrington, and Moffitt) and the "life-history" ones (Laub and Sampson), just as in the United States. This is of considerable interest, since it is a reminder of the eternal question of individual versus social (-economic) causes of criminal development, which is also debated in the United States. However, real controversies, such as in the time of Bonger, on whether the object of criminology should be the individual offender or the general phenomenon of crime do not provoke much discussion.

This is not so surprising: the Dutch social sciences in general, including criminology, have been heavily influenced by American theory, research, and research methodology since the 1950s. The American literature is well known, and most hypotheses that are tested are drawn from it. Although this American orientation is comprehensible and useful, an important question is why it dominates and practically excludes other research perspectives. It is as though Dutch criminologists do not realize that the Netherlands belongs first and before all to Europe and that its future lies in Europe and not in the United States.

The question is why we do not much more often consider our crime problems within a European context. Despite some exceptions,[23] one might wonder, for example, where the research is on important issues of crime control, criminal justice, and security in Europe; what might be the explanation for the increasingly repressive tendencies in criminal justice in the Netherlands as in other continental countries; what may be the relationships between crime, migration, and asylum problems in an international and European perspective, and in relation to human rights under the European Convention of Human Rights. Why is there not considerably more comparative research, for example, on differences in law enforcement, services to victims and prisoners, or prevention and aftercare?

All this might stimulate theoretical innovations. As long as Dutch

[23] For example, in the WODC research review of 2003 we found a (legal) study on the influence of European rules on the Dutch criminal justice system. Moreover, participation in the *European Sourcebook* demonstrates interest in crime policies of other European countries.

researchers do not see criminological research in a wider European perspective, it is not likely that we will come up with new insights and instead will continue primarily to follow American developments. This is why we agree with Fijnaut that Dutch criminology is somewhat parochial (Fijnaut 2004) and, we would add, inward-looking.

It is important that Dutch universities not leave the playing field to the two justice-oriented research centers. Fijnaut (2004, p. 6) recommends that the two research centers funded by the Ministry of Justice be eliminated and one big central university center be launched instead. This does not seem to us very realistic, nor desirable. However, the university research centers, whenever possible, should combine their resources and collaborate on original and larger studies, studies that take the European context into account, with a critical view on prevailing policies and a serious reflection on the contributions Dutch and European criminology can make to empirical knowledge and theory.

REFERENCES

Aalberts, Monique M. J. 1989. *Operationeel vreemdelingentoezicht in Nederland*. The Hague: Staatsuitgeverij.

Aletrino, Arnold. 1902. *Handleiding bij de studié der crimineele anthropologie*. Amsterdam: Maas and van Suchtelen.

Bernasco, Willem, Gerben J. N. Bruinsma, and Wim Huisman. 2004. "Ruimtelijke strategieën van misdadigers; sociale relaties voor criminele infrastructuur." *Stedebouw and Ruimtelijke Ordening* 85(3):34–37.

Bernasco, Willem, and F. Luykx. 2003. "Effects of Attractiveness, Opportunity and Accessibility to Burglars on Residential Burglary Rates of Urban Neighborhoods." *Criminology* 41(3):981–1002.

Bernasco, Willem, and Paul Nieuwbeerta. 2003. "Hoe kiezen inbrekers een pleegbuurt? Een nieuwe benadering voor de studie van criminele doelwitselectie." *Tijdschrift voor Criminologie* 45(3):254–70.

Bianchi, Herman. 1956. *Position and Subject-Matter of Criminology: Inquiry concerning Theoretical Criminology*. Amsterdam: Vrije Universiteit Amsterdam.

———. 1961. "Strafsancties en geestelijke gezondheid." Inaugural speech. Vrije Universiteit Amsterdam.

———. 1971. *Stigmatisering*. Deventer: Kluwer.

———. 1974a. "Gouvernementele en non-gouvernementele kriminologie." *Tijdschrift voor Criminologie* 16(5):201–16.

———. 1974b. "Naar een nieuwe fenomenologische criminologie." *Nederlands Tijdschrift voor Criminologie* 16:97–112.

———. 1999. "In redactionele inleiding." *Tijdschrift voor Criminologie* 41: 107–8.

Bijleveld, Catrien, J. Hendriks, and M. Vinke. 2003. "Moeilijke meisjes-de relatie tussen delict-en persoon (lijkheid) skenmerken van delinquente meisjes." *Tijdschrift voor Criminologie* 45(1):53–70.

Block, Rebecca C. R., and Nelleke C. van der Werff. 1991. *Initiation and Continuation of a Criminal Career*. Arnhem: Gouda Quint.

Blokland, Arjan. 2005. "Crime over the Life Course: Trajectories of Criminal Behavior in Dutch Offenders." PhD dissertation, University of Leiden, Department of Psychology.

Bol, Menke W., and Jan J. Overwater. 1984. *Dienstverlening—vervanging van de vrijheidsstraf in het strafrecht voor volwassenen*. The Hague: WODC, Ministry of Justice.

Bonger, Willem A. 1913. *Geloof en misdaad: Een criminologische studie*. Leiden: Brill.

———. 1932. *Inleiding tot de criminologie*. Haarlem: Bohn.

———. 1954. *Inleiding tot de criminologie*. 2nd ed., revised by G. Th. Kempe. Haarlem: De Erven F. Bohn N.V.

———. 1967. *Criminality and Economic Conditions*. New York: Agathon. (Originally published 1905.)

Boutellier, Hans. 2000. *Crime and Morality*. Dordrecht: Kluwer.

———. 2002. *De veiligheidsutopie*. The Hague: Boom.

Bovenkerk, Frank, Mieke Komen, and Y. Yesilgöz. 2003. *Multiculturaliteit in de strafrechtspleging*. The Hague: Boom.

Bovenkerk, Frank, and Y. Yesilgöz. 1998. *De Maffia van Turkije*. Amsterdam: Meulenhoff.

Braithwaite, John. 1989. *Crime, Shame and Reintegration*. Cambridge: Cambridge University Press.

Brants, Chrisje, and J. Silvis. 1987. "Dutch Criminal Justice and a Challenge to Abolitionism." In *The Criminal Justice System as a Social Problem: An Abolitionist Perspective*, edited by J. Blad, H. Van Mastricht, and N. Uitdriks. Rotterdam: Erasmus University.

Bruinsma, Gerben J. N. 1985. "Criminaliteit als sociaal leerproces." Dissertation, Universiteit Twente.

———. 1999. *Criminaliteitsbeeld in Twente in 1995, 1996 en 1997*. Twente: International Politie Instituut Twente.

Bruinsma, Gerben J. N., Henk G. van de Bunt, and Jan P. S. Fiselier. 1990. "Hoe onveilig is Nederland?" *Tijdschrift voor Criminologie* 32(2):138–55.

Bruinsma, Gerben J. N., Henk G. van de Bunt, and Ineke Haen-Marshall. 2001. *Met het oog op de toekomst: Verkenning naar de kennisvragen over misdaad en misdaadbestrijding in 2010*. The Hague: Adviesraad voor Wetenschaps- en Technologiebeleid.

Buikhuisen, Wouter. 1966. "Criminologie en criminologisch onderzoek." Inaugural lecture. Assen: Rijksuniversiteit Groningen.

———. 1986. "Erfelijkheid en criminaliteit." *Nederlands Tijdschrift voor Criminologie* 10:129–43.

Buikhuisen, Wouter, Riekent W. Jongman, and Wim Oving. 1969. "Ongeregistreerde criminaliteit onder studenten." *Nederlands Tijdschrift voor Criminologie* 11:69–89.

Buiks, P. E. J. 1983. *Surinaamse jongeren op de kruiskade.* Deventer: Van Loghum Slaterus.

Burnier, Andreas. 1981. *Een tevreden lach.* Amsterdam: Wetenschappelijke uitgeveris. (Originally published 1965.)

Cloward, R. A., and L. E. Ohlin. 1960. *Delinquency and Opportunity.* New York: Free Press.

Cohen, L. E., and Marcus Felson. 1979. "Social Change and Crime Rate Trends: A Routine Activity Approach." *American Sociological Review* 44: 588–608.

Coleman, J. S. 1972. *Policy Research in the Social Sciences.* Morristown, NJ: General Learning Press.

Decker, Scott H., and Frank M. Weerman, eds. 2005. *European Street Gangs and Troublesome Youth Groups.* Lanham, UK: Altamira.

de Haan, Willem. 1990. *The Politics of Redress—Crime, Punishment and Penal Abolition.* London: Unwin Hyman.

de Keijser, Jan W., and Marijke Malsch. 2002. "Is spreken zilver en zwijgen goud? Spreekrecht en het ontstemde slachtoffer." *Delikt and Delinkwent* 32(1):5–20.

Dessaur, C. I. Ronnie. 1971. *Foundations of Theory Formation in Criminology: A Methodological Analysis.* The Hague: Mouton.

———. 1987. *De rondgang der gevangenen: Een essay over goed en kwaad.* Amsterdam: Querido.

de Tarde, Gabriel. 1890. *Les lois de l'imitation.* Paris: Félix Alcan.

———. 1898. *Les lois sociales: Esquisse d'une sociologie.* Paris: Félix Alcan.

Dijksterhuis, Fokke P. H., and Jan Nijboer. 1990. "Slachtoffer-enquête: Een vergelijking tussen België en Nederland." *Delikt en Delinkwent* 20(7):615–22.

Durkheim, Emile. 1986. *Les règles de la méthode sociologique.* Paris: Presses Universitaires de France. (Originally published 1895.)

Elffers, Henk. 1991. *Income Tax Evasion: Theory and Measurement.* Deventer: Kluwer.

Enquêtecommissie Opsporingsmethoden. 1996. *Inzake opsporing.* The Hague: SDU uitgevers.

European Committee on Crime Problems. 1980. *Report on Decriminalisation.* Strasbourg: Council of Europe.

Felson, Marcus. 1998. *Crime and Everyday Life.* 2nd ed. London: Thousand Oaks.

Fijnaut, Cyrille. 2004. "De criminologie in Nederlands." *Tijdschrift voor Criminologie* 20:5–9.

Fiselier, Jan P. S. 1978. *Slachtoffers van delicten: Onderzoek naar verborgen criminaliteit.* Utrecht: Ars Aequi Libri.

Franke, Herman. 1990*a*. "Misdaadenquête meet slechts gevoeligheid slachtoffers." *De Volkskrant* (May 8).

———. 1990*b*. *Twee eeuwen gevangen.* Utrecht: Het Spectrum.

————. 1990c. "Veilig land maar laat wel je fiets thuis: Nederland en het dri-jfzand van de criminaliteitscijfers." *NRC Handelsblad* (March 31).

Gezik, E. 2002. *Eer, identiteit en moord—een vergelijkende studie tussen Nederland, Duitsland en Turkije.* Utrecht: Nederlands Centrum Buitenlanders/STO.

Goring, C. 1913. *The English Convict: A Statistical Study.* Montclair, NJ: Patterson-Smith.

Gottfredson, Michael R., and Travis Hirschi. 1990. *A General Theory of Crime.* Stanford, CA: Stanford University Press.

Grapendaal, Martin, Ed Leuw, and Hans Nelen. 1995. *A World of Opportunities—Life-Style and Economic Behavior of Heroin Addicts in Amsterdam.* Albany: State University of New York Press.

Hessing, D. J., Henk Elffers, and R. H. Weigel. 1988. "Exploring the Limits of Self-Reports and Reasoned Action: An Investigation of the Psychology of Tax Evasion Behavior." *Journal of Personality and Social Psychology* 54:405–13.

Hirschi, Travis. 1969. *Causes of Delinquency.* Berkeley: University of California Press.

Hulsman, Loek. 1978. "The Relative Mildness of the Dutch Criminal Justice System: An Attempt at Analysis." In *Dutch Law for Foreign Lawyers,* edited by D. Fokkema, W. Chorus, and E. Hondius. Deventer: Kluwer.

————. 1981. "Penal Reform in the Netherlands: Bringing the Criminal Justice System under Control." *Howard Journal* 20:150–59.

Hulsman, Loek, and J. Bernat de Célis. 1982. *Peines perdues: Le système pénal en question.* Paris: Centurion.

Junger-Tas, Josine. 1979. "Wetenschap en beleid." *Justitiële Verkenningen* 7: 4–30.

————. 1993. "Evaluatieonderzoek ten behoeve van justitieel beleid." In *Rekenschap-evaluatieonderzoek in Nederland: De stand van zaken,* edited by Marianne Donker and Jan Derks. Utrecht: Nederlands Centrum voor Volksgezondheid.

————. 1994. *Alternatives to Prison Sentences: Experiences and Development.* Amsterdam: Kugler.

Junger-Tas, Josine, Ineke Haen-Marshall, and Denis Ribeaud. 2003. *Delinquency in an International Perspective: The International Self-Reported Delinquency Study.* New York: Criminal Justice Press.

Junger-Tas, Josine, and Joke S. E. Holten-Vriesema. 1978. *Relatie tussen de primaire politie-opleiding en de polite-prakti—eindrappor.* The Hague: Staatsuitgeverij.

Junger-Tas, Josine, Marianne Junger, and Els Barendse-Hoornweg. 1985. *Juvenile Delinquency II: The Impact of Judicial Intervention.* The Hague: WODC, Ministry of Justice.

Junger-Tas, Josine, Marianne Junger, and Marjan Sampiemon. 1983. *Juvenile Delinquency: Backgrounds of Delinquent Behavior.* The Hague: WODC, Ministry of Justice.

Junger-Tas, Josine, J. L. F Maarten, Petra M. Cruyff, Jansen van de Looij, and Fred Reelick. 2003. *Etnische minderheden en het belang van binding.* The Hague: SDU uitgevers.

Junger-Tas, Josine, Gert-Jan Terlouw, and Malcolm W. Klein, eds. 1994. *Delinquent Behavior among Young People in the Western World: First Results of the International Self-Reported Delinquency Study*. New York: Kugler.

Kaufman, W. J., and H. T. Verbraeck. 1986. *Marokkaan en verslaafd: Een studie naar randgroepvorming, heroïnegebruik en criminalisering*. Utrecht: Afdeling Onderzoek ROVU, Gemeente Utrecht.

Kelk, Constantijn. 1983. "The Humanity of the Dutch Prison System and Prisoners' Consciousness of Their Legal Rights." *Contemporary Crises* 7: 155–70.

Kempe, Gerrit Th. 1938. *Criminaliteit en kerkgenootschap*. Utrecht: Willem Pompe Instituut.

———. 1952. "Criminologie in existentialistische doorlichting." *Tijdschrift voor Strafrecht* 61:166–86.

———. 1957. "50 jaar criminologie in Nederland (1907–1957)." In *Psychiatrisch-juridisch gezelschap gedenkboek 1907–'57*. Amsterdam: F. van Rosen.

———. 1976. *Inleiding tot de criminologie*. Haarlem: De Erven F. Bohn N.V.

Kleemans, Edward R., Ellen A. I. M. van den Berg, and Henk G. van de Bunt. 1998. *Georganiseerde criminaliteit in Nederland*. The Hague: WODC, Ministry of Justice.

Klein, Malcolm W. 1994. "Epilogue." In *Delinquent Behavior among Young People in the Western World: First Results of the International Self-Report Delinquency Study*, edited by Josine Junger-Tas, Gert-Jan Terlouw, and Malcolm W. Klein. Amsterdam: Kugler.

Lacassagne, Jean-Alexandre. 1878. *Précis de médecine judiciaire*. Paris: G. Masson.

———. 2001. *Etude médico-légale: Complémentaire de la question de survie. Affaire Tarbé des sablons*. Lyon: Storck. (Originally published 1890.)

Laub, John H., and Robert J. Sampson. 2003. *Shared Beginnings, Divergent Lives: Delinquent Boys to Age 70*. Cambridge, MA: Harvard University Press.

Lemert, Edwin. 1967. *Human Deviance, Social Problems and Social Control*. Englewood Cliffs, NJ: Prentice Hall.

Leuw, Ed, Catrien Bijleveld, and A. Daalder 2003. "Seksuele delinquenten (inleiding)." *Tijdschrift voor Criminologie* 45(4):330–38.

Leuw, Ed, and Ineke Haen-Marshall, eds. 1994. *Between Prohibition and Legalization: The Dutch Experiment in Drug Policy*. Amsterdam: Kugler.

Malsch, Marijke, and I. Freckelton. 2005. "Expert Bias and Partisanship: A Comparison between Australia and the Netherlands." *Psychology, Public Policy and Law* 11:42–61.

Mayhew, Pat, and Jan J. M. van Dijk. 1997. *Crime Victimisation in Eleven Industrialised Countries: Key Findings from the 1996 International Crime Victims Survey*. The Hague: WODC, Ministry of Justice.

Miedema, Siep. 2002. "Onderzoek nader onderzocht: Een vergelijkende analyse van etnografisch onderzoek naar de relatie tussen etniciteit, groepsvorming en delinquentie bij jongens." *Tijdschrift voor Criminologie* 44(2): 150–61.

Ministry of Justice. 1977. *Memorie van toelichting—begroting 1977*. The Hague: Ministry of Justice.

———. 1985. *Society and Crime: A Policy Plan for the Netherlands*. The Hague: Ministry of Justice.

Moffitt, Terrie E. 1993. "Adolescence-Limited and Life-Course Persistent Anti-social Behavior." *Psychological Review* 100:674–701.

Moffitt, Terrie E., Avshalom Caspi, Michael Rutter, and Phil A. Silva. 2001. *Sex Differences in Antisocial Behavior*. Cambridge: Cambridge University Press.

Muller, Nico. 1908. *Biografisch-aetiologisch onderzoek over recidive bij misdrijven tegen den eigendom*. Amsterdam: Universiteit van Amsterdam.

Nagel, Willem H. 1949. *De criminaliteit van Oss*. The Hague: Rijksuniversiteit Groningen.

———. 1963. "De Utrechtse School." *Tijdschrift voor Strafrecht* 72:322–55.

———. 1965. *Het voorspellen van crimineel gedrag: Een rapport uitgebracht aan het Ministerie van Justitie*. The Hague: Staatsuitgeverij.

Nieuwbeerta, Paul, Arjan A. J. Blokland, and Catrien Bijleveld. 2003. "Lange termijn recidive van daders van seksuele delicten." *Tijdschrift voor Criminologie* 45(4):369–77.

Nijboer, Jan A. 1975. *Voorspellen van recidive*. Assen: Van Gorcum.

Nijboer, Jan A., René Hesseling, and Monica Smit. 2001. "Mensensmokkel en mensenhandel." *Tijdschrift voor Criminologie* 43(4):24–30.

Nuyten-Edelbroek, Liesbet G. M., and Arnold Slothouwer. 1988. *Een blik op de toekomst van het CRI: Verslag van een onderzoek bij politie en Openbaar Ministerie*. The Hague: Staatsuitgeverij.

Polder, Wim, and Fransje J. C. Van Vlaardingen. 1992. *Preventiestrategieën in de praktijk: Een meta-evaluatie van criminaliteitspreventie projecten*. Arnhem: Gouda Quint.

Pompe, Willem. 1935. *Handboek van het Nederlandse strafrecht* (rev. in 1959). Zwolle: Tjennk Wittink.

———. 1946. *Het nieuwe tijdperk in het recht*. Amsterdam: Vij Nederland.

Rovers, Ben. 1999. "Veertig jaar Tijdschrift voor criminologie in cijfers: 1959–1999." *Tijdschrift voor Criminologie* 41(2):123–38.

Sampson, Robert J., and John Laub. 1993. *Crime in the Making: Pathways and Turning Points through Life*. Cambridge, MA: Harvard University Press.

Sampson, Robert J., S. W. Raudenbusch, and Felton Earls. 1997. "Neighborhoods and Violent Crime: A Multilevel Study of Collective Efficacy." *Science* 277:914–18.

Shaw, Clifford, and Henry McKay. 1942. *Juvenile Delinquency and Urban Areas*. Chicago: University of Chicago Press.

Spickenheuer, Hans P. L. 1977. *Het reclasseringswerk: De tijdsbesteding*. The Hague: Staatsuitgeverij.

Steenhuis, Dato W. 1972. *Rijden onder invloed*. Assen: van Gorcum.

Steinmetz, S. R. 1892–94. *Ethnologische studien zur erster entwicklung der strafe*. Leiden: van Doesburgh.

———. 1893. "Suicide among Primitive People." *American Anthropologist* 7: 53–60.

———. 1907*a*. *De studie der volkenkunde.* The Hague: Nijhoff.

———. 1907*b*. *Wat is sociologie: Openbare les.* Leiden: van Doesburgh

———. 1908. *De betekenis der volkenkunde van mensch en maatschappij.* The Hague: Nijhoff.

van de Bunt, Henk G. 1992. *Organisatiecriminaliteit.* Arnhem: Gouda Quint.

———. 2002. "Diamanten." *Tijdschrift voor Criminologie* 44(4):319–27.

van de Bunt, Henk, Cyrille Fijnaut, Frank Bovenkerk, and Gerben J. Bruinsma. 1996. "De georganiseerde criminaliteit in Nederland." *Tijdschrift voor Criminologie* 38(2):102–19.

van de Bunt, Henk G., and Wim Huisman. 2004. "Organisatiecriminaliteit." *Tijdschrift voor Criminologie* 46(2):106–20.

van der Heiden-Attema, N., and Bouke S. J. Wartna. 2000. *Recidive na verblijf in een JBI: Geregistreerde criminaliteit onder jongeren uit een justitiële behandelinrichting.* The Hague: WODC, Ministry of Justice.

van der Laan, Peter H. 1991. *Experimenteren met alternatieve sancties voor jeugdigen.* Arnhem: Gouda Quint.

van Dijk, Jan J. M. 1982. "Verschillen en overeenkomsten tussen praktische en academische criminologie." *Justitiële Verkenningen* 6:5–24.

van Dijk, Jan J. M., Pat Mayhew, and Martin Killias. 1990. *Experiences of Crime across the World: Key Findings of the 1989 International Crime Survey.* Deventer: Kluwer.

van Dijk, Jan J. M., Irene Sagel-Grande, and Leo G. Toornvliet. 2002. *Actuele criminologie.* The Hague: SDU/Vermande.

van Heerikhuizen, Bart. 1987. *W. A. Bonger/socioloog en socialist.* Groningen: Wolters/Noordhoff.

van Kerckvoorde, Jaak. 1995. *Een maat voor het kwaad? Over de meting van criminaliteit met behulp van officiële statistieken en door middel van enquêtes.* Leuven: Universitaire Pers Leuven.

van Kesteren, John, Pat Mayhew, and Paul Nieuwbeerta. 2000. *Crime Victimisation in Seventeen Industrialised Countries.* The Hague: WODC, Ministry of Justice.

van Koppen, Peter J. 2004. *Paradoxen van deskundigen: Over de rol van experts in strafzaken.* Deventer: Kluwer.

van Ruller, Simon. 1988. "Ideeën over misdaadbestrijding in de jaren dertig." *Tijdschrift voor Criminologie* 30(2):98–109.

van Swaaningen, René. 1991. "Abolitionisme." *Tijdschrift voor Criminologie* 33(4):355–61.

van Weringh, Koos J. 1967. *Het maatschappij beeld van Abraham Kuyper.* Assen: van Gorcum.

———. 1971. "Heeft onze maatschappij de criminaliteit die zij verdient?" Inaugural lecture. Universiteit van Amsterdam.

———. 1978. *Onrust is van alle tijden: Opstellen over criminaliteit in Nederland.* Amsterdam: Der Arbeiders-pers Meppel.

―――. 1986. *De afstand tot de horizon/verwachting en werkelijkheid in de Nederlandse criminologie.* Amsterdam: de Arbeiderspers.

van Wilsem, Johan. 2001. "Verschillen in slachtofferschap van criminaliteit tussen 27 landen." *Justitiële Verkenningen* 43(2):158–81.

―――. 2004. "Criminal Victimization in Cross-National Perspective: An Analysis of Rates of Theft, Violence and Vandalism across 27 Countries." *European Journal of Criminology* 1(1):89–111.

Veendrick, L. 1976. *Verborgen en geregistreerde kriminaliteit in Groningen.* Groningen: Kriminologisch Instituut Rijksuniversiteit Groningen.

Vervaele, John A. E., A. H. Klip, A. J. Berg, N. M. Dane, and O. J. D. M. L. Jansen. 2001. *Administratieve en strafrechtelijke samenwerking inzake fraudebestrijding tussen justitiële en bestuurlijke instanties van de EU-lidstaten.* The Hague: WODC, Ministry of Justice.

Wartna, Bouke S. J. 1999. *Recidive onderzoek in Nederland.* WODC Onderzoeknotitie. The Hague: WODC, Ministry of Justice.

―――. 2000. "Recidiveonderzoek en survival analyse." *Tijdschrift voor Criminologie* 42(1):2–21.

―――. 2004. *Bekenden van justitie.* Meppel: Boom Juridische uitgeverij.

Wartna, Bouke S. J., M. Tollenaar, and M. Blom. 2005. *Recidive 1997.* The Hague: WODC, Ministry of Justice.

Webley, P., H. S. J. Robben, H. Elffers, and D. J. Hessing. 1991. *Tax Evasion: An Experimental Approach.* Cambridge: Cambridge University Press.

Weigel, R. H., D. J. Hessing, and Henk Elffers. 1987. "Tax Evasion Research: A Critical Appraisal and Theoretical Model." *Journal of Economic Psychology* 8:215–35.

Welters, L. A. 1978. "Beleid ten aanzien van onderzoek en onderzoek voor beleid." *Beleid en Maatschappij* (1):8–18.

Werdmölder, Hans. 1986. *Van vriendengroep tot randgroep: Marokkaanse jongeren in een oude stadswijk.* Amsterdam: Het Wereldvenster.

Winkel, Frans W., and L. Koppelaar. 1991. "Rape Victims' Style of Self-Presentation and Secondary Victimization by the Environment: An Experiment." *Journal of Interpersonal Violence* 6:29–41.

Winkel, Frans W., L. Koppelaar, and A. Vrij. 1988. "Creating Suspects in Police-Citizen Encounters: Two Studies on Personal Space and Being Suspect." *Social Behaviour* 3:307–19.

Winkel, Frans W., and A. Vrij. 1990. "Fear of Crime and Mass Media Crime Reports: Testing Similarity Hypotheses." *International Review of Victimology* 1:251–66.

Wolfgang, Marvin E., Robert M. Figlio, and Thorsten Sellin. 1972. *Delinquency in a Birth Cohort.* Chicago: University of Chicago Press.

Zwanenburg, M. A. 1977. *Prediction in Criminology.* Nijmegen: Dekker and van de Vegt.

Edward R. Kleemans

Organized Crime, Transit Crime, and Racketeering

ABSTRACT

When organized crime reached the political agenda in the early 1990s, it was framed in terms of "Mafia-type" organizations and infiltration in (local) governments, geographical areas, and economic sectors (racketeering). This conception contradicted the phenomenon: the primary business of organized crime is more fittingly described as "transit crime," as opposed to the control of economic sectors or regions. Criminal groups should be viewed as "criminal networks" (instead of as pyramidal structures), as can be seen in several illegal activities: drug trafficking, human trafficking for sexual exploitation, smuggling of illegal immigrants, arms trafficking, and trafficking in stolen vehicles. The misconception of the nature of organized crime put criminal investigation strategies on the wrong track, but the changing view of organized crime is mirrored by a change in criminal investigation strategies. Flexible "prompt intervention" strategies are more common, as an alternative to the large-scale and lengthy "long-haul" strategies of the past. Both covert policing and infiltration and uncontrolled deliveries (of drugs) were regulated or forbidden and displaced by increasing reliance on "unobtrusive" methods of gathering evidence such as wiretapping and bugging. These methods may be effective in cases of transit crime. The innovative administrative approach may be more effective against racketeering than against transit crime.

In many European countries, with the exception of Italy, organized crime has only recently begun to be viewed as a serious problem, and its place on the political agenda and in public debate has been significant only since the late 1980s (Fijnaut and Paoli 2004, p. 603). For a

Edward R. Kleemans is a senior researcher at the Research and Documentation Centre (RDC/WODC) of the Ministry of Justice, the Netherlands. I am grateful to all those who commented on earlier drafts of this essay, particularly Michael Tonry, Catrien Bijleveld, three anonymous reviewers, the participants of the Crime and Justice conference in Leiden in April 2005, Wendy de Jong-Ward, Karla van Leeuwen-Burow, and the members of the Organized Crime Monitor research group.

163

long time, Dutch criminologists, as well as policy makers, regarded organized crime as a predominantly foreign phenomenon (see, e.g., Fijnaut 1984, 1985). The world of serious crime, however, gradually transformed in the 1970s and 1980s as a result of the large quantities of drugs being bought, sold, and trafficked through the Netherlands. In those decades several native Dutch and Surinamese offenders made huge profits trafficking cannabis and cocaine internationally. They invested their returns in real estate and small businesses.

At the end of the 1980s, the Amsterdam police tried to draw attention to the problem of organized crime by privately briefing members of Parliament and public prosecutors in confidence. In addition, a team of crime analysts attempted to take stock of all criminal groups in the Netherlands in 1988 by sending out questionnaires to police forces in the country asking if they were aware of criminal groups that met one or more of the following five criteria: engaged in several illegal activities (drugs, weapons, fraud, and so on), had a hierarchy and a fixed division of tasks, employed an internal positive or negative sanctioning system, laundered money with the aid of experts, and used corruption. Although the confidential report contained only three groups believed to meet all five criteria, the sheer number (189) of criminal groups— meeting at least one of these criteria—attracted extensive media attention (Fijnaut et al. 1998, pp. 10–13). The impression was that the problem of organized crime had been grossly underestimated. This idea was reinforced by several incidents, in particular by the killing of Klaas Bruinsma—an alleged Mafia don—in 1991.

The initial disbelief gave way to a sense of urgency. In 1992 the Dutch government issued an ambitious memorandum titled "Organized Crime in the Netherlands: An Impression of Its Threat and a Plan of Action" (Ministerie van Justitie/Ministerie van Binnenlandse Zaken 1992). With the benefit of hindsight, the problem of organized crime was somewhat overstated. According to the memorandum, organized crime was on the verge of infiltrating economic sectors and political institutions and was a major threat to the integrity of Dutch society. A firm preventive and law enforcement approach was promulgated, laying the foundation for a number of legislative changes in later years, for instance, provisions designed to reach the financial resources of organized crime (confiscation of criminal assets and requiring financial institutions to report unusual transactions). In addition, new investigation methods were introduced and interregional investigation squads (IRTs) were established to combat organized crime. In 1994, the reorganization of the Dutch Police Service reached completion, joining municipal and deconcentrated police forces together nationally into twenty-five regional forces and one national force that provides support services. The IRTs were joint investigation teams made up from several regional police forces.

In December 1993, however, the "IRT affair" emerged with the sudden dismantling of the Amsterdam-Utrecht IRT. According to the authorities in Amsterdam, the IRT had been dismantled because of the use of unacceptable investigation methods. In the media, however, suggestions of a dispute regarding the jurisdiction over the team and even accusations of corruption in Amsterdam were made. The dispute between Amsterdam and Utrecht about the real reasons for the dismantling of the IRT escalated further and resulted in the appointment of a fact-finding committee of independent experts in March 1994, a parliamentary fact-finding committee in October 1994, and eventually a full-fledged Parliamentary Inquiry Committee on Criminal Investigation Methods (Parlementaire Enquêtecommissie Opsporingsmethoden [PEO] 1996).

One of the conclusions of the PEO was that the IRT had used unacceptable investigative methods—several tons of drugs had been imported under the supervision of the authorities, in the hope that some informers would move to the top of criminal organizations. In the end, however, it was questioned whether the authorities were running the informers, or vice versa (Parlementaire Enquêtecommissie Opsporingsmethoden 1996). According to the committee, this investigative method was unacceptable in a constitutional democracy, as the uncontrollability of the method constituted a serious threat to the integrity of government. Furthermore, the committee made a thorough inquiry into several criminal investigation methods—observation techniques, the use of informers, covert policing and infiltration, and intelligence. The main conclusions were that there was a legal vacuum concerning criminal investigation methods, that the organization of the criminal justice system was inadequate, and that the command and control of criminal investigations should be improved. As a result of the 1996 report, there have been several reforms of the Dutch criminal justice system, including important legislation concerning the use of criminal investigation methods.

A positive side effect of the PEO was its encouragement to empirical research on organized crime. Until then, very little was known, apart from some pioneering work by the Central Criminal Intelligence Service and the Research and Documentation Centre (Wetenschappelijk Onderzoek- en Documentatiecentrum [WODC]) of the Ministry of Justice (van Duyne, Kouwenberg, and Romeijn 1990). For this reason, the committee appointed an external research group chaired by Professor Fijnaut to make an inquiry into the nature, seriousness, and scale of organized crime in the Netherlands. The extensive research report of the Fijnaut research group was published as an appendix to the report of the committee in 1996 (Fijnaut et al. 1996, 1998). The research findings modified the exaggerated image of organized crime of the early 1990s. According to the Fijnaut research group, there was no evidence of an octopus-like criminal syndicate in the Netherlands. Furthermore, it was clear that no criminal groups at national or local levels had gained control of legitimate sectors of the economy by taking over crucial businesses or trade unions (racketeering; see, e.g., Gambetta 1993; Jacobs 1999; Jacobs and Peters 2003; Paoli 2003). Hence, the problem of organized crime in the Netherlands was viewed as essentially different from the situation in Italy or the United States. However, the picture sketched by the Fijnaut research group was not all that reassuring: extensive networks were involved in organized crime, the prevalence of certain immigrant groups in drug trafficking was worrying, and certain criminal groups had made substantial investments in real estate, in particular in Amsterdam's red-light district. After publication of the Fijnaut group's report in 1996, the minister of justice promised the Dutch Parliament to report periodically on the nature of organized crime in the Netherlands. To meet this need for information, WODC started the Organized Crime Monitor, an ongoing systematic analysis of closed police investigations of criminal groups. Major reports to Parliament were published in 1999 and 2002 (Kleemans, van den Berg, and van de Bunt 1998; Kleemans, Brienen, and van de Bunt 2002).

Three lines of investigation can be distinguished in empirical Dutch studies of organized crime. First, the extensive use of case studies sometimes combined with interviews of criminal justice experts. It is important to note that—compared to other countries—Dutch criminal investigations provide a great deal of "objective" evidence on offender behavior, due to the extensive use of wiretapping, observation techniques and other special investigative methods, and the absence of plea bargaining. Researchers have access to the original police files and can to a large extent check the files themselves. Major examples of this line of research are studies carried out by van Duyne, Kouwenberg, and Romeijn (1990), van Duyne (1995), the Fijnaut research group (Fijnaut et al. 1996, 1998) and the Organized Crime Monitor research group (Kleemans, van den Berg, and van de Bunt 1998; Kleemans, Brienen, and van de Bunt 2002). Analyses have also been made of specific cases such as murders and liquidations (van de Port 2001) and of specific aspects of organized crime, such as revenues, expenditures, and investments (van Duyne et al. 2001; Meloen et al. 2003). Finally, both researchers and journalists have conducted detailed $N = 1$ case studies. An important example of this line of research is a detailed analysis of a network of Dutch drug traffickers by Klerks (2000).

Many of these studies were carried out or facilitated by WODC or police institutions. Compared to other countries, law enforcement institutions in the Netherlands are generally quite willing to cooperate in empirical research. Some special investigation squads have even developed strategic alliances with universities, resulting in public reports about, for instance, organized crime in Amsterdam (Huisman, Huikeshoven, and van de Bunt 2003), human trafficking (Interregionaal Recherche Team Noord- en Oost-Nederland 1997), eastern European organized crime (Kernteam Noord- en Oost-Nederland 1999, 2001; Korps Landelijke Politiediensten 2004a, 2005a), and Turkish organized crime (Korps Landelijke Politiediensten 2004b). Although most reports by law enforcement institutions are still confidential, there are more and more classified and nonclassified versions. A nonclassified national threat assessment was published in 2004, one year after the formation of a national criminal investigation squad—a merger of the former interregional investigation squads (Dienst Nationale Recherche Informatie 2004).

The second line of research consists of ethnographic studies into organized crime. Bovenkerk has conducted several interesting ethnographic studies, including a biography of a Dutch female go-between in the drug trade (Bovenkerk 1995), a study of Turkish organized crime (Bovenkerk and Yesilgöz 1998), and a study on the cultivation of cannabis (Bovenkerk and Hogewind 2003). Other representatives of this line of research are Zaitch (2002a, 2002b), who conducted ethnographic research into Colombian drug traffickers; Siegel (2005), who did ethnographic research within the Russian community in the Netherlands; Gruter and van de Mheen (2005), who interviewed participants in cocaine distribution networks; and Engbersen's research group (fieldwork into illegal immigrants and the informal sector in the Netherlands; see Engbersen, van der Leun, and de Boom, this volume). Compared to case studies, the ethnographic approach has the potential to provide important complementary insights into (the context of) organized crime. Some "ethnographic" researchers have also discovered the empirical richness of Dutch police investigations (e.g., Staring et al. 2005).

The third line of research concerns evaluations of policy measures to combat organized crime. In 2000, important legislation concerning special investigative methods was enacted as a result of the IRT affair and the final report of the Parliamentary Inquiry Committee. This legislation, called the BOB Act, which regulates methods such as covert policing and infiltration, observation, bugging, and wiretapping, was evaluated by WODC (Bokhorst, de Kogel, and van der Meij 2002; Beijer et al. 2004). Research has also reviewed the effectiveness of wiretapping (e.g., Reijne, Kouwenberg, and Keizer 1996; Beijer et al. 2004; De Poot et al. 2004) and covert policing and infiltration (Kruissink, van Hoorn, and Boek 1999). From an international perspective, it is unusual to carry out research on such highly sensitive topics and publicly report the results (Fijnaut and Paoli 2004, pp. 1040–41). Other researchers have examined preventive strategies toward organized crime (e.g., Lankhorst and Nelen 2003, 2004; van de Bunt and van der Schoot 2003; Zoomer, Nieuwkamp, and Johannink 2004; Huisman et al. 2005). Finally, anti–money laundering efforts and asset forfeiture are much-researched areas (e.g., Terlouw and Aron 1996; Nelen and Sabee 1998; Faber and van Nunen 2002, 2004; Meloen et al. 2003; Nelen 2004; Schaap Bruin van Vliet 2004).

This essay elaborates on the main results of empirical research into organized crime and organized crime policies in the Netherlands (for an overview of European and American literature, see, e.g., Abadinsky [2002], Albanese [2004], and Fijnaut and Paoli [2004]). In Section I, I summarize the key research findings on the nature of organized crime. When the problem of organized crime reached the political agenda in the early 1990s, it was viewed in terms of "Mafia-type" organizations and infiltration in (local) governments, geographical areas, and economic sectors (racketeering). After assessing the evidence of corruption, violence, and intimidation, and the intertwining between organized crime and the legal economy, I conclude that this concept actually contradicted with the way this phenomenon manifested itself in this country. An alternative concept is therefore introduced, now widely accepted in policy and research circles in the Netherlands. Put simply, the primary business of organized crime is "transit crime" (instead of controlling economic sectors or regions), and the nature of criminal groups should be conceived as "criminal networks" (instead of pyramidal structures). Section II elaborates on these main points, focusing on several specific illegal activities: drug trafficking, human trafficking for sexual exploitation, smuggling of illegal immigrants, arms trafficking, and trafficking in stolen vehicles.

Section III describes major changes in organized crime policies over the past two decades. The misconception of the nature of organized crime undoubtedly increased awareness of the problem and stimulated the emergence of several preventive strategies, yet it put criminal investigation strategies on the wrong track. The changing view of the nature of organized crime is mirrored by a change in investigative strategies. Flexible "prompt intervention" strategies are more common, as an alternative to the large-scale and lengthy "long-haul" strategies of the past. Arrests and seizures in criminal networks are no longer postponed or prevented at any cost but are—on the contrary—sometimes deliberately used to gather evidence against the prime suspects. Furthermore, both covert policing and infiltration and uncontrolled deliveries (of drugs) were—as a result of the IRT affair—strictly regulated or forbidden and made way for an increasing reliance on "unobtrusive" methods of gathering evidence such as wiretapping and bugging. The empirical evidence available suggests that these methods may still be effective in cases of transit crime, primarily because communication between the main suspects is essential and (traceable) communication methods can be only partly replaced by meetings in person. A third change in criminal investigation strategies was (increasing use of) cross-border police investigations, paralleled by a centralization of police capacity used for fighting transnational organized crime.

Finally, attention is paid to the emergence of preventive strategies and particularly to the administrative approach, both on a local level (Amsterdam) and on a national level. Although this innovative approach has many positive aspects, empirical research shows that two main lessons can be learned. The first is that the administrative approach may be more effective against racketeering than against transit crime. Because international illegal markets are not regulated by (local) governments, the opportunities for an administrative approach to make a difference are rather limited: it cannot target the primary business but can focus only on investments and the legal entities offenders use for facilitating their criminal activities. The second lesson is that the administrative approach is highly dependent on information from law enforcement (about criminal activities) and tax authorities (about legal and illegal activities). The essay concludes with a discussion of policy and research implications (Sec. IV).

I. The Nature of Organized Crime

When the issue of organized crime reached the political agenda in the early 1990s, the threat of organized crime was framed in terms of Mafia-type organizations in Italy or the United States, which had gained control of certain economic sectors or regions, acting as "alternative governments" (for an overview of very similar developments in some other European countries, see Fijnaut and Paoli [2004, pp. 239–62, 603–21]). Organized crime groups were portrayed as bureaucracies with a pyramidal structure—a strict hierarchy, with a clear division of tasks and an internal sanctioning system (cf. Cressey 1969, criticized, e.g., by Albini 1971; Ianni and Reuss-Ianni 1972; Smith 1975; Chambliss 1978; Block and Chambliss 1981; Moore 1987; Potter 1994; see for an overview Paoli [2002]). Corruption, racketeering, and infiltration in economic sectors were viewed as major threats of organized crime. Controlling certain regions or economic sectors, organized crime was believed to make a profit by taking over two traditional state monopolies—the use of violence and taxation. In the international literature, this is referred to as "racketeering" (see, e.g., Gambetta 1993; Jacobs 1999; Jacobs and Peters 2003; Paoli 2003).

This conception of organized crime is not in line with the empirical facts. In this section, I first assess the evidence of corruption, violence, and intimidation (Sec. I.A) and the facts about relations between organized crime and the legal economy (Sec. I.B). In Sections I.C and I.D, I introduce an alternative concept of organized crime, which is now commonly accepted in policy and research circles. This is that the primary business of organized crime is more fittingly described as "transit crime" (as opposed to controlling economic sectors or regions) and that criminal groups are best viewed as "criminal networks" rather than as pyramidal structures.

A. Corruption, Violence, and Intimidation

In the early 1990s, the sense of urgency was reinforced by several confrontations between criminal groups and the public authorities. These confrontations were partly the result of the sudden police interest, after years of leniency, in some major drug traders in the vicinity of Amsterdam. The Fijnaut research group described several counterstrategies of these groups: countersurveillance, intimidation, corruption, and, to a lesser extent, media manipulation and the use of influential people to counterbalance potential interventions. These counterstrategies, however, were apparently confined to lower-level employees of the official agencies most directly involved in combating organized crime, especially the police and the customs services. It was concluded that there was no evidence of the use of either corruption or intimidation in order to gain control over any of the important government services, let alone the major official bodies or authorities (Fijnaut et al. 1996, 1998).

Recently, the use of intimidation and violence again attracted extensive media attention. First, the public prosecutor who was investigating several contract killings of well-known, alleged gangsters stepped down after serious death threats. Although intimidation of public prosecutors is a matter of serious concern, at the moment there is no clear evidence that this problem is widespread. A second wave of media attention resulted from killings of well-known real estate agents, a lawyer, and several well-known, alleged gangsters.

Leistra and Nieuwbeerta (2003, p. 128) estimate the number of contract killings in the Netherlands at roughly fifteen to twenty per year, although such an estimate is highly dependent on often missing information about victims, offenders, and motives. Van de Port (2001) investigated fifty cases of a wide variety of killings in the criminal milieu, ranging from murders related to organized crime to escalations between petty thieves and paranoid outcasts. He strongly opposes the view that these killings are the outcome of rational calculations and shows how easily—in a world of fear, uncertainty, rumor, and accusation—emotions, fear, and distrust can lead to an escalation of violence (see also Bovenkerk 2005).

After the Fijnaut research group that devoted much attention to counterstrategies, the follow-up studies of the Organized Crime Monitor investigated both counterstrategies and evasive strategies (Kleemans, van den Berg, and van de Bunt 1998; Kleemans, Brienen, and van de Bunt 2002). Where criminal justice intervention was strong and highly visible, several counterstrategies such as countersurveillance and corruption were used. Yet many criminal groups, particularly those involved in smuggling illegal immigrants and human trafficking for sexual exploitation, tried to avoid rather than seek confrontation with the authorities. Corruption was mainly found in cases in which there was an explicit need for corruption: when groups needed licenses, visas, or forged documents; when groups wanted to evade surveillance (border controls, brothel checks, and so on); or when groups needed information about ongoing investigations or imminent police actions. Cases of corruption more than incidentally emerged from a combination of social relations and (partly) common interests.

Huberts and Nelen published an extensive study on corruption in the Netherlands (2005). They conclude that research on criminal cases and convictions under the corruption articles in the penal code supports the image that the corruption problem in the Netherlands is limited. Each year about fifty investigations on alleged corruption are conducted, resulting on average in twenty-seven convictions, of which only eight result in prison sentences. The authors argue, however, that these cases may be only the tip of the iceberg. A survey among government agencies shows that, within the whole public sector, each year about 130 internal investigations are conducted into alleged integrity violations. Per 1,000 employees, these numbers range from about 0.1 for the judiciary and 0.2 for the police to 0.3 for municipalities. The major activities concern tendering, purchasing goods and services, internal management of goods and money, (how to deal with) confidential information, and—to a lesser extent—providing subsidies, licenses, passports, and visas. Politicians or governors were hardly ever involved, except in some small local municipalities. Most investigations concerned lower-level employees (Huberts and Nelen 2005).

Police corruption is not currently an issue in the Netherlands, and it has only incidentally been of public concern in the past (van de Bunt 2003). In 1993, Fijnaut investigated fourteen cases of police corruption and concluded that there was no evidence of a widespread problem (Fijnaut 1993). These findings were corroborated by Lamboo et al. (2002) in their study of the prevalence of integrity violations within the Dutch forces. The number of investigated cases of bribery was very low. In the period 1999–2000, only twenty-five such allegations of corruption were investigated by the police internal affairs units, and only a few of those produced sufficient evidence to bring these cases before the public prosecutor. Furthermore, Nelen and Nieuwendijk (2003) concluded that allegations of police corruption mostly concerned supplying confidential police information to the criminal milieu, drug trading, and issuing temporary residence permits to foreigners. According to Huberts and Naeyé (2005), only 1.5 percent of all internal investigations pertain to corruption and only 0.2 percent to accepting gifts and discounts. Many internal investigations (22 percent) concern allegations of unacceptable private behavior (drugs and alcohol use, domestic violence, and private contacts with offenders).

Van Ruth and Gunther Moor (1997) investigated the informal exchange of police information with third parties, including the criminal milieu. They concluded that the exchange of information with the criminal milieu was mostly influenced by family ties, friendship, and bribery and that both personal factors and hobbies of police officers may increase risk. Two categories of police officers were believed to run a higher risk of corruption—foreign-born police officers and police officers in criminal intelligence agencies and alien registration offices.

Alleged cases of customs corruption are mainly connected to Amsterdam-Schiphol Airport (Nelen and Nieuwendijk 2003). No cases were discovered in the large seaports. The strict passenger and luggage checks by individual customs officers at airports may be offered as a tentative explanation (Kleemans, Brienen, and van de Bunt 2002). In seaports, hiding contraband in containers and lorries is effective enough in itself. Corruption necessarily involves more than one individual and may increase the risk of detection (see also Zaitch 2002a).

The conclusion that government corruption is not currently a big issue in the Netherlands affirms the general conclusions reached by Transparency International (2005) on the reputation of the Netherlands. On the basis of a very broad definition of corruption (the abuse of public office for private gain), the Netherlands is time and again ranked in the Corruption Perception Index as one of the least corrupt governments on the planet.

B. Organized Crime and the Legal Economy

One of the major conclusions of the Fijnaut research group was that no criminal groups at either a national or local level had gained control of legitimate sectors of the economy by taking over crucial businesses or trade unions (racketeering; Fijnaut et al. 1996, 1998). The research group singled out the theoretically most vulnerable economic sectors for an extensive audit: sectors related to the trade in illegal goods and services (transport, harbors, the automobile sector, slot machines, and the hotel, restaurant, nightclub, and pub sector) and industries controlled by organized crime in other countries, such as the construction industry and the waste disposal industry. Attention was also paid to the garment industry, the insurance industry, the wildlife sector, the smuggling of nuclear material, money laundering, and the role of lawyers, notaries public, and accountants. To assess the situation at the local level too, in-depth studies were carried out in Amsterdam and three other cities (Arnhem, Nijmegen, and Enschede).

Although the Fijnaut research group found no evidence of significant criminal infiltration, there were some indications of criminal infiltration in the transport sector, as well as in the hotel, restaurant, nightclub, and pub sector. The transport sector is crucial for the transportation of drugs by sea, air, and land. Criminal groups hire, buy, or set up their own haulage companies to import and export drugs. They use Amsterdam-Schiphol Airport and the port of Rotterdam for the same purpose, sometimes getting ample help from insiders (airport personnel in particular). There was, however, no evidence that criminal groups played a permanent role of any significance in the transport sector, let alone that they had it under their control. The scale of investments in the hotel, restaurant, nightclub, and pub sector in some cities, in particular in the red-light district of Amsterdam, was more worrying. By investing in real estate, criminal groups created a certain kind of private territory as well as an infrastructure for other illegal activities, such as selling drugs, laundering money, and installing illegal slot machines (Fijnaut et al. 1996, 1998).

This does not mean, however, that economic sectors are not subject to all kinds of fraud, causing a great deal of economic damage to governments and businesses. In the last decade considerable empirical evidence has been generated of value added tax (VAT) fraud, evasion of taxes on highly taxed goods (e.g., oil, tobacco, and alcohol), counterfeiting (e.g., textiles, CDs, CD-ROMs, and DVDs), European Community fraud (e.g., meat and dairy products and import and export quotas), financial fraud, and so on (van Duyne, Kouwenberg, and Romeijn 1990; van Duyne 1995, 2003; Aronowitz, Laagland, and Paulides 1996; Kleemans, van den Berg, and van de Bunt 1998; Kleemans, Brienen, and van de Bunt 2002). In 2002 a parliamentary inquiry committee investigated fraud, corporate crime, and illegal price-fixing in the construction industry (Parlementaire Enquêtecommissie Bouwnijverheid 2002).

The Organized Crime Monitor studies corroborated the main conclusion of the Fijnaut research group (Kleemans, van den Berg, and van de Bunt 1998; Kleemans, Brienen, and van de Bunt 2002). In the extensive case studies, hardly any evidence was found of protection, political corruption, illegal manipulation of political decisions, or infiltration in trade unions and economic sectors. Rather than controlling certain regions or certain sectors of the economy, criminal groups use the legal infrastructure and legal commodity and money flows. Because the Netherlands is an important logistical node in Europe (Amsterdam-Schiphol Airport and the port of Rotterdam), this also creates an excellent opportunity structure for organized crime (see below). Economic sectors are used to commit or to conceal crimes or to spend criminal proceeds. Companies sometimes facilitate organized crime activities knowingly or unknowingly. In general, criminal justice policies are a trade-off between economic interests and criminal justice interests (see also Zoomer, Nieuwkamp, and Johannink 2004). For the National Threat Assessment (Dienst Nationale Recherche Informatie 2004), an in-depth study was carried out on the use of infrastructure for transnational criminal activities. In addition to the well-known conclusions concerning both Amsterdam-Schiphol Airport and the large seaports (and related companies), attention was paid to blind spots such as railway transport and inland shipping.

Criminal proceeds are spent on expensive lifestyles, investments in valuable objects, companies, and real estate. Meloen et al. (2003) investigated fifty-two "big" asset forfeiture cases (exceeding 1 million Dutch guilders, or 450,000 euros) and concluded that—contrary to popular belief—most of the money is not spent but saved or invested in companies and real estate. Most of these investments are in sectors familiar to the criminal groups, such as bars, hotels and restaurants, prostitution, cars, and transport. Both the nature and location of the investments are largely influenced by the "cognitive map" of the offenders. Offenders tend to invest in their country of origin—native Dutch offenders in the Netherlands, Turkish offenders in Turkey, and so on. When money was invested in other countries, this often could be explained by close personal contacts or the logistics of criminal activities (Kleemans, Brienen, and van de Bunt 2002; Meloen et al. 2003).

C. Transit Crime

The concept of organized crime as an alternative government, controlling certain regions or economic sectors, is at odds with the empirical facts. The nature of organized crime in the Netherlands might be more fittingly described as transit crime—criminal groups are primarily involved in international illegal trade, using the same opportunity structure that facilitates legal economic activities. The major business of organized crime groups in the Netherlands boils down to international smuggling activities—drug trafficking, smuggling illegal immigrants, human trafficking for sexual exploitation, arms trafficking, trafficking in stolen vehicles, and other transnational illegal activities, such as money laundering and evasion of taxes (e.g., cigarette smuggling and European Community fraud). The Netherlands can be either a country of destination, a transit country, or, especially in the case of synthetic drugs, a production country (Kleemans, Brienen, and van de Bunt 2002; Kleemans 2004).

Recent estimates of the Central Bureau of Statistics (CBS) give some idea of the scale of the trade in illegal goods and services in the illegal economy of the Netherlands (Smekens and Verbruggen 2004). No doubt one must be very careful with these estimates, as it is very difficult to measure the illegal economy. Besides, the focus of CBS is primarily on economic added value. It includes illegal goods and services such as drugs, prostitution, illegal gambling, fencing, illegal activities of specialized job services, and illegal copying and counterfeiting but does not include smuggling illegal immigrants, weapons, cigarettes, fireworks, and endangered species. Because there is already an explicit estimate of "black" legal activities in the national accounts, these are also excluded. According to CBS estimates for 2001, the total added value of the aforementioned activities amounts to 3.3 billion euros, which is less than 1 percent of the gross domestic product. About 1.96 billion euros (60 percent) concerns drugs, while prostitution yields 660 million euros; illegal gambling, 140 million euros; fencing, 50 million euros; illegal activities of specialized job services, 520 million euros; and illegal copying and counterfeiting, 100 million euros. According to these CBS figures, importing and exporting drugs are major illegal activities. The domestic consumption of ecstasy (XTC) and amphetamines, for instance, is estimated at 40 million euros, while their export is estimated at 320 million euros. The domestic consumption of heroin and cocaine is estimated at 430 million euros, import, at 720 million euros, and export, at 1.16 billion euros. Finally, domestic cannabis consumption is estimated at 600 million euros, while import of cannabis is estimated at 230 million euros and export at 810 million euros (Smekens and Verbruggen 2004). In the cannabis sector, rapid import substitution has taken place since the 1980s (Jansen 2002). Imports from Pakistan, Lebanon, and Morocco have been replaced by locally grown cannabis. Nowadays, about three-fourths of the cannabis sold in the Netherlands is locally produced *nederwiet*, which is also exported (for a description of the rise of the cultivation of cannabis in the Netherlands, see Bovenkerk and Hogewind [2003]).

Profitability is why transit crime seems to be the major activity of Dutch organized crime. The Dutch wholesale price for cocaine, for instance, is about ten times the wholesale price in Colombia (van der Heijden 2001, p. 42; Zaitch 2002*b*). Also, exporting cocaine from the Netherlands to other European countries can be very lucrative because of substantial price differences (Farrell, Mansur, and Tullis 1996; Farrell 1998; van der Heijden 2001, p. 42). The same applies to exporting synthetic drugs to other European countries, the United States, Australia, New Zealand, and Japan (van de Bunt, Kunst, and Siegel 2003). The average production costs of an XTC tablet amount to 56 eurocents, while average selling prices in the Netherlands amount to 3.50 euros. Selling prices are much higher in many other European countries, particularly in Norway and Italy (about 20 euros per XTC tablet), in most American cities and states (20–30 euros), in Australia and New Zealand (about 30 euros), and in Japan (25–50 euros; Korps Landelijke Politiediensten 2005*b*, pp. 75–87). According to a recent United Nations Office on Drugs and Crime report, the Netherlands and Belgium are the main source countries of XTC (2005, pp. 15, 108, 115). Handsome profits can also be made by smuggling illegal immigrants and highly taxed goods (e.g., cigarettes, alcohol, and oil) and from VAT fraud and E.U. fraud (see, e.g., van Duyne 1993, 1995).

Another reason for the apparent dominance of transit crime in

Dutch organized crime might be that the regulation of vices such as gambling, prostitution, and drugs has traditionally been quite tolerant (see Buruma, in this volume). Perhaps (partial) government regulation of these sectors has to a certain extent prevented the monopolization of the exploitation of these vices by organized crime groups as in other countries such as the United States.

Finally, some major factors facilitating control over certain regions or economic sectors, which have been present in other countries, have been absent in the Netherlands for a long time, particularly "weak government" and opportunities—by manipulating elections—to gain access to positions of power in the police, politics, unions, or (local) government (Kleemans, Brienen, and van de Bunt 2002, p. 141).

Compared with countries such as Italy and the United States, the opportunities for organized crime groups to get control of certain regions or economic sectors have always been quite low in the Netherlands, while the opportunity structure for transit crime is excellent. More generally, Fijnaut and Paoli (2004, pp. 614–16) state that in most western European countries the ability of traditional organized crime groups to infiltrate the legitimate economy and corrupt civil and political institutions has been grossly overstated, with the exception of in Italy and Turkey.

D. Criminal Networks

In the Netherlands, pyramidal structures with a strict hierarchy, a clear division of tasks, and an internal sanctioning system (e.g., Cressey 1969) are the exception rather than the rule. The term "criminal networks" is far better suited for describing the actual structure of cooperation (Kleemans, Brienen, and van de Bunt 2002). Offenders cooperate in certain projects, yet the structure of cooperation is fluid and changes over time. Although the initial concern in many European countries was largely dictated by fear of the expansion of the Italian Mafia and the Italian Mafia model to the rest of Europe, empirical research in these countries leads to very similar conclusions (Fijnaut and Paoli 2004, pp. 607–10).

Social relations form the basis for criminal cooperation (Kleemans and van de Bunt 1999). Family, friends, and acquaintances work together and introduce each other to third parties. In this way, offenders not only find new opportunities but also solve problems of cooperating in an environment that is dominated by distrust, suspicion, and potential deceit. Although the stakes are high, the rules and mechanisms that make transactions in the legal world so much easier are absent: entering into contracts, paying via the official banking system, and—in the case of disagreement—availing of mediation or the courts (e.g., Reuter 1983; Potter 1994). Social relations enhance the conditions for cooperation in such a hostile environment. Parties have information about past behavior and have invested in their relationship (shadow of the past). At the same time, they know that they probably will meet again in the future (shadow of the future; for an overview, see, e.g., Granovetter [1985], Coleman [1990], and Buskens [1999]).

The flexibility of networks is also the foundation for their development. People come into contact with organized crime through their social relations. In the beginning they are very dependent on the resources (money, knowledge, and contacts) of other people. Yet over time, this dependency declines and people start their own projects, subsequently attracting people from their own social environment again. This social snowball effect gives a better description of the dynamics of organized crime than the traditional view of "recruitment"—criminal organizations recruiting "outsiders" who start by doing the "dirty jobs" and who are able to climb the hierarchical ladder by proving their capability (Kleemans, van den Berg, and van de Bunt 1998; Kleemans and van de Bunt 1999).

Criminal networks and flexibility do not imply, however, that there are no hierarchical or dependency relations among offenders. The same individuals often emerge as the main "nodes" in networks of alternating composition, because many offenders are dependent on their scarce resources such as money, knowledge, and contacts. In many of the cases of the Organized Crime Monitor, we found that major "nodal" offenders often operate on an international or interethnic level or somewhere between the underworld and the legitimate world (Kleemans, Brienen, and van de Bunt 2002; van de Bunt and Kleemans 2004). This might be because geographical and/or social barriers create "structural holes" in social networks (e.g., Burt 1992, 2000, 2005; Morselli 2001, 2005), particularly between different countries, different ethnic groups, and the underworld and the legitimate world. Few people are in a position to bridge these structural holes. The illegal character of the activities presupposes a high level of mutual trust; offenders who can bridge these structural holes have all kinds of strategic opportunities to make a profit. They are the ones who make the connections between networks that would otherwise have remained apart. Because trust is so important, these connections are often based on family ties or other strong social bonds.

"Facilitators" such as underground bankers (see, e.g., Passas 1999, 2005), money exchangers, and document forgers can also be considered as nodes in networks, because several groups consistently use their illegal services. Generally, these service providers are far removed from the crimes under investigation and, therefore, are not identified as a primary target. Nevertheless, by providing crucial services, they perform an important function for diverse criminal groups. The position of the service provider is influenced by both scarcity and the function of these services in the logistical chain of certain criminal processes (cf. Sieber and Bögel 1993; Huisman, Huikeshoven, and van de Bunt 2003).

II. Illegal Activities

The literature on organized crime contains a recurring discussion over whether organized crime should be defined in terms of characteristics of groups or of criminal activities (for an overview, see Paoli [2002]). In the Netherlands, organized crime is mainly distinguished from terrorism, corporate crime, group crime, and other types of crime by the characteristics of the groups involved. Following the Fijnaut research group and the Parliamentary Inquiry Committee (Parlementaire Enquêtecommissie Opsporingsmethoden 1996; Fijnaut et al. 1998) in the Netherlands, groups are considered as organized crime groups when they are focused primarily on obtaining illegal profits, systematically commit crimes with serious damage for society, and are relatively capable of shielding their criminal activities from the authorities. Shielding illegal activities from the authorities is possible by various strategies: using corruption, violence, intimidation, storefronts, communication in codes, countersurveillance, media manipulation, and the use of experts such as notaries public, lawyers, and accountants.

Defining organized crime in terms of the characteristics of the groups involved implies that not all groups that are active in certain illegal or legal markets can be considered as organized crime groups. One example is the drugs market, where several offenders and groups that may be active in the retail market often cannot be considered as organized crime groups. Another example is the broad variety of fraudulent activities, some committed by organized crime groups (involving legal businesses as well); many of these fraudulent activities committed by legal businesses can be better characterized as corporate crime (see van de Bunt and Huisman, in this volume).

The research group Fijnaut concluded that the main activities of organized crime groups in the Netherlands concerned providing goods and services at illegal markets (Fijnaut et al. 1996, 1998). As Dutch studies on such activities are abundant, I restrict my attention to the following illegal activities, leaving out many details: drug trafficking, human trafficking for sexual exploitation, smuggling of illegal immigrants, arms trafficking, and trafficking in stolen vehicles.

A. Drug Trafficking

The Netherlands is an important transit country for drugs in Europe (e.g., van der Heijden 2001, 2003; Kleemans, Brienen, and van de Bunt 2002; Zaitch 2002b; Europol 2005; United Nations Office on Drugs and Crime 2005; for a review of European literature on upper-level drug trafficking, see Dorn, Levi, and King [2005]). In Section I, I discussed both the scale and the profitability of international trafficking in cocaine, heroin, synthetic drugs, and cannabis. I also described the excellent opportunity structure for international trade (Amsterdam-Schiphol Airport and the ports of Rotterdam and Amsterdam). International drug trafficking makes use of the same opportunity structure that facilitates legal economic activities.

The Netherlands also provides a good social opportunity structure for international drug trafficking (Fijnaut et al. 1998, pp. 83–87). The major immigrant groups that came to the Netherlands in the 1960s and 1970s originated from drug-producing or exporting countries such as Surinam, the Netherlands Antilles, Aruba, Morocco, and Turkey. A major amount of the heroin for the European market now comes from Turkey; Surinam, the Netherlands Antilles, and Aruba link Colombia and its cocaine to Europe; and Morocco has developed into the leading hashish producer. Because migration has created strong social ties between the Netherlands and the countries of origin, this constitutes a fertile breeding ground for international drug trafficking.

The role of native Dutch offenders was initially restricted to investments and transport. In the early 1970s, Dutch seamen, engaged in hydraulic engineering projects near Dubai, made contact with Pakistani hashish dealers. As a result, several Dutch trailer park residents funded large shipments of hashish from Pakistan to Europe and North America (Fijnaut et al. 1998, p. 74). Later on, native Dutch offenders also became heavily involved in the production and export of synthetic drugs (e.g., Moerland and Boerman 1998; Korps Landelijke Politiediensten 2005*b*; Neve et al. 2005) and in the cultivation of cannabis (Bovenkerk and Hogewind 2003).

The major drugs traded are logically connected to both established contacts and the availability of particular kinds of drugs in the countries of origin. Consequently, Turkish offenders play a major part in transnational heroin trafficking from Turkey to Europe (Korps Landelijke Politiediensten 2004*b*), and Latin American offenders, particularly Colombian, Surinamese, and Antillean immigrants, are heavily involved in cocaine trafficking (Korps Landelijke Politiediensten 2004*c*). But the case studies of the Organized Crime Monitor urge us to reconsider the traditional view that certain ethnic groups specialize in particular kinds of drugs: native Dutch offenders trafficking in hashish and synthetic drugs to the exclusion of everything else; Colombians, in cocaine; Moroccans, in hashish; and Turks, in heroin. The reality of Dutch organized crime is far more varied than the picture of "ethnic specialization" suggests, because offenders from various ethnic backgrounds work together and offenders trade in several different kinds of drugs (Kleemans and van de Bunt 1999; Dienst Nationale Recherche Informatie 2004).

The case studies show the social logic of international drug trafficking: over and over again family ties and bonds of friendship are the foundation for criminal cooperation (Kleemans, van den Berg, and van de Bunt 1998). Criminal cooperation, however, is not built so much on ethnicity as it is on social relationships among several individuals. People cooperate because they are family or because they originate from the same village. Often this means that they have the same ethnicity, because ethnicity affects social relations. Therefore, a certain degree of ethnic homogeneity in criminal cooperation is to be expected. Yet the blending of ethnic groups in Dutch society is mirrored by a more heterogeneous composition of criminal networks.

Another reason for more ethnic heterogeneity is the transnational character of drug trafficking and the strategic advantages that arise from bridging "structural holes" between different ethnic groups and different countries. In many cases, the prime suspects were interethnic "brokers," for instance, linking Colombian cocaine traffickers to Dutch producers of synthetic drugs. Such an interethnic link may have been created by migration, marriage, or a temporary stay in, for instance, the Netherlands Antilles (Kleemans, Brienen, and van de Bunt 2002).

The good social infrastructure of the Netherlands for international drug trafficking attracts offenders from many other countries. In particular, the multicultural and liberal city of Amsterdam might be viewed as a marketplace for international drug trafficking (Huisman, Huikeshoven, and van de Bunt 2003). In ethnographic research, foreign criminal entrepreneurs speak highly of the many opportunities to do business in relative anonymity with other people from all over the world (Zaitch 2002a; Blickman et al. 2003, p. 54). Huisman, Huikeshoven, and van de Bunt (2003) characterize Amsterdam as a full-service market, attracting buyers and sellers but also providing contacts for logistical facilities such as transport, housing, commercial property, and financial services.

B. Human Trafficking for Sexual Exploitation

Dutch criminal law makes a distinction between smuggling illegal immigrants and human trafficking for sexual exploitation (e.g., Bureau Nationaal Rapporteur Mensenhandel 2005a, pp. 3–7). Although women who are forced into prostitution have often also been smuggled to the Netherlands, the emphasis of the offense is on sexual exploitation.

Extensive research has been done on forced prostitution (e.g., Fijnaut et al. 1996, 1998; Interregionaal Recherche Team Noord- en Oost-Nederland 1997; Kleemans, van den Berg, and van de Bunt 1998; Bureau Nationaal Rapporteur Mensenhandel 2002a, 2002b, 2005a, 2005b; van Dijk 2002; Hopkins 2005). Van Dijk (2002) estimated that in 2000 there were about 3,500 victims of "forced prostitution," which is about 20 percent of the total estimated number of prostitutes working in the Netherlands. The Dutch National Rapporteur on Trafficking in Human Beings, which has reported annually on this topic since 2002, uses data from a national victim support organization (Bureau Nationaal Rapporteur Mensenhandel 2005b, pp. 3–4). In 2003, the majority of (possible) victims originated from central and eastern Europe (52 percent), in particular Bulgaria, Romania, Ukraine, the Russian Federation, and Lithuania. Other regions of origin are Africa (25 percent), Asia (6 percent), Latin America and the Caribbean (6 percent), the Netherlands (4 percent), and other western European countries (2 percent).

Van Dijk (2002, pp. 69–102) provides an overview of the offenders involved, based on an analysis of 521 suspects arrested in the period 1997–2000. Three-fourths of the suspects are males and one-fourth are females. Females sometimes play a prominent role, particularly in Nigerian trafficking networks. Some have been victims of forced prostitution themselves before becoming involved as offenders. The suspects were born in the Netherlands (28 percent), Yugoslavia (13 percent), Nigeria (8 percent), Turkey (7 percent), Bulgaria (4 percent), Morocco (5 percent), Albania (4 percent), the Czech Republic (3 percent), Germany (3 percent), and other countries (25 percent). Recent data for the period 2000–2003 suggest that the main countries of birth are the Netherlands (27 percent), Bulgaria (10 percent), Albania (8 percent), Nigeria (6 percent), Turkey (6 percent), Romania (5 percent), and former Yugoslavia (4 percent; Bureau Nationaal Rapporteur Mensenhandel 2005*b*, p. 51). Most suspects cooperate with offenders from various countries of origin and ethnic groups, although some groups have a clear ethnic profile (i.e., Albanians, Nigerians, and Turks; van Dijk 2002).

Van Dijk (2002) distinguishes among three categories of offenders. The first is "solo offenders," who have forced one or more girls into prostitution. Sometimes the girls are recruited abroad, but more often they are simply "bought" from other pimps or recruited in the Netherlands. Solo offenders generally operate a solo business, although in some cases they get some help from assistants. A substantial part of the solo offenders are "lover boys," who seduce vulnerable girls and gradually move them into (forced) prostitution (see also Bureau Nationaal Rapporteur Mensenhandel 2005*a*, p. 50). Facts and figures about this phenomenon and in-depth studies of the backgrounds of lover boys have recently been published (Bovenkerk et al. 2004; Terpstra, van Dijke, and van San 2005; van Dijke and Terpstra 2005).

The second category, self-supporting criminal groups, control the entire process—from recruitment to prostitution—and have no established contacts with other offenders or groups involved in trafficking in women. The main suspects are often in charge of a brothel or sex club in the Netherlands. If victims are recruited abroad, members of the group transport the victims themselves, mostly using a family contact of the main suspect or his or her partner living abroad. These groups are built around active, entrepreneurial offenders and can be described as "ego networks" (e.g., Klerks 2000).

The third category might be described as "criminal macronetworks" (Klerks 2000): a fluid criminal infrastructure, in which many people are connected via one or more intermediaries, although there are clusters based on geographical proximity, family ties, friendships, commercial circuits, and similarity in activities (e.g., Feld 1981). In trafficking networks, clusters mostly evolve around recruitment in particular countries, sometimes around transport, and around forced prostitution in the Netherlands. A great number of people are involved, in particular in the countries in which victims are recruited.

Victims are bought and sold again and the turnover rate is high. Many victims report that they have worked in various cities in the Netherlands and in other countries in the European Union (particularly Germany, Belgium, Spain, and Italy). In the police investigations analyzed, some victims were active in street prostitution or escort services, but most worked in brothels or in window prostitution. Forty clubs were owned by trafficking suspects, twenty-seven clubs cooperated (the owners usually turned a blind eye), and twenty-one clubs were used by traffickers (the owners being unaware). People renting rooms in window prostitution were never directly involved in trafficking. They rented rooms to pimps, without checking whether prostitutes were illegal or exploited (van Dijk 2002, pp. 99–102).

In October 2000, new legislation came into force, lifting the ban on brothels. Brothels in which adult prostitutes work voluntarily are no longer prohibited. At the same time, legislation on unacceptable forms of prostitution has become more stringent, and the government plans to exercise more control over the sex industry. The first evaluation of this policy change points at a slight improvement in the position of prostitutes (Daalder 2002, 2004). Yet lifting the ban could lead to displacement of the punishable forms of prostitution to the unregulated sector. A final evaluation, to be carried out in 2006, may provide an answer to this question.

In 2005, legislation on forced prostitution was extended to other forms of "modern slavery." Van der Leun and Vervoorn (2004) reviewed the evidence that these phenomena, particularly forced or compulsory labor and trafficking in human organs, exist in the Netherlands. The authors concluded that there is little solid evidence that trafficking in human organs occurs in the Netherlands. Illegal labor occurs on a substantial scale, and low wages and poor health and safety conditions are common in certain sectors. Yet, according to the authors, this does not necessarily imply that the restrictions on free will are harsh enough to warrant calling it "modern slavery" (van der Leun and Vervoorn 2004).

C. Smuggling Illegal Immigrants

Smuggling rings provide a most wanted connection between poor or dangerous countries (e.g., Iran, Iraq, Afghanistan, India, China, and several African countries) and affluent, democratic countries such as the member states of the European Union, Canada, the United States, and Japan. The Netherlands is an important transit country for the United Kingdom, Scandinavian countries, and the United States (Informatie- en Analysecentrum Mensensmokkel 2001; Dienst Nationale Recherche Informatie 2005). The main reasons for the attractiveness of the Netherlands as a transit country are Amsterdam-Schiphol Airport, the multiethnic character of the Netherlands, and the country's asylum policy, which—until recently—made a short stay in asylum facilities very easy. Yet starting a new life and making a living without being noticed by the authorities is quite difficult in a small and densely populated country with many housing, work, and tax registries, which have recently become increasingly interconnected (see Engbersen et al. 2002).

Dutch asylum policy has become increasingly strict in recent years. Therefore, the Netherlands is more important as a transit country than as a country of destination. People often enter the Netherlands by air—via Amsterdam-Schiphol Airport, but also nearby Belgian or German airports—or by land, taking a mainly eastern route (eastern Europe, Austria, and Germany) or southern route (Italy, France, and Belgium). For smuggling illegal immigrants, the European Union is virtually borderless, apart from some physically isolated countries such as Greece, the United Kingdom, and Ireland. The main borders are the "blue borders" (the Mediterranean, the Channel, and the Atlantic Ocean) and the borders between E.U. and non-E.U. countries.

An analysis of ten police investigations from the Organized Crime Monitor shows that the illegal market for smuggling illegal immigrants is based mainly on symbiosis among offenders, smuggled illegal immigrants, and their families (Kleemans and Brienen 2001; Kleemans and van de Bunt 2003). Often, smuggling is fostered by mutual consent and mutual benefit. In contrast to cases concerning trafficking in women for sexual exploitation, smuggled people are very often better characterized as clients than as victims. Although these clients are very dependent and, thus, potentially highly vulnerable, smuggling rings have a clear interest in keeping their clients satisfied because satisfied clients or their family members introduce new customers. In migrant communities, communication about trafficking is relatively open, and advertising by word of mouth is a common way of attracting new clients.

The prime suspects in the cases analyzed very often had social ties with both the countries of origin and the countries of destination. Traffickers and clients often share the same ethnic background, and before they started smuggling, many traffickers have been smuggled to the Netherlands themselves. Smuggling networks emerged in which the organizers of (sub)routes are the major players. The prime suspects are not distant masterminds but are often involved in the day-to-day activities (Kleemans and van de Bunt 2003). The cases studied also illuminate the crucial role of forged documents (Informatie- en Analysecentrum Mensensmokkel 2001; Dienst Nationale Recherche Informatie 2005). Forged documents make the logistics of smuggling much less complicated, because smuggled immigrants can simply travel by airplane. The core of these smuggling rings can be relatively small, consisting of a few people in the country of origin, (possibly) a transit country, and the country of destination. Many prime suspects are also closely involved in forging documents (Kleemans and van de Bunt 2003).

Without forged documents, the journey becomes much longer and much more complicated because of additional barriers, transfers, and stops. Smuggling rings then have to use local knowledge and local contacts in the transit countries, making the chain much longer and the coordination between the links of the chain much more complicated. Sometimes these chains are coordinated from start to finish, but in other instances clients are successively passed through the hands of groups that are only very loosely connected.

Some cases, especially those regarding smuggling of Chinese, diverge from this general picture of symbiosis and reciprocity, as immigrants are threatened, taken hostage, and sometimes physically abused (e.g., Soudijn 2001; Dienst Nationale Recherche Informatie 2005; Staring et al. 2005). Staring et al., analyzing eleven police investigations into smuggling illegal immigrants in the Rotterdam area, make the interesting observation that there might be a link between several types of organizations and the way in which clients are treated. In the analyzed cases, there appears to be a relationship between threatening smuggled immigrants and command and control structures in smuggling organizations, that is, between external and internal threats. The command and control starts in the countries of origin, extends to the families of smuggled immigrants, and lasts until smuggled immigrants have reached their final destination and have paid off their debts. Immigrants smuggled by more horizontal organizations, however, are rarely controlled and are able to negotiate destinations, travel conditions, and prices. The prices are relatively low, and sometimes immigrants are smuggled under "no cure, no pay" conditions. The ethnic homogeneity of horizontal organizations is high, while the command and control organizations involve offenders with more diverse ethnic backgrounds (Staring et al. 2005).

Soudijn (2006) carried out an extensive study into human smuggling of Chinese, analyzing eighty-eight Dutch court files in the period 1996–2003. These cases primarily dealt with smuggling Chinese migrants out of the Netherlands, the United Kingdom being the predominant country of destination. About a quarter of the suspects were nonethnic Chinese, often acting as large-scale transporters, whereas 13 percent of all smugglers were ethnic Chinese women, some of them playing a very important part. According to Soudijn (2006), no evidence was found of a central organization controlling—either from the Netherlands or abroad—any (let alone all) smuggling operations. The diversity found in smugglers and (large and relatively smaller) smuggling groups additionally made it implausible that there was overall control. Although some smuggling groups were responsible for the smuggling of hundreds of people, at the same time there were many others active, each independently using different methods and strategies. Because these smuggling groups act autonomously, a good reputation is essential. Violence within smuggling groups did occur, but not on a structural basis. Although several beatings and three homicides were recorded over an eight-year period, these should not be seen as evidence of strict discipline but as a consequence of fear and marital infidelity. The smuggling groups mostly concentrated on smuggling and did not display heterogeneity in criminal behavior. No evidence was found of smugglers selling migrants into prostitution or forcing clients into narcotics trafficking or robberies. In general, smuggled Chinese work very hard in the illegal labor sector, which could sometimes end in exploitation. There was no evidence, however, that large-scale smuggling groups were directly involved in this exploitation. On the contrary, only small-scale smugglers directly employed illegal migrants (Soudijn 2006).

It is interesting to note that many of these conclusions drawn from police and court files are very similar to findings from field interviews (Zhang and Gaylord 1996; Zhang and Chin 2002; Pieke et al. 2004) using diametrically different sources and focusing on source or destination countries (China and the United States). Still, there are two distinctive additional observations. First, there is the presence of non-ethnic Chinese, often acting as large-scale transporters. Field interviews would miss such an observation because such research is generally focused on Chinese smugglers and the Chinese community. Second, the Chinese smuggling scene in the Netherlands does not consist of individuals who form temporary business alliances (Zhang and Chin 2002). This might be an adequate description when the whole smuggling route is taken under consideration, because different stages of the journey are taken care of by different smuggling groups. Groups in the Netherlands take on assignments from several organizers abroad, and different alliances are continued if smuggling operations run smoothly. Rather than by central coordination, smuggling is harmonized by looser organizations through social networks. Yet on a local level, police and court files show much more cohesion, because the relationships among offenders can be relatively stable. The Chinese smugglers not only are bound by instrumental relationships but also display certain mutual affective interactions that result in strong cohesion (see also Bruinsma and Bernasco 2004). These bonds do not indicate flexibility and fluidity but durability and consistency. Furthermore, large-scale smuggling groups handle a continuous flow of migrants waiting to be smuggled, which makes it important to have reliable people at hand and to construct some division of labor (Soudijn 2006).

D. Arms Trafficking

After the report of the Fijnaut research group in 1996 (Fijnaut et al. 1996), a number of studies have examined the illegal arms trade and illegal weapons in the Netherlands (Maalsté et al. 2002; Spapens and

Bruinsma 2002*a*, 2002*b*, 2004; Bruinsma and Moors 2005). According to official registrations, 1,777 illegal firearms were seized by the Dutch police in 2003, which amounts to eleven firearms per 100,000 inhabitants. Seizures were relatively high in the most urbanized areas (Amsterdam, Rotterdam, and The Hague). Although the registration of seized firearms is problematic, the number of people possessing an illegal weapon was estimated at 54,000. The seized firearms had been produced in countries such as Italy, Germany, Belgium, the United States, former Yugoslavia, and several former Eastern Bloc countries (Bruinsma and Moors 2005).

On the basis of several (contestable) assumptions, Spapens and Bruinsma (2004) estimate that every year 10,000–15,000 illegal weapons are transported into the Netherlands. Countries of origin are mainly Portugal, Germany, Belgium, and former Eastern Bloc countries, particularly former Yugoslavia, the Czech Republic, and Hungary.

The profits made are relatively modest, especially compared to the drugs trade. Interviews with prisoners by Maalsté et al. (2002) led to the conclusion that middlemen earn about 25–75 euros per firearm, and large-scale traders, about 225 euros per weapon. These earnings are quite modest, which might explain why those involved often combine their illegal weapons trade with other illegal activities (drug trafficking in particular).

Spapens and Bruinsma (2004) report that—next to some major importers—most weapons are smuggled in small shipments (five to thirty weapons) by relatively small groups and that use is often made of regular trade and traffic. Weapons are sold only to persons who belong to the criminal milieu and can be trusted not to attract police attention. Contacts and negotiations occur at regular meeting places (e.g., bars, [illegal] casinos, fitness centers, the car business), but delivery generally takes place at other spots.

About 20 percent of all confiscated illegal firearms originate from former Eastern Bloc countries (Spapens and Bruinsma 2002*a*). Police investigations into arms trafficking from these countries reveal that the groups involved are relatively small and that the importer is the key figure in these groups. This person is able to obtain illegal firearms in one of the former Eastern Bloc countries involved and has a network of people in the Netherlands who sell these arms on the criminal market. The actual smuggling of batches of five to thirty firearms is done by couriers, recruited in the country of origin. Most of the importers are also involved in other types of criminal activities (Spapens and Bruinsma 2002*a*).

E. Trafficking in Stolen Vehicles

In the international literature, little is known about trafficking in stolen vehicles and the involvement of organized crime groups (for an overview, see Clarke and Brown [2003]). Until recently the same conclusion could be drawn for the situation in the Netherlands. In 2005 an in-depth study into this topic was published, based on analysis of twenty-three recent police investigations into vehicle trafficking, using the method of the Organized Crime Monitor (Ferwerda et al. 2005).

The number of stolen vehicles declined from 30,000 in 2003 to 25,600 in 2005. About three-fourths of the stolen vehicles are cars, stolen either for the use of vehicle parts (stripping) or to give the cars a new identity and a new owner. Compared to ten years ago, the cars stolen today are relatively luxurious, new, and expensive (Ferwerda et al. 2005, pp. 19–21).

In 1996, when the Fijnaut research group analyzed this phenomenon, it was largely unknown which groups and persons were responsible for the various parts of the process: stealing cars, changing the vehicle identification numbers, switching parts, changing identification numbers, forging registration papers, and exporting cars. Most of the police files analyzed by the research group Fijnaut involved Dutch groups of car thieves and a few groups from eastern Europe (Russia, Latvia, Ukraine, and former Yugoslavia; Fijnaut et al. 1996, 1998).

In 2005, both expert interviews and the police investigations analyzed suggested that the major countries of destination for stolen cars have shifted from eastern European countries to countries in northern and western Africa (Ferwerda et al. 2005, pp. 94–95). Also, the criminal groups and networks involved seem to have changed. Offenders from eastern Europe no longer play a prominent role, although there are still eastern European groups committing hit-and-run car theft, to meet the continuing high demand for vehicle parts in eastern European countries (Korps Landelijke Politiediensten 2004*a*, 2005*a*). Ferwerda et al. (2005, pp. 34–59, 86–104) distinguish between nationally oriented groups that sell stolen vehicles and vehicle parts locally, regionally, or nationally and international groups consisting of offenders of various ethnic backgrounds selling stolen vehicles and vehicle parts both in the Netherlands and abroad. Two-thirds of the groups analyzed are internationally oriented, especially targeting northern and western African markets. While selling vehicle parts is a major activity of the nationally oriented groups, the international groups focus mainly on exporting cars, particularly very expensive and exclusive cars (e.g., sports utility vehicles). The groups and networks can be described as fluid and dynamic with (small groups of) nodal offenders. The nodal offenders are mainly (international) brokers and fences for the more expensive cars, which they obtain from different car-stealing groups (Ferwerda et al. 2005, pp. 34–59, 86–104).

Because stolen vehicles frequently have to find their way back into the legitimate world, legal businesses are often involved. Analyzing 355 police investigations regarding the involvement of legal businesses, Moerland and Boerman (1999, p. 155) conclude that groups active in trading stolen vehicles are very strongly focused on the legal car business. In the twenty-three cases that were analyzed by Ferwerda et al. (2005, pp. 42–43), nine legal car businesses were involved—knowingly or unknowingly—reselling stolen cars or vehicle parts. Also, four breakers' yards were used both for temporarily hiding stolen cars and for selling vehicle parts. In three cases, there were indications that civil servants provided access to confidential information (e.g., registration numbers); two cases involved a corrupt customs officer in Africa.

III. Organized Crime Policies

This section describes the major changes in organized crime policies over the past two decades and elaborates on the change in criminal investigation strategies, the extension and regulation of special investigation methods, and the emergence of preventive strategies.

A. Criminal Investigation Strategies

The changing view on the nature of organized crime in the Netherlands is mirrored by a change in criminal investigation strategies. In the early 1990s, when the IRTs were set up, the image of pyramidal organizations was largely reflected in large-scale and long-term investigations aimed at putting the leaders of these organizations behind bars, sometimes using intrusive investigation methods such as covert policing and infiltration and uncontrolled deliveries of drugs. Since preliminary arrests and seizures might endanger the ultimate aim of the investigation, these were postponed until leaders could be arrested.

Such strategies are expensive and may yield very low returns, both in the short run and in the long run. Because it is hard to gather evidence without arrests and seizures, there is increasing pressure to get involved in the criminal milieu and in criminal activities, protecting informers, infiltrators, and ongoing investigations. The IRT affair was a clear example of the drawbacks of such strategies.

After the IRT affair, both covert policing and infiltration and uncontrolled deliveries were strictly regulated or forbidden. Police investigations increasingly relied on unobtrusive methods of gathering evidence such as the extensive use of wiretapping and—since 2000—bugging. In the main, observing criminal activities replaced getting heavily involved in the criminal milieu.

Another major change during the last decade was the increasing use of flexible prompt intervention strategies, an alternative to the large-scale and lengthy police investigations of the past. Arrests and seizures in criminal networks were no longer postponed or prevented at any cost but were—on the contrary—sometimes used deliberately to gather evidence against the prime suspects (Kleemans and Kruissink 1999). Prompt interventions are now often combined with a more long-term investigation strategy.

The third major change in criminal investigation strategies was (increasing use of) cross-border police investigations, paralleled by a centralization of police capacity used for fighting transnational organized crime. The setting up of IRTs between 1993 and 1995 was the first step in this development, earmarking roughly 2 percent of the Dutch police force for investigations that—although often linked to certain cities and regions—go beyond the immediate interests of the regional police forces. An evaluation concluded that these teams performed reasonably well in certain respects (Klerks et al. 2002). The teams were allowed to devote long-term attention to selected geographical regions (Latin America, Turkey, and eastern Europe), infrastructure (Amsterdam-Schiphol Airport and the port of Rotterdam), or specific illegal activities (smuggling illegal immigrants or the production of and trafficking in synthetic drugs). This enhanced coherence and continuity in intelligence and criminal investigations. It also fostered good relationships with foreign police forces (Klerks et al. 2002). However, evaluators were highly critical of the complex and slow decision-making structure concerning the teams, in which too many judicial and administrative authorities were involved. In 2003 these teams were pooled together in the National Criminal Investigation Squad, focusing explicitly on transnational organized crime (Korps Landelijke Politiediensten 2003). Priority areas of investigation are trafficking in cocaine, heroin, and synthetic drugs (including the production of synthetic drugs), smuggling illegal immigrants, trafficking in human beings for (sexual) exploitation, money laundering, arms and explosives, and terrorism (Openbaar Ministerie 2004).

B. Special Investigation Methods

After the IRT affair, the Parliamentary Inquiry Committee entered at length into the use of several criminal investigation methods: observation techniques, the use of informers, covert policing and infiltration, and intelligence. The main conclusions were that there was a legal vacuum concerning criminal investigation methods, that the organization of the criminal justice system was insufficient, and that the command and control of criminal investigations should be enhanced.

In 2000, the Act on Special Investigative Police Powers (BOB Act) came into force. The three main aims of this law were to codify certain methods of investigation that carry risks for the integrity of the investigation or that violate the fundamental rights of citizens; to enhance the central authority in criminal investigations of the public prosecutor, by making the use of special investigative powers dependent on authorization by the public prosecutor or—in cases of particularly invasive powers (wiretapping and bugging)—the examining magistrate; and to monitor criminal investigations, by requiring reports of the special investigative powers used and, in principle, accountability at trial for their deployment.

The BOB Act regulates the following special investigative police powers: systematic observation, requests for telecommunications data, the recording of telecommunications (wiretapping), the recording of confidential communications (bugging), the entering of private property, three "undercover powers" (infiltration, buying illegal goods or substances, and providing illegal services), and the systematic gathering of intelligence. The act also regulates the use of civilians (informers) in criminal investigation, their deployment in systematically gathering intelligence, illegal goods or substances purchases, illegal services provision, and infiltration by civilians. Although the act itself does not specifically forbid the use of civilians in infiltration operations, the existence of such a prohibition can be inferred from the legislative debate.

The BOB Act has been evaluated in two phases (Bokhorst, de Kogel, and van der Meij 2002; Beijer et al. 2004). The final evaluation was based on legal literature, case law, parliamentary documents, interviews with 110 practitioners, (quantitative) information concerning the deployment of certain methods, and six case studies on bugging (a newly introduced special investigative power). It is concluded that both the role of the public prosecutor and transparency have been enhanced. Yet transparency also implies a big administrative burden for the police, especially with regard to the (extensive) use of wiretapping.

Respondents are positive about the opportunities that bugging affords, although they observe problems regarding the long period of preparation it can require, limited capacity, and the (technological and procedural) impossibility of listening directly to recorded conversations. Bugging is used in particular if no (further) results are to be expected from other methods such as wiretapping and observation. The case studies show that bugging contributes significantly to investigations. Not only are its direct results important, they are especially so in conjunction with intelligence obtained by means of other methods of investigation.

Particular problems with the BOB Act are still connected to the very roots of the IRT affair—uncontrolled deliveries and the use of informers and undercover police activities. One problem concerns the fact that the interests of the investigation may clash with the duty to confiscate illegal goods, if one knows where such goods or substances can be found. In practice, different ways have been developed to avoid as much as possible the undesirable consequences of unduly early confiscation. This sometimes damages the efficacy of the investigation when, for instance, police teams avoid wiretapping certain suspects in order not to get too much clear evidence on specific illegal activities.

A more important problem concerns the use of informers and undercover police activities. First of all, the BOB Act is supposed to regulate systematic intelligence gathering by civilians. Yet, in many instances, transparency and protecting the identity of informers are conflicting interests. As a result, the term "systematic" is interpreted by practitioners in such a way as to cover barely any action on the part of a civilian. Moreover, as soon as an informer looks as though he is engaging in systematic activities, these activities are immediately curtailed. As a result, the work of the Criminal Intelligence Division with informers takes place almost entirely outside of the context of the BOB Act.

Furthermore, in regulating undercover police activity, the Parliament opted for a threefold division in powers: systematic intelligence gathering, purchasing illegal goods or substances and rendering illegal services, and infiltration. These investigative methods are assumed to be of a successively invasive nature, and the requirements with regard to their deployment are therefore increasingly strict. The research, however, shows that, in practice, the first two methods can be combined to allow for invasive undercover investigations that are nevertheless not regarded as infiltration (Beijer et al. 2004).

In addition to the extensive evaluation of the BOB Act, research has been carried out into the effectiveness of investigation methods such as infiltration, wiretapping, and other more traditional policing methods (Reijne, Kouwenberg, and Keizer 1996; Kleemans, van den Berg, and van de Bunt 1998; Kruissink, van Hoorn, and Boek 1999; De Poot et al. 2004). Kruissink, van Hoorn, and Boek conducted a unique study of twelve infiltration cases in 1996. The remarkable conclusion was that only one case evolved as planned and generated evidence that could be used in court. This case involved a criminal who bought confidential police material from a corrupt police officer. Four cases were largely conducted as planned and produced some results, yet they did not generate substantive evidence. The other seven cases produced no results at all. Of course, one could question whether the only relevant result of an infiltration operation is generating evidence that can be used in court. Sometimes infiltration may contribute indirectly to this ultimate goal by leading a police investigation in the right direction. Moreover, the reason police teams start thinking about infiltration may be the same reason why such an operation fails: these cases are complex and the suspects involved shield their activities quite effectively against the authorities. The main problem, according to Kruissink, van Hoorn, and Boek, is getting into contact with the main suspect. For outsiders such as police agents, this may be very difficult, and contacts with middlemen may prove futile, because they are unable to introduce the police agents to the main suspect or they have fallen out with him in the meantime. The comparative advantage of insiders may explain why the only effective infiltration case concerned a (criminal) citizen, exactly the kind of operation that was banned after the IRT affair. In March 2003, by the way, this explicit ban on deploying civilian infiltrators was toned down. Deploying civilian infiltrators is still highly restricted but can be permitted under very exceptional circumstances, for instance during investigations into terrorism.

Studies into other investigative methods reveal that wiretapping especially is quite effective in generating both guiding information and evidence that can be used in court (e.g., Reijne, Kouwenberg, and Keizer 1996; Kleemans, van den Berg, and van de Bunt 1998; De Poot et al. 2004). Reijne, Kouwenberg, and Keizer provided some evidence regarding the effectiveness of wiretapping and the extensive use of wiretapping by the Dutch police service. The evaluation of the BOB Act contains some figures for the period 2000–2003, which show that wiretapping is most frequently used, followed by systematic observation, and that other BOB methods such as bugging and infiltration lag far behind (Beijer et al. 2004, pp. 147–55). The forty case studies of the second sweep of the Organized Crime Monitor give some indications of the effectiveness of wiretapping (Kleemans, Brienen, and van de Bunt 2002, pp. 88–91). Wiretapping, whether or not combined with other methods, in three-quarters of the cases substantially contributed to the evidence that could be used in court, despite the commonly used communication in codes. In a large number of cases, significant evidence was also gathered by static or dynamic observation (cameras and tracking equipment). The third largest contribution to the evidence was provided by statements from suspects and witnesses.

Thus, the available evidence suggests that quite "traditional" policing methods may still be effective in cases of organized crime. The main reason wiretapping generates much evidence, particularly in cases of transnational crime, is that communication by the main suspects is essential in these cases. Because people live in different countries, they have to communicate by phone, fax, or e-mail, and this (traceable) communication can only be partially replaced by meetings in person. Furthermore, communication by business partners and co-offenders may also generate evidence against prime suspects. Finally, seizures and arrests may turn the relatively comfortable and strategic position of a broker sour. When problems arise, he is the one who gets called about what went wrong, who is responsible, and who is going to pay the debts. Indispensability forces action and communication—and can be monitored by wiretapping and observation (Kleemans, Brienen, and van de Bunt 2002, pp. 53–56).

C. Preventive Strategies

Preventive strategies to tackle organized crime have been heavily influenced by a meeting in 1990 between members of the New York State Organized Crime Task Force and Dutch police officials, public prosecutors, and researchers (Fijnaut and Jacobs 1991; Jacobs 1999). During this conference, attention was paid not only to repressive strategies for combating organized crime but also to the preventive approach advocated by the New York State Organized Crime Task Force. Since then, several initiatives have been launched in the Netherlands, addressing governments, citizens, and organizations, to make them responsible for reducing the opportunities for organized crime. The kind of opportunities that facilitate organized crime have been described by van de Bunt and van der Schoot (2003). This study, based on comparative analysis of criminal investigations in the Netherlands, Italy, Hungary, and Finland, distinguishes among three categories of preventive measures: reducing the demand for illegal products and services, increasing the responsibility and defensibility of facilitators in the licit environment (most notably public officials and professionals), and reducing the availability of tools in the licit environment (e.g., forged documents, legal persons, and traditional and nontraditional financial services). Furthermore, unambiguous legislation and regulation, efficient law enforcement, and exchange of information between agencies are viewed as necessary conditions for effective prevention (van de Bunt and van der Schoot 2003, pp. 25–32).

Levi and Maguire (2004) have presented an overview of successful and less successful preventive initiatives in Europe. In this section, I cannot provide a full account of all the preventive measures taken in the Netherlands (for an overview, see, e.g., van de Bunt [2004, pp. 691–701]; Zoomer, Nieuwkamp, and Johannink [2004]). I will, for instance, not devote much attention to anti–money laundering efforts and the proceeds-of-crime approach (including asset forfeiture; e.g., Keyser-Ringnalda 1994; Terlouw and Aron 1996; Nelen and Sabee 1998; Mul 1999; van Duyne et al. 2001; Faber and van Nunen 2002, 2004; Meloen et al. 2003; Nelen 2004; Schaap Bruin en van Vliet 2004). Considerable research has been done on these issues, yet anti–money laundering efforts are not unique to the Netherlands, and the rather negative findings regarding the results of the proceeds-of-crime approach are very similar to conclusions in the international literature (e.g., Levi and Osofsky 1995; Gradowski and Ziegler 1997;

Kilchling 2002; Naylor 2002; Reuter and Truman 2004; Levi and van Duyne 2005). Because of space limitations, I also will not elaborate on research on the role of legal professions such as lawyers, notaries public, real estate agents, tax consultants, and accountants (e.g., Fijnaut et al. 1996, 1998; Lankhorst and Nelen 2003, 2004; Levi, Nelen, and Lankhorst 2004). Instead, I focus on two initiatives: the administrative approach in Amsterdam and the BIBOB (Bevordering Intergriteits-beoordelingen door het Openbaar Bestuur) Act, an act on integrity screening by government agencies.

The administrative approach in Amsterdam was a response to the alarming conclusions of the Fijnaut research group regarding the situation in Amsterdam and in particular with regard to Amsterdam's red-light district. In this so-called Wallen area, criminal organizations built up positions of economic power in real estate, bars, and restaurants, and it was questioned whether the local government had lost control of the situation (Fijnaut et al. 1996, 1998).

Therefore, firm preventive action was taken on at least three fronts (for an overview, see Fijnaut [2001]). First, steps were taken in the civil service to enhance the awareness of risks of corruption and fraud, and a special integrity bureau was set up to investigate reports of suspected cases of fraud or corruption. An evaluation study by Nelen (2003) concluded that the majority of reports involved suspicions of theft and fraud by employees and only a small part (11 percent) concerned corruption.

Second, public tendering was increasingly scrutinized by a screening and audit bureau in order to prevent participation by companies with criminal connections. Van der Wielen (2001) concluded that 20 percent of the total amount of screenings resulted in the exclusion of companies from public tendering procedures. The main reason for exclusion turned out to be insufficient information or lack of financial guarantees, while only some cases concerned possible involvement of criminal money.

Third, in 1997 the Wallen project was launched, which focused on the problems in Amsterdam's main red-light district. This project was later extended to other parts of the city: the so-called van Traa project, named after the chairman of the Parliamentary Inquiry Committee. The activities and results of both projects have been evaluated by Huisman et al. (2005) over the period 1999–2004. Many activities have been carried out since 1997: fifty-six properties have been bought and sold by the local government in order to give them a bona fide exploitation, four illegal casinos have been closed, legal instruments have been developed and used to refuse or suspend licenses for bars and restaurants, various bars and restaurants have been closed temporarily, ownership and financing structures of several streets and branches have been traced, screening procedures for licenses have been developed (in the context of the BIBOB Act), and several activities have been carried out to improve cooperation with local authorities (local districts) and law enforcement. Huisman and his coauthors' main conclusion is that this innovative administrative approach should be continued, although many lessons can be learned from the experiences of the van Traa project.

First, the project is partly inspired by the preventive approach of the New York State Organized Crime Task Force (Jacobs 1999). Yet the situation in Amsterdam is entirely different from the situation in New York. In New York, the main activities of mobsters pertained to racketeering in legal markets such as the construction industry, the garment industry, and the waste-haulage industry. In Amsterdam (and the Netherlands in general), the main activities do not involve racketeering but transit crime. Because international illegal markets are not regulated by local authorities, the opportunities for an administrative approach to have any effect are rather limited. Interventions can mainly focus on investments and the legal entities offenders use for facilitating their criminal activities.

Second, the administrative approach turns out to be highly dependent on information from law enforcement (about criminal activities) and tax authorities (about legal and illegal business activities). Without this information, suspicions about properties, businesses, or businessmen can never be validated. In Amsterdam, the police were highly reluctant to provide law enforcement information, and the tax authorities even retreated after some time, because the van Traa project was not part of their core activities. Therefore, Huisman et al. (2005) advised giving law enforcement the lead and focusing on an administrative follow-up.

Third, the van Traa project was subject to considerable net widening. All kinds of activities were carried out. Many also targeted neighborhood conditions, yet in the end it was not clear exactly how these activities were related to the original background of the project: combating organized crime.

On a national level, the administrative approach is manifested in the BIBOB Act (2003). This act provides a legal basis to refuse or withdraw permits, licenses, grants, and subsidies from applicants when there is a serious threat of criminal abuse. Local governments and other agencies may seek advice from a special BIBOB Bureau, part of the Ministry of Justice. This bureau has access to both police intelligence and criminal and tax records and delivers written advice, indicating if there is a serious threat of criminal abuse. Whether this advice is followed or disregarded is entirely at the discretion of the requesting agency.

The BIBOB Act will be evaluated in 2006. A preliminary study suggests that the expectations about the number of requests should be quite moderate (Eiff et al. 2003). In a survey of 712 potential requesting agencies, only 11 percent of the respondents indicate that they have encountered situations of criminal abuse in the past. One-third of the agencies reveal that they do not know whether such situations have ever occurred. One expert meeting suggests potential negative side effects, such as lengthy procedures, higher administration costs, and legalism, according to Eiff et al. One last important question concerns the quality of the advice. Is the information at the national level sufficient to prevent too many false positives and false negatives?

IV. Conclusion

The framing of the problem of organized crime in terms of "Mafia-type" organizations and infiltration in (local) governments, geographical areas, and economic sectors misperceived what was going on in the Netherlands. Although this misconception undoubtedly increased awareness of the problem and stimulated the emergence of several preventive strategies, criminal investigation strategies were put on the wrong track. It is now commonly accepted that the primary business of organized crime pertains to transit crime (instead of controlling economic sectors or regions) and that the nature of criminal groups might be better conceived as criminal networks (instead of pyramidal structures; see also Korps Landelijke Politiediensten 2003).

The main implications for empirical research and public policy stem from the very fact that the Netherlands is an important transit country, yet this does not imply that this small country is center stage. For empirical research, it means that more energy must be devoted to the transnational aspects of organized crime. Because case studies are our primary sources of knowledge, researchers should recognize that some police investigations are restricted to local groups, while others cross borders and illuminate the transnational aspects of the problem.

It may prove worthwhile to change perspective radically. Instead of studying organized crime through the looking glass of national police investigations—therefore concluding that the Netherlands is center stage—researchers could examine the problem from the perspective of source countries such as Colombia: How does Colombian cocaine reach European markets? And what role does the Netherlands play (e.g., Zaitch 2002*a*, 2002*b*)? It may also imply studying problems in other countries, say, corruption in eastern European countries or the intertwining between organized crime and economic sectors in countries of the former Soviet Union (e.g., Kernteam Noord- en Oost-Nederland 1999, 2001; Korps Landelijke Politiediensten 2004*a*). In order to understand transnational organized crime, this may be as important as studying our more "local" manifestations.

Another important area for research—also from a theoretical point of view—is criminal careers in organized crime. Much research has been done into careers in traditional crime and juvenile delinquency (see Weerman, in this volume). Yet very little is known about adult offenders and careers in organized crime (see, e.g., Morselli 2001, 2003, 2005; Dorn, Levi, and King 2005). Ongoing research into approximately 1,000 suspects of the first eighty cases of the Organized Crime Monitor already shows that some characteristics of these suspects differ substantially: about three-quarters of the suspects are in their thirties, forties, or even fifties, and no suspects younger than eighteen are involved. How have these careers developed? Were people recruited? Or are other mechanisms involved? Exactly what is the role of social relations and the snowball effect of social relations in organized crime networks (Kleemans and van de Bunt 1999)? What part is played by facilitating environments?

The development of XTC production in the Netherlands may provide an interesting case for such research. From a theoretical point of view, it might prove worthwhile to make use of findings from very different fields of research, showing, for example, the salience of existing, similar businesses for the emergence of new businesses (e.g., Sörenson and Audia 2000). Personal contacts and geographical proximity foster opportunities to acquire the necessary knowledge, to create or develop the necessary social relationships, and to gain confidence in the prospect of starting a new business. How well may this Silicon Valley hypothesis fit the emergence of XTC production?

In-depth research into criminal careers, criminal networks, and criminal markets might also provide more elaborated insights into criminal markets and the roles of cooperation and competition. In both economics and sociology, several authors have paid attention to the roles of social relations and social capital in economic markets (e.g., Granovetter 1985; Coleman 1990; Burt 1992, 2005; Guillén et al. 2002). Findings from this emerging field of "economic sociology" are highly relevant for research into illegal markets, because economic behavior in criminal markets is subject to very different constraints than in legal markets (e.g., Reuter 1983; Potter 1994). How do suppliers and buyers search and find each other in illegal markets? How do they cooperate or compete? And how do they deal with the risks of deception and betrayal and with the risks of law enforcement? These questions can also be applied to criminal groups, going beyond the rather one-sided conceptions of either individual, rational entrepreneurs or cohesive criminal organizations—leaving little room for individual behavior and internal dynamics. The issue of searching for suitable co-offenders, raised by Tremblay (1993), should be further explored against the background of illegal markets, where the financial stakes are high. Yet the rules and mechanisms that make transactions in the legal world so much easier are absent: entering into contracts, paying via the official banking system, and—in the case of disagreement—the availability of mediation or the courts (e.g., Reuter 1983; Potter 1994).

A final area of research that deserves more· attention is the effectiveness of law enforcement and law enforcement methods. Many discussions about law enforcement methods are purely normative. Very little is known about effectiveness (what works?) or even about basic empirical questions such as how law enforcement methods are actually employed, which is crucial for designing effective laws and effective command and control structures. Such research, in which the Netherlands has a modest yet quite unique research tradition, could extend purely normative discussions about "law enforcement in the books" to more balanced discussions about "law enforcement in action."

Salient policy questions for the near future stem from two important new insights and developments. The first insight has already been mentioned in this essay. If organized crime should be characterized mainly as transit crime, this implies for policy makers that checking outgoing traffic and exports is at least as significant as checking incoming traffic and trade flows (see also van de Bunt and Kleemans 2004). It also means that discussions about policy measures and priorities in law enforcement become transnational as well. Policy measures in other countries could prevent transit crime more effectively than policy measures in one's own country. And law enforcement priorities are not an entirely national affair anymore. Although the Netherlands has some history in trying to decide rationally on national priorities in combating organized crime (e.g., Openbaar Ministerie 2004), transit crime substantially limits the degree of freedom in national decision making and forces other countries' priorities to be incorporated in national debates.

Another important development since 2001 is the emergence of the problem of terrorism, which is partly combated by law enforcement measures (see, e.g., Muller, Spaaij, and Ruitenberg 2003; Buruma 2005). Since the IRT affair, a lot of effort has been put into enhancing the transparency of the deployment of criminal investigation methods. Some criminal investigation methods were highly restricted or banned, such as the deployment of civilian infiltrators. In March 2003, however, the explicit ban on deploying civilian infiltrators was eased. Deploying civilian infiltrators is still highly restricted but is allowed under highly exceptional circumstances, for instance during investigations into terrorism. Furthermore, several requirements for the use of special investigation methods have become less restrictive and investigative powers have been expanded. Finally, information from the Secret Service can now be admitted in court.

An important policy question for the future will be how the criminal justice system will deal with these new "nontransparencies." Another policy question will concern the effectiveness of law enforcement in combating terrorism. The combat of organized crime has introduced the notion of proactive policing. Contrary to traditional reactive policing, which is primarily instigated by victim reports or criminal events such as murders or rapes, proactive policing is mainly induced by law enforcement information and law enforcement priorities. In proactive policing, gathering evidence about past behavior of offenders is steadily replaced by gathering evidence on the current and future behavior of offenders. In substantive law this development was paralleled by criminalizing preparatory actions and membership of a criminal organization—followed now by criminalizing preparatory actions, conspiracy, membership of an organization with a terrorist intention, and recruitment for the jihad. In organized crime cases, however, much evidence in court is still mainly based on information on the actual behavior of offenders, wiretapping, seizures, house searches, and statements from suspects and witnesses. In terrorism investigations, the basic tension between proactive policing and clear evidence is stretched even further, as investigations primarily focus on future behavior that has to be prevented at any cost—law enforcement thereby destroying its own evidence of terrorist intentions materializing into concrete terrorist actions. How much evidence will be needed of terrorist preparatory activities? How much weight will judges attach to transparency? How successful will law enforcement be in gathering such evidence? Will it stand up in court? Two decades after the IRT affair, the criminal justice system is put to another severe test.

REFERENCES

Abadinsky, H. 2002. *Organized Crime*. New York: Wadsworth.
Albanese, J. S. 2004. *Organized Crime in Our Times*. 4th ed. Cincinnati: Anderson.
Albini, J. 1971. *The American Mafia: Genesis of a Legend*. New York: Appleton.
Aronowitz, A. A., D. C. G. Laagland, and G. Paulides. 1996. *Value-Added Tax Fraud in the European Union*. New York: Kugler.
Beijer, A., R. J. Bokhorst, M. Boone, C. H. Brants, and J. M. W. Lindeman. 2004. *De Wet Bijzondere Opsporingsbevoegdheden: Eindevaluatie* [The Special Investigative Police Powers Act: Final evaluation]. The Hague: Boom Juridische Uitgevers.
Blickman, T., D. J. Korf, D. Siegel, and D. Zaitch. 2003. *Synthetic Drugs Trafficking in Amsterdam*. Amsterdam: Transnational Institute.
Block, A. A., and W. J. Chambliss. 1981. *Organizing Crime*. New York: Elsevier.
Bokhorst, R., C. de Kogel, and C. van der Meij. 2002. *Evaluatie van de Wet BOB: Fase 1* [Evaluation of the BOB Act: Phase 1]. The Hague: Boom Juridische Uitgevers.
Bovenkerk, F. 1995. *La bella Bettien* [The beautiful Bettien]. Amsterdam: Meulenhoff.
———. 2005. *Bedreigingen in Nederland* [Threatening in the Netherlands]. Amsterdam: Augustus.
Bovenkerk, F., and W. Hogewind. 2003. *Hennepteelt in Nederland: Het probleem van de criminaliteit en haar bestrijding* [Cannabis cultivation in the Netherlands: The problem of the criminal activity and its containment]. Zeist: Uitgeverij Kerckebosch.
Bovenkerk, F., M. van San, M. Boone, T. Boekhout van Solinge, and D. J.

Korf. 2004. *"Loverboys" of modern pooierschap in Amsterdam* ["Loverboys" or modern pimps in Amsterdam]. Utrecht: Willem Pompe Instituut voor Strafrechtswetenschappen.

Bovenkerk, F., and Y. Yesilgöz. 1998. *De Maffia van Turkije* [The Turkish Mafia]. Amsterdam: Meulenhoff.

Bruinsma, G., and W. Bernasco. 2004. "Criminal Groups and Transnational Illegal Markets: A More Detailed Examination on the Basis of Social Network Theory." *Crime, Law, and Social Change* 41:79–94.

Bruinsma, M. Y., and J. A. Moors. 2005. *Illegale vuurwapens: Gebruik, bezit, en handel in Nederland* [Illegal firearms: Use, possession, and trafficking in the Netherlands]. Tilburg: IVA.

Bunt, H., D. Kunst, and D. Siegel. 2003. *XTC over de grens: Een studie naar XTC-koeriers en kleine smokkelaars* [XTC across borders: A study into XTC couriers and minor smugglers]. The Hague: Boom Juridische Uitgevers.

Bureau Nationaal Rapporteur Mensenhandel. 2002*a. Mensenhandel: Eerste rapportage van de Nationaal Rapporteur* [Trafficking in human beings: First report of the National Rapporteur]. The Hague: Bureau Nationaal Rapporteur Mensenhandel.

———. 2002*b. Mensenhandel: Aanvullende kwantitatieve gegevens: Tweede rapportage van de Nationaal Rapporteur* [Trafficking in human beings: Second report of the National Rapporteur]. The Hague: Bureau Nationaal Rapporteur Mensenhandel.

———. 2005*a. Trafficking in Human Beings: Third Report of the National Rapporteur.* The Hague: Bureau Nationaal Rapporteur Mensenhandel.

———. 2005*b. Trafficking in Human Beings, Supplementary Figures: Fourth Report of the National Rapporteur.* The Hague: Bureau Nationaal Rapporteur Mensenhandel.

Burt, R. S. 1992. *Structural Holes.* Cambridge, MA: Harvard University Press.

———. 2000. "The Network Structure of Social Capital." In *Research in Organizational Behavior*, edited by R. I. Sutton and M. Staw. Greenwich, CT: JAI.

———. 2005. *Brokerage and Closure: An Introduction to Social Capital.* Oxford: Oxford University Press.

Buruma, Y. 2005. *De dreigingsspiraal: Onbedoelde neveneffecten van misdaadbestrijding* [The spiral of threat: Unanticipated side effects of combating crime]. The Hague: Boom Juridische Uitgevers.

———. In this volume. "Dutch Tolerance: On Drugs, Prostitution, and Euthanasia."

Buskens, V. 1999. *Social Networks and Trust.* Utrecht: Interuniversity Center for Social Science Theory and Methodology.

Chambliss, W. J. 1978. *On the Take: From Petty Crooks to Presidents.* Bloomington: Indiana University Press.

Clarke, R. V., and R. Brown. 2003. "International Trafficking in Stolen Vehicles." In *Crime and Justice: A Review of Research*, vol. 30, edited by Michael Tonry. Chicago: University of Chicago Press.

Coleman, J. S. 1990. *Foundations of Social Theory*. Cambridge, MA: Harvard University Press.

Cressey, D. R. 1969. *Theft of the Nation: The Structure and Operations of Organized Crime in America*. New York: Harper & Row.

Daalder, A. L. 2002. *Het bordeelverbod opgeheven: Prostitutie in 2000–2001* [Lifting the ban on brothels: Prostitution in 2000–2001]. The Hague: Wetenschappelijk Onderzoek- en Documentatiecentrum.

———. 2004. *Lifting the Ban on Brothels: Prostitution in 2000–2001*. The Hague: Wetenschappelijk Onderzoek- en Documentatiecentrum.

De Poot, C. J., R. J. Bokhorst, P. J. van Koppen, and E. R. Muller. 2004. *Rechercheportret: Over dilemma's in de opsporing* [A portrait of detective work: Dilemmas in police investigations]. Deventer: Kluwer.

Dienst Nationale Recherche Informatie. 2004. *Nationaal dreigingsbeeld zware of georganiseerde criminaliteit: Een eerste proeve* [National threat assessment on serious or organized crime]. Zoetermeer: Korps Landelijke Politiediensten–Dienst Nationale Recherche Informatie.

———. 2005. *Mensensmokkel in beeld, 2002–2003* [People smuggling: The picture, 2002–2003]. Zoetermeer: Korps Landelijke Politiediensten.

Dorn, N., M. Levi, and L. King. 2005. *Literature Review on Upper Level Drug Trafficking*. Home Office Online Report 22/05. London: Home Office.

Eiff, V. L., D. A. van Steensel, M. A. Luursema, and A. J. van den Berg. 2003. *Voorstudie evaluatie Wet BIBOB* [Preliminary study evaluation BIBOB Act]. Utrecht: Berenschot.

Engbersen, G., R. Staring, J. van der Leun, J. de Boom, P. van der Heijden, and M. Cruijff. 2002. *Illegale vreemdelingen in Nederland: Omvang, herkomst, verblijf en uitzetting* [Illegal immigrants in the Netherlands: Amount, origin, stay, and expulsion]. Rotterdam: Rotterdams Instituut voor Sociaal-wetenschappelijk BeleidsOnderzoek.

Engbersen, Godfried, Joanne van der Leun, and Jan de Boom. In this volume. "The Fragmentation of Migration and Crime in the Netherlands."

Europol. 2005. *2005 EU Organised Crime Report: Public Version*. The Hague: Europol.

Faber, W., and A. van Nunen. 2002. *Het ei van Columbo? Evaluatie van het Project Financieel Rechercheren* [The egg of Columbo? Evaluation of the Financial Investigation Project]. Oss: Faber Organisatievernieuwing.

———. 2004. *Uit onverdachte bron: Evaluatie van de keten ongebruikelijke transacties* [From an unsuspected source: Evaluation of the system concerning the reporting of unusual transactions]. The Hague: Boom Juridische Uitgevers.

Farrell, G. 1998. "Routine Activities and Drug Trafficking: The Case of the Netherlands." *International Journal of Drug Policy* 9(1):21–32.

Farrell, G., K. Mansur, and M. Tullis. 1996. "Cocaine and Heroin in Europe, 1983–93: A Cross-National Comparison of Trafficking and Prices." *British Journal of Criminology* 36(2):255–81.

Feld, S. L. 1981. "The Focused Organization of Social Ties." *American Journal of Sociology* 86:1015–35.

Ferwerda, H., N. Arts, E. de Bie, and I. van Leiden. 2005. *Georganiseerde autodiefstal: Kenmerken en achtergronden van een illegale branche in beeld gebracht* [Organised car theft: Characteristics and backgrounds of an illegal branch]. Amsterdam: Uitgeverij SWP.

Fijnaut, C. 1984. "De uitdaging van de georganiseerde misdaad" [The challenge of organized crime]. *Delikt en Delinkwent* 14:581–84.

———. 1985. "Georganiseerde misdaad: Een onderzoeksgerichte terreinverkenning" [Organized crime: A research-oriented exploration of the field]. *Justitiële Verkenningen* 11:5–42.

———. 1993. *Politiële corruptie in Nederland* [Police corruption in the Netherlands]. Arnhem: Gouda Quint.

———, ed. 2001. *De bestuurlijke aanpak van (georganiseerde) criminaliteit in Amsterdam* [The administrative approach toward (organized) crime in Amsterdam]. Amsterdam: Directie Openbare Orde en Veiligheid Gemeente Amsterdam.

Fijnaut, C., F. Bovenkerk, G. Bruinsma, and H. van de Bunt. 1996. "Eindrapport onderzoeksgroep Fijnaut." App. 7 in *Inzake opsporing: Enquête opsporingsmethoden* [Final report of the Fijnaut research group. App. 7 in Concerning investigation: Inquiry into criminal investigation methods], edited by Parlementaire Enquêtecommissie Opsporingsmethoden. The Hague: Sdu Uitgevers.

———. 1998. *Organized Crime in the Netherlands*. Boston: Kluwer Law International.

Fijnaut, C., and J. Jacobs. 1991. *Organized Crime and Its Containment: A Transatlantic Initiative*. Deventer: Kluwer Law and Taxation.

Fijnaut, C., and L. Paoli. 2004. *Organised Crime in Europe: Concepts, Patterns, and Control Policies in the European Union and Beyond*. Dordrecht: Springer.

Gambetta, D. 1993. *The Sicilian Mafia: The Business of Private Protection*. Cambridge, MA: Harvard University Press.

Gradowski, M., and J. Ziegler. 1997. *Geldwäsche, Gewinnabschöpfung: Erste Erfahrungen mit den neuen gesetzlichen Regelungen* [Money laundering: First experiences with the new legislation]. Wiesbaden: Bundeskriminalamt.

Granovetter, M. 1985. "Economic Action and Social Structure: The Problem of Embeddedness." *American Journal of Sociology* 91:481–510.

Gruter, P., and D. van de Mheen. 2005. *Cocaïnehandel in Nederland: Impressies van deelnemers aan drugsdistributienetwerken* [Cocaine dealing in the Netherlands: Impressions from participants in drugs distribution networks]. Rotterdam: Instituut voor Verslavingsonderzoek.

Guillén, Mauro F., Randall Collins, Paula England, and Marshall Meyer, eds. 2002. *The New Economic Sociology: Developments in an Emerging Field*. New York: Russell Sage Foundation.

Hopkins, R. 2005. *Ik laat je nooit meer gaan: Het meisje, de vrouw, de handelaar en de agent* [I will never let you go: The girl, the woman, the trafficker, and the police agent]. Breda: Uitgeverij De Geus.

Huberts, L. W. J. C., and J. Naeyé. 2005. *Integriteit van de politie: Wat we weten op basis van Nederlands onderzoek* [Integrity of the police: What do we know from Dutch research?]. Zeist: Uitgeverij Kerckebosch.

Huberts, L. W. J. C., and J. M. Nelen. 2005. *Corruptie in het Nederlandse openbaar bestuur: Omvang, aard en afdoening* [Corruption in Dutch government: Extent, nature, and settlement]. Utrecht: Uitgeverij Lemma BV.

Huisman, W., M. Huikeshoven, H. Nelen, H. van de Bunt, and J. Struiksma. 2005. *Het van Traa-project: Evaluatie van de bestuurlijke aanpak van georganiseerde criminaliteit in Amsterdam* [The van Traa project: Evaluation of the administrative approach toward organized crime in Amsterdam]. The Hague: Boom Juridische Uitgevers.

Huisman, W., M. Huikeshoven, and H. van de Bunt. 2003. *Marktplaats Amsterdam: Op zoek naar de zwakste schakel in de logistiek van criminele processen aan de hand van Amsterdamse rechercheonderzoeken* [Marketplace Amsterdam: Searching for the weakest link in the logistics of criminal processes based on an analysis of police investigations in Amsterdam]. The Hague: Boom Juridische Uitgevers.

Ianni, F. A. J., and E. Reuss-Ianni. 1972. *A Family Business: Kinship and Social Control in Organized Crime*. London: Routledge & Kegan Paul.

Informatie- en Analysecentrum Mensensmokkel. 2001. *Dreigingsbeeld mensensmokkel, 2000* [Threat analysis concerning smuggling illegal immigrants, 2000]. Zoetermeer: Informatie- en Analysecentrum Mensensmokkel.

Interregionaal Recherche Team Noord- en Oost-Nederland/Internationaal Politie Instituut Twente. 1997. *Mensenhandel vanuit Centraal- en Oost-Europa* [Human trafficking from central and eastern Europe]. Nijverdal: Interregionaal Recherche Team Noord- en Oost-Nederland.

Jacobs, J. B. 1999. *Gotham Unbound: How New York City Was Liberated from the Grip of Organized Crime*. New York: New York University Press.

Jacobs, J. B., and E. Peters. 2003. "Labor Racketeering: The Mafia and the Unions." In *Crime and Justice: A Review of Research*, vol. 30, edited by Michael Tonry. Chicago: University of Chicago Press.

Jansen, A. C. M. 2002. "De economie van de cannabissector" [The economy of the cannabis sector]. *Economisch Statistische Berichten* 87(4354):276–78.

Kernteam Noord- en Oost-Nederland. 1999. *Oost-Europese georganiseerde criminaliteit: Een bedreiging voor Nederland?* [Eastern European organized crime: A threat to the Netherlands?]. Nijverdal: Kernteam Noord- en Oost-Nederland.

———. 2001. *Algemene criminaliteitsbeeldanalyse: Oost Europa, 2000–2001* [General crime analysis: Eastern Europe, 2000–2001]. Nijverdal: Kernteam Noord- en Oost-Nederland.

Keyser-Ringnalda, L. 1994. *Boef en buit: De ontneming van wederrechtelijk verkregen vermogen* [Felon and loot: Seizing and confiscating the proceeds of crime]. Arnhem: Gouda Quint.

Kilchling, M., ed. 2002. *Die Praxis der Gewinnabschöpfung in Europa* [The practice of seizing and confiscating the proceeds of crime in Europe]. Freiburg: Edition Iuscrim.

Kleemans, E. R. 2004. "Crossing Borders: Organised Crime in the Netherlands." In *Organised Crime in Europe: Concepts, Patterns, and Control Policies in the European Union and Beyond*, edited by C. Fijnaut and L. Paoli. Dordrecht: Springer.

Kleemans, E. R., and M. E. I. Brienen. 2001. "Van vriendendienst tot slangenkop: Een analyse van tien opsporingsonderzoeken naar mensensmokkel" [From kind turns to snakeheads: An analysis of ten police investigations into smuggling illegal immigrants]. *Tijdschrift voor Criminologie* 43(4):350–59.

Kleemans, E. R., M. E. I. Brienen, and H. G. van de Bunt. 2002. *Georganiseerde criminaliteit in Nederland: Tweede rapportage op basis van de WODC-monitor* [Organized crime in the Netherlands: Second report based upon the WODC-monitor]. The Hague: Wetenschappelijk Onderzoek- en Documentatiecentrum.

Kleemans, E. R., and M. Kruissink. 1999. "Korte klappen of lange halen? Wat werkt bij de aanpak van georganiseerde criminaliteit?" [Prompt intervention strategies or long-haul strategies? What works in combating organized crime?]. *Justitiële Verkenningen* 25(6):99–111.

Kleemans, E. R., and H. G. van de Bunt. 1999. "The Social Embeddedness of Organized Crime." *Transnational Organized Crime* 5(2):19–36.

———. 2003. "The Social Organisation of Human Trafficking." In *Global Organized Crime: Trends and Developments*, edited by D. Siegel, H. van de Bunt, and D. Zaitch. Boston: Kluwer Academic.

Kleemans, E. R., E. A. I. M. van den Berg, and H. G. van de Bunt. 1998. *Georganiseerde criminaliteit in Nederland: Rapportage op basis van de WODC-monitor* [Organized crime in the Netherlands: Report based upon the WODC-monitor]. The Hague: Wetenschappelijk Onderzoek- en Documentatiecentrum.

Klerks, P. P. H. M. 2000. *Groot in de hasj: Theorie en praktijk van de georganiseerde criminaliteit* [Big in hashish: Theory and practice of organized crime]. Antwerp: Kluwer Rechtswetenschappen.

Klerks, P. P. H. M., C. In 't Velt, A. van Wijk, M. Scholtes, P. Nijmeijer, and J. van der Velde. 2002. *De voorhoede van de opsporing: Evaluatie van de kernteams als instrument in de aanpak van zware georganiseerde criminaliteit* [The advance guard of criminal investigation: Evaluation of the special investigation squads]. Apeldoorn: Nederlandse Politie Academie.

Korps Landelijke Politiediensten. 2003. *Opsporen en tegenhouden van georganiseerde criminaliteit: Richtinggevend document voor de nationale recherche* [Investigating and stopping organized crime: Vision of the national criminal investigation squad]. Driebergen: Korps Landelijke Politiediensten.

———. 2004a. *Misdaad zonder grenzen: Criminaliteitsbeeld; Oost-Europa, 2002–2003* [Crime without borders: Crime assessment; Eastern Europe, 2002–2003]. Driebergen: Korps Landelijke Politiediensten, Dienst Nationale Recherche.

———. 2004b. *Criminaliteitbeeldanalyse: Turkse georganiseerde criminaliteit in Nederland, 2002–2003* [Crime assessment: Turkish organized crime in the Netherlands, 2002–2003]. Driebergen: Korps Landelijke Politiediensten, Dienst Nationale Recherche.

————. 2004c. *Criminaliteitsbeeldanalyse: Latijns-Amerika, 2002–2003* [Crime Assessment: Latin America, 2002–2003]. Driebergen: Korps Landelijke Politiediensten, Dienst Nationale Recherche.

————. 2005a. *Eindrapportage van het project Polaris: Mobiel banditisme uit Polen en Litouwen* [Final report of the Polaris project: Mobile banditry from Poland and Lithuania]. Driebergen: Korps Landelijke Politiediensten.

————. 2005b. *Criminaliteitsbeeldanalyse: Synthetische drugs, 2002–2004* [Crime analysis: Synthetic drugs, 2002–2004]. Driebergen: Korps Landelijke Politiediensten.

Kruissink, M., A. van Hoorn, and J. Boek. 1999. *Infiltratie in het recht en in de praktijk* [Undercover policing and infiltration in law and practice]. The Hague: Wetenschappelijk Onderzoek- en Documentatiecentrum.

Lamboo, T., J. Naeyé, A. Nieuwendijk, and M. van der Steeg. 2002. "Politie neemt integriteitsschendingen serieus" [The police take integrity violations seriously]. *Tijdschrift voor de Politie* 64(10):4–11.

Lankhorst, F., and H. Nelen. 2003. *Dilemmas Facing the Legal Professions and Notaries in Their Professional Relationship with Criminal Clients: Falcone Project, National Report of the Netherlands.* Amsterdam: Vrije Universiteit.

————. 2004. "Professional Services and Organised Crime in the Netherlands." *Crime, Law, and Social Change* 42:163–88.

Leistra, G., and P. Nieuwbeerta. 2003. *Moord en doodslag in Nederland, 1992–2001* [Murder and manslaughter in the Netherlands, 1992–2001]. Amsterdam: Prometheus.

Levi, M., and M. Maguire. 2004. "Reducing and Preventing Organised Crime: An Evidence-Based Critique." *Crime, Law, and Social Change* 41:397–469.

Levi, M., H. Nelen, and F. Lankhorst. 2004. "Lawyers as Crime Facilitators in Europe: An Introduction and Overview." *Crime, Law, and Social Change* 42:117–21.

Levi, M., and L. Osofsky. 1995. *Investigating, Seizing, and Confiscating the Proceeds of Crime.* London: Home Office.

Levi, M., and P. C. van Duyne. 2005. *Drugs and Money: Managing the Drug Trade and Crime Money in Europe.* London: Routledge.

Maalsté, N., P. Nijmeijer, and M. Scholtes. 2002. *De vuurwapengedetineerde aan het woord: Daderonderzoek naar achtergronden en motieven van vuurwapenbezit, vuurwapengebruik en vuurwapenhandel* [Talking to prisoners detained for firearms: The backgrounds and motives of possession and use of firearms and arms trade]. The Hague: Eysink, Smeets, and Etman.

Meloen, J. D., R. Landman, H. de Miranda, J. van Eekelen, and S. van Soest, with the assistance of P. C. van Duyne and W. van Tilburg. 2003. *Buit en besteding: Een empirisch onderzoek naar de omvang, de kenmerken en de besteding van misdaadgeld* [Proceeds and spending: An empirical analysis of the extent, the characteristics, and the spending of criminal proceeds]. Zoetermeer: Nationale Recherche Informatie.

Ministerie van Justitie/Ministerie van Binnenlandse Zaken. 1992. *De georganiseerde criminaliteit in Nederland: Dreigingsbeeld en plan van aanpak* [Organized crime in the Netherlands: Threat analysis and a plan of action]. The Hague: Ministerie van Justitie/Ministerie van Binnenlandse Zaken.

Moerland, H., and F. Boerman. 1998. *De opsporing van synthetische drugs* [Investigating synthetic drugs]. Deventer: Gouda Quint.

———. 1999. *Georganiseerde misdaad en betrokkenheid van bedrijven* [Organized crime and the involvement of legal businesses]. Deventer: Gouda Quint.

Moore, M. H. 1987. "Organized Crime as a Business Enterprise." In *Major Issues in Organized Crime Control*, edited by H. Edelhertz. Washington, DC: U.S. Government Printing Office.

Morselli, C. 2001. "Structuring Mr. Nice: Entrepreneurial Opportunities and Brokerage Positioning in the Cannabis Trade." *Crime, Law, and Social Change* 35(3):203–44.

———. 2003. "Career Opportunities and Network-Based Privileges in the Cosa Nostra." *Crime, Law, and Social Change* 39(4):383–418.

———. 2005. *Contacts, Opportunities, and Criminal Enterprise.* Toronto: University of Toronto Press.

Mul, V. 1999. *Banken en witwassen* [Banks and money laundering]. Arnhem: Gouda Quint.

Muller, E. R., R. F. J. Spaaij, and A. G. W. Ruitenberg. 2003. *Trends in terrorisme* [Trends in terrorism]. Alphen aan den Rijn: Kluwer.

Naylor, R. T. 2002. *Wages of Crime: Black Markets, Illegal Finance, and the Illegal Economy.* Ithaca, NY: Cornell University Press.

Nelen, H. 2003. *Integriteit in publieke functies* [Integrity in public office]. The Hague: Boom Juridische Uitgevers.

———. 2004. "Hit Them Where It Hurts Most? The Proceeds-of-Crime Approach in the Netherlands." *Crime, Law, and Social Change* 41:517–34.

Nelen, H., and A. Nieuwendijk. 2003. *Geen ABC: Analyse van Rijksrechercheonderzoeken naar ambtelijke en bestuurlijke corruptie* [No ABC: An analysis of corruption investigations]. The Hague: Boom Juridische Uitgevers.

Nelen, J., and V. Sabee. 1998. *Het vermogen te ontnemen: Evaluatie van de ontnemingswetgeving* [Evaluation of the law on seizing assets]. The Hague: Wetenschappelijk Onderzoek- en Documentatiecentrum.

Neve, R. J. M., M. M. J. van Ooyen-Houben, J. Snippe, B. Bieleman, A. Kruize, and R. V. Bijl. 2005. *Samenspannen tegen XTC: Tussentijdse evaluatie van de XTC-nota* [Conspiring against XTC: Midterm evaluation of the XTC policy plan]. The Hague: Wetenschappelijk Onderzoek- en Documentatiecentrum.

Openbaar Ministerie. 2004. *De strafrechtelijke aanpak van georganiseerde misdaad in Nederland, 2005–2010* [The criminal justice approach toward organized crime in the Netherlands, 2005–2010]. The Hague: Openbaar Ministerie.

Paoli, L. 2002. "The Paradoxes of Organized Crime." *Crime, Law, and Social Change* 37:51–97.

———. 2003. *Mafia Brotherhoods: Organized Crime, Italian Style.* New York: Oxford University Press.

Parlementaire Enquêtecommissie Bouwnijverheid. 2002. *De bouw uit de scha-*

duw [The construction industry out of the shadow]. The Hague: Sdu Uitgevers.

Parlementaire Enquêtecommissie Opsporingsmethoden. 1996. *Inzake opsporing: Enquête opsporingsmethoden* [Concerning investigation: Inquiry into criminal investigation methods]. The Hague: Sdu Uitgevers.

Passas, N. 1999. *Informal Value Transfer Systems and Criminal Organizations: A Study into So-Called Underground Banking Networks.* The Hague: Wetenschappelijk Onderzoek- en Documentatiecentrum.

———. 2005. *Informal Value Transfer Systems and Criminal Activities.* The Hague: Wetenschappelijk Onderzoek- en Documentatiecentrum.

Pieke, F. N., P. Nyíri, M. Thuno, and A. Ceddagno. 2004. *Transnational Chinese: Fujianese Migrants in Europe.* Stanford, CA: Stanford University Press.

Potter, G. W. 1994. *Criminal Organizations: Vice, Racketeering, and Politics in an American City.* Prospect Heights, IL: Waveland.

Reijne, Z., R. F. Kouwenberg, and M. P. Keizer. 1996. *Tappen in Nederland* [Wiretapping in the Netherlands]. Arnhem: Gouda Quint.

Reuter, P. 1983. *Disorganized Crime: Illegal Markets and the Mafia.* Cambridge, MA: MIT Press.

Reuter, P., and E. M. Truman. 2004. *Chasing Dirty Money: The Fight against Money Laundering.* Washington, DC: Institute for International Economics.

Schaap Bruin en van Vliet. 2004. *Evaluatie grote ontnemingszaken* [Asset seizures: An evaluation of big cases]. Capelle aan den IJssel: Schaap Bruin en van Vliet.

Sieber, U., and M. Bögel. 1993. *Logistik der organisierten Kriminalität* [Logistics of organized crime]. Wiesbaden: Bundeskriminalamt.

Siegel, D. 2005. *Russische bizniz* [Russian business]. Amsterdam: Meulenhoff.

Smekens, M., and M. Verbruggen. 2004. *De illegale economie van Nederland* [The illegal economy of the Netherlands]. Voorburg: Centraal Bureau voor de Statistiek.

Smith, D., Jr. 1975. *The Mafia Mystique.* New York: Basic Books.

Sörenson, O., and G. Audia. 2000. "The Social Structure of Entrepreneurial Activity: Geographic Concentration of Footwear Production in the United States, 1940–1989." *American Journal of Sociology* 106(2):424–62.

Soudijn, M. 2001. "Gijzeling: Een onderbelichte kant bij de mensensmokkel van Chinezen" [Taking hostages: An underexposed side of smuggling illegal Chinese immigrants]. *Tijdschrift voor Criminologie* 43(4):360–67.

———. 2006. *Chinese Human Smuggling in Transit.* The Hague: Boom Juridische Uitgevers.

Spapens, A. C., and M. Y. Bruinsma. 2002*a*. *Smokkel van handvuurwapens vanuit voormalige oostbloklanden naar Nederland* [Trafficking of small firearms from former Eastern Bloc countries to the Netherlands]. Tilburg: Instituut voor Sociaal Wetenschappelijk Beleidsonderzoek en Advies.

———. 2002*b*. *Vuurwapens gezocht: Vuurwapengebruik, -bezit, en handel in Nederland, 1998–2000* [Searching for firearms: The possession and use of firearms and arms trade in the Netherlands, 1998–2000]. Tilburg: Instituut voor Sociaal Wetenschappelijk Beleidsonderzoek en Advies.

————. 2004. *Illegale vuurwapens in Nederland: Smokkel en handel* [Illegal weapons in the Netherlands: Trafficking and trade]. Zeist: Uitgeverij Kerckebosch.

Staring, R., G. Engbersen, H. Moerland, N. de Lange, D. Verburg, E. Vermeulen, and A. Weltevrede. 2005. *De sociale organisatie van mensensmokkel* [The social organization of trafficking in human beings]. Zeist: Uitgeverij Kerckebosch.

Terlouw, G., and U. Aron. 1996. *Twee jaar MOT: Een evaluatie van de uitvoering van de wet Melding Ongebruikelijke Transacties* [Evaluation of the law on reporting unusual transactions]. Arnhem: Gouda Quint.

Terpstra, L., A. van Dijke, and M. van San. 2005. *Loverboys: Een publieke zaak* [Loverboys: A public matter]. Amsterdam: Uitgeverij SWP.

Transparency International. 2005. "Transparency International Corruption Perceptions Index 2005." http://www.transparency.org.

Tremblay, P. 1993. "Searching for Suitable Co-offenders." In *Routine Activity and Rational Choice: Advances in Criminological Theory*, vol. 5, edited by R. V. Clarke and M. Felson. New Brunswick, NJ: Transaction.

United Nations Office on Drugs and Crime. 2005. *World Drug Report, 2005.* Vienna: U.N. Office on Drugs and Crime.

van de Bunt, H. G. 2003. "Police Corruption in the Netherlands." In *Police Corruption: Challenges for Developed Countries, Comparative Issues and Commissions of Inquiry*, edited by M. Amir and S. Einstein. Huntsville, TX: Office of International Criminal Justice.

————. 2004. "Organised Crime Policies in the Netherlands." In *Organised Crime in Europe: Concepts, Patterns, and Control Policies in the European Union and Beyond*, edited by C. Fijnaut and L. Paoli. Dordrecht: Springer.

van de Bunt, H. G., and W. Huisman. In this volume. "Organizational Crime in the Netherlands."

van de Bunt, H. G., and E. R. Kleemans. 2004. "Transnational Organized Crime: New Directions for Empirical Research and Public Policy." In *Punishment, Places, and Perpetrators: Developments in Criminology and Criminal Justice Research*, edited by G. Bruinsma, H. Elffers, and J. de Keijser. Cullompton, U.K.: Willan.

van de Bunt, H. G., and C. van der Schoot, eds. 2003. *Prevention of Organised Crime: A Situational Approach*. Cullompton, U.K.: Willan.

van de Port, M. 2001. *Geliquideerd: Criminele afrekeningen in Nederland* [Contract killings in the Netherlands]. Amsterdam: Meulenhoff.

van der Heijden, T. 2001. *De rol van Nederland in de Europese cocaïnehandel* [The role of the Netherlands in the European cocaine trade]. Driebergen: Korps Landelijke Politiediensten.

————. 2003. *De Nederlandse drugsmarkt: Een poging tot kwantificering van import, export, productie en consumptie van verdovende middelen* [The Dutch drugs market: An attempt to estimate import, export, production, and consumption of drugs]. Zoetermeer: Korps Landelijke Politiediensten.

van der Leun, J. P., and L. Vervoorn. 2004. *Slavernijachtige uitbuiting in Nederland: Een inventariserende literatuurstudie in het kader van de uitbreiding van de strafbaarstelling van mensenhandel* [Modern slavery in the Netherlands: A review of the literature]. The Hague: Boom Juridische Uitgevers.

van der Wielen, L. 2001. "De screenings- en bewakingsaanpak: Een instrument in de criminaliteitsbestrijding." In *De bestuurlijke aanpak van georganiseerde criminaliteit in Amsterdam*, edited by C. Fijnaut. Amsterdam: Directie Openbare Orde en Veiligheid.

van Dijk, E. 2002. *Mensenhandel in Nederland, 1997–2000* [Trafficking in human beings in the Netherlands, 1997–2000). Zoetermeer: Korps Landelijke Politiediensten.

van Dijke, A., and L. Terpstra. 2005. *Loverboys: Feiten en cijfers, een quick scan* [Loverboys: Facts and figures]. Amsterdam: Uitgeverij SWP.

van Duyne, P. C. 1993. "Organized Crime Markets in a Turbulent Europe." *European Journal on Criminal Policy and Research* 1:10–30.

———. 1995. *Het spook en de dreiging van de georganiseerde misdaad* [The phantom and threat of organized crime]. The Hague: Sdu Uitgevers.

———. 2003. "Organizing Cigarette Smuggling and Policy Making, Ending up in Smoke." *Crime, Law, and Social Change* 39(3):285–317.

van Duyne, P. C., R. F. Kouwenberg, and G. Romeijn. 1990. *Misdaadondernemingen: Ondernemende misdadigers in Nederland* [Crime enterprises: Entrepreneurial offenders in the Netherlands]. Deventer: Gouda Quint.

van Duyne, P. C., M. Pheijffer, H. G. Kuijl, A. Th. H. van Dijk, and G. J. C. M. Bakker. 2001. *Financial Investigation of Crime: A Tool of the Integral Law Enforcement Approach*. The Hague: Koninklijke Vermande.

van Ruth, A., and L. Gunther Moor. 1997. *Lekken of verstrekken? De informele informatie-uitwisseling tussen opsporingsinstanties en derden* [Informal exchange of information between investigation departments and third parties]. Ubbergen: Uitgeverij Tandem Felix.

Weerman, F. M. In this volume. "Juvenile Offending."

Zaitch, D. 2002*a*. "From Cali to Rotterdam: Perceptions of Colombian Cocaine Traffickers on the Dutch Port." *Crime, Law, and Social Change* 38(3): 239–66.

———. 2002*b*. *Trafficking Cocaine: Colombian Drug Entrepreneurs in the Netherlands*. The Hague: Kluwer Law International.

Zhang, S., and K. L. Chin. 2002. "Enter the Dragon: Inside Chinese Human Smuggling Organizations." *Criminology* 40(4):737–67.

Zhang, S. X., and M. S. Gaylord. 1996. "Bound for the Golden Mountain: The Social Organization of Chinese Alien Smuggling." *Crime, Law, and Social Change* 25(1):1–16.

Zoomer, O., S. Nieuwkamp, and R. Johannink. 2004. *Economische belangen: Barrières voor preventie en bestrijding van (georganiseerde) criminaliteit?* [Economic interests: Barriers for preventing and combating (organized) crime?]. Dordrecht: Stichting Maatschappij, Veiligheid en Politie Producties.

Henk van de Bunt and Wim Huisman

Organizational Crime in the Netherlands

ABSTRACT

Academic discussions in the Netherlands about the nature and ambiguity of white-collar and corporate crime have dragged on for years. Empirical research started relatively late. Studies that address explanations mostly focus on the criminology of the market or the corporation. Although major incidents of organizational crime stir punitiveness, most corporate law-breaking is dealt with by a strategy of regulatory enforcement based on promoting compliance and stimulating self-regulation. A typical Dutch manifestation of organizational crime is the high level of entanglement of business and public administration.

Dutch society can be rather tolerant toward deviancy and crime. The Netherlands may seem overregulated, but there is also an aversion to "going by the book," not so much out of respect for alternative opinions and conduct, but because of financial considerations. Law enforcement is costly and can lead to counterproductive effects that result in additional expenses. The Dutch policies of condoning vices such as drugs, pornography, prostitution, and gambling, for example, are often based on such cost-benefit calculations rather than on moral considerations.

This essay deals with misconduct by corporations, including commercial, nonprofit, and governmental organizations, and with the regulation of corporate behavior in the Netherlands. For a long time, organizational crimes were handled pragmatically. The authorities, and

Henk van de Bunt is professor of criminology, Erasmus University, Rotterdam. Wim Huisman is an associate professor in the Department of Criminal Law and Criminology, Free University, Amsterdam.

the public, were not always wholly unsympathetic to crimes committed by legitimate organizations, as long as their activities benefited the economy and promoted employment. During the period of postwar reconstruction and ensuing years of growing prosperity (1945–65), there was a blind spot toward crime and deviancy in the business community.

From the 1970s onward, this pragmatic attitude changed. The unbridled growth in employment, income, and government spending of the 1950s and 1960s came to an end. Budget deficits rose substantially as a result of lower tax proceeds and increased public spending. In this economic climate, organizational crime was recognized as a problem. Attention focused on tax evasion and improper use of government funds (e.g., subsidies, social security benefits). Combating fraud directed *against the government* quickly became a political priority, and the use of criminal law in relation to tax fraud was considered effective and appropriate. However, as time went by, interest in tax fraud waned, and other types of organizational crimes, such as environmental crimes (1980s) and crimes against financial integrity (1990s), came within the purview of the criminal courts.

Despite these changes over time, a considerable degree of constancy can be observed in the Dutch approach to regulating corporations. There is intensive government intervention, reflected in detailed regulations, development of policies on subsidies, and willingness to experiment with new, alternative approaches such as self-regulation. However, the government exercises restraint in enforcing the rules: enforcement is mostly aimed at persuasion and reaching consensus. Possibly counterproductive regulatory approaches and implementation of far-reaching sanctions are generally avoided.

Criminological interest in the regulation of corporate behavior was late in coming. In 1984, the Dutch association of criminologists (Nederlandse Vereniging voor Kriminologie) organized a conference on "white-collar crime." The organizers observed that white-collar criminality had gained momentum since 1980. They pointed to sensational cases handled by the police and the public prosecutor that were widely reported in the press. They noted that science should not lag behind (Berghuis, Brants, and Willemse 1984, p. i). These cases concerned well-known Dutch persons. In 1976 it was alleged that the late Prince Bernard, the then-queen's husband, had tried to influence government decision making regarding military contracts.

This was done in exchange for $1.1 million he received from the Lockheed Company. In 1983 a police raid on a respectable Dutch bank, Slavenburg's Bank, attracted wide public attention. The chief executive officer (CEO) and his board members were convicted of approving fraud and facilitating money laundering. At the same time, another notorious scandal emerged. The deputy director of the Dutch Public Pension Fund (at the time one of the largest public pension funds in the world) was prosecuted for taking bribes. Several years later he was acquitted.

What has been achieved in the twenty years since that first conference on white-collar crime? What is now known about organizational crime, how is it defined, and what are the most significant empirical and theoretical findings? What more do we need to know, and what should our research agenda for the future look like? These are the questions we examine in this essay. We discuss relevant Dutch work on organizational crime, ranging from empirical studies to findings of parliamentary committees and regulatory agencies. Existing knowledge about organizational crime and the effects of regulatory enforcement leaves much to be desired. The debate on regulation of corporate behavior is bogged down in ideology, with little reference to results of empirical research. More research needs to be done on the assumptions about corporate behavior that underlie positions of policy makers and regulatory agencies. It is often posited that corporations are amoral, rational calculators, but the available empirical data point in another direction. Dutch criminologists paint a picture of failing and incompetent organizations as the principal lawbreakers.

In this essay, we present an analysis of organizational crime in the Netherlands and of responses to it. Section I describes how Dutch criminology first became aware of organizational crime. Section II sketches the current scale and nature of the problem. Section III discusses different explanations of organizational crime, using empirical data thus far collected. In Section IV we discuss responses to organizational crime in the Netherlands. Section V deals with a typical Dutch phenomenon in the field of organizational crime: the entanglement of corporations and government. In the various sections, gaps in criminological knowledge are highlighted. We conclude with a plea for more focused research and for more interdisciplinary collaboration. In Section VI we sketch a research agenda for the near future.

I. The Awakening of Dutch Criminology

Criminological interest in organizational crime arose in the early 1980s, but conceptual tools and the expertise necessary to investigate it were lacking. It is hardly surprising that in those early days Dutch criminologists relied heavily on the Anglo-Saxon literature and on concepts and issues that had long been part of the literature on white-collar crime. Equally unsurprisingly, the first-generation Dutch publications focused on why organizational crime became a research issue so late. Why was it that the criminal justice system had suddenly "discovered" organizational crime as a problem? Was a criminal approach even desirable?

Behind these questions lay some confusion and even embarrassment. Adopting a criminal law approach to organizational crimes ran counter to prevailing criminological views on administration of criminal justice. Studies conducted by, among others, the criminological research group headed by Riekent Jongman (1981) in Groningen demonstrated that class bias was at work at different stages of the criminal justice system (police patrol, prosecution, and sentencing). Why did a judicial system accustomed to focusing on crimes of the powerless suddenly begin paying attention to influential adversaries?

In those days, left-wing criminologists and criminal lawyers advocated limited use of criminal law (Hulsman 1986). Paradoxically, in the Netherlands, as in the United Kingdom and the United States, the Left has supported a criminal law approach to corporate crime even though it has rejected punitiveness as an approach to conventional crime (Simpson 2002). In its view, the criminal law approach to crime meant dealing with symptoms rather than underlying social causes. The stigma attached to a criminal conviction would affect an individual offender's chances of reintegration into society. The experts agreed on the direction criminal policies should take, namely toward decriminalization and alternative sanctions. The anomalous move against reputable companies rekindled doubts about the appropriateness of decriminalization. Would it not serve the public interest to stigmatize companies that had so far managed to hide their harmful actions behind all kinds of rationalizations?

Many first-generation commentators were intrigued and inspired by these questions and ambivalences. They did not primarily focus on empirical research on organizational crime or on possible explanations, but on the social impact of this type of criminality and on the pros and cons of the criminal justice approach. An example is the article "Zwarte toga's contra witteboorden" ("Black robes against white collars") by Henk van de Bunt and Theo de Roos in the left-wing legal journal *Recht en Kritiek* (1983). They argued in favor of the criminal justice approach to white-collar crimes because of its symbolic value. In their view, this enforcement strategy was best suited to expose the seriousness and the damaging nature of the violation of organizational rules.

Chrisje Brants was one of the first scholars to try to explain the growing interest in fraud and white-collar crime in the Netherlands by using theoretical notions about the role of the media. She pointed to the social construction of fraud and the mechanisms of "convergence" and "amplification of deviance." Once a concept such as "fraud" or "illegal contractors" becomes broad enough to encompass a great number of concrete events (convergence) and gains prominence in the media, reports on the problem increase in number and the problem itself seems to grow in size (amplification of deviance). An important precondition was constant interaction between the media and the police and the Public Prosecutor's Office. These "primary definers" feed the media, and vice versa (Brants and de Roos 1984). Brants later examined the "social construction of fraud" in more detail in her doctoral thesis (Brants and Brants 1991).

With hindsight of twenty years, it is striking that Brants explained the late discovery of a hidden problem in the Netherlands by applying a conceptual framework used by, among others, Stanley Cohen (1977) and Stuart Hall (1978) to explain the overreporting of everyday crime problems (e.g., disorderly and violent behavior, mugging). It is doubtful whether increased criminalization of organizational deviance can be attributed to the role of the media. It seems more likely that societal factors account for the criminal justice system's growing interest in organizational crimes. The criminalization of tax fraud in the 1980s can probably be traced to budget deficits rather than to the construction of a social problem in the media.

Many Dutch authors in the 1980s adopted the term "white-collar crime" from Edwin Sutherland (1949), while at the same time distancing themselves from his definition. They argued that his definition was too vague and would lead to constant arguments over what types of behavior could be classified as white-collar crime (Brants-Langeraar 1981; Berghuis, Brants, and Willemse 1984, p.

3). Chrisje Brants and Kees Brants were critical that Sutherland did not take into account differences between organizations and natural persons (Brants and Brants 1991). Taking up this argument, Henk van de Bunt proposed the term *organisatiecriminaliteit* (organizational crime) to describe "crimes committed individually or in a group by members of a reputable and bona fide organization in the course of their organizational duties" (1992, p. 12). In its turn, this term and its definition drew criticism (van den Berg 2002), but the term "organizational crime" took hold. The battle over the definition of white-collar crime is largely a thing of the past, and most Dutch criminological publications on organizational crime focus on describing and analyzing the phenomenon. It took until the 1990s before criminological research took off. Interest in government intervention in the corporate domain is also increasing within public administration, but there has been little collaboration with criminologists. In this essay we include the results of public administration research into regulation of corporate behavior.

Empirical and theoretical criminological research in the 1990s did not concern itself with debates, definitions, or whether rule violations outside the domain of criminal law should be considered part of criminology's sphere. Another issue, organized crime, was put high on the political and academic agenda. In academic and policy debates, organizational crime and organized crime are seen as separate phenomena. Although this is the dominant view in mainstream criminology, the distinction is contested by some researchers (van Duyne 1996). The emergence of organized crime as a problem led to clarification of the definition of organizational crime. Organizational crime is generally viewed as crime committed by otherwise reputable and bona fide organizations, such as the police, commercial organizations, or legitimate nonprofit organizations. Organized crime, by contrast, is generally defined as crime committed by social groups that have no reason to exist apart from their criminal activities. These groups are primarily involved in the illegal trade; they often make use of the logistical facilities provided by the legitimate world but can be distinguished from legitimate companies (Fijnaut et al. 1998). Of course, this distinction between organizational crime and organized crime does not preclude the existence of grey areas and overlaps.

II. Scale and Nature

It is difficult to estimate the scale of organizational crime. Organizational crime varies from governmental crimes to business crimes. Both police violence and environmental crimes can be counted as organizational crimes. Estimates of the occurrence of these phenomena stem from different sources of varying quality. But even an assessment of the frequency of a specific type of organizational crime is almost impossible.

A. Scale and Sources

The usual problems criminologists have trying to establish the scale of criminality are especially pressing concerning organizational crime. Cases officially recorded by the police and other regulatory agencies do not tell us much about the extent of the problem. The "dark figure" for unknown organizational crime is probably higher than for ordinary crimes because organizational crime is generally less visible (Croall 1993) and harder to recognize. Official records of organizational crime reflect the expertise and the priorities of the official agencies more than in relation to criminal offenses involving victims or witnesses. These agencies usually have more than one way to act on their suspicions. A tax inspector, for instance, can respond to incorrect tax returns by simply "adjusting" the estimated business turnover. In 2003, this happened in 5 percent of all cases, and the Treasury collected an extra 12.984 million euros (Belastingdienst 2003, pp. 26–27). The Treasury is primarily interested in collecting taxes, not in investigating tax fraud. This pragmatic policy unfortunately does not help much in establishing the reliability of the official registration of tax crimes.

Two years ago, the Dutch Auditor General (Algemene Rekenkamer) stated that it was impossible to assess the effectiveness of the fight against fraud in the Netherlands because of shortcomings in the records of tax fraud and social security fraud (Algemene Rekenkamer 2004). Official statistics of other departments suffer from similar problems (Huisman and Niemeijer 1998).

A variety of methods have been used to estimate the numbers. Leo Huberts (1992) polled town clerks and city managers on the scale of corruption, and van der Hoeven et al. (2003) organized expert meetings on the occurrence of organized fraud in the public health sector. The results were not encouraging. Van der Hoeven and his colleagues found that experts were unable to assess even roughly the frequency of organizational crime in the public health sector, which has a budget of 44 billion euros. The experts agreed that the sector offered ample opportunity for organized fraud.

Our assumption that the dark number must be high is strengthened by the outcomes of intensive monitoring operations. Some years ago, for example, the Dutch labor inspectorate revisited 327 employers that had been fined for hiring employees without the necessary documents. Before the fines were actually collected, one-third (34 percent) of the companies were using illegal workers again (Algemene Rekenkamer 2004, p. 51). The numbers indicate the persistent and probably widespread character of organizational crime.

There is another reason for caution when it comes to estimating the scale of organizational crime. It is not altogether clear what the numbers actually mean, or what units should be counted. Are we really interested in the number of rule violations, or in the number of violators? A few years ago, for example, the full extent of antitrust crimes in the Dutch construction industry became clear. Construction firms systematically arranged among themselves how to submit tenders for a contract, who would be awarded the contract, and for what price (Enquêtecommissie Bouwnijverheid 2003). There was never real competition, and these practices had probably been going on for decades, despite a ban in 1986 and the enactment in 1998 of the new Dutch Competition Act (*Mededingingswet*) that expressly affirmed the prohibition of all kinds of setoffs with other companies, related to market sharing, price-fixing, and mutual compensation. Now, does it make any difference in a case like this, whether the law was broken 100,000 times or ten times that number? It is much more important to determine how the conspiracy was organized than to waste energy trying to assess accurately the number of violations.

B. Nature and Sources

To explore qualitative questions on the nature of organizational crime, Dutch criminologists can draw on sources other than official statistics.

First, committees of inquiry have provided an abundance of empirical material. In the past few decades, parliamentary inquiries were conducted into questionable subsidies to the shipbuilding industry (Enquêtecommissie RSV 1984), organized crime (Enquêtecommissie Opsporingsmethoden 1996), and antitrust practices in the construction industry (Enquêtecommissie Bouwnijverheid 2003). The proceedings were held in public, all evidence was given under oath, and reports were published in full. Since these committees of inquiry were authorized to ask for confidential reports and information, their findings provide in-depth views of the modus operandi of rule violators and their strategies of concealment.

Apart from parliamentary inquiries, the past few years have seen reports by committees investigating controversial incidents, such as the disaster in Enschede in which an explosion at a fireworks plant killed twenty-two people (Commissie onderzoek Vuurwerkramp 2001), and the previously mentioned report by the Dutch Auditor General on the effectiveness of the government's policies to combat fraud. These committees do not have the wide investigative powers possessed by parliamentary inquiry committees, but they produce useful information.

Second, police files and court decisions often contain interesting data. In the Netherlands, academic researchers are allowed access to police files on offenders (natural as well as legal persons). An example is the research project "Monitor on Organised Crime," which studies the files of police investigations into major criminal organizations (van de Bunt and Kleemans 2004). The WODC (the Research and Documentation Center of the Dutch Ministry of Justice) decided to apply the same research methods to organizational crime. In 1998, a research project was launched to analyze forty-one cases of organizational crime on the basis of police files (van den Berg 2002). Several other studies, such as Alexis Aronowitz's empirical research into the world of international value-added tax fraud (Aronowitz, Laagland, and Paulides 1996) and a case study of an environmental crime (Eshuis and van den Berg 1996), were also mainly based on extensive study of police files.

Third, a number of criminological researchers have tapped into new and more direct sources of knowledge, including interviews with experts (Huberts 1992; van der Hoeven et al. 2003). Recently, Gudrun van de Walle (2003) conducted interviews with managers, physicians, national health services, and victims in order to find out more about organizational crime in the pharmaceutical industry. Wim Huisman (2001) interviewed company representatives about the observance of regulations relating to the environment and working conditions. This research shows that it is not only possible, but highly informative, to interview persons closely associated with the phenomenon. As long as the questions are straight and to the point, this method seems to produce better results than having the experts assess—or guess—the scale of organizational crime in a particular sector. Much more can be done in this area. For instance, the example of Marshall Clinard (1983), who conducted interviews with recently retired company directors, is definitely worth following in the Netherlands.

What conclusions can be drawn? Marcus Felson has pointed to the existence of fallacies about crime resulting from selective media coverage (Felson 1998). The media have a tendency to concentrate on serious, exceptional crimes, simply because they are more newsworthy than ordinary crimes. A steady dose of reports on the unusual can lead the average citizen to mistake the exception for the rule. This is how fallacies emerge. Felson's warning certainly applies to organizational crime, where the media focus on the big scandals and much less on daily transgressions. Books on corporate crime, such as *Dirty Business* by Maurice Punch (1996), lead one to suspect that criminologists also suffer from this fallacy.

The reality of organizational crime is different. The majority of organizational crime cases handled by the Dutch police and other regulatory agencies involve relatively minor offenses. A formal distinction can be made between crimes and minor offenses (*overtredingen*). It is possible in the Netherlands to prosecute and punish corporations (legal persons) for crimes and minor offenses. The majority of cases handled by the Public Prosecutor and the judge are against natural persons (individuals). However, 6.3 percent of all the decisions made in 2004 were against corporations.

Most organizational crimes do not consist of traditional crimes such as fraud, theft, extortion, and swindles, but in an overwhelming majority violations of traffic law and other regulatory laws. The same applies to the minor offenses recorded by the Public Prosecutor's Office. In 2004, 10.1 percent of all decisions pertained to corporative crimes (complaints against legal persons). Once again the mass of cases are relatively small infractions, such as undue delay in providing a regulatory agency with information or not observing maximum driving hours. In theory, the use of criminal law is often presented as the final remedy, but in practice these minor offenses are frequently punished. The punishment of these routine crimes and minor offenses does not generate publicity, and the sanctions are as routinely imposed as they are accepted. The situation is, of course, fundamentally different when it comes to sensational incidents that could tarnish the reputation of an organization. Stories about such major incidents draw a great deal of attention from the public, but they do not do justice to the empirical reality of organizational crime.

It is often stated in the relevant literature that organizational crimes are technically complicated and difficult to evaluate from a moral perspective (Yeager 1995; Hutter 1997). Supposedly, both perpetrators and enforcers suffer from moral ambivalence regarding the illicit nature of organizational crimes. The two major scandals in recent Dutch history, however—the accounting fraud at Ahold, a multinational supermarket and food services company (Ondernemingskamer 2004), and the antitrust case in the construction industry (Enquêtecommissie Bouwnijverheid 2003)—were fairly straightforward, both factually and morally. The CEO of Ahold overstated sales and earnings in order to boost the share price. Ahold consolidated into its financial statements 100 percent of the sales and earnings of several joint ventures that it did not completely control. Ahold stated to the outside world that it had control over these companies, but side letters, which were kept from the public, made it clear that the company did not have the control that would allow for a consolidation.

The antitrust case provides a detailed description of how construction firms knew about each other's interest in a particular public tender, how they met, and how they decided which would get the contract, and at what price. This company then divided a certain amount of money among the other firms participating in the tender. It was all very simple, leaving the intriguing question of how hundreds of construction firms managed to operate in this way for such a long time without the relevant authorities finding out (Enquêtecommissie Bouwnijverheid 2003).

On the basis of her analysis of forty-one cases, Ellen van den Berg (2002) concluded that the offenses committed were "relatively simple." The perpetrators may have used sophisticated tricks, but they were transparent to anyone slightly familiar with the subject matter. This is not, of course, to say that organizational crimes are committed in broad daylight. After all, Ahold's side letters were not available to the public. The argument is that these crimes are not necessarily technically complicated or hard to evaluate from a moral point of view. Organizational crime usually boils down to perpetrators who benefit from fraud at the expense of consumers, the Treasury, society, public health, the environment, or competitors. There is not much room for moral ambiguity.

The immorality or punishability of some types of corporate offenses can be disputed. The perpetrators of the construction industry fraud often came up with rationalizations and justifications. The most frequent justification was that fierce competition would endanger the stability of the market and threaten the survival of large construction companies (van den Heuvel 2004, p. 130). Van den Berg also observed that many perpetrators' ideas about their culpability differed vastly from the views held by those enforcing the law (van den Berg 2002, pp. 74 et seq.).

III. Explanations

Dutch studies of organizational crime are highly influenced by American, British, and Australian predecessors. These Anglo-Saxon studies pointed out the significance of the fact that the crimes are committed in the context of an organization. Many criminologists argue that corporate crime should be studied in the light of organizational sciences. After all, findings on "normal" organizational behavior could also apply to deviant corporate behavior. "Corporate crime is *organizational* crime, and explaining it requires an *organizational* level of analysis" (Kramer 1982, p. 79). These organizational studies show how organizational characteristics or shortcomings lie at the root of corporate crime. Other studies show how the characteristics of the branch or market, or even unclear regulations and inadequate enforcement, can create opportunities for corporate crime.

Neal Shover and Chris Bryant (1993) argue that explanations for organizational crime can be found on several aggregate levels: the micro level of the individual employee or manager, the meso level of the organization, and the macro level of the branch of industry. A relevant question on the macro level is whether differences between branches or markets can explain differences in the occurrence of organizational crime. Several studies were conducted in the Netherlands into criminogenic opportunity structures in different branches and economic sectors. Given these criminogenic characteristics, the question arises whether differences between organizations can explain differences in behavior on the meso level. So far, a small number of Dutch studies have focused on criminogenic traits of organizations. At the micro level, are personal traits of members of an organization relevant to the occurrence or absence of organizational crime?

A. Branches of Industry

Criminality is often viewed as the result of supply and demand in a criminal market. Economic sectors are examined for weaknesses and vulnerability to crime. In a particular market or branch, certain factors may be present that make rule violation attractive or facilitate such behavior. In a criminogenic market or branch, there is ample opportunity to violate the rules, the risk of getting caught is minimal, and there is little need for justification (Faber 1998, p. 243).

Various sectors of the Dutch economy have been examined in this way, for instance by the parliamentary inquiry committee on organized crime (Bruinsma and Bovenkerk 1996). Several studies have shown the presence of factors facilitating environmental crime within the waste disposal industry (van Vugt and Boet 1994; van den Berg 1995; Bruinsma 1996b; van den Anker and Hoogenboom 1997; Huisman 2001). Payment is made as soon as the waste is handed over to the disposal firms, motivating them to process the waste as cheaply as possible. The rules relating to waste products are complex, and the market is badly regulated. Partly as a consequence, enforcement of the regulations is poor. Some firms hold monopoly positions; others control several, or all, links in the disposal chain. Effective monitoring of the industry is hard to achieve, and illegal practices are easily covered up. This combination of factors offers ample opportunity to commit violations with impunity.

The car trade is another industry investigated within the framework of the parliamentary inquiry "Investigating Methods." Analogous to the findings by Needleman and Needleman (1979), Gerben Bruinsma (1996c) concluded that the Dutch car trade is characterized by fierce competition between garages and by pressure on dealers and garages from the manufacturers to achieve sales targets. To sell enough new cars, many dealers are forced to accept losses, which must somehow be compensated. The result is that customers are overcharged for repairs, service, and used cars.

The Dutch construction industry has been investigated more than once. In the 1980s, illegal contracting sparked an investigation. The sector was investigated a second time within the framework of the parliamentary inquiry "Investigating Methods" (Bruinsma 1996d). As part of the parliamentary inquiry Bouwnijverheid, van den Heuvel (2003) prepared a criminological analysis of the sector. Illegal pricing practices were widespread. Almost every construction firm participated. There was institutional collusion between government institutions and the industry, as became apparent from favors secretly granted to certain firms and the condoning of guaranteed minimum prices. Grat van den Heuvel (2004) mentions a certain "branch culture" in which participants have a tendency to bend the authorities to their will and regarded themselves as above the law.

As we discuss in Section IV, the integrity of the financial sector and the stock market came into question as the result of a number of scandals and criminal investigations. Reputable stockbrokers and financial institutions were suspected of tax fraud, insider trading, money laundering, and corruption. Studies by Bob Hoogenboom (Hoogenboom, Mul, and Wielinga 1995; Hoogenboom 1996) point to strong interdependence between investors and brokers, the absence of formal control mechanisms and procedures (until recently), and a culture of greed and mutual trust guaranteed to cover up misconduct.

Other markets in which criminogenic risk factors are present include road transport (Projectgroep Wegtransport en Criminaliteit 1996) and the shipping fuel market (Inspectie Milieuhygiëne 1997, p. 333). There is the same pattern of poor regulation, unclear definitions, untransparent markets, poor enforcement, and high disposal costs of specific products. Faber (1997) demonstrated that marine insurance fraud (scuttling, the deliberate sinking of a vessel in order to collect the insurance) is made possible by criminogenic opportunity structures in the Dutch marine insurance market. Opportunities arise because this is largely an informal market, based on mutual trust, and because of the structure of the market, which is dominated by a limited number of agents and brokers and in which principals and underwriters never meet in person.

All these studies document recurring criminogenic characteristics. First, there is poor regulation and poor enforcement. In some branches of industry there is a definite blurring of moral standards. The waste disposal industry is a good example. In the early years there was a lot of easy money to be made, and the relevant environmental regulations were fragmented, changed rapidly, and were rarely enforced. Insiders describe this period as a "Wild West situation." It attracted a certain type of entrepreneur who did not much care for rules and regulations (Huisman 2001).

Second, the prevailing standards within the sector, for instance, relating to competition, safety, or the environment, may deviate from the formal standards. On the basis of the investigations of the parliamentary inquiry committee Bouwnijverheid, Hertogh (2005) described the emergence within the Dutch construction industry of a culture that did not disapprove of violations of rules competition. Informal rules on the private distribution of contracts were considered more important than formal rules against these practices. These issues point to the importance of the government's role in creating criminogenic situations.

Third, criminogenic characteristics can be connected with the structure of the market and relations between different parties. Mutual interdependence can upset a system of checks and balances. Certain markets are dominated by a small number of large players. Major companies with a significant market share have more to lose and are less inclined to violate the rules than marginal companies about to go under. Small or marginal firms in road transport and waste disposal are usually the first to resort to illegal means (Bovenkerk and Lempens 1996; Bruinsma 1996a).

B. Criminogenic Organizations

A macro approach, however, could not explain why—given a certain opportunity structure—some corporations take advantage of these opportunities and others do not. The macro perspective does not explain differences in compliance between corporations in the same branch of industry. To understand these differences, we need to examine organizational characteristics and the immediate environment. In several Anglo-Saxon studies, general organizational characteristics such as organizational strategy, organizational structure, and organizational culture have been related to organizational crime (Clinard and Yeager 1980; Box 1983; Vaughan 1983; Passas 1990; Simpson 1993; Cohen 1995; Slapper and Tombs 1999). Specific organizational characteristics that concern regulatory compliance are business ethics and environmental and safety management.

Often corporations are viewed as amoral, rational actors. However, most corporations comply with regulations, although violation would be more profitable. This might indicate that most corporations do not calculate costs and benefits on purely financial grounds, but also take account of moral considerations (Kagan and Scholz 1984; Paternoster and Simpson 1993, 1996; Simpson, Piquero, and Paternoster 2002). Several Dutch studies stress the moral side of corporate actors and seek explanations in internal norms and values (Huisman 2001), neutralizations (van den Berg 2002; van den Heuvel 2003), and social responsiveness (van de Bunt 1992).

The only Dutch study devoted solely to the explanation of corporate (non)compliance is the dissertation by Wim Huisman (2001). Huisman reports on an empirical study of the background factors of differences in compliance with environmental and safety and health regulations by corporations in two branches of industry. He conducted case studies of seven companies with excellent compliance records and seven that structurally violated regulations. The "good" and the "bad" companies differed on several points.

Companies with a low level of compliance focused on maximizing profits in the short term or trying to minimize costs because of losses. Several companies demonstrated a certain level of incompetence to comply with regulations because they lacked the knowledge and skills to do so. Finally, these companies were characterized by a culture of noncompliance, which attached little value to regulatory compliance and was facile in its ability to justify violations.

By contrast, the companies with high levels of compliance chose to comply because they recognized the long-term costs of noncompliance and because they considered it to be a social responsibility. They also invested in the knowledge and skills required for regulatory compliance, mostly by maintaining an environmental and safety management system. These companies had a culture of compliance whose norms and values uphold those established by regulation and support occupational safety and care for the environment.

Huisman shows the complex interaction between organizational and environmental characteristics. As administrative, business, and social environments differ from one corporation to the next, differences in compliance between corporations can be partly attributed to environmental conditions. There are no simple explanations for why a corporation may or may not comply with a particular regulation. "Seemingly obvious motives for corporate lawbreaking, such as the desire for profits or disagreement with regulations, cannot be disentangled from the context in which these motives evolve. Regulatory compliance is the result of a complex of conditions that reinforce or counteract each other, conditions which—depending on the circumstances—create motives or opportunities for compliance or violation" (Huisman 2001, p. 580).

Huisman's study shows that safety concerns, care for the environment, and compliance with the law weigh heavily in the decision-making processes of corporations with good compliance performances. These companies are inspired not only by financial motives (the benefits of regulatory compliance in the long term are estimated to be higher than the quick benefits of rule violation), but also by moral considerations. There is a high degree of norm internalization: the value of the environment and the importance of safe working conditions are recognized both in the boardroom and on the shop floor.

On the basis of her analysis of forty-one cases of organizational crime, Ellen van den Berg (2002) puts profit into perspective as the main motive for organizational crime. When financial motives are involved, a quick profit is rarely the goal. More often, violations are committed to avoid bankruptcy, to obtain a dominant market position, or to strengthen the company's market position. One of van den Berg's findings is that organizational criminality can be an emotional act, an observation that runs counter to conventional ideas about calculating perpetrators. In van den Berg's cases, managers are sometimes motivated by feelings of resistance (anger, frustration) or feelings of invulnerability (hubris). Neutralization plays an important role. Van den Berg came across every classical type of neutralization during her research: denial of the seriousness of the matter, appeal to a higher loyalty, and denial of the criminal nature and intent of the offenses.

Neutralizing culpability serves as a way to deny responsibility or shift the blame onto others. The everyday nature or the necessity of the offenses is stressed, and the victim's actions, the practices of law enforcement agencies, or the law itself is called into question. In the construction fraud case, a number of contractors defended their behavior by saying that they were interested only in strengthening the company's position and in boosting the national economy. The illegal funds were there to fall back on in hard times. Because no one had lined his or her own pockets and there were no physical victims, several offenders openly wondered whether secret price-fixing and rigging bids for contracts should be classified as offenses. According to Grat van den Heuvel (2004), these arguments are strongly reminiscent of what

Gilbert Geis (1967) observed in his studies of price-fixing for heavy electrical equipment in the United States forty years ago.

Henk van de Bunt (1992) takes the inadequate social responsiveness of organizations as a starting point to explain organizational crime. Social responsiveness is a particular aspect of organizational culture, relating to an organization's ability to take into account the feelings and expectations of the external environment. From this perspective, organizational criminality is the result of a lack of social responsiveness, a communication breakdown between an organization and its environment. A socially responsive organization will try to anticipate the effect of its actions on the outside world and is therefore better able to calculate the risks and costs involved in possible rule violations than "autistic" organizations that are blind to the outside world and therefore more liable to commit grave errors.

Another significant factor emerging from the research is the level of competence of a company. Huisman observed a high level of norm internalization and professionalism within the companies that demonstrated good compliance performance. Sufficiently qualified personnel, state-of-the-art equipment, and maintenance of environmental and safety management systems enabled these companies to operate by the rules. Conversely, negligence and ignorance were typical of companies that failed to comply with regulations. Huisman describes three possible scenarios: companies that are unaware of the regulations, companies that know the regulations but do not know how to comply, and companies that know the regulations and know how to comply but lack the means to do so. In the cases described by Ellen van den Berg (2002), overdue maintenance, technical failure, miscommunication, and blocked channels of communication emerged as possible causes of organizational criminality.

While most Dutch legal academics still portray organizations as economic actors, acting from the *need of greed* (de Lange 1992; Blomberg and Michiels 1997; Faure and Visser 2004, p. 68), most criminologists now paint a picture of failing, unresponsive organizations as the ones violating the rules. Dutch research findings do not fit the classical image of a rational organization driven by purely economic motives.

C. Managers and Employees

Organizational crimes are committed by individuals, albeit on behalf of organizations. Little is known about the personal characteristics of persons who commit organizational crimes. In the United States, research has been conducted on the personal characteristics of white-collar criminals, but not within the setting of an organization (Hagan and Kay 1990; Weisburd, Chayet, and Waring 1990; Weisburd et al. 1991; Benson 2001). As yet, similar research from the Netherlands is not available, with the possible exception of the work of van den Berg (2002), who mentioned some characteristics of the perpetrators in the criminal files she studied. They were mainly middle-aged men in executive positions, and though one-third of the forty-one suspects in these cases had a criminal record, none saw themselves as criminals.

Insofar as individual perpetrators are depicted in the Dutch studies, two types of offenders can be discerned. First, there are employees carrying out the orders of their superiors. Their involvement in organizational criminality can be explained by loyalty or pressure. Possible motives to break the law for the benefit of their employer include personal ambition, a tendency to identify with the goals of the organization, or fear of negative consequences if they refuse to follow an instruction. When practices have become normal procedure within an organization, employees may be unaware that they are breaking the law (Huisman and Niemeijer 1999). Roland Eshuis and Ellen van den Berg (1996, p. 61) described how employees of Tanker Cleaning Rotterdam (TCR) were conditioned by various mechanisms of transference and internalization to participate in environmental crimes. Bruinsma (1996a) showed how employee loyalty in the waste disposal sector was exacted through relatively high wages, extra bonuses, and intimidation. People were hired who would otherwise have had difficulty finding jobs, because of a low level of education or a police record.

Second, there are the executives. Research into the ethical dilemmas facing managers, such as that conducted by Clinard (1983), has not yet been duplicated in the Netherlands. To the extent that the views and personal characteristics of individual managers are discussed, the emphasis is on their ambivalent attitudes toward rule compliance (Huisman 2001; van den Berg 2002). From the behavior of the managers in the cases she studied, van den Berg drew tentative conclusions about psychological characteristics contributing to organizational criminality, such as a lack of interest in problems within the organization.

One question is whether the personality of the offender is important. The perpetrators of organizational crimes strongly deny its relevance.

They are joined by many academic researchers who emphasize that the behavior of individual offenders is largely dictated by the organizational context within which they operate. Most cases of organizational crime cannot be explained by the "perverse personalities of their perpetrators" (Braithwaite 1984, p. 2). In this view, employees and managers are actors taking on a role, under conditions created by the organization. The bonds between the employee and the organization are crucial. The more a person feels involved in the organization and identifies with its interests, the lower the threshold to breaking the law on behalf of the organization. The motives and rationales of the individual are therefore difficult to separate from the organizational context. Contemporary research into the causes of organizational crime focuses mainly on the conditioning effects of the organization. This type of research "encourages us to look not so much at 'bad' people but more at how the condition of work shapes moral consciousness and how ordinary people are induced in an organizational setting to violate laws and rules" (Punch 1996, p. 239).

D. Political Economy

These three levels of analysis may not provide a complete explanation of organizational crime. A fourth level is the political economy as a whole. Changes in the national political economy may also shape patterns of organizational lawbreaking. Dutch criminology has hardly addressed this level.

Often a historical explanation is given for Dutch governmental policies regarding business: for centuries the inhabitants of the Netherlands ("the Low Countries") had to work together to empolder land and maintain dikes in order to keep the water out, otherwise all would drown. This need for cooperation is commonly said to have shaped Dutch civil society. Issues are resolved by negotiation and settlement rather than by conflict. In the 1990s, this Dutch form of public governance was labeled the "polder model" (Delsen 2000). It represented organized cooperation among the Dutch government, employers, and labor unions, aimed at reaching agreements rather than allowing conflict (Léonard 2005). The model gained official status in the 1992 report of the Dutch Social Economic Council "Convergentie en overlegeconomie" ("The economy of convergence and consultation") (Sociaal Economische Raad 1992).

For years this model of public governance was praised, including by the former American president Bill Clinton. But did it have negative side effects? What might be the criminogenic effects of the polder model? Van den Heuvel argues that close relations between Dutch government and Dutch business can easily lead to collusion (van den Heuvel 1998). That could partly be an explanation for malpractice in the construction industry (van den Heuvel 2003). Another possible example: the Dutch government showed a more lenient reaction to accounting fraud cases than the United States did. In the United States, these cases resulted in very strict legislation under the Sarbanes-Oxley Act, whereas the Dutch authorities responded by asking a private commission of captains of industry to write a code of conduct for Dutch corporations (Commisie Tabaksblat 2003). Subsequently, a law was enacted that does not require corporations to follow it, but only that they explicitly indicate in their annual reports when they do not.

IV. Responses to Organizational Crime

This section focuses on formal reactions to organizational crime in the Netherlands. First, the regulation of corporations in the past three decades is considered. Second, law enforcement practices are considered. A connecting thread may be discerned over three decades. Little criminal law enforcement and a steadily increasing application of administrative sanctions can be said to have taken place. As a result of catastrophes and scandals, calls are occasionally made for more frequent checks and stronger criminal consequences for breaching the rules. But these incidents do not appear to have lasting effects. Finally, we discuss problems that occur in practice and the results of enforcement.

A. Regulating Business

The history of corporate regulation is characterized by a series of oppositions. An unmistakable strengthening and expansion of rules and sanctions are evident regarding the behavior of corporations. However, a tendency to dispense with rules may also be perceived, along with a strategy of inducing companies to comply with the norms not as a result of command-and-control but through consultation and negotiation.

1. *Criminal Law.*   Since 1976, corporate criminal liability has been part of the Netherlands Criminal Code. Section 51 provides that all

offenses may be committed by both natural and legal persons.[1] Corporate criminal liability had existed since 1950 in the Economic Offenses Act. If an act is committed by a corporation, a sanction may be imposed on the corporation or on those natural persons who committed the offense or who instructed others to do so. Despite the legislation, the Supreme Court indicated that a corporation can be only an indirect offender. Liability must be traced back to natural persons who act on behalf of the corporation. Criminal proceedings can also be taken against the management of the organization for organizational crimes when managers were aware that criminal offenses had taken place and declined to take the opportunity to put a stop to them. In practice, this means that criminal liability of managers is limited if offenses occur in the organization outside their sight and knowledge (de Doelder and Tiedemann 1996).

Corporations may in principle be liable for any criminal offense in the criminal code. It is, for example, possible to institute proceedings against corporations for manslaughter when employees are killed because of negligence. Other provisions of the criminal code, such as fraud, bribery, fiddling the books, and false bankruptcy, are also applicable to organizational behavior. Ordinary criminal sanctions (with the exception of a prison sentence) may be imposed.

The criminal code contains no crimes that can be committed only by legal persons such as corporations. In addition, shortly after World War II, the Economic Offenses Act (WED) was enacted, specifically designed for regulating business in many areas, such as occupational safety, agriculture, financial transactions, and market regulation (competition). These laws belong to the period of the postwar reconstruction, in which public administration had a strong influence on the organization of social-economic relations in society in the Netherlands. Nearly all these regulatory laws contained criminal provisions. Sometimes the laws contemplated penal sanctions, in most cases because they had been classified under the WED. The WED, a catchall, describes a large number of regulatory acts in Section 1 and provides that intentional violations are crimes. The punishments authorized are far from slight. For instance, the WED authorizes shutting down an en-

---

[1] A number of years ago, the Supreme Court made an exception for public service organizations that fulfill an exclusive public service, such as the fire brigade and the police. These organizations cannot have criminal proceedings brought against them. Individual members of these organizations may be liable for the crimes they commit.

terprise, maximum prison sentences from six months to six years, and fines up to 0.5 million euros.

2. *Administrative Law.* Compliance with regulatory laws may also be enforced with administrative sanctions. Government and its regulatory agencies can react to violations. These administrative sanctions are radical in nature. A corporation's license may be withdrawn or the changed situation (environmental damage, demolition) that resulted from the violation may have to be restored to the former situation at the corporation's own costs.

For a long time, it was not possible for public administrators to impose financial sanctions. This meant a stark choice between issuing a series of warnings, one after another, and applying heavy administrative sanctions with far-reaching consequences. Because the development of a system of administrative enforcement lagged behind, the strategy used to enforce these regulatory laws was primarily criminal in character. As we show below, the prosecution of these offenses has traditionally received little priority.

Since the 1950s, a marked criminalization of corporate behavior can therefore be said to have taken place. Not only was criminal liability introduced for corporations, but regulatory laws also provided penal sanctions. The proposition advanced by critical criminologists that the criminal law is a faithful reflection of power relations in society and, in particular, that only the behavior of citizens from lower social classes is liable to punishment is—in the Netherlands—completely incorrect. The opposite is true: many more activities subject the behavior of corporations to punishment (van de Bunt 1992, p.12).[2]

Only in the last two decades has the application of administrative sanctions been extended. New administrative sanctions—the "penalty payment" and the "administrative fine"—were introduced. The penalty payment requires a company to pay a certain price to the regulator when it does not take the desired action within a certain period, such as taking safety measures or undoing environmental damages. The penalty payment is authorized in nearly sixty laws (concerning the regulation of corporate behavior in sectors such as food, environmental protection, and tax). The penalty payment system enables the regulator

[2] This is not to deny that there are major differences in the nature and degree of the maintenance of law and order with regard to the behavior of the higher and lower social classes.

to add force to its warnings. Should the violation of rules continue despite warnings, the violator will be required to pay.

The introduction of the administrative fine gives regulators the capacity to punish violations of regulatory laws with fines. In contrast to the criminal fine, which is imposed by a judge, the public administration may impose its own sanctions. The person receiving an administrative fine may appeal to an administrative judge, who will evaluate the decision. From the perspective of enforcers, administrative sanctioning is more efficient than criminal sanctions (Hartmann and Rogier 2004).

Other administrative sanctions have been introduced such as a "naming and shaming" sanction in the Environmental Care Act. The names of companies that violate environmental legislation by polluting the environment may be publicly exposed.

The introduction of these new administrative sanctions means that the credibility of administrative enforcement of regulatory laws has significantly increased. At the same time, the new sanctions are punitive. Because of this, the distinction between administrative and penal enforcement of laws has become blurred.[3] Administrative law enforcement is traditionally seen as aimed primarily at achieving *compliance* with the law, whereas criminal sanctions are based on the idea of *deterrence* (Reiss and Tonry 1993). Because of the expansion of punitive administrative sanctions, such a distinction has little meaning.[4]

Administrative enforcement has been strengthened in other ways. In some recent acts containing prohibitive rules, violations are threatened exclusively with administrative sanctions. An illustration is the new Competition Act of 1998, which prohibits, among other things, price-fixing. The predecessor act authorized penal sanctions and was far less explicit and strict than the current law. Under the new law, stiff fines for price-fixing have been imposed on hundreds of construction com-

---

[3] This was even further reinforced because new sanctions were introduced into the criminal code that were consensual in character. The most important example is the "transaction," an agreement between the suspect and public prosecutor, in which the prosecutor promises not to continue with proceedings if the suspect agrees to pay a certain sum or keeps to some other conditions.

[4] The European Court of Human Rights treats the administrative fine as the equivalent of a criminal charge. These sanctions fall under the scope of Section 6 of the European Convention on Human Rights. This means that administrative and penal sanctions cannot be simultaneously imposed for the same offense because they are both regarded as punitive.

panies. The amount of money involved is high: 700 million euros. Only ten perpetrators were brought to the criminal court.

3. *Deregulation and Self-Regulation.* Another relevant development is a "battle" between regulation and deregulation. There are pressures toward far-reaching regulation of corporate behavior, for example, under the influence of the European Union. As a consequence of European directives and regulation, new areas were regulated and existing regulations were tightened. Economic competition offers an example. Existing national regulations not in line with much stricter European regulations were tightened: for example, the new Competition Act with its stricter regulations regarding economic competition (Mok 2004). Recommendations of the Financial Action Task Force (FATF)—via a European directive—led to obligations for financial service providers in the fight against money laundering.[5] Obligations regarding the reduction of the discharge of dangerous materials into the atmosphere, stemming from the Kyoto agreement, have led the Dutch business world to introduce a system of marketable emission rights.

However, since the 1980s, a strong countercurrent of "deregulation" and self-regulation has flowed. Politicians and policy makers agreed that in many areas there were too many regulations and that regulations were unclear, were subject to different interpretations, and contained contradictions (Bovens 1990; Eijlander, Gilhuis, and Peters 1993). These shortcomings could result in low levels of compliance and lack of enforcement. Deregulation was considered a solution to compliance problems. The government has acted on the idea. It eliminated 190 regulations, particularly in the area of financial reports and labor conditions. In populist language, there is talk of a "reduction of irritating and contradictory regulation" (Eerste Kamer 2004–5, p. 2).

An important part of the antiregulation movement is discovery of the meaning of self-regulation. Garland (1996) argues that governments confronted with their impotence in solving problems can go in two directions: *denial*, deny their impotence and suggest that the problems can be solved by taking hard measures; or *adaptation*, adapt to the existing situation and involve others in solving the problems. Self-

[5] An interesting difference is that the FATF and the European directives require an obligation to report *suspected* transactions, whereas the Netherlands legislation poses the much wider obligation to give notification of *unusual* transactions, which entails considerable administrative obligations for financial service providers (Mitsilegas 2003; van der Schoot 2006).

regulation by policy makers and enforcers can be interpreted as a form of adaptation.

This "adaptation" was first expressed in 1988 by a committee of academics in an influential report on regulation. The committee suggested a retreat from repressive styles of regulation and pleaded for greater confidence in the self-regulating capacities of society. The report received much positive response, and the ideas were adopted in government policies. This ideology was further expressed by the Ministry of Justice in the policy paper *Zicht op wetgeving* ("View on legislation," 1992): "In the preparation of legislation, the aim is to find the right balance between the responsibility of the government and of society. Forms of government-controlled self-regulation will be used whenever possible."

To stimulate self-regulation, several regulatory instruments were developed. These instruments are a clear example of promoting responsibility, one of Garland's strategies of adaptation. Instead of detailed command-and-control regulation, organizations must comply with "open" norms such as "duty of care provisions."[6] Another popular instrument is the covenant. A covenant is a "gentleman's agreement" between a government agency and a sector or branch of industry to attain common goals. The contents of a covenant can include that the sector promises to fulfill certain agreements (e.g., concerning environmentally friendly packaging material). The benefit for the government is that if the effort is successful, more may be achieved than by enforced regulation. The benefit for corporations is that they avoid inconvenient regulation.

In the domains of environmental care and occupational safety and health, new regulation was directly connected to self-regulation. A 1999 policy plan by the Ministry of Environmental Affairs contemplated issuing companies a license "on central issues" instead of a traditional permit with many detailed regulations. In its "environmental management system," the license holder should explain how general regulations are observed (Ministerie van VROM 1999).

The strategy of self-regulation works on the assumption that corporations are socially responsible. Self-regulation sits well with current international trends in the business world in which there is much talk

---

[6] A duty of care provision is a relatively general formulated duty (of care) that represents a certain responsibility of the person or organization to whom the norm refers and that can be enforced through administrative or criminal law (Visser 2001).

about social responsiveness and corporate ethics. These trends characterize Dutch business (Kaptein 1998). Concerns for the social and environmental impact of corporate behavior and about the public image of good corporate citizenship have encouraged the development of corporate governance and integrity management.

Other developments in corporate governance incorporating self-regulatory ideas are striking. A committee of representatives from the business world was given the assignment of developing a code of behavior for corporate governance (Commissie Tabaksblat 2003). The cabinet decided to include in the act an obligation that businesses quoted on the stock exchange that do not comply with the corporate governance code must explicitly mention this in their annual reports.

In the area of regulating business there are thus both an expansion of regulation and sanctions and a strong undercurrent of deregulation, including self-regulation. Both styles of regulation reinforce each other. It is not a zero-sum game, but an addition, which leads to an increase in social control (van Stokkom 2004, p. 43).

B. Enforcement in Practice

Relationships between government and business in the Netherlands have never been based on hostility. Neither are they characterized by a sharp conflict of interests. Enforcement in practice has never really been a matter of command-and-control regulation, although the many regulatory laws with penal sanctions and punitive administrative sanctions might seem to suggest otherwise. Empirical research into twenty-eight regulatory agencies showed that almost all used a cooperative enforcement style. Most of the agencies used only administrative sanctions. Only six were also geared toward criminal prosecution (Algemene Rekenkamer 1989).

A pioneering study by Marius Aalders (1984) showed that inspectors from an environmental agency generally used a cooperative enforcement strategy. This strategy relied mainly on consultation and negotiation rather than on formal legal actions. Persuasion was seen as more effective to generate compliance than forced regulation. Aalders observed the drawbacks of this friendly manner of enforcement. Reluctant companies appeared capable of violating the law over the long term, without this resulting in the government taking decisive measures. Once the official measures of administrative sanctions were adhered to, administrators usually hesitated to take more decisive action because of their consequences. Even judicial decisions against companies some-times were not enforced.

What is known about the law in action? First we discuss criminal law enforcement, then administrative law enforcement.

1. *Criminal Law in Action.* Violations of regulatory acts and the criminal code by corporations are seldom discovered and acted on by the police. The regulatory agencies are authorized to conduct inves-tigations in their specific areas. In the main, it is therefore these ser-vices that refer cases to the public prosecutor. The number of criminal sanctions imposed on corporations is low.

In recent decades, however, a number of large cases have been tack-led by the Public Prosecutor's Office and have had a great impact on public opinion and governmental policy. These included the cases of environmental pollution by the corporations Uniser and TCR, in which the managers of these waste-processing companies were con-victed for illegal disposal of chemical waste. Other major cases involved fraud, such as the money-laundering schemes of Slavenburg's Bank in the 1980s, securities fraud at the Amsterdam Securities Exchange, and insider trading by well-known captains of industry in the 1990s and, more recently, the accounting fraud by Ahold and widespread price-fixing in the construction industry. The role of criminal prosecution is limited, but its strong symbolism offers considerable influence. (These cases are discussed later in this subsection and in Sec. V.)

Research into the administration of criminal justice concerning or-ganizational crime has been undertaken by, among others, Henk van de Bunt and Hans Peek (1987) and by Hans Nelen and Vincent Sabee (1998). These projects revealed that criminal justice agencies found it difficult to cope with complex organizational crime. The heavier bur-den of proof required by criminal law and unclear rules have taken their toll. In a recent analysis of efforts to combat fraud, the Dutch auditor general confirmed that an insufficient level of investigation and prosecution still exists (Tweede Kamer 2004–5).

Despite these difficulties, the police and the Public Prosecutor's Of-fice have shown interest in containing organizational crime since the early 1970s. In the past three decades, there even have been "flare-ups" of certain forms of organizational crime.

In the 1970s, the problem of tax fraud attracted interest from the criminal justice system. For the first time since World War II, the public began to distrust and criticize the business world and the government. In this climate, organizational crime was recognized as "crime." The focus was on subcontractors in the construction industry. Some of them recruited workers without bothering with contracts or taxes. In one major case in 1972 (the Papa Blanca case), four illegal contractors deprived the state of 70 million euros over a period of ten years. They were sentenced to long prison terms (Sleurink 1982).

Partly as a result of this scandal, tax fraud received a great deal of attention. Combating fraud directed specifically against the government became a political priority, and criminal law was considered an effective instrument in relation to tax fraud. In 1983, the government stated that effective measures to combat fraud were among the most important objectives of government policy.

In the same year, the Netherlands Fiscal Intelligence and Investigation Agency (FIOD) and the Public Prosecutor's Office took the unusual step of raiding the head office of the Slavenburg Bank. This reputable financial institution was suspected of assisting the transfer of "black-market money" to foreign bank accounts. The prosecutor's office set its sights high and charged the chairman of the board and other board members with criminal offenses committed by subordinates employed in local branches. They were eventually acquitted. Only the most junior manager in the hierarchy, who was relatively close to the actual events, was convicted (Brants 1994).

After these spectacular cases, the number of cases sent by the FIOD to the Public Prosecutor's Office has remained at a constant, relatively low level. It concerns about 600 criminal cases annually, which amount to 0.2 percent of the cases sent by police and regulatory agencies to the Public Prosecutor.[7] The great majority of violations of tax law are handled using administrative sanctions.

From the late 1970s onward, other forms of organizational crime became targets for criminal prosecution. Several incidents of environmental criminality put this type of organizational crime high on the political agenda. The most notorious was the Uniser affair. Uniser was a company that pretended to process chemical waste but dumped the waste in the waterways. The case led to criminal charges, and in 1981 the five company directors were sentenced to prison terms of between seven and thirty months (Brants and de Roos 1984, pp. 216 et seq.). A number of years later this case was surpassed as far as seriousness

---

[7] It is not clear what the ratio is between natural and legal persons; an unknown number of the 600 cases are not organizational crimes, but tax fraud committed by individuals.

was concerned by the TCR case. The perpetrators in the notorious TCR case, discussed in the next section, received prisons terms varying from one to six years.

Until the 1990s, the enforcement of environmental laws by criminal sanctions was considered complementary to administrative regulation (National Environmental Plan [Tweede Kamer 1993–94, p. 191]). The Public Prosecutor's Office (1994) assumed an autonomous role for the enforcement of environmental law. In its view, the use of criminal law was no longer limited to more serious environmental crimes. Despite these intentions, the number of criminal law proceedings has remained small. In 2003, for example, the Public Prosecutor's Office prosecuted only a small number of organizational crimes: 14,615 cases of organizational crimes were recorded; only a small number (955) were brought before the criminal court (Eggen and van der Heide 2005).

In the 1990s, organized crime and the integrity of financial markets were the subjects of great attention. In particular, combating money laundering led to concerns about the integrity of financial markets. In 1995, a new law regulating the securities market was enacted. A special authority was also created to monitor compliance. The activities of this authority, combined with a zealous fraud prosecutor, led to a number of cases of insider trading in which well-known captains of industry were suspected. The climax was a raid on the Amsterdam Stock Exchange in 1997 by the police, the tax authorities, and the Public Prosecutor's Office. This operation "Clickfonds" led to many indictments of brokers and their clients on suspicion of front-running, falsifying documents, and tax evasion. Front-running and other forms of securities fraud proved very hard to prove, and most of the suspects were acquitted.

After these spectacular flare-ups of attention to organizational crime from the criminal justice system, calm appears to have resumed. In a recent policy plan, the Public Prosecutor's Council (Openbaar Ministerie 2004) stressed the moral ambiguity of organizational crime, concluding that inspection agencies and administrative law enforcement agencies have the first responsibilities. According to the council, criminal law has only a subsidiary role in the most serious cases when punitive sanctions are needed.

2. *Administrative Law in Action.*   In 1998, results appeared of extensive empirical research into enforcement in practice in ten fields of regulation, including waste products, airplane noise, and labor condi-

tions (Michiels 1998). The researchers interviewed representatives of regulatory agencies, studied documents, and gained insight into these services' cases. Although differences were observed in enforcement in the diverse areas, the researchers drew some general conclusions. The agencies interviewed believed that their surveillance of the behavior of corporations was deficient and that they were unable to carry out sufficient visits and inspections. The second unpleasant conclusion was that even when there was sufficient supervision and illegal situations were discovered that were not stopped, insufficient sanctions were imposed and enforced (Michiels 1998 p. 48). Moreover, the majority of violations discovered ceased during the supervision phase. The number of administrative sanctions was low in all ten regulatory areas (p. 49).

Michiel's study suggests that inadequate enforcement results from insufficient expertise, poor regulation, and lack of manpower. The chances of detecting offenses and punishing offenders are very small. Partly elaborating on these findings and on research conducted by foreign scholars such as Hawkins (1984), Kagan and Scholz (1984), Braithwaite (1985), and Hutter (1997), several empirical studies in the Netherlands on law enforcement in a number of regulatory areas came to the same conclusions, particularly concerning environmental regulation (Blomberg and Michiels 1997; Wiering 1999).

Recently, van de Peppel and Herweijer (2002) conducted surveys of enforcement officers employed by environmental agencies. Their main findings are that there is a lack of inspection and sanctions are not applied. The main problem is limited capacity. The frequency of inspections is not sufficient. On average, a company that falls under the authority of a public body is inspected once in four years. Van de Peppel and Herweijer estimate that 10–15 percent of companies operate without necessary permits. Too often companies are notified of inspections, so they can prepare themselves. Considerable time passes between the detection, the warning, the second inspection, the threat of sanctioning, and the actual issuance of the sanction. In many cases, public authorities show leniency and give violating companies a second or third chance. Van de Peppel and Herweijer find that the enforcement is not credible and that spontaneous compliance by other corporations is undermined. Even more, they suggest that there is no threat of sanctions when violations continue and that even when sanctions are imposed, only a small fraction are carried out.

This research on the shortcomings of law enforcement by administrative agencies has led to a number of recommendations to improve regulatory enforcement. In many areas, projects have been established to professionalize the enforcement process, install procedures, draft action plans, and make better use of existing instruments.

V. Interdependency between Public Administration and Corporations

The Dutch system has produced a host of rules and regulations, but in the end often fails to enforce them. This is not the result only of administrative incompetence, but also of a lack of will. Lex Michiels points to insufficient motivation on the part of the government to force corporations to comply with the law as one of the causes of nonenforcement (Michiels 1998). The reason is that Dutch government bodies are in many ways dependent on corporations. The government is not only enforcer but also client, customer, or even partner and often needs corporations' assistance to realize its goals. The result is an opaque web of shared interests and secret understandings. A cynical hypothesis perhaps, but the small number of cases of corruption by public authorities in the Netherlands may well be related to widespread collusion: it is not necessary to bribe enforcers and other public authorities in the Netherlands because they are predisposed to keep in mind the interests and views of corporations.

The establishment of Tanker Cleaning Rotterdam was subsidized by the Dutch government. In the mid-1980s, it provided the company with 8 million euros to set up machinery to process ships' waste. The government itself created the market, by requiring large tankers to use the services of tank cleaning companies such as TCR. Vast amounts of money were spent creating a nationwide network of companies for collecting and processing waste from ships. TCR was the key player. The government granted licences to TCR and a small number of other companies to operate, and other firms were denied entry into the market. A detailed study into ten years of inadequate public controls on TCR, carried out from a public administration perspective, revealed that the government was afraid to clamp down hard for fear of damaging the network as a whole. One striking conclusion was that the credulous government agencies were no match for the "unheard-of impudence" of the TCR management (ten Heuvelhof, de Bruijn, and Luigies 1996, p. 102). In contacts with government agencies the company was represented by persons well respected in business and political circles (Eshuis and van den Berg 1996; ten Heuvelhof, de Bruijn, and Luigies 1996).

The TCR case illustrates how governments actively engaged in creating markets and supporting corporations become involved in the process and are thereby disinclined to intervene. This case was not an isolated instance. Lex Michiels concluded that "one of the causes of non-enforcement that should not be underestimated lies in the fact that the enforcer often has no interest in enforcing" (1998, p. 55).

Recently, research into the nature and scale of price-fixing and cartels in the construction industry has demonstrated again how strongly government agencies and companies are sometimes intertwined. The parliamentary committee mentioned "collusion" as one of the major problems. Examples were found of government agencies commissioning major construction projects that eliminated competition by putting out projects to private tender only. Certain local construction companies were secretly favored, on the basis of an appeal to the need for regional employment. In several cases government agencies gave preferential treatment to companies by accepting overpriced bids. Individual civil servants and public authorities were not averse to accepting small gifts. The Parliamentary Inquiry Commission described this culture of "grease and feasts" as widespread. Only four cases of corruption, with traceable services rendered in return, were uncovered (Enquêtecommissie Bouwnijverheid 2003; van den Heuvel 2004; Vulperhorst 2005).

The committee arrived at the conclusion that government bodies should be put at a distance in their relations with corporations. It also advocated a "new realism," in which the different responsibilities are clearly demarcated (Enquêtecommissie Bouwinijverheid 2003, p. 296).

VI. The Research Agenda

We still know very little about the effects of regulation of corporate behavior. Bas van Stokkom (2004, p. 9) reached the same conclusion in a comprehensive meta-evaluation of research into the effectiveness of enforcement styles. In view of low risks of arrest and imposition of sanctions, expectations regarding effectiveness should not be high.

Despite this, enforcers in the Netherlands seem to know exactly what to do. Vigorous claims have been made about the appropriateness of particular enforcement strategies. The concepts of responsive regulation and the enforcement pyramids of Ayres and Braithwaite (1992) are very influential, possibly because they are consistent with the Dutch propensity always to steer a middle course, in this case between self-regulation and command-and-control regulation.[8]

An example of adoption of Braithwaite's ideas can be seen in an enforcement memorandum of the Inspectorate of the Ministry of Transport and Communications (Inspectie van Verkeer en Waterstaat 2005). This inspectorate is responsible for regulations regarding transport by road, rail, sea, and air. The memorandum emphasizes the importance of understanding an organization's motives for noncompliance and suggests that there is a fitting intervention for every motive. A complete toolbox is required to respond adequately to rule violations, including both soft interventions (information, advice, and warnings) and hard interventions (administrative fines, suspension of licenses, and criminal prosecution). The ministry explicitly uses Ayres and Braithwaite's intervention pyramid.

This kind of planning unintentionally reveals the need for more empirical insight into corporate behavior, particularly into the conditions
• leading up to rule violations. Without better evidence, every discussion of the effectiveness of approaches to regulation of corporate behavior must be built on quicksand. In the worst case, these discussions end in ideological debates without reference to empirically grounded evidence (Ponsaers 2004, p. 179).

What should research on organizational crime in the Netherlands for the next ten years look like?

We need to know more about the nature and scale of organizational crime. Knowledge is fragmented and limited to certain branches of industry in which scandals have occurred. But what about levels of compliance in other branches of industry? Do other branches have widespread and structurally embedded—yet undiscovered—forms of lawbreaking such as the construction industry had regarding competition regulation? A starting point could be data collected by inspection and law enforcement agencies that regulate business, such as the Environmental Inspection Agencies, the Occupational Safety and Health Inspection Agency, the Authority Financial Markets, the Netherlands

---

[8] This regulatory model is endorsed in several Dutch criminological studies on the regulation of corporate behavior (van de Bunt 1992; van den Heuvel 1998; van de Bunt and Huisman 1999; Ponsaers and Hoogenboom 2004; van Stokkom 2004).

Competition Authority, and the Inspectorate of the Ministry of Transport and Communications. These data could show levels of compliance in many branches of industry and many fields of regulation. It would be interesting to assess how regulatory violations are spread across branches of industry, between corporations within the same branch, and across different kinds of regulation.

It will remain uncertain to what extent these figures document the scale of corporate offending and to what extent they document the enforcement priorities of these agencies. For that reason, field work is also necessary. By interviewing corporate officials and studying internal documents, one can make assessments of corporations' compliance performance and how this relates to organizational characteristics and environmental conditions. When we have established levels of compliance, we should look for explanations for differences. The case of the construction industry teaches us to look at reasons why widespread lawbreaking can remain hidden for so long.

Most Dutch literature on the causes of organizational crime is influenced by Anglo-Saxon research. Implicitly, it is assumed that the same explanations are to be found. This may not be true. Dutch criminologists should wonder whether there are distinctive features of Dutch organizational crime. These could be found on the level of the national political economy or the Dutch business culture. For instance, what might be the criminogenic effects of the Dutch polder model, the organized cooperation between the Dutch government, employers, and labor unions aimed at reaching agreements and avoiding conflict (Léonard 2005)? Van den Heuvel relates collusion between Dutch business and government regulators to the tradition of the polder model, which is partly an explanation for malpractice in the construction industry (van den Heuvel 2003). Another possible example: the Dutch government responded more leniently to the accounting fraud cases than the United States did. In the United States these cases resulted in very strict legislation, whereas Dutch authorities responded by creating a private commission of captains of industry to write a code of conduct for Dutch corporations (Commisie Tabaksblat 2003). More empirical research is needed on the consequences of the polder model and its criminogenic effects.

European unification and the globalization of markets challenge Dutch firms to expand abroad. On international markets the regulatory framework may be less or more demanding. In what way does this influence attitudes and behavior? Does this lead to feelings of anomie that could result in lawbreaking or unethical behavior? Empirical research on Dutch corporations that cross national boundaries and are active in, for instance, emerging markets in eastern Europe and Asia should attempt to answer these questions.

Almost all research on organizational crime assumes that explanations are not to be found at the level of the individual employee or manager. It is widely accepted that organizational factors determine which individuals will commit violations on behalf of the organization. But is this true? A recent report on accounting fraud at well-known and respectable corporations emphasizes that in all cases new and ambitious CEOs set extremely demanding targets, while also displaying risky behavior in other aspects of life, such as showing off with beautiful young new wives (Cools 2005).

By conducting intensive case studies and in-depth interviews with managers who did and did not break the law within the same position or situation, we could gain insight into the personal factors that play a role in the occurrence of organizational crime.

Research questions also have to be addressed to topics of regulation and regulatory enforcement. There is much research into the competence of agencies, which regularly concludes that they suffer from a lack of professionalism and manpower. This type of research should not be given priority. It is much more interesting to look at the behavior of enforcers in another way.

Given the entanglement between the regulators and the regulated, it is important to carry out research into the risks of certain regulatory styles. How can enforcers retain their independence and integrity without adopting a businesslike control-and-command approach? Since many regulatory agencies have shifted strategies to emphasize self-regulation and horizontal control, it is important to understand whether this approach leads to better compliance and under what circumstances.

Braithwaite's model of responsive regulation is very influential. However, the approach's effectiveness has not been tested, at least not in the Netherlands. The underlying assumptions are taken for granted and never questioned. But how well do they apply in the Dutch situation? The model prescribes that enforcement processes start with advising, instructing, and convincing corporations, but the practice in many fields is that minor offenses are dealt with by criminal law.

Inspections by regulatory agencies increasingly are based on risk assessments. Almost all inspection agencies are developing risk assessment tools. These tools should be critically studied. Our first impression is that most of these tools are based on one-sided economic models of corporate decision making. Research on organizational crime, however, shows that other factors influence organizational compliance, such as business culture and social responsiveness, which are much harder to determine. It would be useful to see how these criminological considerations could be included in risk assessment models.

Research into the due process character of administrative regulation warrants support. In recent years, administrative agencies have been equipped with more powers and a wide range of possibilities to administer sanctions (e.g., administrative fines), but how just have the actions of these pseudo-judges been? What are the enforcement policies of new administrative agencies that impose these sanctions? And what are the effects? Empirical studies should uncover the decision-making criteria for issuing sanctions. Here too lies a challenge for criminologists: to break free from their fixation on criminal regulation (Ponsaers 2004, p. 179).

REFERENCES

Aalders, Marius V. C. 1984. *Industrie, milieu en wetgeving: De Hinderwet tussen symboliek en effectiviteit.* Amsterdam: Kobra.
Algemene Rekenkamer. 1989. *Bijzondere opsporingsdiensten en handhaving.* The Hague: SDU uitgevers.
———. 2004. *Fraudebestrijding: Stand van zaken 2004.* The Hague: SDU uitgevers.
Aronowitz, Alexis A., Desiree C. G. Laagland, and Gerard Paulides. 1996. *The Detection and Settlement of VAT Fraud in Four Countries: Addendum to the Report Value-Added Tax Fraud in the European Union.* The Hague: WODC, Ministry of Justice.
Ayres, Ian, and John Braithwaite. 1992. *Responsive Regulation: Transcending the Deregulation Debate.* New York: Oxford University Press.
Belastingdienst. 2003. *Beheersverslag 2003.* The Hague: Ministry of Finance.
Benson, Michael L. 2001. *Crime and the Life Course.* Los Angeles: Roxbury.
Berghuis, Bert A. C., Chrisje H. Brants, and Hans M. Willemse. 1984. *Witteboorden-criminaliteit.* Nijmegen: Ars Aequi Libri.
Blomberg, Aletta B., and Felix C. M. A. Michiels. 1997. *Handhaven met effect:*

Een empirisch-juridische studie naar de mogelijkheden voor een effectieve hand-having van het milieurecht. The Hague: VUGA.

Bovenkerk, Frank, and Ankie Lempens. 1996. "De branche van het wegtransport." In *Deelonderzoek II: Branches*, edited by Gerben J. N. Bruinsma and Frank Bovenkerk. The Hague: SDU uitgevers.

Bovens, Marcus A. P. 1990. *Verantwoordelijkheid en organisatie: Beschouwingen over aansprakelijkheid, institutioneel burgerschap en ambtelijke ongehoorzaamheid.* Zwolle: W. E. J. Tjeenk Willink.

Box, Steven. 1983. *Power, Crime and Mystification.* London: Tavistock.

Braithwaite, John. 1984. *Corporate Crime in the Pharmaceutical Industry.* London: Routledge & Kegan Paul.

————. 1985. *To Punish or to Persuade.* Albany: State University of New York Press.

Brants, Chrisje H. 1994. "The System's Rigged—or Is It? The Prosecution of White Collar and Corporate Crime in the Netherlands." *Crime, Law and Social Change* 21:103–25.

Brants, Chrisje H., and Kees L. K. Brants. 1991. *De sociale constructie van fraude.* Arnhem: Gouda Quint.

Brants, Chrisje H., and Theo de Roos. 1984. "De strafzaak Uniser in de spiegel van de persverslagen." In *Grenzen en mogelijkheden, opstellen over en rondom de strafrechtspleging*, edited by Constantijn Kelk. Nijmegen: Ars Aequi Libri.

Brants-Langeraar, Chrisje H. 1981. "Over het begrip white collar crime." *Tijdschrift voor Criminologie* 23(4):224–35.

Bruinsma, Gerben J. N. 1996a. *Beelden van criminaliteit.* Arnhem: Gouda Quint.

————. 1996b. "De afvalverwerkingsbranche." In *Deelonderzoek II: Branches*, edited by Gerben J. N. Bruinsma and Frank Bovenkerk. The Hague: SDU uitgevers.

————. 1996c. "De autobranche en (vracht) autocriminaliteit." In *Deelonderzoek II: Branches*, edited by Gerben J. N. Bruinsma and Frank Bovenkerk. The Hague: SDU uitgevers.

————. 1996d. "De bouwnijverheid." In *Deelonderzoek II: Branches*, edited by Gerben J. N. Bruinsma and Frank Bovenkerk. The Hague: SDU uitgevers.

Bruinsma, Gerben J. N., and Frank Bovenkerk. 1996. "Deelonderzoek II: Branches." In *Inzake opsporing: Enquête opsporingsmethoden, eindrapport.* Parlementaire Enquêtecommissie Opsporingsmethoden. The Hague: SDU uitgevers.

Clinard, Marshall B. 1983. *Corporate Ethics and Crime: The Role of Middle Management.* Beverly Hills, CA: Sage.

Clinard, Marshall B., and Peter C. Yeager. 1980. *Corporate Crime.* New York: Free Press.

Cohen, David V. 1995. "Ethics and Crime in Business Firms: Organizational Culture and the Impact of Anomie." In *The Legacy of Anomie Theory*, edited by Freda Adler and William S. Laufer. New Brunswick, NJ: Transaction.

Cohen, Stanley. 1977. *Folk Devils and Moral Panics: The Creation of the Mods and the Rockers.* Oxford: Blackwell.

Commissie Tabaksblat. 2003. *De Nederlandse Corporate Governance Code: Beginselen van deugdelijk ondernemingsbestuur en Best Practice bepalingen.*

Cools, Kees. 2005. *Controle is goed. Vertrouwen nog betar. Over bestuurders en corporate governance.* Assen: Koninklijke van Gorcum.

COV (Commissie Onderzoek Vuurwerkramp). 2001. *De vuurwerkramp.* The Hague: SDU uitgevers.

Croall, Hazel. 1993. "Business Offenders in the Criminal Justice Process." *Crime, Law and Social Change* 20:359–72.

de Doelder, Hans, and Klaus Tiedemann. 1996. *Criminal Liability of Corporations.* Dordrecht: Kluwer Law International.

de Lange, Anton. 1992. "Sancties in het milieurecht in rechtseconomische perspectief." *Delikt en Delinkwent* 1992:323–38.

Delsen, Leonardus W. M. 2000. *Exit poldermodel? Sociaal-economische ontwikkelingen in Nederland.* Assen: van Gorcum.

Eerste Kamer. 2004–5. *Vermindering administratieve lasten: Nu volle kracht vooruit.* 29 515, no. 59.

Eggen, Anton Th. J., and Wieger van der Heide. 2005. *Criminaliteit en rechtshandhaving 2004: Onwikkelingen en samenhangen.* The Hague: Boom Juridische uitgevers.

Eijlander, Philip, Pieter C. Gilhuis, and Johannes A. F. Peters. 1993. *Overheid en zelfregulering: Alibi voor vrijblijvendheid of een prikkel tot actie?* Zwolle: W. E. J. Tjeenk Willink.

Enquêtecommissie Bouwnijverheid. 2003. *De bouw uit de schaduw; Bijlage 2: Aard en omvang van onregelmatigheden in de Bouwnijverheid.* Tweede Kamer, 2002–3, 28 244, no. 9. The Hague: SDU uitgevers.

Enquêtecommissie Opsporingsmethoden. 1996. *Inzake opsporing: Enquête Opsporingsmethoden, eindrapport.* The Hague: SDU uitgevers.

Eshuis, Roland J. J., and Ellen A. I. M. van den Berg. 1996. *Dossier TCR: Tien jaar schone schijn.* The Hague: WODC, Ministry of Justice.

Faber, Eeuwke. 1997. "Shipping and Scuttling: Criminogenesis in Marine Insurance." *Crime, Law and Social Change* 27(2):111–35.

———. 1998. "Criminelen en kooplieden-de Amsterdamse beursfraude." In *Crimineel jaarboek 1998*, edited by John R. Blad, Jacco Boek, Marc Bosch, Eeuwke Faber, Pieter Ippel, and Pieter Wiewel. Nijmegen: Ars Aequi Libri.

Faure, Michael G., and Marjolein J. C. Visser. 2004. "Law and Economics of Environmental Crime." In *New Perspectives on Economic Crime*, edited by Hans Sjorgen and Goran Skogh. Cheltenham, UK: Elgar.

Felson, Marcus. 1998. "Fallacies about Crime." In *Crime and Everyday Life.* London: Sage.

Fijnaut, Cyrille J. C. F., Frank Bovenkerk, Gerben J. N. Bruinsma, and Henk G. van de Bunt. 1998. *Organized Crime in the Netherlands.* The Hague: Kluwer Law International.

Garland, David. 1996. "The Limits of the Sovereign State: Strategies of Crime Control in Contemporary Societies." *British Journal of Criminology* 36: 445–71.

Geis, G. 1967. "The Heavy Electric Equipment Antitrust Case of 1961." In

Criminal Behaviour Systems: A Typology, edited by Marshall B. Clinard and Richard Quinney. New York: Holt, Rinehart and Winston.

Hagan, John, and F. Kay. 1990. "Gender and Delinquency in White-Collar Families: A Power-Control Perspective." *Crime and Delinquency* 36(3):391–407.

Hall, Stuart. 1978. *Policing the Crisis: Mugging, the State, and Law and Order.* London: Macmillan.

Hartmann, Arthur R., and Lodewijk J. J. Rogier. 2004. "Bestuurlijke handhaving in het wetsvoorstel vierde tranche awb." *Nederlands Juristenblad* 36: 1877–82.

Hawkins, Keith. 1984. *Environment and Enforcement: Regulation and the Social Definition of Pollution.* Oxford: Clarendon.

Hertogh, Marc. 2005. "Van naleving naar beleving van regels: Bouwwereld en bouwfraude vanuit een rechtssociologisch perspectief." In *Recht realiseren: Bijdragen rond het thema adequate naleving van rechtsregels*, edited by Thomas Barkhuysen, Willemien den Ouden, and Jaap E. M. Polak. Deventer: Kluwer.

Hoogenboom, A. Bob. 1996. *Beursfraude en (zelf)regulering: Witwassen en handel met voorkennis.* Dordrecht: Stichting Maatschappij en Politie.

Hoogenboom, A. Bob, Vincent Mul, and Allart Wielinga. 1995. *Financiële integriteit.* Arnhem: Gouda Quint.

Huberts, Leonardus W. C. J. 1992. *Bestuurlijke corruptie en fraude in Nederland.* Arnhem: Gouda Quint.

Huisman, Wim. 2001. *Tussen winst en moraal: Achtergronden van regelnaleving en regelovertreding door ondernemingen.* The Hague: Boom Juridische uitgevers.

Huisman, Wim, and Elibert Niemeijer. 1998. *Zicht op organisatiecriminaliteit: Een literatuuronderzoek.* The Hague: SDU uitgevers.

———. 1999. "Organisatiecriminaliteit: Naar een aanpak op basis van inzicht." *Justitiële Verkenningen* 25(2):8–35.

Hulsman, Louk. 1986. *Afscheid van het strafrecht.* Houten: Het Wereldvenster.

Hutter, Bridget M. 1997. *Compliance: Regulation and Environment.* Oxford: Clarendon.

Inspectie Milieuhygiëne. 1997. *Toezichtsactie olievlek: Een beoordeling van de bunkermarkt door de Inspectie Milieuhygiëne en de DCMR milieudienst rijnmond.* Werkdocument 1997/333. The Hague: Inspectie Milieuhygiëne.

Inspectie van Verkeer en Waterstaat. 2005. *Toezicht in beweging: Ontwikkeling in het toezicht van Verkeer en Waterstaat.* The Hague: SDU uitgevers.

Jongman, Riekent. 1981. *Klasse elementen in de rechtsgang.* Groningen: Vakgroep Criminologie Groningen.

Kagan, Robert A., and John T. Scholz. 1984. "The 'Criminology of the Corporation' and 'Regulatory Enforcement Strategies.'" In *Enforcing Regulation*, edited by Keith Hawkins and J. M. Thomas. Boston: Kluwer Nijhoff.

Kaptein, Samuel P. 1998. *Ethics Management: Auditing and Developing the Ethical Content of Organizations.* Dordrecht: Kluwer Academic Publishers.

Kramer, Ronald C. 1982. "Corporate Crime: An Organizational Perspective."

In *White-Collar and Economic Crime: Multidisciplinary and Cross-National Perspectives*, edited by Peter Wickman and Timothy Dailey. Lexington, MA: Lexington.

Léonard, E. 2005. "Governance and Concerted Regulation of Employment in Europe." *European Journal of Industrial Relations* 11:307–26.

Michiels, Felix C. M. A. 1998. *De wet milieubeheer.* Deventer: W. E. J. Tjeenk Willink.

Ministerie van Justitie. 1992. *Zicht op wetgeving.* Kamerstukken II 1990–91, 22 008: 1, 2. The Hague: SDU uitgevers.

Ministerie van VROM. 1999. *Wegwijzer vergunning op hoofdzaken, vergunningverlening op maat.* The Hague: SDU uitgevers.

Mitsilegas, Valsamis. 2003. *Money Laundering Counter-measures in the European Union: A New Paradigm of Security Governance versus Fundamental Legal Principles.* The Hague: Kluwer Law International.

Mok, M. R. 2004. *Kartelrecht Nederland: De mededingingswet, beknopte editie.* Deventer: Kluwer.

Needleman, Martin L., and Carolyn Needleman. 1979. "Organizational Crime: Two Models of Criminogenesis." *Sociological Quarterly* 20:517–28.

Nelen, Hans M., and Vincent Sabee. 1998. *Het vermogen te ontnemen: Evaluatie van de ordeningswetgeving: Eindrapport.* The Hague: WODC, Ministry of Justice.

Ondernemingskamer. 2004. *Beschikking van 6 januari 2005.* Rekestnummer 153/2004.

Openbaar Ministerie. 2004. *Aanpak georganiseerde misdaad.* The Hague: SDU uitgevers.

Passas, Nikos. 1990. "Anomie and Corporate Deviance." *Contemporary Crises* 14:157–78.

Paternoster, R., and Sally S. Simpson. 1993. "A Rational Choice Theory of Corporate Crime." In *Advances in Criminological Theory: Routine Activity and Rational Choice*, edited by Ronald V. Clarke and Marcus Felson. New Brunswick, NJ: Transaction.

———. 1996. "Sanctions, Threats and Appeals to Morality: Testing a Rational Choice Model of Corporate Crime." *Law and Society Review* 30(3):549–83.

Ponsaers, Paul. 2004. "Een van de grote mazen in het controlenet: De bijzondere inspectiediensten." In *Voor een verantwoorde, transparante, democratische politiezor—pour une police responsable, transparente, démocratique*, edited by G. Bourdoux, H. Berkmoes, and A. Vandoren. Brussels: Politeia.

Ponsaers, Paul, and A. Bob Hoogenboom. 2004. "Het moeilijke spel van wortel en stok: Organisatiecriminaliteit en handhavingstrategieën van bijzondere inspectie-en opsporingsdiensten." *Tijdschrift voor Criminologie* 46(2):165–81.

Projectgroep Wegtransport en Criminaliteit. 1996. *Wegtransport en criminaliteit: Verslag van een fenomeenonderzoek naar de relatie tussen het wegvervoer en de georganiseerde misdaad.* Rotterdam: Platform Aanpak Zware Georganiseerde Criminaliteit.

Punch, Maurice. 1996. *Dirty Business: Exploring Corporate Misconduct, Analysis and Cases.* London: Sage.

Reiss, Albert J., and Michael Tonry. 1993. "Organizational Crime." In *Beyond the Law: Crime in Complex Organizations*, edited by Michael Tonry and Albert J. Reiss. Vol. 8 of *Crime and Justice: A Review of Research*, edited by Michael Tonry and Norval Morris. Chicago: University of Chicago Press.

Shover, Neil, and Chris Bryant. 1993. "Theoretical Explanations of Corporate Crime." In *Understanding Corporate Criminality*, edited by M. B. Blankenship. New York: Garland.

Simpson, S. L. 1993. "Strategy, Structure, and Corporate Crime: The Historical Context of Anticompetitive Behavior." In *New Directions in Criminological Theory*, edited by Freda Adler and William S. Laufer. New Brunswick, NJ: Transaction.

Simpson, Sally S. 2002. *Corporate Crime, Law, and Social Control*. Cambridge: Cambridge University Press.

Simpson, Sally S., N. L. Piquero, and R. Paternoster. 2002. "Rationality and Corporate Offending Decisions." In *Rational Choice and Criminal Behavior: Recent Research and Future Challenges*, edited by Alexis R. Piquero and S. G. Tibbets. New York: Routledge.

Slapper, Gary, and Steve Tombs. 1999. *Corporate Crime*. Harlow, UK: Longman.

Sleurink, Hans. 1982. *Hoe fraude de samenleving bedreigt: Het ISMO-rapport*. Arnhem: Gouda Quint.

Sociaal Economische Raad. 1992. *Convergentie en overlegeconomie*. The Hague: SER.

Sutherland, Edwin H. 1949. *White Collar Crime*. New York: Dryden.

ten Heuvelhof, Ernst F., Johan A. de Bruijn, and H. H. Luigies. 1996. *Bestuursrechtelijke handhaving tankcleaning Rotterdam*. Delft: Faculteit der Technische Bestuurskunde.

Tweede Kamer. 1993–94. *Ministerie van VROM 1994, Nationaal Milieu plan*. 23 560, no. 2.

——. 2004–5. *Fraudebestrijding: Stand van zaken*. 29 810, nos. 1, 2.

van de Bunt, Henk G. 1992. *Organisatiecriminaliteit*. Arnhem: Gouda Quint.

van de Bunt, Henk G., and Theo de Roos. 1983. "Zwarte toga's kontra witte boorden?" *Recht en Kritiek* 9(1):6–50.

van de Bunt, Henk G., and Wim Huisman. 1999. "Het kan ook anders: Overwegingen bij de keuze tussen klassiek of alternatief reguleren op milieuterrein." In *De effectiviteit van klassieke en alternatieve reguleringsinstrumenten in milieuhandhaving*, edited by Pieter C. Gilhuis, Ernst F. ten Heuvelhof, and Henk G. van de Bunt. Serie Onderzoek en Beleid, no. 179. The Hague: WODC, Ministry of Justice.

van de Bunt, Henk G., and Edward Kleemans. 2004. "Transnational Organized Crime: New Directions for Empirical Research and Public Policy." In *Punishment, Places and Perpetrators*, edited by Gerben Bruinsma, Jan de Keijser, and Henk Elffers. Devon, UK: Willan.

van de Bunt, Henk G., and J. H. Peek. 1987. *Fraudeofficieren in de opsporing: Beleidsvoornemens en werkwijzen*. Groningen: Wolters Noordhoff.

van de Peppel, Rob A., and Michael Herweijer. 2002. *Zargplicht voor de hand-*

having van milieurecht: Advies van de evaluatiecommissie Wet Milieubeheer. The Hague: ECWM VROM.

van den Anker, Marianne J. J., and A. Bob Hoogenboom. 1997. *Schijn bedriegt: Overheid, bedrijfsleven en gelegenheidstructuren voor milieucriminaliteit op de hergebruikersmarkt.* The Hague: VUGA.

van den Berg, Ellen A. I. M. 1995. *De markt van misdaad en milieu: Deel 1.* The Hague: WODC, Ministry of Justice.

————. 2002. *Organisatiecriminaliteit: Aard, achtergronden en aanpak.* Onderzoeksnotitie no. 8. The Hague: WODC, Ministry of Justice .

van den Heuvel, Grat A. A. J. 1998. *Collusie tussen overheid en bedrijf: Een vergeten hoofdstuk uit de organisatiecriminologie.* Maastricht: Universiteit Maastricht.

————. 2003. *De Bouw uit de schaduw; bijlage 2: Aard en omvang van onregelmatigheden in de Bouwnijverheid.* Parlementaire Enquêtecommissie Bouwnijverheid. Tweede Kamer, 2002–3, 28 244, no. 9. The Hague: SDU uitgevers.

————. 2004. "Nederland als collusieparadijs—de bouwfraude als organisatiecriminologische casus." *Tijdschrift voor Criminologie* 46(2):121–34.

van der Hoeven, G. J., D. Ruimschotel, R. van den Sigtenhorst,and A. J. M. Verkoren. 2003. *Kwetsbaarheid van de zorgsector voor georganiseerde fraude.* Amsterdam: CMC/T11 Co.

van der Schoot, Cathelijne R. A. 2006. *Organised Crime Prevention in the Netherlands.* The Hague: Boom Juridische uitgevers.

van de Walle, Gudrun. 2003. "Conflictafhandeling of risicomanagement? Een studie van conflicten tussen slachtoffers en ondernemingen in de farmaceutische sector." Dissertation, Universiteit Gent.

van Duyne, Petrus C. 1996. *Organized Crime in Europe.* Commack, NY: Nova Science Publishers.

van Stokkom, Bas. 2004. "Goede handhaving: Een inventarisatie van effectieve strategieën." In *Handhaving in den brede.* Expertisecentrum Rechtshandhaving. The Hague: Ministry of Justice.

van Vugt, G. W. M., and J. F. Boet. 1994. *Zuiver handelen in een vuile context.* Arnhem: Gouda Quint.

Vaughan, Diane. 1983. *Controlling Unlawful Organizational Behaviour: Social Structure and Corporate Misconduct.* Chicago: University of Chicago Press.

Visser, M. J. C. 2001. "Zorgplichtbepalingen in het strafrecht." Arnhem: Gouda Quint.

Vulperhorst, Lenny. 2005. *Verzwegen onderneming: Ondernemers, overheid en het einde van het bouwkartel (2001–2005).* Amsterdam: van Gennep.

Weisburd, David, E. F. Chayet, and Elin J. Waring. 1990. "White-Collar Crime and Criminal Careers: Some Preliminary Findings." *Crime and Delinquency* 36(3):342–55.

Weisburd, David, Sally Wheeler, Elin J. Waring, and N. Bode. 1991. *Crimes of the Middle Classes: White-Collar Offenders in the Federal Courts.* New Haven, CT: Yale University Press.

Wiering, Marco. 1999. *Controleurs in context: Handhaving van mestwetgeving in Nederland en vlaanderen.* Lelystad: Vermande.

Yeager, Peter C. 1995. "Management, Morality, and Law: Organizational Forms and Ethical Deliberations." In *Corporate Crime: Contemporary Debates*, edited by F. Pearce and L. Snider. Toronto: University of Toronto Press.

Frank M. Weerman

Juvenile Offending

ABSTRACT

Police statistics and self-report studies on juvenile offending in the Netherlands show nothing startling compared with other Western countries, although levels are somewhat above the means. Official figures reveal a steady increase from the 1960s, especially for violent offenses, a development in line with the general trend in Europe. Self-reports reveal no dramatic changes since the 1990s, although some studies suggest a recent increase. Much youth offending takes place in company, sometimes in the form of troublesome youth groups. These groups are rarely territorial and are less hierarchical and organized than are gangs in the United States. Offending is often an illegal alternative to get income, respect, and status for marginalized or stigmatized youths. Studies on the etiology of youth crime report risk factors and correlates in line with findings throughout the world. Dutch research on juvenile offending is well developed, but some areas need more attention.

In the Netherlands, as elsewhere, rule breaking and doing forbidden things are not atypical adolescent behavior. Self-report studies reveal that the majority of young people break the law at one time or another (Junger-Tas, Haen Marshall, et al. 2003). This is usually relatively harmless, although it can be very troublesome to parents and adults and can be a nuisance. A small but significant part of the juvenile population is involved in more serious crimes. A few percent of the Dutch juveniles report using weapons and committing crimes such as burglaries or robberies. More than 4,000 juveniles end up each year in closed juvenile justice institutions because of their delinquent behavior (see Wittebrood 2003*a*; van der Laan, forthcoming). So, there are two faces of juvenile offending in the Netherlands, relatively minor offending that is not uncommon and more serious delinquency that is less common but not rare.

Frank M. Weerman is senior researcher at the Netherlands Institute for the Study of Crime and Law Enforcement, Leiden.

Offending was not always so widespread. The level of recorded youth crime—and of crime in general—was very low during the 1950s. Since the beginning of the 1960s, the proportion of juveniles interrogated by the police has risen steadily. This mirrored the general crime figures, but, relatively speaking, juvenile offending increased more. The number of juveniles apprehended by the police appears still to be on the increase, especially recently. However, there are no indications that the Dutch level of youth crime is exceptional when seen in an international perspective (Killias 2003). Self-report studies also do not provide evidence of an exceptional level of delinquent behavior among Dutch youths (Junger-Tas, Haen Marshall, et al. 2003). In addition, self-report studies do not show a substantial increase since the early 1990s. This departs from the trend in the police statistics, although self-report studies report peaks and an increase in some offenses in the past few years.

Youth justice in the Netherlands has been characterized as a hybrid between punitiveness and welfare (Junger-Tas 2004). Central elements are the notions that minors are less responsible for their acts (and children not responsible at all), that juvenile delinquents should be protected from adult criminals, and that judicial reactions should contribute to rehabilitation and reeducation. Judicial decisions should be "in the interest of the child" and are made by specialized youth judges. Important policy developments occurred during the 1980s and 1990s. Many diversion programs were initiated in which juvenile offenders were sanctioned outside the justice system. This started with the HALT (Het ALTernatief [the alternative]) sanctions in the 1980s, which have expanded tremendously (Wittebrood 2003a; Junger-Tas 2004). These sanctions are given by the police and involve the waiver of further prosecution; they consist of small restorative tasks (a maximum of twenty hours) or financial compensation. Other alternative sanctions were introduced during the 1980s and 1990s, ranging from unpaid community service and compulsory courses to rehabilitation programs and intensive probation supervision. These are ordered by the judge or proposed by the prosecutor and became formal modes of punishment in the Youth Justice Law of 1995.

Dutch government policies on juvenile offending changed during the 1990s. In the beginning of the 1990s, public concern led to special government attention and to the installation of a special Juvenile Crime Committee (known as the van Montfrans Committee). Its report

(Commissie Jeugdcriminaliteit 1993) and follow-up government papers (Ministerie van Justitie et al. 1998; Ministerie van Justitie 2002, 2003) were very influential. The Juvenile Justice Law of 1995 increased the maximum sanctions for juveniles (from six months' detention to one year; for those aged between sixteen and eighteen, the maximum is two years) and expanded possibilities for the waiver of juveniles to adult courts when the offense or the offender is adult in character. The special position of youths in criminal law remains intact, but the traditional Dutch strategy of minimalistic reactions has been abandoned and replaced by quicker and more punitive responses (Wittebrood 2003*a*; van der Laan, forthcoming). Numerous new intervention strategies have been introduced, for example, the Community That Cares program in which various neighborhood institutes are brought together to promote the prevention of problem behavior and crime (Hawkins 1999; Ince et al. 2004). Prevention measures and the treatment of juvenile offenders continue to be regarded as important.

The general political climate in the Netherlands has changed since the early 1990s. The progressive attitude, tolerance, and mild penal policies that characterized the Dutch climate in the 1970s and 1980s were replaced by stricter and more repressive attitudes. Recently, the Netherlands has seen large shifts in political preferences, and two dramatic political assassinations happened (politician Pim Fortuyn and filmmaker Theo van Gogh). Crime in general, and especially youth crime, are regarded by the public as among the most important political problems, along with differences between ethnic groups and problems with the integration of migrants. This shift in political climate is likely to affect future developments with regard to juvenile offending and youth justice.

Juvenile offending has received a great deal of attention from the research community. Many studies have been conducted on youth crime, juvenile offenders, and juvenile justice interventions. A substantial number of articles, books, and special journal issues have been published (e.g., Angenent 1991; Franke, van der Laan, and Nijboer 1995; Baerveldt and Bunkers 1997; van Acker 1998; Knorth et al. 2003). Research on youth offending has traditionally been conducted by researchers in academic criminology departments. In the past, the Criminology Institute of Groningen University was especially active. Recently, much fundamental research on juvenile offending has been conducted at the Netherlands Institute for the Study of Crime and

Law Enforcement (NSCR) in Leiden (see http://www.nscr.nl). The government-based research department, the Wetenschappelijk Onderzoeks en Documentatie Centrum (WODC; internationally also known as RDC, the Research and Documentation Center), has published many reports and studies on juvenile offending and youth justice interventions (see http://www.wodc.nl). Several commercial research institutes and researchers from police departments in the Netherlands have conducted research on juvenile delinquency.

Systematic empirical research dates back to the 1960s. Many studies were conducted in which classic criminological theories were tested, including Hirschi's social control theory and Sutherland's differential association theory. Most empirical research has been done by criminologists, but researchers in other social science departments, especially sociology and anthropology, have been also active. Many of the latter used qualitative methods to study young offenders from minority groups. Recently, developmental psychologists have also become active (e.g., Koops and Slot 1998; Bongers 2005). They shifted attention to individual and early childhood factors and played an important role in a recent volume on serious and violent delinquency (Loeber, Slot, and Sergeant 2001).

The literature on the context and correlates of juvenile offending is voluminous. To organize this body of research, a distinction is made between qualitative research that is mainly descriptive and ethnographic and quantitative research on the causes and correlates of juvenile offending. Of course, in practice, qualitative and quantitative methods are sometimes combined. Nevertheless, the styles of researchers in the Netherlands with a preference for one method or the other are usually quite different. Qualitative researchers are more interested in obtaining good and realistic descriptions of the lifestyles of young offenders, using in-depth interviews, observations, and ethnographic methods. Quantitative researchers are more focused on significant and generalizable results from large samples from police data, judicial files, and survey data.

This essay offers an overview of Dutch research on juvenile offending (youth crime and delinquency are used as equivalents). I have tried to cover the most important studies and findings from the past twenty-five years and have selected studies that appeared in scientific journals or were published as a book or report by the end of 2005, when this essay was finished. The most important Dutch journals were searched in detail, as well as academic books and research reports from the WODC and several commercial or government research institutes (if they met reasonable methodological standards). I tried to find as many publications by Dutch researchers in international journals as I could but limited these to reports of studies conducted in the Netherlands.

In this essay, I do not give a detailed description of developments with regard to Dutch youth justice and policies to reduce juvenile offending. Recent developments are addressed thoroughly in an earlier volume of *Crime and Justice* (Junger-Tas 2004) and elsewhere (Wittebrood 2003a; van der Laan, forthcoming). I also excluded the many studies focusing on the effects and consequences of prevention and intervention projects and programs.

While writing this essay, I had two goals in mind. First, I wanted to give an impression of Dutch youth crime itself and to address Dutch findings about juvenile offenders and their backgrounds. The implications of these findings may be interesting and are not restricted to the Netherlands, though many of the underlying reports are not published in English. Second, I wanted to characterize Dutch criminological research on juvenile offending and to identify which aspects have received relatively greater and lesser attention than elsewhere.

Juveniles or youths in this essay are defined as persons between twelve and eighteen years old. However, I mention several studies that focus on or include offending by older youths between the ages of eighteen and twenty-five. I do not address studies on the spatial distribution of youth crime, on juvenile sex offenders, and on changes in penal policies that are relevant to juvenile offending.

This essay is organized as follows. In Section I, data on youth crime are presented. The prevalence of juvenile offending is discussed, using different sources of information. Changes over the past decades are addressed, and gender and ethnic differences in delinquency are discussed. Section II addresses studies on characteristics of juvenile offending, on specific offense types, and on offending with others or in groups. Section III addresses the most important qualitative studies. For a large part, these studies focus on ethnic minority youths (and often young adults). Section IV addresses studies on the causes and correlates of juvenile offending. Important studies testing etiological theories and more general or eclectic studies on the correlates of juvenile delinquency are described. More complex studies and analyses about the (causal) role of certain risk factors are highlighted as are studies that focus on the difference in delinquency between boys and girls. Section V summarizes the preceding sections and discusses the nature of Dutch youth crime and youth crime research. Gaps in knowledge are discussed, and suggestions for future research are offered.

I. Prevalence and Changes

Data are available to characterize the prevalence of delinquent behavior among Dutch youths and changes in the level of youth crime. These data show that levels of juvenile offending in the Netherlands are not especially high, though somewhat above the mean level of other Western countries. Important differences exist between boys and girls and between ethnic groups. Police data indicate a steady increase in juvenile delinquency over the long term, especially in violent offenses, but this is not unique to the Netherlands. Different sources of information provide somewhat different images of changes between categories and recent changes in juvenile offending.

A. Sources

Two sources are used to obtain information about the prevalence and changes in juvenile offending: official statistics on offenses committed by minors and self-report studies. I use both.

Official statistics are an obvious source for answering basic questions about juvenile offending. Such data are kept by the Central Bureau of Statistics (CBS) and are published on a regular basis in collaboration with the WODC (e.g., Kruissink and Essers 2001, 2004; van der Heide and Eggink 2003; Blom and Huijbregts 2004; Blom, van der Laan, and Huijbregts 2005). These statistics give information on the number of minors (twelve to seventeen years of age) who come into contact with the police each year for different types of offenses. They are a main source of information about changes in juvenile offending over time, because the statistics have been compiled for decades.

Official data have important drawbacks. Only a small portion of committed offenses are discovered and reflected. Offense categorization by the police is often diffuse and not always reliable. More important, the statistics are not a direct function of the volume of youth crime. They are also dependent on the efforts and priorities of the police, on recording policies, and on changing perceptions of what constitutes certain offense types. Nevertheless, they offer important information as long as we take methodological problems into account.

Self-report studies are also an important source for information. In the United States, self-report methodologies have been used regularly since the 1950s. In the Netherlands, they were introduced to investigate the dark figure of unreported delinquency among a sample of college students (Buikhuisen, Jongman, and Oving 1969). Since the 1970s, self-reports have been used in numerous studies of juvenile delinquency among secondary school students (among many more, see Junger-Tas 1972; Bruinsma 1985, 1992; Nijboer and Dijksterhuis 1987, 1989; Junger 1990; Ferwerda 1992; Junger-Tas 1992; Junger and Haen Marshall 1997; Rovers 1997; Weerman 1998; Baerveldt et al. 2004; Broekhuizen and Driessen 2005; Harland et al. 2005).

Self-reports are also used in long-term projects in which juvenile offending is monitored. The WODC-monitor started during the late 1980s (the last wave was held in 2004) and has been conducted every two or three years since then (e.g., Junger-Tas and Kruissink 1987; Junger-Tas, Kruissink, and van der Laan 1992; van der Laan et al. 1998; Kruissink and Essers 2001, 2004; Blom and Huijbregts 2004; Blom, van der Laan, and Huijbregts 2005). For this survey, about 1,000 (until 2001) or 1,500 youths (in 2004) representing the Dutch minor population were questioned about their offending behavior during visits at home. In the last wave (in 2004) a stratified sample was drawn, and the results were weighted to get a representative picture of offending among youths in the Netherlands. Another monitor is the Student Study, which has been conducted every two or three years since 1990 (the last wave was held in 2002). The Social and Cultural Planning Office (SCP) uses this study to report developments affecting Dutch youths, including their delinquent behavior (Beker, Hoff, and Maas 1998; Wittebrood 2000, 2003b). It is administered by teachers in the classroom. The sample is large, about 10,000 respondents, and the results are weighted to obtain representative estimates. The CBS also conducts self-report surveys (CBS Youth Survey) on a regular basis. This is a survey of about 4,000 youths who are questioned at home, most recently in 2003 (Huls et al. 2001; http://www.cbs.nl). Results are weighted to correct for deviations from the population in the sample distribution.

Self-report surveys offer information about the so-called dark figure of crime and complement police statistics. Juveniles are generally quite willing to reveal information about their behavior, as long as the situation feels safe and anonymous. Nevertheless, there has been a debate in the Dutch research community about the validity and reliability of self-reports. On the basis of a test-retest study, Bruinsma (1994) challenged their use because many respondents answered differently during the retest. Hessing and Elffers (1995) used statistical arguments to challenge the validity of this method. Other researchers argue that the self-report method is more reliable and valid than the critics suggest (Nijboer 1995; van der Heijden, Sijtsma, and 't Hart 1995; Swanborn 1996; see also Haen Marshall 1996; Junger-Tas and Haen Marshall 1999).

B. *Juvenile Offending*

According to the police statistics, nearly 60,000 minor suspects were interrogated by the Dutch police in 2003. Blom and Huijbregts (2004) adjust this figure to 46,000 on the basis of the number of cases officially recorded. This constitutes about 4 percent of the total youth population in that age category. The offenses are most often property crimes (about 45 percent). About 30 percent of these youths were apprehended for vandalism or a public order offense and about 20 percent for a violent offense. Relatively more were apprehended for theft, qualified theft, vandalism, assault, and disturbing the public order. Smaller numbers were apprehended for very serious offenses such as rape (about 200 in 2003), indecent assault (about 500), robberies (2,500 juveniles were held for "theft with violence"), and offenses against life or person, a broad category that includes not only murder but also aggravated assault and attempted murders (about 2,000).

It is difficult to characterize these statistics as "high" or "low." Statistics from the *European Sourcebook* (Killias 2003) indicate how Dutch juvenile offending statistics compare with those from other countries. The sourcebook does not give separate statistics for minors, but calculations can be made of minor offending for countries by the use of data for total offending per 100,000 inhabitants and for the proportion of minor suspects relative to all suspects.

Table 1 shows that the number of apprehended minors per 100,000 inhabitants is higher in the Netherlands than in most other European states, and higher than the mean for all Europe, but is also lower than in several countries, for example, England and Germany. Although we have to keep in mind that countries differ vastly in how minor suspects

TABLE 1

Apprehended Minors per 100,000 Minor Inhabitants, Several
European Countries

	Publication Data Collection		
Country	Total Criminal Offenders per 100,000 Inhabitants	Minors among Offenders (%)	Total Minor Offenders per 100,000 Inhabitants
Netherlands	1,691	17.9	303
Austria	2,531	16.0	405
Finland	6,341	11.7	742
France	1,363	21.3	290
Germany	2,754	19.3	532
Ireland	914	1.5	14
Italy	1,385	2.8	39
Norway	1,667	14.8	247
Spain	514	12.6	65
Sweden	782	11.8	92
Switzerland	786	28.8	226
England and Wales	4,060	11.2	455
Europe (mean)	1,385	12.0	166

SOURCE.—Compiled from data for 1999 in Killias (2003).

are dealt with, the type of offenses that are used as indicators, and the
minimum age of criminal responsibility, these data suggest that the
Netherlands do not stand out in Europe.

Many publications provide self-report statistics about the prevalence
of youth offending. The monitors mentioned above, using representative samples, are the most useful. Studies on etiological questions also
offer information on the prevalence of delinquency among certain categories of youths. Table 2 presents information from a selection of
recent studies in which self-report questions were used. Included in
the table are the monitors (WODC-monitor, SCP Student Survey, and
CBS Youth Survey) and results from the last waves (and from the
WODC-monitor the second-to-last wave also because that wave included questions about more offenses than did the last wave and used
a sample of twelve- to seventeen-year-old youths instead of ten to seventeen-year-olds). Also included is information from the International
Self Report Delinquency (ISRD) study conducted in 1992 (Terlouw
and Bruinsma 1994; Junger-Tas, Haen Marshall, et al. 2003; Barberet
et al. 2004); about 1,000 youths in large and middle-large cities were
questioned at their home addresses. This is not a representative sample,

TABLE 2
Prevalence Statistics, Selection of Dutch Self-Report Studies

	Publication					
	Kruissink and Essers (2004)	Blom et al. (2005)	Wittebrood (2003b)	CBS (2004)	Junger-Tas, Haen Marshall, et al. (2003)	Harland et al. (2005)
Data collection	WODC-monitor 2001	WODC-monitor 2004	Student Survey 2002	Youth Survey 2003	ISRD 1992	NSCR School Study 2002
Sample size (N)	±1,000	±1,500	±10,000	±4,000	±1,000	±2,000
Location of data collection	At home	At home	At school	At home	At home	At school
Sampling focus	Representative	Representative	Representative	Representative	Big and medium cities	Low education, most in cities
Age of respondents	12–17	10–17	12–17	12–17	14–21	13–16
Prevalence of "any offense" (%)	37.3	25.8		51.3	56.3	62.6
Fare dodging (%)	21.3		8.7	25.4	21.2	49.3
Shoplifting (%)	8.1	9.3	14.4	9.5	4.3	15.0
Assault/fighting (%)	11.1		9.3	13.3	10.0	21.4
Wounding someone (%)	12.0	8.9		4.9		8.3
Use of knife/weapon (%)	1.3	.5	6.9	1.0	.7	
Graffiti (%)	9.6	10.5	5.8	10.6	3.4	14.9
Vandalism (%)	11.0	6.5		20.0	13.5	9.8
Bike theft (%)	3.0				5.0	5.8
Burglary (%)	2.9			4.9	1.3	.9

although it is broadly representative of youths living in cities. The table also includes data from the first wave of data collection from the NSCR School Study (Harland et al. 2005). In this study, about 2,000 students from lower levels of secondary schools were questioned by researchers in their classrooms. This also is not a representative sample but represents lower-educated adolescents in the province of South Holland containing relatively many respondents from minority groups and big cities. Students with these characteristics have a relatively high risk of being involved in delinquency.

Table 2 gives data for the total prevalence during the last year ("yes" on any of the delinquency items) and for the prevalence of specific offense types. A caveat is that the studies differ vastly in sampling methodology, the number of delinquency items used, and the wordings of the different delinquency items. Nonetheless, table 2 offers a general impression of prevalence statistics found in Dutch self-report studies.

Table 2 shows quite divergent total prevalence percentages; the reason is that different items and different numbers of them are used in these studies. Despite these differences, a large proportion of respondents, in several studies the majority, report at least one offense. Prevalence statistics for specific offenses in the representative samples are not very different from each other, given the varying wordings and methods that are used. Fare dodging seems to be the most common offense, but other minor offenses are also committed by a substantial proportion of the respondents, varying from 5 to 20 percent. These statistics support the impression that lawbreaking is not uncommon among Dutch youths. The table shows that minor offenses are committed by a small but substantial part of the youth population. The most serious offenses appear to be committed by a small proportion of youths, one or a few percent (about 1 percent for weapon use, 1–3 percent for burglary). The Dutch part of the ISRD study departs a little from the representative monitors: the overall prevalence of any delinquency is quite high, but for some particular offenses (e.g., vandalism), prevalence statistics are lower. The NSCR School Study shows higher percentages of offenders than the three representative studies. The reason is that the sampling strategy aimed at including youths with certain characteristics (lower-educated youths in big or medium-sized cities). These characteristics result in a relatively high risk of becoming delinquent. Nonetheless, the relative order of offenses is comparable with those found in the others: minor offenses (especially fare dodging) are relatively more common among youths, but serious offenses are quite rare.

The ISRD was conducted in several other countries in Europe and in the United States (see Junger-Tas, Haen Marshall, et al. 2003; Barberet et al. 2004), and the project was designed to use similar self-report methodologies in different countries. Although many differences in sampling strategy remained, it can be used to get an impression of the Dutch level of delinquency in comparison to other Western countries. In table 3, results are presented for several countries (largely the same as in table 1) and for the Netherlands.

The findings in table 3 suggest that juvenile offending reported by the respondents in the Dutch sample is neither much lower nor higher than was found in the other samples. This is true for the overall level as well as for specific categories of samples. Unfortunately, the comparison is limited because some samples were country samples, others were at the city level, and some questionnaires were conducted at schools and not at home. There were also small differences in questioning; for example, the English questionnaire did not cover all types of property offenses. A second wave of the ISRD to be held in the near future offers enhanced opportunities for comparison. All the same, table 3 indicates that the self-reported level of delinquency in the Netherlands does not stand out in comparison to other countries, although its figures are not among the lowest. Particularly, property and violent offenses appear relatively highly prevalent, but vandalism and serious offending seem to be relatively less widespread.

C. Changes

Police statistics can be used to get an indication of changes in the volume of juvenile crime, especially long-term changes since these statistics cover several decades. Figure 1 presents long-term changes in youth offenders interrogated by the police from 1960 through 2004. The figure represents changes over the years in the number of apprehended juveniles divided by the total population of juveniles. It is important to make this correction for population size, since this has been fluctuating since 1960.

The number of juvenile suspects has increased steadily to a level about two and a half times higher than in the early 1960s. During the 1960s the level was relatively stable, but, especially between 1975 and 1982, a substantial increase occurred. In the 1980s the level remained

TABLE 3
Prevalence Self-Reports 1992, Several European Countries and the United States

Country	Respondents Reporting Any Delinquency (%)	Respondents Reporting Property Offenses (%)	Respondents Reporting Violent Offenses (%)	Respondents Reporting Vandalism (%)	Respondents Reporting Serious Offenses (%)
Netherlands	56.3	28.0	21.2	13.5	9.1
Belgium (Liège)	59.8	27.1	16.8	21.0	11.1
Finland (Helsinki)	67.7	32.9	14.7	16.3	9.0
Germany (Mannheim)	45.3	20.7	11.7	7.3	3.7
Ireland (Belfast)	45.0	29.1	13.1	19.7	13.4
Italy (three cities)	62.3	3.8	12.4	14.3	2.6
Portugal	54.3	21.4	18.1	16.3	9.9
Spain	54.2	19.7	21.8	20.4	10.4
Switzerland	65.4	29.5	16.4	18.2	6.1
United Kingdom: England and Wales	35.1	16.4	13.5	5.2	13.6
United States (Omaha, NE)	59.2	37.6	27.1	15.0	15.3

SOURCE.—Junger-Tas, Marshall, et al. 2003.

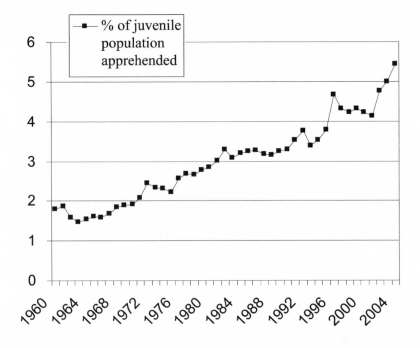

FIG. 1.—Changes between 1960 and 2004 in the proportion of juveniles apprehended and interrogated by the police. Source: Calculated by the author from Dutch police data.

stable, fluctuated in the beginning of the 1990s, and jumped and peaked in 1996. Many authors (e.g., Junger-Tas 2004; van der Laan, forthcoming) attribute this steep rise to the introduction of the new juvenile justice law in 1995 that changed police recording policies. Certain minor offenses, followed by a HALT-sanction (a form of diversion), were held out of the statistics before 1996 but were afterward included. After 1996, the proportion of interrogated juvenile offenders stabilized at a slightly lower level than in 1996 but higher than in the early 1990s.

In the last three years for which information is available (2002–4), there has been a sizable increase in the number of juvenile offenders, to even higher levels than in 1996. It is unclear to what extent this relates to real changes in juvenile offending. The increase may result in part from the introduction of police performance contracts, which led to pressure on the police to "produce" more. That juvenile offending has become a priority in policing may also have contributed to the increase.

The statistics on recorded juvenile offending further show that violent crimes and vandalism–public order offenses increased since the early 1990s, whereas property offenses changed little. In 2002–4, threats, theft with violence (robberies), simple thefts, public order offenses, and vandalism have increased. Many of these changes, however, may be attributed to policy changes (e.g., the increase in "public order" offenses and threats). Nonetheless, the increase in violent offending and robbery among juveniles during the 1990s is marked and seems too large to attribute completely to changes in policy.

The various self-report delinquency monitors also offer information about changes in juvenile offending. This information is a valuable complement to police statistics because self-reports are less influenced by policy changes and recording practices, although results may be influenced by fluctuations in sampling methodology. The Student Survey and the WODC-monitor show a relatively stable level of offending over the past ten to fifteen years, with no spectacular increases or decreases since the beginning of the 1990s (Wittebrood 2003b; Kruissink and Essers 2004). In the WODC-monitor, prevalence statistics seem to have increased for some offenses in the second-to-last wave in 2001; in the last wave, the prevalence seemed quite stable for most offenses. The Student Survey reveals that the proportion of students reporting violent offenses has increased somewhat since 1994, but property offending has decreased. The WODC-monitor also shows a somewhat higher prevalence for many offenses in 1996 than in other years, which seems to confirm the peak in the police figures, although less dramatically. Self-report statistics from the CBS (http://www.cbs.nl) for the years 1997, 2001, and 2003 show that general prevalence among twelve- to seventeen-year-old respondents was highest in 2001 but decreased somewhat in 2003. The same pattern is found for most specific offenses.

In general, self-report studies suggest that delinquent behavior among young people has not changed since the early 1990s. This differs from the pattern found in the police statistics. However, the monitors also indicate that some offenses, especially violent crimes, were increasing recently, which confirms the recent increases on violent offending found in the police statistics. The WODC-monitor suggests not only that the peak in 1996 was a recording effect but that something really happened in that year. The CBS self-report statistics for 2001 and 2003, however, depart from police statistics. In general, though, there are multiple indications of a recent increase in (violent) juvenile offending. Further research is needed to determine whether the most recent rise reflects a real increase in youth crime or merely changes in juvenile justice or registration policies. Developments in juvenile offending remain unclear.

D. Gender Differences

Like elsewhere, boys in the Netherlands are more involved in crime than girls, especially with respect to serious, violent, and persistent offending. The most recent police statistics show that 84 percent of offenders questioned were boys (Blom and Huijbregts 2004; van der Laan, forthcoming). Police statistics also suggest that the recidivism rate is higher for boys. There appear, however, to be no differences in the age of first arrest (Mertens, Grapendaal, and Docter-Schamhardt 1998).

The proportion of girls questioned has grown slowly but steadily: from about 10 percent during the 1960s to the beginning of the 1980s to 13 percent in the 1990s to 16 percent in the early years of the twenty-first century. This increase was apparent for property offenses (the proportion of girls changed from 12.5 percent in 1980 to 21 percent in 2003) and for violent offenses (from 4 to 15 percent). Whether this means that girls are catching up (Angenent 1991) or that an important gender gap still remains (Bouw 1995) is a matter of interpretation.

Self-report studies give a different picture. Although these studies confirm that boys are more involved in delinquency than girls, the differences are less marked than in police statistics. How much difference there is depends on the type of offense that is considered. For serious and violent offenses, the differences are substantial. For example, in the WODC-monitor, the Student Survey, and the NSCR School Study, boys report involvement in street fights or injuring about twice as often as girls and vandalism about three times as often. This is a clear difference, but the ratio is less than in the police statistics. For some offenses, however, there seem to be few or no distinctions. In the last wave of the WODC-monitor, the two sexes did not differ substantially on petty offenses such as fare dodging, shoplifting, and graffiti. Similar results were found in the NSCR School Study: girls and boys were equally involved in graffiti, shoplifting, and fare dodging.

Differences are more noticeable when very serious offenses, such as robberies and burglaries, are considered. In the NSCR School Study, about 1.5 percent of boys admitted such offenses, whereas only a few girls were involved (0.1 percent for burglary, 0.3 percent for robbery). These findings suggest that serious offending among girls is rare, though not absent. In certain cases, girls can be very violent and criminal (see, e.g., the cases described in Mertens, Grapendaal, and Docter-Schamhardt [1998]). However, among girls, serious offending seldom lasts long. A five-year longitudinal study using self-report methods (Nijboer 1997) found that the involvement of girls in serious delinquency usually lasted only one year, significantly shorter than the average for boys. On the basis of police records in two big cities, Mertens, Grapendaal, and Docter-Schamhardt (1998) also report that girls end delinquent behavior earlier than boys do.

E. Offending and Ethnicity

For a long time, police statistics were not very informative about the relationship between ethnicity and juvenile offending. Only the native country of suspects was registered, but not their ethnicity (which is officially forbidden to prevent ethnic discrimination). That was a major problem because many youths are second-generation ethnic minorities: they were born in the Netherlands, but their parents come from abroad. Because of this, studies on ethnicity and crime must use sources of police data other than the official statistics compiled by the Dutch Central Bureau of Statistics. However, it was possible with the identification system used by the police (HKS) to estimate involvement in delinquency among different ethnic groups (van der Hoeven 1985; van Hulst and Bos 1994; Korf, Bookelman, and de Haan 2001). Local studies and reviews of these studies (Leuw 1997; Junger, Wittebrood, and Timman 2001; Driessen et al. 2002) show that juveniles from certain ethnic categories are disproportionately represented in youth crime. Moroccan and Antillean youths appear to be overrepresented the most (about three to five times), and Surinamese youths also are overrepresented (about two times). Members of certain relatively recent ethnic minority groups (refugees and asylum seekers) appear to be overrepresented in police data, although there are vast differences between countries (Kromhout and van San 2002). There are also ethnic minorities in the Netherlands that are not overrepresented. Examples are juveniles originating from eastern Asian countries and Hindustan youths with a Surinamese background.

A recent study explored the relationship between ethnicity and offending in more detail. All data from the HKS system from 2002 were combined with demographic data in the population register obtained via the CBS (Blom et al. 2005). A distinction was made between first-generation ethnic minority youths, second-generation youths with two foreign parents, and second-generation youths with one Dutch parent and one parent from an ethnic minority. This study confirmed the overrepresentation of some minority youths: while 1.3 percent of all Dutch youths were recorded as a suspect, this was true of 3.1 percent of the ethnic minority youths. Moroccan and Antillean youths appeared relatively often as suspects. Both first- and second-generation, but mainly male, Moroccan youths were overrepresented (10.4 percent of the first-generation boys, 7.6 percent with one Moroccan parent, and 11.9 percent with two Moroccan parents). For Antillean youths, both boys and girls were overrepresented, but the first generation more than the second (13.7 percent of the first-generation boys and 4.5 percent of the first-generation girls). Second-generation boys from Turkey and both generations of Surinamese boys were overrepresented to a lesser extent, and high percentages were also found for some other smaller ethnic groups, for example, second-generation youths from Yugoslavia and from some African countries. Youths with Asian, Eastern European, and South or Central American background either were not clearly overrepresented or were underrepresented.

Blom et al. (2005) conducted multivariate analyses in which the effect of ethnicity was controlled by the background variables of socioeconomic status (SES), gender, age, household composition, and neighborhood. The effects of ethnicity decrease when controlled for by these variables, especially when the SES of parents is taken into account. The amount of variance in whether an individual is a suspect or not, explained by ethnic background, is only 4 percent. However, the effects of ethnicity are still substantial, even when controlled for by different risk factors. The greatest effects were found for having an Antillean (first generation), Moroccan, or Yugoslavian (second generation, two parents) background. In the model that includes most variables, odds ratios were found about 3 and 4, indicating that youths from these ethnic minorities have a three to four times higher chance of being a suspect, controlling for background demographic variables.

Self-report studies are another possible source for exploring the relationship between ethnicity and juvenile offending. Unfortunately, many studies in the Netherlands long used samples consisting predominantly of ethnically Dutch youths. Recently, sampling strategies focus more often on including juveniles from a foreign ethnic background. In the last waves of the WODC-monitor, for example, a larger number of ethnic minorities was included than before (Kruissink and Essers 2004; Blom, van der Laan, and Huijbregts 2005). This study did not find large differences between Dutch youths and juveniles from ethnic minorities. Junger-Tas, Cruyff, et al. (2003) used data from a youth survey in Rotterdam to compare the delinquency scores of different ethnic categories. This study was conducted in 1997 among more than 4,000 third-grade students from secondary schools, mainly aged fourteen and fifteen. The sample offers a good representation of different ethnic categories and educational levels in Rotterdam. The researchers found that respondents with Antillean and Cape Verdean (a substantial minority group in Rotterdam) backgrounds were more involved in delinquent behavior than were juveniles from other descents. Both the Antillean and Cape Verdean boys and girls had relatively high scores. Among the other ethnic categories, Moroccan and Surinamese juveniles had relatively high scores. Turkish and Dutch juveniles had the lowest. Also in the NSCR School Survey, Antillean juveniles appeared to be relatively more involved in offending than were other juveniles, for both boys and girls (Harland et al. 2005). However, respondents from other ethnic minorities did not report more offenses than Dutch youths, and Turkish and Moroccan respondents (boys as well as girls) reported fewer. The same result was found in a recent survey using a multiethnic sample of almost 700 (mainly twelve-year-old) children in the last year of primary school in Rotterdam (Broekhuizen and Driessen 2005). The Moroccan respondents reported slightly fewer offenses than the other ethnic categories, and the Cape Verdean and Antillean respondents slightly more minor and property offenses, but the differences were small.

Junger, Wittebrood, and Timman (2001) conducted secondary analyses of three self-report studies to explore the overrepresentation of juveniles from ethnic minority groups among serious and violent offenses. They concluded that over the whole range, ethnic minority youths had (in varying degrees) higher prevalence figures for serious property and violent offenses than Dutch youths. Antillean youths, especially boys and girls, had higher prevalence figures, and in two studies the Moroccan boys had higher rates than the Dutch boys.

A less recent study revealed that there may be problems with the use of self-report methods among certain ethnic minority categories (Junger 1989; Junger and Zeilstra 1989). Researchers compared self-reports with police records. In some cases a discrepancy was found between both sources, most often among Moroccan and Turkish respondents. Involvement of Turkish and Moroccan juveniles was similar to that of Dutch youths when self-report data were used, but they were more involved in delinquency when police records were used. These findings suggest that self-reports from Turkish or Moroccan youths were less reliable than those from other juveniles (at least at the time of that study). This may be why Moroccan youths in several studies report fewer, not more, offenses than other ethnic groups. However, the results reflect a real lower level of delinquency among young Moroccans at school. Older juveniles and youths absent from school may be responsible for their overrepresentation in police statistics.

II. Characteristics of Juvenile Offending

Statistics on juvenile offending do not reveal how these offenses take place. Studies in which certain offenses are described and in which juvenile offending in groups is analyzed give a more complete picture. Categories of offenders can be distinguished on the basis of differential motivations and experience. A large fraction of youth crime takes place in social company, sometimes in the form of troublesome youth groups. These groups sometimes incorporate elements from the American gang culture, but there are major differences between troublesome Dutch youth groups and American gangs.

A. Specific Offenses

Several studies have focused on particular offenses (e.g., robberies) or groups of offenses (e.g., violence). Some included juvenile offenders (together with young adults) and are informative about the motivations and backgrounds of young offenders and about their modus operandi.

A few studies in the 1990s focused on robbery (either street robberies or holdups in a store or bank). Kroese and Staring (1993) interviewed young and adult prisoners convicted for robbery. They distinguished three types of robbers: beginners, who usually chose easy objects that pay less; professionals, who chose more difficult but also more rewarding targets; and desperate robbers, who committed a robbery as a way of solving financial problems. Juvenile robbers were typically beginners. Most did not have the experience to be a professional. De Haan (1993) distinguished four types of motivations: to get money to buy drugs; to get money because there are no other means of income; as an instrument to obtain easy or a lot of money; and as recreation, to get excitement and kicks. Those with the last motivation appeared usually to be young, but juveniles were also found in the other categories. These studies suggest that street robberies, especially grabbing bags from old ladies, are looked down on by many offenders. Nevertheless, many young beginners use this technique. Bank robberies are regarded as more honorable and as a way to obtain status.

Gruter and Kruize (1995) focused on young robbers in big cities (fifteen to twenty years old). They analyzed criminal records and conducted interviews. Most respondents told the interviewers that they started offending when they were between ten and fourteen years old. In this period they usually committed petty offenses such as shoplifting and bike theft, but their offending pattern progressed quickly. These robbers were characterized as versatile offenders involved in a wide range of property offenses during their careers. More than half also sold small amounts of drugs, and robberies were sometimes a means of getting investment money. Gruter and Kruize found that there is not always a development from petty offending to robberies; some of the respondents started with robberies and committed simple thefts later on. Young offenders made the step toward robbery when they were mentally ready for it, and some were ready early in life. Some young robbers offended because they had no other means of living, but drug use was seldom the primary reason. The versatile and frequent offenders usually had a mixture of recreational and instrumental motives.

Several studies examined violent behavior in general. This issue has received a lot of attention, following increasing public concern about street violence (often referred to as "senseless violence"). Several theoretical publications and reflections were published on this issue (Franke, Wilterdink, and Brinkgreve 1991; Hoogerwerf 1996; de Haan et al. 1999; van den Brink 2001). A few empirical studies were conducted in which small numbers of violent juveniles were interviewed (Ferwerda and Beke 1995; Bol et al. 1998). These and other studies (e.g., Ferwerda 1992) suggest that violent behavior is sometimes quite normal for juveniles under certain circumstances. One of these circumstances is going out during the weekend, when young people hang out in city centers and sometimes use large amounts of alcohol. For some youths, fighting on the street is part of a good night out, and they use every excuse to do it. This category of violent offenders often become victims of violence themselves (Ferwerda 1992). Although many of these fights result from impulses, often committed under the influence of alcohol, sometimes a certain amount of planning is involved. Some violent offenders said that they were aware of the risks of being apprehended and therefore tried to plan fights at certain locations (Ferwerda and Beke 1995). Others said that violent behavior can be a way to gain dominance over the street (Bol et al. 1998).

B. Kids and Groups

Many juvenile offenses are committed in company (cf. Hakkert 1998; Weerman 2001, 2003). In several studies in the 1990s, researchers collected data on the proportion of co-offending in juvenile crime. Studies based on police records usually find that offenses are committed by two or more persons in the majority of the cases (Ferwerda, Bottenberg, and Beke 1999). Hakkert et al. (1998) used data from the WODC self-report monitor to study co-offending among juvenile offenders. These data confirmed that the majority of juvenile offenses are committed by more than one person (see also Hakkert 1998). Co-offending seems to decrease with age, but there were no obvious differences between boys and girls in their rate of co-offending or the number of accomplices.

The rate of co-offending appears highest for vandalism and public order disturbances, and the average number of co-offenders is highest for these offenses (Hakkert et al. 1998; Ferwerda, Bottenberg, and Beke 1999). Assaults and fighting are relatively more often committed by lone offenders, but when there is group fighting the number of co-fighters is often relatively high (five to ten). Property offenses are most often committed by two to four juvenile offenders. Usually, offending groups are not stable; they change from offense to offense. The findings about co-offending among juveniles in the Netherlands do not depart much from findings in other countries (see Reiss 1988; Warr 2002).

Several studies have been conducted on troublesome youth groups. The research department of the Hague police used a questionnaire for police workers to make an inventory of youth groups in public areas that caused problems for the police (Gruter, Baas, and Vegter 1996). Three types of troublesome youth groups were distinguished: both-ersome groups of youths who hang around and are annoying but do not commit offenses, nuisance (or, better, "light delinquent") groups that commit petty crimes and are threatening toward people on the street, and criminal groups that commit different kinds of light and serious offenses. Beke, van Wijk, and Ferwerda (2000) adopted this strategy to study the prevalence and characteristics of these youth groups in five middle-sized cities. A considerable number (generally ten to twenty) of these groups were present in each city. They were not limited to deteriorated neighborhoods but were present throughout the city, although the most troubled neighborhoods had relatively more nuisance and criminal youth groups. The groups mostly numbered ten to twenty, and very large groups (more than forty) were rare. Beke, van Wijk, and Ferwerda conducted a network analysis using the police files of the members of the youth groups. Many groups consisted of two or more subgroups that differed in severity of offending. Many group members co-offended with juveniles who did not belong to the groups on the street.

Dutch criminologists long disagreed over whether there are youth "gangs" in the Netherlands. Some authors used the label quite easily, without discussing the criteria to call a group a gang (Sansone 1992; Werdmölder 1997). Others emphasized the differences between these "gangs" and gangs in the United States (van Gemert 1995; van Oosterwijk, Gruter, and Versteegh 1995) or assumed that juveniles using gang colors and symbols were merely imitating the American examples (Ferwerda, Versteegh, and Beke 1995). Recently, some authors adopted the definition developed by the Eurogang Program (see van Gemert and Fleisher 2004, 2005; Decker and Weerman 2005; Esbensen and Weerman 2005). According to this definition, groups may be called a gang or a troublesome youth group (depending on the preference of the researcher) when it is a durable street-oriented youth group whose identity includes illegal behavior.

During the 1990s, certain youth groups in the Netherlands (especially in The Hague) adopted gang clothes and symbols of the American Crips (and their counterparts, the Bloods). They wore blue (or red) colors, used American gang terms, and tried to get a dangerous reputation (van Oosterwijk, Gruter, and Versteegh 1995). This phenomenon was initiated by one delinquent group of Surinamese youths and was later imitated by many other youths from different backgrounds, and also by groups that were not delinquent or dangerous (van Stapele 2003). Nowadays, the Crips symbols are not widespread; other examples have taken their place.

Van Gemert (1998a, 2001) conducted a small case study on three delinquent Crips groups, using information from police records and informants. The youths from two of these gangs committed robberies to prove themselves and to gain status in the group. Group pressure and gang culture stimulated offending in these cases. The role of group processes also emerged from an ethnographic study of a large group of Moroccan boys between the ages of sixteen and twenty (van Gemert and Fleisher 2004, 2005). This was an extremely troublesome group that had conflicts with the neighborhood and in some cases also intimidated police officers. Some persons in this group committed robberies and other offenses. The group did not have special clothes or rules and was not territorial. Group members were egalitarian and said that they did not have a leader and also would not obey others in the group; in practice, some persons clearly had higher status than others. Although this group clearly does not fit stereotypes about gangs, van Gemert and Fleisher conclude that this group is a gang, according to the Eurogang definition.

Esbensen and Weerman (2005) used quantitative survey data to compare troublesome Dutch youth groups with American youth gangs. The results indicated that several percent of the respondents in both countries belonged to a gang or a troublesome youth group. The level of delinquency of Dutch and American members of these groups was remarkably similar: these juveniles committed four to five times more offenses than respondents who were not in a gang or troublesome youth group. The risk factors correlated with membership in a gang or troublesome youth group appeared to be the same in both countries (e.g., weak bonds with parents and school, higher impulsivity, and more risk seeking). But there were large differences between the United States and the Netherlands in the characteristics of these groups. The Dutch groups were smaller and much less organized. Only a minority of the Dutch youths reported that their group had formal leaders, or special rules, symbols, or clothing; these characteristics were found in a large majority of the American cases.

III. Qualitative Research

Ethnographic research relevant to understanding juvenile offending is usually broad in scope, describing the whole complex of attitudes, ideas, and behavioral patterns of different categories of youths. Some studies aim at giving insight into the culture and lifestyles of youths in general, of which offending may or may not be a part. Many other studies focus on understanding the lives and backgrounds of ethnic minority youths. These lives often include delinquent behavior, but this is usually interpreted in a broader context. It appears that offending can be an alternative life strategy for marginalized or stigmatized youths, an alternative way to earn a living and gain respect and status.

A. Lifestyles and Subcultures

During the 1960s and 1970s, a time when young people developed their own subcultures and sometimes rebelled against society, youth culture and lifestyle became an important field of research (Abma 1986). An early criminological example was the study by Buikhuisen (1965) of a group that was called "nozems" at that time. Buikhuisen and colleagues used interviews with closed and open items, employed psychological instruments, and conducted participant observation in a cafeteria and during New Year's Eve. One of Buikhuisen's conclusions was that provocative behaviors he observed should not be seen as rebellious, but as leisure activity.

Miedema et al. (1986), Miedema and Eelman (1987), and Janssen (1988) studied lifestyles of poorly educated youths. Using in-depth interviews, they tried to reconstruct discourses and different types of lifestyles. Their approach was to view delinquency as part of a coherent pattern of attitudes and activities, instead of as an isolated phenomenon. Most of their respondents were "respectable" youths who believed that delinquent behavior was generally inappropriate. In the lifestyles of what the researchers called "cultural rebellions" and of working youths who went out on the weekend, delinquent behavior was incidental and acceptable under certain circumstances. In the lifestyles of "marginal" youths, lawbreaking was acceptable because they were raised with (or developed) a them-and-us view of society.

B. Ethnic Minority Youths and Young Adults

A substantial number of studies have been conducted on ethnic minority youths (a comprehensive review is found in Driessen et al. [2002]). Many were ethnographic, aimed at gaining insight into lifestyles and circumstances. In varying degrees they were aimed at getting a better understanding of offending by minority youths. Some of these studies date back to the 1970s and 1980s, but most appeared in the past fifteen years. During this period, there was increasing awareness and recognition that juveniles from some ethnic groups were overrepresented in the crime figures.

Buiks (1983) studied a group of addicted young people from Surinam (aged fifteen to thirty, in a deteriorated Rotterdam neighborhood). He interviewed informants and respondents from the area to understand the origins of this marginalized group, their lifestyles, and "ethnic patterns" of thinking and acting. Another book about marginal young Surinamese people (in Amsterdam, mainly aged fourteen to twenty-two) was published by Sansone (1992), based on a long period of fieldwork in youth centers, education centers, and other meeting places. Both Buiks and Sansone view deviant lifestyles among young Surinamese as survival strategies. One is symbolic (being like rasta). But another involves "hosselen" (hustling), doing all kinds of small street jobs and trades to get money, a way of living that is common in Surinam. Many of these "hossels" appear to be illegal or semilegal, for instance, smuggling and trading small amounts of drugs and selling stolen goods. "Hossels" provide a good alternative to regular work and gave the Surinamese of this generation the freedom that they were used to.

Werdmölder (1986, 1990, 1997) studied marginal Moroccan boys in Amsterdam. His research subjects were fourteen to twenty-two years of age, migrated to the Netherlands from Morocco in their childhood, and were often involved in delinquency and aggressive behavior. The group met in a youth center, and Werdmölder worked as a bartender to establish contact. He provides a vivid impression of this group and the development of the group members over several years. He describes a process of isolation and ongoing marginalization that resulted from poor integration and hostile reactions from the neighborhood. A more recent ethnographic study on Moroccan immigrant boys was conducted by van Gemert (1998b) in Rotterdam. He observed and in-terviewed Moroccan boys and informants in a neighborhood center. His description of Moroccan culture explains the background of certain key elements (especially a lack of norm internalization and an attitude of distrust) in the behavior of Moroccan boys in the Netherlands. In Moroccan families, unwanted behaviors are often prevented by pun-ishment without explanation. Moroccan children learn by "trial and error," and that may explain why they often test the limits of adults and try to find out what they can do without being corrected. Van Gemert also believes that there is a high level of distrust among Mor-occan people in the Netherlands, a cultural feature that originally de-veloped in the harsh circumstances of rural life in Morocco. This ex-plains why there is a remarkable lack of coordination and cooperation between young Moroccan offenders, who seem to assume that every-one tries to get the best for himself.

Van San (1998) studied the delinquent behavior of Antillean boys (fourteen to seventeen years old). She interviewed sixty boys (offenders and nonoffenders) and thirty mothers and conducted observations of two Antillean families. The interviews were aimed at understanding the boys' and their mothers' perceptions of the background and causes of their delinquent behavior. The boys said that offending, in particular stealing, was common in the poor Antillean neighborhoods where they grew up and that all of their friends did it. Violence appeared to be legitimated by honor and masculinity, and these legitimations were used by the boys and their mothers. Many Antillean boys seemed to be normalized to react strongly and stab a person with a knife when being challenged or insulted. Van San analyzed the role of one-parent, matrifocal families in which most Antillean boys grew up and con-cluded that single parenthood in itself is not criminogenic, but, rather, the deprived circumstances of these mothers is. As a result, Antillean boys and their mothers attached a great deal of meaning to status sym-bols such as expensive clothes and shoes to keep their reputations high.

These influential studies, and other qualitative studies about offend-ing among ethnic minority youths (Kaufman and Verbraeck 1986; Bo-venkerk 1992; van Hulst and Bos 1994; Coppes, De Groot, and She-raazi 1997; Kemper 1999), provide insights into the cultural backgrounds of these youths and the meanings of offending for them. In general, these studies suggest that delinquent behavior is often a survival strategy of marginalized or stigmatized groups. For many, offending is an alternative to earning a living and a way to get respect and status. Some authors, however, warn against exclusive ethnic explanations of certain behavior patterns. Miedema (2002), for example, argues that many elements in the behavior of offenders and offending groups in different ethnic categories are manifestations of a wider street or youth culture.

IV. Causes and Correlates

Quantitative studies on juvenile offending usually focus on causes and correlates. Quite a few are informed by particular criminological theories, others using a broader eclectic or multiple risk factor approach. These studies report many risk factors and correlates that match findings in research throughout the world. Some investigate more thoroughly the roles of parents, schools, and peers and analyze interactions among them. Several focus on explanations of gender differences in juvenile offending.

A. Testing Classic Etiological Theories

Several studies have tested or developed etiological theories. They use interviews or questionnaires, employ self-report methodology, and aim at understanding individual differences in offending.

Junger-Tas (Junger-Tas 1972, 1976, 1983; Junger-Tas, Junger, and Barendse-Hoornweg 1985) was among the first to use self-report methods to test theoretical assumptions about juvenile offending. In her studies from the 1970s, interviews with adolescents in a Belgian city were used to test hypotheses from several criminological theories, especially from a control perspective. The studies from the early 1980s were conducted among a large group of Dutch adolescents and aimed at investigating the backgrounds of delinquents and the impact of judicial reactions. In her dissertation from 1972, Junger-Tas used the literature from early control theorists such as Nye and Reckless. Later in her career, she adopted Hirschi's social control theory and became a strong proponent of this theory in the Netherlands. She found many correlations of self-reported delinquent behavior with social control variables such as attachment to parents, supervision of parents, motivation for school, and unconventional attitudes toward delinquent behavior. Poor integration in the family and failure at school were the strongest correlates in these studies. Having delinquent friends and "negative" leisure activities were strongly related to delinquency, but these variables were interpreted as an effect of poor integration in the family and school. A combined index measured the overall concept of "social integration" and correlated strongly with delinquent behavior; changes in this index were correlated with changes in the frequency of offending (Junger-Tas, Junger, and Barendse-Hoornweg 1985).

During the 1980s, social control theory became quite popular in Dutch criminology and won strong advocates (Junger 1989, 1990; Rutenfrans and Terlouw 1996). The theory was used by policy makers as a foundation for an influential government paper (Commissie Kleine Criminaliteit 1985). Bruinsma (1981) was more critical. On the basis of survey data from secondary school students, he used path analysis to test parts of the theory. He found that attachment to friends had a positive effect on delinquency and also that the explained variance was much higher for respondents from higher social economic backgrounds than for lower-class respondents. Bruinsma concluded that the social control theory did not do well in comparison with other major theories.

Bruinsma (1985) elaborated and tested a version of differential association theory on a sample of high school students (see also Bruinsma 1992). Path analyses resulted in significant effects for most elements of the theory. For example, contacts with deviant parents and friends were related to communication about criminal techniques, to deviant definitions (an index of the acceptability of deviant behavior in general), and to deviant definitions on less adherence to law-conforming norms. This variable was directly related to the frequency of delinquent behavior. Bruinsma controlled his results for gender and social class and also contrasted the results with hypotheses derived from rival theories. He concluded that differential association theory was supported over the other theories. In a secondary analysis of these data, Fiselier and Verschuren (1988) used structural equation modeling (LISREL) further to scrutinize and advance Bruinsma's model. In general, the model was supported, but it appeared that improvements were possible. One of the modifications was to add a feedback effect of delinquent behavior on contacts with deviant peers; another was to add an extra effect of criminal techniques on delinquency via the perception of criminal opportunities. The authors concluded that their modified model had a better fit to the data than the original one. They interpret their modifications as consistent with differential association theory and see their model as a better representation of the social learning perspective than Bruinsma's original model.

In the late 1980s and in the 1990s, the social control perspective continued to be important in theory-driven research. Baerveldt (1990) formulated a modified version for his study of the role of schools in the prevention of crime. Apart from the assumption that social bonds, especially bonds with schools and teachers, are negatively related to delinquency, he assumed that some bonds were related to more delinquency, such as having delinquent peers in one's social network at school. Both assumptions were supported by the results of a survey among secondary school students.

Rutenfrans and Terlouw (1994) adopted Hirschi's theory in its original form in a study of life events, social control, and delinquency. They used data from a study in the city of Utrecht that was primarily designed to track the social and psychological development of youths (the WIL-study; see Meeus and 't Hart 1993). A sample of more than 3,000 youths and young adults were interviewed two times at home, in 1991 and 1994. The sample was not representative of young people in the Netherlands: it was a subsample of a panel for a telephone interview study and consisted almost completely of native Dutch respondents. Effects on delinquency were found for indicators of attachment, commitment, involvement, and belief: the elements of social control theory. The absence of delinquency was predicted well by social control variables. However, the predictive value of low-level social control was limited: weak bonds often were not correlated with high levels of delinquency.

Junger and colleagues (Junger and Zeilstra 1989; Junger 1990; Junger and Polder 1992; Junger and Haen Marshall 1997) explored the usefulness of social control theory for explaining differences in delinquency among several ethnic groups. Dutch, Surinamese, Moroccan, and Turkish boys were interviewed. Many indicators for attachment, commitment, and involvement were related to delinquency. In a multivariate analysis, the strongest effects were found for conventional beliefs, the supervision of parents, school conflicts, and unconventional leisure activities. Most of these effects were significant for each of the groups, with relatively small differences in strength. Junger concluded that the theory is valid for different ethnic groups. She also tested assumptions from rival theories and concluded that social control theory was superior as an explanation for delinquency differences within and between ethnic groups.

Weerman (1998) investigated elements from social control theory in a follow-up of a sample of juvenile detainees and secondary school students. Conventional and unconventional social bonds were distinguished, as were different bonding mechanisms and several change mechanisms. Correlations were found between social control variables (family bonds and supervision, school attachments and commitment, and beliefs) and delinquency, and between changes in social bonds and changes in delinquency. A cluster analysis was conducted, using five factors that correlated most strongly with delinquency (see also Weerman 1996). Respondents with an accumulation of weak conventional bonds and strong relationships with delinquent peers were very often serious delinquents, whereas those with a mix of conventional and unconventional bonds were partly minor and partly serious delinquents. Other patterns resulted in either no or only light delinquent behavior.

Luijpers (2000) added elements about identity development to social control theory. He assumed that an increased intention to explore and experiment in early adolescence is related to the beginning of delinquency and that a strengthening of conventional bonds toward the end of adolescence is related to desistance. Data from two studies were used to analyze the usefulness of this approach. The results were mixed: in one study a correlation was found between exploration in adolescence and delinquency, but not in the other.

Recently, Junger-Tas and colleagues used social control theory to analyze differences among ethnic minority youths (Junger-Tas, Cruyff, et al. 2003). Social control variables were combined with information on negative life events, social contexts, and psychological well-being. They used data from a youth survey in Rotterdam (the Rotterdam Jeugdmonitor) to test their theoretical model. In that study, information was gathered for several age groups between one and eighteen years of age to make an inventory of well-being and problem behavior in Rotterdam. The researchers used a subsample of more than 4,000 fourteen- to fifteen-year-old students from thirty-three schools, a representative sample of that age group in the city. Correlates of delinquency were quite similar for six ethnic groups. At the same time, social bonds appeared to be weaker for several ethnic minority groups in comparison with Dutch respondents: they had on average more problematic family situations, less supervision and support, and more problems at school. The number of negative life events and living in a poor neighborhood were clearly related with ethnicity. These results suggest that social control variables combined with other contextual factors can explain an important part of ethnic differences in delinquency.

Gottfredson and Hirschi's (1990) general (self-control) theory of crime did not receive as much attention in the Netherlands as social control theory did, though it was the subject of two studies that appeared during the 1990s. Junger et al. (1995) investigated the relationship between accidents and delinquency as an indirect test of the theory (which states that low self-control enhances reckless behavior and offending). Rutenfrans and Terlouw (1996) used several other indirect indicators of low self-control, such as frequent dating, low dedication for schoolwork, financial problems, and having one-night stands. Both studies used data from the longitudinal WIL-study. In multivariate analyses, accidents and most of the other indirect indicators of low self-control appeared to have significant effects on delinquent behavior, which was interpreted as important support for the general theory of crime. However, the indirect behavioral indicators of these studies are often regarded as inferior to attitudinal scales (see Pratt and Cullen 2000). In a recent study, conducted in the Netherlands and three other countries, self-control theory was tested using the attitudinal measurement method (Vaszony et al. 2001). This study showed that different dimensions of self-control (especially impulsivity and risk seeking) had effects on different types of deviance and delinquency in samples from all participating countries.

These and other Dutch studies in which constructs from criminological theories are used generally result in the replication of findings from research in other countries (especially the United States). They show that major criminological perspectives are valid not only elsewhere but also in the Netherlands. However, although the number of studies is substantial, etiological research on juvenile offending remains limited. While Hirschi's social control theory (1969) received a lot of attention in empirical research, other important leading theories in criminology were never the subjects of empirical testing in the Netherlands, for example, Akers's social learning theory (1973) and Agnew's general strain theory (1992). And self-control theory, which has been tested repeatedly in the United States (Gottfredson and Hirschi 1990), was investigated only three times in the Netherlands.

The Dutch debate about etiological theories has been quite vivid.

Apart from empirical research, discussion papers and theoretical discussions have appeared in the literature (e.g., Jongman 1981; Rutenfrans 1983; Bruinsma 1985; van der Hoeven 1987; Angenent 1991; Rovers 1998; Völker and Driessen 2003; see also van der Laan 2004). An important element in the debate is the question of whether and how the integration of influential theories is possible (see de Haan 1998).

B. Other Studies

Many other studies on causes and correlates have been conducted. Some aimed at exploring the relation of delinquency with a list of risk factors, for example, different personality factors (Hauber, Toornvliet, and Willemse 1986) or school factors and truancy (Dijksterhuis and Nijboer 1984). Some aimed at exploring the relationship of offending with psychiatric or developmental psychological factors (Scholte 1993; Doreleijers 1995). Others referred to criminological theories but used them eclectically, combining elements from a wide array of theories (Markus 1995; Hendriks-Elzes 1997). Recently, studies use a risk factor approach or follow the recent expansion of developmental criminology (van der Heiden-Attema and Bol 2000; Bongers 2005; van Dam 2005; see also Loeber and Slot, in this volume).

An interesting large-scale study was conducted at Groningen University during the 1980s and 1990s to increase insights into the role of (secondary) education and delinquency (Nijboer and Dijksterhuis 1989; Ferwerda 1992; Dijksterhuis 1993; Nijboer 1993, 1997). The researchers formulated a theoretical model in which elements from different theories and approaches were combined. A five-year longitudinal study was conducted in which a purposive sample of about 500 respondents were questioned yearly over five years. The data indicated that several family and school factors, peer influences, and two personality indexes (disinhibition and also thrill and adventure seeking) had strong predictive value. Exploratory LISREL analyses suggested that the most important factors were family climate factors, motivation for school work, and misbehavior at school.

As a part of this study, Ferwerda (1992) conducted qualitative interviews with a subsample of high-risk boys. Despite their high-risk characterizations, some respondents had not offended at all, others had committed only petty offenses, and some had developed more serious forms of delinquency. The offenders had a more negative attitude toward school and were more impulsive and thrill seeking. The most serious offenders planned their offenses more carefully, were primarily motivated by prospects for gain, and committed offenses alone or with a trusted companion. Some of the petty offenders desisted, but others were increasingly delinquent. Most of the high-risk boys preferred a conventional future above a criminal one. Only a small proportion were expected to develop a criminal career, in particular those who were instrumental in their offending behavior.

Beke and Kleiman (1993) conducted a survey of adolescents and young adults in which they made a distinction between what they called "hard-core" delinquents and "joiners." These labels have been adopted by policy makers and the Dutch Ministry of Justice, although they are a bit misleading ("hard-core" delinquents committed two or more serious offenses, "joiners" only one or less serious offenses, but both can be in the center or periphery of a group). There were substantial differences between the two categories. On average, the most serious delinquents had the weakest bonds with parents and school and were more oriented toward their peers. They also were less bonded to conventional norms and often believed that violence and other offenses were acceptable. On the basis of interviews with a subsample of offenders, the researchers concluded that serious delinquents were often more instrumental in their offending and more often planned their offenses ahead of time. The less seriously delinquent respondents appeared to commit their offenses more often impulsively.

Several studies were based on delinquent samples or used case files. Ploeg and Scholte (1990; see also Scholte 1993) used a small sample of apprehended youths to test a "psycho-social" model to explain differences in the level of delinquency. They combined insights from criminology and developmental psychology and distinguished risk factors in the domains of family, school, peers, and the personality of the offender (e.g., low self-esteem). Being in a deviant peer group and being raised in a family with poor socialization practices appeared to have the strongest effects on delinquency. Low self-esteem appeared to correlate with vandalism, but high self-esteem with fighting behaviors.

Doreleijers (1995) studied offenders taken into custody from a (child) psychiatric perspective and used information from diagnostic examinations and instruments. He aimed to get insight into disorder prevalence among Dutch detained juvenile offenders, according to the standard psychiatry manual DSM III. The majority of juvenile detainees were diagnosed as having one or more types of psychiatric disorders, such as attention deficit disorder, antisocial behavior disorders, affective disorders, and drug use. Although these disorders include offending behavior, the study made clear that psychological disfunctioning was overrepresented among detained juvenile offenders, even though often it was not diagnosed or treated.

Van der Heiden-Attema and Bol (2000) used records and files about juveniles (ten to eighteen years old) investigated by a youth care organization because of personality problems or because of antisocial or delinquent behavior. A large number of risk and protective factors were related to the prevalence and seriousness of offending during a follow-up period of five years. Those juveniles who became delinquents appeared to be exposed to different risk factors than those who developed other problems. The most serious delinquents started earlier and had committed offenses more frequently in the past. But most of the risk factors found for the early starters were not different from the ones for youths who became delinquent later in their lives, though early starters were exposed to them at an earlier stage. Several other studies in which a developmental perspective was used are discussed in Loeber, Slot, and Sergeant (2001).

Many correlates and risk factors are repeatedly found among causes and correlates of juvenile offending, and they are not divergent from what is found in the international research (see, e.g., Hawkins et al. 1998; Loeber, Slot, and Sergeant 2001; Thornberry and Krohn 2003). The most frequently mentioned risk factors are in the area of family (weak bonds with parents, poor supervision, and poor socialization practices), school (especially low school motivation, truancy), and leisure time and peers (deviant peer group, "negative" leisure activities such as hanging round and alcohol or drug use). Personal risk factors were found in some of the studies, such as thrill and adventure seeking. Having unconventional norms and using neutralization techniques were correlated with delinquency. Some risk factors known from international research are relatively underinvestigated in the Netherlands; they include a high level of impulsivity, attention deficit disorder, low intelligence quotient, and being in a gang. But there are no indications that there are different risk factors in the Netherlands than in other Western countries.

In several of the studies a distinction is made between minor offenders and serious delinquents. Several authors observe qualitative differences between the two delinquent categories. In general, they conclude that minor delinquents commit their offenses more or less impulsively and in the company of peers, whereas the more serious offenders operate in a more deliberate and planned fashion. However, it is unknown yet how valid this distinction is, and the possibility of more types of juvenile offenders is relatively unexplored.

C. The Role of Risk Factors

Not all correlates and risk factors have causal influence (cf. Farrington 2000). Many may merely be covariates or effects of delinquency. For example, having nonconventional values and norms and delinquent behavior may be seen as two related phenomena that sometimes are considered as tautological. In his longitudinal data, Nijboer (1997) found indications that the adoption of delinquent norms often follows offending. Engels et al. (2004) investigated causal relationships between attitudes and delinquent behavior using the longitudinal data of the Utrecht WIL-study. They found that attitudes had an effect on later delinquency only for respondents who were not delinquent at the beginning of their adolescence. For those already delinquent, no influence of attitudes was found; delinquency seemed instead to have a further deteriorating effect on moral attitudes.

Dutch researchers are aware of the difference between establishing a correlation or identifying a risk factor and imposing causal influence. They devote more or less effort to evaluating the exact role of different risk factors in the causal process. Particularly, the most important social areas of young people, family, school, and peers, have been subjects of several detailed analyses.

The roles of family and parenting are taken into account in many studies. Multivariate analyses give varying results with regard to the relative contributions of family factors to delinquency, but there is always an effect of one or more family factors. Nijboer (1997) found that structural family factors (broken home, number of children, or family SES) had small effects on delinquency and only through parenting style and the social bonds of juveniles with their parents. The latter variables had an important but indirect effect via school and peer factors. This is in line with international research that finds that structural family factors such as family size and being in a broken home appear to be less important than parenting style indicators such as low supervision and a lack of warmth in the family (see, e.g., Wells and Rankin 1991).

An interesting study on the role of parents in combination with the role of romantic relationships was recently published by Meeus, Branje, and Overbeek (2004). They used the longitudinal Utrecht WIL-study to analyze whether an intimate partner moderates delinquency or even takes over the role of parents in late adolescence. Among older respondents who did not have a partner at all during a period of six years, having lots of support from parents had an inhibiting effect on delinquency. Among those who did have a partner during the research period, there was no effect from the bond with parents. Instead, support from the partner had a negative effect on delinquency.

Little research in the Netherlands has focused on parenting style and delinquency. The relation between parenting and problem behavior in general has received attention (see Deković 1999). In the Nijmegen study, children and their parents were interviewed to study family and parenting characteristics and the development of behavior from childhood into young adulthood (Gerris et al. 1993). This Nijmegen study, together with the WIL-study from Utrecht, was used in a secondary analysis in Loeber, Slot, and Sergeant (2001). In both studies, the parent-child interaction is studied in more detail than in most criminological research. Elements from the parent-child interaction were clearly correlated with violent behavior (for more details, see Loeber and Slot, in this volume). Hoeve et al. (2004) used the Nijmegen study to study the influence of family factors in childhood on delinquency during young adulthood. They also used data from the Pittsburgh Youth Study to make comparisons between the United States and the Netherlands. Hoeve et al. found that most family and parenting factors did not have long-term effects on delinquency in young adulthood, but the effects of low supervision in the American study and of low order and structure in the household in the Nijmegen study were significant and substantial. In the Nijmegen study, there was also a significant enhancing effect on later delinquency of being in a family with an authoritarian parenting style, although only for girls.

Several Dutch studies focused on the role of school in juvenile offending. One of the main goals of the Groningen longitudinal study was to investigate the potential criminogenic influence of education (Nijboer and Dijksterhuis 1989; Dijksterhuis 1993; Nijboer 1997). Although many school factors were related to delinquency, the role of school was less important than was expected. The LISREL analyses suggested that the effects of many school factors decreased when other factors were taken into account. School failure was related to offending, but the main reason was that school failure was influenced by inadequate parenting styles that had an (indirect) effect on delinquent behavior. School bonding had no direct effect, but an indirect effect through the motivation for school. And labeling by teachers appeared to be a result of misbehavior at school instead of a causal factor for delinquent behavior. School motivation and misbehavior at school—measured by getting punished by teachers—appeared to have the strongest effects on delinquency.

Baerveldt's study (1990, 1992) investigated the influence of several school factors on juvenile delinquency, not only individual characteristics but also characteristics of the participating schools, such as school atmosphere, quality ambitions, teacher attitudes, and features of the lessons. The analyses showed only weak or no effects of these school characteristics, but the individual bond with school had an important effect. There were almost no added effects of schools on delinquency when individual differences were taken into account. Differences between classes explained a small but significant part of the variance. Baerveldt concluded that the role of school characteristics with regard to juvenile offending is absent or at the most very small.

A number of studies focused on delinquent peers. Bruinsma (1985, 1992) distinguished several aspects of peer influences: frequency of contacts, identification with friends, communication about criminal techniques, and priority of deviant contacts. Most had a separate effect on delinquency. A high frequency of contacts with deviant friends had an indirect effect through the acquisition of positive definitions of deviant behavior and through communication about criminal techniques. Weerman (1998) suggested that the frequency of contacts is especially important. The quality of the bond with friends and the importance attached to the opinion of friends was unrelated to delinquency, but the amount of time spent with friends was highly correlated. However, this was only for those respondents who had delinquent friends. Juveniles who spend a great deal of time with delinquent friends appeared often to be serious offenders.

Broekhuizen and Driessen (2005) found a correlation between frequency of contact and delinquency in their study of twelve-year-old school youths in Rotterdam. They distinguished between contacts with peers at school, in the family, in leisure organizations, in the neighborhood, and in peer groups on the street. The delinquency of friends in each of these areas was correlated with the individual's delinquent behavior. Each area had its separate effects in a multivariate analysis with these different peer networks together. The effects from neighborhood friends and peer groups are stronger than from peers elsewhere, and a high amount of overlap between different peer networks is related to delinquent behavior.

Baerveldt used social network methods to study the relation between delinquent peers and delinquency (Baerveldt 1990, 1992; Baerveldt, Vermande, and van Rossem 2000; Baerveldt et al. 2004). High school students were asked to select peers from a numbered list of fellow students, and both the respondents and the nominated peers were questioned about offending. This may be more valid than the usual method of asking respondents about their peers, in which friends may be perceived as more similar than they are in reality. Baerveldt suggested that peer networks at school are less homogeneous in their offending behavior than is often thought. In one of the studies, similarity in behavior was not higher for more intimate relations between students but rather somewhat lower than for relatively superficial contacts.

Social network methods are also used in a study (based on data from the NSCR School Study) by Weerman and Smeenk (2005), in combination with the usual method of asking youths about their friends. The association between friends' and the respondent's delinquency was much lower than had been found with the usual method, suggesting that the relation had been overestimated in the past. Many respondents had one or two best friends with delinquency levels that were lower than those of their friends in general. The level of best friends' delinquency levels mattered apart from the general delinquency level of all friends. Another analysis of these data showed that delinquent and nondelinquent students did not exclusively hang out with each other at school (Weerman, Bijleveld, and Averdijk 2005). Visual representations of the school networks showed a mixed picture: apart from a few cliques and groupings of students with similar behavior, nondelinquents, minor delinquents, and serious delinquents have many contacts with each other.

De Kemp et al. (2004) used social network data on high school students who chose each other as best friends to investigate the effects of parenting variables, delinquent best friends, and delinquent behavior.

The investigators used longitudinal data on twelve- to thirteen-year-old students collected in three waves with gaps of half a year. There were clear relationships between delinquent behavior, best friends' delinquency, and three parenting variables: support, monitoring, and psychological (manipulative) control. Structural equation modeling showed significant causal effects of the three parenting variables on subsequent offending. However, the results also suggested that the relationship between best friends' delinquency and that of the respondent was mainly the result of selection processes. Being delinquent had an independent effect on friends' delinquency in a subsequent wave but not the other way around. It is unclear, however, if this is an artifact of the restriction of the sample to mutual friendships: in this analysis, selection effects might be the same as influence effects from the respondent on the best friends' delinquency. More longitudinal research using social network methods is needed to understand the causal effects of delinquent peers in combination with other factors.

D. The Gender Gap

The finding that boys are relatively more often involved in delinquency than girls has long received attention. A number of studies and a special journal issue on the subject appeared during the 1980s (Rutenfrans 1983, 1989; Bontekoe 1984; Bruinsma and Lissenberg 1987). The debate was vivid. Some authors adopted biological views, others stressed the greater significance of social relationships for women, and still others viewed the different crime rates among girls and boys as a result of different gender identities and morals (see Bouw 1991). Some authors adopted social control theory as a general explanation of differences between boys and girls. The discussion paralleled the international debate between those who believe that general theories are valid for both sexes and those who advocate gender-specific theorizing (cf. Moffitt et al. 2001; Lanctôt and Le Blanc 2002).

Several empirical studies have sought to explain differences between boys and girls. In the 1980s, several studies appeared in which correlates of delinquency were compared. Junger-Tas (1983) found that the relation between family integration and delinquency was less strong for girls than for boys. Bruinsma (1985) reported that attachment with peers was more strongly related to delinquency for girls than for boys. Hauber, Toornvliet, and Willemse (1986) found mainly similarities between boys and girls. The results from their multivariate analyses were comparable for boys and girls, which made them conclude that there is no need for separate explanations of offending for boys and girls. Dijksterhuis and Nijboer (1987) contested this conclusion and stressed the differences in the results of Hauber, Toornvliet, and Willemse. They also presented results from their own study that revealed differences in correlates for boys and girls. For example, conflicts at school are important only for girls, whereas school motivation is the most important school factor for boys, but not for girls.

A few recent Dutch studies on juvenile offending make explicit comparisons between boys and girls with respect to the effects of various variables on delinquency. Junger-Tas, Ribeaud, and Cruyff (2004) used data from the ISRD and from a study in Rotterdam. They found that similar background and social control variables were correlated with delinquency for boys and girls. These factors also partly explained the difference in delinquency levels between boys and girls. However, while direct parental control had the strongest effects in boys, female delinquency seemed to be affected more by family composition and psychological well-being. The authors concluded that direct controls may be more important for boys and emotional controls more important for girls, which parallels conclusions from international research. Van der Rakt, Weerman, and Need (2005) used data from the NSCR School Study. They found some remarkable differences. Bonding with school had the strongest effect for boys, whereas the bond with parents was most important for girls. Moreover, the mean delinquency level in the class social network was significant for girls but not for boys. For boys, the number of chosen friends among students and the number of female friends had stronger effects. The authors suggested that it may be the company of friends in itself that stimulates delinquent behavior through status and ridicule mechanisms in boys (at least at school). For girls, being like other students at school may be more important.

V. Conclusions

I return to the two aims set out in the beginning of this essay. First, I address the question of whether there are distinctive characteristics of juvenile offending in the Netherlands in comparison with other countries. Second, I discuss the nature of Dutch research on juvenile offending.

In general, we have a great deal of information about the prevalence and level of Dutch juvenile offending. Police statistics make clear that about 4 percent of Dutch juveniles are interrogated by the police each year. Statistics from the *European Sourcebook* (Killias 2003) do not indicate that the Netherlands stands out in this respect; the official crime figures for youth crime are slightly higher than in some other countries, but not the highest. Self-report studies show that the majority of Dutch juveniles commit offenses at some point in their adolescence. Percentages for separate minor offenses are typically 5–20 percent, and for separate serious offenses 1–3 percent. Findings from the ISRD study suggest again that the Netherlands does not stand out in comparison with other countries. Most countries have lower levels of self-reported juvenile offending than the Netherlands, but a number of countries have higher levels.

The percentage of juveniles interrogated by the police in the Netherlands has risen steadily since the beginning of the 1960s, with stronger increases at the end of the 1970s and in the mid-1990s. In the last three years for which information is available, the percentage has increased again, and violent offenses especially have become more common. Part of this increase, however, may result from major changes in police strategies and policies, and it is unclear to what extent the increases reflect a real change in juvenile offending. Self-report studies suggest that juvenile offending as a whole did not change dramatically in recent years, but the figures here contradict each other. More research is needed to get a better insight.

The long-term changes in juvenile offending and the more recent increase in violent offending among juveniles are in line with trends in other European countries (Pfeiffer 1998; Killias et al. 2004). This suggests that the increase in juvenile offending in the Netherlands is not specifically Dutch but instead follows a European trend. It is unclear, however, what caused the changes and fluctuations. Research aimed at understanding the mechanisms behind long-term changes in the level of juvenile offending in a country or in Europe is scarce.

Many different risk factors and correlates have been found in a large number of Dutch studies aimed at the causes and the etiology of youth crime. These are not very different from findings in research throughout the world (Hawkins et al. 1998; Loeber et al. 1998; Farrington 2000; Thornberry and Krohn 2003). There are no indications that the mechanisms behind juvenile offending are different in the Netherlands.

It may be possible that certain factors are more important in the Netherlands than in countries in other parts of Europe (Barberet et al. 2004).

As elsewhere, the majority of youth offending takes place in company. There are also troublesome youth groups in many Dutch cities, and in the past some have adopted American gang clothes and symbols. Comparison of troublesome Dutch youth groups with American and European examples of youth gangs suggests that offending behaviors and risk factors are not very different (Klein et al. 2000; Esbensen and Weerman 2005). However, Dutch gangs and troublesome youth groups are rarely territorial and are less hierarchical than elsewhere, especially the United States. Possibly, the Dutch preference for equality and compromise is manifested in an aversion to leadership among offenders in groups.

The first thing that stands out with regard to Dutch research on juvenile offending is that there has been so much. Many efforts have been made to estimate the prevalence of offending among Dutch juveniles, and several monitors have been used to report on trends and changes in youth crime. As far as I know, only the United Kingdom has been monitoring juvenile offending as thoroughly with the use of self-report methodology. The amount of research into the causes and correlates is also high. Dutch researchers have conducted many studies. Usually these have been published in Dutch, but several researchers have found their way into international journals and outlets. Of course, the studies of the past twenty-five years vary greatly in thoroughness and quality (I left out many relatively weak studies). It is also clear, with a few exceptions, that Dutch research has not been at the forefront of the international criminological community for a long time. Nevertheless, most studies meet the standards of good empirical research, and, especially since the 1990s, Dutch research has become more advanced and more internationally oriented. The body of research on juvenile offending in the Netherlands is voluminous and of high quality in comparison with that in most other countries in Europe.

A great deal of attention has been given to differences between ethnic groups. Several qualitative studies have been conducted on groups. A number of quantitative studies compared the effects of variables between different groups. This is understandable in light of the large share of ethnic minorities in the youth population, especially in the cities. Research on the role of ethnicity in youth offending has been stimulated by increasing recognition during the 1990s, partly led by research findings, that juveniles from some groups were overrepresented in the crime figures.

Many questions remain unanswered. We do not know to what extent ethnic minority youths commit more offenses than youths of Dutch origin, because self-report studies contradict each other on this issue. There is also a lack of consensus about the explanation for the overrepresentation of juvenile offenders among certain groups. Qualitative researchers stress the importance of the marginalized positions of many ethnic minority youths and focus on cultural elements and lifestyles. Quantitative researchers usually adopt a universal explanation of offending and argue that ethnic minority youths are relatively more exposed to certain risk factors or explanatory variables, especially from a social control perspective. What has been lacking is a systematic combination of the findings and perspectives from both qualitative and quantitative researchers. A combination of research methods and data sources would be useful.

There has recently been an increase in interest in group offending. Several studies on co-offending and troublesome youth groups have been conducted, although this research is modest in comparison with the large body of gang research in the United States. Attention to this subject has been fed partly by an influential government paper in which juvenile crime is mentioned as a focus of policy and research (Commissie Jeugdcriminaliteit 1993). Experience with several remarkable examples of troublesome youth groups has led to several publications in this field. For a long time, there was discussion of whether these groups were gangs or not. Recently, some authors adopted the approach suggested by the Eurogang Network (see Decker and Weerman 2005) to call these groups either a troublesome youth group or a gang, as long as they are durable, street-oriented, and involved in illegal activity. This solution might be helpful in future research on the role of these groups in juvenile offending.

There has been much interest in theory testing and theory development. Several studies have been conducted to test or expand classic criminological theories, and theoretical essays have been published regularly. Nevertheless, the attention has been relatively one-sided. Hirschi's social control theory has been the subject of most etiological studies, but other perspectives and theories have been absent or have received much less attention. An important reason for this is that the theory was an important foundation for a very influential government report about petty crime (Commissie Kleine Criminaliteit 1985). Another factor might have been the popularity of the theory at the WODC, the research institute of the Dutch government that was dominant in Dutch criminology over a long period. But the great amount of attention can also be traced to an influential Dutch researcher, Josine Junger-Tas, who introduced and studied the theory. Her close colleagues have stepped into her footsteps.

Apart from studies aimed at theory testing and development, many others have been conducted on the causes and correlates of juvenile delinquency. Some combined existing theories in more or less eclectic models; others were focused on the establishment of risk factors and correlates. Many distinguish between minor offenders and serious or "hard-core" delinquents. This may reflect a general Dutch attitude to distinguish between those offenders who are really harmful and those who display behavior that is relatively normal for the life periods young people are in. The distinction between the two types of delinquents has not been linked much to the dual taxonomy of Moffitt (1993), in which life course persistent and adolescent-limited offenders are distinguished (but see Donker et al. [2003] and Donker [2004] for a study of young adults using the distinction). An important reason for this is that most studies have been cross-sectional or were only short-term longitudinal, which makes it difficult to reproduce trajectories over time. Further, it is unclear if the distinction between two subcategories is enough, or if more than two types of juvenile offenders should be distinguished, for example, offender groups in the three trajectories distinguished by Loeber (1997) or even more types of offenders. Research on these issues would give a more nuanced understanding of the backgrounds of juvenile offenders in the Netherlands.

Several longitudinal studies have examined the development of juvenile offending in the Netherlands. Most used a limited period of follow-up. Some had several waves. Only a few were aimed at the study of delinquency. Most were conducted for other reasons. Although the existing longitudinal studies have produced interesting findings, they are still limited if we compare them with long-lasting longitudinal studies in the United Kingdom, and especially the United States (see Thornberry and Krohn 2003). The Dutch government has never funded a large research program like the combination of three longitudinal studies (in Seattle, Rochester, NY, and Pittsburgh) in the

United States. Although several longitudinal projects have recently been started, there is no large longitudinal project focused primarily on the development of juvenile offending.

Dutch research has produced a large body of knowledge about the correlates and risk factors for juvenile offending. These factors are comparable to those found elsewhere. However, despite this knowledge, few insights are available with regard to the roles of all these factors. Researchers often seem to be satisfied with a list of correlates, without understanding the larger theoretical framework in which they have a role. Because of this, a lot remains to be learned about the processes by which risk factors are connected to juvenile delinquency.

Despite the fact that there has been a wealth of Dutch research on juvenile offending, much remains to do. First, it would be wise to combine different sources of information on the prevalence and development of youth offending. Police statistics and self-reports depart from each other in their conclusions; it would be wise to link them and discover how each of them is biased. One possibility is to gather police information on respondents in self-report studies and, vice versa, to investigate the self-reports and characteristics of those who are apprehended or detained. Such a combination of methods and sources is especially important to gain more insight into the level of delinquent behavior among ethnic minority youths, about whom diverging findings are reported.

Further, it is very important to continue and intensify studies aimed at understanding delinquent behavior among different categories of youths (ethnic minorities, boys, and girls) and to explain these differences. The efforts that have been made to do this should be applauded, but they are limited in scope and perspective. What is needed is a combination of quantitative and qualitative methods, using data from different sources and informed by different perspectives, that contrast different explanations with each other. Such a broad strategy is especially important with regard to the subject of delinquency among ethnic minorities. This is an issue that is central to the Dutch political debate at the moment, and opinions and decisions should be informed by valid and reliable research findings.

Dutch research on juvenile offending also needs expansion with regard to the perspectives and theories that are used. As we have seen, several criminological perspectives have not been tested or have received relatively little attention. A few areas of research have long been neglected in the Netherlands, for example, the role of troublesome youth groups and of personality and biological factors. More research is also needed that goes beyond the establishment of correlates and risk factors to disentangle causal processes and interaction effects. It would be wise to combine such fundamental etiological research with efforts made by colleagues from abroad and aim for comparable methods and measurements. More generally, international comparative research is important for learning more about typically Dutch elements in juvenile offending and their backgrounds and for finding out which factors and processes are universal.

Last but not least, it is important to collect and analyze more long-term longitudinal data about the development of juvenile offending. A study comparable to several influential projects conducted abroad (like those in Seattle, Rochester, and Pittsburgh) would be ideal. But using longitudinal data that have been collected or will be collected to answer important criminological questions is very useful already. These analyses can focus on searching for different trajectories, such as the ones proposed in Moffitt's (1993) and Loeber's (1997) models. It is unclear how valid these models are in the Dutch situation. Furthermore, longitudinal research can shed more light on the causes and contexts of starting a criminal career, the escalation toward more frequent and severe offending, and desistance, or the cessation of offending among juveniles. Such information is crucial to develop effective prevention and intervention strategies.

REFERENCES

Abma, Ruud. 1986. "Cultuur en tegencultuur in het Nederlandse jeugdonderzoek: Een historisch overzicht." In *Beelden van de jeugd*, edited by M. Mathijssen and F. van Wel. Groningen: Wolters-Noordhoff.
Agnew, Robert. 1992. "Foundation for a General Strain Theory of Crime." *Criminology* 30:47–87.
Akers, Ronald L. 1973. *Deviant Behavior: A Social Learning Approach*. Belmont, CA: Wadsworth.
Angenent, Huub. 1991. *Achtergronden van jeugdcriminaliteit*. Houten-Diegem: Bohn Stafleu van Loghum.
Baerveldt, Chris. 1990. *De school: Broedplaats of broeinest? Een vergelijkend onderzoek naar de rol van de school bij de bestrijding en verspreiding van kleine criminaliteit van leerlingen*. Arnhem: Gouda Quint.

————. 1992. "Schools and the Prevention of Petty Crime: Search for a Missing Link." *Journal of Quantitative Criminology* 8:79–94.

Baerveldt, Chris, and Hans Bunkers, eds. 1997. *Jeugd en cel: Over justitiële inrichtingen, jongeren en jongvolwassenen.* Utrecht: De Tijdstroom.

Baerveldt, Chris, Marjolein Vermande, and Ronan van Rossem. 2000. "Over vrienden die het ook doen: De kleine criminaliteit van scholieren en hun sociale netwerken." *Sociale Wetenschappen* 43:7–26.

Baerveldt, Chris, Marjolein Vermande, Ronan van Rossem, and Frank Weerman. 2004. "Students' Delinquency and Correlates with Stronger and Weaker Ties: A Study of Students' Networks in Dutch High Schools." *Connections* 26:11–28.

Barberet, R., B. Bowling, J. Junger-Tas, C. Rechea-Alberola, J. van Kesteren, and A. Zurawan. 2004. *Self-Reported Juvenile Delinquency in England and Wales, the Netherlands and Spain.* Helsinki: European Institute for Crime Prevention and Control.

Beke, B. M. W. A., and W. M. Kleiman. 1993. *De harde kern in beeld: Jongeren en geweldscriminaliteit.* Utrecht: Sociaal Wetenschappelijke Pers.

Beke, B. M. W. A., A. van Wijk, and H. B. Ferwerda. 2000. *Jeugdcriminaliteit in groepsverband ontrafeld: Tussen rondhangen en bendevorming.* Amsterdam: Sociaal Wetenschappelijke Pers.

Beker, M., S. J. M. Hoff, and C. J. Maas, with the assistance of J. Boelhouwer. 1998. *Rapportage jeugd 1997.* Rijswijk: Sociaal Cultureel Planbureau.

Blom, M., and G. L. A. M. Huijbregts. 2004. *Monitor jeugd terecht 2004.* The Hague: Wetenschappelijk Onderzoeks en Documentatie Centrum.

Blom, M., J. Oudhof, R. V. Bijl, and B. F. M. Bakker. 2005. *Verdacht van criminalitei: Allochtonen en autochtonen nader bekeken.* The Hague: Wetenschappelijk Onderzoeks en Documentatie Centrum/Centraal Bureau voor de Statistiek.

Blom, M., A. M. van der Laan, and G. L. A. M. Huijbregts. 2005. *Monitor jeugd terecht 2005.* The Hague: Wetenschappelijk Onderzoeks en Documentatie Centrum.

Bol, M. W., G. J. Terlouw, L. W. Blees, and C. Verwers. 1998. *Jong en gewelddadig: Ontwikkeling en achtergronden van de geweldscriminaliteit onder jeugdigen.* The Hague: Wetenschappelijk Onderzoeks en Documentatie Centrum.

Bongers, Ilja L. 2005. *Pathways to Deviance: Developmental Trajectories of Externalizing Problems in Dutch Youth.* Rotterdam: Optima Grafische Communicatie.

Bontekoe, Elisabeth H. M. 1984. "Criminaliteit en geslacht." *Tijdschrift voor Criminologie* 26:18–31.

Bouw, Caroline. 1991. "Meisjes en misdaad." In *Het is meisjes menens: Inleiding meisjesstudies,* edited by I. van der Sande. Amersfoort: Acco.

————. 1995. "Misdadige meisjes." *Tijdschrift voor Criminologie* 37:124–37.

Bovenkerk, Frank. 1992. "Criminaliteit van Marokkaanse jongens." In *Hedendaags kwaad: Criminologische opstellen,* edited by Frank Bovenkerk. Amsterdam: Meulenhoff.

Broekhuizen, J., and F. M. H. M. Driessen. 2005. *Van je vrienden moet je het hebben: Criminaliteit onder jongeren: Structuur of cultuur?* Utrecht: Bureau Driessen.

Bruinsma, Gerben J. N. 1981. "De controletheorie van Travis Hirschi: Toetsing van een causaal model." In *Grenzen van de jeugd*, edited by Lodewijk Gunther Moor, Albert Hauber, Richard Landman, Jan Nijboer, and Sietse Steenstra. Utrecht: Ars Aequi Libri.

———. 1985. *Criminaliteit als sociaal leerproces: Een toetsing van de differentiële associatietheorie in de versie van K.-D. Opp.* Arnhem: Gouda Quint.

———. 1992. "Differential Association Theory Reconsidered: An Extension and Its Empirical Test." *Journal of Quantitative Criminology* 8:29–50.

———. 1994. "De test-hertest betrouwbaarheid van het meten van jeugdcriminaliteit." *Tijdschrift voor Criminologie* 36:218–35.

Bruinsma, Gerben J. N., and E. Lissenberg. 1987. "Vrouwen als daders." *Tijdschrift voor Criminologie* 29:11–25.

Buikhuisen, Wouter. 1965. *Achtergronden van het nozemgedrag.* Assen: Van Gorcum.

Buikhuisen, Wouter, R. W. Jongman, and W. Oving. 1969. "Ongeregistreerde criminaliteit onder studenten." *Tijdschrift voor Criminologie* 11:69–89.

Buiks, P. E. J. 1983. *Surinaamse jongeren op de kruiskade: Overleven in een etnische randgroep.* Deventer: Van Loghum Slaterus.

Commissie Jeugdcriminaliteit (Commissie van Montfrans). 1993. *Aanpak jeugdcriminaliteit: Met de neus op de feiten.* The Hague: Staatsuitgeverij.

Commissie Kleine Criminaliteit (Commissie Roethof). 1985. *Eindrapport.* The Hague: Staatsuitgeverij.

Coppes, R., F. De Groot, and A. Sheraazi. 1997. *Politie en criminaliteit van Marokkaanse jongens: Een praktijkonderzoek.* Deventer: Gouda Quint.

Decker, Scott H., and Frank M. Weerman, eds. 2005. *European Street Gangs and Troublesome Youth Groups: Findings from the Eurogang Program of Research.* Walnut Creek, CA: Alta Mira.

de Haan, W. 1993. *Beroving van voorbijgangers: Rapport van een onderzoek naar straatroof in 1991 in Amsterdam en Utrecht.* The Hague: Ministerie van Binnenlandse Zaken.

———, ed. 1998. "Theoretische integratie." Special issue, *Tijdschrift voor Criminologie* 40, no. 2.

de Haan, W., E. F. A. E. de Bie, C. Baerveldt, C. Bouw, Th. A. P. Doreleijers, H. B. Ferwerda, J. M. A. Hermanns, and P. H. van der Laan. 1999. *Jeugd en geweld: Een interdisciplinair perspectief.* Assen: Van Gorcum.

De Kemp, Raymond A. T., Ron H. J. Scholte, Geertjan Overbeek, and Rutger C. M. E. Engels. 2004. "Opvoeding, delinquente vrienden en delinquent gedrag van jongeren." *Pedagogiek* 24:262–78.

Deković, M. 1999. *Opvoedingsproblemen in de (pre)adolescentie: Implicaties voor onderzoek en hulpverlening.* Amsterdam: Vossiuspers.

Dijksterhuis, Fokke P. H. 1993. "Onderwijs als bron voor delinquentie." In *De armen van vrouwe justitia*, edited by Riekent W. Jongman. Nijmegen: Ars Aequi Libri.

Dijksterhuis, Fokke P. H., and Jan A. Nijboer. 1984. "Spijbelen en delinquent gedrag: De signaalwaarde van spijbelen." *Tijdschrift voor Criminologie* 26: 32–45.

———. 1987. "Meisjes en jongensdelinquentie: Dezelfde etiologische processen?" *Tijdschrift voor Criminologie* 29:104–10.

Donker, Andrea. 2004. "Precursors and Prevalence of Young-Adult and Adult Delinquency." PhD dissertation, Universiteit Leiden.

Donker, Andrea, Wilma H. Smeenk, Peter H. van der Laan, and Frank C. Verhulst. 2003. "Individual Stability of Antisocial Behavior from Childhood to Adulthood." *Criminology* 41:593–610.

Doreleijers, Theo A. H. 1995. *Diagnostiek tussen jeugdstrafrecht en hulpverlening.* Arnhem: Gouda Quint.

Driessen, F. M. H. M., B. G. M. Völker, H. M. Op den Kamp, A. M. C. Roest, and R. J. M. Moolenaar. 2002. *Zeg me wie je vrienden zijn: Allochtone jongeren en criminaliteit.* Zeist: Kerckebosch.

Engels, Rutger C. M. E., Eric Luijpers, Johannes Landsheer, and Wim Meeus. 2004. "A Longitudinal Study of Relations between Attitudes and Delinquent Behavior in Adolescents." *Criminal Justice and Behavior* 31:244–60.

Esbensen, Finn-A., and Frank M. Weerman. 2005. "A Cross-National Comparison of Youth Gangs and Troublesome Youth Groups in the United States and the Netherlands." *European Journal of Criminology* 2:5–37.

Farrington, David P. 2000. "Explaining and Preventing Crime: The Globalization of Knowledge." *Criminology* 38:1–24.

Ferwerda, Henk B. 1992. *Watjes en ratjes: Een longitudinaal onderzoek naar het verband tussen maatschappelijke kwetsbaarheid en jeugdcriminaliteit.* Groningen: Wolters-Noordhoff.

Ferwerda, Henk B., and Balthazar M. W. A. Beke. 1995. "Een tip van de sluier: Overwegingen van geweldplegers." *Tijdschrift voor Criminologie* 37:43–53.

Ferwerda, Henk B., M. Bottenberg, and B. M. W. A. Beke. 1999. *Jeugdcriminaliteit in de politieregio Zaanstreek-Waterland: Een onderzoek naar omvang, aard, spreiding en achtergronden.* Arnhem/Middelburg: Advies-en Onderzoeksgroep Beke.

Ferwerda, Henk B., Peter Versteegh, and Balthazar Beke. 1995. "De harde kern van jeugdige ciminelen." *Tijdschrift voor Criminologie* 37:138–52.

Fiselier, J. P. S., and P. J. M. Verschuren. 1988. "De differentiële associatietheorie als verklaring van crimineel gedrag." *Tijdschrift voor Criminologie* 30: 203–19.

Franke, H. J., P. van der Laan, and J. Nijboer, eds. 1995. "Zin en onzin over jeugdcriminaliteit." Special issue, *Tijdschrift voor Criminologie* 37, no. 2.

Franke, H. J., N. A. Wilterdink, and C. Brinkgreve, eds. 1991. "Alledaags en ongewoon geweld." Special issue, *Amsterdams Sociologisch Tijdschrift* 18, no. 3.

Gerris, J. R. M., D. A. A. M. Boxtel, A. A. Vermulst, J. M. A. M. Janssens, R. A. H. van Zutphen, and A. J. A. Felling. 1993. *Parenting in Dutch Families.* Nijmegen: University of Nijmegen.

Gottfredson, Michael R., and Travis Hirschi. 1990. *A General Theory of Crime.* Stanford, CA: Stanford University Press.

Gruter, Paul, M. Baas, and D. Vegter. 1996. *Problematische jeugdgroepen in de regio Haaglanden: Een inventarisatie onder wijkagenten en jeugdrechercheurs.* The Hague: Politie Haaglanden, Bureau Analyse en Research.

Gruter, Paul, and Peter Kruize. 1995. "Tussen geldgebrek en tijdverdrijf: Jonge overvallers in de Haaglanden." *Tijdschrift voor Criminologie* 37:257–22.

Haen Marshall, Ineke. 1996. "De methode van zelfrapportage: Aanzet tot een rationele benadering." *Tijdschrift voor Criminologie* 38:2–20.

Hakkert, Alfred. 1998. "Group Delinquency in the Netherlands: Some Findings from an Exploratory Study." *International Review of Law, Computers and Technology* 12:453–74.

Hakkert, Alfred, A. van Wijk, H. Ferwerda, and T. Eijken. 1998. *Groepscriminaliteit: Een terreinverkenning op basis van literatuuronderzoek en een analyse van bestaand onderzoeksmateriaal, aangevuld met enkele interviews met sleutelinformanten en jongeren die tot groepen behoren.* The Hague: Ministerie van Justitie.

Harland, Paul, Peter H. van der Laan, Wilma H. Smeenk, and Frank M. Weerman. 2005. *Wangedrag en delinquentie op school . . . en daarbuiten: Prevalentie, ontwikkeling en samenhang.* The Hague: Boom Juridische Uitgevers.

Hauber, A. R., L. G. Toornvliet, and H. M. Willemse. 1986. "Persoonlijkheid en criminaliteit bij scholieren." *Tijdschrift voor Criminologie* 28:92–106.

Hawkins, J. David. 1999. "Preventing Crime and Violence through Communities That Care." *European Journal of Criminal Policy and Research* 7:443–58.

Hawkins, J. David, T. Herrenkohl, D. P. Farrington, D. Brewer, R. F. Catalano, and T. W. Harachi. 1998. "A Review of Predictors of Youth Violence." In *Serious and Violent Juvenile Offenders*, edited by Rolf Loeber and David P. Farrington. Thousand Oaks, CA: Sage.

Hendriks-Elzes, G. 1997. *Problematisch gedrag onder jongeren: Op zoek naar predictoren van spijbel-, verslavings- en wetsovertredend gedrag.* Groningen: Wolters-Noordhoff.

Hessing, D. J., and H. Elffers. 1995. "De validiteit van de self-report methode in onderzoek naar regelovertredend gedrag." *Tijdschrift voor Criminologie* 37:55–70.

Hirschi, Travis. 1969. *Causes of Delinquency.* Berkeley: University of California Press.

Hoeve, Machteld, Wima Smeenk, Rolf Loeber, Magda Stouthamer-Loeber, Peter van der Laan, Jan Gerris, and Judith Semon Dubas. 2004. "Opvoeding en delinquent gedrag bij jongvolwassen mannen." *Tijdschrift voor Criminologie* 46:347–60.

Hoogerwerf, Anton. 1996. *Geweld in Nederland.* Assen: Van Gorcum.

Huls, F. W. M., M. M. Schreuders, M. H. ter Horst-van Breukelen, and F. P. van Tulder. 2001. *Criminaliteit en rechtshandhaving 2000: Ontwikkelingen en samenhangen.* The Hague: Wetenschappelijk Onderzoeks en Documentatie Centrum.

Ince, Deniz, Marleen Beumer, Harrie Jonkman, and Mieke Vergeer. 2004. *Veelbelovend en effectief: Overzicht van preventieprojecten en—programma's in de domeinen gezin, school, kinderen en jongeren, wijk.* Utrecht: Nederlands Instituut voor Zorg en Welzijn.

Janssen, Otto. 1988. "Criminaliteit en levensstijlen van jongeren." *Tijdschrift voor Criminologie* 30:189–202.

Jongman, Riekent W. 1981. "(Jeugd)criminaliteit als verzet tegen de ongelijkheid." In *Grenzen van de jeugd*, edited by Lodewijk Gunther Moor, Albert Hauber, Richard Landman, Jan Nijboer, and Sietse Steenstra. Utrecht: Ars Aequi Libri.

Junger, Marianne. 1989. "Discrepancies between Police and Self-Report Data for Dutch Racial Minorities." *British Journal of Criminology* 29:273–83.

———. 1990. *Delinquency and Ethnicity: An Investigation on Social Factors Relating to Delinquency among Moroccan, Turkish, Surinamese and Dutch Boys.* Deventer: Kluwer.

Junger, Marianne, and Ineke Haen Marshall. 1997. "The Interethnic Generalizability of Social Control Theory: An Empirical Test." *Journal of Research in Crime and Delinquency* 34:79–112.

Junger, Marianne, and Wim Polder. 1992. "Some Explanations of Crime among Four Ethnic Groups in the Netherlands." *Journal of Quantitative Criminology* 8:51–78.

Junger, Marianne, Gert-Jan Terlouw, Peter van der Heijden, and Chris Rutenfrans. 1995. "Zelfcontrole, ongevallen en criminaliteit." *Tijdschrift voor Criminologie* 37:2–21.

Junger, Marianne, Karin Wittebrood, and Reinier Timman. 2001. "Etniciteit en ernstig en gewelddadig crimineel gedrag." In *Ernstige en gewelddadige jeugddelinquentie: Omvang, oorzaken en interventies*, edited by Rolf Loeber, N. Willem Slot, and Joseph A. Sergeant. Houten: Bohn Stafleu van Loghum.

Junger, Marianne, and M. Zeilstra. 1989. *Deviant gedrag en slachtofferschap onder jongens uit etnische minderheden.* The Hague: Ministerie van Justitie.

Junger-Tas, Josine. 1972. *Kenmerken en sociale integratie van jeugddelinkwenten.* Brussels: Studiecentrum voor Jeugdmisdadigheid.

———. 1976. "Achtergronden van delinkwent gedrag: Een onderzoek naar verborgen ciminaliteit in een Belgische stad." *Tijdschrift voor Criminologie* 18: 217–37.

———. 1983. *Jeugddelinquentie: Achtergronden en justitiële reactie.* The Hague: Wetenschappelijk Onderzoeks en Documentatie Centrum.

———. 1992. "An Empirical Test of Social Control Theory." *Journal of Quantitative Criminology* 8:9–28.

———. 2004. "Juvenile Justice in the Netherlands." In *Youth Crime and Youth Justice: Comparative and Cross-National Perspectives*, edited by Michael Tonry and Anthony N. Doob. Vol. 31 of *Crime and Justice: A Review of Research*, edited by Michael Tonry. Chicago: University of Chicago Press.

Junger-Tas, Josine, M. Cruyff, P. van de Looij-Jansen, and F. Reelick. 2003. *Etnische minderheden en het belang van binding: Een onderzoek naar antisociaal gedrag onder jongeren.* Houten/The Hague: Bohn Stafleu van Loghum/SdU/ Koninklijke Vermande.

Junger-Tas, Josine, and Ineke Haen Marshall. 1999. "The Self-Report Methodology in Crime Research." In *Crime and Justice: A Review of Research*, vol. 25, edited by Michael Tonry. Chicago: University of Chicago Press.

Junger-Tas, Josine, Ineke Haen Marshall, Denis Ribeaud, and Martin Killias. 2003. *Delinquency in an International Perspective: The International Self-Reported Delinquency Study (ISRD)*. The Hague: Kugler.

Junger-Tas, Josine, Marianne Junger, and E. Barendse-Hoornweg. 1985. *Jeugddelinquentie II: De invloed van justitieel ingrijpen*. The Hague: Wetenschappelijk Onderzoeks en Documentatie Centrum.

Junger-Tas, Josine, and Maurits Kruissink. 1987. *Ontwikkeling van de jeugdcriminaliteit*. The Hague: Staatsuitgeverij.

Junger-Tas, Josine, Maurits Kruissink, and Peter H. van der Laan. 1992. *Ontwikkeling van de jeugdcriminaliteit en de justitiële jeugdbescherming: Periode, 1980–1990*. Arnhem: Gouda Quint.

Junger-Tas, Josine, Denis Ribeaud, and Maarten J. L. F. Cruyff. 2004. "Juvenile Delinquency and Gender." *European Journal of Criminology* 1:333–75.

Kaufman, P., and H. Verbraeck. 1986. *Marokkaan en verslaafd: Een studie naar randgroep-vorming, heroinegebruik en criminalisering*. Utrecht: Gemeente Utrecht.

Kemper, Ellie. 1999. *Water in de thee: Een onderzoek naar criminaliteit van Turkse jongens in Deventer*. The Hague: Koninklijke de Swart.

Killias, Martin, ed. 2003. *European Sourcebook of Crime and Criminal Justice Statistics—2003*. Meppel: Boom Juridische Uitgevers.

Killias, Martin, Sonia Lucia, Philippe Lamon, and Mathieu Simonin. 2004. "Juvenile Delinquency in Switzerland over 50 Years: Assessing Trend beyond Statistics." *European Journal on Criminal Policy and Research* 10:111–22.

Klein, Malcolm W., Hans-Jörgen Kerner, Cheryl L. Maxson, and Elmar G. M. Weitekamp. 2000. *The Eurogang Paradox: Street Gangs and Youth Groups in the U.S. and Europe*. Dordrecht: Kluwer-Plenum.

Knorth, Erik J., Tom A. van Yperen, Peter H. van der Laan, and Gerda Vlieger-Smid. 2003. "Gedrag gekeerd? Interventies in de jeugdzorg bij antisociaal gedrag en jeugdcriminaliteit." Special issue, *Kind and Adolescent* 22, no. 4.

Koops, W., and W. Slot, eds. 1998. *Van lastig tot misdadig*. Houten: Bohn Stafleu van Loghum.

Korf, Dirk J., George W. Bookelman, and Tjalling de Haan. 2001. "Diversiteit in criminaliteit: Allochtone arrestanten in de Amsterdamse politiestatistiek." *Tijdschrift voor Criminologie* 43:230–59.

Kroese, G. J., and R. H. J. M. Staring. 1993. *Prestige, professie en wanhoop: Een onderzoek onder gedetineerde overvallers*. Arnhem: Gouda Quint.

Kromhout, M., and M. van San. 2002. *Schimmige werelden: Nieuwe etnische groepen en jeugdcriminaliteit*. The Hague: Boom Juridische Uitgevers.

Kruissink, M., and A. A. M. Essers. 2001. *Ontwikkeling van de jeugdcriminaliteit: Periode, 1980–1999*. The Hague: Wetenschappelijk Onderzoeks en Documentatie Centrum.

———. 2004. *Zelfgerapporteerde jeugdcriminaliteit in de periode, 1990–2001*. The Hague: Wetenschappelijk Onderzoeks en Documentatie Centrum.

Lanctôt, Nadine, and Marc LeBlanc. 2002. "Explaining Deviance by Adolescent

Females." In *Crime and Justice: A Review of Research*, vol. 29, edited by Michael Tonry. Chicago: University of Chicago Press.

Leuw, Ed. 1997. *Criminaliteit en etnische minderheden: Een criminologische analyse.* The Hague: Ministerie van Justitie.

Loeber, Rolf. 1997. "Ontwikkelingspaden en risicopatronen voor ernstige jeugddelinquentie en hun relevantie voor interventies: Nooit te vroeg en nooit te laat." Inaugural lecture. Amsterdam: Vrije Universiteit.

Loeber, Rolf, David P. Farrington, Magda Stouthmer-Loeber, Terrie E. Moffitt, and Avshlom Caspi. 1998. "The Development of Male Offending: Key Findings from the First Decade of the Pittsburgh Youth Study." *Studies on Crime and Crime Prevention* 7:141–71.

Loeber, Rolf, and Wim Slot. In this volume. "Serious and Violent Juvenile Delinquency: An Update."

Loeber, Rolf, N. W. Slot, and J. A. Sergeant, eds. 2001. *Ernstige en gewelddadige jeugddelinquentie: Omvang, oorzaken en interventies.* Houte: Bohn Stafleu van Loghum.

Luijpers, Eric. 2000. *Intentie tot exploratie, sociale binding en delinquent gedrag van Nederlandse jongeren.* Delft: Eburon.

Markus, Judith. 1995. *Doen ze het of doen ze het niet? Recidivisme bij mannelijke delinquenten: Een prospectief onderzoek.* Enschede: Copy Print 2000.

Meeus, Wim, Susan Branje, and Gert Jan Overbeek. 2004. "Ouders, partner en criminaliteit: Longitudinale studie naar veranderingen in relationele steun en criminaliteit in adolescentie en jonge volwassenheid." *Tijdschrift voor Criminologie* 46:37–55.

Meeus, Wim, and H. 't Hart. 1993. *Jongeren in Nederland.* Amersfoort: Academische Uitgeverij.

Mertens, Nicole, Martin Grapendaal, and B. J. W. Docter-Schamhardt. 1998. *Meisjescriminaliteit in Nederland.* The Hague: Wetenschappelijk Onderzoeks en Documentatie Centrum.

Miedema, Siep. 2002. "Etnografisch onderzoek naar de relatie tussen etniciteit, groepsvorming en delinquentie bij jongens." *Tijdschrift voor Criminologie* 44: 150–61.

Miedema, Siep, and N. Eelman. 1987. *Over pumps en punks: Een kwalitatief onderzoek naar levensstijlen van meisjes uit de lagere sociaal-economische strata.* Groningen: Criminologisch Instituut.

Miedema, Siep, H. Jonkman, and O. J. A. Janssen, with the assistance of W. Hartholt. 1986. *Respectabiliteit en deviantie in levensstijlen: Een kwalitatief onderzoek naar de leefwerelden van oud-leerlingen met een lbo-opleiding en vroegtijdige schoolverlaters in de tertiaire socialisatiefase.* Groningen: Criminologisch Instituut.

Ministerie van Justitie. 2002. *Vasthoudend en effectief.* The Hague: Ministerie van Justitie.

———. 2003. *Jeugd terecht.* The Hague: Ministerie van Justitie.

Ministerie van Justitie, Binnenlandse Zaken, Onderwijs, Sociale Zaken en Volksgezondheid, Welzijn en Cultuur. 1998. *Vier jaar van montfrans: Uitvoering plan van aanpak jeugdcriminaliteit.* The Hague: Ministeries van Justitie,

Binnenlandse Zaken, Onderwijs, Sociale Zaken en Volksgezondheid, Welzijn en Cultuur.

Moffitt, Terrie E. 1993. "Adolescence-Limited and Life-Course Persistent Antisocial Behavior: A Developmental Taxonomy." *Psychological Review* 100: 674–701.

Moffitt, Terrie E., A. Caspi, M. Rutter, and P. A. Silva. 2001. *Sex Differences in Antisocial Behaviour*. Cambridge: Cambridge University Press.

Nijboer, Jan A. 1993. "Onderwijs en delinquentie: Voorlopige balans." In *De armen van vrouwe justitia*, edited by Riekent W. Jongman. Nijmegen: Ars Aequi Libri.

———. 1995. "Het meten van delinquentie door middel van self-report." *Tijdschrift voor Criminologie* 37:273–80.

———. 1997. *Delinquentie en dwang: Ontwikkeling van delinquent gedrag bij leerlingen van het voortgezet onderwijs*. Groningen: Rijksuniversiteit Groningen.

Nijboer, Jan A., and Fokke P. H. Dijksterhuis. 1987. "De relaties tussen delinquentiepatronen en school—en achtergrondfactoren bij meisjes en jongens." *Tijdschrift voor Criminologie* 29:156–73.

———. 1989. *Ontwikkelingen in delinquent gedrag van scholieren: Eerste ronde*. Groningen: Criminologisch Instituut.

Pfeiffer, Christian. 1998. "Juvenile Crime and Violence in Europe." In *Crime and Justice: A Review of Research*, vol. 23, edited by Michael Tonry. Chicago: University of Chicago Press.

Ploeg, J. D., and E. M. Scholte. 1990. *Lastposten of slachtoffers van de samenleving*. Rotterdam: Lemniscaat.

Pratt, Travis C., and Francis T. Cullen. 2000. "The Empirical Status of Gottfredson and Hirschi's General Theory of Crime: A Meta-analysis." *Criminology* 38:931–64.

Reiss, A. J., Jr. 1988. "Co-offending and Criminal Careers." In *Crime and Justice: A Review of Research*, vol. 10, edited by Michael Tonry and Norval Morris. Chicago: University of Chicago Press.

Rovers, Ben. 1997. *De buurt een broeinest: Een onderzoek naar de invloed van woonomgeving op jeugdcriminaliteit*. Nijmegen: Ars Aequi Libri.

———. 1998. "Theoretische integratie van Hirschi en Merton." *Tijdschrift voor Criminologie* 40:151–65.

Rutenfrans, Chris J. C. 1983. "Hirschi, Opp en vrouwencriminaliteit." *Tijdschrift voor Criminologie* 25:82–89.

———. 1989. *Criminaliteit en sexe: Een verklaring voor de verschillen inj het criminele gedrag van vrouwen en mannen*. Arnhem: Gouda Quint.

Rutenfrans, Chris J. C., and Gert-Jan Terlouw. 1994. *Delinquentie, sociale controle en "life events": Eerste resultaten van een longitudinaal onderzoek*. Arnhem: Gouda Quint.

———. 1996. "Zelfcontrole en delinquent gedrag." *Tijdschrift voor Criminologie* 38:64–76.

Sansone, Livio. 1992. *Schitteren in de schaduw: Overlevingsstrategieën, subcultuur en etnische identiteit van Creoolse jongeren uit de lagere klasse in Amsterdam: 1981–1991*. Amsterdam: Het Spinhuis.

Scholte, Evert M. 1993. "Psychosociale achtergronden van delinquentie bij jeugdigen." In *Criminaliteit als politiek probleem*, edited by Jan A. Nijboer, A. C. Berghuis, F. P. H. Dijksterhuis, M. M. Kommer, C. J. C. Rutenfrans, and H. Timmerman. Arnhem: Gouda Quint.

Swanborn, Peter G. 1996. "Argumenten en misverstanden rondom de kwaliteit van self-report data." *Tijdschrift voor Criminologie* 38:284–89.

Terlouw, Gert-Jan, and Gerben J. N. Bruinsma. 1994. "Self-Reported Juvenile Delinquency in the Netherlands: Results from the Dutch Survey for the ISRD Project." In *Delinquent Behavior among Young People in the Western World*, edited by Josine Junger-Tas, Gert-Jan Terlouw, and Malcolm W. Klein. Amsterdam: Kugler.

Thornberry, Terence P., and Marvin D. Krohn. 2003. *Taking Stock of Delinquency: An Overview of Findings from Contemporary Longitudinal Studies*. New York: Kluwer Academic/Plenum.

van Acker, Juliaan. 1998. *Jeugdcriminaliteit: Feiten en mythen over een beperkt probleem*. Houten: Bohn Stafleu van Loghum.

van Dam, Coleta. 2005. *Juvenile Criminal Recidivism: Relations with Personality and Post Release Environmental Risk*. Nijmegen: Radboud Universiteit Nijmegen.

van den Brink, Gabriël. 2001. *Geweld als uitdaging: De betekenis van agressief gedrag bij jongeren*. Utrecht: Nederlands Instituut voor Zorg en Welzijn.

van der Heide, W., and A. Th. J. Eggink. 2003. *Criminaliteit en rechtshandhaving 2001: Ontwikkeling en samenhangen*. The Hague: Wetenschappelijk Onderzoeks en Documentatie Centrum.

van der Heiden-Attema, N., and M. W. Bol. 2000. *Moeilijke jeugd: Risico—en protectieve factoren en de ontwikkeling van delinquent gedrag in een groep risicojongeren*. The Hague: Wetenschappelijk Onderzoeks en Documentatie Centrum.

van der Heijden, P. G. M., K. Sijtsma, and H. 't Hart. 1995. "Self-report delinquentie-schalen zijn nog steeds betrouwbaar." *Tijdschrift voor Criminologie* 37:71–77.

van der Hoeven, Erik. 1985. *Allochtone jongeren bij de jeugdpolitie I*. The Hague: Coördinatiecommissie Wetenschappelijk Onderzoek Kinderbescherming.

———. 1987. "Maatschappelijke bindingen van jongeren en 'veel voorkomende criminaliteit.'" *Tijdschrift voor Criminologie* 29:215–43.

van der Laan, André M. 2004. *Weerspannigheid en delinquentie: Een toetsing van Sherman's "defiance"-theorie als een algemene verklaring voor de averechtse werking van sanctioneren*. Nijmegen: Wolf Legal.

van der Laan, Peter H. Forthcoming. "Juvenile Delinquency and Juvenile Justice in the Netherlands." In *Juvenile Justice in Different Countries*, edited by Josine Junger-Tas and Scott H. Decker. Leusden: Springer.

van der Laan, Peter H., A. A. M. Essers, G. L. A. M. Huijbregts, and E. C. Spaans. 1998. *Ontwikkeling van de jeugdcriminaliteit: Periode, 1980–1996*. The Hague: Wetenschappelijk Onderzoeks en Documentatie Centrum.

van der Rakt, Marieke, Frank Weerman, and Ariana Need. 2005. "Delinquent gedrag van jongens en meisjes: Het anti(sociale) kapitaal van vriendschaps-relaties." *Mens en Maatschappij* 80:328–52.

van Gemert, Frank. 1995. "Amerikaanse gangs en Nederlandse jeugdbendes." In *Preventie van jeugdcriminaliteit in een grote stad*, edited by E. Rood-Pijpers, B. Rovers, F. van Gemert, and C. Fijnaut. Arnhem: Gouda Quint.

———. 1998*a*. *Crips in drievoud: Een dossieronderzoek naar drie jeugdbendes*. Amsterdam: Regioplan Onderzoek Advies en Informatie.

———. 1998*b*. *Ieder voor zich: Kansen, cultuur en criminaliteit van Marokkaanse jongens*. Amsterdam: Het Spinhuis.

———. 2001. "Crips in Orange: Gangs and Groups in the Netherlands." In *The Eurogang Paradox: Street Gangs and Youth Groups in the U.S. and Europe*, edited by Malcolm W. Klein, Hans-Jörgen Kerner, Cheryl L. Maxson, and Elmar G. M. Weitekamp. Amsterdam: Kluwer.

van Gemert, Frank, and Mark Fleisher. 2004. *In de greep van de groep: Een onderzoek naar een Marokkaanse problematische jeugdgroep*. Amsterdam: Regioplan Beleidsonderzoek.

———. 2005. "In the Grip of the Group." In *European Street Gangs and Troublesome Youth Groups: Findings from the Eurogang Program of Research*, edited by Scott H. Decker and Frank M. Weerman. Walnut Creek, CA: Alta Mira Press.

van Hulst, H., and J. Bos. 1994. *Pan i rèspèt: Criminaliteit van geïmmigreerde Curaçaose jongeren*. Utrecht: Onderzoeksbureau OKU.

van Oosterwijk, Chris, Paul Gruter, and Peter Versteegh. 1995. *Haagse jeugd-bendes—Amerikaanse gangs*. The Hague: Bureau Analyse en Research Politie Haaglanden.

van San, Marion. 1998. *Stelen en steken: Delinquent gedrag van Curaçaose jongens in Nederland*. Amsterdam: Het Spinhuis.

van Stapele, Saul. 2003. *Crips.nl*. Amsterdam: Vassallucci.

Vaszony, A. T., L. E. Pickering, M. Junger, and D. Hessing. 2001. "An Empirical Test of a General Theory of Crime: A Four-Nation Comparative Study of Self-Control and the Prediction of Deviance." *Journal of Research in Crime and Delinquency* 38:91–131.

Völker, Beate, and Frans Driessen. 2003. "Delinquent gedrag, netwerken en sociaal kapitaal: Een netwerktheoretisch perspectief op criminaliteit van jongeren." *Tijdschrift voor Criminologie* 45:271–85.

Warr, Mark. 2002. *Companions in Crime: The Social Aspects of Criminal Conduct*. Cambridge: Cambridge University Press.

Weerman, Frank M. 1996. "Combinaties van bindingsfactoren en delinquent gedrag." *Tijdschrift voor Criminologie* 38:44–63.

———. 1998. *Het belang van bindingen: De bindingstheorie als verklaring van verschillen en veranderingen in delinquent gedrag*. Groningen: Universiteit Groningen.

———. 2001. *Samenplegen: Over criminele samenwerking en groepsvorming*. Nijmegen: Ars Aequi Libri.

———. 2003. "Co-offending as Social Exchange: Explaining Patterns in Co-offending." *British Journal of Criminology* 43:398–416.

318   Frank M. Weerman

Weerman, Frank M., Catrien C. J. H. Bijleveld, and Margit Averdijk. 2005. "Netwerken en netwerkposities van delinquente en niet-delinquente jongeren." *Tijdschrift voor Criminologie* 47:24–41.

Weerman, Frank M., and Wilma Smeenk. 2005. "Peer Similarity in Delinquency for Different Types of Peers: A Comparison Using Two Measurement Methods." *Criminology* 43:499–524.

Wells, L. E., and J. H. Rankin. 1991. "Families and Delinquency. A Meta-analysis of the Impact of Broken Homes." *Social Problems* 38:71–93.

Werdmölder, Hans. 1986. *Van vriendenkring tot randgroep: Marokkaanse jongeren in een oude stadswijk*. Houten: Het Wereldvenster.

———. 1990. *Een generatie op drift: De geschiedenis van een Marokkaanse randgroep*. Arnhem: Gouda Quint.

———. 1997. *A Generation Adrift: An Ethnography of a Criminal Moroccan Gang in the Netherlands*. The Hague: Kluwer Law International.

Wittebrood, Karin. 2000. "Probleemgedrag onder jongeren." In *Rapportage jeugd 2000*, edited by Karin Wittebrood and Saskia Keuzenkamp. The Hague: SCP.

———. 2003*a*. "Juvenile Crime and Sanctions in the Netherlands." *Journal of Contemporary Criminal Justice* 19:435–53.

———. 2003*b*. "Preventieve en strafrechtelijke interventies ter voorkoming van jeugdcriminaliteit." In *Rapportage jeugd 2002 (landelijke jeugdmonitor)*, edited by Elke Zeijl. The Hague: SCP.

Catrien Bijleveld

Sex Offenders and Sex Offending

ABSTRACT

The prevalence of victimization by sex offenders in the Netherlands is comparable to that of other European countries. For 100 years, there have been major fluctuations in prosecutions for sexual acts against minors. Prosecution and sentencing patterns have been fairly stable in recent years. The likelihood that a prosecuted case results in a sanction has increased considerably for cases involving sexual assault or offenses against minors because relatively more cases are sent on for trial. Treatment modalities are varied. Almost half of convicted offenders enroll in ambulatory treatment. Most victims are (very) young and female. Offenders are almost all male. Much sex offending takes place within the family. Perpetrators tend to be opportunistic and not to specialize in sex offending. Recidivism to a sex offense is much lower than to other offenses. There have been many studies on special subgroups of dangerous sex offenders. Among juveniles, group sex offenders are a significant subgroup. There have been few broad studies on the etiology of sex offending or on risk factors. There have been no studies on treatment effectiveness, though there is a clear association between the risk of recidivism and failure of treatment.

Sybine Jansons, a thirteen-year-old girl from Maarn, was sexually abused and murdered in 1999. Her body was found five weeks after her disappearance in the river De Grote Heycop, close to Kockengen. Evidence quickly pointed to a man who since her disappearance had raped a stewardess and attempted to rape another girl. He had been driving around various parts of the Netherlands trying to lure young girls into his blinded van and had approached several women at the Schiphol Airport parking lot telling them his car had broken down and

Catrien Bijleveld is senior researcher at the Netherlands Institute for the Study of Crime and Law Enforcement, Leiden, and professor of criminology at the Free University Amsterdam. Thanks are due to Harm Aten, Harry Huys, Paul Smit, Jos van Emmerik, Jan Hendriks, Victor van der Geest, and Miriam Wijkman.

asking for a ride. Sybine Jansons' rape and murder occurred two months after his release from prison after serving nine years for rape. The perpetrator, Martin C., was sentenced to seventeen and a half years' imprisonment and to a secure hospital order. In 2004 he confessed to Sybine's rape and murder.

Martin C. is for many the prototypical sex offender. He was dangerous and predatory and was an extremely active, almost compulsive, sex offender. Sybine's case and her murderer, however, are exceptional and extremely rare. Most sex offenses in the Netherlands, as in other countries, are committed by offenders known to the victims. Many victims are young children, mostly girls. Offenders, predominantly male, tend to be generalists rather than specialists, and there is wide variety in motives for offending, as well as a great variety in types of sex offenses. Although sex offenses can be traumatic experiences for victims, there is generally little risk of physical harm. Some behaviors, such as sexual acts with a child, have always been labeled and treated as sex offenses, but other acts now seen as abusive have not always been regarded as such and correspondingly reported or prosecuted with vigor. Sexual acts, sexuality, and sexual mores are subject to evolving societal norms regarding what is appropriate and healthy. More than other kinds of behavior that may be labeled criminal, much of sex offending occurs in the family, a realm into which many believe the state should not intrude. Because sex offenses generally occur in one-on-one situations and because often it is lack of consent of one of the parties rather than the act itself that makes the behavior criminal, sex offenses are notoriously difficult to prove. Because of the humiliation involved or because victims are often too young or dependent, sex offenses are among the most underreported of crimes.

This essay reviews data and research findings on sex offending and sex offenders in the Netherlands. As in other countries, sex offenses are fairly prevalent. At least one in six women is at some point confronted with unwanted sexual approaches or acts forced upon them. When men are victims, in about 10 percent of cases, this happens mostly when they are boys. Offenders are predominantly males, of whom an important part are juveniles. Most victims know their offender. Often he is their caretaker, opportunistically choosing a weak and available victim. Most offenders are generalists, and recidivism rates are lower than is commonly assumed. Treatment is often administered as part of a sanction. Chances that sanctions will be imposed for sexual assault and offenses against minors have recently increased greatly. Wide differences exist in offenders' motives and the kinds of offenses they commit. A small but dangerous and persistent group of chronic, mainly pedosexual offenders has been studied extensively. These offenders may be violent, be diagnosed with paraphilias, and act from motives related to personality or psychiatric disorders, and they present a real physical risk to their victims. This small group is notoriously hard to treat and may be treated under a secure hospital order (TBS). Juvenile sex offenders have been studied in-depth in the Netherlands, adult offenders less so.

Section I summarizes sex offending laws and policies since 1985, outlining the criminal code for all sex offenses and focusing on hands-on offenses (i.e., sex offenses entailing physical contact with a victim). Section II discusses the prevalence of sex offending, presenting data on recorded crime, victimization, prosecution, sentencing, and treatment. Subsections discuss juvenile and female offenders. Section III details research findings over the past twenty-five years on sex offenders and offending. First, victim studies are discussed, disaggregating findings, whenever possible, by age and sex of the victim. Next follow studies on offenders and on the etiology of offending. Categories of sex offenders that have been studied particularly extensively, such as pedophiles and juvenile sex offenders, figure prominently. Finally, criminal careers of sex offenders are discussed. Section IV ends with policy recommendations and a research agenda.

I. Sex Offending Laws and Policies, 1985–2005

The Dutch Criminal Code in 2006 contained several articles on sex offenses. With minor changes, these had been in effect since 1991, when major changes were made. Previous major changes took place in 1911 and briefly during the Second World War, when the German occupiers criminalized homosexual acts between men (but not between women). Some smaller changes took place before 1991.

Sex offenses in the Dutch Criminal Code fall under a section entitled *Misdrijven tegen de zeden* (crimes against morality). This title illustrates that sex offenses used to be seen predominantly as offenses against good taste, or morality, or as simply indecent. Over the years, sex offenses (and particularly those entailing force or against vulnerable victims) have increasingly become viewed as violent offenses. The Appendix lists all hands-on sex offenses and the corresponding maximum sanctions; the Netherlands has no statutory minimum penalties. The offenses listed in the Appendix have been counted as sex offenses in the Netherlands since 1982. In most statistics, these are disaggregated into rape, sexual assault, and a category labeled "other sex offenses," predominantly composed of hands-on sex offenses with young or child victims.

Articles 239, 240 (not in the Appendix), and 250 are hands-off sex offenses. Article 239 concerns exhibitionism, popularly known in English as "flashing" and in Dutch as "pencil peddling." Even though still under the crimes against morality title, exhibitionism is a hybrid. Since 1982 it has been counted as a public order offense, but exhibitionists are viewed (and treated) as a particular kind of sex offender.

Articles 240, 240a, and 240b are articles concerning pornography, 240b addressing child pornography. This article was changed substantially in 2002. Before then, offenders who owned or offered child pornography could be found guilty only if the pictures were real, depicting actual children and actual situations. The rationale was to protect children from abuse, inasmuch as filming or photographing children performing or suffering sexual acts harms them. However, with the advent of modern computer technology, defendants increasingly claimed that the images were manipulated, or even constructed, and therefore did not depict or harm real children in real situations. This placed a large burden of proof on the prosecutors. This article was extended to cover manipulated images. In addition, provisions allowing possession of such items were eliminated. Prosecution for possession of a single child pornographic item seldom occurs, however.

A further recent criminalization of child pornography followed from Dutch ratification of the Convention on Cybercrime and a framework decision by the Council of Europe on combating sexual exploitation of children and child pornography. In 2002, the age of children depicted in child pornography was increased from sixteen to eighteen; this follows from ratification by the Netherlands of the International Labour Organization treaty on child labor.

Article 242 is the article concerning rape. Until 1991, rape entailed forcible sexual intercourse with a woman unmarried to the perpetrator. Only women could be raped, and a woman could not be raped by her husband. The scope of this article was much extended in 1991. The offense was made gender-neutral (as were all sex offenses) in 1991, and rape was defined to include sexual penetration of any bodily orifice. Men could legally be a victim of rape, women could be raped by their own husbands, and rape could take place with instruments other than the male sexual organ. In the famous *Tongzoen* (wet kiss) case (NJ, 1994, 379, dd. 22 April 1994), the Supreme Court found guilty of rape a man who forced his tongue into the mouth of another man. The changes should have facilitated prosecutions for acts previously not falling under the article (such as penetration of a boy victim or rape of a woman by her husband), but much of the definitional widening was undone by a stricter judicial interpretation of the elements of the offense by judges, particularly the stricter delineation of the *dolus* (intent) requirement (Kool 2003).

Article 246 is the article pertaining to sexual assault (literally "indecent assault"). Its definition was widened in 1991. Threat of force is no longer necessary; other circumstances can constitute a threat (such as blackmail). This has been interpreted to apply to threats that would make the victim submit to acts to which he or she otherwise would not have submitted.

Articles 243–249 describe sexual acts that are punishable because the victims are unable to determine or express their will because of impairment, young age, or unequal power relations between perpetrator and victim. These articles are meant to protect vulnerable victims. Articles 243, 244, and 245 prohibit sexual penetration of persons unable to determine or make known their will (243), children under age twelve (244), and children between ages twelve and sixteen (245). Article 247 encompasses all these categories of victims, but the sexual acts need not entail sexual penetration. Articles 248, 248b, and 248c list aggravating circumstances or particular sexual acts involving minors. Article 249 covers abusive sexual acts with persons entrusted to one's care or under one's authority, such as children, patients, and subordinates. Article 250 forbids forcing persons to undergo or perform sexual acts. The legal changes since 1991 have not led to major changes in prosecution policies or to quantitative changes. By 1994 more cases than before 1991 were initiated under articles 244 and 245, and fewer under 247, which points to a qualitative shift. Quantitatively, this does not make a difference, but it does mean that more cases are prosecuted for offenses subject to heavier maximum sentences (de Savornin Lohman et al. 1994, p. 200).

Since 1991, a number of additional changes have been made, most notably an extension on September 1, 1994, of the statute of limitations for offenses against children. It no longer starts from the day of commission of the offense, but from the day the victim turns eighteen. This extended period was made retroactive. In addition, a previously shorter limitations period for the prosecution of juvenile sex offenders was retracted. By an amendment of November 7, 2002, the period of registration of offenses in judicial records, which was twenty years for all offenses, or until the right to prosecute ceased or the defendant died, was extended to "until death" for all sex offenses under articles 240b–250 (Alwin 1994; Boelrijk 1996). Finally, the jurisdiction of Dutch courts was extended to cover sex offenses involving child victims committed abroad. This was done to combat the trade in child pornography and sex tourism.

In 1907, the first municipal police unit specializing in "moral" offenses (*Zedenpolitie*, literally translated as the "morals squad," but perhaps better understood as the vice squad) was established in Rotterdam. The Hague followed suit in 1912 and Amsterdam in 1920. These departments were established because of growing concern about loosening morals in the larger cities. From the start, these teams focused on prostitution, dangerous abortion practices, and serious neglect of youth. From 1930, special sex offending teams focused on abortion, adultery, sale of contraceptives to those under eighteen, exhibitionism, transvestism, child abusers, and to a lesser extent victims of rape and incest (Visser 1984). By the 1960s and 1970s the Zedenpolitie had become much more specialized and professionalized. In the police reorganization in 1994, the Zedenpolitie was dissolved. This is generally recognized to have been a mistake. A lot of expertise was lost, and the aim that every police officer have the specialized skills and expertise to deal with sex offending proved unrealistic (de Savornin Lohman et al. 1994).

The College of Procurors General (the policy and steering body of the prosecution service) includes a Landelijke Expertisegroep Bijzondere Zedenzaken (National Expert Group on Exceptional Sex Offending Cases). It supports the police for specified cases of sexual abuse (see http://www.om.nl/pg/documents/zedenzaken.pdf). The prosecutor handling a case must consult this committee when there are very young victims, when retrieved memory plays a role, or when the abuse appears ritualistic (such as with voodoo or satanic rites). Prosecutors may also ask advice from this committee whenever they feel that is expedient. The committee consists of a dozen specialists: a psychologist, an experimental psychologist, an education specialist, a therapist specializing in sex offending, a number of detectives specializing in sex offenses, and a number of specialists in homicide and sex offending from the KLPD, the federal police service. The committee meets whenever advice is sought on a particular case. About half of the cases pertain to offenses in the categories for which advice is mandatory.

The Netherlands does not have community notification laws. Since early 2001, the prosecution service, as an experiment, has notified victims of sex offenders upon their request when a sex offender has completed his sentence and will return to the community. Policy makers in the Netherlands believe that community notification will lead to stigmatization and ostracism and may thus even increase the risk of recidivism. Reintegration, with the police being aware of a sex offender's presence, the offender knowing that the police are aware of his presence, and the offender not allowed to work in high-risk functions such as with young children, is believed to create a better environment for the prevention of recidivism (Leuw 2000).

Since 1996, the Netherlands has experienced twenty-six incidents of hostile actions toward pedosexual offenders following their return to their community after completing their sentences. The incidents mostly involved breaking up and destroying offenders' living quarters, smearing paint on their houses, or demolishing their cars. However, assaults have also taken place, and two incidents ended in the death of the offender. The municipal police are always notified when a pedosexual offender is released; when unrest is expected, the prosecution service may also notify the mayor. Pedosexual offenders are often advised to change their place of residence.

Since February 2005, those convicted for an offense that carries a maximum sentence of at least four years and who have been given a sanction or a measure[1] for that offense can be required to supply DNA to be fed into a large DNA database. People suspected of such offenses are also requested to supply DNA, which will be removed if they are acquitted. The database is being filled in a stepwise fashion. Since the law came into force, so far only violent and sex offenders have been

---

[1] The Netherlands authorizes sanctions and measures. Both are imposed for an offense. A sanction is intended as a punishment and must be proportionate to the seriousness of the offense. A measure may be intended to reduce the risk of recidivism and as such may be treatment (other examples are victim compensation or the recapture of criminal profits). A measure need not be proportional to the seriousness of the offense.

asked to supply DNA. In about half a year, 10,000 profiles were added to the database, of whom about one-fifth were convicts and four-fifths were defendants. A number of cold cases have been solved with the aid of DNA. Only in one case (Marianne Vaatstra, who was raped and murdered close to a center for asylum seekers in Friesland) has DNA material found on the body of the victim been used to determine racial characteristics of the perpetrator: in her case this showed that the probable perpetrator was Caucasian.

II. The Prevalence of Offending, Sanctions, and Measures

The present Dutch Criminal Code came into effect in 1886. Much of its structure has remained the same, although some offenses have been added, some have been deleted, and quite a few have been changed. Until 1886, the Netherlands had the French Code Napoléon, which had articles pertaining only to exhibitionism and sexual assault. Sexual assault was a much wider category of socially unacceptable sexual behavior and included rape. Exhibitionism was likely not the offense it is these days, comprising the much broader category of indecent exposure of bodily parts, and not what it predominantly is today, exposing the genitalia.

The first year for which data are available is 1882. No statistics were published for the years 1944–45. No statistical information for the year 1974 is available. Figure 1 shows convictions per 100,000 population combining numbers for rape, sexual assault, and "other sex offenses" (mainly sex offenses against children and adolescents). For a while homosexual acts with juveniles (under the age of twenty-one) constituted an offense; this is no longer regarded a sex offense, but it is counted for those years under the category other sex offenses. The data do not always measure precisely the same categories, the measurements fluctuating among measurements of convicted persons and convicted cases (see the legend to fig. 1). Strictly speaking, the various years cannot be compared; for instance, a person convicted twice of a sex offense in one year counts as one in 1895 (when convicted persons were counted) but as two in 1897 (when convictions were counted). Keeping in mind these incongruities, one can interpret the figure with some caution.

Over the years, the number of convictions has risen steadily. There was a sudden dip during the First World War (1914–18) and a second

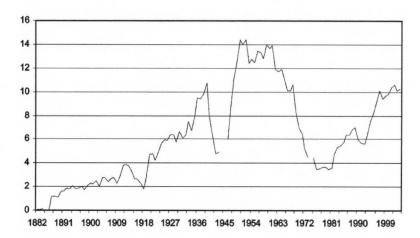

FIG. 1.—Yearly numbers of convictions (and comparable statistics) for sex offenses (rape, sexual assault, and offenses pertaining to the current category of other sex offenses) per 100,000 population. Source: From 1882–1981 CBS Statistical Yearbooks: 1882–95, convictions; 1896–1957, convicted persons; 1958–60, convictions; 1961–63, convicted persons; 1964–68, convictions; 1969–81, convicted persons. From CBS and CBS/WODC Criminaliteit en Rechtshandhaving, 1982–2004: convictions in first instance.

dip during the Second World War (in the Netherlands 1940–45). During those years (especially World War I) the courts' attention was diverted to offenses related directly to matters of state security. By 1950 the long-term rise stopped. After a plateau around thirteen convictions per 100,000 population until 1964, the curve slowly started to descend and plummeted after 1968. It reached a low of 3.5 per 100,000 population between 1976 and 1980. Then, around 1981–82, it started to climb again. There is a dip around 1992–93 because the entire records system of the prosecution service and the courts was computerized, leading to delays and data loss. The curve ends at around ten convictions for sex offenses per 100,000 population by 2004.

Why did convictions for sex offenses rise through 1950? Second, why did the rise stop by 1950? Why did the curve descend after 1964 and drop like a log in 1968, more than halving in four years? Why did the rates climb again after 1982?

When the Dutch Criminal Code was written in the 1880s, the prevailing liberal opinion was that the state should be restrained in interfering in the area of sexuality, since that domain was considered preeminently private. The minister of justice formulated this as follows:

"It is not the task of the criminal law to protect individuals against their freely chosen moral corruption" (Memorie van Toelichting, as reported in Kool [1999, p. 41]). Supplying commercial pornography to minors was a criminal offense, as well as sex with minors, sexual assault, and sex in power relations. Rape outside of marriage was a criminal offense.

In 1911 a number of fairly large changes were made in the sex offending laws, including criminalization of abortion, the seduction of minors of immaculate reputation, pornography in general, the sale of contraceptives to minors, brotheling, pimping, abortion, trafficking in women, and homosexual acts between an adult and a minor (the age limit then being twenty-one). The background general concern was about the corruption of morals. The law increasingly was viewed as an instrument to improve the moral standing of the population. By 1911, the chambers of Parliament had become more representative of society with many more religious parties becoming important, particularly calling for a halt to brothels as hotbeds of moral corruption. Although a few more changes were made in the sex offending laws, this protectionist view prevailed until around the 1960s (Tomesen 1993; Kool 1999, chap. 3).

Although there is little empirical evidence to support this, this prevailing view of the law as an instrument to combat moral (and sexual) corruption is generally viewed as the most likely explanation for the rising trend in sex offenses in the Netherlands through mid-century. By 1950, the majority of sex offending convictions (84 percent) were for exhibitionism and cases involving sexual acts with minors or children (Frenken 1984).

This trend reversed in the 1960s, and by 1982, rape and sexual assault constituted 60 percent of all convictions (Frenken 1984). In the 1960s, the pendulum had begun to swing back, and sex offending laws became—if not in the statutes, then in their application—much more liberal. According to Frenken, acts previously considered as sex offenses were de facto decriminalized since they were far less often reported, were less often recorded, were more often dismissed, and more often resulted in acquittal. In 1969, the sale of contraceptives to minors was decriminalized. In 1971 adultery (art. 241) was finally decriminalized, as were sexual acts between adults and persons of the same sex aged between sixteen and twenty (art. 248ter).

Figure 2 gives absolute numbers for the same data as figure 1 dis-

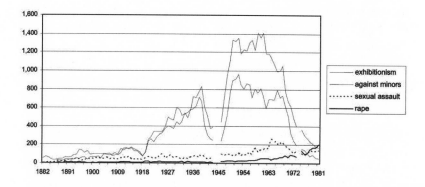

Fig. 2.—Yearly absolute numbers of convictions, respectively convicted persons disaggregated for rape, sexual assault, offenses pertaining to the current category of other sex offenses, and exhibitionism. Source: From 1882–1981 CBS Statistical Yearbooks: 1882–95, convictions; 1896–1957, convicted persons; 1958–60, convictions; 1961–63, convicted persons; 1964–68, convictions; 1969–81, convicted persons.

aggregated for the various types of sex offenses, up to 1981. Exhibitionism is added for illustrative reasons, although it was not included in figure 1.

Figure 2 shows that not all crimes developed similarly. From 1882 to 1981 the number of convicted rapists increased yearly, from the first four rapes in 1887 to around twenty-five rapists a year in 1950, to eighty from 1970, to 200 in 1982. The trend for sexual assaults is different: it climbed slowly to a high of 168 in 1968, then decreased. Most marked, however, is the huge increase and subsequent drop in what are currently labeled other sex offenses, mainly offenses against children and juveniles and other vulnerable persons. These climbed to almost 1,400 per year between 1959 and 1961, decreased to a little over 1,000 per year by 1968, tumbled within four years to less than half that number, and decreased further. In another five years they were down to a quarter of the high point, and by 1981 they were down to just 170 per year. Exhibitionism was added for illustrative reasons since it follows the same trend.

After 1960 there was a huge drop in the prosecution and conviction of exhibitionism and sexual acts with children and juveniles. Whether that is due to more dismissals or reluctance to report such offenses to the police remains to be determined. What exhibitionism and the other sex offenses have in common, however, is that they generally do not involve force (some offenses with children between twelve and sixteen may be entirely consensual) and both implicate "indecency." Given the widespread sexual liberalization of the 1960s and the stress on people's rights to express themselves as they wanted as long as they did not harm others, it is not remarkable that these offenses were less often viewed as criminal. In the 1960s, the foundation Valentijn sought to have sexual acts between adults and children over twelve years decriminalized (see Brongersma 1984), and letters to the editor could be read in free-thinking media arguing that sex with an older person might be healthy for children.

At the same time, sexual acts involving force were increasingly viewed as sex offenses. Research and the feminist movement showed that sexual relations between men and women not only were a private matter but were inseparable from prevailing social and power relations between the sexes. There was a movement away from the view that the "indecency" of an act made it punishable to the view that what made the behavior criminal was that it was not voluntary. The study by Draijer (1988) had an immense impact in showing that sexual acts with children and adolescents were fairly prevalent, often occurred against the will of the child, and sometimes had a highly detrimental effect. This drew attention to the need to protect weaker members of society who by age or impairment were unable to determine or express their will. This embodied a major conceptual shift from sex offending laws that preserved and enforced the morals of the population to laws that protected individuals from violation of their physical and sexual integrity.

A. Victimization, 1975–2004

Two sources of yearly victimization data on sex offenses are available: the Statistics Netherlands Victim Survey and the International Crime Victims Survey.

The Research and Documentation Center (WODC) of the Netherlands Ministry of Justice started a victim survey in 1973, which was transferred to Statistics Netherlands (CBS) in 1980. The format changed several times. The first occurred when CBS assumed responsibility in 1980, first administering it yearly and then biyearly. The survey changed format again in 1992, and in 1997 it changed format yet again as it became part of a wider survey called POLS (Permanent Onderzoek Leefsituatie or Permanent Study on Living Conditions).

This wider survey is administered continuously. The recall period in POLS thus differs for respondents surveyed at different times throughout the year. This causes the POLS prevalence data to be a priori incongruent with those generated by other victim surveys.

In 1975, the survey asked about *handtastelijkheden buiten*, best translated as "pawing outside"; the question was phrased as "Has someone outside, for instance on the street, ever touched you in a sexual manner?" From 1980 it also asked about *handtastelijkheden binnen*, best translated as "pawing inside the home." The questions were rephrased as "Has someone in your own or someone else's home, in a café or bar or somewhere else in a closed space, touched you against your will in a sexual manner?" for the incidents occurring inside and as "Has someone in the street, in a park or somewhere else outside, touched you against your will in a sexual manner?" for the incidents occurring in public spaces. Such incidents reported by respondents are named "sexual incidents." As the two prevalence rates are simply added, and respondents may have experienced both, there can be some double counting.

These questions remained in the survey until 1992 and were administered to both male and female respondents. Between 1992 and 1997, the survey asked only females whether they were victims of a sexual offense. Such incidents are labeled "sex offenses." The question was phrased as "People sometimes touch others or grab them for sexual reasons in a really offensive way. This can happen any place: in someone's home, at the workplace, in the street, et cetera. Has this happened . . . to you?" From 1997 onward, the victim survey asked men and women whether they were a victim of a sexual offense during the past year. The sample size for the entire victimization survey is around 10,000, with a response rate hovering around 55 percent. Administration is face-to-face, and the sample is persons drawn from municipal registers. Respondents for the questions on sexual incidents and offenses are fifteen years or older, with a sample size somewhat smaller.

A second source of victimization data is the International Crime Victims Survey (ICVS; van Dijk, Mayhew, and Killias 1990; van Kesteren, Mayhew, and Nieuwbeerta 2000). In the ICVS, female respondents are asked the following question: "Men sometimes grab or touch women in a really offensive way, or assault them for sexual reasons. This can happen either at home or elsewhere, for instance in a pub, the street, school, on public transport, on the beach, or at one's work-

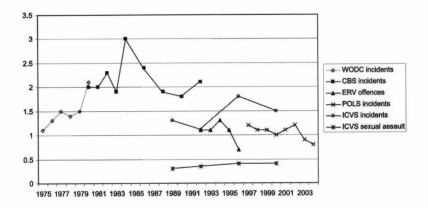

FIG. 3.—Yearly victimization rates of sexual incidents and sex offenses according to the various victim surveys. Source: CBS and van Kesteren, Mayhew, and Nieuwbeerta (2000).

place. . . . has anyone done this . . . to you? Please take your time to think about it." The ICVS sample size for the Netherlands is approximately 2,000 and the response rate is close to 60 percent. The survey is administered by telephone, with sample members selected using random digit dialing. Respondents are fifteen years or older. See also Wittebrood (2006).

Figure 3 shows yearly victimization rates measured by these two surveys. Victimization is computed as the percentage of respondents; for the ICVS, reported percentages are the percentage of female respondents, which for comparability reasons have been divided by two, giving roughly the percentage for all respondents.

Given that victimization percentages are low, that the ICVS sample is relatively small, and that the other survey formats changed a number of times, it is hard to compute trends for separate categories of offenses. The WODC result rises suddenly in the last year because incidents inside the home were included. Victimization by sexual incidents remained relatively stable, although the curves are jagged. Those from the various surveys match reasonably well. While the WODC survey started out with approximately 1 percent of respondents reporting victimization by a sexual incident in the past year, this percentage is around 1.5 percent for the ICVS. Victimization by sex offenses is much lower, around 0.7 percent as measured by the ICVS. Because of small sample sizes and because sexual incidents are less well reported in victim surveys than other incidents are (Fisher and Cullen 2000), these figures should be regarded as suggestive. No clear trends appear in the data.

Victimization by sexual incidents and offenses in the Netherlands is comparable to that in other countries included in the ICVS. In 1989 and 1992, the average for sexual incidents in all industrialized countries was 2.4 percent for female respondents; the Netherlands hovered around that figure with 2.6 and 2.2 percent. Average percentages for 1996 and 2000 were 2.4 percent and 1.7 percent; figures for the Netherlands were higher, with 3.6 percent and 3.0 percent, and appear to be somewhat on the rise. For sexual assaults the Netherlands has a slightly lower prevalence of victimization than the average (on average, 0.7, 1.0, 0.8, and 0.7 for the various survey years, with the Netherlands reporting 0.6, 0.6, 0.7, and 0.8).

The Statistics Netherlands survey asks about a wider category of offenses, which may explain why these figures are slightly higher for 1997–2004. Brouwers and Smit (2005) estimate that 8 percent of sexual incidents reported in the Statistics Netherlands 1997–2004 victim surveys are classified by respondents as an (attempted) sexual assault or rape; Wittebrood (2006) using the same data estimates that 2 percent are completed offenses and 7 percent are attempts. This translates into 15,000–16,000 offenses per year (Brouwers and Smit 2005). Respondents report that 22 percent of these offenses were reported to the police, and for two-thirds a statement was signed, meaning that these incidents should appear as recorded in the statistics. This translates into approximately 2,000 recorded (including attempted) sexual assaults and rapes with adult (over age fifteen) victims per year. Wittebrood suspects that respondents in victim surveys underreport sexual incidents and offenses. If one takes into account child victims, the approximately 4,500 police-recorded sexual assaults and rapes per year are not inconsistent with this estimate.

Police records cannot be made to match perfectly with victim survey estimates since no victims under fifteen are interviewed and sex offenses against children can also be recorded under rape or assault; there are numerous other smaller inconsistencies. A major problem is that victim surveys miss out on children. Daalder and Essers (2003) found that 63 percent of all sexual offending cases registered at the prosecutor's office in the Netherlands involve children under sixteen as victims. There are, however, no sexual abuse victimization monitoring instruments in the Netherlands. Medical personnel are not under legal obligation to report suspected cases of sexual abuse. Personnel of institutions in which such abuse takes place are obliged to report.

Yearly rates in the victim surveys for reporting sex offenses to the authorities vary quite a bit, probably because of instability as a result of the relatively low base rates. The average reporting rate between 1995 and 2004 is almost 9 percent; the average recording rate is a little over 4 percent. De Savornin Lohman et al. (1994) report that two-thirds of all reported offenses are recorded. As Brouwers and Smit (2005) state, 22 percent of the more serious sexual offenses are reported. For the ICVS, yearly reporting rates hover around 15 percent; this is around the cross-national average. In general, reporting rates for other offenses in the Netherlands are somewhat higher than international averages. Thus, according to the victim surveys, between 85 and 91 percent of all sexual incidents go unreported. In the Netherlands, almost 96 percent of all sexual incidents go unrecorded for the age group fifteen and over. The 15,000–16,000 serious sexual offenses per year should probably be multiplied by a factor of at least two to include children. This would amount to a conservative estimate of 30,000 serious sex offenses per year or almost 200 per 100,000 population.

The CBS surveys for 1997–2004 show that about one in seven incidents for victims aged fifteen or over takes place in a house (the victim's or another house); one in six in the street; one in four in a café, bar, or restaurant; another one in four at work or school; and the remainder in other locations. Given the relatively small samples and the low prevalence of victimization by sexual offending in the surveys, no disaggregated information is published by offense type or by perpetrator.

B. Police-Recorded Sex Offenses, 1985–2004

The number of police-recorded sex offenses has increased over the past twenty years.[2] In 2004, the police recorded approximately 1,800 rapes, 2,700 sexual assaults, and 2,200 other sexual offenses. The last are mainly offenses against children and juveniles.

The number of recorded rapes increased by 48 percent from 1985 to 2004; as figure 4 shows, the increase was fairly gradual. The 30

---

[2] CBS is currently revising counting procedures for police data, and the data analyzed here have been supplied by WODC on the basis of CBS data under that provision.

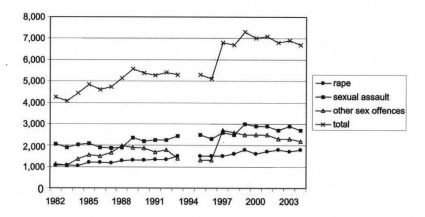

FIG. 4.—Yearly police recorded numbers of sex offenses for rape, sexual assault, and other sex offenses. Source: WODC until 1994, CBS/WODC from 1995.

percent growth for sexual assault was also quite gradual, whereas the category other sex offenses exhibited a level change in 1996–97—a jump of a staggering 140 percent. This jump is also evident quite clearly in the total numbers of recorded sex offenses; it is unknown to what this jump is to be attributed. Broadly speaking, the total number of sex offenses grew from a little under 4,000 sex offenses a year to around 5,500 between 1985 and 1993, and from 1997 to 2004 it hovered around 7,000 sex offenses a year. This translates to around 42 recorded sex offenses per 100,000 population for those latter years.

Figure 5 depicts recorded sex offenses as a percentage of all violent crimes (i.e., including sex offenses) and as a percentage of all recorded crimes. As figure 5 shows, recorded sex offenses are a fairly stable proportion of all recorded offenses. The hump (due to the 140 percent jump in registered other sex offenses) is clearly visible, but otherwise the figure hovers a little under 0.5 percent until 1996 and around 0.6 percent from 1996 onward. Sex offenses constitute an ever-decreasing proportion of all violent offenses: from a little over 13 percent in 1985 to a little under 6 percent in 2004, a 50 percent decrease. This is due to recorded violent offenses rising faster than sex offenses.

The clearance rate for sexual assault has remained more or less the same from 1985 to 2004, hovering around 40 percent (see fig. 6). Clearance rates for rape and other sex offenses have decreased considerably. Rape has decreased from a level around 64 percent between

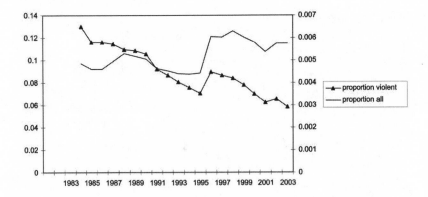

FIG. 5.—Total number of registered sex offenses as a proportion of total number of registered offenses and as a proportion of total number of violent offenses. Source: WODC until 1994, CBS/WODC from 1995.

1985 and 1993 to a rate around 56 percent since. For the category other sex offenses, the line is much more jagged, but overall the decrease is even more marked: from around 75 percent between 1985 and 1989 to a little under 60 percent by 2004.

The decreasing clearance rates have offset the increased numbers of recorded sex offenses only a little: while the increase of recorded cases was around 38 percent, in cleared cases an increase of 36 percent remained. However, if one compares the number of suspects of sex offenses identified over the years (something different is being measured, so the comparison is in principle flawed), the number of suspects averaged over the number of cleared cases has increased considerably. By 1994 a little under 0.9 suspects per cleared sex offense was measured; from 1996 onward this number was around 1.16 suspects. This rise can be explained by many things. It may simply be that more suspects are interrogated, that offenses are recorded differently in the police records, or that sex offenses are more often committed by several perpetrators.

C. Convictions, 1982–2004

Since 1982, the prosecution service has had the authority to impose noncustodial sanctions and fines. From 1982, not only judges' verdicts but also prosecutorial decisions must be taken into account. Prosecutors may dismiss cases for policy reasons or for technical reasons; the

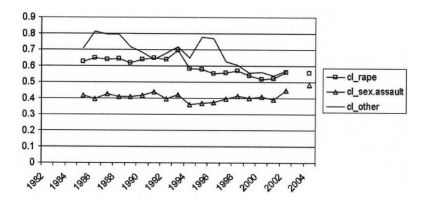

FIG. 6.—Yearly clearance rates for rape, sexual assault, and other sex offenses. Source: WODC until 1994, CBS/WODC from 1995.

latter occurs mainly when prosecutors assess the proof to be insufficient and expect the case to end in acquittal if they proceed. Second, prosecutors may dismiss cases upon certain conditions to be met by the defendant, such as submitting to the supervision of a therapist. Third, prosecutors may impose fines or community service; the defendant must agree; if not, the case is brought to court (for more information, see Bijleveld and Smit [2005]).[3]

Conviction data from 1982–2004 are discussed here. Judicial data systems were computerized in the early 1990s; this was a major operation. For prosecution service statistics, the years 1991 and 1992 are considered so unreliable that they are not reported. One must interpolate the data for those years. Dispositions in first instance are given, that is, either by the prosecutor or by a judge, in the court, as is customary in Dutch statistics.

Tables 1, 2, and 3 give yearly numbers of sex offending cases (for rape, sexual assault, and other sex offenses) recorded by the police, numbers of suspects, numbers of sex offending cases registered at the prosecution service, and yearly numbers of cases dealt with by prosecutors and courts. These include completed and attempted offenses. Cases, which may contain several offenses, are generally registered under the label of the offense that potentially bears the heaviest sentence.

[3] Transactions are counted as conditional policy dismissals (*sepot onder voorwaarden*) and prosecutorial sanctions (*transacties*).

TABLE 1
Yearly Dispositions of Rape (Article 242 Criminal Code)

	Police-Recorded Cases	Suspects	Prosecution Registered Cases	Total Dispositions	Prosecutorial Dispositions	Dismissals	Technical Dismissals	Policy Dismissals	Prosecutorial Sanctions	Court Dispositions	Guilty Verdicts	Acquittals	Probability of Sanction Given Disposition
1982			567	496	229	200 (87%)	146 (64%)	54 (24%)	0 (0%)	267 (54%)	256 (96%)	10 (4%)	.52
1983			692	616	314	282 (90%)	207 (66%)	75 (24%)	0 (0%)	302 (49%)	277 (92%)	19 (6%)	.45
1984			648	602	299	263 (88%)	187 (63%)	76 (25%)	1 (0%)	303 (50%)	279 (92%)	23 (8%)	.47
1985	1,213	861	837	660	373	334 (90%)	256 (69%)	78 (21%)	1 (0%)	287 (43%)	257 (90%)	24 (8%)	.39
1986	1,210	897	826	699	369	335 (91%)	273 (74%)	62 (17%)	5 (1%)	330 (47%)	289 (88%)	28 (8%)	.42
1987	1,193	783	769	701	386	353 (91%)	290 (75%)	63 (16%)	4 (1%)	315 (45%)	249 (79%)	43 (14%)	.36
1988	1,287	865	822	749	408	383 (94%)	310 (76%)	73 (18%)	8 (2%)	341 (46%)	284 (83%)	37 (11%)	.39
1989	1,336	774	753	691	385	349 (91%)	299 (78%)	50 (13%)	4 (1%)	306 (44%)	257 (84%)	42 (14%)	.38
1990	1,331	812	774	620	365	348 (95%)	303 (83%)	45 (12%)	0 (0%)	255 (41%)	204 (80%)	42 (16%)	.33
1991	1,348	760	713	585	360	336 (93%)	294 (82%)	44 (12%)	1 (0%)	225 (38%)	183 (81%)	37 (16%)	.31

1992	1,348	860	745	600	**355**	**324** (91%)	**284** (80%)	**43** (12%)	**1** (0%)	245 (41%)	196 (80%)	35 (14%)	.33
1993	1,496	915	**880**	633	350	309 (88%)	277 (79%)	42 (12%)	**1** (0%)	283 (45%)	248 (88%)	28 (10%)	.39
1994	1,541	951	1,015	756	385	360 (88%)	322 (84%)	38 (10%)	2 (0%)	371 (49%)	325 (88%)	36 (10%)	.43
1995	1,413	1,066	1,117	884	476	450 (94%)	408 (86%)	42 (9%)	6 (1%)	408 (46%)	352 (88%)	50 (12%)	.40
1996	1,427	1,040	1,048	804	404	391 (95%)	361 (89%)	30 (7%)	1 (1%)	400 (50%)	329 (86%)	63 (16%)	.41
1997	1,526	1,032	979	767	362	336 (97%)	305 (84%)	31 (9%)	1 (0%)	405 (50%)	337 (82%)	61 (15%)	.44
1998	1,626	1,076	904	706	314	286 (93%)	256 (84%)	30 (9%)	1 (0%)	392 (53%)	335 (83%)	55 (15%)	.48
1999	1,775	1,146	975	687	278	247 (91%)	220 (82%)	27 (10%)	2 (0%)	409 (56%)	337 (85%)	65 (14%)	.49
2000	1,648	1,016	921	754	379	344 (89%)	317 (79%)	27 (10%)	4 (1%)	375 (60%)	294 (82%)	70 (16%)	.40
2001	1,725	1,055	935	698	312	273 (91%)	253 (84%)	20 (7%)	3 (1%)	386 (50%)	328 (78%)	50 (19%)	.47
2002	1,801	1,132	939	757	319	277 (88%)	251 (81%)	26 (6%)	4 (1%)	438 (55%)	367 (85%)	64 (13%)	.49
2003	1,700		866	680	284	241 (88%)	221 (79%)	20 (8%)	4 (1%)	396 (58%)	367 (84%)	64 (15%)	.49
2004	1,800	1,300	1,064	729	296	277 (87%)	221 (78%)	20 (7%)	6 (1%)	396 (58%)	335 (85%)	55 (14%)	.50
						247 (85%)	230 (78%)	17 (6%)	5 (2%)	433 (59%)	351 (81%)	77 (18%)	.49

SOURCE.—1982–90 and 1994–2004: CBS; 1991–93: de Savornin Lohman et al. (1994); registered cases, 1982–92: de Savornin Lohman et al. (1994); police-recorded cases and suspects: WODC.

NOTE.—Numbers in parentheses are percentages of prosecutorial dispositions for all categories except court dispositions (percentages of total dispositions) and guilty verdicts and acquittals (percentages of court dispositions). Bold numbers have been interpolated.

TABLE 2
Yearly Dispositions of Sexual Assault (Article 246 Criminal Code)

	Police-Recorded Cases	Suspects	Prosecution Registered Cases	Total Dispositions	Prosecutorial Dispositions	Dismissals	Technical Dismissals	Policy Dismissals	Prosecutorial Sanctions	Court Dispositions	Guilty Verdicts	Acquittals	Probability of Sanction Given Disposition
1982			606	510	368	313 (85%)	105 (29%)	208 (57%)	0 (0%)	142 (28%)	129 (91%)	12 (8%)	.25
1983			575	602	425	340 (80%)	124 (29%)	216 (51%)	4 (1%)	177 (29%)	161 (91%)	12 (7%)	.27
1984			531	530	357	291 (82%)	82 (23%)	209 (59%)	5 (1%)	173 (33%)	168 (97%)	5 (3%)	.33
1985	2,075	713	524	487	314	254 (81%)	93 (30%)	161 (51%)	8 (3%)	173 (36%)	160 (92%)	7 (4%)	.34
1986	1,907	691	516	481	301	254 (84%)	91 (30%)	163 (54%)	9 (3%)	180 (37%)	162 (90%)	14 (8%)	.36
1987	1,900	656	561	518	317	251 (79%)	126 (40%)	125 (39%)	12 (4%)	201 (39%)	183 (91%)	9 (4%)	.38
1988	1,922	702	553	524	370	298 (81%)	151 (41%)	147 (40%)	11 (3%)	154 (29%)	134 (87%)	14 (9%)	.28
1989	2,380	728	624	560	378	312 (83%)	166 (44%)	146 (39%)	20 (5%)	182 (33%)	166 (91%)	14 (8%)	.33
1990	2,231	747	606	540	368	305 (83%)	156 (42%)	149 (40%)	24 (7%)	172 (32%)	153 (89%)	14 (8%)	.33
1991	2,443	648	610	554	368	303 (82%)	162 (44%)	142 (39%)	24 (7%)	186 (34%)	169 (91%)	11 (6%)	.35

1992	2,257	745	619	542	**368**	**301** (82%)	**168** (46%)	**136** (37%)	**24** (7%)	174 (32%)	149 (86%)	13 (7%)	.32
1993	2,424	746	**621**	553	369	301 (82%)	175 (47%)	126 (34%)	**25** (7%)	184 (33%)	169 (92%)	9 (5%)	.35
1994	2,245	789	623	587	407	348 (82%)	200 (47%)	148 (34%)	25 (7%)	180 (33%)	158 (92%)	19 (5%)	.31
1995	2,434	1,034	675	559	359	295 (86%)	188 (49%)	107 (36%)	36 (6%)	200 (31%)	174 (88%)	23 (11%)	.38
1996	2,244	1,004	705	675	408	328 (82%)	199 (52%)	129 (30%)	53 (10%)	267 (36%)	241 (87%)	23 (12%)	.44
1997	2,523	1,189	767	702	406	302 (80%)	207 (49%)	95 (32%)	60 (13%)	296 (40%)	273 (90%)	17 (9%)	.47
1998	2,469	1,194	721	651	359	264 (74%)	178 (51%)	86 (23%)	53 (15%)	292 (42%)	261 (92%)	28 (6%)	.48
1999	2,959	1,427	844	657	317	213 (74%)	145 (50%)	68 (24%)	67 (15%)	340 (45%)	301 (89%)	33 (10%)	.56
2000	2,896	1,419	793	792	404	267 (67%)	166 (46%)	101 (21%)	76 (21%)	388 (52%)	342 (89%)	39 (10%)	.53
2001	2,853	1,311	826	825	435	252 (66%)	166 (41%)	86 (25%)	113 (19%)	390 (49%)	340 (88%)	46 (10%)	.55
2002	2,737	1,398	877	834	381	207 (58%)	138 (38%)	69 (20%)	106 (26%)	453 (47%)	386 (87%)	59 (12%)	.59
2003	2,900		810	832	369	227 (54%)	139 (36%)	88 (18%)	95 (28%)	463 (54%)	402 (85%)	51 (13%)	.60
2004	2,700	1,500	839	804	369	194 (62%)	115 (38%)	79 (24%)	123 (26%)	435 (56%)	388 (87%)	43 (11%)	.64
						(53%)	(31%)	(21%)	(33%)	(54%)	(89%)	(10%)	

SOURCE.—1982–90 and 1994–2004: CBS; 1991–93: de Savornin Lohman et al. (1994); registered cases, 1982–92: de Savornin Lohman et al. (1994); police-recorded cases and suspects: WODC.

NOTE.—Numbers in parentheses are percentages of prosecutorial dispositions for all categories except court dispositions (percentages of total dispositions) and guilty verdicts and acquittals (percentages of court dispositions). Bold numbers have been interpolated.

TABLE 3
Yearly Dispositions of Other Sex Offenses (Articles 243, 244, 245, 247, 248ter, and 249 Criminal Code)

	Police-Recorded Cases	Suspects	Prosecution Registered Cases	Total Dispositions	Prosecutorial Dispositions	Dismissals	Technical Dismissals	Policy Dismissals	Prosecutorial Sanctions	Court Dispositions	Guilty Verdicts	Acquittals	Probability of Sanction Given Disposition
1982			608	599	411	380 (92%)	125 (30%)	255 (62%)	0 (0%)	188 (31%)	178 (95%)	9 (5%)	.30
1983			545	580	397	361 (91%)	110 (28%)	251 (63%)	0 (0%)	183 (32%)	173 (95%)	9 (5%)	.30
1984			651	586	370	334 (90%)	103 (28%)	231 (62%)	5 (1%)	216 (37%)	206 (95%)	6 (3%)	.36
1985	1,550	1,008	815	732	454	406 (89%)	151 (33%)	257 (57%)	10 (2%)	278 (38%)	267 (96%)	7 (3%)	.38
1986	1,497	998	873	839	456	463 (1,02%)	176 (39%)	233 (51%)	8 (2%)	383 (46%)	359 (94%)	15 (4%)	.44
1987	1,711	1,139	982	862	475	414 (87%)	219 (46%)	195 (41%)	11 (2%)	387 (45%)	353 (91%)	16 (4%)	.42
1988	2,011	1,409	1,167	1,012	521	475 (91%)	277 (53%)	198 (38%)	9 (2%)	491 (49%)	449 (91%)	33 (7%)	.45
1989	1,945	1,075	994	1,042	539	486 (90%)	293 (54%)	193 (36%)	10 (2%)	503 (48%)	457 (91%)	41 (8%)	.45
1990	1,893	1,158	973	982	534	496 (93%)	316 (59%)	180 (34%)	12 (2%)	448 (46%)	417 (93%)	30 (7%)	.44
1991	1,683	940	883	942	509	469 (92%)	305 (60%)	164 (32%)	13 (3%)	433 (46%)	376 (87%)	30 (7%)	.41

1992	1,789	1,032	803	892	**484**	**441** (91%)	**295** (61%)	**148** (31%)	**14** (3%)	408 (46%)	363 (89%)	**30** (7%)	.42
1993	1,380	871	**1,039**	904	459	416 (91%)	285 (62%)	131 (29%)	**14** (3%)	445 (49%)	401 (90%)	**31** (7%)	.46
1994	1,506	879	1,274	1,092	504	472 (91%)	320 (62%)	152 (29%)	15 (3%)	588 (49%)	555 (90%)	31 (7%)	.52
1995	1,090	804	1,236	1,243	562	523 (94%)	381 (63%)	142 (30%)	9 (3%)	681 (54%)	625 (92%)	50 (5%)	.51
1996	1,094	881	1,281	1,270	494	444 (93%)	336 (68%)	108 (25%)	17 (2%)	776 (55%)	695 (94%)	65 (7%)	.56
1997	2,637	1,822	1,225	1,390	587	493 (90%)	363 (68%)	130 (22%)	19 (3%)	803 (61%)	744 (90%)	56 (8%)	.55
1998	2,546	1,658	1,160	1,167	439	358 (84%)	280 (62%)	78 (22%)	17 (3%)	728 (58%)	674 (93%)	48 (7%)	.59
1999	2,530	1,540	1,100	1,191	437	364 (82%)	282 (64%)	82 (18%)	18 (4%)	754 (62%)	682 (93%)	64 (7%)	.59
2000	2,535	1,583	1,031	1,182	436	361 (83%)	273 (65%)	88 (19%)	15 (4%)	746 (63%)	679 (90%)	58 (8%)	.59
2001	2,492	1,447	1,068	1,171	417	328 (83%)	256 (63%)	72 (20%)	29 (3%)	754 (63%)	677 (91%)	68 (8%)	.60
2002	2,301	1,381	954	1,120	395	315 (79%)	223 (61%)	78 (17%)	41 (7%)	725 (64%)	645 (90%)	68 (9%)	.61
2003	2,700		932	1,037	319	258 (80%)	195 (56%)	53 (20%)	29 (10%)	718 (65%)	639 (89%)	72 (9%)	.64
2004	2,200	1,400	925	1,011	284	238 (81%)	179 (61%)	53 (17%)	19 (9%)	727 (69%)	654 (89%)	68 (9%)	.67

SOURCE.—1982–90 and 1994–2004: CBS; 1991–93: de Savornin Lohman et al. (1994); registered cases, 1982–92: de Savornin Lohman et al. (1994); police-recorded cases and suspects: WODC.

NOTE.—Numbers in parentheses are percentages of prosecutorial dispositions for all categories except court dispositions (percentages of total dispositions) and guilty verdicts and acquittals (percentages of court dispositions). Bold numbers have been interpolated.

343

It may thus be that more sex offenses were actually registered but are invisible since they are "hidden" under the label of a heavier offense in the same case. The numbers of cases each year do not match the numbers of cases disposed of, since cases take some time from registration to disposition. In addition, there may be mismatches, since cases registered by the prosecution, for instance under rape, may appear in court statistics as a sexual assault when the judge concluded that penetration could not be proved or that an offense did not involve force under one of the articles governing other sex offenses.

There is a clear trend in the data: overall the number of cases registered for prosecution rose. For rape (table 1) the rise was 88 percent (but, leaving aside 2004, which may be an anomaly, the rise is 53 percent); for sexual assault, 38 percent (table 2); and for other sex offenses, 52 percent (table 3).

While the offenses prosecuted under the articles for sex with minors involve young victims, one cannot be sure that sexual assault prosecutions involve only adult victims. Sex offenses involving young victims can also be prosecuted as rapes or sexual assaults; one reason to do so is that a rape verdict carries a heavier sentence.

While the numbers of sex offending cases rose over the past twenty-three years, the prosecution service itself disposed of slightly decreasing numbers of cases each year. The overall rise was allocated to the courts. Of the cases that the prosecution service disposed of in the 1980s, almost 90 percent ended in dismissal, a percentage that decreased steadily to 70 percent by 2004. Policy dismissals decreased even more, and technical dismissals increased. The number of sex offending cases for which the prosecutor hands out fines or sanctions increased as well.

When rape, sexual assault, and other sex offenses are looked at separately, the pictures vary. Over the course of the years, more rape cases (see table 1) have been dealt with by the courts (from around 50 percent to around 60 percent); if cases are dismissed, technical reasons were increasingly cited; the number of cases dismissed for policy reasons decreased from almost a quarter to just 6 percent by 2004. However, the likelihood that the defendant is convicted by the courts decreased substantially from around 95 percent in 1982 to 80 percent by 2004. By that year about one in six cases ended in acquittal. This is a high figure for the Netherlands (on average, 2 percent). When one considers both prosecutorial dispositions and court sanctions, the likelihood that a rape disposition resulted in a sanction did not rise from

1982 to 2004: it decreased from around .50 in 1982 to about .30 in 1990/91 and then rose to almost 1982 levels. These low years saw relatively many (technical) prosecutorial dismissals.

Table 2 gives the same data for sexual assaults. The number of dispositions in this category also rose over the years. The shift from prosecutorial to court disposition is much larger, from almost 30 percent of sexual assault cases dealt with by the courts in 1982 to approximately 55 percent in 2004. As with rape, the absolute numbers of cases dealt with by the prosecution—with a little fluctuation—remained almost the same. The likelihood that the prosecution dismissed a case decreased sharply: from 85 percent to 50 percent. The decrease is mainly due to fewer policy dismissals: from 57 percent in 1982 to around 20 percent after 2000. The probability of a guilty verdict remained fairly stable, just under 90 percent. Chances of acquittal fluctuated a bit, rising slightly but mainly hovering between 7 and 10 percent. When one considers prosecutorial and court dispositions together, the likelihood that a sexual assault disposition resulted in some kind of sanction more than doubled from .25 in 1982 to .64 in 2004. The rise is due to the accumulated effect of fewer policy dismissals coupled with more prosecutorial sanctions and larger numbers of cases dealt with by the courts and ending in a guilty verdict.

For the other sex offenses, involving mainly sex offenses against minors, the same trend is prominent. More and more cases were dealt with by the court: from around 30 percent in 1982 to more than 70 percent in 2004; the absolute number of cases dealt with by the prosecutor decreased. As with rape and sexual assault, the percentage of policy dismissals decreased considerably from a little under 60 percent in 1982 to a little under 20 percent in 2004. Technical dismissals rose from 35 percent in 1982 to about 60 percent toward the end of the series. Prosecutorial sanctions increased. The likelihood of conviction by a judge decreased slightly, and chances of acquittal rose. When prosecutorial and court sanctions are combined, the likelihood that a prosecution for a sex offense involving a child victim resulted in some kind of sanction more than doubled, rising from 30 percent in 1982 to 67 percent in 2004. This is mainly due to larger numbers being referred to the courts.

For each type of sex offense, increasing numbers of cases were processed by the criminal justice system. The prosecution dealt with the same numbers of cases (or fewer cases), but the caseloads of the courts rose. Prosecutors generally tended to dismiss cases more often for technical reasons and less often for policy reasons. Particularly for sexual assault and sex offenses against children, prosecutors have increasingly sanctioned these cases themselves.

At the beginning of the period examined in this subsection, sex offenses were typically seen as offenses that were inopportune to prosecute. However, since 1982, cases have been dismissed increasingly for technical reasons and less for policy reasons, and those considered fit for prosecution are increasingly sent on to the courts. For rape, policy dismissal rates always were very low and remained very low (around 5 percent). By 2004, policy dismissal rates for the other sex offenses and for sexual assaults were still above the average for all offenses registered at the prosecutor's office (on average, in 2004, 11 percent of registered cases were dismissed for policy reasons and another 11 percent for technical reasons [Eggen and van der Heide 2005]). Chances of conviction in court were high and highest for rape; however, they were much lower than average chances of conviction for other offenses.

D. Sanctions and Measures, 1994–2004

Perpetrators may receive various sanctions or measures, although it is also possible to be found guilty without the imposition of punishment. Offenders may be sanctioned by a fine, detention, or community service. Such community service orders (*taakstraf*) are divided into orders that involve some kind of volunteer work (*werkstraf*, literally "work punishment") or a treatment-like modality (*leerstraf*, literally "learning punishment"). Prosecutors may also impose such sanctions as a condition for dismissal. Community service orders and fines may be imposed by a prosecutor or a judge; sentences that involve incarceration may be imposed only by a judge.

Table 4 lists the yearly probabilities of custodial sentences for rape, sexual assault, and the category of other sex offenses, conditional on disposition of the case and conditional on a court guilty verdict for that offense. It also gives average sentence lengths of custodial sentences.

From 1994 onward, almost two-thirds of court verdicts for rape entailed a custodial sanction; this percentage has remained fairly stable. For sexual assault, the percentage is much lower: one in four verdicts for sexual assault produces a custodial sentence; this percentage also appears fairly stable. For sex offenses involving child victims, the prob-

TABLE 4
Probability of Custodial Sanction Given Disposition

	Rape			Sexual Assault			Other Sex Offenses		
	Probability of Custodial Sentence Given Court Guilty Verdict	Probability of Custodial Sentence Given Disposition	Average Sentence Length	Probability of Custodial Sentence Given Court Guilty Verdict	Probability of Custodial Sentence Given Disposition	Average Sentence Length	Probability of Custodial Sentence Given Court Guilty Verdict	Probability of Custodial Sentence Given Disposition	Average Sentence Length
1994	.70	.30	452	.23	.06	154	.40	.21	321
1995	.66	.26	451	.25	.08	193	.39	.20	318
1996	.73	.30	433	.18	.06	160	.37	.20	332
1997	.69	.30	469	.23	.09	203	.35	.19	314
1998	.67	.32	484	.09	.04	166	.34	.19	304
1999	.64	.31	461	.23	.11	175	.28	.16	302
2000	.65	.25	466	.21	.09	135	.31	.18	303
2001	.65	.30	423	.24	.10	135	.35	.20	306
2002	.66	.32	525	.18	.08	144	.36	.20	277
2003	.68	.34	521	.21	.10	183	.38	.23	272
2004	.63	.30	489	.24	.11	160	.41	.27	325

SOURCE.—CBS; custodial sentences and sentence length: WODC/CBS.

ability of a conviction resulting in a custodial sentence has been a little over one in three since 1994 but may have increased lately.

As the percentage of cases sent to court differs for the various offense types, the likelihood of a disposition ending up in a custodial sentence likewise differs (other sanctions and measures may also be added to a custodial sentence). Approximately three in ten rape cases disposed of end in a custodial sentence. For sexual assault, the chance of detention has risen, with some ups and downs, from around 7 percent in the mid-1990s to around 10 percent more recently. The rise is not due per se to a greater chance of detention given conviction, but to the larger numbers of cases being sent to the courts. For sex offenses involving children, there is a small rise in the likelihood of incarceration: from under 20 percent in the mid-1990s to 25 percent more recently. As with sexual assault, the rise is due to the larger numbers of cases sent on to the courts.

Sentence length is fairly stable for all three offenses. Average sentence length is greatest for rape, the average custodial sentence being about fifteen months, although sentence lengths may have increased somewhat lately. Average sentence length for sexual assault is a little under six months and fluctuates a bit but does not show a clear trend. Average sentence length for the other sex offenses is fairly stable at approximately ten months. Approximately 5 percent of the Dutch prison population is incarcerated for a sex offense (Tubex 2006).

The probability of a sanction given a recorded offense by the police increased from around 15 percent from 1985 to 1993 to around 20 percent between 1998 and 2004, a 30 percent increase. The probability of a sanction given a suspect increased from around 30 percent from 1985 to 1993 to around 35 percent between 1998 and 2004.

Over the years, the police have identified more offenders per case, of whom it referred fewer for prosecution. This by itself offset to a certain extent the increased likelihood of a sanction given disposition, mainly because the prosecution referred more cases to the courts for disposition, both relatively and absolutely. While the quantitative cause of these rising sanctioning rates can be pinpointed, it is hard to explain it, since the properties of the various cases processed and through different stages of the system are unknown. First, the prosecution decided to leave fewer cases unprosecuted. Next, as an explanation for increased technical dismissals, the prosecution service may have selected from an increasing supply of cases those it considered easiest to prove, and thus attractive to prosecute, discarding by technical dismissal potentially less "successful" cases. Prosecutors may also have proceeded with those that it considered most serious and thus warranting prosecution and punishment (or another intervention), which would explain the rising acquittal rates. The chances of detention given a guilty verdict have hovered around 40 percent and may have decreased a bit.

E. Treatment

Judges and prosecutors may impose treatment. Prosecutors may do so as a sentence by itself (for instance, a *leerstraf*) or conditionally, accompanying a conditional dismissal. Treatment for sex offenders can be provided in an ambulatory setting or residentially. An important form of residential treatment for sex offenders is the entrustment order (*terbeschikkingstelling* or TBS). Ambulatory treatment is mainly provided by a small number of forensic clinics. Exact numbers are not available.

Treatment for sex offenders has changed substantially since the late 1980s, when cognitive behavioral techniques became more prevalent and popular. The prevailing idea had been that sex offenders suffer from a personality disorder, mental illness, or paraphilia that required treatment. Since the early 1990s, however, specialists have differentiated responses: cure should be sought for some, but for others prevention of relapse might suffice. For these latter offenders, the motto "not cure but control" was adopted.

Treatment is routinely provided in homogeneous groups sorted by the type of sex offense. Child abusers are treated in one group, "incest-opa's" (incest-granddads) in another, and compulsive assaulters in another. Special groups exist for sex offenders with below-average intelligence (IQ score 70–85). Ambulatory treatment generally continues one to two years. The content varies widely depending on the type of sex offender and the etiology of risk factors. All treatment is modular. Treatment is provided by De Waag, with seven branches in the west of the Netherlands, and in several other centers (such as Tender in Deventer, DOK in Rotterdam, and the Forensic Outpatient Clinic in Amsterdam). From the capacity of these institutions it can be estimated that about 300 adult sex offenders a year enroll for ambulatory treatment. Such group treatment is available only for men. Treatment of a female sex offender must be done on an individual basis.

Hormonal treatment is provided for a small number of obsessive child abusers (no data are available: estimates are that not more than 5 percent of treatment involves hormones, with Androcur most often administered). Antidepressants that suppress libido, such as selective serotonin reuptake inhibitors (SSRI), are also prescribed. Medication is generally not prescribed as treatment per se but to enable particularly obsessive sex offenders to participate in therapy. While these forms of "chemical castration" thus may be prescribed in exceptional cases, until 1968 sex offending males could be castrated. Between 1938 and 1967, 381 men who had received a TBS order for sex offending were castrated, mostly for homosexual acts with children or minors (Beyaert 1986; van der Meer 2005). Castration was carried out only with the offender's consent and was not allowed when it appeared that the offender agreed only in order to be able to return home. Half of these surgical castrations took place between the end of World War II and 1967. Research on recidivism reported methodologically unsound but fairly average reoffending rates (between 1.3 and 3 percent for the Netherlands) relative to—methodologically noncomparable—studies from other countries. Feelings of frustration and anger increased after castration (Beyaert 1986).

Especially for violent and sexual crimes, TBS orders are given in combination with a prison sentence (van Emmerik 1989). An entrustment order can be imposed for crimes carrying a maximum statutory penalty of at least four years' imprisonment if hospital care is deemed necessary to protect other people, the general public, or property and if the offender cannot be held (fully) accountable for his acts. The TBS order is imposed on an estimated fifty sex offenders a year (Dienst Justitiële Inrichtingen [DJI], 2006: http://www.dji.nl). The order lasts for two years but may be extended. In practice, the average confinement for those released from entrustment orders by 1998 was five to six years (Leuw 1999, p. 28). The average length of stay has recently increased considerably.

By 2004, judges imposed over 300 TBS measures yearly—not only for sex offenses. Only a little over eighty terminate each year. Thus the TBS population expands. According to DJI, by early 2005, around 1,500 persons were detained under a TBS order. Almost all TBS detainees have committed aggressive offenses. Almost 30 percent of the TBS population is there for at least one sex offense. In principle, the TBS order includes treatment. Some TBS detainees, however, are untreatable, but remain too dangerous to release. For these, a long-stay institution has been created inside the clinic Veldzicht: former TBS detainees are not treated but receive only nursing care, a much less expensive form of care. Additional long-stay facilities were being built in 2007. Over half of the long-stay Veldzicht population is made up of sex offenders (de Kogel and Verwers 2003). While 9 percent of the general TBS population is diagnosed with a sexual disorder, 43 percent of the long-stay population is diagnosed with a sexual disorder. This illustrates how this category of violent sex offenders is relatively harder to treat. Most of these sexual disorders entail pedophilia.

Taken together, approximately 350 (300 ambulatory plus fifty TBS orders) of 900 convicted adult sex offenders each year are enrolled in some form of treatment.

F. Special Groups: Juvenile and Female Offenders

Males constitute the bulk of the general offender population, and this is truer for sex offending. Prosecution data show a disproportionately low and qualitatively different involvement of females in sex offenses (personal communication with G. Beijers, 2006). For the years 1994 to mid-2005, 2.4 percent of sex offending cases handled by the prosecution service involved female defendants. Females' offense patterns are different than males': for males, 23 percent of sex offenses were rapes; for women, this was 12 percent. Twenty-four percent of male sex offenders were prosecuted for sexual assault, compared with 9 percent of females. Female defendants were somewhat less often involved in offenses against children/minors (41 percent against 47 percent females); for child pornography the distribution was similar (3.4 percent females against 3.9 percent males). A staggering 34 percent of all female cases involved prosecution for pimping (art. 250) compared with only 3.4 percent of male defendants. Adult female sex offenders thus are most often prosecuted for sex offenses against children/minors (around 40 percent) and pimping (around one-third of cases). Rape and sexual assault are infrequent.

Women's cases are more often dismissed than men's, but their chances of acquittal are about equal (both 11 percent). Cases with a male perpetrator have a higher chance of conviction (50 percent against 37 percent). One possible explanation is that cases with females more often involve types of offenses especially likely to be dismissed. This is not the case: for pimping, women's chances of technical dismissal are lower than men's (14 percent against 27 percent). Another possibility is that women are more often accomplices; however, women are identified as accomplices in less than 2 percent of cases. This small percentage cannot explain the big difference in chances of dismissal.

A sizable proportion of sex offenders are juveniles. At the police level, for which data are available from 1995 to 2004, about one in eight is a juvenile. For offenses against children or minors, the proportion is almost 9 percent, for rape it is approximately 11 percent, and for sexual assault it is 16 percent. With regard to the prosecution level, the proportion of cases with juvenile defendants is substantially higher. Even though suspects at the police level and cases at the prosecution level cannot strictly speaking be compared, it nonetheless appears that juveniles are disproportionately more often prosecuted than adults. While 12 percent of suspects of a sex offense at the police level are juveniles, this increases to 21 percent at the prosecution level. One explanation may be that these juveniles are judged to be more in need of a tailored intervention. For rape the increase is from 11 to 17 percent, for sexual assault from 16 to 33 percent, and for offenses involving minors from 9 to 16 percent. These percentages have been fairly stable in recent years.

Among cases disposed of, the numbers for 1995–2004 are approximately the same for rape as for prosecutions, with about one in six dispositions involving a juvenile perpetrator. For sexual assault, the juvenile proportion is larger again, around 40 percent of cases. For sexual offenses involving child victims, the proportion of dispositions involving a juvenile is about 20 percent.

For sex offenses with juvenile perpetrators, the same general trend appears as described above. Overall, the number of dispositions involving juvenile defendants is increasing, with the increase being handled by the courts. The numbers are small, but this appears most marked for sexual assaults and child abuse. No data are available on sanctions imposed on juveniles by the prosecution service. However, given that the prosecution service handles around 250 juvenile sex offender dispositions per year, of which some are dismissals, a crude but conservative estimate is that 100 sex offending cases with a juvenile offender are disposed of each year with a sanction or a (conditional) treatment measure or are dismissed under (treatment) conditions.

Between 1995 and 2004, a little over 600 registered sex offending cases each year involved a juvenile defendant. Of these, six to seven cases per year involved an adolescent female sex offender (Hendriks and Bijleveld 2006), around 1 percent. Girls thus constitute only a very small fraction of known juvenile sex offenders.

Because of low absolute numbers, it is hard to draw conclusions on sentencing trends for juveniles. Guilty verdicts in the courts for juveniles hover around 83 percent for rape and around 90 percent for sexual assault and for sex offenses involving children (Eggen and van der Heide 2005). Juvenile rapists are sentenced to detention in 33 percent of guilty verdicts. For sexual assault and offenses involving children, the percentage of those detained was about 14 percent from 1995 to 2004. Juveniles sentenced to detention for rape received on average five months. For sexual assault this was a little over three months, and for sex offenses involving child victims around three and a half months. There is no discernible trend in these data. These figures are much lower for juveniles than for adults: the likelihood of a custodial sentence is much lower, and custodial sentences are much shorter.

Juvenile sex offenders may be sentenced to a custodial sanction or to a community service order or *werkstraf* (which is a noncustodial sanction). No data are obtainable on the number of community service orders for juvenile sex offenders. The prosecutor may also impose *leerstraf*, noncustodial sanctions, which implies that a training course must be completed. Dismissals may be conditioned on such ambulatory courses or treatment.

While not treatment per se, the training courses are meant to be beneficial. The Rutgers/NISSO foundation and De Waag offer a *leerstraf* on sexuality, in which in ten sessions juvenile sex offenders discuss sexuality, intimate relations, condom use, and the like. Rutgers/NISSO and De Waag also offer a twenty-five-session Relapse Prevention course. Juvenile sex offenders may also receive social skills training (SoVa training). These awareness-raising/educational courses may be imposed only on non–child abusers and first-time sex offenders. Numbers could not be obtained, but from the capacity of these courses it can be estimated that around 100–120 juvenile sex offenders follow these training courses yearly.

A juvenile sex offender may receive ambulatory treatment. Ambulatory treatment is predominantly provided by De Waag. From capacity it can be estimated that around seventy-five juvenile sex offenders enroll each year for treatment. Treatment is modular. The modules developed by De Waag (Hendriks, Bullens, and van Outsem 2002) are also used (in translation) in Sweden, Germany, Switzerland, and

France. They deal with the objectives of treatment and the disadvantages of sex offending for the perpetrator and the victim. Following this the five G's are discussed: *gebeurtenissen* (events), *gedachten* (thoughts), *gevoelens* (feelings), *gedrag* (behavior), and *goedpraters* (excuses). Cognitive distortions are explored, as are behavioral alternatives to offending (short-term, when confronted with a situation that could develop into an offense, and long-term, for instance planning to stay away from young children). Social skills training is an integral component. The program is multifocal since it includes practical preventive guidelines and training, behavioral alternatives, attempts to increase understanding of the offending behavior and its consequences, and attempts to increase protective skills.

A juvenile sex offender can receive residential treatment as a measure. Most who receive such measures are treated at Harreveld, which specializes in juvenile sex offenders (around twenty convicted juvenile sex offenders per year). A few places are available at Groot Emaus for those with impaired intellectual functioning. Harreveld offers treatment for child abuse and opportunistic (i.e., mainly peer abusing) offenses. Apart from living in a group-based living environment, treatment is individually tailored (Hendriks and Bijleveld 2005*a*). The order under which such treatment takes place is the PIJ measure (PIJ is short for placement in an institution for juveniles). The measure in principle lasts two years and may be extended twice. Juveniles may also be treated under a civil law order, for instance when the family background of the juvenile is considered inadequate or damaging, or when the offender is under the age of criminal responsibility (twelve).

Juveniles seldom receive hormonal treatment because regular medication can affect bone development in immature children. Such medication can be prescribed only when it has been established with certainty that the juvenile offender's body is fully developed. Medication in such cases is the same as for adults. Antidepressants such as SSRI can be prescribed with fewer restrictions.

Of around 325 convicted juvenile sex offenders per year, plus an unknown number of policy dismissals (estimated at 100), approximately 200 are enrolled in some form of treatment or a training course. Thus not only are juveniles more often prosecuted than adults, but when prosecuted and convicted, treatment and training are more often (in an estimated 50 percent of cases) imposed than for adult sex offenders (about 40 percent of cases). Detention, however, is much less likely, and when it is imposed, it is much shorter. This is not surprising given the rationales underlying juvenile criminal law and its different sanctioning system (Junger-Tas 2004).

III. Sex Offenders and Sex Offending

Most empirical research on sex offending and offenders focuses on a few themes. Traditionally, much research was carried out by psychiatrists and psychologists, most of it clinically oriented and not aiming at broad generalizations. The WODC has carried out broader studies focusing on profiles of sex offenders or particular groups such as pedosexual offenders. A number of authors have written about juvenile sex offenders. A number of studies have been conducted to estimate the prevalence of sexual victimization. Scattered empirical work exists on pedophilia, sexual abuse of boys, long-term risks of recidivism, and adolescent female sex offenders. There are strikingly few broad encompassing studies. Most studies are small, focusing on special groups. The Netherlands is not unique in this, and the objects of study may show such great variation that sweeping generalizations would be unfounded. There has been little theorizing. Many articles published in Dutch journals reiterate Anglo-Saxon findings and mainstream theories and are not discussed here.

In this section the available empirical studies are organized as follows. First, victimization studies are discussed, disaggregating studies by the age and sex of the victim. Next studies on offenders are examined, focusing on types of sex offenders that have been studied more extensively, such as pedophiles and juvenile sex offenders. The section ends with studies on the criminal careers of sex offenders.

A. Victims

The most influential study of victims and offenders of sex offenses and sexual abuse is by Nel Draijer (1988). It generated a storm of protests and indignation but was a landmark in that it showed (what had until then been asserted mainly by feminist groups) that sexual abuse of women and girls is widespread and that the perpetrators are mainly men with whom the victims stand in a relation of unequal power. The study appeared at a time when general acceptance of the idea that all consensual sexual acts are legitimate was waning. The public, parents, and criminal justice officials were coming to recognize that children may not always be able to choose such acts or be in a position to refuse them and that the very idea of consent may be irrelevant in their cases. The study showed how damaging such sexual acts can sometimes be. It appeared in a period that was receptive to its findings.

Draijer (1988) conducted face-to-face interviews with 1,054 women between twenty and forty years of age, representatively selected from all over the Netherlands. The 49 percent response rate was not exceptionally low for the Netherlands. Analysis of nonresponders showed that women acutely suffering from the effects of sexual abuse may have disproportionately refused to cooperate. If so, Draijer noted, the findings probably underestimate prevalence and underrepresent serious cases. Her study focused on sexual abuse of girls by relatives. She used a fairly narrow definition of abuse: only hands-on abuse was counted. Thus a father's masturbating in front of his daughter did not count as sexual abuse.

One in six women (15.6 percent) had been abused sexually by a relative. One in four had been abused by a nonrelative, excluding forced sex and other sexual incidents during dating. Almost one in three had experienced unwanted sexual contact before age sixteen, varying from touchings to rape. One in fourteen had been abused by more than one perpetrator. No increase in such victimization was reported over the years. In 99 percent of cases of abuse within the family, the perpetrator was male. Brothers and uncles were reported most often. Four percent of respondents had been sexually harassed by their fathers before age sixteen. In one in three cases ($N = 165$) the sexual abuse was a once-only incident; in repeat-abuse cases, it lasted an average of four years ($N = 100$). When multiple family members ($N = 43$) were abused, the perpetrator was in most cases a father or grandfather. In half of father-daughter incest cases ($N = 31$), the child was also physically abused (by the father or the mother).

About 50 percent of all sexual incidents were rated to be serious or very serious, entailing sexual penetration or attempts; sexual contacts with fathers were prevalent here. One in ten to fifteen women witnessed a serious and damaging form of sexual abuse by relatives.

Most women resisted sexual abuse as children, although strong emotional pressures made this difficult. Those who had undergone more serious sexual abuse especially often reported dissociative and other defensive coping reactions. Only one in five reported the incidents as a child to her mother. Younger respondents had more often reported the incidents; supportive reactions were related to less traumatization.

Families in which sexual abuse took place were characterized by affective neglect and parental unavailability. Family characteristics explained about a quarter of the variation in the prevalence of incest.

Women abused as a child by a family member reported more psychological and psychosomatic complaints than women who had not been abused. It is unknown whether this was a selection effect, with victims chosen by perpetrators because of their vulnerability. The sexual abuse contributed to these complaints, independently of the effect of other family risk factors. Over half of abused respondents reported complaints. About one in seven did not report elevated symptoms. Sexual abuse by non–family members had an independent additive effect on complaint levels.

Draijer showed that 97 percent of cases of abuse by family members were not reported to the police. Abuse by others went unreported in 93 percent of cases. The closer the perpetrator was to the victim, the lower the likelihood of reporting to the police. Respondents in such cases indicated that they had not known whether what was happening to them was normal or not or had been afraid that the family would be broken up if the father were sent to prison. However, the likelihood of reporting increased as the abuse was more serious. In most cases, the abuser was the father and both sexual and physical abuse took place; most abusive fathers were heavy drinkers. Eight percent of the most serious cases of sexual abuse by family members were reported to the police.

Many of Draijer's central findings were corroborated by others. In a study of fifty incest victims who had sought counseling (recruited through calls in newspapers) and incest counselors (response rate 71 percent, covering 116 victims), Frenken and van Stolk (1987) had previously reported that fathers and stepfathers were predominantly the perpetrators. The sexual abuse reported typically took place over four to five years, with a starting age between 8.5 and 9.6 years; 78 percent of the abuse was very serious. Victims' families were characterized by emotional neglect, marital problems, disturbed communication, parentification, and oftentimes physical abuse. Fathers were typically authoritarian and tyrannical, mothers distant and emotionally unapproachable. In 50 percent of cases, mothers knew about the incest. Most victims (60 percent) had been referred by someone outside the incestuous family. For thirty-one of the 116 victims, the incest was ongoing when the referral took place. In two-thirds of cases, the counselors did not manage to stop the incest. This happened only when the police or medical doctors were called in. Most victims reported a range of psychological and psychosomatic complaints, including depression, phobias, nervousness, dislike of sex, and problems with intimacy. Frenken and van Stolk suggest that the high prevalence and seriousness of complaints are due to the particular sample (victims who had sought help). They estimate that 15 percent of victims experience such prolonged and serious victimization that damage, such as emotional problems, including dissociative disorders and post-traumatic stress disorder, is inevitable.

Using victim survey data from Statistics Netherlands for respondents aged fifteen and over, Brouwers and Smit (2005) reported that 22 percent of rapes and sexual assaults are reported to the police and 6 percent of all other sexual incidents. Thus the more serious incidents are more often reported. The most important reason victims give for reporting is that they want the perpetrators punished (Wittebrood 2006).

Leuw, Bijl, and Daalder (2004), studying court files on pedosexual offenses, found that 80 percent of perpetrators of pedosexual offenses are close relatives of the victim. Only in 10 percent of cases are victim and perpetrator completely unacquainted. They also showed that the younger the victim, the closer the relationship with the perpetrator. In more than a third of cases, the father or someone acting in that role is the perpetrator.

In a sample of 278 court and prosecution cases between 1993 and 1999, Daalder and Essers (2003) found that 64 percent of victims were under sixteen years and 40 percent were younger than twelve. In 46 percent of cases, the perpetrator was a member of the nuclear family or a family friend. Wittebrood (2006) reported that respondents in victim surveys knew their offender in 56 percent of cases by name or face and in 7 percent of cases only by face, meaning that the perpetrator was completely unknown in only one-third of cases.

These divergent findings are not implausible. Respondents are assumed to overreport cases of sexual abuse by strangers in such surveys, but such cases are harder to solve (cf. Hazelwood and Schippers [1995], who found that 80 percent of all reported rapes with an unknown perpetrator go unsolved), and there may be differential prosecution effects. It seems safe to conclude that the majority of victims of sex offenses in the Netherlands are children and that the majority of perpetrators are their caretakers and close relatives or friends.

Studies of domestic violence and violence against adult women have shown, as with underage girls, that physical and sexual violence are linked. Among women physically abused by a partner, Römkens (1992) showed that 60–65 percent of those suffering serious repeat victimization had also been raped or sexually assaulted. Van Dijk et al. (1997) also reported that physical and sexual violence are related. Over 90 percent of women in domestic violence shelters are victims of sexual violence; in all shelter facilities for women in the Netherlands, the percentage is 49 percent (Keuzenkamp and Oudhof 2000). A sizable fraction of the most serious and extended cases of sexual violence occur against the backdrop of seriously dysfunctional and violent families.

Other studies have shown that men and boys are also victimized by sex offenses, though less often than females. Offending against boys and men takes different forms. The Statistics Netherlands surveys show that 90 percent of adult victims of sexual incidents are women (Wittebrood 2006). For children this ratio may be different. The *Zedenalmanak* (2003, pt. II) reports that 33 percent of recorded victims of child sexual abuse in the Netherlands are boys; this implies 9–10 percent of all boys in the Netherlands. Qualitative work suggests that boys are more often abused outside of the family, by teachers and coaches, and more often by groups of perpetrators and by perpetrators close to them in age (*Zedenalmanak* 2003). Abused boys may be younger than abused girls (Dijkstra 1995). Vennix (1984) reported in a study of 250 men that 4 percent of boys had been sexually abused by a male perpetrator and 1 percent by a female perpetrator, none of them (remarkably) a family member. From an unrepresentative sample of thirty-two boys who had called the *Kindertelefoon* (the children's helpline) in Groningen regarding a problem with sexual abuse, Drion (1989) reports that seventeen had been abused within the family, eight by the mother, and six by an older sister. In twenty-eight cases, the perpetrator was a woman. In twenty cases, the abuse had occurred several times. As this very small sample is unrepresentative, no other conclusions can be drawn except that sexual abuse of boys by female family members does happen. As Dijkstra (1995) notes, while it must be assumed that the majority of perpetrators are male, most clinical descriptions focus on mothers as perpetrators. One reason may be the taboo on homosexuality, added on to the incest taboo, leading to even grosser underreporting.

Daalder and Essers (2003) report that 81 percent of victims in sex offending cases are female and 19 percent male. Almost all male victims are underage. Leuw, Bijl, and Daalder (2004) report that 20–25 percent of victims of pedosexual offenses are male; just 2 percent of pedosexual offenders are female. Offenses in which a non–family member is a perpetrator are more likely to be reported. Because boys are more likely to be victimized by non–family members, these diverse findings are not inconsistent.

Studies on sexual victimization of boys report that boys abused by men may also have problems with their sexual orientation. Victims sometimes question whether they have become homosexual because they were abused by a man or whether they were selected for the abuse because they were recognized as being homosexual. Particularly when they feel that they did not resist enough or became sexually aroused, the abuse may be viewed as a sign of latent homosexuality. In addition, since males are socialized to be strong and independent and to be the dominant partner in sexual relations, a boy reporting abuse by a female may be met with disbelief: a real man would never let such a thing happen (Dijkstra 1995), or a real man would have enjoyed it. Similar, reverse, problems with sexual orientation may occur when a boy is abused sexually by a female and did not enjoy the acts; boys have been reported to express fear that they must be gay because they did not enjoy sex with a female (Gianotten 1988). Remarkably, some boys abused by females report their abuse in active terms ("I am sleeping with my mother"), whereas girls frame it in passive terms ("My father harasses me") (Drion 1989). It seems reasonable to estimate that one in ten victims of sexual violence is male, that male victimization is concentrated in the childhood years, that most perpetrators are male and less often family members, and that abused men may suffer additional problems with their sexual identity.

Although a relative wealth of studies exists on incest victims and victims of child sexual abuse, no general studies or studies geared to other groups of victims could be located. Wittebrood (2006) notes that the average cost of a sexual incident for a victim is €936, falling in between the costs of "theft from car" and "threat" and at around 70 percent of the cost of assault; this necessarily refers mostly to adult women and to less invasive events. No data are available on the cost of childhood sexual abuse. Studies are lacking on the cost for other special groups, such as rape victims and victims of group sex offending. Sex offending victims appear especially unfortunate: for no victim type is the chance of revictimization within a year by the same offense so high (Wittebrood 2006).

B. Offenders

Most sex offenders in the Netherlands, as in other countries, are male. Little research has been carried out on female sex offenders. The exceptions are Hendriks and Bijleveld's (2006) study of adolescent female sex offenders and Wijkman and Bijleveld's (2007) study of prosecuted female sex offenders. Discussion in this subsection, with that exception, applies only to males.

Only a few studies describe population samples of offenders. Most studies focus on convicted or suspected offenders, since no self-report studies contain questions on sexual abuse. A sizable number of the studies pertain to special groups of offenders such as TBS convicts, who include the most serious of the offender population and are thus not at all representative. Brouwers and Smit (2005) report that the average age of suspects of sexual offenses is thirty-two years. In 2004, one in four suspects questioned by the police for a sex offense was a juvenile; for all offenses together this ratio is one in six. Thus juveniles are relatively overrepresented among sex offenders. They are even more overrepresented among robbers and for some public order offenses. Juveniles are particularly prominent concerning sexual assault offenses.

Overall, three-quarters of suspects were born in the Netherlands: 60 percent of rapists and 83 percent of offenders of child sexual abuse. Suspects from the Netherlands Antilles, Surinam, and (not northern) Africa are prominent among rapists. Sex offenders from Morocco are more prominent in sexual assault cases. Weapons are very rarely used. Daalder and Essers (2003) report, from their representative sample of court files of all hands-on sex offenses, that sex offenders are markedly older than other offenders. Juveniles constitute 18 percent of defendants (13 percent for all other prosecuted offenses). The age distribution is bimodal: there is a peak for juveniles and another peak between twenty-five and forty-five years of age. Older offenders are almost exclusively child abusers, some of them so-called "incest-grand-dads" who abused first their own children (often without police notification or judicial reaction) and then abuse their children's children. In such cases, prosecution of the earlier abuse may finally occur. In many cases involving child sexual abuse by a parent, police notification often takes place only years after the victim has left the family home, or when the victim later develops psychological or psychosomatic problems.

Daalder and Essers (2003) show that one in ten sex offenders has an alcohol problem; there is no noteworthy addiction to drugs or gambling. The personality characteristics do not point to a particular profile. There is diversity in intelligence, education, and social status, although a sizable group have a very low intelligence and appear unaware of the damage they are doing. Many defendants grew up in unstable or unsafe families. Sometimes offenders grew up in households in which sexual abuse was endemic. Many come from multiproblem families in which the children are both neglected and physically abused, parents are abusive toward each other, or parents are addicted to alcohol.

About half of Daalder and Essers' sample denied the sex offense from beginning to end of the prosecution and trial phase. A quarter confessed all offenses, and a quarter confessed some offenses or certain elements. Only 24 percent of cases contained only one sex offense. In one in three cases, the abuse had gone on for a long time (mostly child abuse), and it could not be determined how many offenses had taken place.

Child abusers differed in modus operandi and sexual preference; some had a sexual preference for prepubertal children, boys or girls. However, by far the majority of offenses against children were committed by situational offenders—offenders with a sexual preference for adult men or women, who engaged in temporary sexual relationships with dependent or available children. Such behavior, entailing a situational choice for weak and available victims, also occurs in sexual abuse of mentally handicapped institutionalized persons. Through staff interviews, van Berlo (1995) found that 1.2–2.5 percent of the mentally handicapped in institutions had been sexually abused in the preceding two years. Of those, 78 percent were women and 22 percent men. Abuse usually took place over extended periods. The main abusers were other institutionalized handicapped persons (36 percent), family members (33 percent), and staff (17 percent).

Daalder and Essers (2003) report that sex offenders generally need not use force and that psychological pressure suffices, which is not remarkable since so many victims are children. In one-quarter of child abuse cases, physical force was used. Violence is more often used with older victims (two-thirds of cases), mainly to force the victim to co-operate. In 12 percent of cases, the sex offense was committed by a group of offenders. Bijleveld et al. (2007) argue on the basis of a study of court files and psychological screenings of juvenile sex offenders that the victim in such cases is a priori outnumbered, and instrumental violence is less often needed. They further estimate that one in three prosecuted juvenile sex offending cases involves a group sex offense.

Group sex offending is, however, not exclusively a juvenile thing. Eighteen percent of sex offending cases registered at the prosecutor's office involve a juvenile suspect; if one in three involves a group of-fense, 6 percent of all cases would entail juvenile group sex offending. Since 12 percent of registered cases involve group sex offending, the remaining 6 percent of cases involve adult offenders.

Leuw, Bijl, and Daalder (2004) investigated socioeconomic and per-sonal problems of delinquents who committed more serious pedosexual offenses. Though the information in their subsample ($N = 101$) of court files was often incomplete, family psychopathology appeared fairly prevalent (40 percent), and a minority of families were middle-class families. About half of offenders were unemployed. Within the group of prosecuted sex offenders Daalder and Essers (2003) previously studied, about a third had an alcohol problem. For 20 percent, deviant sexual development had been reported. Only one in four had a clear sexual preference for children.

Daalder and Essers described several characteristic elements in of-fense scripts. Although physical violence was used in only one in seven serious pedosexual offenses, the child was generally forced or lured to cooperate. Offenders used two strategies: rewarding the child with presents, privileges, or attention or making the child appear complicit in the abuse (an "accomplice"). The latter strategy was used in a third of cases, particularly when the child was somewhat older. Children were given money for the fair, for example, and a kiss or sexual fondling "bought." All this may generate very complicated and pathological family dynamics. The child has been victimized and made powerless, but the child's sexual relevance for the perpetrator and the risk of disclosure make the child extremely powerful.

When the child is made coresponsible for the offense, two different mechanisms may operate. The offender may use "blaming the victim" as a cognitive distortion to be able to cope better with feelings of guilt and shame. Such blaming can also be used to exert control and power. The perpetrator elicits feelings of guilt and responsibility in the child to ensure further availability and prevent disclosure. This mechanism may cause extensive psychological confusion and damage.

The role of the mother can cause additional damage: in 20–29 percent of cases in which a father or a father figure committed the abuse, the mother allowed the abuse to happen. In 30–43 percent of cases the mother blamed the victim. The mother is often caught in a serious conflict of loyalty and may feel guilty herself if sexual relations between herself and the abuser are not what she feels they should be. In 30 percent of cases, it appeared as though perpetrating uncles and family friends capitalized on the emotional liability or low intelligence of the mother and thus her incapacity to intervene.

When serious pedosexual offending takes place within the family context, the father is mostly a dominant and antisocial father figure. Some of these fathers are true tyrants who claim sexual rights in all females in the family. In this situation the mother often appears powerless and may blame or punish the children.

A second subtype is the psychologically unstable, weak, and dependent father figure. Victims are then usually much younger, around five years. The husband does not maintain sexual relations with his wife and keeps the abuse secret. The sexual abuse is a safe, infantile substitute for a mature sexual relation.

A third subtype is the exploitative intruder. Here a family friend has an almost natural right to be with the family. This "uncle" often helps the family with support or money and exploits a weak and insecure, sometimes conflicted, isolated family. In some cases, the parents allow the abuse to continue because of the advantages the family friend brings.

Most extreme is a fourth subtype of abuse when children are abused by the parents themselves and are also offered to others. Frenken and van Stolk (1987) describe such an extended family in which nearly every family member had sex with other family members and sexual acts with children were sold by fathers to "customers" in a bar that family members frequented. Sons had sex with their mothers and daughters with their mother's boyfriend. This pattern is based on openly deviant norms and values that are accepted as normal and acceptable within the structure of family and family friends. Most sexual relations are obtained through emotional blackmail, by giving children rewards: candies, marbles, and the like. In Frenken and Stolk's case study, boys were rewarded less than girls and young children less than older children. Leuw, Bijl, and Daalder (2004) observe that such situations are encountered only in extremely marginalized families, poor, violent, and intellectually backward, mostly over several generations, and that such cases are rare.

Bijleveld and Hendriks (2007) showed that 16 percent of fathers and 3 percent of mothers had been convicted for at least one sex offense in a sample of parents ($N = 359$) of residentially treated juvenile sex offenders. If a child was sexually abused by the father, the mother was a co-offender in 25 percent of cases. If a child was sexually abused by the mother, the father participated in six of seven cases. Women (or mothers) appear more often to be accomplices to the pedosexual offenses of their partners than vice versa. Further research is needed to establish this.

Leuw, Bijl, and Daalder (2004) also distinguish various types of offenders in pedosexual homosexual delinquency. The offenses are much rarer. There are the escort service kinds of offenses: the adolescent victims are offered money for sexual services, and some say that they were simply interested in the money. Another type is the offender who invites victims to a permissive "boys' paradise": boys are offered computer and Internet facilities, toys, free drinks, and chips. Sex films may also be shown.

Leuw et al. show that pedosexual offenses ending in the death of the victim are extremely rare. Physical harm to the victim seldom occurs, although it is more likely if the offender is unknown to the victim.

In a study of a small group of convicted, very serious and thus atypical, sexually aggressive TBS offenders ($N = 20$), van Beek (1999) developed a typology of rapists, according to the scripts of their offense. The first category is the sexualizing offender, who was rejected and sexually abused as a child. This offender has a negative self-image, and his attachment style is anxious-ambivalent insecure. He was bullied and excluded by his peers. From early puberty onward he commits sex offenses, first hands-off and later hands-on. Offenses are planned beforehand and embody long-existing fantasies.

The second category, the antisocial offender, is the victim of inconsistent, violent educational surroundings. His attachment style is anxious-avoidant insecure. He was aggressive in school, bullied his peers, and has a positive to superior self-image. He had delinquent friends and committed various other serious offenses from an early age on. His sexual offenses are impulsive and opportunistic. He has no empathy for his victims.

The third category, the avenging offender, was physically abused as a child. He was bullied in school but denies or suppresses his aggression. His style is submissive and conformist. Aggression is the main motive of his offenses. His victims run the highest risk of harm or death.

Van Beek's typology shows some similarities but also significant differences from a previously employed typology by van Marle, van Putten, and de Ridder (1995) based on a larger sample of 161 sex offenders. Van Marle et al. identified "pure" sex offenders, who commit only sex offenses, and "antisocial" sexually violent offenders, whose sex offending is part of a generally antisocial, violent, and delinquent lifestyle.

Van Marle et al.'s pure sex offender most resembles van Beek's sexualizing rapist, but committed other offenses as well, albeit generally less serious and less violent ones. The pure sex offender could as such not be validated. In addition, van Beek found only one dominant mother in his sample of sex offenders, whereas van Marle et al. found that one in four sexually violent offenders had a dominant mother. However, van Marle et al. had studied a different sample (sex offenders admitted to the Pieter Baan Centrum for observation, of whom half had had a TBS order imposed) whereas van Beek studied TBS convicts only.

Second, as van Beek notes, there may be a different theoretical orientation. Van Marle is a psychiatrist and may have been more psychodynamically oriented, and emphasizes the role of the mother in the psychological and sexual socialization of the child; van Beek is a cognitive behavioral therapist and focuses more on the father as a model for the male child.

Finally, van Beek found clear differences in sexual preferences between sexualizing and the antisocial rapists, which van Marle et al. did not. Van Beek concluded that for all types of offenders, physical abuse by the father, having been bullied at school, isolation from peers, sexual abuse, developmental factors, and strong sexualization (for the sexualizing rapists) or delinquent peers and general criminalization of his lifestyle (for the antisocial rapists) were strong causal factors. Alcohol and drugs (for the antisocial and avenging rapists), the inability to make (sexual) contact (for the sexualizing rapists), and a problematic course of relationships (for the avenging rapists) are strong disinhibiting factors; for all types cognitive distortions play a prominent role.

Van Beek argues that offense scripts, which he frames as a third explanatory layer, have so far been developed for sexualizing rapists only. He argued that treatment should be geared to the typology into which the rapist fits; for instance, sexualizing rapists should be trained in improvement of their self-image and reducing their tendency to overcontrol. For antisocial rapists, the focus should be more on controlling their impulses and increasing empathy.

Jan Hendriks' (2006) study of juvenile sex offenders presented a somewhat different classification system. He based his typology on psychological screening files or penitentiary treatment files of about 500 male juvenile sex offenders. These contained self-reported and official data on sex offending. The sample is not representative of all juvenile sex offenders since it contains those whose offenses were so serious or whose behavior was so problematic that psychological screening or residential treatment was warranted. Hendriks classified them into "group sex offenders," solo "peer abusers," and solo "child abusers." All were under age eighteen when their sampling offense was committed, and some were even under twelve and had been referred for psychological screening because of sex offending. All had confessed to or been convicted of at least one hands-on sex offense. Having a victim five years younger than himself classified an offender as a child abuser.

Hendriks had two rationales for this classification. First, group sex offenders must be distinguished from those committing solo offenses. Because of the presence of co-offenders, the numerical preponderance of offenders over the victim, particular motives (male bonding, collective expression of male dominance, and rivalry), and the need to cross fewer psychological barriers than a solo offender, it is likely that group sexual offenders on average have different backgrounds and personality structures than solo offenders. Second, those who abuse much younger children can be supposed to have distinctive characteristics. This may be related to the presence of pedophilia. Social isolation from peers or inadequate social skills may equally well explain why some youngsters offend against children.

Hendriks showed in various studies that clear and interpretable differences exist among subtypes of juvenile sex offenders. Around 5 percent were so-called mixers in that they committed various types of offenses and were thus unclassifiable. Solo offenders scored significantly higher on neuroticism, impulsivity, and sensation seeking, but lower on sociability. The solo offenders were more often recidivists for sexual offenses and were more often themselves victims of sexual offenses. Solo offenders were significantly older than juveniles who committed offenses in groups (Bijleveld and Hendriks 2003).

Within the group of solo sex offenders, juvenile child molesters reported higher levels of neurotic instability, had experienced more social problems, and had been bullied more often at school than offenders who sexually assaulted same-age or older victims. Child molesters also reported a more negative self-image. They were younger when referred for screening but had committed more sex offenses, more often against males than females (Hendriks and Bijleveld 2004).

Group offenses almost always included at least one rape (88 percent of cases), compared with 37 percent of child abusers who had raped their victims and 37 percent of solo peer abusers. Group offenders were on average fourteen years old and their victims thirteen years old (Bijleveld et al. 2007). Solo child abusers averaged fourteen years and three months old, solo peer abusers fourteen years and nine months. Thus the peer abusers are the oldest group. To commit their offenses they need to subdue a victim who may be as old and strong as they are. Victims of peer abusers resisted significantly more often than child victims did. Child abusers were more often of ethnic Dutch descent than the other groups (see Hendriks 2006).

Using Hendriks' and additional data on a small number of juveniles who had committed hands-off sex offenses ($N = 510$), Hissel et al. (2006) investigated whether juvenile sex offenders can be classified as specialists and generalists, as did a typology put forward by van Wijk (2000) for juvenile sex offenders. Van Wijk distinguished between antisocial or criminal sex offenders (rapists and assaulters) and sexualizing offenders (incest offenders, child abusers, and exhibitionists). His two types of juvenile sex offenders resemble van Beek's antisocial and sexualizing adult sex offenders (van Beek 1999).

Bruinsma (1996) had earlier proposed a marginally different typology. He distinguished juvenile sex offenders into opportunistic, premeditating, and situational offenders. Situational offenders may commit a sex offense only once but not recidivate. Opportunistic offenders commit sex offenses as part of a fairly extensive criminal career; an opportunistic sex offender simply grabs, emotionally and materially, what he stumbles upon. Such an offender may come upon a woman in the course of a burglary and decide he wants sex with her. A premeditating sex offender, by contrast, carefully plans his offenses, in practical terms and as part of his fantasies. This type of offender has the highest risk of recidivism. Bruinsma's opportunistic offender thus has a sizable overlap with van Wijk's antisocial sex offender, and his premeditating sex offender almost equates with van Wijk's sexualizing offender.

Implicit in these typologies is that the sex offenses for opportunistic/antisocial offenders occur as a by-product of the criminal career, whereas for the premeditating/sexualizing offender, sex offenses are his core business. The latter type is thus a specialist and the first a generalist. As both van Wijk and Bruinsma note, it is often presumed that specialists offended against children and generalists against their peers.

Employing latent class analysis, Hissel et al. (2006) first showed that specialists and generalists are empirically distinguishable. Within the group of juvenile offenders, many are starters; a fairly large group of first offenders also had to be distinguished, since they could not be classified as generalists or specialists. A tiny fourth group of exhibitionists was also distinguished. Hissel et al. showed that specialists were more often victims of bullying, and generalists were characterized by worse family environments: parents were more often divorced, addicted, and unemployed. Generalists had more often been physically abused and neglected. Hissel et al.'s analysis thus shows that those who specialize in sex offenses do not have a particular profile, but those whose sex offending is part of a general criminal lifestyle score high on well-known risk factors for serious delinquency. Hissel et al.'s analysis also showed that the overlap between specialization in sex offending and offending against children was less than is commonly assumed: only two-thirds of specialists were child abusers, and, conversely, 30 percent of child abusers were generalists who had committed numerous other, serious, offenses as well.

Bijleveld et al. (2007) studied juvenile group sex offenses from reconstructions based on court files for forty-two different offender groups with ninety-one total offenders. Perpetrators generally had below-average intelligence and otherwise a fairly average personality profile. Offenders from non–ethnic Dutch backgrounds were overrepresented. They often came from broken families, in which unemployment, abuse, and neglect were common. These offenders thus resemble serious juvenile offenders. The average group size was four, and the groups were accidental; they could not be characterized as gangs.

Offenses were generally not planned. In some cases, offenders had agreed among themselves to have sex with a victim, though without discussing how to arrange it. In other cases, offenders seemed to know what was going to happen without discussing it beforehand. In one-third of the groups, a leader orchestrated the offense. Either group members were instrumental in enabling the group to complete the offense, or they functioned as an audience. The primary focus seemed to be to force a girl to have sex with the group, with the public group-wise humiliation and debasement of the victim being important features. The offense was often regarded as entertainment and not referred to by the offenders as an offense, even though groups took precautions against disclosure.

In most situations at least one vaginal rape took place. In many cases the victim was threatened, even after completion of the offense. Victims were generally girls from the offenders' social networks. Offenders tend to pick victims with little social support, who had trouble at home, or had only this group of boys to fall back on in their neighborhood.

While it had often been suggested in the Dutch media that group sex offenses by juveniles are a relatively new phenomenon, other Dutch and European studies (Oseretzky 1929; Drukker 1937; Phillip 1962; Parrot and Guitton 1963) show that group sex offenses by juveniles have probably always been fairly prevalent.

It had also been suggested that overrepresentation of ethnic minorities may explain these offenses as stemming from non-Western conceptions of women as articles for exploitation. As Hendriks and Bijleveld (2007) point out, however, the fairly large percentage of non-ethnic-minority offenders speaks against the image of women that these offenders hold being particularly non-Western. Hendriks and Bijleveld note from clinical practice that many group sex offenders distinguish girls into "dirty" girls and "respectable" girls, and that while respectable girls must be respected, dirty girls may be used as one pleases.

In an analysis of one group sex offending case in Rotterdam, van Leiden and Jakobs (2005) studied a group of twenty-one mainly Cape Verdian and Antillean juveniles who had committed various group sex offenses with a total of eight victims. They also analyzed case files of relatives and previous contacts of these juveniles with the Council for Youth Protection. A smaller nucleus of four juveniles was responsible for most of the sex offenses committed by groups made up of twenty-one offenders. The offenders came from a single socioeconomically marginalized neighborhood. Their families were criminally active and rife with problems such as divorce and educational deficits. The offenders had low intelligence and inadequate conscience formation and were highly impulsive and aggressive. Most had committed previous offenses. The offenders had—from a European perspective—deviant images of sexuality and relations between the sexes. The study largely confirmed previous studies on group sex offending by juveniles.

Hendriks and Bijleveld (2006) studied ten adolescent female sex offenders who had been referred for screening with respect to at least one hands-on sex offense. This small, qualitative study, which included about a quarter of all adolescent female sex offenders registered with the prosecution, showed that female adolescent sex offenders generally came from extremely troubled family backgrounds. For instance, for only one of the girls it was certain she had *not* been abused sexually. Neglect and abuse were the rule rather than the exception. Half of the girls had experienced divorces, excessive alcohol use by a family member, and violence between parents. Girls often functioned at below-average cognitive levels. Most scored low to extremely low on measures of self-esteem, and many suffered neurotic complaints. Half were regularly bullied or harassed by their peers. Most had committed their offenses with one or more co-offenders.

Victims were mostly girls, and over half were of primary school age or younger. In nearly all cases, the victim was known to the offender. Over half of the cases involved a single victim. Although a number of offenses occurred in babysitting situations and involved fondling or excessive sexual experimentation, the majority of offenders used considerable or serious violence: hitting, kicking, or threatening the victim. A number of the offenses resembled "reprisals" for incidents such as purportedly kissing boyfriends, in which the sexual element seemed of little importance, the sexual assault functioning as a means of violence and humiliation.

These girls' offenses thus bear similarity to those committed by male juvenile group sex offenders. However, the sometimes serious violence could be caused by a selection process involved in diagnostic referrals since perhaps only the most serious cases of girl sex offenders are referred for prosecution. In comparison with male offenders, these girls seemed to function less effectively at nearly every level. A possible explanation is that young women commit sexual abuse only when they start to suffer serious behavioral and psychological problems. The threshold for males would then be lower. Other similarities exist between boys and girls who commit sex offenses. For instance, the victims tend to be of primary school age, the social skills of both groups are underdeveloped, and offenders have often been bullied. The female offenders are most similar to the adolescent male offenders who abuse young children.

Bijleveld and Hendriks (2007) studied 185 juvenile male sex offenders treated in the Harreveld residential setting. They investigated the extent to which the parents had committed sex offenses and whether sexual abuse had taken place within the family. The penitentiary's treatment files contained self-reported and official data and were supplemented with the parents' and their sex offending children's rap sheets. Risk factors for victimization by sexual abuse were investigated. Juvenile sex offenders from incestuous families were shown to be at an increased risk of abusing children themselves (rather than peers). Children who were victims of incest or whose younger siblings were, were at higher risk of committing incest themselves. Juvenile sex offenders whose fathers committed sex offenses against them during their childhood were also at higher risk of committing similar offenses themselves.

Almost half of the sex offenders studied had been abused sexually, and another 10 percent may have been. Almost one in five was probably a victim of incest. The prevalence of paraphilia was not significantly increased among incest victims. The critical factor in committing sex offenses against children appears to be not so much being a victim oneself, but growing up in a family in which sexual abuse occurs. The father in particular seems to play a crucial role. There were no differences between risks for children of biological and nonbiological (foster or step-) parents. No indications were found that a child's risk of becoming a victim of sexual abuse is increased by the mother having been an incest victim, or by sexually abused mothers choosing sexually abusive partners. The findings support theories that posit that sexual abuse is transmitted via social learning, that is, via role modeling on the father.

C. Criminal Careers

There have been few studies in the Netherlands on sexual recidivism of sex offenders. A number have retrospectively examined criminal careers of sex offenders, mainly using police databases. Juvenile sex offenders' criminal careers have been studied more extensively.

The WODC publishes regular overviews of the recidivism rates of special groups of offenders. The 2005 overview gave general and special recidivism rates of all those registered for a sex offense with the Dutch prosecution service in 1997 (Wartna, Tollenaar, and Blom 2005). Over a period of seven years, over 14 percent of adult sex offenders reoffended to a sex offense. General reoffending was 36 percent. For juveniles, the recidivism pattern is reversed: sex offending recidivism was much lower at 8 percent, but general recidivism, at 55 percent, was much higher. Thus juveniles appear to be much more active criminally, with sex offenses more often once-only offenses. Unfortunately, the WODC did not disaggregate offenders with regard to their type of sex offense. On the basis of the literature, it may be supposed that reoffending patterns for child abusers are different from those for rapists.

Looking back at careers of all those registered for a sex offense with the Dutch Prosecution Service, Brouwers and Smit (2005) concluded that 38 percent of sex offenders in any year are first offenders. For about 40 percent of sex offenders, a sex offense was their first registered offense. Using police data, Bijleveld, Meijer, and Prins (2000) concluded that only one in eight of those registered for a pedosexual offense in police databases had a previous registration for a pedosexual offense. Using police data from the Haaglanden police area for 1988–97 for offenders aged twelve to twenty-five years, van Wijk and Ferwerda (2000) concluded that sex offenders also commit non–sex offenses: only one in eight of their offenses was a sex offense. Brouwers and Smit (2005) reported that 57 percent also commit non–sex offenses; when first offenders are excluded, only 6.5 percent had a career with sex offenses only. This is not evenly distributed over types of sex offenders: rapists particularly often committed other offenses, whereas child abusers were more often first offenders or specialized in sex offenses.

The sex offender who commits only sex offenses is fairly rare. Such offenders are most likely to be pedosexual offenders. Looking in-depth at the criminal careers of pedosexual offenders at the police level for the whole of the Netherlands over 1996–2002, Leuw, Bijl, and Daalder (2004) noted that 63 percent were first offenders, 10 percent had earlier been registered for a pedosexual offense, and one in four had previously been registered for other offenses. Those suspected of sexual intercourse with juveniles between twelve and sixteen years of age were most criminally active outside of sex offending. Of all offenses pedosexual offenders were convicted of over their life course, only 46 percent were non–sex offenses. Using a representative sample of court files for pedosexual offenses ($N = 101$), Leuw, Bijl, and Daalder reported that pedosexual offenders most often started careers at age thirty-one, that they start pedosexual careers at age thirty-five, and that 42 percent has already committed other offenses before the first pedosexual offense.

Nieuwbeerta, Blokland, and Bijleveld (2003) followed all 488 sex offenders registered for a sex offense with the Central Prosecution Service in 1977. Forty percent had committed offenses previously. The average age of sex offenders was not significantly different from that of other offenders. If one counts only reconvictions and labels cases as they were registered if the case was not disposed of, 71 percent recidivated over twenty-five years. Recidivism to a sex offense was 29 percent, which included 30 percent to exhibitionism, 29 percent to rape or sexual assault, and 30 percent to sex offenses against children or minors. General recidivism was highest among rapists and sexual assaulters (76 percent). Recidivism to any sex offense was 40 percent for exhibitionists, 24 percent for rapists/sexual assaulters, and 28 percent for those who sexually offended against children. When hands-off reoffending is excluded, the corresponding rates were 13 percent for exhibitionists, 21 percent for rapists/sexual assaulters, and 24 percent for those who had sexually offended against children. On the basis of survival curves, rapists/sexual assaulters generally recidivated most and fastest. For sexual reoffending, exhibitionists recidivated most and fastest, although mostly for hands-off offenses. Sex offenders against children continued recidivating longest. These studies point to little evidence of specialization: most sex offenders are versatile, generalists rather than specialists.

Looking at special groups, Wartna, el Harbachi, and van der Knaap (2005) reported that 11 percent of those receiving a TBS order for at least one sex offense and who were released between 1994 and 1998 ($N = 57$)—after an exposure period of about ten years—recidivated to a sex offense. This compares favorably to the recidivism rate reported in the survival curves of Nieuwbeerta, Blokland, and Bijleveld's study, where around 20 percent had recidivated after ten years. General recidivism among former TBS sexual offenders was 42 percent after ten years. Van Emmerik and Brouwers (1989) reported that a third of the entire cohort of former TBS convicts released between 1979 and 1983 had reoffended to a new sex offense by 1988 (after approximately seven years).

TBS clinics have, however, become more restrictive in releasing patients from treatment, implying that reoffending statistics are improving at the price of increasing numbers of TBS detainees being kept locked away. Van Emmerik and Brouwers show that by 1988 the duration of the TBS order for sexual offenders was more than eight and a half years compared with around five years for other TBS offenders. For a subgroup ($N = 123$) of sex offenders with a TBS order treated in one particular clinic, de Vogel et al. (2003) reported that there were clear differences in sexual reoffending risk between different types of sex offenders. The average reoffending risk after twelve years was 39 percent. For those who completed treatment successfully, the risk was 22 percent. For noncompleters (who left the clinic contrary to the advice of treatment staff, generally on a legal technicality), the risk was more than double at 48 percent. Even more striking were differences between rapists and different types of child abusers: 33 percent of rapists reoffended to a sex offense compared with 59 percent of child abusers and 89 percent of extrafamiliar abusers of boys. The general reoffending rate was 74 percent. Thus, even among the special group of serious and disturbed sex offenders with a TBS order, many qualify as generalists.

Only one experimental study looked into the effectiveness of treatment for sex offenders. Ruddijs and Timmerman (2000) reported on a small-scale study in which first-time sex offenders ($N = 56$) who received out-patient treatment were matched with first-time offenders not in treatment. Matching variables were age, date of admission, previous sex offending, type of sex offending, type of sanction, and age and sex of the victim. The average period over which offending could occur was apparently seven years, though this is not clear. Mainly because of very small numbers (5 percent recidivism in the treatment group [$N = 3$] and a 2 percent relapse in the control group [$N = 1$]), no treatment effect could be shown.

Hendriks and Bijleveld (2005*a*) analyzed recidivism rates of 114 juveniles treated for at least one hands-on sex offense at the Harreveld residential institution. Using the same criteria as Nieuwbeerta, Blokland, and Bijleveld (2003), they found a 10 percent sex offending recidivism rate for a follow-up period of six and a half years. Recidivism to a sex offense was related to the choice of a very young victim, to the choice of a female victim outside of the offender's family, and to the absence of truancy. Recidivism to a sex offense occurred quickly: 90 percent of eventual sexual recidivists recidivated within three years after termination of treatment. General recidivism was 60 percent. Violent recidivism was 21 percent and was related to high impulsivity, an active criminal career, the choice of an unknown victim, better social skills, and non-Dutch ethnicity.

Van der Geest, Bijleveld, and Wijkman (2005) compared the recidivism rates of these residentially treated juvenile sex offenders with those of 270 residentially treated non-sex-offending male juveniles; over a similar exposure period, the latter group recidivated to a sex offense in 1.5 percent of cases. The risk of recidivism to a sex offense is thus clearly increased for the juvenile sex offenders (10 percent compared with 1.5 percent), though in absolute terms it is not very high.

Studying 325 male juvenile sex offenders who had received either ambulatory treatment or no treatment, Hendriks and Bijleveld (2005*b*) found a recidivism rate to a new sex offense of 8 percent for a follow-up period of six and a half years. Sex offending recidivism rates were 10 percent for group sex offenders, 8 percent for child abusers, and 8 percent for peer abusers. Those who had not completed treatment had the highest recidivism rate: 19 percent. For those who completed treatment, the rate was 4 percent; for those who had not been assigned to treatment, the rate was 9 percent.

Hendriks (2006) explains this by observing that treatment is generally assigned to offenders deemed to have an increased risk of recidivism to sex offending. Treatment is designed to bring that risk down. Those not perceived as having an increased risk are not assigned treatment. If treatment functions as desired, treated offenders should converge to the risk level of those who did not need treatment. Studying 510 juvenile sex offenders, most of whom had previously been studied by Hendriks, Hissel et al. (2006) found that specialists, generalists, and first offenders did not differ in their reoffending rates to a sex offense.

General and violent recidivism was higher for generalists than for first offenders and specialists.

Thirteen percent of adult female sex offenders convicted for at least one hands-on sex offense in the Netherlands ($N = 128$) recidivated to a new sex offense over a median follow-up period of eight years (Wijkman and Bijleveld 2007).

IV. Policy and Research Implications

A number of conclusions can be drawn. First, sex offending is fairly common. A sizable proportion of women are confronted with unwanted sexual approaches and touchings or have sexual acts forced on them. Men may also be victimized, although the circumstances in which abuse occurs differ. Offenders are predominantly adult males. Women are responsible for only a fraction of hands-on sex offenses, but juveniles are responsible for a sizable proportion of recorded sex offenses. The majority of offenders are known to the victim. In around half of cases that become known to the criminal justice system, the offender is the caretaker of the child victim. It thus appears that sex offenders predominantly choose weak and available victims. Much offending appears situational, with offenders opportunistically making use of situations that present themselves. Much abuse may be a surrogate for lacking essential fulfilling elements in offenders' lives such as a satisfactory relationship with an adult. Part of the offending takes place in situations of inebriation or by offenders addicted to alcohol. Sex offenders are more often generalists than specialists. There is generally very little evidence for paraphilias. For many, the sex offense is a once-only occurrence or an offense that recurs sporadically in a general antisocial lifestyle. Much sex offending should be regarded as the by-product of an ineffective, emotionally unsatisfactory, and marginalized existence, and at times even of an ordinary life in which children and women are viewed as objects on which sexual urges can be acted out.

There is huge variation in types of offenders and offenses and in their seriousness. There is huge variation in the criminal careers of offenders, with most being generalists, some of them petty offenders, some with more serious and violent criminal careers (notably rapists), and a small fraction specializing in sex offenses. Not all specialists are child abusers. Nor are all child abusers specialists.

And there is huge variation in the backgrounds of offenders. There is Dutch evidence of a small but dangerous and persistent group of chronic sex offenders. These are the offenders to whom TBS orders may be given, who choose victims from outside their own families, who are violent, some of whom are diagnosed with paraphilias, who may act out of motives related to personality or psychiatric disorders, and who present physical risks to their victims. Sybine Jansons' murderer belongs to this group. Within this group, the extrafamiliar child abusers stand out, and among them, those offenders who abuse boys, or boys and girls. This group is notoriously difficult to treat. Much Dutch research has focused on this group. This group is most thoroughly observed in treatment settings (and can thus be studied easiest) and presents the greatest risk and possibility of damage to the victims. Unfortunately, this group is not representative of most sex offending.

Sex offending seldom comes by itself. Particularly for offenders who commit violent or brutal offenses, there appear to be associations with alcohol abuse by the offender, physical abuse of other family members, and abusive and dysfunctional families. When sexual abuse takes place within families, the fathers are the most serious and chronic offenders. If transmission of particular forms of sexual abuse takes place, behavior is modeled on the father. As sexual victimization occurs more frequently, is more intrusive, and stretches out over longer periods of time, the damage to victims increases. In such cases, the sexual abuse is also more often accompanied by other forms of abuse. Such sexual abuse is often a by-product of a generally abusive childhood. It has an independent detrimental effect. Since Draijer's (1988) study, no replications have been carried out. Studies of more prevalent forms of sexual abuse are needed.

Victim surveys do not indicate that sexually unwanted behavior is on the rise. The prevalence of victimization of rape and assault is even harder to assess because of small numbers and short time series. The historical overview in Section I showed that the assessment and treatment of various forms of sexual behavior are subject to prevailing norms that may change widely over time. However, sanctioning chances for sexual assault and offenses against children have increased dramatically. This warrants explanation, which requires detailed information on sex offending cases: the properties of cases cleared, cases sent on for prosecution, cases resolved by the prosecution, and cases sent on to the courts differ. Differences exist between the prosecution outcomes of adult males, females, and juveniles. Adult women are often sanctioned. Juveniles' cases are more often prosecuted, more treatment is imposed, and sentences are shorter.

Most studies in the Netherlands suffer from unavoidable methodological limitations. First sex offenses are probably the worst reported and recorded offenses. It is therefore risky to base conclusions on any reoffending study based on reconvictions. If only 22 percent of offenses are reported and the possibility of a sanction given recording is around 20 percent, almost all the relevant behavior is missed. There is no easy solution because few offenders (and in all likelihood respondents) are eager to disclose sex offenses. This calls for methodologically sophisticated self-report studies on sex offending, using randomized response to counter offender reluctance to report sex offending.

Many studies have been unable to relate the risk of sex offending to characteristics of the offender. Part of the reason may be that not enough pertinent characteristics were studied, but part of it is that sex offenders are identified after they enter the criminal justice system. Those offenders who pose large risk of recidivism are treated to reduce that risk of reoffending, and those whose risk is deemed acceptable remain untreated. The one consistent risk factor in all studies, on juveniles and adults and across various subgroups, is whether treatment was terminated prematurely or ended unsatisfactorily. The Netherlands has a remarkable dearth of studies on treatment effectiveness. It is high time that the effectiveness of the many different treatment modalities in the Netherlands, particularly for juvenile sex offenders, be evaluated in true experimental designs. This requires support from policy makers and the judiciary.

Are there any other policy implications? First and foremost, as described in Section II, the research findings need to be related to the increasing severity of policy measures. Recently, rules provide that registrations of sex offenses against children will not be erased during the lifetime of the offender. This means that a thirteen-year-old who commits a sex offense against a child may be unable to work as a teacher for the rest of his life. Policy makers should consider whether there is sufficient empirically assessed risk in juvenile sex offenders to justify such policies.

Next, enormous attention is paid to the serious subgroup of offenders against extrafamiliar young children. The empirical evidence indicates that other kinds of sex offenders cause a greater risk to society in terms of the risk of reoffending combined with their sheer numbers. Most notably, the juvenile group sex offenders stand out as a neglected category. More systematic psychological screening of group sex offenders might mitigate some of these risks.

The Netherlands does not have community notification equivalent to American "Megan's laws." The studies outlined above show that this is empirically defensible. Given that 88 percent of pedosexual offenders in any year are unknown to the police (Bijleveld, Meijer, and Prins 2000), there would be limited practical use of such a notification system, other than quietening the conscience of the police and soothing the public.

There have been very few studies on the etiology of sex offending, since there have been hardly any studies on more "ordinary" offenders such as rapists. Why men rape, whom they rape, when they rape, and how rapes connect to an antisocial lifestyle all warrant more research and systematic attention. Many sex offenders come from dysfunctional families in which either there is extensive exposure to sex (offending) or the family is an extremely closed system with no outlets for sexual expression. Many adult offenders are believed to have started offending when they were adolescents. To study the etiology of such factors, long-term prospective studies are needed among risk groups in which self-report data are gathered. While Sybine Jansons' rape and murder are among the worst imaginable offenses, it is the widely prevalent, seemingly mundane sex offenses against children and the more run-of-the-mill, seemingly sexually normal, opportunistic sex offender who warrants research attention.

APPENDIX
Sex Offenses in the Dutch Criminal Code

242 *Rape (Verkrachting)*. He who through violence or another matter or threat with violence or with another matter forces someone to undergo acts that consist of or partially consist of the sexual penetration of the body will be punished as guilty of rape with a prison sentence of twelve years maximum or a fine of the fifth category.[4]

243 *Intercourse with a will-deficient (Gemeenschap met een wilsonbekwame)*. He who commits, with someone of whom he knows that he is in a condition of unconsciousness or physical inability, or suffers such an in-

---

[4] The minimum fine in the Netherlands is €2. The maxima are as follows: for fines of the second category, €2,250; for fines of the third category, €4,500; for fines of the fourth category, €11,250; and for fines of the fifth category, €45,000.

sufficient development or sickly disturbance of his mental capacities that he is unable to determine his will in this regard or make it known or put up resistance against it, acts that consist of or partially consist of the sexual penetration of the body will be punished with a prison sentence of eight years maximum or a fine of the fifth category.

244   *Intercourse with a child under the age of twelve (Gemeenschap met een kind beneden 12 jaar).* He who commits, with someone below the age of twelve years, acts that consist of or partially consist of the sexual penetration of the body will be punished with a prison sentence of twelve years maximum or a fine of the fifth category.

245   *Intercourse with a person under the age of sixteen (Gemeenschap met een persoon beneden 16 jaar).* He who commits, with someone who has reached the age of twelve years but has not yet reached the age of sixteen years, outside of marriage, lascivious acts that consist of or partially consist of the sexual penetration of the body will be punished with a prison sentence of eight years maximum or a fine of the fifth category.

246   *Indecent assault (Feitelijke aanranding der eerbaarheid).* He who through violence or another matter or threat with violence or with another matter forces someone to commit or to allow lascivious acts will be punished as guilty of actual sexual assault with a prison sentence of eight years maximum or a fine of the fifth category.

247   *Lechery with an unconscious person or a mentally handicapped person or child (Ontucht met bewusteloze, geestelijk gestoorde of kind).* He who commits, with someone of whom he knows that he is in a condition of unconsciousness, impaired consciousness, or physical inability or who suffers from an impaired mental development or disease-like disturbance of his mental capacities such that he is unable or not fully able to determine his will on this matter or make that will known or resist, or with someone below the age of sixteen outside of marriage lecherous acts, or seduce the latter person to commit such acts or endure such acts with a third person is punished with a prison sentence of six years maximum or a fine of the fourth category.

248   *Increased penalties (Gevallen van strafverzwaring).*
       1. When one of the acts described in the articles 240b, 243, 245, 246, 247, 248a, 248b, and 249 results in severe physical injury or when from these acts life danger is to be feared, a prison sentence of maximum twelve years or a fine of the fifth category will be imposed.
       2. When one of the acts described in the articles 240b, 243, 245, 246, 247, 248a, 248b, and 249 results in death, a prison sentence of maximum fifteen years or a fine of the fifth category will be imposed.

248a   *Inciting a juvenile to lechery (Uitlokken van een minderjarige tot ontucht).* He who through gifts or promises of money or goods, abuse of power from a particular relation, or by misleading a person of whom he knows or reasonably must suspect that this one has not reached the age of eighteen yet purposely incites to commit lecherous acts or to endure such acts from him is punished with a prison sentence of four years maximum or a fine of the fourth category.

248b *Lechery with a juvenile between the ages of sixteen and eighteen years (Ontucht met persoon tussen de 16 en 18 jaar).* He who commits lechery with someone who offers himself as available for committing sexual acts with a third person against payment and who has reached the age of sixteen but not yet the age of eighteen is punished with a prison sentence of four years maximum or a fine of the fourth category.

248c *Being present at the commission of lecherous acts by juveniles (Aanwezigheid bij plegen ontuchtige handelingen door minderjarigen).* He who is purposely present at the commission of lecherous acts by a person of whom he knows or reasonably must suspect that this one has not reached the age of eighteen yet, or at the showing of images of such acts in a locality designated for that purpose, is punished with a prison sentence of four years maximum or a fine of the fourth category.

249 *Lechery with abuse of authority (Ontucht met misbruik gezag).*

1. He who commits lecherous acts with his underage child, stepchild, or foster child, his pupil, a juvenile entrusted to his care, education, or vigilance, or his underage servant or subordinate is punished with a prison sentence of six years maximum or a fine of the fourth category.

2. With the same punishment will be punished (1) the civil servant who commits lechery with a person under his authority or entrusted or commended to his vigilance; (2) the manager, physician, teacher, functionary, overseer, or employee in a prison, state institution for child care, orphanage, hospital, or charitable institution who commits lechery with someone admitted there; (3) the person who, working in health or social care, commits lechery with someone who has entrusted himself as patient or client to him.

250 *Forcing someone to commit sexual acts with a third person against payment (Dwingen tot seksuele handelingen met een derde tegen betaling).*

1. Punished will be (1) with imprisonment of four years maximum or a fine of the fourth category he who purposely causes or promotes the commission of adultery with a third person by his underage child, stepchild, or foster child, his pupil, a juvenile entrusted to his care, education, or vigilance, or his underage servant or subordinate; (2) with imprisonment of three years maximum or a fine of the fourth category he who, outside of the cases mentioned under (1), purposely causes or promotes the commission of adultery with a third person by an underage person whose juvenile status he knows or reasonably should suspect.

2. When the perpetrator makes a habit of the commission of these acts, the punishment can be increased by a third.

REFERENCES

Alwin, L. 1994. "Verjaringstermijnen zedendelicten verruimd" [Expiry period sex offenses extended]. *Algemeen Politieblad* 16:12–14.

Beyaert, F. H. L. 1986. "Castratie 1985/1986" [Castration 1985/1986]. *Delikt and Delinkwent* 16:362–66.

Bijleveld, C. C. J. H., and Jan Hendriks. 2003. "Juvenile Sex Offenders: Differences between Group and Solo Offenders." *Psychology, Crime and Law* 9: 237–45.

Bijleveld, C. C. J. H., and Joyce Hendriks. 2007. "Gezin en seksueel misbruik" [Family and sexual abuse]. *Tijdschrift voor Criminologie* 49:122–35.

Bijleveld, C. C. J. H., R. F. Meijer, and L. Prins. 2000. "Verdachten van een pedoseksueel delict: Een verkenning op basis van politiegegevens 1998" [Suspects of a pedosexual offense: An exploration of police data]. *Justitiële Verkenningen* 26:119–24.

Bijleveld, C. C. J. H., and P. R. Smit. 2005. "Crime and Punishment in the Netherlands, 1980–1999." In *Crime and Punishment in Western Countries, 1980–1999*, edited by Michael Tonry and David P. Farrington. Vol. 33 of *Crime and Justice: A Review of Research*, edited by Michael Tonry. Chicago: University of Chicago Press.

Bijleveld, C. C. J. H., F. Weerman, D. Looije, and Jan Hendriks. 2007. "Group Sex Offending by Juveniles: Coercive Sex as a Group Activity." *European Journal of Criminology* 4:5–31.

Boelrijk, M. 1996. "Verjaring seksuele delicten gepleegd door minderjarigen" [Expiry of sex offenses by juveniles]. *Nederlands Juristenblad* 71:1412–13.

Brongersma, E. 1984. "Seksualiteit en wetgeving" [Sexuality and lawmaking]. In *Strafbare seksualiteit: Opvattingen en aanpak van politie, justitie en hulpverlening* [Punishable sexuality: Views and handling by police, justice, and aid organizations], edited by J. Frenken and J. Doomen. Deventer/Zwolle: Van Loghum Slaterus/Tjeenk Willink.

Brouwers, M., and P. R. Smit. 2005. "Seksuele delinquentie; de prevalentie door de jaren heen" [Sex offending; prevalence over the years]. *Justitiële Verkenningen* 31:37–47.

Bruinsma, F. 1996. *De jeugdige zedendelinquent: Diagnostiek, rapportage en behandeling* [The juvenile sex offender: Diagnosis, screening, and treatment]. Utrecht: SWP.

CBS (Centraal Bureau voor de Statistiek). 1882–1981. *Statistisch jaarboek* [Statistical yearbook]. Voorburg: CBS.

Daalder, A., and A. Essers. 2003. "Seksuele delicten in Nederland" [Sex offenses in the Netherlands]. *Tijdschrift voor Criminologie* 45:354–68.

De Kogel, C. H., and C. Verwers. 2003. *De longstay afdeling van Veldzicht: Een evaluatie* [Veldzicht's long-stay ward: An evaluation]. Series Onderzoek en Beleid no. 207. The Hague: Boom Juridische Uitgevers/WODC.

de Savornin Lohman, J., W. M. E. H. Beijers, C. P. van Gelder, M. J. H. Goderie, S. M. A. Nieborg, and R. A. L. Rijkschroeff. 1994. *Betere en adequatere bescherming door de nieuwe zedelijkheidswetgeving? Evaluatieonderzoek naar de effecten en de doelbereiking van de nieuwe zedelijkheidswetgeving* [Better and more adequate protection because of the new sex offending laws? Evaluation study of the effects and effectiveness of the new sex offending laws]. Utrecht: Verwey-Jonker Instituut.

de Vogel, V., C. de Ruiter, D. van Beek, and G. Mead. 2003. "De waarde van gestructureerde risicotaxatie: Een retrospectief onderzoek bij behandelde seksuele delinquenten" [The value of structured risk assessment: A retrospective study of treated sex offenders]. *Maandblad voor Geestelijke Volksgezondheid* 58:9–29.

Dijkstra, S. 1995. "Onderzoek naar seksueel misbruik van jongens" [Research into sexual abuse of boys]. *Jeugd en Samenleving* 3:115–27.

Draijer, N. 1988. *Een lege plek in mijn geheugen: Seksueel misbruik van meisjes door verwanten* [An empty place in my memory: Sexual abuse of girls by relatives]. The Hague: Ministerie van Sociale Zaken en Werkgelegenheid.

Drion, N. 1989. "Jongens als slachtoffer van seksueel misbruik" [Boys as victims of sexual abuse]. *Maandblad Geestelijke Volksgezondheid* 44:159–64.

Drukker, L. 1937. *De sexueele criminaliteit in Nederland 1911–1930* [Sex offending in the Netherlands, 1911–1930]. The Hague: Martinus Nijhoff.

Eggen, A. Th. J., and W. van der Heide. 2005. *Criminaliteit en rechtshandhaving* [Crime and law enforcement]. Voorburg/The Hague: CBS/WODC.

Fisher, B. S., and F. T. Cullen. 2000. "Measuring the Sexual Victimization of Women: Evolution, Current Controversies and Future Research." http://www.ncjrs.gov/criminal_justice2000/vol_4/04g.pdf.

Frenken, J. 1984. "Seksuele criminaliteit: Enkele feiten en achtergronden" [Sex crimes: Facts and backgrounds]. In *Strafbare seksualiteit* [Punishable sexuality], edited by J. Frenken and J. Doomen. Deventer/Zwolle: Van Loghum Slaterus/W.E.J. Tjenk Willink.

Frenken, J., and B. van Stolk. 1987. "Incestslachtoffers en hulpverleners" [Incest victims and aid workers]. *Maandblad voor Geestelijke Volksgezondheid* 42: 1203–20.

Gianotten, W. 1988. "Jongens en mannen als slachtoffer van incest en ander seksueel misbruik" [Boys and men as victims of incest and other sexual abuse]. In *Op gebaande paden? Ontwikkelingen in diagnostiek, hulpverlening en preventie met betrekking tot seksueel misbruik van kinderen* [Well-trodden paths? Developments in diagnostics, aid, and prevention regarding the sexual abuse of children], edited by H. Baartman. Utrecht: SWP Press.

Hazelwood, R. R., and C. Schippers. 1995. "Hulpmiddel in zedenzaken: Gedragskundige recherche-advisering" [Aid in sex-offending cases: Behavioral detecting advice]. *Modus* 4:4–7.

Hendriks, J. 2006. *Jeugdige zedendelinquenten: Een studie naar subtypen en recidive* [Young sex offenders: A study of subtypes and recidivism]. Utrecht: Forum Educatief.

Hendriks, J., and C. C. J. H. Bijleveld. 2004. "Juvenile Sex Offenders: Differences between Peer Abusers and Child Molesters." *Criminal Behavior and Mental Health* 14:238–50.

———. 2005a. "Recidive van jeugdige zedendelinquenten na residentiële behandeling." *Tijdschrift voor Seksuologie* 29:150–60.

———. 2005*b*. "Recidive van jeugdige zedendelinquenten: Poliklinisch behandelden versus niet-behandelden." *Tijdschrift voor Seksuologie* 29:215–25.

———. 2006. "Adolescent Female Sex Offenders—an Exploratory Study." *Journal of Sexual Aggression* 12:31–41.

———. 2007. "Groepszedendaders: Profielen, delicten en recidive." In *Facetten van zedencriminaliteit*, edited by A. van Wijk, R. A. R. Bullens, and P. van den Eshof. Amsterdam: Elsevier.

Hendriks, J., R. Bullens, and R. van Outsem. 2002. *Handboek behandeling van jeugdige zedendelinquenten* [Handbook treatment of juvenile sex offenders]. Utrecht: Forum Educatief.

Hissel, S., C. C. J. H. Bijleveld, J. Hendriks, B. Jansen, and A. Collot d'Escury-Koenigs. 2006. "Jeugdige zedendelinquenten: Specialisten, generalisten en 'First offenders.'" *Tijdschrift voor Seksuologie* 30:215–25.

Junger-Tas, J. 2004. "Youth Justice in the Netherlands." In *Youth Crime and Youth Justice: Comparative and Cross-National Perspectives*, edited by Michael Tonry and Anthony N. Doob. Vol. 31 of *Crime and Justice: A Review of Research*, edited by Michael Tonry. Chicago: University of Chicago Press.

Keuzenkamp, S., and K. Oudhof. 2000. *Emancipatiemonitor 2000* [Emancipation monitor 2000]. The Hague: Statistics Netherlands and Sociaal Cultureel Planbureau.

Kool, R. S. B. 1999. *De strafwaardigheid van seksueel misbruik* [On punishing sexual abuse]. Deventer: Gouda Quint.

———. 2003. "Vrijheid, blijheid? Over het dilemma van de strafbare seksualiteit" [Free and happy? On the dilemma of punishable sexuality]. *Tijdschrift voor Criminologie* 45:338–53.

Leuw, Ed. 1999. *Recidive na de tbs: Patronen, trends en processen en de inschatting van gevaar* [Recidivism after TBS: Patterns, trends, and processes and risk assessment]. Series Onderzoek en Beleid no. 182. The Hague: WODC.

———. 2000. *Registratie en monitoring van pedoseksuele delinquenten* [Registration and monitoring of pedosexual delinquents]. The Hague: WODC.

Leuw, Ed., R. V. Bijl, and A. Daalder. 2004. *Pedoseksuele delinquentie: Een onderzoek naar prevalentie, toedracht en strafrechtelijke interventies* [Pedosexual offending: A study into prevalence, characteristics, and criminal law interventions]. Series Onderzoek en Beleid no. 220. The Hague: Boom Juridische Uitgevers/WODC.

Nieuwbeerta, P., A. Blokland, and C. C. J. H. Bijleveld. 2003. "Lange termijn recidive van daders van seksuele delicten" [Long-term recidivism of sex offenders]. *Tijdschrift voor Criminologie* 45:369–77.

Oseretzky, N. J. 1929. "Sie Sexualkriminalität der Minderjährigen." *Monatschrift für Kriminalpsychologie und Strafrechtsreform* 20:705–32.

Parrot, Ph., and R. Guitton. 1963. "Étude clinique des complots: Délits commis en bande" [The clinical study of "complots": Offenses committed in a group]. *Clinical Revue de Neuropsychiatrie Infantile* 11:385–90.

Phillip, E. 1962. "Jugendliche Gruppentäter bei Sexualdelikten" [Juvenile group offenders in sex offenses]. *Jahrbuch für Jugendpsychiatrie und ihre Grenzgebieten* 3:116–19.

386   Catrien Bijleveld

Römkens, R. G. 1992. *Gewoon geweld? Omvang, aard, gevolgen en achtergronden van geweld tegen vrouwen in heteroseksuele relaties* [Some violence? Prevalence, characteristics, consequences, and background to violence against women in heterosexual relationships]. Amsterdam: Swets and Zeitlinger.

Ruddijs, F., and H. Timmerman. 2000. "The Stichting Ambulante Preventie Projecten Method: A Comparative Study of Recidivism in First Offenders in a Dutch Outpatient Setting." *International Journal of Offender Therapy and Comparative Criminology* 44:725-39.

Tomesen, W. B. M. 1993. "Honderd jaar zedelijkheidswetgeving: De eenzijdige debatten tussen liberalen en moralisten" [One hundred years of sex offending laws: The one-sided debates between liberals and moralists]. *Trema* 5: 181-83.

Tubex, H. 2006. "De juridische en strafrechtelijke bemoeienis met plegers van seksueel geweld/misbruik: Een overzicht van de Belgische en Nederlandse situatie" [The legal and criminal law engagement with perpetrators of sexual violence/abuse: An overview of the Belgian and Dutch situation]. *Tijdschrift voor Seksuologie* 26:105-14.

van Beek, D. J. 1999. *De delictscenarioprocedure bij seksueel agressieve delinquenten* [The crime script procedure in sexually aggressive offenders]. Deventer: Gouda Quint.

van Berlo, W. 1995. *Seksueel misbruik bij mensen met een verstandelijke handicap: Een onderzoek naar omvang, kenmerken en preventiemogelijkheden* [Sexual abuse of people with a mental handicap: A study into prevalence, properties, and prevention]. Delft: Eburon.

van der Geest, V., C. C. J. H. Bijleveld, and M. Wijkman. 2005. *Delinquentie na behandeling: Een verkennend onderzoek naar geregistreerde justitiecontacten, persoonlijke en omgevingskenmerken van jongeren uit een behandelinrichting* [Delinquency after treatment: An exploratory study of registered crime, personal, and background characteristics of juveniles from a judicial institution]. Report no. 2005-4. Leiden: NSCR.

van der Meer, Th. 2005. "Castration and the Making of Real Men: Eugenic Anxiety, Sexual Pathology and the Castration of Sex Offenders in Holland, 1938-1968." Mosse Lecture, International Institute for Social History, October 19.

van Dijk, J. J. M., P. Mayhew, and M. Killias. 1990. *Experiences of Crime around the World: Key Findings from the 1989 International Crime Survey*. Deventer/Boston: Kluwer.

van Dijk, T., S. Flight, E. Oppenhuis, and B. Duesmann. 1997. *Aard, omvang en hulpverlening van huiselijk geweld* [Characteristics, prevalence, and aid in domestic violence]. Rijswijk: Intomart.

van Emmerik, J. L. 1989. *Tbs en recidive: Een vervolgstudie naar de recidive van ter beschikking gestelden van wie de maatregel is beëindigd in de periode 1979-1983* [TBS and recidivism: A follow-up study on recidivism of TBS convicts whose measure ended 1979-1983]. Series Onderzoek en Beleid no. 95. Arnhem: Gouda Quint.

van Emmerik, J. L., and M. Brouwers. 1989. "Ter beschikking gestelde seksuele delinquenten: Enkele kwantitatieve gegevens over hun delictgedrag." *Tijd-schrift voor Criminologie* 31:215–28.

van Kesteren, J., P. Mayhew, and P. Nieuwbeerta. 2000. *Criminal Victimization in Seventeen Industrialised Countries: Key Findings from the 2000 International Crime Victims Survey.* Series Onderzoek en Beleid no. 187. The Hague: WODC.

van Leiden, I., and J. Jakobs. 2005. *Groepszedenmisdrijven onder minderjarigen: Een analyse van een Rotterdamse casus* [Group sex offenses among juveniles: Analysis of a Rotterdam case]. Arnhem: Advies- en Onderzoeksgroep Beke.

van Marle, H. J. C., C. M. van Putten, and M. J. J. de Ridder. 1995. "De zedendelinquent in het Pieter Baan Centrum" [The sex offender in the Pieter Baan Center]. *Tijdschrift voor Psychiatrie* 37:285–98.

van Wijk, A. Ph. 2000. *Een verkennend onderzoek naar jeugdige zedendelinquenten* [An exploratory study into juvenile sex offenders]. Arnhem/Amsterdam: Advies-en Onderzoeksgroep Beke/VU.

van Wijk, A. Ph., and H. Ferwerda. 2000. "Criminaliteitsprofielen van zeden-delinquenten" [Crime profiles of sex offenders]. *Maandblad Geestelijke Volks-gezondheid* 55:1131–45.

Vennix, P. 1984. "Incestueus of niet, wat maakt het uit?" [Incestuous or not, what does it matter?] In *Incest, feiten, achtergronden en hulpverlening—een sym-posium,* edited by J. Frenken and C. van Lichtenburcht. Utrecht-Zeist: Ned-erlandse Vereniging voor Seksuologie—Nederlands Instituut voor Sociaal Sexuologisch Onderzoek.

Visser, A. C. 1984. "Veranderend denken over wetstoepassing bij seksuele de-licten" [Changing views on the application of the law for sex offenses]. In *Strafbare seksualiteit: Opvattingen en aanpak van politie, justitie en hulpverlening* [Punishable sexuality: Views and handling by police, justice, and aid orga-nizations], edited by J. Frenken and J. Doomen. Deventer/Zwolle: Van Loghum Slaterus/Tjeenk Willink.

Wartna, B. S. J., S. el Harbachi, and L. M. van der Knaap. 2005. *Buiten be-handeling: Een cijfermatig overzicht van de strafrechtelijke recidive van ex-terbe-schikkinggestelden* [Out of treatment: A numerical overview of the criminal recidivism of ex–TBS convicts]. Series Onderzoek en beleid no. 227. The Hague: Boom Juridische Uitgevers, WODC.

Wartna, B. S. J., N. Tollenaar, and M. Blom. 2005. *Recidive 1997: Een cijfer-matig overzicht van de strafrechtelijke recidive van volwassen en jeugdige daders* [Recidivism 1997: A numerical overview of the criminal recidivism of adult and juvenile offenders]. Series Onderzoek en Beleid no. 230. The Hague: Boom Juridische Uitgevers, WODC.

Wijkman, M. D. S., and C. C. J. H. Bijleveld. 2007. *Vrouwelijke zedendelin-quenten* [Female sex offenders]. NSCR report no. 2007-1. Leiden: NSCR.

Wittebrood, K. 2006. *Slachtoffers van criminaliteit: Feiten en achtergronden* [Vic-tims of crime: Facts and backgrounds]. The Hague: Sociaal en Cultureel Planbureau.

Zedenalmanak. 2003. http://www.huiselijkgeweld.nl/publicaties/handboeken/zedenalmanak.html

Godfried Engbersen, Joanne van der Leun, and Jan de Boom

The Fragmentation of Migration and Crime in the Netherlands

ABSTRACT

International migration processes have drastically changed the face of Dutch society. Following changes in migration patterns, the research on migrants and crime is developing into two distinct lines of research. The postcolonial guest worker migrations from the 1950s and 1960s and subsequent family reunification led to attention to problems of crime among second-generation youngsters. More recently, asylum migration (peaking in the 1990s) and irregular migration generated problems of crime among first-generation asylum seekers and immigrants without a residence status. These groups are much more fragmented than the preceding immigrant groups, and their societal position is even more vulnerable. Findings in both fields make clear that research on immigrants and crime should take into account the changing contexts of reception and incorporation. The role of the state has become crucial in understanding some of the patterns found.

On May 6, 2002, the Netherlands was shocked by the brutal murder of Pim Fortuyn, just nine days before national elections. A few days earlier, Fortuyn's Rotterdam-based political party had made its unexpectedly successful first appearance in local politics. Fortuyn's spectacular rise to prominence cannot be understood without his sharp criticism of Dutch multicultural society. Fortuyn called for the Dutch borders to be closed. "This country is full," he said. "I think 16 million

Godfried Engbersen is professor of theoretical sociology at Erasmus University of Rotterdam, the Netherlands. Joanne van der Leun is associate professor of criminology at Leiden University, the Netherlands. Jan de Boom is researcher at the Rotterdam Institute for Social Policy Research, the Netherlands.

Dutchmen are about enough" (Volkskrant 2002). He pleaded for the assimilation of ethnic minorities already present. Moreover, according to Fortuyn, Islam was a "backward religion."

After Fortuyn's violent death, Ayaan Hirsi Ali, a liberal-conservative Dutch politician with a Somali background, became a prominent spokeswoman for the critics of multiculturalism. She heavily criticized the suppression of women in Muslim communities and occasionally extended her criticism to Islam in general. She and Dutch film director Theo van Gogh made a controversial film called *Submission*. It featured four partially nude women in long, dark, transparent veils, with Koran texts written in calligraphy on their bare skin. In November 2004, Mohammed B., a young man of Moroccan origin, murdered van Gogh, allegedly because he considered the film an insult to Islam. These violent incidents and the ensuing public debates contributed to a public climate in which skepticism about or plain criticism of multiculturalism became common.

It would be incorrect, however, to assume that the position of immigrants in Dutch society was given much attention only after these murders. In the 1990s and around the turn of the century, there had been fierce public debates on Dutch multicultural society. Furthermore, migration and integration policy in the Netherlands has changed dramatically over the past thirty years. Three phases can be differentiated in Dutch immigrant incorporation policies or what is now called "integration policies" (Engbersen 2003a). In each phase different aspects of integration were emphasized. In the first phase (1980s), the emphasis was on self-organization and the cultural dimension of integration (e.g., arrangements for education in the minorities' own languages). This emphasis was in line with the Dutch tradition of "pillarization" (i.e., compartmentalization along sociopolitical lines). There were special arrangements for immigrants, fully financed by the state, such as Muslim and Hindu schools, and broadcasting and political consultation facilities for migrant communities. The immigrant incorporation policy aimed at mutual adaptation in a multicultural society with equal opportunities for Dutch people and ethnic minorities (WRR 1979). The central idea of "integration while preserving ethnic identity" was soon criticized because it strengthened the isolated, unemployed, and segregated position of many first- and second-generation immigrants in the 1980s.

Next, in the 1990s and onward, in the second phase, the emphasis was on reducing unemployment and welfare dependency, particularly through improving labor market participation. Integration was interpreted as equal participation in the major social institutions (WRR 1989).

The millennium change brought another change in tone and idiom (the third phase). Now, active citizenship with a strong emphasis on the social obligations of citizenship and individual responsibility of citizens became the main goal. More attention was paid to the moral dimension of integration. Integration policies became strongly related not only to issues such as shared norms about the rule of law and the obligation to learn the Dutch language and know something about Dutch culture, but also to social problems of public order and crime. Particularly after the 2002 elections, marked by the rise and death of Fortuyn, integration became a key issue, and integration and migration policies were redefined.

This new approach is also reflected in changes in immigration law with regard to family migration, labor migration, and asylum migration. Stricter income and age criteria are now set for marital migration.[1] Marital migrants also need to pass a Dutch language test containing 500 common Dutch words before they are allowed to come. Restrictive measures are taken with regard to labor migration. Employers must first turn to their own labor supply, that is, within the national borders or within the European Economic Area, before they may hire labor migrants (Roodenburg, Euwals, and ter Rele 2003). In 2000 the Dutch state adopted a more restrictive and efficient Aliens Act to limit the number of asylum seekers and to simplify and accelerate the asylum procedure. Significant aspects of this new act are the elimination of the possibility of administrative review of a decision made by the immigration authorities and the accelerated asylum procedure. Furthermore, various measures were taken to fight illegal or undocumented migration. Crucial in this respect is the exclusion of illegal immigrants from public services and the formal labor market. In addition, the capacity of the aliens police and the labor inspection

[1] The Aliens Act 2000, enacted in 2001, introduced various measures to limit marital migration and family reunification. In 2003, the following new measures were introduced: the minimum age for marital migration was raised from eighteen to twenty-one (also to prevent forced marriages); the minimum income requirement for marital migration was increased from 100 percent to 120 percent of the official minimum income level; the partner already living in the Netherlands has to have adequate housing (stipulated for marital migrants entering the country and those who apply for a permanent residence permit).

was increased to combat illegal labor and illegal stay. Moreover, special detention centers were built for illegal migrants and asylum seekers who have exhausted all legal remedies. These two groups now constitute an increasing part of the prison population. An estimated 10 percent of prisoners have committed migration offenses. The majority are detained because of illegal residence or illegal work (in the Netherlands, unlawful stay and illegal work are not considered criminal offenses). Expectations are that the proportion of migrants who committed migration offenses in the total prison population will increase.

The debates on multiculturalism, the changing policy paradigms on integration, and the changes in immigration law and enforcement policies show that the Netherlands has become a country of immigration. For decades, the Netherlands was a "reluctant country of immigration" (Cornelius, Martin, and Hollifield 1994; Muus 2004). Although the Netherlands has had a positive immigration surplus since the early 1960s, successive governments continued to deny officially that the Netherlands was a country of immigration. Only in 1998 did the Dutch government officially acknowledge that the Netherlands has become an immigration country. This reticence was partly reflected by the social sciences research agenda on migration and crime. Only at the end of the 1980s was the first serious research on ethnic minority groups and crime carried out (see Junger 1990; Bovenkerk 1991). Compared to other European countries, however, the Netherlands was quick in breaking the taboo on social sciences research into issues concerning migration and crime.

This essay provides an overview of the research on relations between migration and crime with a special emphasis on the last ten years. An analytical distinction is made between two lines of research. The first consists of research on immigrants with strong residence and citizenship statuses. This involves in particular crime patterns among the largest immigrant groups in Dutch society (Turks, Moroccans, Surinamese, and Antilleans). These groups reflect the colonial past of the Netherlands and the period in the 1960s when the Netherlands actively recruited guest laborers in the Mediterranean. Some other migrant groups that came to the Netherlands in the past fifteen years (e.g., immigrants from Somalia and Ghana) show a rather strong involvement in crime. Dutch statistics, based on police records, reveal that, on average, males in migrant groups are suspected of having been involved in crime two and one-half times as much as males in the native population. Females score low across the board, but the rate for females with an immigrant background is almost three times higher than for females in the native population. Problems arise for Moroccan and Turkish boys of the second generation and Antillean suspects and newer groups of first-generations (Blom et al. 2005).

The second line of research concerns "new" groups of immigrants with a weaker residence status, such as asylum seekers and illegal immigrants. This second line of research emerged by the end of the 1990s. This research reflects the increasing plurality and fragmentation of the categories of migrants who are on the move and increased irregularization of migration. The Netherlands is confronted with an influx of asylum seekers from central and eastern Europe (from former Yugoslavia and the former Soviet Union), Asia (from China, Iran, and Iraq), and Africa (Somalia, Ghana, and Sierra Leone) and with a growing number of irregular immigrants. Dutch statistics show that these groups are more involved in certain types of crime than the native population. Another significant finding is that the exclusionary policy with regard to illegal migrants has led to forms of "subsistence crime" (income-generating crimes such as theft and burglary). It must be said, however, that there are also substantial differences in the involvement in crime among asylum seekers and irregular immigrants. Some groups are more involved than others. New immigrant groups that are not embedded in well-established ethnic communities score particularly high in this respect.

To understand the differences between immigrant groups, it is important to make a distinction between groups with a strong citizenship status and groups with a weak citizenship status. The first group has full access to all the social rights of an advanced welfare state and the second group only to a limited extent or not at all. The theory of differential opportunity structures (Merton 1996) offers a first device for understanding some of the fundamental differences in legitimate and illegitimate opportunities that different groups of immigrants face in Dutch society. It also offers a theoretical framework that helps explain differences in criminal involvement. A related perspective is offered by migration theories on differences in the context of reception (Portes and Rumbaut 1990). However, to understand the different patterns of criminal behavior among immigrant groups, including transnational forms of crime, we need to develop more specific theories.

There are two policy implications of the research on migration and crime. First, the socioeconomic integration of regular migrants needs to be accelerated and improved. More attention must be paid to improving the educational and labor market opportunities of these groups, particularly of the young members of migrant groups. Second, the Dutch state has to rethink some of its restrictive policies because of the criminal effects it produces. For example, the expansion of labor migration programs (temporary as well as permanent) would enable some irregular laborers to reside and work legally. Similarly, the selective regularization of irregular migrants and groups of asylum seekers could help in this regard.

Before summarizing the principal findings in both lines of research in Sections II and III, we provide a brief sketch of the Netherlands as a multicultural country, indicating the main trends in international migration that have had a massive impact on the composition of the Dutch population and of the major cities (Sec. I). Over a few decades the Netherlands has changed from a relatively homogeneous society into a thoroughly heterogeneous one. The incorporation of a continuous stream of new immigrants is not unproblematic because dominant integration mechanisms (through formal labor and the welfare state) have become partially embroiled in crisis, and crime may be seen as a symptom of these difficulties. We refer here to high unemployment figures among young migrants, which have risen to over 30 percent, as well as to the exclusion of migrant groups from the welfare state. We go deeper into this in the final section (Sec. IV).

I. Immigrants in the Netherlands

After the Second World War, the Netherlands was a country of emigration. Officially encouraged by the state-sponsored emigration policy of the Dutch government, many Dutch citizens emigrated to typical immigration countries such as Australia, Canada, and New Zealand and to a lesser extent to Brazil and South Africa. Between 1946 and 1969, nearly half a million Dutch citizens left the Netherlands. In the same period the Netherlands experienced a massive influx of repatriates and Eurasians from the former Dutch East Indies (now Indonesia) after Indonesia's independence in 1949. More than fifty years later (in 2003), 400,000 people in the Netherlands either had been born in Indonesia or had at least one parent who had been born there. The integration of repatriates from Indonesia is often presented as a role model for successful assimilation. However, many were well educated; most spoke Dutch and had been educated in a school system that was almost the same as that of the mother country. Furthermore, 5 percent of all newly built houses in the 1950s were put at their disposal to speed their assimilation. They also profited from the postwar economy, which reached full employment in the 1960s. An indicator of their integration is that the intermarriage rate is extremely high (Entzinger 1995, p. 343).[2]

A new pattern occurred in the early 1960s with the arrival of guest workers from the Mediterranean. As the term guest worker implies, they were expected to stay in the Netherlands temporarily and to return to their countries of origin once they had done their jobs. This myth of immigrants returning home dominated official Dutch thinking on immigration and immigrant integration for many years (van Amersfoort 1982; Muus 2004). When guest workers started bringing their families to the Netherlands, it began to dawn on the Dutch that many were going to stay. This became even clearer when, around and after Surinam's independence in 1975, major flows of postcolonial immigrants from Surinam began to arrive in the Netherlands. In the 1970s, almost half of the foreign-born immigrants to the Netherlands came from just five countries: Turkey, Morocco, Surinam, Netherlands Antilles, and Indonesia (see table 1). In the 1990s, the percentage of these five immigrant groups steadily declined to less than 25 percent of new foreign-born immigrants. Since then, the percentage of these more or less traditional immigrant groups has remained steady at a much lower level. The percentage of immigrants from other E.U. countries in the total immigrant population in the Netherlands remained around 20 percent. This means that the percentage of immigrants arriving from the other countries increased from 30 percent in the early 1980s to more than 55 percent in the first years of the twenty-first century.

---

[2] Indonesia's independence also led to the arrival of 12,500 Ambonese or Moluccans. Most were Moluccan military who had served in the Dutch colonial army and were not demobilized when the Republic of South Moluccas declared independence from the new republic of Indonesia in the 1950s. This placed those soldiers who were still serving in the colonial army in a very difficult position. The Dutch government decided to bring these soldiers and their families to the Netherlands. Upon arrival the Moluccans were demobilized and housed in camps, segregated from Dutch society. This policy underlined the temporary character of their stay and enabled these groups to preserve their own group identity. However, their stay became permanent when the South Moluccas' independence from Indonesia proved utopian. In the 1970s Moluccan youngsters committed a series of terrorist acts. The Moluccan actions were a form of political, separatist terrorism. The aim was an independent republic in the Moluccas (Janse 2005).

TABLE 1

Immigration to the Netherlands by Country of Birth, 1970–2004: Five-Year Averages

	1970–74	1975–79	1980–84	1985–89	1990–94	1995–99	2000–2004
Total	89,100	97,600	79,400	90,600	114,600	111,300	117,200
Born in the Netherlands	24,700	23,800	21,800	21,900	23,400	23,500	21,500
Foreign-born	64,500	73,800	57,600	68,700	91,200	87,800	95,700
European Union	12,000	15,300	13,500	15,200	19,100	19,200	19,800
Turkey	9,200	11,600	7,600	8,600	8,900	5,500	5,800
Morocco	3,700	6,900	7,000	7,200	7,100	4,600	4,700
Surinam	11,800	14,600	6,700	5,100	7,400	3,500	3,400
Netherlands Antilles	1,900	3,100	3,100	6,300	5,000	5,700	6,400
Indonesia	2,700	2,800	2,300	1,800	1,700	1,500	1,800
Other countries	23,100	19,500	17,400	24,600	41,900	47,800	53,800
As Percentage of Foreign-Born Immigrants							
European Union	18.7%	20.8%	23.5%	22.1%	20.9%	21.9%	20.7%
Turkey	14.3	15.8	13.2	12.5	9.8	6.3	6.0
Morocco	5.8	9.3	12.1	10.5	7.8	5.2	4.9
Surinam	18.3	19.8	11.6	7.4	8.1	4.0	3.5
Netherlands Antilles	2.9	4.2	5.5	9.1	5.5	6.4	6.6
Indonesia	4.2	3.7	4.0	2.6	1.9	1.7	1.9
Other countries	35.8	26.5	30.3	35.8	46.0	54.5	56.3

SOURCE.—Statistics Netherlands (http://www.cbs.nl).

Table 1 describes the immigration flows to the Netherlands. We now discuss the stock of foreign nationals and immigrants living in the Netherlands. Before providing these Dutch data, we need to discuss definitions. How are foreign nationals and immigrants defined and counted? In Dutch statistics, persons are considered immigrants or nonnative Dutch residents if at least one parent was born abroad. This type of registration facilitates tracing migrants who acquired Dutch citizenship by birth (from the Netherlands Antilles) and second-generation migrants. This is also important for gaining insight into second-generation migrants' involvement in crime. In this essay we refer to Dutch residents with non-Dutch citizenship as "foreign nationals." When we speak of immigrants, we mean not only foreign-born residents but also their offspring born in the Netherlands (in accordance with the official Dutch definition).

Finally, the official Dutch statistics draw a distinction between nonnative residents from "Western" and from "non-Western" countries. Western countries include all countries in Europe (excluding Turkey), North America, Oceania, Indonesia, and Japan. Non-Western countries include Turkey and countries in Africa, South America, and Asia, except Indonesia and Japan. The latter two countries are grouped with the Western countries on the basis of their socioeconomic and sociocultural positions. Table 2 provides an overview of the composition of the Dutch population on the basis of five-year averages. This shows the steady increase of migrants from non-Western countries such as Turkey, Morocco, Netherlands Antilles, and Surinam. It also shows a strong increase in the number of nonnatives from 1.9 million in 1985–89 to 2.9 million in 2000–2004. In the same period the native Dutch population was more or less stable. The increase in the number of nonnative residents is mainly due to the growing influx from central and eastern European and from non-Western countries. The number of nonnative residents from various non-Western countries also grew rapidly from 700,000 in 1985–89 to more than 1.5 million in 2000–2004. On January 1, 2005, roughly 1.7 million non-Western and 1.4 million nonnative people were living in the Netherlands. About 40 percent of the non-Western and 60 percent of the Western population are second-generation (Snel, de Boom, and Engbersen 2005).

Table 3 provides a detailed overview of the current composition of the Dutch population, showing that the Dutch population has become more diverse. Besides the five major migrant groups and migrants from

TABLE 2
Nonnative Population in the Netherlands by Ethnic Origin, 1972–2004: Five-Year Averages (in Thousands)

	1972–74	1975–79	1980–84	1985–89	1990–94	1995–99	2000–2004
Total	13,383	13,806	14,264	14,624	15,123	15,580	16,081
Native	12,121	12,347	12,544	12,705	12,880	13,015	13,134
Nonnative	1,262	1,460	1,720	1,919	2,242	2,564	2,947
Western countries	1,075	1,116	1,152	1,185	1,261	1,335	1,399
Indonesia	...	...	...	...	...	408,000	400,000
Non-Western countries	187	344	568	734	982	1,229	1,548
Turkey	38	77	137	170	232	281	330
Morocco	24	45	90	131	188	234	284
Netherlands Antilles	24	32	47	62	83	91	122
Surinam	62	122	179	212	252	286	314
Other non-Western	39	68	116	159	226	338	497
			As Percentage of Nonnative				
Western countries	85.2%	76.5%	67.0%	61.8%	56.2%	52.1%	47.5%
Indonesia	...	...	...	...	...	15.9	13.6
Non-Western countries	14.8	23.5	33.0	38.2	43.8	47.9	52.5
Turkey	3.0	5.2	8.0	8.9	10.3	11.0	11.2
Morocco	1.9	3.1	5.2	6.8	8.4	9.1	9.6
Netherlands Antilles	1.9	2.2	2.7	3.2	3.7	3.5	4.1
Surinam	4.9	8.4	10.4	11.0	11.2	11.1	10.7
Other non-Western	3.1	4.6	6.8	8.3	10.1	13.2	16.9

SOURCE.—Statistics Netherlands (http://www.cbs.nl).

the old E.U. countries, there are now also substantial numbers of migrants from Poland, former Yugoslavia, the former Soviet Union, Iraq, China, Afghanistan, and Iran. There are also a number of smaller migrant groups from Somalia, Ghana, Egypt, Vietnam, Pakistan, and Hong Kong. Today, there are a total of fifty-six immigrant groups of at least 4,000 persons in the Netherlands (Blom et al. 2005).

A. Pluralization and Fragmentation

The new migration of the past fifteen years differs from that in the more distant past. It is characterized by new geographical patterns of migration and new types of immigrants with different or no residence statuses (asylum seekers, temporary labor migrants, and illegal immigrants). The new geography of migration relates to the increased long-distance migration to the Netherlands from a growing number of countries. In addition, the traditional migration direction from south to north is complemented by migration flows from east to west. The traditional labor immigrants, family immigrants, and people from former colonies and their offspring, all of whom had strong residence statuses, are increasingly being supplemented with new categories of immigrants. First of all, there are *asylum seekers*, whose numbers—with all fluctuations—increased strongly during the period 1990–2004 (see table 4). After a period of relatively high numbers of asylum requests, the number of asylum applications started to fall at the end of the year 2000. From the end of 2001 the rate of this reduction accelerated. Since then the numbers have fallen every year. In 2004 the number of requests dropped below 10,000, the lowest number in more than a decade. Several Dutch politicians have claimed the reduction as an effect of the Aliens Act 2000 that came into effect on April 1, 2001. Table 4 reveals that asylum migrants are mostly from former Yugoslavia, the former Soviet Union, Turkey, Afghanistan, Iraq, Iran, Sri Lanka, Angola, Somalia, and Sierra Leone.

Cohort studies show that the approval percentage was 47 percent for asylum seekers who submitted their requests in 1994. For those who submitted their requests in 2001, the figure was 16 percent (see table 5) There are considerable differences. Asylum seekers from countries such as Iraq and Afghanistan have a high approval percentage, whereas asylum seekers from other countries have a low or a variable approval percentage. It is clear, however, that the larger part of the asylum requests are rejected. In Section IV we argue that approxi-

TABLE 3

Nonnative Population in the Netherlands by Ethnic Origin, 1995–2004: Two-Year Means (Selection 15,000+)

	Absolute Numbers					As a Percentage of the Nonnative Population	
	1995–96	1997–98	1999–2000	2001–2	2003–4	1995–96	2003–4
Total	15,530,000	15,707,000	15,926,000	16,149,000	16,282,000		
Native Dutch	13,004,000	13,047,000	13,103,000	13,147,000	13,176,000		
Nonnative	2,527,000	2,660,000	2,823,000	3,002,000	3,105,000		
From Western countries	1,330,000	1,348,000	1,377,000	1,411,000	1,422,000	52.7	45.8
Germany	410,000	405,000	400,000	395,000	388,000	16.2	12.5
United Kingdom	66,000	67,000	71,000	75,000	76,000	2.6	2.5
Belgium	111,000	112,000	113,000	113,000	113,000	4.4	3.6
Poland	26,000	28,000	30,000	33,000	38,000	1.0	1.2
Yugoslavia (former)	58,000	62,000	69,000	75,000	76,000	2.3	2.5
Soviet Union (former)	14,000	19,000	26,000	37,000	43,000	.6	1.4

United States	23,000	25,000	27,000	29,000	30,000	.9	1.0
Indonesia	411,000	407,000	405,000	402,000	397,000	16.3	12.8
From non-Western countries	1,196,000	1,312,000	1,446,000	1,590,000	1,684,000	47.3	54.2
Turkey	276,000	295,000	314,000	336,000	355,000	10.9	11.4
Morocco	229,000	247,000	267,000	290,000	311,000	9.1	10.0
Somalia	22,000	27,000	29,000	28,000	23,000	.9	.8
South Africa	10,000	11,000	13,000	15,000	15,000	.4	.5
Ghana	13,000	14,000	16,000	18,000	19,000	.5	.6
Cape Verde	17,000	18,000	18,000	19,000	20,000	.7	.6
Egypt	12,000	13,000	15,000	17,000	18,000	.5	.6
Surinam	283,000	294,000	306,000	318,000	327,000	11.2	10.5
Netherlands Antilles and Aruba	88,000	96,000	112,000	127,000	131,000	3.5	4.2
Iraq	14,000	26,000	36,000	42,000	43,000	.5	1.4
Afghanistan	6,000	14,000	24,000	33,000	37,000	.3	1.2
China	24,000	27,000	31,000	37,000	43,000	1.0	1.4
Iran	18,000	21,000	24,000	27,000	29,000	.7	.9
Vietnam	13,000	14,000	15,000	16,000	18,000	.5	.6
Pakistan	14,000	15,000	16,000	18,000	18,000	.6	.6
Hong Kong	17,000	17,000	18,000	18,000	18,000	.7	.6

SOURCE.—Statistics Netherlands (http://www.cbs.nl).

TABLE 4

Asylum Requests in the Netherlands by Country of Nationality, 1991–2004: Two-Year Means

	1991–92	1993–94	1995–96	1997–98	1999–2000	2001–2	2003–4
Total	20,985	43,990	26,060	39,830	43,310	25,623	11,592
Yugoslavia (former)	4,175	11,815	4,060	6,060	7,110	1,516	518
Soviet Union (former)	820	3,065	1,785	2,595	4,860	2,563	1,008
Romania	1,310	1,925	255	70	75	47	27
Czechoslovakia (former)	320	460	205	365	930	301	124
Turkey	815	630	695	1,180	1,885	1,019	376
Afghanistan	325	2,015	2,465	6,520	4,725	2,346	590
Iran	1,515	4,345	2,110	1,465	2,040	1,092	503
Iraq	725	3,045	3,405	8,970	3,245	1,176	2,258
Syria	395	330	285	645	960	422	209
China	770	885	475	1,040	1,320	622	280
Sri Lanka	1,425	1,855	1,400	1,275	910	487	86
Algeria	115	830	545	675	535	265	88
Angola	140	955	580	490	1,890	3,001	274
Nigeria	485	195	505	345	265	479	319
Somalia	2,980	4,860	2,720	2,030	2,425	818	622
Sierra Leone	15	90	320	435	1,655	2,013	226

Sudan	95	210	630	1,280	1,560	691	274
Congo	390	1,745	605	735	390	511	148
Other	4,170	4,735	3,015	3,655	6,530	6,257	3,666

As Percentage of Total Asylum Requests

Yugoslavia	19.9%	26.9%	15.6%	15.2%	16.4%	5.9%	4.5%
Soviet Union (former)	3.9	7.0	6.8	6.5	11.2	10.0	8.7
Romania	6.2	4.4	1.0	.2	.2	.2	.2
Czechoslovakia (former)	1.5	1.0	.8	.9	2.1	1.2	1.1
Turkey	3.9	1.4	2.7	3.0	4.4	4.0	3.2
Afghanistan	1.5	4.6	9.5	16.4	10.9	9.2	5.1
Iran	7.2	9.9	8.1	3.7	4.7	4.3	4.3
Iraq	3.5	6.9	13.1	22.5	7.5	4.6	19.5
Syria	1.9	.8	1.1	1.6	2.2	1.6	1.8
China	3.7	2.0	1.8	2.6	3.0	2.4	2.4
Sri Lanka	6.8	4.2	5.4	3.2	2.1	1.9	.7
Algeria	.5	1.9	2.1	1.7	1.2	1.0	.8
Angola	.7	2.2	2.2	1.2	4.4	11.7	2.4
Nigeria	2.3	.4	1.9	.9	.6	1.9	2.7
Somalia	14.2	11.0	10.4	5.1	5.6	3.2	5.4
Sierra Leone	.1	.2	1.2	1.1	3.8	7.9	1.9
Sudan	.5	.5	2.4	3.2	3.6	2.7	2.4
Congo	1.9	4.0	2.3	1.8	.9	2.0	1.3
Other	19.9	10.8	11.6	9.2	15.1	24.4	31.6

SOURCE.—Statistics Netherlands (http://www.cbs.nl).

403

TABLE 5

Percentage of Asylum Requests Granted in the Netherlands Cohort, 1994–2003: Top Ten Countries, 1994–2003

	1994	1995	1996	1997	1998	1999	2000	2001	2002	2003
Iraq	82.8	86.9	77.6	70.9	36.1	26.6	20.0	15.9	30.9	24.0
Afghanistan	78.0	71.9	84.0	82.6	71.9	55.0	54.6	26.5	12.0	13.4
Yugoslavia	28.0	22.0	15.2	8.6	21.0	55.4	10.4	5.7	5.1	5.7
Bosnia-Herzegovina	80.3	77.0	64.7	21.3	12.5	8.6	9.3	5.7	.5	.9
Somalia	56.7	50.0	57.9	52.3	42.1	28.4	19.0	11.7	12.7	18.0
Iran	39.9	33.0	31.5	31.3	29.9	17.8	12.9	12.1	9.5	9.8
Angola	37.4	27.2	19.8	23.4	36.8	34.5	29.2	10.1	13.1	7.9
Turkey	32.2	26.8	18.3	10.2	12.5	7.9	4.0	4.1	8.2	2.3
Sri Lanka	14.9	8.4	8.0	9.2	13.3	12.1	6.0	9.0	8.9	3.2
Sierra Leone	54.9	34.8	27.9	39.1	45.3	50.5	48.4	43.8	17.4	5.6
Total	43.0	42.2	44.5	48.4	34.1	29.8	19.9	14.6	10.9	12.3

SOURCE.—Ministry of Justice, Immigration and Naturalization Service (2005).

mately 20 percent of the rejected asylum seekers remain in the Netherlands.

Second, besides the large influx of asylum seekers, there is an increase in the number of *temporary labor immigrants* (ACVZ 2004). Table 6 shows the countries of origin for labor migrants who came to the Netherlands with a temporary work permit. More than two-thirds of temporary labor migrants came from Western countries (particularly the new E.U. member states). Furthermore, the number of temporary labor migrants from eastern European countries increased sharply in recent years. Most temporary work permits are issued for low-qualified professions. In 2004 almost half of all temporary work permits were issued for agricultural and horticultural work. Other lower-qualified occupations that attract a relatively large number of labor migrants are industrial production jobs and jobs in the transport and hotel and catering industries.

Third, there is the relatively new type of immigrants known as *undocumented* or *illegal immigrants*. In the Dutch context, undocumented immigrants are commonly labeled illegal immigrants. We define illegal immigrants as people who stay in the country without official permission to do so at the time of the research, regardless of whether they entered the country legally and regardless of whether they are economically active. Many came to the Netherlands on tourist visas and stayed; others crossed the border illegally or became illegal when they were refused refugee status (Burgers and Engbersen [1999] 2003; Sta-

TABLE 6

Number of Temporary Work Permits (WAV) Granted in the Netherlands by Nationality, 1996–2004 (Absolute Numbers; Selection 500+ in 2004)

	1996	1997	1998	1999	2000	2001	2002	2003	2004
Total	9,173	11,062	15,181	20,816	27,678	30,153	34,558	38,036	44,113
Western countries				11,994	16,234	17,633	20,175	22,663	32,538
Europe							14,893	17,222	28,303
New E.U. countries							9,400	12,542	24,424
Poland	735	928	1,184	1,501	2,497	2,831	6,572	9,511	20,190
Czechoslovakia (former)	174	256	282	606	1,058	1,673	1,494	1,653	2,690
Hungary	275	349	502	662	718	1,063	1,000	953	1,080
Other Europe							5,492	4,680	3,877
Soviet Union (former)	287	193	299	2,121	3,572	3,784	3,309	2,547	1,741
Romania				458	643	741	860	1,095	1,300
Other Western countries	1,945	2,275	2,603	5,556	6,186	5,980	5,295	5,443	4,235
United States	949	893	871	2,822	3,133	2,918	2,594	2,564	2,024
Japan	146	148	211	890	945	909	1,008	1,204	823
Indonesia				482	547	799	795	872	578
Non-Western countries				8,695	11,229	12,245	14,015	14,977	11,312
Sierra Leone				31	81	222	1,047	1,252	560
China	578	489	512	701	980	1,161	1,741	2,253	2,402
India	390	519	830	901	1,006	974	776	845	1,050
Iraq	12	30	964	1,520	1,627	1,176	782	786	663
Afghanistan	8	15	238	651	580	699	974	1,008	555

SOURCE.—Centre for Work and Income, the Netherlands.

TABLE 7

Estimation of Population of Illegal Immigrants in the Netherlands
by Year and Nationality (Absolute Numbers)

	1997	1998	1999	2000	2001	2002	2003*
Total	194,332	180,294	144,558	162,868	192,604	206,247	158,581
Turkey	41,098	32,250	8,104	16,136	38,112	15,250	12,255
North Africa	12,091	7,811	8,626	7,011	6,707	8,721	6,930
Other Africa	22,549	25,422	21,525	17,355	27,517	35,734	27,680
Surinam	4,734	5,457	4,983	3,716	913	1,293	971
Western Europe	24,250	19,850	18,913	17,638	14,013	17,700	13,288
Eastern Europe	44,788	45,013	47,563	53,438	61,213	88,938	68,213
Asia	31,840	31,652	27,632	30,972	30,086	21,094	20,304
South and Central America	9,766	10,630	4,859	11,267	6,642	14,800	7,362
North America/ Oceania	626	726	449	1,517	487	1,006	407

SOURCE.—Leerkes et al. (2004).
* Based on incomplete data.

ring 2001). The dividing lines between asylum seekers, commuting immigrants, and illegal immigrants are sometimes diffuse. Polish immigrants, for instance, who work in agriculture are commonly regarded as illegal immigrants, although coming from an E.U. member state, they do not need a visa to stay in the Netherlands (but they do have to meet certain criteria; e.g., they must have a work permit). In the same vein, asylum seekers are often confused with illegal immigrants, whereas they lose their residence rights only when they are rejected and refuse to leave. There are no official registrations of illegal immigrants, and we cannot fall back on census data. Van der Heijden and Cruijff (2004) used apprehension data[3] to estimate that, in the period 1997–2003, between 150,000 and 200,000 illegal immigrants were residing annually in the Netherlands. Table 7 gives a rough indication of the composition of the illegal population (Leerkes et al. 2004), al-

[3] The estimate was based on the capture-recapture method: a methodology derived from biology that can also be used in human population research when dealing with unknown populations. The data can be based either on observations by two or more independent bodies or on continuously collected data such as investigation data in criminology. Police records can be seen as continuously collected data, and they satisfy the requirements of this method to a certain extent. Van der Heijden et al. (2003) have elaborated a model that obviates the violations of the general assumptions as far as possible.

though it must be emphasized that this picture is based on inherently selective police data.

The preceding overview makes clear that the composition of the Dutch population has become much more diverse. The five major migrant groups (Indonesians, Surinamese, Antilleans, Turks, and Moroccans) have been augmented by a number of other migrant groups from all parts of the world. In addition, there was an influx of people with a temporary residence status (temporary workers), an insecure status (asylum seekers still awaiting a decision), and no residence status (illegal immigrants). How these changes in the composition of migration stocks and flows affect patterns of settlement is dealt with below.

B. Spatial Concentration and Integration

Migration has a considerable impact on large cities. Non-Western immigrants in particular congregate in urban areas. Only 13 percent of the total Dutch population live in the four major cities (Amsterdam, Rotterdam, The Hague, and Utrecht) compared to 40 percent of non-Western immigrants. In 2017 the number of non-Western immigrants (first- and second-generation) will constitute a majority of Rotterdam's population. In Amsterdam this will be the case in 2030 (Engbersen, Snel, and Weltevrede 2005). These figures do not take into account that—on the basis of analysis of police files—also approximately half of illegal immigrants reside in the four major cities (Engbersen, Staring, and van der Leun 2002).

Immigrants often find themselves in the lower ranks of society. Although many non-Western immigrants managed to improve their labor market position in the 1990s, many remain in a weak position. Non-Western immigrants participate less in the formal labor market, are unemployed more often, and receive social security benefits more often than native Dutch inhabitants. Moreover, non-Western immigrants who are employed tend to be overrepresented in unskilled or semiskilled jobs that are flexible and often insecure. Former guest workers and their families from Turkey and Morocco have a persistent weak labor market position more often than postcolonial immigrants from Surinam and people from the Netherlands Antilles (SCP 2003). The high risk of unemployment can be partly attributed to low educational qualifications of specific immigrant groups. Yet, recent data also show that between 25 and 40 percent of immigrants with a refugee status, who are often much better educated, are also unemployed (Mattheijer 2000).

Snel, de Boom, and Engbersen (2005) present five factors that together explain the weak labor market position of non-Western immigrants: lack of individual qualifications (education, work experience, and command of Dutch), labor queueing (non-Western immigrants at the back of the supply queue because employers view them as the least productive), industrial restructuring (the disappearance of industrial work), cultural factors (low labor force participation among Turkish and Moroccan women), and discrimination (immigrant workers have a higher risk of unemployment than native workers who have similar individual characteristics such as education) (see also Veenman 2003). Public attention that focused on the disadvantaged labor market position of immigrants is gradually being replaced by concerns over alternative careers in crime, which we address in the next section.

II. Non-Western Immigrants, Crime, and Criminal Justice

The link between migration and crime is anything but new. It is one of the classical topics addressed by social scientists and criminologists, in particular in countries with a long-standing immigration history. Traditional questions are whether or not (certain groups of) migrants are more involved in crime than nationals and how these differences can be explained (Savona and Goglio 1996). Conventional wisdom presumes a law-abiding first generation of immigrants and a more crime-prone second generation. The idea is that first-generation migrants tend to have preferences and expectations in line with their experiences in their home country, whereas their offspring take nonmigrants as their reference group. In this sense, integrating into the receiving society can stimulate crime. Yet, theoretical explanations are contradictory since a high involvement in crime is also often seen as a lack of integration or assimilation (Junger-Tas 2002). As can easily be derived from Merton's work—he does not refer to immigrants but to people in the lower strata of society in general—blocked mobility may drive immigrants to alternative routes to success (Merton 1957). These alternative routes may be stimulated by the formation of subcultures with divergent norms (O'Kane 1992). More recent "segmented assimilation" researchers in the United States (Portes and Zhou 1993; Portes and

Rumbaut 2001) contend that the growth of immigrant communities can result in both higher and lower levels of crime than in the general population depending on the "modes of incorporation" in the receiving society. Different groups in different periods face different opportunity structures (see Engbersen and van der Leun 1998). We return to this in the last section.

Much of the Dutch criminological literature on marginal groups including immigrant groups is based on the theory of social control as elaborated by Hirschi (Hirschi 1969; Junger-Tas 2002) and to a lesser extent the work of Merton on anomie, under the label of "strain theory" (Merton 1957; Junger 1990; Jongman, Weerman, and Kroes 1991). Crime has primarily been linked to a (perceived) lack of integration into the mainstream of the receiving society (Angenent 1997; Leuw 1997), a lack of social control and parental supervision, and a lack of acceptance of Western norms (Junger-Tas et al. 2003). These explanations are mainly confirmed for lower-educated youngsters (primarily boys) from the traditional immigrant groups. The explanations increasingly fall short now that immigration has become more fragmented and now that, as a result of better transport and communication means, immigrants can live in Dutch society and remain culturally and politically connected to their country of origin.

Moreover, it has become clear that integration is all but a linear process. The second generation is not per se more integrated than the first, for instance. Recently, cultural explanations have been brought back into the debate by ethnographic researchers such as van Gemert (1998) and van San (1998). Van Gemert stresses a culture in which honor and especially distrust play an important role in the everyday life of young Moroccans, who are one of the major problem groups in the Netherlands at the moment. Van San concludes on the basis of fieldwork among Antillean boys, another problem group, and their mothers that "respect" is crucial for them. The neutralization techniques that they collectively adopt make them believe that they are not doing anything wrong when using knives to restore their respect. The anthropologist and criminologist Bovenkerk warns against essentialist views on culture and ethnicity in case studies such as these (Bovenkerk 2003; Bovenkerk and Yesilgoz 2004) and stresses that cultural and structural factors influence each other in dynamic ways.

The available studies, summarized below, show differential patterns of arrests that only partially confirm the conventional wisdom just described. This spurred interest in the bias of police data and in particular the likelihood of being apprehended because of "foreign" appearances. In the remainder of this section we elaborate on selective crime enforcement, immigrants as suspects, victimization and fear of crime, and detention and imprisonment.

A. Selective Law Enforcement?

After heated discussions in the 1980s, it is now more or less accepted that some immigrant groups are overrepresented in certain forms of crime and that this overrepresentation cannot be explained solely on the basis of selective data. It is important to note, however, that a very small minority of the population comes into contact with the police as suspects. There is a large "dark number." According to estimations by van der Heide and Eggen (2003, p. 199), there were 4.65 million crimes committed against civilians in the Netherlands in 2001, of which only 1.6 million (34 percent) were reported to the police and for which 277,000 suspects were registered. Among these "known suspects" registered by the Dutch police, 2.2 percent came from immigrant groups and 0.9 percent of all inhabitants came from a nonimmigrant background (Blom et al. 2005, p. 85).[4] We go into these data with more detail below.

In addition, it must be noted that police data, crime registrations, and judicial system data are selective because they depend on police policies and routines and complex decision-making processes (Sampson and Lauritsen 1997). The national police database on suspects (HKS), which is a main source of information, does not comprise information of special investigation services; therefore, street crimes are overrepresented and white-collar crimes underrepresented. Furthermore, vulnerable groups in general run a relatively high risk of attracting the attention of the police and the public. Police statistics represent particular acts committed by the less powerful, which in turn tend to be

---

[4] These data are based on a national database of the Dutch police force (HKS) in combination with the Social Statistical Database of Statistics Netherlands (CBS), which also contains information from the municipal personal records database. The national database of suspects contains information on reporting of crime and personal information on the suspects of these crimes. One or more official reports may be made against a single suspect in one year, and an official report may in turn involve several offenses. The information includes persons who are at least twelve years old and are named as suspects in a report of a crime. The HKS contains information on the type of offense, but also personal information such as date of birth, sex, country of birth, and nationality (see Blom et al. 2005, pp. 83–85).

the types of crimes that most common people think of when they speak of crime. This makes crimes committed by immigrants highly visible (see Jongman, Weerman, and Kroes 1991; see also Sec. IIB).

The Dutch Aliens Act and Identification Act were intended to prevent discrimination against non-Western immigrants. According to some authors, this aim has succeeded (Aalberts 1990; Junger-Tas 1997; Boekhoorn, Speller, and Kruijssen 2004); others doubt that (den Boer 1995). For instance, it has been reported that negative stereotyping of non-Western immigrants is not uncommon among Amsterdam police officers (Esmeijer and Luning 1978). Non-Western immigrants appear to be stopped by the police more often than Dutch citizens (Junger-Tas and van de Zee-Nefkens 1977; Bovenkerk 1991). Junger (1990) maintained that ethnic selectivity by the police is usually not racist. It rather arises from the desire to optimize the "organizational output" under conditions of limited resources. Police officers tend to monitor groups they suspect of crime. These practices probably inflate the figures on crime involvement of immigrants and ethnic minorities. In a literature review study, Rovers (1999) concludes that there is no ground to assume a selective approach at the stage of arrest toward individuals from a migrant background.

Recently, Wittebrood (2004) used a multilevel research design to examine ethnic differences in crime *registration*. Her findings confirm that ethnic bias does not have unidirectional effects. All else being equal, the chance that the police register a crime reported by a crime victim depends on the type of neighborhood in which the crime victim lives. In poor (immigrant) neighborhoods, reports are more often registered (which suggests that poor neighborhoods are controlled more intensely). However, police officers are less likely to register offenses reported by members of non-Western immigrant groups in comparison with Dutch crime reporters (since most crime is "intra-ethnic," this practice contributes to the underestimation of ethnic minorities' crime involvement).

There is a broad consensus that selective law enforcement influences but does not cause ethnic differences in crime. Van San and Leerkes (2001) have given four arguments for this position. First, ethnic differences are quite substantial, even when age, degree of urban settlement, and socioeconomic position are controlled for.[5] Second, discrim-

---

[5] This finding is confirmed in a recent study by Blom et al. (2005).

ination and selectivity do not explain the (substantial) group differences from one ethnic minority to the other with regard to crime rates and types of crimes committed. Third, some (white) minorities (Yugoslavians, Russians) are less easily identified by the police than "visible minorities" (Antilleans, Moroccans) but are nevertheless prominent in crime figures. Fourth, ethnic bias cannot explain differential offending within ethnic groups. For instance, Moroccan and Turkish girls are significantly less involved in crime than their Dutch counterparts. Self-report studies among young members of immigrant groups also find higher rates for non-Western immigrants than for indigenous Dutch youths. For instance, young non-Western immigrants more often report having committed violent offenses and offenses against property than do indigenous youngsters (Wittebrood 2003).[6] Selective law enforcement strategies by the police can therefore overstate but not explain differences in crime patterns for immigrant groups (Haen Marshall 1997; Tonry 1997; van San and Leerkes 2001; see also Sec. IIB).

It is not clear if or to what extent recent anti-immigration sentiments have affected relations between immigrants and the police, which were traditionally relatively good. A study on the discriminatory nature of immigration control by the aliens police (mainly targeted at illegal immigrants) concludes that recent policy changes have not resulted in "indication of serious violations of the non-discriminatory nature" of the surveillance of foreign nationals. Yet, targeted actions aimed at combating overpopulation and public nuisances in certain urban areas do indicate "that the boundaries of the law are being explored" (Boekhoorn, Speller, and Kruijssen 2004, p. 212).

B. Immigrant as Suspects

Contrary to what is often thought, Dutch research in this field started to develop relatively early. The first reports date back to the 1970s and 1980s, focusing on Moluccan youngsters and Surinamese drug dealers, and part of the stream of publications since then has been commissioned by the national government (for an overview, see, e.g., Leuw [1997]). Early studies in the Dutch context showed that boys of Ambonese (Indonesian) origin were more often registered as crime suspects than Dutch boys (Buikhuisen and Timmerman 1971). Van Amersfoort and Biervliet (1977) reported similar findings for Surinam-

---

[6] Evidence in this field is not conclusive, though (see Junger-Tas 1997).

ese boys. After a period of silence surrounding these issues, they have become widely discussed predominantly since the 1990s. A number of studies since then recognize a significant overrepresentation of Moroccan and Antillean youngsters in recorded crime (Junger and Zeilstra 1989; Junger 1990; Werdmölder 1991; Bovenkerk 1992; van Hulst and Bos 1993; Werdmölder and Meel 1993; Junger-Tas 1997; Leuw 1997; van Gemert 1998; van San 1998). More recently, attention has started to shift to "newer" groups such as Africans, eastern Europeans, and Cape Verdeans (Kromhout and van San 2003). At first sight, the general findings are in line with the conventional wisdom of the law-abiding first generation and the more crime-prone second generation. As in many countries, however, this does not apply to all groups of immigrants. An exception that has attracted attention is the relatively low level of arrests of Turkish youngsters, who grow up under circumstances that are to a large extent similar to those of Moroccan youngsters (Junger 1990). More generally, the available studies show differential patterns of arrest: certain groups have below-average offender rates, whereas other groups score much higher than "autochthonous" inhabitants.

In contrast to some years ago (see Junger-Tas 1997), more data are available by nationality and country of birth. On the basis of these data, the Ministry of Interior Affairs published an influential report on crime in relation to the integration of ethnic minorities in 1996, studying the nature, scope, and causes of crime in ethnic minority groups (Ministry of Interior Affairs 1997). The report focused on Turkish, Moroccan, Antillean, and Surinamese suspects. It confirmed popular beliefs that minorities, especially Moroccans, were disproportionately active in crime. This finding held when socioeconomic factors were controlled for. Among juveniles between twelve and seventeen years old, nearly all immigrant groups are recorded as suspects relatively more frequently than persons of Dutch origin, and a comparable picture was obtained for people aged eighteen to nineteen years. There are some notable exceptions: the first-generation Indonesians and western Europeans and first- and second-generation Asian immigrants. It is often assumed that the low criminal involvement of Asian migrants is related to a high level of social control within their communities and a strong emphasis on upward mobility through education.

Police data for 2002 show that 37.5 percent of all recorded suspects of a crime living in the Netherlands are of foreign origin (including

TABLE 8

Suspect Rates per Capita in the Netherlands, Year 2002,
by Background, Generation, and Sex

	Total	Male	Female
Total	1.2	2.0	.4
Native Dutch	.9	1.6	.3
Immigrant	2.2	3.8	.7
First generation	2.3	3.9	.8
Western	1.3	2.1	.5
Non-Western	2.9	4.9	.9
Second generation	2.1	3.6	.6
Western	1.3	2.2	.5
Non-Western	4.0	7.1	.9

SOURCE.—Blom et al. (2005, p. 31).
NOTE.—Standardized by age and sex. Total of the population group
is 100 percent.

those of the second generation). The proportion of these persons in
the suspect population is therefore almost twice as high as the share
of immigrants among the Dutch population. The highest suspect rates
per capita are found among first- (4.9) and second-generation (7.1)
male migrants from a non-Western background. Rates for so-called
Western migrants are very close to those of the native Dutch. In all
groups, rates for women are considerably lower than for men, with the
highest found among non-Western migrants (Blom et al. 2005, p. 31);
see table 8.

Within immigrant groups, the percentage of suspects (people identified by the police as suspects within the year 2002) among the first
generation is somewhat higher than among the second generation.
This does not hold for Moroccans and Turks, however, among whom
the second generation is suspected of crimes more often than the first
generation.

How can the high rates for some groups be explained? The relationship with integration is important but much more complex than is
often assumed. Some groups are very well integrated, like Surinamese
migrants, and still show relatively high crime rates. Other groups are
not very well integrated, like many Chinese immigrants, but demonstrate no significant crime problem. It is clear that social position and
cultural factors are often interrelated. Regardless of ethnicity, many
poorly educated and unemployed youngsters are demoralized and turn
away from conventional society (Leuw 1997). Within some groups,

however, this leads to crimes and in others to a much lesser extent. The literature focuses strongly on Moroccan boys and, besides structural problems of low education and high unemployment, emphasizes feelings of being caught between the modern Western culture and the more collectivist culture of their own ethnic group (Gijsberts 2004), particularly because the gap between parents and children in the pace of modernization appears to be wide (Distelbrink and Pels 2002). These feelings may feed criminal behavior. Furthermore, many Moroccan parents feel that the behavior of their children outside the private realm is not their business, leading to a lack of parental control especially on boys. Additionally, feelings of deprivation and disappointment about not succeeding in Dutch society also provide fertile ground for deviant behavior (van Gemert 1998). The stigmatization of the Moroccan population, in particular, already leads to the withdrawal of this group into their own community: a recent survey demonstrates that second-generation Moroccans have begun to identify more with their own group in recent years (Dagevos and Schellingerhout 2003).

For the Caribbean boys from the Dutch Antilles the situation is somewhat different. Since the second half of the 1980s the Netherlands has faced the problem of first-generation Antillean youngsters with a very low level of education, insufficient command of Dutch, a high proportion of teenage mothers and one-parent families, unemployment, debts, and criminal behavior. The problems are found mainly in a few municipalities in which a large proportion of Antilleans in the Netherlands live. Their problems largely stem from a lack of perspective, but according to van San (1998), the problems are also culturally reproduced because many boys grow up in single-parent families with mothers who do not reject the criminal behavior of their sons. For both Moroccans and Antilleans, feelings of alienation appear to be worsened through stigmatization and discrimination.

Apart from police data and crime patterns, data are weak. In large longitudinal surveys, immigrants have so far been underrepresented or even left out, resulting in a lack of longitudinal information on the development of criminal careers of immigrant boys. An exploratory study found that social perspectives (education, jobs) together with significant others (parents and partners) are important in preventing some immigrant youngsters who are engaged in crime from pursuing a further criminal careers (Beke et al. 1998), but these broad conclusions cannot explain differences between groups.

TABLE 9

Suspects of Crime in the Population and Asylum Migrants in the Netherlands by Age, Sex, and Ethnic Origin (%)

	12–17 Years		18–24 Years		25–44 Years		45– Years		
	Male	Female	Male	Female	Male	Female	Male	Female	Total
A. Population (2002)									
Total	2.8	.6	5.0	.7	2.5	.5	.9	.2	1.2
Native	2.0	.5	3.8	.5	1.9	.4	.8	.2	.9
Nonnative	5.7	1.3	8.6	1.4	4.6	.9	1.5	.3	2.5
Netherlands Antilles and Aruba	10.1	3.1	13.0	3.7	11.9	3.2	5.3	1.2	6.6
Morocco	11.0	2.0	17.9	2.1	7.0	.9	1.4	.2	5.0
Surinam	6.7	2.0	11.1	2.1	7.5	1.4	3.8	.7	4.0
Yugoslavia (former)	5.4	1.9	8.3	1.7	4.7	1.2	2.2	.7	2.9
Soviet Union (former)	4.0	1.2	10.6	2.6	6.4	1.6	2.7	.9	3.2
Turkey	5.0	.7	8.9	.7	5.4	.5	1.6	.2	2.9
Iraq	5.5	.5	7.9	1.2	3.6	1.0	1.9	.3	2.9
Iran	5.3	1.0	9.3	1.6	4.8	1.1	2.8	1.1	3.5
Afghanistan	2.6	.3	5.5	.5	2.9	.6	1.3	.3	2.1
Sri Lanka	2.2	.5	5.6	.4	3.7	.5	1.7	.6	2.2
China	1.5	.6	1.7	.9	1.8	.7	1.1	.3	1.1
Algeria	10.6	3.8	15.1	2.3	5.7	1.2	4.1	.3	5.1
Somalia	8.4	2.9	11.3	1.8	6.2	1.5	2.4	.2	4.8
Angola	5.5	2.1	9.8	3.1	8.0	2.5	7.7	1.1	5.7
Sierra Leone	6.7	3.2	6.6	2.8	5.4	1.9	n.a.	n.a.	5.6
Nigeria	6.1	1.8	8.5	3.3	5.8	2.3	2.3	1.2	4.4
Ethiopia	9.2	1.2	12.9	1.4	4.6	.7	2.1	.6	3.7
B. Asylum Migrants (2004)									
Total	5.8	1.2	8.7	2.0	5.0	1.4	2.2	.7	4.0
Yugoslavia (former)	5.3	.8	4.7	1.7	4.6	.8	1.2	.2	2.5
Soviet Union (former)	7.3	1.3	15.3	3.0	9.5	3.1	4.4	2.3	5.9
Turkey	3.8	2.3	5.8	2.5	3.7	1.5	4.2	.0	3.4
Iraq	4.9	.7	10.4	.7	4.4	.8	1.4	.3	3.4
Iran	4.2	1.2	12.9	1.5	5.7	1.4	2.8	1.1	4.2
Afghanistan	3.4	.6	6.7	.9	3.9	.7	2.1	.2	2.7
Sri Lanka	2.0	.0	4.1	.0	3.1	.4	3.3	.0	2.1
China	7.2	1.6	3.3	1.2	2.2	1.2	5.6	.0	2.5
Algeria	25.0	10.0	18.1	.0	9.1	.0	.0	.0	9.0
Somalia	5.7	1.8	6.2	1.3	4.5	.9	1.2	.0	3.0
Angola	9.9	2.6	10.2	2.9	7.1	2.0	12.0	6.9	7.1
Sierra Leone	11.8	5.0	9.3	2.8	6.7	1.8	.0	.0	7.1
Nigeria	17.6	4.5	15.8	3.4	6.2	1.1	9.5	.0	6.8
Ethiopia	6.5	1.5	4.3	1.3	2.8	1.3	6.5	.0	2.5

SOURCE.—Population: Blom et al. (2005); asylum migrants: de Boom, Engbersen, and Leerkes (2006).

Although problems with youngsters with Moroccan and Antillean backgrounds attract most of the attention, the 2002 police data also show that less well-known groups of immigrants display much higher crime rates than natives (table 9). They come from countries such as Algeria, Somalia, Angola, Sierra Leone, Nigeria, Ethiopia, former Yugoslavia, the former Soviet Union, Iraq, and Iran (see also Blom et al.

2005). These data demonstrate that the fragmentation of migration is also leading to a fragmentation of crime patterns (see also Kromhout and van San 2003). These newer groups have received very little scholarly attention so far.

Many of the newer groups are made up of people with a typical *asylum background* (immigrants from Angola, Sierra Leone, and the former Soviet Union) and in other groups include many *illegal immigrants* (Cape Verdeans and Algerians). In other words: these groups have different legal and social statuses and fall under our second line of research (see Sec. III).

C. Victimization and Fear of Crime

The criminologist de Haan concluded in 1997 that victimization of immigrants and fear of crime were blind spots in the Dutch literature (de Haan 1997), and to a certain extent this still holds true. Given the substantial number of studies on minority offending, the scarcity of academic research on victimization and fear of crime among immigrants and ethnic minorities in the Netherlands is remarkable. In the early 1990s, researchers of the Ministry of Justice (1993) pioneered the topic and reported elevated victimization rates for minorities in urban areas. As their findings were severely criticized for ignoring "neighborhood effects," the claims were withdrawn in 1994 (see Lempens, Öntas, and Bovenkerk 1997, p. 359). Later studies tend to find lower levels of victimization among non-Western immigrants than among native Dutch, but they often question the validity of their claims. In 1997, Lempens, Öntas, and Bovenkerk reported that non-Western immigrants were underrepresented among the clients of organizations that support crime victims, which they attributed to selection effects rather than actual differences in ethnic victimization rates. A complication is that large surveys often compare immigrants concentrated in cities with autochthonous Dutch who live more widely dispersed over the country. Recent information on immigrants and natives in urban settings suggests that non-Western immigrants are not more likely than autochthonous Dutch to become victims of crime. For most groups the level of victimization is somewhat lower (Wittebrood 2006). Local surveys of youngsters in Rotterdam confirm these findings (Gemeente Rotterdam 2004).

In an overview of the available studies, higher victimization rates sometimes found may occur because non-Western immigrants live spatially segregated in the Netherlands with high concentrations in disadvantaged urban areas (van der Wouden and Bruijne 2001). For similar reasons it is probable that ethnicity correlates with fear of crime. First, we know that anxiety strongly declines with increased socioeconomic position of neighborhoods in general and individual households in particular and also increases with the degree of urbanization (Wittebrood 2001). Yet, outcomes of a local survey held in Rotterdam[7] show the opposite. About 36 percent of respondents from Surinamese, Antillean, Turkish, Moroccan, and Cape Verdean backgrounds report that they sometimes feel unsafe, against 45 percent of the native Dutch inhabitants. Moroccans score very low, with 23 percent, and Turkish respondents score very close to the native population (Gemeente Rotterdam 2004). Again, it seems more reliable to compare outcomes within cities than on a national level, and when this is done, victimization rates are comparatively low. However, it is true that we know very little about group differences in responding to survey questions on feelings of safety or fear of crime (Junger-Tas et al. 2003, p. 85).

D. Detention and Imprisonment

Apart from crime rates and shares of suspects, detention figures can also be taken as an indicator of a crime problem among immigrants, although selectivity causes a more serious bias than at the stage of arrest (Rovers 1999). Nonetheless, a high number of foreign-born people in prisons and detention centers was observable in the 1980s, and the overrepresentation has become much more acute. Whereas Dutch penal policy has long been characterized as relatively lenient with low incarceration rates, the rate of imprisonment is rapidly rising. In ten years' time the number of prisoners has almost doubled (Centraal Bureau voor de Statistiek [CBS] [http://www.cbs.nl]). On September 30, 2004, 16,455 people were imprisoned (approximately 0.1 percent of the population). For 1994 this figure was only 8,740. The share of first- and second-generation immigrants in prison is also on the rise (see Wacquant 2005a, 2005b). Official data on imprisonment, however, distinguish only foreign-born or, in other words, first-generation immigrants. Between 1994 and 2004, the percentage of prisoners born in the Netherlands fell from 50 to 45 percent (among whom are second-generation immigrants). While less than 10 percent of the Dutch pop-

---

[7] The report was based on a large (N = 12,000) representative sample of the Rotterdam population (Gemeente Rotterdam 2004).

ulation is foreign-born, more than half of the prison population is foreign-born (table 10). According to 2005 figures by the CBS, relatively large groups come from Surinam, the Dutch Antilles, Morocco, Turkey, Algeria, and the former Republic of Yugoslavia. Rates per capita are especially high for Algerians, Antilleans, and Surinamese (see table 10).

Most prisoners have been sentenced for violence and theft, and immigrants are no exceptions in this regard. However, a disproportionate share of foreign-born prisoners have been sentenced on the basis of drug laws (predominantly production, trafficking, and sale). For example, in 2004 more than one-third of the sentences of Surinamese (35 percent) and Antilleans (38 percent) related to drug offenses, compared with 15 percent for native inmates. The rise of the share of foreign-born prisoners since 1994 is partly due to enhanced enforcement of antidrug laws; between 1994 and 2004 the number of prisoners sentenced under drug laws rose by 240 percent from 1,355 in 1994 to 3,255 in 2004 (2005 figures from the CBS).

The sociologist Koopmans (2003b) has attempted to compare the available figures on the prison population internationally and concludes that the overrepresentation of foreign-born inmates is much higher in the Netherlands than in countries such as Great Britain, Germany, or France. In Germany, 27 percent of the prison population in 1997 was of non-German descent, whereas 53 percent of inmates in the Netherlands in 1998 were foreign-born[8] (Koopmans 2003a). According to Koopmans, these—and other unintended outcomes of a "soft" approach such as high unemployment and a high rate of school dropouts—can be attributed to the failure of Dutch integration policies. Koopmans, however, does not differentiate between reasons for detention. It is likely that the high involvement of certain migrant groups in drug-related offenses, for instance, has more to do with the position of the Netherlands as a transit country for drugs than with "soft" integration policies.

Part of the rise of the foreign-born prison population is also caused by the exclusionary Dutch alien policy that targets unwanted (illegal) immigrants, who are increasingly being detained[9] (van Kalmthout

[8] Here, the common definition of "allochtonous" is not used, Therefore, second-generation migrants are invisible in detention statistics.
[9] Illegal residence is not a criminal offense according to Dutch law. Detention is an administrative measure for foreigners awaiting expulsion.

TABLE 10
Prison Population in the Netherlands

	Prison Population			Population			Prison Population as a Percentage of the Population		
	1995	2000	2004	1995	2000	2004	1995	2000	2004
Total	10,330	11,760	16,455	15,493,889	15,863,950	16,305,526	.07	.07	.10
Netherlands	5,115	5,310	7,330	14,086,803	14,307,613	14,569,399	.04	.04	.05
Foreign-born	5,215	6,450	9,125	1,407,086	1,556,337	1,736,127	.37	.41	.53
Europe	1,305	1,510	2,095	552,427	589,479	650,689	.24	.26	.32
Turkey	520	565	640	167,498	178,027	195,937	.31	.32	.33
Yugoslavia (former)	155	145	255	43,779	50,535	54,493	.35	.29	.47
America	2,010	2,260	3,320	311,012	358,381	400,394	.65	.63	.83
Surinam	1,075	985	1,415	180,961	184,979	190,104	.59	.53	.74
Netherlands Antilles	660	930	1,415	62,498	76,276	89,657	1.06	1.22	1.58
Africa	1,390	1,750	2,330	229,057	263,469	304,869	.61	.66	.76
Morocco	840	860	1,050	140,728	152,693	168,528	.60	.56	.62
Algeria	275	340	360	2,861	3,707	4,013	9.61	9.17	8.97
Asia	445	770	970	302,422	332,113	366,043	.15	.23	.26
Oceania/unknown	60	160	410	12,168	12,895	14,132	n.a.	n.a.	n.a.

SOURCE.—Statistics Netherlands, processed by authors.

2005). Illegal immigrants are by definition the products of legislation that aims at controlling migration (Engbersen and van der Leun 2001). In recent years, controls have been intensified, and in particular, detention figures have risen quickly, as we discuss in the next section.

The increase in Dutch prison capacity and the strong increase in the number of prisoners in custody for drug crimes and breaking immigration laws indicate that the policies of tolerance are weakening. A similar tendency has been discussed with regard to integration politics. As a result of these changes in the political climate, Dutch immigration and immigrant integration policies have become more restrictive and exclusionary. This paradigm shift in migration and integration policies is accompanied by an increased xenophobic discourse by national and local politicians and the media (van Meeteren 2005). Another effect is the fragmentation of immigrant statuses. In Section III we shift attention to newer groups of immigrants with less stable statuses.

III. Asylum Seekers, Illegal Immigrants, and Crime

The changes in international migration that we discussed in Section I are being mirrored in research on new groups of immigrants and crime. In addition to publications on former guest workers and postcolonial immigrants and their offspring, attention is increasingly given to research on immigrants with a weak residency status (asylum seekers) or without status (illegal immigrants). The substantial inflow of asylum seekers from all parts of the world since the 1980s and the growing concerns about irregular or illegal migration in particular during the 1990s have stimulated three new subfields of study: First, in the study of the possible relations between asylum migration and crime, attention is primarily paid to those groups of asylum seekers that remain in the asylum procedure for a long time. Second, the study of the social construction of illegality and the interrelatedness of illegality and crime is receiving attention. Third, an increasing amount of attention is being paid to the social organization of illegal immigration, the smuggling and trafficking of human beings (see Kleemans's contribution in this volume). Analogous to what happened in the 1990s (Bovenkerk and Yesilgoz 2004, p. 85), Dutch researchers seem quick to study these issues empirically in comparison to their counterparts in surrounding countries.

These new areas of attention are the result of changing migration patterns and changes in asylum and illegal immigrant policies. Substantial changes have taken place in both policy areas. A crucial problem of the pre-2000 Dutch asylum policy was the lengthiness of the procedure. It often took years before a final decision was made, especially if asylum seekers appealed against negative decisions of the immigration authorities or continued the procedure in an effort to obtain better status. The 2000 Aliens Act aimed to shorten the asylum procedures in the following three ways. First, in principle the immigration authorities issue a decision on an asylum request within six months. This is not a strict requirement, but one that an effort is made to meet. An important measure to simplify and accelerate the asylum procedure was to set up so-called application centers, where a first assessment of an asylum request is to be made within forty-eight "process hours" (which takes a maximum of about five days). Asylum seekers rejected at the application center have to leave the Netherlands immediately. Furthermore, criteria were formulated on which countries could be considered safe. A country is considered safe if it has signed the relevant human rights agreements and abides by them. Asylum seekers from countries considered safe according to the formal criteria are not immediately rejected. There is always an assessment of each individual case. A precondition is that asylum seekers can make a plausible case that their personal safety is at risk in their home country.

Second, the Aliens Act 2000 eliminated the option of an administrative review of a decision by the immigration authorities. Asylum seekers have the opportunity to lodge an appeal to a court, followed by an appeal to the Council of State, the highest Dutch administrative appeal board, which is required to make a decision within six months. In principle, the asylum seeker can remain in the Netherlands pending an appeal decision, though not in the case of a decision on a further appeal. If the asylum appeal is rejected, the alien no longer has a right to make use of a reception center or of the other facilities and has to leave the Netherlands. No separate appeal is possible against the termination of the reception facilities, since this is a part of the negative decision on the asylum application itself.

The third and final important change in the 2000 Aliens Act pertains to different asylum statuses. Prior to the act, the Netherlands had various asylum statuses with different rights and privileges depending on the grounds for asylum. As of April 1, 2001, every asylum seeker whose asylum request is approved receives the same temporary residence permit, regardless of the grounds for asylum. Each asylum seeker who is admitted first receives a temporary residence permit for a maximum of three years, which can later be converted into a permanent residence permit (in 2004 this was changed to five years). Uniform rights and facilities are attached to this single status. All asylum migrants who have been admitted to the Netherlands (status holders) have the same rights with regard to employment, social security, family reunification, study and study grants, refugee passports, and so forth. During the asylum procedure, asylum seekers have a right to be housed at a reception center or elsewhere. However, the basic principle is that asylum seekers remain outside society. Asylum seekers have only a limited right to engage in paid employment and no access to the Dutch social security system. Instead, there are pocket money arrangements at the application centers. The idea is that asylum seekers have to be kept outside Dutch society as long as their asylum request has not been approved. Integration into Dutch society would only make it harder for them to leave again.

A final "spearhead" of the new asylum and immigration policy is the return policy, which is based on the premise that asylum seekers who have finalized their legal proceedings are responsible for their own return to their country of origin. The idea is that the asylum seekers managed to get to the Netherlands on their own initiative and must therefore return on their own initiative as well. Asylum seekers who have finalized their legal proceedings become illegal and must leave the Netherlands. The starting point is that it is prohibited to stay illegally in the Netherlands. After every negative decision in the procedure, asylum seekers are reminded of their responsibility and encouraged to make preparations for their return. It cannot be established how many asylum seekers actually leave the country or remain without a valid residence permit (that is to say, are "illegal").[10]

The following changes have recently been made in illegal immigrant policy. First, the Dutch state tries to block access to the formal labor market through high employer sanctions and by laying a protective ring of documentary requirements around the formal labor market, blocking access to stable tax-paid jobs. Since 1991, it is impossible for illegal aliens in the Netherlands to register in the population register

[10] The only available data refer to voluntary return with help from the International Organization for Migration. In 2004 this organization supported 3,714 individuals with their return, which was an increase of 28 percent as compared to 2003.

and thus obtain a social-fiscal number, the "entry ticket" to formal work. Dutch document requirements make it very difficult for illegal aliens to get a job in the legal, regular economy (van der Leun and Kloosterman 2006). Second, the Dutch state tries to exclude irregular immigrants from public services (welfare, social security, health care, education, and public housing). In 1998, the Benefit Entitlement (Residence Status) Act came into force (van der Leun 2003). This act aims at preventing the continuation of unlawful residence and at preventing people without valid documents from building up a quasi-legal position (Minderhoud 2004). This act was to ensure that only immigrants with residence permits could obtain social security and other social rights. This act is also known as the "Linking Act" because immigration service registration files, census bureau data, fiscal identification agency data, and social security and social assistance data can all be cross-checked to verify the validity of immigrants' residence and work status.

Third, the Dutch state is intensifying instruments of detention and expulsion. Detention and deportation are regarded as the final stages of an effective illegal aliens policy. The legal basis of alien detention differs in the European countries. In Belgium, France, Germany, and to some extent England, illegal residence is punishable. The penalty usually consists of imprisonment or a fine. In the Netherlands, illegal residence as such is not punishable (ACVZ 2002). The most important reason for nonpenalization is that this can prolong illegal residence (Minderhoud 2004). Irregular immigrants can be detained and expelled on the basis of the Dutch Aliens Act. Most of the incarcerated immigrants have not committed any crimes. They break the rules by being in a country without the necessary documents; in a legal sense, detention is an administrative matter, not a penal measure. The Netherlands has seven special deportation centers for apprehended illegal immigrants and failed asylum seekers. These deportation centers focus on efficiently organizing forced return programs and establishing the identities and nationalities of the apprehended "unidentifiable" immigrants. Under the Aliens Act 2000, it has become easier to arrest and detain illegal immigrants. On September 30, 2004, the number of immigrants held in custody because of immigration laws (1,655) had almost *quadrupled* since 1994 (425). This increase was also partly enabled by the construction of special deportation centers at Schiphol Airport and Rotterdam Airport. Approximately half of the immigrants are in custody for less than seven days (ACVZ 2002, p. 23). These are immigrants who are easy to expel. On average, however, not only are illegal immigrants more often detained than in previous years, but the average length of detention has also risen significantly. A substantial share of the detained illegal immigrants have not committed any criminal offense; for those who have, the offenses are mainly minor (van Kalmthout 2005). Between 2000 and 2001, of the almost 20,000 custodies that ended, well over 60 percent ended in expulsion. This means that a large number of illegal immigrants returned into Dutch society because there was no prospect of deportation (ACVZ 2002, p. 23). Engbersen, Staring, and van der Leun (2002) and van Kalmthout (2005) find that less than half of the apprehended and detained illegal immigrants are effectively expelled, and van Kalmhout finds that, in contradiction to what the political rhetoric suggests, the share of effective expulsions has been decreasing over the years. Illegal immigrants are therefore increasingly detained, but their detention is not per se followed by an expulsion. As a consequence, many irregular immigrants are sent back to the streets.

The asylum and immigration policy developments outlined above have had various consequences. The old asylum procedure created a very extensive group of asylum seekers who had to wait for years for the final decision. This group had a very weak legal position and a poor income position. The new asylum procedure primarily creates large numbers of rejected asylum seekers (see table 5). However, the Netherlands does not expel most individuals, but merely orders them to leave the country promptly, and there is no way to estimate how many former asylum seekers remain illegally. The policy toward irregular immigration has the effect that it increasingly forces irregular immigrants underground because legal avenues toward formal work or public assistance are blocked.

The changes in Dutch immigration control policies demonstrate that nation-states are key institutions in the structuring of class and social order. States have a legitimate monopoly over the control of movement and the distribution of citizenship rights and are therefore a decisive factor in the allocation of life chances to social groups and classes (Torpey 1998; Engbersen 2003*b*). States are also crucial institutions in defining what are legitimate and illegitimate *actions* and what are legitimate or illegitimate *beings* (Bauman 2004). Criminologists mainly discuss the role of the state in the literature on the functioning of the criminal justice system and the rise of the penal state (see Tonry 1995;

Wacquant 2001) and to a limited extent when studying state crimes and human rights violations (Cohen [1993] 2003). In criminology, little attention has been paid to immigration control policies and the social consequences they have on crime rates among specific groups of asylum seekers and undocumented or irregular immigrants (see also Wacquant 2005a, 2005b). This has changed over the past ten years, as far as the Netherlands is concerned.

In order to explain the criminal practices of asylum seekers and irregular immigrants, researchers in this new field use theories from several disciplines, such as migration studies, urban studies, anthropology, criminology, and sociology. Hirschi's (1969) social control theory, which was much used in Dutch migrant studies in the 1980s (see Sec. II), is less suitable for research on such new immigrant groups. In terms of methodology, the research also deviates from that on legally admitted immigrants groups, since it is mainly based on analyses of aliens police registrations and ethnographic research among specific populations. For obvious reasons, large-scale surveys are not undertaken because a sample base is lacking. In this section we elaborate on asylum and crime, irregular migration and crime, and some fundamental policy and research issues.

A. Asylum and Crime

In early 2001, Jacques Wallage, the mayor of Groningen (a town in the north of the Netherlands), caused considerable commotion by declaring that the crime rate among asylum seekers in the Groningen region was five times as high as that among the regular Groningen population. The same had already been stated in various nonpublic police reports. These police studies also suggested the presence of organized crime, for example, the trade in stolen goods, in which criminal organizations make strategic use of asylum seekers. These would be recruited in asylum seekers' centers. Furthermore, specific criminal activities would be organized from these centers. A study by de Haan and Althoff (2002) in the Groningen region produced a different impression. The key finding, based on analyses of police registrations, file analyses, and interviews with key informants, was that asylum seekers living in asylum seekers' centers committed thefts (from shops) and minor aggressive offenses in particular. Property offenses were committed outside the asylum seekers' center, and the police overestimated their number. The aggressive offenses occurred mainly within the walls of the asylum seekers' center, and the police underestimated their number. De Haan and Althoff explained these offense patterns on the basis of the opportunity structure for asylum seekers (ban on labor participation, little money, and chronic boredom) and the problematic living conditions at such centers (see Goffman 1968), where people of many different nationalities occupy a limited space for a long period, which increases the risk of friction. Another finding was that there was no concrete evidence of "supra-individual crime" organized by asylum seekers from residence centers. De Haan and Althoff concentrated on those asylum seekers who stayed in the asylum seekers center, and not on those who went to live in other types of housing, which may have caused a certain bias toward law-abiding persons.

The results of the Groningen study partially correspond with those of the studies by Snel et al. (2000) and van San, Snel, and Boers (2002) among young Yugoslavs with an asylum background. These studies, based on an analysis of police statistics and interviews with young Yugoslavs, were meant to establish whether there was an organized Yugoslav burglary ring, as suggested in some police studies. This proved not to be the case. Yet unlike de Haan and Althoff's (2002) study, these studies showed a strong involvement in crime among this group of young Yugoslavs. In 2000, the police suspected more than one in ten people in the eighteen to twenty-four age group from former Yugoslavia of having been involved in some criminal offense, for the most part robberies and burglaries. Striking also is the large involvement of specific groups in serious violent offenses such as armed robbery, threatening behavior, bodily harm, kidnapping, and murder. Similar patterns emerged from qualitative research among forty detained Yugoslavs. One-quarter of the young respondents (under age thirty) were suspected of or had been convicted of attempted or actual homicide or manslaughter. However, these offenses are not representative of all the suspects from former Yugoslavia. Interviewing respondents in prison almost automatically entails an overrepresentation of serious offenders.

Snel et al. (2000) and van San, Snel, and Boers (2002) explain that this strong involvement in crime has to do with the young Yugoslavs' poor integration into Dutch society—they constitute a first generation—in combination with other factors. This poor integration finds expression in high unemployment figures, but also in the illegal position of some respondents (they were refused as asylum seekers). The other factors are the exclusionary effect of the asylum procedure, violent war experiences, and the visibility and presence of crime in the Yugoslav community. Finally, the studies show that some young Yugoslavs make strategic use of their reputation for violence to take over a specific part of the criminal market. Van San and Snel (2004) show that the respondents use and manipulate their own "culture" in a creative way to achieve certain aims. According to Bovenkerk, Siegel, and Zaitch (2003, p. 36), ethnicity—like culture—is not a behavioral determinant in itself. Instead, people construct their own culture and strategically use the prevailing stereotypes around them for different audiences. They would be wise to keep a low profile when faced with law enforcement agencies. In criminal circles, however, they can make the most of their violent reputation. There is a very shadowy blend of images and reality here, and it is not inconceivable that the images will become reality at some point simply because all the parties treat them as such (see van de Port 2001; Bovenkerk, Siegel, and Zaitch 2003).

A large-scale research program under way in the Netherlands focuses on the relations between asylum migration and crime (de Boom, Engbersen, and Leerkes 2006). Within the framework of this program, a national database of all asylum seekers who applied for asylum in the Netherlands in the period 1989–2004 ($N = 400,000$) and a national database of suspects from the twenty-five regional police files were linked. The latter database contains all persons who were suspected of having committed an offense in the period 1996–2004 ($N = 1,080,000$). One of the key questions is whether asylum seekers are more involved in crime than the general population. To be able to answer this question, a distinction is made between asylum seekers who are in the Netherlands legitimately (asylum seekers whose request has been granted or who are still awaiting the [final] decision) and the group of asylum seekers whose request has been refused. Of the asylum migrants whose asylum request was granted, 3.4 percent were suspected of being involved in crime; of the asylum seekers who are still waiting for the (final) decision of their request, an average of 5.4 percent were suspected of criminal involvement in 2004. These results indicate that asylum seekers are more involved in crime than the regular Dutch population (the involvement of the total population in the Netherlands in 2004 was about 1.2 percent). However, the differences are smaller than many populist Dutch politicians had anticipated.

When making such a comparison, controlling for age and sex is essential, because there are more young males in the asylum population than in the regular population and young males are usually the most involved in criminal behavior. When one controls for both variables, the outcome is that asylum migrants are more involved in crime than the total Dutch population, but less than some of the regular migrant groups such as Antilleans and Moroccans (see table 9). Again, differences between groups of asylum seekers are substantial. Asylum migrants from the former Soviet Union (5.9 percent), Algeria (9 percent), and Sierra Leone (7.1 percent) are suspected of crimes relatively more often than asylum migrants from countries such as Sri Lanka (2.1 percent), China (2.5 percent), and Ethiopia (2.5 percent). We may therefore conclude that the involvement in crime of asylum seekers who are legally in the Netherlands in 2004 was between 3.4 percent (asylum seekers with a residence permit) and 5.4 percent (asylum seekers still awaiting a decision).

The majority of requests for asylum are turned down, and the percentage is increasing every year (see table 5), which raises the question as to what extent rejected asylum seekers come into contact with crime. The answer is difficult because it is not clear what proportion of asylum seekers actually leave the Netherlands and what proportion stay illegally. If one assumes that almost no rejected asylum seekers have left the country, only a small percentage (1.8 percent) are involved in crime. The Ministry of Justice, however, assumes that about 90 percent of the rejected asylum seekers leave the country (ACVZ 2005). Following this logic, 18 percent would be involved in criminal activities (de Boom, Engbersen, and Leerkes 2006).

On the basis of the capture-recapture method (van der Heijden and Cruijff 2004), a more reliable estimate of the number of rejected asylum seekers residing in the Netherlands can be made. Using apprehension data, van der Heijden and Cruijff estimated that, in 2002, approximately 210,000 illegal immigrants were residing in the Netherlands. About 11 percent (24,000 persons) of those illegal immigrants are rejected asylum seekers. From this number it follows that approximately 20 percent of the rejected asylum seekers stay in the country and about 10 percent of rejected asylum seekers are involved in criminal activities.

Explaining the differences in crime patterns among different groups requires substantive in-depth research that systematically takes into account their citizenship status; their migration history and experiences; their physical, human, and social capital; and the responses from the wider society (including educational institutions and employers). The concept of the "differential opportunity structure" as developed in several empirical studies on different groups of illegal immigrants may be a useful conceptual tool for understanding these group differences. These studies argue that differential access to legitimate and illegitimate opportunities explains group-specific involvement in crime.

B. Irregular Migration and Crime

With the increase in irregular migration, a new dimension has been added to the immigrant crime debate, due to the characteristics of the social position of illegal immigrants (van der Leun 2003). Almost all research on migration and crime—from the early Chicago School to the present—is focused on *legitimate* groups that engage in *illegitimate* activities but are allowed to stay in the territory of a nation-state. This is also the case for asylum seekers. The groups under study may differ in spatial concentration, social organization, human capital, social bonds, self-control, illiteracy, group discrimination or stigmatization, and levels of violence and crime, but they have at least one thing in common: none of these groups has an illegal status. However, illegality with respect to illegal immigrants is not attached to a kind of illegitimate *activity*, but to a state of *being* illegitimate (see Schinkel 2005). Immigrants are classified by the state as illegal if they lack a valid legal residence permit. In some European countries, being illegal is defined as a crime and is punishable as such. This is not the case in the Netherlands. Illegal residence is a misdemeanor, and the main sanction is detention or expulsion. The steep increase in the number of illegal immigrants in the prison population shows the growing importance of detention as a strategy for immigration control. A substantial fraction have not committed crimes. This illustrates how the state influences the life chances of illegal immigrants in two ways: first, by classifying certain immigrants as illegal and, second, by combating illegal residence with exclusionary policies. This raises the question whether the social construction of illegality itself can generate specific types of subsistence crime: crimes committed in order to stay and to live in a country (Albrecht 2002). The exclusion of illegal immigrants from legitimate means of survival (work and public services) could push illegal immigrants toward income-generating criminal activities in order to reside in the Netherlands.

Various Dutch studies on irregular migration based on police data and ethnographic research reveal three major empirical findings. First, the police data show a strong increase in crime as a reason for apprehension (Engbersen, van der Leun, and Leerkes 2004; Leerkes et al. 2004). Over a period of almost seven years (1997–2003), the apprehension data on illegal immigrants show a marked rise in the categories of minor offenses and serious offenses. In 1997, nearly 30 percent of the illegal immigrants who were apprehended came into contact with the police for criminal offenses (and not for infractions of the aliens laws or labor laws or for misdemeanors). This number had risen to about 45 percent in 2003. This strong increase cannot be solely explained by a general trend in stricter law enforcement, in which, because of societal pressure, the police are generally more active in crime detection and in registering their findings. If this were true, this should also be visible in the regular police data for 1997–2003. But this is not the case (Engbersen, van der Leun, and Leerkes 2004). Another explanation is that the police are more active in tracking down illegal immigrants than before, which also increases the number of apprehended illegal immigrants arrested for criminal activities. This is not very likely because most criminal illegal immigrants are arrested by police officers working for basic police units, who do not know beforehand whether they are dealing with illegal immigrants or not. Yet, in cases in which the police are actively searching for people, this may be the case. That there has been a significant rise in the number of people arrested for the possession of false documents and people who have been declared "undesirable aliens" does point to selective and more active enforcement by the police. However, if the figures on these reasons for arrest are excluded from the overall figures, the rise in criminal offenses as a reason for apprehension is still very strong. This strong rise indicates that the restrictive aliens policy is affecting the illegal immigrants' residence strategies. In the recent past (before 1991), illegal immigrants had relatively easy access to the formal labor market and some public services (Engbersen 1999; Minderhoud 2004). This has now become much more difficult (van der Leun and Kloosterman 2006). As a result, illegal immigrants who stay in the Netherlands develop forms of subsistence crime, as becomes clear from the offenses they are arrested for. The increase in criminal offenses for which they were apprehended mainly includes theft and the use of false documents. These are crimes that are directly related to the precarious position of illegal immigrants who are excluded from public services and the labor market. The aim of these offenses is to acquire money (theft) or to enter the labor market (false documents).

Second, some groups of illegal immigrants are more involved in crime than others. Newer groups of illegal immigrants (e.g., from Angola, Iran, Somalia, and to a lesser extent from former Yugoslavia and the former Soviet Union) resort more to crime than illegal immigrants from Turkey or Surinam. In accordance with previous findings, North Africans (Moroccans and Algerians) are also overrepresented in apprehension statistics (Engbersen, Staring, and van der Leun 2002). These differences can be partly explained by the results of several ethnographic studies in Amsterdam, Rotterdam, Utrecht, and The Hague, which show that illegal immigrants from countries of origin that are frequently mentioned in police statistics in relation to crime are rather vulnerable with respect to their social embeddedness (Burgers and Engbersen [1999] 2003; Engbersen et al. [1999] 2003; Leerkes et al. 2004). They often occupy uncertain and marginal positions in the formal and informal housing, labor, and marriage markets. Illegal immigrants from these countries cannot rely on well-rooted communities to provide jobs, housing, documents, and legal marriage partners. These groups therefore seem much more disposed to forms of subsistence crime than illegal immigrants from Turkey or Surinam, who can fall back on large, well-established, and close-knit communities. However, it must be noted that even among illegal immigrants from Turkey or Surinam, involvement in crime is on the rise.

Third, although illegal immigrants are generally involved in petty crime such as theft, there are also patterns of criminal specialization. Typically, the offense patterns of particular illegal immigrants reflect the offense patterns of their legal compatriots. Just like legal Turkish suspects (Bovenkerk 1998; Bovenkerk and Junger-Tas 2000), illegal Turkish immigrants are more often apprehended for violent offenses than suspects from other countries of origin. Just like legal suspects from South America (including Surinam), illegal immigrants from South America are apprehended for cocaine trafficking relatively often (ISEO 2002). Illegal immigrants from eastern European countries, former Yugoslavia in particular, are often apprehended for theft and burglary, whereas their involvement in drug trafficking appears to be limited (see Snel et al. 2000; van San, Snel, and Boers 2002). Illegal Moroccans have a disproportionate share in theft with violence and the trafficking of marijuana (van Gemert 1998; ISEO 2002). The share of document fraud suspects is much higher among illegal immigrants from several African and Asian countries than among suspects originating from non-African countries (van San and Leerkes 2001). These findings indicate considerable similarities among legal and illegal immigrants from a particular origin with regard to the type of crimes committed. Leerkes (2005) assumes that the criminal involvement of legal immigrants influences the delinquent behavior of illegal immigrants. The illegal immigrants' likelihood of a criminal career in the Netherlands partially depends on the prevalence of crime among legal immigrants and their crime specializations (see also Zaitch 2002). This implies that the risk of illegal immigrants becoming involved in crime in the Netherlands not only is influenced by changing state policies with regard to illegal residence but also depends on the prevalence of crime among established immigrants in the Netherlands and the types of criminal activities they engage in. However, the interrelation between legal and illegal immigrants cannot explain the sharp increase in crime among illegal immigrants, since the figures on the criminal involvement of legal suspects have not increased according to the available data. Rather, it partially explains the types of crimes that groups of illegal immigrants will resort to in order to stay in the country.

To explain these three empirical findings, Dutch researchers make use of social theories on immigration control policies and citizenship (Andreas and Snyder 2000; Guiraudon and Joppke 2001; Cornelius et al. 2004); structural constraints and opportunity structures (Cloward and Ohlin 1960; Merton 1996); social capital (Bourdieu 1983; Portes 1998); and informal economies in global cities (Hughes [1951] 1994; Sassen 1991). These theoretical strands have been incorporated into Engbersen and van der Leun's (1995, 1998, 2001) theoretical reformulation of the concept of the differential opportunity structure. They argue that the opportunity structure of undocumented immigrants can be divided along three institutional dimensions.

The first is the degree of access to the legitimate, formal institutions of a nation and welfare state, such as the labor market, education, housing, and health care. Before 1990, illegal immigrants had easy access to the labor market and some public services. After 1990, this became much more difficult, particularly after 1998. It is only with the aid of false or borrowed documents that illegal immigrants can now gain access to formal institutions.

The second dimension is the degree of access to informal, partly illegitimate, institutions, such as the informal economy, the informal housing sector, the informal marriage market, and the informal networks of family, friends, and relatives in the Netherlands. The size and significance of the informal networks in which the illegal immigrants are embedded are major indicators of the social capital that illegal immigrants are able to mobilize.

The third is differential access to illegitimate institutions, such as criminal economies and networks. Different groups of illegal immigrants seem to have access to different networks of crime, whereas others have no access at all. This in line with Cloward and Ohlin's (1960) observation that in order to explain the delinquent behavior of groups, one has to take into account not only their (non-) access to legitimate opportunities but also their (non-) access to illegitimate opportunities.

The conceptual framework of the differential opportunity structure offers an explanation for the rise in crime among illegal immigrants and for differences in the patterns of involvement in criminal behavior. Immigrants who have little or no access to formal and informal institutions and who cannot fall back on a community sufficiently well established to provide jobs, housing, and relevant documentation (passports, health insurance, and social security numbers) face stronger pressures to turn to illicit means. And immigrants who have access to specific criminal economies, such as the drug economy, are more likely to become active there.

This framework also offers an opportunity to analyze the effects of restrictive policy. Dutch policy is aimed at closing off the illegal immigrants' access to the labor market and public services (the first dimension). However, empirical studies show that ethnic communities in which illegal immigrants are embedded mediate the effects of these exclusionary state policies. Some communities are able to provide proper support (jobs, housing, money, documents, or a partner) to illegal immigrants; other communities are too small and fragmented to provide support to illegal compatriots (the second dimension). This clearly affects the risk that illegal immigrants become involved in crime. Furthermore, ethnic communities also seem to shape the access to specific criminal "institutions" or economies in which legal immigrants operate (the third dimension). This implies that the illegal immigrants' chances of a criminal career in the Netherlands do not vary exclusively with the tightening of state policies on illegal residence, but also with the prevalence of crime among established immigrants in the Netherlands and with the types of crimes they tend to engage in.

C. Unintended Consequences and Political and Ethical Aspects

The study of the interrelation between illegality and crime reveals that restrictive migration and aliens policies generate unintended effects (Engbersen 2001; Kyle and Koslowski 2001; Bigo 2004). As a consequence of this policy, the number of illegal immigrants in Europe and the Netherlands has increased, simply because more unwanted immigrants are classified as illegal (Castles and Miller 1994). The restrictive policy also contributes to forms of subsistence crime among illegal immigrants. Finally, because of the intensification and modernization of border control (Fortress Europe), immigrants have become more dependent on professional smugglers to reach Europe (Ruggiero 1997). It is becoming increasingly difficult for unwanted immigrants simply to cross a border themselves. The professionalism of some illegal immigration networks thereby legitimizes new far-reaching measures. This creates a border control race in which national states call into being a professional illegal immigration industry (Miller 2001, p. 329). Thus the criminalization of migration leads to the creation of criminal organizations (see Kleemans, in this volume). So far, these research results have had no effect on the Dutch aliens policy, which is becoming even more restrictive.

A second point for discussion brought forward by the study of crime patterns among illegal immigrants and asylum seekers relates to the political and ethical aspects of research. The current debate has echoes of the debate held in the Netherlands in the late 1980s in reaction to the first studies on migration and crime. Scientific research on delinquency and the ethnic origins of offenders was for a long time regarded as a risky undertaking. Some argued that this kind of social research stigmatizes the migrant groups involved and puts them at risk, whereas others thought that the police statistics used in this kind of research were unreliable. These arguments are also heard in the current debate (Groenendijk and Böcker 1995; Böcker and Groenendijk 1996; Westerink 2005). It is also argued that social-scientific research may have serious repercussions for very vulnerable groups (illegal immigrants) and that linking files on aliens (asylum seekers and illegal immigrants) with police files is contrary to data protection legislation. Others argue that solid and systematic social research liberates these controversial issues from the dilemma between taboo and dramatization (Burgers 1996). If new social issues such as irregular migration and delinquency are considered taboo for social research, little will be known about them. And it is precisely this unfamiliarity with new issues (as products of structural changes in international migration, urban labor markets, and state policies) that often results in these issues being dramatized once they feature in the public arena. Estimates in the media of the number of illegal immigrants are usually exaggerated, and the same goes for popular views on illegality, asylum, and crime. Social-scientific research may enfeeble incorrect mythologization and is also critical in laying bare the consequences of the "criminalization of migration" (Bauman 1998, 2004; Bigo 2004; Wacquant 2005b).

IV. Conclusion

Over the past twenty-five years, migration processes have drastically changed the face of Dutch society. This essay has presented the results of two lines of research that stem from different migration movements. First is the postcolonial migration and guest worker migration from the 1950s and 1960s. The subsequent family reunification migration led to the problem of crime among *second*-generation youngsters from Morocco and to a lesser extent Turkey and among first-generation Antilleans. Second is the asylum migration and irregular migration from the 1980s and 1990s, which generated problems of crime among *first*-generation asylum seekers and illegal immigrants.

What do we now know about the interactions between immigration and crime in relation to *regular* immigrants? Contrary to what is often maintained, the Netherlands has a tradition of research on the relations between migrants and crime. This research is seriously biased since it focuses much more on immigrants (first- and second-generation) as suspects of crime than as victims of crime. To summarize the literature on offending, first, recent research based on police data confirms an overrepresentation of migrants in crime. Police records reveal that, on average, male migrants are suspected of having been involved in crime two and one-half times as much as males in the native population, and the females three times as much as native females. The highest crime rates are found among male migrants who are classified as non-Western.

Second, the conventional wisdom of a law-abiding first generation and more problematic second generation is not confirmed in general. In the case of Turkish and more in particular Moroccan boys, "typical" second-generation problems do play a role, but other groups of second-generation migrants, such as Asians, show very low crime rates. Among Antilleans, the most problematic group consists of first-generation immigrants who come to the Netherlands with very low qualifications and a lack of prospects.

Third, the focus on crime patterns among the largest immigrant groups in Dutch society (Turks, Moroccans, Surinamese, and Antilleans), four groups that reflect the colonial past of the Netherlands and the period in the 1960s when guest laborers were recruited from the Mediterranean, no longer suffices. Some smaller migrant groups that came to the Netherlands in the past fifteen years (e.g., from the Dominican Republic, Somalia, and Ghana) show a strong involvement in crime as well.

Fourth, official data on imprisonment, concerning only foreign-born or first-generation immigrants, show that between 1994 and 2004 the percentage of prisoners born in the Netherlands decreased from 50 to 45 percent (including also second-generation immigrants). Where less than 10 percent of the Dutch population is foreign-born, more than half of the prison population is foreign-born. According to 2005 figures from the CBS, large groups come from Surinam, the Dutch Antilles, Morocco, Turkey, Algeria, and the former Republic of Yugoslavia. Rates per capita are especially high for Algerians, Antilleans, and Surinamese.

Finally, as to explanations, it is clear that a lack of integration can cause crime problems but falls short as the main explanation. Some well-integrated groups show high crime rates and other less well-integrated groups display no crime problem at all. It is clear, though, that social position and cultural factors are often interrelated and work to the detriment of many young non-Western males. Regardless of ethnicity, being poorly educated and being unemployed are strong risk factors for youngsters, who easily become demoralized and turn away from conventional society, in particular when parental control and prospects for the future are lacking.

What do we know about interactions between immigration and crime in relation to *irregular* immigrants? First, Dutch research has demonstrated the relation between migration statuses and crime. Immigrants who have a weak status (asylum seekers) or no status (irregular immigrants) are more involved in crime than social groups with a strong residence status. This finding is typical of a northern European welfare state that is not losing control over its border but, on the contrary, is able to exclude immigrants very effectively from its formal economy and public services (Torpey 2000; van der Leun 2003). Second, some irregular immigrants are more involved in crime than others. These differences can be explained by the immigrants' differential opportunity structures. A crucial factor is access to ethnic social networks (social capital). These networks have strategic weight for getting access to formal or informal institutions (for jobs, housing, partners, and documents) and specific forms of criminal specializations. However, and this is a third relevant finding, many new immigrants from countries that have no colonial or economic ties with the Netherlands are not able to rely on established ethnic communities and have to fend for themselves. These groups are more likely to develop criminal activities. A final finding is that Dutch society pays a price for the effective exclusion of irregular immigrants and the time-consuming asylum procedure. Because of specific contextual circumstances, asylum procedures take a long time, generating small-property and minor aggression offenses. And the exclusion of irregular migrants from labor and public services has caused them to go even deeper underground and into criminal behavior.

These Dutch findings demonstrate that immigration control policies have unforeseen outcomes and unintended side effects. In future, irregular migrants have to participate in various informal economies or develop criminal activities in order to be able to stay in the Netherlands. These findings exemplify that it is important to consider policy options that may have a decriminalizing effect. First, the expansion of (temporary or permanent) foreign worker programs might enable immigrants to work legally and help to counteract the development of informal economies. Naturally, this is offset by the risk of low-skilled labor migrants establishing themselves permanently in the Netherlands—as was the case on a large scale in the 1960s and 1970s—and becoming permanently dependent on the welfare state. A second option is selective regularization of illegal immigrants. Over the past few years sizable regularization programs have been carried out in Italy, Spain, Greece, and Portugal and to a rather limited extent in France, Belgium, and the United Kingdom (Levinson 2005). Regularization is a radical measure for controlling illegality, but it is a difficult policy operation. There is the problem of developing criteria that will lead to new distinctions within the illegal population between those who do and those who do not meet the criteria (akin to the classical distinction between the deserving and undeserving poor). And there is also the problem that new groups of irregular migrants are attracted because regularization is taking place. Various international examples have revealed that regularization programs—usually presented as one-off solutions—are seldom what they claim to be (Cornelius et al. 2004; OECD 2004). Nevertheless, selective regularization can—in the short term—reduce public order problems and incorporate into Dutch society groups that are de facto already integrated. Other policy options include systems of earned regularization to legalize irregular migrants and realistic return programs that stimulate people to go back voluntarily, in a sustainable manner. The mission for smart immigration and public order policies seems to lie primarily in finding the right balance between various policy strategies. Central to this is designing a restrictive migration policy including an effective return policy. But alongside selective legalization, forms of labor migration could be incorporated into immigration control policies in order to prevent a sizable illegal underclass from developing, which could pose a threat to public order.

The two lines of research make clear that the contexts of reception (see Portes and Rumbaut 1990) of immigrants have changed dramatically over the past decades. The postcolonial immigrants and first generation of guest workers had no difficulties finding industrial jobs. For current asylum seekers and irregular immigrants, that has now become very difficult. Asylum seekers have only very limited access to the formal labor market, even when they have acquired refugee status, and illegal immigrants are in principle banned from the labor market. The same goes for the first generation of guest workers who became unemployed en masse in the 1980s and for groups of semi- and unskilled immigrants of the second generation. The security of a steady job is replaced by job insecurity. This job insecurity is reflected in the growth of unemployment, poorly paid part-time jobs, temporary employment contracts, and workfare-like programs.

Incorporation into the welfare state has also become more problematic. In the recent past, countries such as the Netherlands, Germany, and France included immigrants (especially guest workers) in the welfare state by giving them comprehensive social rights and limited political rights (Guiraudon 2002, p. 150). This incorporation process is now being questioned because many low-skilled immigrants (first- and second-generation) are unable to find and keep a job and rely instead on welfare state provisions (see Roodenburg, Euwals, and ter Rele 2003). Furthermore, there is a strict exclusion of unwanted immigrants by means of a restrictive migration policy. Nevertheless, groups of irregular immigrants succeed in passing the European borders. They manage to climb over the wall around the West (Andreas and Snyder 2000) but then come up against a second wall: the wall around the welfare state (Engbersen 2003*b*).

This essay has demonstrated that the changed national and international contexts play a limited role in current scientific explanations of crime patterns among first- and second-generation immigrants in the Netherlands. Dutch research is mainly aimed at delinquent juveniles of Moroccan, Antillean, and, recently, Yugoslav origins. Little research has been conducted on new aspects of crime resulting from the changing migration streams and integration patterns, the consequences of the changing perception of migrants, and the intended and unintended consequences of migration control and public order policies.

Five themes deserve to be placed on the future research agenda. Some of these are being developed; others still need to be explored.

A. Comparative Research on Integration Processes and Crime

Systematic and comparative research into the differences in crime patterns of migrant groups in relation to integration needs to be done. The Research and Documentation Center of the Ministry of Justice (WODC) and CBS have taken important steps toward creating a national monitoring instrument that can be used to trace the integration over time of first- and second-generation people of non-Dutch origin (irregular immigrants are of course not included). However, this instrument is based on a limited number of indicators (labor market position, social security and social assistance, and police records). There is limited or no information on crucial indicators such as educational background, social capital, and experiences of discrimination. Additional surveys and qualitative research are therefore essential as an addition to this monitoring instrument. Moreover, more energy should be put into including representative numbers of respondents with an immigrant background in longitudinal surveys, victimization surveys, and surveys on feelings of safety. Additional research will also be required with regard to irregular migrants who have not been registered in the regular population statistics in the Netherlands.

B. Transnational Crime

Processes of globalization bring with them forms of cross-border crime. For a research agenda on migration and crime, the increase in human trafficking and human smuggling is of interest. International and Dutch research projects show that both large-scale professional organizations and small-scale, familial organizations are involved in human trafficking and human smuggling. Both types of organizations are hard to combat, the first because of their professional nature and the second because of the legitimate use they make of their (transnational) social networks. The transnational social capital of ethnic communities makes it possible to trespass borders easily and remain in the shadow of ethnic communities. Dutch research on human smuggling shows that three dimensions are essential for understanding the social organization of human smuggling: the extent of coordination (division of labor and specialization and differentiation of tasks), the degree of domination (authority structures and internal control mechanisms), and the structure of (transnational) social networks in which human smuggling is embedded (Staring et al. 2005). However, this research was based on in-depth study of police investigation files, whereas multi-sided research is needed in order to understand the smuggling processes from sending to receiving countries.

C. Import Crime

There are indications that some migrant groups were already criminally active before they came to the Netherlands or that they came to the Netherlands because of perceived opportunities for criminal activity. This is known as import crime. Bovenkerk (2002, p. 235) differentiates between direct and indirect import of crime. Direct import involves migrants who built up a criminal career in their own country or elsewhere and continue this career in the Netherlands. It also involves migrants who came to the Netherlands specifically to commit specific crimes (e.g., drug trafficking, car trafficking, and theft). Indirect import of crime involves migrants who display behavior that is to a certain extent authorized within their own cultural context but falls under the criminal law in the Netherlands (e.g., avenging the family honor and possession of firearms). In view of the war situation in their country, for instance, firearms had become part of the basic necessities of life for many migrants from former Yugoslavia. Furthermore, the expansion of the European Union to twenty-four member states enables migrants from central and eastern Europe to travel to the Netherlands and possibly also commuter crime. These phenomena of direct and indirect import crime have not yet been systematically researched.

D. State Classifications and Crime

In the Netherlands, there is a long-standing tradition of research into the relation between socioeconomic position or class and crime. This tradition needs to be supplemented with further research into the relation between citizenship status and crime, including the unintended consequences of immigration control policies. In more abstract terms, this involves the relation between social classifications and life chances (Dahrendorf 1979). In a globalized world, having the right documents is a crucial condition for social and geographical mobility. Those who do not have the right documents run the risk of being declared illegal, being pushed to the margins, and sometimes also becoming involved in certain forms of crime (Bauman 2004; Wacquant 2005a, 2005b).

E. Effects of Public Hostility

Over the past five years, the political and social climate in the Netherlands with regard to migrants has changed dramatically as a result of major international events (terrorist attacks in the United States, Spain, and the United Kingdom) and major domestic events (the assassinations of Pim Fortuyn and Theo van Gogh). These events created considerable tensions between immigrants and native Dutch, particularly in the major cities. Large groups of Dutch people assume that some immigrant groups are by definition criminal, even though most have never been in contact with the police (Bovenkerk 2003). No systematic research has yet been conducted into the consequences of the changing social climate in terms of the increased sense of insecurity among migrants (especially with an Islamic background) or its impact on discrimination practices of the police, the judiciary, and employers. Nor has systematic research been conducted into the consequences in terms of possible processes of political radicalization and for the migrants' identity development. Finally, it is important to conduct research into the effects of the current social climate with regard to migrants on the sense of insecurity among Dutch citizens. Will the Netherlands become a more divided society? Or will the political parties and civil society succeed in spanning the gaps between the different groups in Dutch society?

Research on these five themes will infuse Dutch criminology with theories and empirical findings from other disciplines and international criminology. Not only will it provide new theoretical impulses to Dutch criminology, but it will also lead to more diverse methodologies. Describing and analyzing patterns of crime requires a broad and contemporary arsenal of research methods including ethnographic work and longitudinal studies. Research on these five themes will inevitably lead to the conclusion that the once-renowned Dutch toleration and multicultural society have lost their innocence. The Netherlands has changed from a reluctant country of immigration into a true country of immigration.

REFERENCES

Aalberts, M. 1990. *Politie tussen discretie en discriminatie* [Police between discretion and discrimination]. Arnhem: Gouda Quint.

ACVZ (Dutch Advisory Committee on Aliens Affairs). 2002. *Vreemdelingen in bewaring* [Aliens in detention]. The Hague: ACVZ.

———. 2004. *Regulering en facilitering van arbeidsmigratie* [Regulation and facilitation of labor migration]. The Hague: ACVZ.

———. 2005. *Terugkeer: De nationale aspecten* [Return: National aspects]. The Hague: ACVZ.

Albrecht, H. J. 2002. "Fortress Europe? Controlling Illegal Immigration." *European Journal of Crime, Criminal Law and Criminal Justice* 10(1):1–22.

Andreas, P., and T. Snyder. 2000. *The Wall around the West: State Borders and Immigration Controls in North America and Europe*. New York: Rowman & Littlefield.

Angenent, H. 1997. *Criminaliteit van allochtone jongeren: Feiten, oorzaken en achtergronden* [Crime among nonnative juveniles: Facts, causes and backgrounds]. Baarn: Intro BV.

Bauman, Z. 1998. *Globalization: The Human Consequences*. Cambridge: Polity.

———. 2004. *Wasted Lives: Modernity and Its Outcasts*. Cambridge: Polity.

Beke, B., H. Ferwerda, P. van der Laan, and A. van Wijk. 1998. *De dunne draad tussen doorgaan en stoppen: Allochtone jongeren en criminaliteit* [The thin line between progressing and stopping: Nonnative juveniles and crime]. Utrecht: SWP.

Bigo, D. 2004. "Criminalisation of Migrants: The Side Effect of the Will to Control the Frontiers and the Sovereign Illusion." In *Irregular Migration and*

Human Rights: Theoretical, European, and International Perspectives, edited by Barbara Bogusz, Ryszard Cholewinski, Adam Cygan, and Erika Szyszczak. Leiden: Martinus Nijhof.

Blom, M., J. Oudhof, R. V. Bijl, and B. F. M. Bakker. 2005. *Verdacht van criminaliteit: Allochtonen en autochtonen nader bekeken* [Suspected of crime: A closer look at immigrants and native Dutch]. Voorburg, The Hague: CBS/WODC.

Böcker, A., and K. Groenendijk. 1996. "Vuile handen of verbrande vingers? Een antwoord op Burgers" [Dirty hands or burned fingers: A reply to Burgers]. *Migrantenstudies* 12(1):27–31.

Boekhoorn, P., T. Speller, and F. Kruijssen. 2004. "Commissie Evaluatie Vreemdelingenwet 2000–2004." In *Evaluatie vreemdelingenwet 2000, terugkeerbeleid en operationeel vreemdelingentoezicht* [Commission Evaluation Aliens Law, 2000–2004]. The Hague: Boom Juridische Uitgevers.

Bourdieu, P. 1983. "The Forms of Social Capital." In *Handbook of Theory and Research for the Sociology of Education*, edited by John G. Richardson. New York: Greenwood.

Bovenkerk, F. 1991. "Het vraagstuk van de criminaliteit der Marokkaanse jongens" [The problem of crime among Moroccan boys]. *De Gids* 150(12):8–28.

———. 1992. *Hedendaags kwaad, criminologische opstellen.* [Contemporary evil: Criminological essays]. Amsterdam: Meulenhoff.

———. 1998. *De maffia van Turkije* [The Turkish Mafia]. Amsterdam: Meulenhoff.

———. 2002. "Essay over de oorzaken van allochtone misdaad" [Essay on the causes of immigrants' crime]. In *Nederland multicultureel en pluriform? Een aantal conceptuele studies, in NWO-reeks sociale cohesie in Nederland*, edited by Jan Lucassen and Arie de Ruijter. Amsterdam: Aksant.

———. 2003. "Taboe in de criminology" [Taboo in criminology]. *Proces: Tijdschrift voor berechting en de reclassering* 82(5):242–51.

Bovenkerk, F., and J. Junger-Tas. 2000. *De oorzaken van criminaliteit onder etnische minderheden: Twee invalshoeken* [The causes of crime among ethnic minorities]. The Hague: NWO.

Bovenkerk, F., D. Siegel, and D. Zaitch. 2003. "Organized Crime and Ethnic Reputation Manipulation." *Crime, Law and Social Change* 39(1):23–37.

Bovenkerk, F., and Y. Yesilgoz. 2004. "Crime, Ethnicity and the Multicultural Administration of Justice." In *Cultural Criminology Unleashed*, edited by J. Farrell. London: Glasshouse.

Buikhuisen, W., and H. Timmerman. 1971. "Criminaliteit onder Ambonezen" [Crime among Ambonese]. *Tijdschrift voor Criminologie* 13:73–83.

Burgers, J. 1996. "Natte vingers en vuile handen; over het schatten van het aantal illegale vreemdelingen. Een reactie op Böcker en Groenendijk" [Wet fingers and dirty hands: Estimating the number of illegal immigrants. A reply to Böcker and Groenendijk]. *Migrantenstudies* 12(1):14–26.

Burgers, J., and G. Engbersen. 2003. *De Ongekende Stad 1: Illegale vreemdelingen in Rotterdam* [The Unknown City I: Illegal immigrants in Rotterdam]. Amsterdam: Boom. (Originally published 1999.)

Castles, S., and M. Miller. 1994. *The Age of Migration: International Population Movements in the Modern World*. Basingstoke, UK: Macmillan.

Cloward, R., and L. Ohlin. 1960. *Delinquency and Opportunity Structure: A Theory of Delinquent Gangs*. New York: Free Press.

Cohen, S. 2003. "Human Rights and Crimes of the State: The Culture of Denial." In *Criminological Perspectives: Essential Readings*, edited by E. Mclaughlin, J. Muncie, and G. Hughes. London: Sage. (Originally published 1993.)

Cornelius, W. A., P. L. Martin, and J. F. Hollifield. 1994. *Controlling Immigration: A Global Perspective*. Stanford, CA: Stanford University Press.

Cornelius, W., T. Tsuda, P. Martin, and J. Hollifield. 2004. *Controlling Immigration: A Global Perspective*. 2nd ed. Stanford, CA: Stanford University Press.

Dagevos, J., and R. Schellingerhout. 2003. "Sociaal-culturele integratie" [Social cultural integration]. In *Rapportage minderheden 2003 onderwijs, arbeid en sociaal-culturele integratie*, edited by J. Dagevos, M. Gijsberts, and C. van Praag. The Hague: Sociaal en Cultureel Planbureau.

Dahrendorf, R. 1979. *Life Chances: Approaches to Social and Political Theory*. Chicago: University of Chicago Press.

de Boom, J., G. Engbersen, and A. Leerkes. 2006. *Asielmigratie en criminaliteit* [Asylum migration and crime]. Rotterdam: Risbo/Erasmus University.

de Haan, W. 1997. "Minorities and Crime in the Netherlands." In *Minorities and Crime: Diversity and Similarity across Europe and the United States*, edited by I. Haen Marshall. New York: Sage.

de Haan, W., and M. Althoff. 2002. *Vreemd en verdacht: Een verkennend onderzoek naar criminaliteit in en om asielzoekerscentra* [Strange and suspect: An exploratory research into crime in and around asylum centers]. Groningen: University of Groningen.

den Boer, M. 1995. "Moving between Bogus and Bonafide: The Policing of Inclusion and Exclusion in Europe." In *Migration and European Integration: The Dynamics of Inclusion and Exclusion*, edited by R. Miles and D. Tränhardt. London: Pinter.

Distelbrink, M., and T. Pels. 2002. "Normatieve oriëntaties en binding" [Normative orientations and bonding]. In *De toekomst in meervoud: Perspectief op multicultureel Nederland*, edited by J. Veenman. Assen: Van Gorcum.

Engbersen, G. 1999. "The Undocumented Outsider Class." In *European Societies: Fusion or Fission?* edited by T. Boje, B. van Steenbergen, and S. Walby. London: Routledge.

———. 2001. "The Unanticipated Consequences of Panopticon Europe: Residence Strategies of Illegal Immigrants." In *Controlling a New Migration World*, edited by Virginie Guiraudon and Christian Joppke. London: Routledge.

———. 2003*a*. "Spheres of Integration: Towards a Differentiated and Reflexive Ethnic Minority Policy." In *Identity and Integration: Migrants in Western Europe*, edited by Rosemarie Sackmann, Bernhard Peters, and Thomas Faist. Aldershot/Burlington, UK: Ashgate.

————. 2003*b*. "The Wall around the Welfare State: International Migration and Social Exclusion." *Indian Journal of Labor Economics* 46(3):479–95.

Engbersen, G., E. Snel, and A. Weltevrede. 2005. *Sociale herovering in Amsterdam en Rotterdam: Een verhaal over twee wijken* [Social recapture in Amsterdam and Rotterdam: A tale of two neighborhoods]. Amsterdam: Amsterdam University Press.

Engbersen, G., R. Staring, and J. P. van der Leun. 2002. "Illegal Immigrants in the Netherlands." In *Migration, Immigrants and Policy in the Netherlands: Report for the Continuous Reporting System on Migration (SOPEMI) of the Organisation of Economic Co-operation and Development (OECD)*, edited by G. Engbersen, E. Snel, J. de Boom, and E. Heyl. Rotterdam: Risbo/Erasmus University.

Engbersen, G., and J. P. van der Leun. 1995. "Illegale vreemdelingen en criminaliteit: De differentiële kansenstructuur van illegalen" [Illegality and criminality: The differential opportunity structure of undocumented immigrants]. *Tijdschrift voor Criminologie* 37(3):238–56.

————. 1998. "Illegality and Criminality: The Differential Opportunity Structure of Illegal Immigrants." In *The New Migration in Europe: Social Constructions and Social Reality*, edited by K. Koser and H. Lutz. London: Macmillan.

————. 2001. "The Social Construction of Illegality and Criminality." *European Journal on Criminal Policy and Research* 9(1):51–70.

Engbersen, G., J. P. van der Leun, and A. Leerkes. 2004. "The Dutch Migration Regime and the Rise in Crime among Illegal Immigrants." Paper presented at the fourth annual conference of the European Society of Criminology, Global Similarities, Local Differences. Amsterdam, August 25–28.

Engbersen, G., J. P. van der Leun, R. Staring, and J. Kehla. 2003. *De Ongekende Stad II: Inbedding en uitsluiting van illegale vreemdelingen* [The Unknown City II: Embeddedness and exclusion of illegal immigrants]. Amsterdam: Boom. (Originally published 1999.)

Entzinger, H. 1995. "East and West Indian Migration to the Netherlands." In *The Cambridge Survey of World Migration*, edited by Robin Cohen. Cambridge: Cambridge University Press.

Esmeijer, L., and M. Luning. 1978. "Surinamers in de ogen van de Amsterdamse politie" [Surinamese in the eyes of the Amsterdam police]. In *Omdat zij anders zijn patronen van rasdiscriminatie in Nederland* [Because they are different: Race discrimination in the Netherlands], edited by F. Bovenkerk. Meppel: Boom.

Gemeente Rotterdam. 2004. *Veiligheidsindex* [Safety index]. Rotterdam: Gemeente Rotteram.

Gijsberts, M. 2004. "Minderheden en integratie" [Minorities and integration]. In *Sociaal Cultureel Rapport 2004*. The Hague: Sociaal Cultureel Planning Bureau.

Goffman, E. 1968. *Asylums: Essays on the Social Situation of Mental Patients and Other Inmates*. Harmondsworth, Middlesex, UK: Penguin.

Groenendijk, K., and A. Böcker. 1995. "Het schatten van de onschatbaren; aantallen illegalen, beeld van een categorie of van de schatter" [Counting the uncountable: Reflection of a category or of the estimator?]. *Migranten-studies* 11:117–28.

Guiraudon, V. 2002. "Including Foreigners in National Welfare States: Institutional Venues and Rules of the Game." In *Restructuring the Welfare State: Political Institutions and Policy Change*, edited by Bo Rothstein and Sven Steinmo. New York: Macmillan.

Guiraudon, V., and C. Joppke. 2001. *Controlling a New Migration World.* London: Routledge.

Haen Marshall, I. 1997. *Minorities, Migrants, and Crime Diversity and Similarity across Europe and the United States.* New York: Sage.

Hirschi, T. 1969. *Causes of Delinquency.* Berkeley: University of California Press.

Hughes, E. C. 1994. "Bastard Institutions." In *Everett C. Hughes on Work, Race, and the Sociological Imagination*, edited by Lewis Coser. Chicago: University of Chicago Press. (Originally published 1951.)

ISEO (Instituut voor Sociologisch-Economisch Onderzoek). 2002. *Integratie-monitor 2002* [Integration Monitor 2002]. Rotterdam: ISEO.

Janse, R. 2005. "Fighting Terrorism in the Netherlands: A Historical Perspective." *Utrecht Law Review* 1(1):55–67.

Jongman, R., F. Weerman, and L. Kroes 1991. "Maatschappelijke marginaliteit en criminaliteit" [Social marginality and crime]. *Tijdschrift voor Criminologie* 33(1):29–41.

Junger, M. 1990. *Delinquency and Ethnicity: An Investigation on Social Factors Relating to Delinquency among Moroccan, Turkish, Surinamese and Dutch Boys.* Deventer: Kluwer.

Junger, M., and M. Zeilstra. 1989. Deviant gedrag en slachtofferschap onder jongens uit etnische minderheden [Deviant behavior and victimization among ethnic minority boys]. Arnhem: Gouda Quint.

Junger-Tas, J. 1997. "Ethnic Minorities and Criminal Justice in the Netherlands." In *Ethnicity, Crime, and Immigration: Comparative and Cross-National Perspectives*, edited by Michael Tonry. Vol. 21 of *Crime and Justice: A Review of Research*, edited by Michael Tonry. Chicago: University of Chicago Press.

———. 2002. "Etnische minderheden, maatschappelijke integratie en criminaliteit: Een theoretisch raamwerk" [Ethnic minorities, social integration, and crime]. In *Nederland multicultureel en pluriform: Een aantal conceptuele studies*, edited by J. Lucassen and A. de Ruijter. Amsterdam: Aksant.

Junger-Tas, J., M. J. L. F. Cruijff, P. M. van de Looij-Jansen, and F. Reelick. 2003. *Etnische minderheden en het belang van binding: Een onderzoek naar antisociaal gedrag onder jongeren* [Ethnic minorities and the significance of attachment]. The Hague: SDU/Koninklijke Vermande.

Junger-Tas, J., and A. A. van de Zee-Nefkens. 1977. *Een observatie-onderzoek naar het werk van de politie-surveillance* [An observational research into police surveillance]. The Hague: WODC.

Kleemans, Edward R. In this volume. "Organized Crime, Transit Crime, and Racketeering."

Koopmans, R. 2003*a*. "Good Intentions Sometimes Make Bad Policy: A Comparison of Dutch and German Integration Policies." In *The Challenge of Diversity: European Social Democracy Facing Migration, Integration, and Multiculturalism*, edited by René Cuperus, Karl A. Duffek, and Johannes Kandel. Innsbruck: Studien Verlag.

———. 2003*b*. "Het Nederlandse integratiebeleid in internationaal vergelijkend perspectief: Etnische segregatie onder de multiculturele oppervlakte" [The Dutch integration policy from an international comparative perspective]. In *Politiek in de multiculturele samenleving, Beleid en Maatschappij jaarboek 2003*, edited by H. Pellikaan and M. Trappenburg. Amsterdam: Boom.

Kromhout, M., and M. van San. 2003. *Schimmige werelden: Nieuwe etnische groepen en jeugdcriminaliteit* [Shadow worlds: New ethnic groups and juvenile delinquency]. The Hague: Boom Juridische Uitgevers.

Kyle, D., and R. Koslowski. 2001. *Global Human Smuggling: Comparative Perspectives*. Baltimore: Johns Hopkins University Press.

Leerkes, A. 2005. "Embedded Crimes? On the Overlapping Patterns of Delinquency among Legal and Illegal Immigrants in the Netherlands." *Netherlands' Journal of Social Sciences* 40(1):3–22.

Leerkes, A., M. van San, G. Engbersen, M. Cruijff, and P. van der Heijden. 2004. *Wijken voor illegalen: Over ruimtelijke spreiding, huisvesting en leefbaarheid* [Neighborhoods for illegal immigrants: Spatial concentration, housing, and residential livability]. The Hague: SDU Uitgevers.

Lempens, A. L. Assa, G. Öntas, and F. Bovenkerk. 1997. *Slachtofferhulp aan allochtonen* [Victim support for the nonnatives]. The Hague: Ministry of Justice.

Leuw, E. 1997. *Criminaliteit van etnische minderheden: Een criminologische analyse* [Crime among ethnic minorities: A criminological analysis]. The Hague: WODC.

Levinson, A. 2005. *The Regularization of Unauthorized Migrants: Literature Survey and Country Case Studies*. Oxford: University of Oxford, Centre on Migration, Policy and Society.

Mattheijer, M. 2000. *De toelating van vluchtelingen in Nederland en hun integratie op de arbeidsmarkt* [The admission of refugees and their labor market integration]. AIAS Research Report no. 2. Amsterdam: University of Amsterdam.

Merton, R. K. 1957. *Social Theory and Social Structure*. New York: Free Press.

———. 1996. "Opportunity Structure." In *On Social Structure and Science*, edited by Piotr Sztompka. Chicago: University of Chicago Press.

Miller, M. J. 2001. "The Sanctioning of Unauthorized Migration and Alien Employment." In *Global Human Smuggling: Comparative Perspectives*, edited by David Kyle and Rey Koslowski. Baltimore: Johns Hopkins University Press.

Minderhoud, P. 2004. "Coping with Irregular Migration: The Dutch Experience." In *Irregular Migration and Human Rights: Theoretical, European and International Perspectives*, edited by Barbara Bogusz, Ryszard Cholewinski, Adam Cygan, and Erika Szyszczak. Leiden: Martinus Nijhoff.

Ministry of Interior Affairs. 1997. *Criminaliteit in relatie tot de integratie van etnische minderheden* [Crime in relation to the integration of ethnic minorities]. The Hague: Ministry of Interior Affairs/Ministry of Justice.

Ministry of Justice. 1993. *Integrale veiligheidsrapportage* [Coordinated safety policy]. The Hague: SDU.

Ministry of Justice, Immigration and Naturalization Service. 2005. *Cohortanalyse Asielprocedure 1994–2003* [Cohort-analysis asylum procedure 1994–2003]. *Peildatum* 31 maart 2004. The Hague: Ministry of Justice.

Muus, P. 2004. "The Netherlands: A Pragmatic Approach to Economic Needs and Humanitarian Considerations." In *Controlling Immigration: A Global Perspective*, 2nd ed., edited by Wayne A. Cornelius, Takeyuki Tsuda, Philip L. Martin, and James F. Hollifield. Stanford, CA: Stanford University Press.

OECD. 2004. *Trends in International Migration: Annual Report 2003*. Paris: OEDC.

O'Kane, J. M. 1992. *The Crooked Ladder: Gangsters, Ethnicity and the American Dream*. New Brunswick, NJ: Transaction.

Portes, A. 1998. "Social Capital: Its Origins and Applications in Modern Sociology." *Annual Review of Sociology* 24:1–24.

Portes, A., and R. G. Rumbaut. 1990. *Immigrant America: A Portrait*. Berkeley: University of California Press.

———. 2001. *Legacies: The Story of the Immigrant Second Generation*. Berkeley: University of California Press.

Portes, A., and Min Zhou. 1993. "The New Second Generation: Segmented Assimilation and Its Variants among Post-1965 Immigrant Youth." *Annals* 530:74–96.

Roodenburg, Hans, Rob Euwals, and Harry ter Rele. 2003. *Immigration and the Dutch Economy*. The Hague: Netherlands Bureau for Economic Policy Analysis.

Rovers, Ben. 1999. *Klassenjustitie: Een overzicht van onderzoek naar selectiviteit in de Nederlandse strafrechtsketen* [Class justice: A literature review on selectivity in the Dutch criminal justice system]. Rotterdam: Erasmus University, Department of Criminal Law and Criminology.

Ruggiero, V. 1997. "Trafficking in Human Beings: Slaves in Contemporary Europe." *International Journal of the Sociology of Law* 25:231–44.

Sampson, Robert J., and Janet L. Lauritsen. 1997. "Racial and Ethnic Disparities in Crime and Criminal Justice in the United States." In *Ethnicity, Crime, and Immigration: Comparative and Cross-National Perspectives*, edited by Michael Tonry. Vol. 21 of *Crime and Justice: A Review of Research*, edited by Michael Tonry. Chicago: University of Chicago Press.

Sassen, S. 1991. *The Global City: New York, London, Tokyo*. Princton, NJ: Princeton University Press.

Savona, E., and S. Goglio. 1996. "Migration and Crime." Trans Crime Working Paper no. 3, Trento University.

Schinkel, Willem. 2005. "Aspects of Violence." PhD dissertation, Erasmus University Rotterdam, Department of Sociology.

SCP (Social Cultural Panning Office). 2003. *Rapportage minderheden 2003: On-*

derwijs, arbeid en sociaal-culturele integratie [Report on ethnic minorities: Education, labor, and social-cultural integration]. The Hague: SCP

Snel, E., J. de Boom, J. Burgers, and G. Engbersen. 2000. *Migratie, integratie en criminaliteit: Migranten uit voormalig Joegoslavië en de voormalige Sovjet-Unie in Nederland* [Migration, integration, and crime: Immigrants from former Yugoslavia and Russia in the Netherlands]. Rotterdam: Risbo/Erasmus University.

Snel, E., Jan de Boom, and Godfried Engbersen. 2005. *Migration, Immigrants and Policy in the Netherlands: Report for the Continuous Reporting System on Migration (SOPEMI) of the Organization of Economic Co-operation and Development (OECD)*. Rotterdam: Risbo/Erasmus University.

Staring, R. 2001. *Reizen onder regie: Het migratieproces van illegale Turken in Nederland* [Organized migration: The migration process of illegal Turks in the Netherlands]. Amsterdam: Het Spinhuis (Aksant).

Staring, R., G. Engbersen, H. Moerland, N. E. de Lange, D. A. Verburg, E. H. Vermeulen, and A. Weltevrede. 2005. *De sociale organisatie van mensensmokkel* [The social order of human smuggling]. Amsterdam: Kerckebosch.

Tonry, M. 1995. *Malign Neglect: Race, Crime, and Punishment in America*. Oxford: Oxford University Press.

———, ed. 1997. *Ethnicity, Crime, and Immigration: Comparative and Cross-National Perspectives*. Vol. 21 of *Crime and Justice: A Review of Research*, edited by Michael Tonry. Chicago: University of Chicago Press.

Torpey, J. 1998. "Coming and Going: On the State Monopolization of the Legitimate 'Means of Movement.'" *Sociological Theory* 16(3):239–59.

———. 2000. "States and the Regulation of Migration in the Twentieth-Century North Atlantic World." In *The Wall around the West: State Borders and Immigration Controls in North America and Europe*, edited by P. Andreas and T. Snyder. Lanham, MD: Rowman & Littlefield.

van Amersfoort, H. 1982. *Immigration and the Formation of Minority Groups: The Dutch Experience, 1945–1975*. Cambridge: Cambridge University Press

van Amersfoort, J., and W. Biervliet 1977. *Criminaliteit van minderheden: De bedreigde burger* [Criminality among minorities: The threatened citizen]. Utrecht: Spectrum.

van de Port, M. 2001. *Geliquideerd: Criminele afrekeningen in Nederland* [Liquidated: Criminal liquidations in the Netherlands]. Amsterdam: Meulenhoff.

van der Heide, W., and A. Th. J. Eggen. 2003. *Criminaliteit en rechtshandhaving 2001: Ontwikkelingen en samenhangen* [Criminality and law enforcement: Trends and coherences]. The Hague: WODC.

van der Heijden, Peter G. M., Rami Bustami, Maarten J. L. F. Cruijff, Godfried Engbersen, and Hans C. van Houwelingen. 2003. "Point and Interval Estimation of the Population Size Using the Truncated Poisson Regression Model." *Statistic Modelling* 3(4):305–22.

van der Heijden, P., and M. Cruijff. 2004. "Een raming van het aantal illegalen in Nederland." In *Wijken voor illegalen: Over ruimtelijke spreiding, huisvesting en leefbaarheid* [Neighborhoods for illegal immigrants: Spatial concentration, housing, and residential livability], edited by A. Leerkes, M. van San, G. Engbersen, M. Cruijff, and P. van der Heijden. The Hague: SDU Uitgevers.

van der Leun, J. P. 2003. *Looking for Loopholes: Processes of Incorporation of Illegal Immigrants in the Netherlands.* Amsterdam: Amsterdam University Press.

van der Leun, J. P., and R. C. Kloosterman. 2006. "Going Underground: The Labor Market Position of Undocumented Immigrants in the Netherlands." *Tijdschrift voor Economische en Sociale Geografie* [Journal of Economic and Social Geography] 97(1):59–68.

van der Wouden, R., and E. Bruijne. 2001. *De stad in de omtrek: Problemen en perspectieven van de vier grootstedelijke gebieden in de Randstad* [The city in its surrounding: Problems and perspectives of the four large urban areas in the "Randstad"]. The Hague: Sociaal en Cultureel Planbureau.

van Gemert, F. 1998. *Ieder voor zich: Kansen, cultuur en criminaliteit van Marokkaanse jongen* [Every man for himself: Opportunities, culture, and crime of Moroccan boys]. Amsterdam: Het Spinhuis.

van Hulst, H., and J. Bos. 1993. *Pan i réspét: Criminaliteit van geïmmigreerde Curaçaose jongeren* [Crime among immigrated youngsters from Curacao]. Utrecht: OKU.

van Kalmthout, A. M. 2005. "Vreemdelingenbewaring." In *Detentie: Gevangen in Nederland* [Detention of foreigners in the Netherlands], edited by E. Muller and P. C. Vegter. Alphen aan den Rijn: Kluwer.

van Meeteren, M. 2005. "Discoursen van integratie: De omslag in het politieke debat over integratie in Nederland" [Discourses of integration: The turn in the political debate on integration]. Unpublished master's thesis, Erasmus University Rotterdam, Department of Social Sciences.

van San, M. 1998. *Steken en stelen: Delinquent gedrag van Curaçaose jongens in Nederland* [Stealing and using knives: Delinquent behavior of boys from Curaçao in the Netherlands]. Amsterdam: Het Spinhuis.

van San, M., and A. Leerkes. 2001. *Criminaliteit en criminalisering: Allochtone jongeren in Belgie* [Crime and criminalization: Young immigrants in Belgium]. Amsterdam: Amsterdam University Press.

van San, M., and E. Snel. 2004. "Using Myths: Former Yugoslav Perpetrators and Violence." *Crime, Law and Social Change* 41:195–208.

van San, M., E. Snel, and R. Boers. 2002. *Woninginbrekers en zware jongens: Daders uit voormalig Joegoslavië in beeld* [Burglars and heavy criminals: Offenders from former Yugoslavia]. Apeldoorn: Politie & Wetenschap.

Veenman, J. 2003. "Discriminatie op de arbeidsmarkt" [Discrimination on the labor market]. *Beleid en Maatschappij* 30:90–100.

Volkskrant. 2002. "Fortuyn: Grens dicht voor Islamiet" [Fortuyn: Close the border for the Islamite]. February 9.

Wacquant, L. 2001. "The Advent of the Penal State Is Not a Destiny." *Social Justice* 28(3):1–9.

———. 2005*a*. *Deadly Symbiosis: Race and the Rise of Neoliberal Penality.* Cambridge: Cambridge University Press.

———. 2005*b*. "Enemies of the Wholesome Part of the Nation: Postcolonial Migrants in the Prisons of Europe." *Sociologie* 1(1):31–51.

Werdmölder, H. 1991. "Marokkaanse jongeren, delinquentie en dreigende uitzetting" [Moroccan boys, delinquency, and the threat of expulsion]. *Tijdschrift voor Criminologie* 33(3):166–73.

Werdmölder, H., and P. Meel. 1993. "Jeugdige allochtonen en criminaliteit: Een vergelijkend onderzoek onder Marokkaanse, Turkse, Surinaamse en Antilliaanse jongens" [Allochthonous boys and crime: A comparative study among Moroccan, Turkish, Surinamese, and Antillean boys]. *Tijdschrift voor Criminologie* 35(3):252–76

Westerink, Harry. 2005. "Wetenschappers in dienst van het beleid tegen 'illegalen'" [Scientists in service of policies against illegal immigrants]. *Agora: Ontmoetingsplatform voor Wetenschap en Samenleving op Het Gebied van de Ruimtelijke Ordening* 21(1):20–23

Wittebrood, K. 2001. "Onveiligheidsbeleving en slachtofferschap in westerse geïndustrialiseerde landen" [Feelings of unsafety and victimization in the Netherlands]. *Tijdschrift voor Criminologie* 43:144–57.

———. 2003. "Juvenile Crime and Sanctions in the Netherlands." *Journal of Contemporary Criminal Justice* 19:435–53.

———. 2004. "Van delictmelding tot officiële aangifte—sprake van sociale ongelijkheid?" [Recording of reported crimes: Social inequality?]. *Tijdschrift voor Criminologie* 46:56–71.

———. 2006. *Slachtoffers van criminaliteit: Feiten en achtergronden* [Victims of crime: Facts and backgrounds]. The Hague: SCP.

WRR (Netherlands Scientific Council for Government Policy). 1979. *Etnische minderheden* [Ethnic minorities]. The Hague: SDU Uitgevers.

———. 1989. *Allochtonenbeleid* [Allochtonous policy]. The Hague: SDU Uitgevers.

Zaitch, D. 2002. *Trafficking Cocaine: Colombian Drug Entrepeneurs in the Netherlands.* Amsterdam: Kluwer International Law.

Gerben J. N. Bruinsma

Urbanization and Urban Crime: Dutch Geographical and Environmental Research

ABSTRACT

Despite particular features of Dutch cities and society, the overall outcomes of Dutch geographical and environmental research fit well with the
early Chicago school's geographical perspective on criminology. Residents
in rural areas are less confronted with crime because of higher levels of
social cohesion and informal social control and lower offender rates in a
well-ordered physical surrounding. Criminals live more frequently in cities
in which their crimes are concentrated in city centers and their surroundings. The greater the distance to the city center, the less crime occurs. A
recent revival in Dutch environmental and geographical criminological research yields outcomes that correspond well with recent developments in
social disorganization theories of neighborhoods.

Criminologists focus on three strongly interrelated subjects: the description and explanation of the origins of crime; the distribution of
crime across society; and the effects of law enforcement on crime,
criminals, and society. Concerning the first subject, criminologists address the central questions why people, groups, organizations, and governments commit crimes (or do not). For centuries, numerous theories
have been suggested, criticized, elaborated, corroborated, and rejected
to answer those questions. Concerning the third subject, research focuses on the working and effectiveness of laws and law enforcement

Gerben J. N. Bruinsma is director of the Netherlands Institute for the Study of Crime
and Law Enforcement (NSCR) and is professor of criminology at the Faculty of Law,
Leiden University. He is grateful for comments and suggestions from anonymous reviewers, editors Michael Tonry and Catrien Bijleveld, Rolf Loeber, and Per-Olof Wikström. The NSCR's librarian, Peter van der Voort, provided invaluable assistance. The
author finished this essay while a visiting fellow at the Institute of Criminology, Cambridge, and is grateful for the institute's hospitality.

on the emergence and prevention of crime and the correction of criminals.

The second subject, the distribution of crime, encompasses three main topics: How and why crime is *geographically* distributed across society, how and why crime is distributed over *time* in society, and how and why crime is *socially* distributed across society. Insight into the geographical, temporal, and social distributions of crime, victimization, and criminals is important from the perspective of law enforcement and essential for understanding the roots of crime. Differences in crime distributions reflect causal mechanisms that generate crime by people in different social contexts because "concentrations of crime in time and space are not random, but reflect individuals, their decisions, their ecological assessment of places, and their actions" (Brantingham and Brantingham 1999, p. 23).

In the history of criminology, three periods of attention to the spatial distribution of crime can be distinguished. During the period of the cartographic or classical school in the nineteenth century, pioneers such as Guerry (1833), Quetelet (1847), and Fletcher (1848, 1849) for the first time empirically investigated differences in crime rates between geographical areas. Among other things they found, contrary to their expectations, more property crimes in wealthier regions than in poorer ones. In the same century, Emile Durkheim questioned how and why rapid socioeconomic changes in European societies caused by industrialization and urbanization fragmented people's social ties, leaving more scope for deviation from social norms (Durkheim [1893] 1964).

The second period of ecological research occurred at the University of Chicago in the first decades of the twentieth century, where a wide range of innovative research was devoted to a city that had transformed in a few decades from a small settlement into a metropolis of a million people (Park and Burgess [1925] 1967). Guided by the notion of social disorganization, they studied the distribution of crime, criminals, and psychopathological deviance across the city and uncovered delinquent areas in which crime and criminals were predominant. They identified structural factors responsible for that clustering. Park ([1925] 1967), Burgess ([1925] 1967), Shaw (1929), Wirth ([1938] 1964), and Shaw and McKay (1942) influenced all subsequent geographical research in criminology. However, from the 1960s through the 1980s, interest in geographical criminology diminished (Sampson 1986).

Renewed interest in geographical and environmental research can be observed in criminology and in crime analyses of the police (Reiss and Tonry 1986; Bursik and Grasmick 1993; Bottoms and Wiles 2002; Wikström and Sampson 2003). Police forces needed more information on the distribution of types of crimes in their districts, and criminologists (inspired by rational choice theories) were keener on specifics and details of the crimes they studied (Moerland and Rovers 2000). In the Netherlands, criminologists initiated descriptive crime-mapping activities for the Dutch police that stimulated new and innovative geographical research on target selection by offenders, mobility of offenders, and the origins of hot spots in crime in urban environments.

This essay surveys Dutch geographical and environmental criminology. It shows that Dutch geographical research roughly reflects the international research agenda albeit with a time lag of years. Dutch geographical environmental research has mostly been guided by original ideas of the Chicago school, with some recent studies inspired by theoretical developments in the international literature on social disorganization. Recent findings indicate that residents in rural areas are less confronted with crime because of higher levels of social cohesion and informal social control, resulting in lower offender rates in a well-ordered physical surrounding. Criminals, including chronic offenders, more often live in cities. Crime sites in the Netherlands are concentrated in city centers and their surroundings. Shopping districts, theaters, cinemas, bars, restaurants, discotheques, and railway and bus stations are concentrated in these central areas, attracting large numbers of tourists, daily visitors, travelers, and offenders. Studies on specific types of crimes, especially residential burglary, demonstrate a similar zone pattern in Dutch cities as was shown by Burgess (1967) for Chicago. The greater the distance to the city center, the less crime occurs. In a few peripheral suburban neighborhoods in large cities, crime places have emerged in recent years. Research outcomes match theories of the earlier Chicago school. Past and recent research identifies persistent crime places and persistent high-offender neighborhoods (delinquent areas). These neighborhoods do not necessarily contain high numbers of ethnic minorities as is often assumed in policy and in much research.

Studies that combine individual properties with structural neighborhood factors in multilevel models show mixed results, sometimes indicating that the impact of neighborhood characteristics on crime is low and sometimes showing that these aggregate properties have significant independent effects on crime. Informal social control and social cohesion of neighborhoods seem to mediate influences of other neighborhood characteristics. Studies of neighborhoods with economic and housing improvements show that social dynamics of a neighborhood are additional factors influencing higher crime rates. The theoretical concepts used in Dutch disorganization research are not well elaborated empirically. Concepts were borrowed from American environmental research without considering whether they could be applied in the same empirical sense in Dutch cities (Bruinsma et al. 2004). Most Dutch geographical and environmental research is cross-sectional, not allowing proper causal inferences because the time ordering of the variables remains unknown. To study the effects of changes in society on crime, longitudinal (preferably historical) data are more appropriate. Most Dutch environmental research is descriptive (correlating descriptive factors). Theory tests and promising methodological improvements are of recent date.

Section I of this essay addresses the relationship between the level of urbanization and crime. Pioneers in Dutch criminology tried to unravel how and why there was less crime in rural areas than in urban settings. Most studies were descriptive and guided by data whose reliability and validity must be seriously questioned. Recent data, however, still indicate considerable differences in crime and victimization rates across levels of urbanization.

Sections II and III are dedicated to Dutch geographical and environmental criminological research on the distribution of crime within urban settings, most of it recent. Section II opens with a brief description of Dutch cities to provide an interpretive frame for valuing and grasping Dutch outcomes. Results of qualitative research on crimes and criminals in cities are included. Criminals use the urban space to organize their criminal activities. Research in other countries, especially in the United States and Great Britain, demonstrates further spatial concentrations in crime having to do with characteristics of the crime location. Factors such as buildings, roads, canals, and squares and social factors influence the decision processes of offenders to commit their crimes at that location and on that particular target or victim (Brantingham and Brantingham 1991, 1999; Bottoms and Wiles 1992; Rengert 2004). Section II then considers three topics: mapping of crime places in Dutch cities, social disorganization, and mobility of offenders.

Section III provides a brief summary of major conclusions and characteristics of Dutch geographical and environmental criminology and discusses central elements of a research agenda for coming years.

A few additional prefatory comments may be useful. Most Dutch geographical and ecological research uses official (police) data. Their deficiencies and advantages are well known and are not repeated here. Dutch police forces have recently collected additional data on crime, criminals, and victims. Most of these data are based on victims' reports to the police and some on police investigations. Geographical software such as Geographic Information Systems (GIS) has been introduced in most regional forces to support intelligence-led policing and regional and local safety policies.

I discuss many studies using data from the Politiemonitor Bevolking. This is a nationwide population survey of about 80,000 residents of the Netherlands on social safety that has been carried out by the regional police forces and the Ministry of Internal Affairs. People are interviewed by telephone on victimization by a limited number of (traditional) crimes, on feelings of insecurity, on opinions about the police, and on measures people take to prevent victimization. Like police data, Politiemonitor Bevolking data have well-known drawbacks and advantages (for an overview see Vanderveen [2006]).

Geographical criminological research is mostly quantitative by nature. However, I also examine results from qualitative research on crimes and criminals in cities. Observational and ethnographic studies or research using extensive police investigation analyses can shed important light on urban and rural crime.

I. Urbanization and the Spatial Distribution of Crime

The relationship between urbanization and crime rates has long been recognized by criminologists. The descriptive studies of the cartographic or statistical school in the nineteenth century (Guerry 1833; Quetelet 1847; Fletcher 1848, 1849) documented the empirical regularity of crime. Durkheim (1964) was one of the first scholars to address the crime problem in densely populated areas of countries at a theoretical level. On the basis of the underlying assumption that long-term social and economic changes disorganize and disrupt social relations, he suggested that urban environments loosen ties between people and thereby facilitate deviation from rules of society. According to Wirth

(1964), special urban characteristics such as size, density, heterogeneity, and impersonality are responsible for a mode of living that generates more crime. Clinard (1942, p. 203) elaborated that view by arguing that there is more crime in densely populated areas than in scarcely populated rural areas because of urban characteristics such as mobility, impersonal relations, differential association, limited participation in community organizations, organized crime cultures, and a criminal type in the life experience of offenders. Wirth theorized that normative consensus and primary group controls were undermined by the increasing size, density, and heterogeneity of cities. He viewed urbanism as a way of life: "The close living together and working together of individuals who have no sentimental and emotional ties foster a spirit of competition, aggrandizement, and mutual exploitation. Formal controls are instituted to counteract irresponsibility and potential disorder" (1964, p. 74). Urbanism can be studied in his view as a physical or ecological structure, as a system of social organization, and as a set of attitudes and beliefs that lead to collective behavior. The underlying theoretical model for the urbanization hypothesis implies that increasing urbanization causes less integration among people and as a consequence generates less informal social control. Less integration and less informal control explain higher levels of crime, disorder, victimization, and fear of crime (Wikström 1991; Wikström and Dolmén 2001, p. 123).

Another perspective in criminology emphasized the opportunity structure cities offer to potential offenders (Cohen and Felson 1979; van Dijk 1991; Glaeser and Sacerdote 1999). Urban environments have more suitable targets, and people are more tempted in cities than in rural areas to commit crimes. These factors combined with a lack of informal guardianship in urban environments explain higher crime rates.

Others, however, challenged these theoretical models. Johnson (1992) offered sociohistorical arguments that cities are not necessarily dangerous or highly criminal-prone environments. After investigating rural-urban differences in crime during the late nineteenth and early twentieth centuries in Germany, he concluded that the influence of factors such as the size of the urban population, population density, and population growth was low (sometimes even negative), whereas the percentage of ethnic minorities and death and poverty rates correlated strongly with the level of crime.

Long-term historical research on violent crime (Spierenburg 1996; Eisner 2003) supported Johnson's analysis. Historical data showed that (violent) crime levels in the Netherlands (Spierenburg 1996) and in Europe more generally (Eisner 2003) have declined since the Middle Ages despite urbanization over the centuries. That is why Eisner strongly advocated the ideas of the sociologist Norbert Elias (1976), who argued that long-term processes over centuries are responsible for increasing levels of self-control in the population. These changes resulted in the internalization of social control and the pacification of interactions in public places that in turn produced fewer violent crimes. Crime data from different countries fit Elias's theory, but a solid test of it is still lacking in Dutch criminology (Eisner 2003).

The growing urbanization in the Netherlands in the nineteenth and twentieth centuries[1] received little theoretical or empirical attention from Dutch criminologists. The reason for this is unknown but may have to do with difficulty getting access to historical crime data and with the assumption that the Netherlands is so densely populated and highly urbanized that there are no important differences in crime between cities and rural areas. In the years before and after the Second World War (1930–50), only a few studies on urbanization and crime or criminals were carried out. Most were predominantly descriptive and in line with mainstream Dutch sociology of these days (sociography). Kempe and Vermaat (1938) investigated the distribution of crimes in Drenthe, one of the most sparsely populated and rural provinces, situated in the northeast. They studied the crime statistics of Drenthe for the years 1920–34, analyzed official files of entire families, and interviewed those families and key figures in local communities. Although the overall level of crime was relatively low compared with other parts of the country, in the rural areas violent crimes were more common: "the aggressive criminality is the ordinary criminality of the people . . . . It is there that even various popular customs encourage the aggressive criminality" (p. 155). "Economic" crimes (we would call them property crimes) were more prevalent in the three municipalities

---

[1] The Netherlands is one of the highest densely populated countries in the world (479 per square kilometer) and one of the most urbanized. In the last fifty years of the twentieth century, the Dutch population increased from 10 million to more than 16 million people. Of those, 16.3 million Dutch men and women, about 5 percent, live in small villages with fewer than 5,000 people, 25 percent in small towns between 5,000 and 50,000, and more than 70 percent in cities over 50,000 (of whom nearly 10 percent live in the four largest cities in the western Netherlands).

of the province. Property crime offenders were characterized by illiteracy, illegitimacy, alcoholism, and recidivism. Most were young, unmarried men with irregular jobs. As was taken for granted those days, the authors predicted that when "urban civilization" penetrated deeper into the rural areas, the extent of violent crime would decrease and the number of property crimes would increase. The considerable amount of violent crimes could be explained partly by old popular morals favoring violence as a means of conflict solution that "were considered as laws not a very long time ago and are still kept up by many" (p. 156). Kempe and Verlaat also observed that small houses and bad housing conditions contributed to a relatively high number of sex crimes and low levels of sexual morality with many promiscuous relationships within and across families.

More than a decade later, van Rooy (1949) demonstrated that the amount of property crimes is relatively higher in larger municipalities, whereas personal crimes such as violence were more present in rural areas. He attributed these differences between cities (especially Nijmegen) and rural areas to processes of loosening traditional and personal ties within communities in larger cities. He argued that the informal social controls of rural areas were not as effective as in municipalities. The theoretical influence of Durkheim's theories is manifest. The prevalence of more violence in rural areas was argued to result from families living together in relative isolation, which was an important breeding ground for personal conflicts and tensions. Van Rooy predicted that differences in crime rates between rural and urbanized areas would diminish over time as they came to resemble each other more.

A famous early study was executed by Willem Nagel, a PhD student, who later became professor of criminology at Leiden University. He studied crime in the small city of Oss, located in the eastern part of the Netherlands (Nagel 1949). He described the history of Oss, the exploitation of its population by a dominating and powerful meat factory, and factors responsible for increasingly high crime rates (including violence) from 1899 through the 1940s. He studied the economic, social, and cultural causes of crime and effects of alcoholism. Consistent with the theories of Durkheim and Wirth, Nagel concluded that a speedy transition from a rural to an industrial society had sharpened conflicts between people: for Nagel those conflicts were the breeding ground of all kinds of crime. In contrast to other early Dutch research,

Nagel did not find a low level of violent crimes in the city of Oss compared with the surrounding rural areas.[2]

The research presented thus far indicated that a relationship between urbanization and crime might exist in the Netherlands, but that relationship needs to be explored empirically with more solid data.

As can be observed in table 1,[3] there is a relationship between recorded crime[4] and the level of urbanization in the Netherlands in the ten years of data shown: the higher the level of urbanization, the more crime. The police figures differ significantly between small towns and large cities: yearly about 4,500 crimes per 100,000 inhabitants were recorded in 1995–2004 in more rural areas, villages, and towns up to 20,000 inhabitants. In cities with more than 100,000 inhabitants, the number of recorded crimes is 12,000 per year, and in the four largest cities the annual number is about 16,000. These numbers imply that the large cities confronted about four times more crimes than the rural areas did. Although the period 1995–2004 is relatively short, the differences in recorded crimes per 100,000 residents among the different levels of urbanization were relatively stable. The unequal distribution of crimes across the country is consistent with the expectations of urbanization theory.

Past research on urbanization and crime in the Netherlands found that in rural areas violent crimes were more common and in urban environments property crimes were more predominant. Recent official data on violent and property crimes[5] do not confirm this distribution of the two types of crimes in modern society. In the four largest cities, the numbers of violent *and* property crimes are roughly five times higher than in rural areas. Smaller urban environments also show relatively higher violent and property crime numbers.

One of the few recent geographical studies on the relationship between urbanization and homicide supported these figures (Nieuwbeerta

---

[2] Oss was an atypical town because of its history and the composition of its population. The lack of comparable urban studies, however, prevents a generalization of Nagel's findings.

[3] For this paper the data have been collected from different sources. Only data after 1995 were available on this subject.

[4] By recorded crimes is meant all crimes that became known to the police in that year by reporting of civilians and organizations or by police investigation.

[5] According to the definitions of Bureau Statistics Netherlands, *violent* crimes consist of rape, sexual assault, and other sexual offenses; theft with violence; extortion; assault; manslaughter; and homicide. Under *property* crimes are all kinds of theft, burglary and breaking and entering, embezzlement, forgery, and fencing (Eggen and van der Heide 2005).

TABLE 1

Recorded Total Violent and Property Crimes per 100,000 Inhabitants 12–79 Years Old by Level of Urbanization (1995–2004)

Year	< 20,000	20,000–50,000	50,000–100,000	> 100,000	Four Largest Cities
			Urbanization		
			All Crimes		
1995	4,343	6,339	9,471	11,725	15,802
1996	4,366	6,350	9,299	11,446	14,289
1997	4,449	6,350	9,299	11,611	15,538
1998	4,441	6,084	9,311	11,692	15,377
1999	4,350	6,133	9,350	11,727	17,082
2000	4,325	6,208	9,430	12,316	16,687
2001	4,650	6,295	9,240	12,339	17,691
2002	4,935	6,482	9,518	12,839	18,214
2003	4,885	6,363	9,141	12,393	17,345
2004	4,908	6,501	8,955	11,652	15,794
			Violent Crimes		
1995	190	274	465	588	1,045
1996	202	302	495	629	1,005
1997	254	342	529	712	1,065
1998	266	353	550	694	1,109
1999	286	380	582	768	1,304
2000	276	388	607	841	1,332
2001	327	429	628	902	1,501
2002	347	462	667	968	1,590
2003	354	458	678	1,001	1,579
2004	384	502	707	1,018	1,563
			Property Crimes		
1995	2,990	4,428	6,772	8,700	12,397
1996	2,866	4,190	6,441	8,140	10,687
1997	2,794	4,064	6,218	8,122	11,502
1998	2,703	3,800	6,145	8,296	11,427
1999	2,734	3,787	6,068	8,176	12,432
2000	2,611	3,832	6,120	8,536	12,185
2001	2,764	3,865	5,932	8,541	12,859
2002	2,908	3,915	6,042	8,695	12,979
2003	2,797	3,788	5,716	8,174	12,016
2004	2,755	3,793	5,442	7,414	10,458

SOURCE.—Eggen and van der Heide (2005, p. 353).

and Deerenberg 2005). The researchers analyzed for ten years the data on all 1,956 homicide victims[6] who lived in the Netherlands (homicides of tourists or illegal residents are left out). The researchers used a standardized mortality rate (SMR) to control for the effects of differences in the populations. In the SMR measure, the observed number of homicides per 100,000 in a certain geographical area is divided by the predicted number of homicides per 100,000. In the period between 1995 and 2004, homicides were rare phenomena in rural areas and were concentrated in the largest cities. Citizens of Amsterdam had a 2.56 higher chance of being killed (considering the number of inhabitants and the composition of the population) than others in the Netherlands. Living in the western part of the country or in the four largest cities in general increased one's chance of being killed. Surprisingly, the highest SMRs were observed in three small municipalities (Diemen, Weesp, and Haarlemmerliede) near Amsterdam. The residents of these villages had a three times higher chance of being killed.

Recent police research points at higher levels of urbanization correlating with higher numbers of official recorded offenders per 10,000 inhabitants (van Tilburg, Boerman, and Prins 2002, 2004). Analyses of police records revealed that yearly about 10 percent of all suspects can be labeled as chronic offenders (Grapendaal and van Tilburg 2002). The police researchers differentiated between three types of offenders: *first* offenders (only one crime), *frequent* offenders (from two to eleven crimes in their career), and *chronic* offenders (more than eleven crimes in their career). Almost 60 percent of all chronic offenders were known as drug addicts. Although the national average of chronic offenders was nearly 11 percent, in rural areas (fewer than 5,000 inhabitants) only 3 percent of the offender population could be labeled as such; in the four largest cities, the percentage is 16. In cities with more than 100,000 inhabitants, the percentage of chronic offenders was higher than the national average. In the four largest cities, this category of a relatively small number of offenders was estimated to be responsible for about 20 percent of *all* police arrests in one year (Grapendaal and van Tilburg 2002).

Crime is not the only problem. Sometimes people feel unsafe or perceive their environment as uncomfortable or threatening. In table 2, findings of the Politiemonitor Bevolking of 2004 on these issues are

---

[6] In the Netherlands, the yearly average of homicides committed in the ten years is about 240; that is 1.47 homicides per 100,000 inhabitants.

TABLE 2

Feelings of Insecurity, Perceptions of Troubles, and Physical
Deterioration in One's Own Neighborhood by Level of
Urbanization in 2004

	Number of Inhabitants				
	< 20,000	20,000–50,000	50,000–100,000	> 100,000	Four Largest Cities
% feeling unsafe	19.9	19.9	30.1	30.9	38.9
Trouble (1–10)	1.9	1.9	2.1	2.2	2.6
Physical (1–10)	3.1	3.2	3.6	3.6	4.0

SOURCE.—Ministerie van BZK (2004).
NOTE.—*Insecurity feelings*: measured by feeling unsafe once. *Trouble in neighborhood*: measured by young people hanging around, drunken people in the street, being annoyed, and drugs and addicts present (mean score of 1–10 much). *Physical deterioration*: measured by presence of graffiti, dirt on the street, dog dirt on the pavements, and vandalism of public facilities (mean score of 1–10 much).

presented by the level of urbanization (Ministerie van BZK 2004). Relatively more people living in more urbanized areas felt themselves often unsafe (38.9 percent) than residents of villages or municipalities with fewer than 20,000 inhabitants (19.9 percent). In rural areas and in small towns the percentages of people "feeling unsafe once in a while" increased steadily in the past twelve years, whereas in cities with a population of more than 100,000 (including the largest), these percentages decreased (Ministerie van BZK 2004).

There were, however, only minor differences in people's perceptions of their surroundings. Dutch people generally do not believe they live in areas that can be characterized as seriously in trouble or physically deteriorated. The low scores on both scales indicated general satisfaction about living conditions. People of all levels of urbanization reported in 2003 less trouble and deterioration in their own neighborhoods since 1995 (Ministerie van BZK 2004).Within this small range of variation, people living in villages or small towns experienced the least serious trouble or physical deterioration. People in the country also reported less often avoiding activities as a consequence of feelings of unsafety than people in urban settings. Recent governmental research indicates that perceptions of a comparatively idyllic country life remain present despite all societal changes (SCP 2006). Most people living there felt themselves healthier, safer, and more involved in the community and had larger houses and more space than those living in urban environments. Residents of rural areas were willing to travel greater distances for shopping, recreation, or medical and social services. In these living conditions, crime and feelings of unsafety do not play an important role in daily life.

In this section I have discussed urbanization and crime. Before and after the Second World War, little criminological research was executed on differences in crime between rural and urban areas. Criminologists were handicapped by a lack of solid data on crime and related phenomena. The research revealed significant differences in crime rates that matched with the expectations of urbanization theories of Clinard (1942) and others (Rephann 1999). Although often not explicitly mentioned, Durkheim's ideas were present in every study in presenting and examining the data. Wirth's (1964) ideas implicitly guided the rare empirical research. Loosening ties, less informal social control, and less social integration were considered causal factors of higher crime rates in urban environments. Dutch research indicated that factors such as a high degree of social cohesion, a high level of informal social control, low offender rates, and a less vulnerable and well-ordered physical surrounding were responsible for the lower crime rates in rural areas (SCP 2004). However, all these theoretical suggestions are a posteriori explanations that should be properly tested.

One striking finding in early Dutch research was that violent crimes were more common in rural areas and property crimes were more typical in urban settings. That is no longer true. Higher rates of violent and property crimes, higher victimization rates, and greater feelings of insecurity are more frequently present in urban areas than in rural ones. Higher numbers of offenders live in cities, and chronic offenders are more active in urban settings. Estimates by the Dutch police demonstrate that this small group of chronic offenders can be held responsible for more than 20 percent of all arrests in cities every year.

II. Urban Crime

Crime rates are not evenly distributed over geographical areas in urban settings. Some neighborhoods are more troubled by crime, and even within neighborhoods there are considerable differences between areas as a result of subtle interplays between physical characteristics and people's behaviors. The early Chicago school of sociology stimulated the study of concentrations of crimes in cities all over the world (Park and

Burgess 1967). Burgess (1967) introduced the idea that a city can be ecologically divided into concentric zones with varying crime rates. The highest crime rates were in the transitional zones surrounding business centers. Shaw and McKay (1942) emphasized the process of social disorganization that leads to concentrations of crime. Poverty, residential mobility, ethnic heterogeneity, bad housing, and weak social relations indicating disorganization do not allow stable communities in neighborhoods. After several years of decline, they suggested, a greater number of offenders will settle in such neighborhoods, and this in turn explains the neighborhood's higher crime rates. Their successors have searched for other structural factors to explain differences in crime rates between neighborhoods (van der Voordt and van Wegen 1991; Bursik and Grasmick 1993). The structure and working of (public) housing markets in European cities play a decisive role (Baldwin and Bottoms 1976; Bottoms and Wiles 2002).

The concept of social disorganization has been further elaborated in recent decades (Kubrin and Weitzer 2003). Sampson and Groves (1989) concentrated on the behavioral mechanisms caused by social disorganization. They argued that social disorganization is related to the capacity of a community to carry out (informal) social control on criminal behavior (for instance, the capacity to supervise adolescents [in peer groups] and to exercise better guardianship, such as by recognizing strangers in the neighborhood). Later, Sampson and his colleagues introduced the concept of collective efficacy that integrates and explains the relationships between neighborhood characteristics and crime (Sampson, Raudenbush, and Earls 1997; Morenoff, Sampson, and Raudenbush 2001). The capacity of the neighborhood to organize social cohesion is a precondition for informal social control (Wikström and Dolmén 2001; Wikström and Sampson 2003).

Recent geographical research focuses on the physical properties of specific locations in streets, street corners, squares, and (parts of) entertainment or shopping areas that attract offenders (Brantingham and Brantingham 1991, 1999; Eck and Weisburd 1995; Goeminne, Enhus, and Ponsaers 2003). These properties may be the styles of building, the kind of buildings, the presence of green areas, the street plan, and the presence of physical and social barriers that direct and hinder people in their movement (De Poot et al. 2005). Besides these things, ease of access and attractiveness of spending time there are important considerations for avoiding, crossing, visiting, or staying at a location. Hot spots can vary with the kind of crime, and some hot spots (shopping areas) attract several types of crimes simultaneously.

Dutch geographical research roughly reflects the international research agenda, albeit with time lags. This section is organized as follows. First a description of Dutch cities is presented combined with results of existing qualitative city studies on crime. The rationale is that cities cannot be described only by analytic variables but also by descriptions of urban life in which crime, criminals, and victims play parts. Then, crime-mapping studies on crime places are presented, including some on spatial displacement. Next, research on structural characteristics of neighborhoods reflecting social disorganization is discussed. Finally, a few recent Dutch theory tests on social disorganization, social control, and collective efficacy are discussed.

A. Dutch Cities

As in most European countries, cities in the Netherlands have a long history going back to the beginning of the first century (Maastricht was founded in AD 10, Utrecht in 50, and Nijmegen in 104). Most cities originated in the twelfth and thirteenth centuries.[7] Urbanization accelerated in the nineteenth century because of industrialization. New houses were built around the old centers of settlements. People moved from rural areas to the expanded cities to find jobs in factories. New neighborhoods with cheap housing were built by local governments in the late 1880s and 1890s to accommodate poorly educated and uneducated newcomers. After World War II, a second acceleration in urbanization took place. As a result of reduced need for agricultural workers, coupled with economic growth, and attracted by new jobs and prosperity, rural residents settled in cities. Many blocks of flats with small apartments were hastily built in areas next to the older parts of the cities in the 1950s and the 1960s. Housing was not subjected to the free market because most of the people could not afford a private house. Most neighborhoods in the expanding Dutch cities were planned on the drawing tables of local government authorities.

A third phase in urbanization took place in the 1970s to 1990s. Many people from Mediterranean countries (Morocco, Turkey) and from former colonies (Surinam, Antilles) came to Holland and settled in the

---

[7] With the exception of Almere, which was founded formally in 1984 and built on reclaimed land from the sea. The population increased from zero in 1975 to 170,000 in thirty years.

cities. In the beginning, men arrived alone to find jobs. A decade later their wives and children joined them, allowed by new legislation. Contemporary Dutch cities can be labeled as multicultural with large minority groups (especially Moroccan and Turkish) and with hundreds of other nationalities. Minorities make up about 10 percent of the national population but are concentrated in the larger cities. In Amsterdam about 34 percent of the population consists of ethnic and other minorities; in The Hague, 31 percent; and in Rotterdam, almost 35 percent. Only Utrecht has a relatively low percentage (20.4 percent) of ethnic minorities. Smaller cities have fewer minority residents mainly because of a lack of employment opportunities in the 1960s and 1970s. The tensions between ethnic minorities (especially the Islamic ones) and the original Dutch inhabitants in the cities have become more visible and more pronounced after 9/11 and the killings of two famous Dutch men (a popular politician and a movie director).

Globalization will further change the character of Dutch cities. Religion, for instance, was almost invisible in Dutch cities (many Protestant and Catholic churches were closed), but mosques are being built in several, mainly relatively poor, neighborhoods to serve the increasing numbers of (traditional) Moslems. Despite the high level of urbanization in the Netherlands, there are no metropolises with millions of citizens as in other countries.

The infrastructures of the cities reflect these three phases of urbanization. The older neighborhoods in proximity to the centers mostly originated in the late eighteenth and nineteenth centuries and were partially restored in the 1980s. In these neighborhoods, public housing is the most important instrument of local government for accommodating people who cannot afford private housing. In the suburbs of cities, three types of neighborhoods emerged beginning in the 1960s. In some suburbs, single-family houses have been built (under a mixture of public and private ownership). In others, single houses and villas were built. In the third kind of suburbs, large blocks of apartments were built with few recreational facilities. Those in the last category deteriorate quickly and steadily, with middle-class people leaving and more deprived people moving in. A relatively recent phenomenon in Dutch cities is that some older neighborhoods near the city centers are now "hot," and houses being sold by the large housing agencies are bought up and renovated by well-to-do people or by double-income couples without or with very young children.

TABLE 3

Characteristics of Cities with More than 100,000 Inhabitants.

Cities	Inhabitants 1/1/04	Houses per Hectare	Population per Hectare	Percentage Non-Western	Percentage One-Person Household
Amsterdam	739,104	17.3	33.7	33.9	55.2
Rotterdam	598,923	9.4	19.7	34.6	47.7
The Hague	469,059	23.2	47.8	31.2	48.4
Utrecht	270,244	11.8	27.2	20.4	52.0
Eindhoven	207,870	10.5	23.4	14.4	43.1
Tilburg	198,767	7.0	16.7	13.3	39.7
Groningen	179,185	9.9	21.4	8.9	56.4
Almere	170,704	2.7	6.9	23.1	26.7
Breda	166,035	5.6	12.9	9.9	37.7
Nijmegen	157,466	11.5	20.7	12.0	50.6
Apeldoorn	156,000	1.9	4.8	6.8	32.1
Enschede	152,989	4.5	10.7	13.9	41.5
Haarlem	147,343	20.9	45.9	12.3	43.7
Arnhem	141,601	6.3	13.9	16.7	45.0
Zaanstad	139,774	7.2	16.8	14.8	32.0
's-Hertogenbosch	133,511	6.3	14.6	9.8	37.0
Amersfoort	132,851	8.6	20.8	13.1	34.9
Haarlemmermeer	127,750	2.8	6.9	9.8	26.7
Maastricht	122,183	9.2	20.3	7.1	45.6
Dordrecht	119,649	5.3	12.0	16.3	36.0
Leiden	118,702	21.8	51.3	13.8	50.8
Zoetermeer	114,216	12.9	30.8	14.4	29.7
Zwolle	110,880	4.0	9.3	8.2	38.7
Emmen	108,354	1.3	3.1	3.5	28.3
Ede	105,495	1.2	3.3	6.7	30.0
The Netherlands	16,258,032	1.6	3.9	10.3	34.4

SOURCE.—Web site Bureau Statistics Netherlands.

Table 3 presents statistical characteristics of the twenty-five largest Dutch cities above 100,000. The numbers of inhabitants are rather equally distributed over the cities: Amsterdam is the largest (739,000). The smallest is Ede, situated in the middle of the Netherlands, with a population of 105,000. The big four (each with more than 250,000), as they are called, are Amsterdam, Rotterdam, The Hague, and Utrecht, all in the western part of the country.

There are differences in population density among the twenty-five, even among the four largest. Leiden, The Hague, and Haarlem have the highest population density per hectare. Apeldoorn, Maastricht, and

Almere are less crowded, and citizens in the smallest cities such as Emmen and Ede have the most living space.

The centers are much the same in all Dutch cities. They date from former times (mostly centuries ago) with a mixture of traditional and modern buildings. Streets have irregular forms and are full of shops, bars, and restaurants. Most of the centers are accessible only to pedestrians or bicyclists, and ways through for cars are hard to find. In many cities, canals control the level of groundwater (about 60 percent of the Netherlands is below sea level). Traditional markets are held once or twice a week in or near the city center. Dutch centers are not business districts as in the United States: offices and small businesses are scattered around. Most of the larger business enterprises have moved to industrial and business areas outside the cities near highways. The geographical structure of Dutch cities is almost completely planned by the governments (except for the old centers). In the last twenty-five years of the twentieth century, the Netherlands designed and developed two new cities on land reclaimed from the sea.

Every city has its own comprehensive public transportation system—bus, streetcar, or subway (only in Amsterdam and Rotterdam). Local policy aims at keeping cars out of the centers. Most neighborhoods have a (small) mall for daily shopping. Elementary schools are situated in all neighborhoods, high schools in only a limited number.

Despite governmental efforts to avoid having neighborhoods with economic drawbacks, every city has deprived areas with concentrations of social problems. The differences between neighborhoods are not as extreme as in the United States or in Asia, but borders between neighborhoods function as social barriers for interaction and for local networks (De Poot et al. 2005). It cannot be denied that Dutch cities have a class structure (Brunt 1996; van Beckhoven and van Kempen 2002). People with low incomes are forced to live in more deprived neighborhoods, where relatively cheap public housing is available. Those with higher incomes live in neighborhoods with more luxurious, private houses. Otherwise, people tend also to cluster together for reasons of lifestyle and ethnicity (De Poot et al. 2005). Ethnic minorities like to live in neighborhoods in which neighbors speak their language and share their norms, values, and beliefs and in which they can find support if necessary. Van der Laan (2004) found that residential-spatial segregation of ethnic minorities decreases contacts of ethnic minority people with native inhabitants. She demonstrated a strong relationship between the statistical likelihood of meeting natives and actual contacts of ethnic minorities with indigenous people.

However, not only immigrants tend to cluster together. People in general look for neighborhoods to settle in where they can find people with a comparable lifestyle. The way neighbors dress, the kind of cars they drive, the language they speak, and the kind of houses in the neighborhoods make people feel at home and comfortable in certain neighborhoods (van Beckhoven and van Kempen 2002). All these factors constitute social barriers between neighborhoods. Despite the class structure, there are no slums in Dutch cities, and there are no no-go areas in which police do not dare to show themselves (Fijnaut et al. 1998).

The composition of the populations of the larger Dutch cities is quite comparable: many inhabitants are young (20–30 percent under twenty-four years old), live in one-person households (35–45 percent), are dependent on social welfare (varying from forty to 120 per 1,000 residents) or on scholarships, are above-average unemployed (more than 6 percent), and have a below-average income (25,000 euros). Many but not all larger cities contain a university or a college, which explains the presence of large numbers of young citizens, the high number of one-person households, and the high percentages with low incomes. During recent decades, many young, wealthier families with children left the cities to settle in smaller towns (20,000–50,000 inhabitants) close by in the same region. The older people (age sixty-five and up) stayed behind. Both patterns imply that cities became poorer and more age-segregated in the last twenty years. Residential mobility varies from 10 to 15 percent each year depending on the neighborhood.

One of the characteristics of a megalopolis in the world is that everyday activities continue during the night in a twenty-four-hour economy. In Holland, that is only partly true (Brunt 1996). Nightlife is concentrated in city centers and ends about two or four o'clock in the morning (depending on local policy), and most shops close at six in the evening (only a few remain open until nine or ten). Estimates of homeless people in the Netherlands (including drug addicts, alcoholics, and psychiatric patients) are about 28,000, of whom 6,000 are under eighteen. Most live in the four largest cities, where they have a greater chance of surviving and experience greater tolerance and less social control.

Cities are also characterized and colored by the extent and nature of their crime, criminal infrastructure, vices, and drug markets (Mayhew [1851] 1950; Groen 1962; Park 1967; Haller 1971; Brunt 1996). These phenomena can emerge in larger quantities and qualities only in cities (Wirth 1964). Most citizens are not aware of the presence of organized crime and a vivid drug trade in their city; nevertheless, they have a negative impact on social safety in a city (Bruinsma and van de Bunt 1996; Fijnaut et al. 1998; Kleemans, Brienen, and van de Bunt 2002). Although most organized crime in the Netherlands centers on transnational trade in drugs and other illegal goods, criminal groups have their local bases in cities, and therefore their presence has local consequences (see Kleemans, in this volume). Smuggling goods and persons demands logistical facilities, such as transportation, storage, communication, financing, and labor. Organized crime makes use of the existing legal and spatial structure in cities for criminal activities. Cities such as Amsterdam can be seen as marketplaces in which demand and supply merge, people meet each other in different places, and an excellent infrastructure for distribution of illegal goods exists (Huisman, Huikeshoven, and van de Bunt 2003; Bernasco, Bruinsma, and Huisman 2004). This infrastructure is not unique to the capital city but exists in different qualities and quantities in most Dutch cities (Bruinsma and van de Bunt 1996; Zaitch 2001, 2002; Blickman et al. 2003). Members of organized crime groups live in cities, have their properties there, and have their families and friends around them. There they can find the people to do jobs for them, and there they have formal and informal contacts with local businesses and social and governmental circles. Criminals not only passively look for opportunities to commit crimes, but also are active in establishing a criminal infrastructure facilitating their criminal activities (Klerks and Kop 2004). This encompasses the physical locations and the social structure of the city: locations to meet other criminals (bars, railway stations, hotels, restaurants, and parking places) that are easy to reach to look for cops or unwanted criminal pursuers, to store drugs or money, and to hide people. These locations are elements of illegal constructions but also synergies with legal businesses.

A "facilitating industry" has emerged in Dutch cities consisting of local property companies, car rental agencies, transport companies, real estate brokers, travel agencies, money transfer and exchange offices, administrative offices, financial advisors, and suppliers of chemicals and tablet machines. That explains why, for instance, Ecstacy laboratories are situated in the middles of cities and not in commercial areas or in the country (Blickman et al. 2003; Bernasco, Bruinsma, and Huisman 2004). The criminal infrastructure in cities takes care of the connections of all kinds of offenders. It facilitates the social and economic organization of illegal markets in which a distribution network operates day and night by all kinds of offenders who play their roles and earn money in accordance with their roles.

The criminal infrastructure of cities is not the same as racketeering (Bruinsma and Bovenkerk 1996; Klerks and Kop 2004). Empirical research makes clear that Dutch cities experience hardly any of the racketeering practices that occur elsewhere in the world (Bruinsma and van de Bunt 1996; Fijnaut and Bovenkerk 1996; Fijnaut et al. 1998; Kleemans, Brienen, and van de Bunt 2002), although recent police reports point at systematic extortion of real estate brokers by organized criminals. Economic systems in cities such as the construction industry, the automobile sector, the toxic waste disposal industry, or the garment industry are not systematically under the control of organized crime through use of violence, extortion, and protection. Hotels, restaurants, nightclubs, and bars are in parts of cities in which organized crime patterns go beyond facilitating criminal activities (Bruinsma and Bovenkerk 1996; Fijnaut et al. 1998; Bruinsma 1999*a*).

Although criminal groups are increasingly becoming ethnically mixed, ethnic lines predominate. As a consequence, in ethnic communities a portion of the youngsters (Pennings, Bruinsma, and Weerman 2006) and parts of local business assist organized crime (Fijnaut and Bovenkerk 1996). Money that has been earned in the drug trade was taken to the home countries in the past, but more recently it is often invested in Dutch real estate, the catering industry, and transport companies (Meloen et al. 2003). Investments by criminals in particular neighborhoods and economic activities have serious consequences for economic and social relations in those neighborhoods (Bruinsma and van de Bunt 1996; Fijnaut and Bovenkerk 1996). Successful criminals can attract young, less privileged adolescents in these neighborhoods to start a career in crime (Bruinsma 1999*a*; Pennings, Bruinsma, and Weerman 2006). Bovenkerk and Hogewind (2003) pointed at the large-scale exploitation of the cultivation of marijuana in many houses in particular neighborhoods in cities under the direction of criminal groups. They observed a flourishing cannabis economic system in cities with interwoven relationships between grow shops, coffee shops, and professional and house growers of high-quality Dutch cannabis (see Buruma, in this volume). By *gedogen* of growing of four ornamental plants in each house by law, in certain neighborhoods a great number of families and houses are involved in the soft-drug culture with unavoidable relations with "coffee shops" and organized crime. Business-like growing also takes place in cities accompanied by diverse protection and cover-up activities. In small Dutch cities, similar patterns were observed (Bruinsma 1999*a*; Klerks and Kop 2004).

In Dutch cities, all kinds of drugs can be delivered to anyone who wants them. The daily trade is on the streets, in houses, in railway stations, and in other public places (Kaal and Korf 2003). The presence of large-scale drug-trading groups benefits the use and the streetwise trade in drugs at a relatively low price. Both the use and the street trade can be seen as the capillaries of the transnational drug trade. Drug addicts live in city centers and have a hard time in a very hectic life: "constantly on the lookout for customers, for good dope, or for an opportunity to make money. Moreover, they have to avoid a large police presence as much as possible. For these active participants in the world of drugs, being an addict is more than a full-time job" (Grapendaal, Leuw, and Nelen 1995, p. 97). Most drug addicts need to commit acquisitive crimes to afford their drug use.[8] Most are frequent or chronic offenders concentrating their activities in or near the city center.

The red-light districts of Amsterdam, Arnhem, and The Hague have long been famous throughout the world (Stachhouwer 1950). Behind this image, a world of exploitation exists in which criminals are in charge and earn most of the money. Dutch criminal law that forbids the organization of prostitution was repealed in 2000. Since then, the prostitution sector drifted in two directions: in a nationwide legal sex industry of about 800 companies controlled by administrative and local governmental laws and in an illegal, fragmented underground industry in which prostitutes work in bars, hotels, ordinary apartments, or parking places or in low-end escort services. The second sector is dominated by criminals. Women and men are forced to hustle in the streets, bars, and newly established erotic cafes. This parallel unregulated sec-

---

[8] It must be stressed, however, that self-report research among addicts shows that property crimes constitute only a fraction of the money needed for acquiring their drugs (van der Poel et al. 2003).

tor paradoxically attracts autonomous, self-assured Dutch prostitutes who want their earnings untaxed and to determine their own hours of work. Since the new brothel law of 2000, the trafficking of women from eastern Europe is increasingly in the hands of organized criminals of different nationalities, among them Albanian and Serbian criminals (Nationaal Rapporteur Mensenhandel 2002). Together with their victims, they settle more or less permanently in Dutch cities.

B. Crime Places

Jan Fiselier was one of the pioneers of the revival in empirical geographical research on crime in the Netherlands when he studied the distribution of crime across the city of Nijmegen in the 1960s (Fiselier 1968). He demonstrated that official crime rates in the city center and the surrounding neighborhoods were higher than in other parts of the city. In the center, burglaries and breaking and entering cars were the most common crimes, along with—not surprisingly, as the main shopping area—shoplifting. The suburbs of Nijmegen showed the lowest numbers of crimes. Subsequent research supported his findings. Hesseling (1987) reported that 40 percent of all crimes in Utrecht were committed in the city center and five surrounding neighborhoods. Breaking and entering cars was the most frequently reported crime in the center (shoplifting was not included in his data). Rovers (1996) observed comparable geographical concentrations in Rotterdam for the years 1990–94. He also analyzed police data on juveniles and studied several aspects of the geographical distribution of crime places in general. He observed higher rates for all types of crime in the city center and its surrounding neighborhoods. More burglaries, thefts from and out of cars, and violent robberies were reported there than elsewhere in the city. His study also made clear that the greater the distance of a neighborhood from the city center, the less crime there was. Rovers also reported stable but uneven distributions of violent and property crimes across neighborhoods. Destruction of property, however, was more equally distributed across neighborhoods. The explanation was that juvenile crimes, especially destruction of property, were more concentrated in their own living areas.

In 1996, Fijnaut, Bovenkerk, Bruinsma, and van de Bunt, among other reports, published four reports on organized crime in four cities for the Parliamentary Inquiry Committee (Bruinsma and van de Bunt 1996; Fijnaut and Bovenkerk 1996). They studied the organized crime problem in Amsterdam, Arnhem, Nijmegen, and Enschede in connection with general crime problems. In all four, the distribution of official crime rates across neighborhoods was systematically skewed and quite persistent over time. Most crimes were committed in the city centers and their surrounding neighborhoods.

Musterd, Oostendorf, and Deurloo (2004) replicated this finding eight years later for Amsterdam. However, when they controlled for the type of crime, a more distinct picture of the distribution emerged. Higher numbers of breaking and entering cars occurred at parking places situated all over the city (hot spots). Purse snatching and bicycle theft were typical center crimes, whereas car theft occurred more often in the suburbs. Burglaries were also more decentralized.

Bruinsma (1999a) presented a more detailed description of all kinds of crime (including organized crime and corporate crime) in the Twente police region with an emphasis on the cities of Almelo, Hengelo, and Enschede. The smallest of the three largest cities in the region (Almelo) had the highest crime rate per 10,000 inhabitants. There were considerable differences in crime rates across neighborhoods in the three cities for all types of crime. After the centers, the deprived neighborhoods close to the city center had the highest crime rates of all areas of the region. But even in these neighborhoods crime was not evenly distributed. In each, certain streets and locations could be labeled as hot spots. And these hot spots persisted for years.

This remarkable stability in crime hot spots was also demonstrated over a longer period. Decades after van Rooy (1949) and Fiselier (1968), van Wijngaarden and Boerman (1997) reported almost a replication of their findings in the city of Nijmegen. They were struck that the same neighborhoods surrounding the center showed the highest crime rates. Several generations of criminologists thus demonstrated great stability in crime places in this city. Although they differed in strategy and methodology and all used imperfect police data, their conclusions were strikingly similar: in all these years (1924–95) the hot spots were at the same locations. This is more striking given that all kinds of policy measures have been implemented in these neighborhoods for decades and that large parts of their populations had been replaced by others. New houses, renovation and restoration, financial support, and diverse social policies had altered these problematic neighborhoods (for an alternative explanation, see Stark [1987]).

Geographical criminology also suggests that crime is concentrated near or within public transport facilities (Brantingham and Brantingham 1991). In the Netherlands, there exists no special research on this topic. Most railway and bus stations are, however, part of the city center and contribute to the high crime rates there. Hauber (1977) reported robberies, vandalism, purse snatching, and thefts of luggage as the most common crimes in buses, trains, and subways and in and around railway and bus stations.

These studies indicated that the type of crime may have something to do with the crime location. Kleemans (1996) observed that the chance of being burglarized in the city of Enschede is highest in neighborhoods close to the center and not in the center itself. His study observed the familiar pattern that this chance decreased the greater the distance between the neighborhood and the center. His results matched those in Sheffield (Baldwin and Bottoms 1976). Kleemans attributed the concentrations in residential burglaries to the greater numbers of offenders living in those neighborhoods or their vicinity. Bernasco and Luykx (2002) divided ninety-four neighborhoods in The Hague into seven more or less equal concentric zones and plotted in each neighborhood the risk of being burglarized per 100 houses in the years between 1996 and 2000. The results of their study are presented in figure 1.

The darkest part of the map corresponding with the highest chance of being burglarized contains the center and its surrounding neighborhoods. Shopping and entertainment areas and the two main railway stations are there. Research by Kleemans (1996) and Bernasco and Luykx (2002) demonstrated that Burgess's concentric zone model describes the distribution of residential burglaries in Dutch cities.[9]

Van Wijk and Ferweda (1998) analyzed police data on 152 street robberies and ninety-seven cases of bag snatchings in Tilburg and concluded that 41 percent of street robberies and 46 percent of bag snatchings were committed in the city center, mostly during evening hours. These crimes were also more frequently committed on roads leading to the center from the living areas. Nieuwbeerta and Deerenberg (2005) examined all 1,956 Dutch homicides over ten years (1995–2004) and concluded that the size of the city is an important factor for the geographical distribution of homicides in neighborhoods. In cities with

---

[9] Two neighborhoods seem to deviate from the general pattern. The authors hypothesize that both neighborhoods were in transition periods when newcomers were settling in newly built or renovated houses.

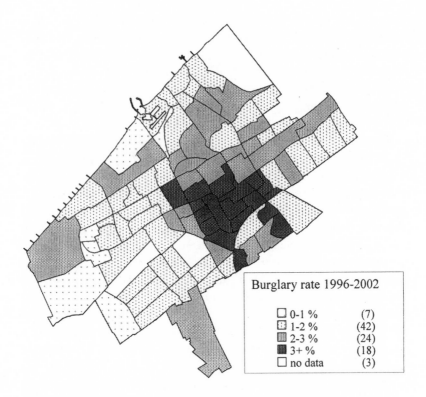

FIG. 1.—Burglary rates in neighborhoods, The Hague, 1996–2000. Source: Bernasco and Luykx (2002, p. 239).

fewer than 50,000 inhabitants, only 20 percent of neighborhoods experienced homicides. In cities with more than 50,000 but fewer than 250,000 inhabitants, homicides occurred in 50 percent of neighborhoods. In the four largest cities, homicides occurred in 70 percent of neighborhoods.

Geographical criminology can encompass displacement studies because they aim at unraveling the spatial behavioral mechanism of people (Eck 1993; Eck and Weisburd 1995; Elffers, Bernasco, and Bruinsma 2005). In this research the spatial effects in criminal behavior are studied after law enforcement or other interventions (preventive as well as repressive) have been carried out. A recent overview demonstrated that little solid displacement research has been done in the Netherlands (Elffers, Bernasco, and Bruinsma 2005, 2006). Most studies have not focused on displacement when studying the effects of crime prevention or other measures, and their results are not solid enough to support inferences on displacement. Criminologists have made use of "natural" experiments to gain insight into spatial displacement. Elffers (2002) and Elffers and Visscher (2002) investigated the hypothesis that strong concentrations of police personnel focusing on public order affairs in a certain neighborhood of The Hague would generate more crime in other neighborhoods. Bruinsma and Luykx (2003) used a quasi-experimental design to study short-term changes in crime rates in surrounding areas after a fireworks explosion in May 2000 destroyed a whole neighborhood in Enschede. These three studies observed small but insignificant spatial displacement effects. Elffers and van Koppen (2003) concluded after studying changes in organization of detective work that they had no effect on the locations of street robberies. Van Wilsem (2003) demonstrated in multilevel analyses of victim survey data small but significant spatial effects of displacement in burglaries when technological prevention was carried out against residential burglary.

C. Social Disorganization

Mapping can show spatial distributions in crime but cannot explain them. Since the mid-1990s, growing numbers of Dutch criminologists have tried to assess the effects of neighborhood characteristics on crime places and the number of offenders living there. Hesseling (1987) had shown that clusters in crime in Utrecht were correlated with a higher level of economic deprivation, a high number of one-person households, and the presence of a higher number of facilities (restaurants, schools, shops, and business companies). Hesseling concluded that concentrations in crime were an expression of the recreational functions of the neighborhood for the city as a whole. Rood-Pijpers et al. (1995) demonstrated that the unequal distribution of crime across three neighborhoods of Rotterdam (Afrikaanderwijk, Hillesluis, and Bloemhof) resulted from social structural neighborhood characteristics such as cultural heterogeneity (another term for ethnic heterogeneity), number of houses per hectare, lack of social control, demographic composition, and percentage of families with social and health problems. Their analyses pointed at two clusters of factors explaining the distributions in crime: an economic cluster (lack of economic sources and multiple financial problems) and a demographic cluster (the larger number of singles in the neighborhood, the higher the residential mobility and the less social control).

Wittebrood (2000) used logistic multilevel analyses on individual survey data of about 200,000 individuals and structural factors of more than 3,700 neighborhoods to show that different levels of violent victimization across neighborhoods depended on sociocultural characteristics (low economic status and residential mobility) and on the ethnic composition of the population. She also demonstrated that the size of the city to which the neighborhood belongs had an additional independent effect on violent victimization rates. Further examinations, however, demonstrated that almost 60 percent of the variance in violent crime rates between neighborhoods could be explained by the individual characteristics of the residents. Men, young people, the unemployed, and the retired have significantly higher chances of being victimized by violence in their own neighborhood.

The economists Musterd, Oostendorf, and Deurloo (2004) explained higher crime rates in the center of Amsterdam by the large numbers of foreign and Dutch tourists and visitors from surrounding areas. In the city center are the shopping areas, the hotel and catering industry, the pubs, the discotheques, and historical spots and museums. Tourists are attractive targets because they are typically prosperous, unfamiliar with the local situation, and more vulnerable in general than local people. In this anonymous public space, potential victims are always present. Looking at the distribution of residential burglaries, they concluded that these crimes are relatively more often committed by offenders who live in the same neighborhood (as Kleemans [1996] and Bernasco and Luykx [2002] did). These neighborhoods are large-scale (public) rental housing areas characterized by anonymity and impersonal nondefensible space awareness.

Van der Leun, Snel, and Engbersen (1998) demonstrated after multivariate analyses of official data of neighborhoods in Utrecht and Rotterdam that the level of deprivation had the largest independent effect on variations in several types of crimes and social disorders. The number of ethnic minorities in the neighborhood was not relevant in all neighborhoods. That to them suggested a more complex model for deprived areas than that advocated by Shaw and McKay (1942). Subsequently, they proposed a situational model in which the demographic and social composition of the resident population, the opportunity structure of the neighborhood, the presence of a criminal circle, and the lack of formal and informal control explain differences in crime rates across areas in cities. They did not test this model empirically but discussed the plausibility of the explanatory power of these factors.

Bernasco and Luykx (2003) proposed six hypotheses relating to attractiveness, opportunity, and accessibility of neighborhoods based on the theories of Sampson and Groves (1989) and of Rengert (1991) and assuming motivated offenders. A high percentage of house ownership, high average estate value, high level of ethnic heterogeneity, high residential mobility, greater proximity to the homes of burglars, and greater proximity to the central business district were correlated with higher numbers of residential burglaries. In line with the ecological tradition in criminology, lack of territoriality and affluence also had strong positive effects on the number of residential burglaries.

The presence of crime depends not only on the opportunity structure of a city but also on the number of offenders living in it. As research has long demonstrated, where offenders live also matters. Criminologists have long demonstrated that offenders do not live randomly in a city (Shaw and McKay 1942). Depending on the kind of crimes they commit, they cluster in certain neighborhoods. Criminals active in financial crimes, tax evasion, or white-collar crimes live in wealthy neighborhoods (and commit their crimes in the business areas of the city during the days). Traditional offenders of crimes such as theft, violence, burglaries, or robberies in public places live in more deprived neighborhoods. Shaw and McKay labeled the latter "delinquent areas" in which delinquent values are passed on in a process of cultural transmission.

Little Dutch research has indicated such specific persistent high-offender neighborhoods. These can be characterized as long-existing working-class neighborhoods, and not only those having high numbers of ethnic minorities. Fiselier (1968) was the first Dutch criminologist who detected specific neighborhoods (in Nijmegen) in which high concentrations of offenders live. Van Wijngaarden and Boerman (1997) demonstrated that these few old and deprived neighborhoods in Nijmegen still have the highest offender rates, but that in the 1990s some suburban neighborhoods contained relatively higher numbers of juvenile delinquents. In The Hague, for instance, two neighborhoods contained the majority of all frequent offenders in the whole city (Duchateau, Ferweda, and Versteegh 2003).

Bruinsma (1997, 1999a) observed in Enschede a few neighborhoods

with persistently high offender rates. Generations of families with recidivists have lived in these "delinquent" neighborhoods, sometimes
close to each other on the same street. In these traditional working-
class neighborhoods in Dutch cities, there is little residential mobility.
These areas were relatively poor with high unemployment rates, the
houses were of varying quality (depending on local urban renewal policy), and most of the time they were situated in proximity to the city
centers. Bruinsma calculated that the standardized offender rates per
neighborhood in Enschede varied from 1 : 11 and 1 : 12 to 1 : 98 or
1 : 138. These figures implied that one of every eleven residents (from
birth to 100 years old) in a neighborhood has been arrested at least
once (among them more frequently) in the previous two and a half
years for committing a crime and were sent to the public prosecutor
for that crime. When all police suspects were taken into account, the
offender rates in the same period increased to 1 : 6 to 1 : 49 across
neighborhoods. These high-offender neighborhoods were not typical
ethnic minority areas.

In most Dutch social disorganization research, multilevel multivariate analyses are applied using structural statistical variables on aggregate levels to correlate with crime and victimization rates in neighborhoods. However, statistical correlation does not always imply causality.
The data show that deprived areas have more crimes than other areas,
but does deprivation lead to crime? We do not know that yet in the
Netherlands, although suggestions have been put forward elsewhere
(Reiss 1986). Recent research has tried to go beyond statistical correlation (Peeples and Loeber 1994).

Rovers (1997) investigated the question whether sociostructural
characteristics of neighborhoods exert an independent influence on juvenile delinquency when individual characteristics are controlled. His
multivariate analyses demonstrated that sociostructural neighborhood
characteristics lose their independent effects on juvenile delinquency
when individual characteristics are controlled. Only the effects of economic deprivation, lack of social control, and a high number of juveniles in the population remained. In a more contextual model, Rovers
mixed these three neighborhood variables with individual variables to
explain self-reported delinquency. Subsequent multilevel analyses
showed that neighborhood variables did not add to the explained variance. All variance in delinquency was accounted for by individual characteristics. This led Rovers to conclude provocatively that living in a

"bad" neighborhood had no effect on the development of juvenile delinquency (see also Wikström and Loeber 2000).

Van Dijk (2005) tested a theoretical model based on the original ideas of the Chicago school as elaborated by Sampson and others (Sampson and Groves 1989; Sampson and Raudenbush 1999; Wikström and Sampson 2003). In his study of 142 neighborhoods (varying from fifty to 500 households) in forty-one areas he used the original survey data of the Sociology Department of the University of Utrecht on social networks and informal social control in neighborhoods and extended the data with victimization rates. Multivariate analyses showed that the level of urbanization, residential instability, the degree of ethnic concentration in the neighborhood, the opportunities to meet neighbors,[10] and the level of informal control had independent effects on the victimization rates of neighborhoods. Informal control has a negative impact. No significant relationships were found for the socioeconomic status of the neighborhood. Residential instability had a negative effect on social cohesion and the level of informal control. According to van Dijk, the data showed that social cohesion and informal control at least partly mediate the effects of structural characteristics such as residential instability and urbanization. Although social cohesion and informal control in a neighborhood were strongly correlated, the effect of social cohesion on victimization disappeared when the level of informal control was added to the model.

Van Dijk's research contradicted some general accepted hypotheses. Propositions such as the higher the neighborhood's ethnic homogeneity, the higher its social cohesion, and the higher the number of public meeting places in the neighborhood, the higher its social cohesion, did not stand the test. Van Dijk (2005, pp. 40–44) tested his theoretical model for property and violent crime rates separately. Compared to the results of the overall test, the level of property crimes was better explained by the level of urbanization, the concentration of ethnic minorities, and the level of informal control (negative impact). For violent crimes, informal control and residential instability were the best predictors whereas the level of urbanization had no significant impact.

Dutch studies of problematic neighborhoods stress the correlation between the presence of large numbers of minority people and crime and disorder. Implicitly, it is assumed that the presence of these groups

---

[10] Indicated by the number of shops, pubs, restaurants, cinemas, schools, sport and recreational facilities, post offices, and public services.

is the cause of crime and disorder (without empirical evidence other than a statistical correlation) or that minority people perceive crime and disorder as normal or at least accept and tolerate them (also without any empirical proof). Bervoets and Stol (2002) interviewed 587 native inhabitants and 310 Moroccan residents (supplemented by more extensive personal interviews with sixteen native and fourteen nonnative adults in three cities) and demonstrated no differences in feelings of insecurity between the two groups. Both expressed their concern about problems in their own neighborhoods. Moroccan and native residents mentioned the presence of Moroccan juveniles hanging out in streets as the most negative livability factors, however, for different reasons. Dutch residents perceived Moroccan adolescents hanging out in the street as a limitation on their own freedom of action and that of their children, whereas Moroccan residents evaluated these youngsters as a corrosion of their own group reputation. More than their native neighbors, the Moroccan residents were concerned about the consequences of the presence of juveniles including the mess, graffiti, and noise. Bervoets and Stol concluded that in ethnically mixed neighborhoods there are ample opportunities for collective efficacy that may lead to more social cohesion and informal social control.

However, improvements in neighborhoods do not necessarily lead to less crime as van Wilsem, Wittebrood, and de Graaf (2003) demonstrated. In neighborhoods in which improvements have taken place because new residents with higher incomes have settled there, an increase in victimization rates was observed. Multilevel analyses of victimization survey data from the 1999 Politiemonitor Bevolking showed that strong socioeconomic improvement of neighborhoods is related to higher victimization risk for theft, violence, and vandalism. City-level characteristics (e.g., population size) were also associated with victimization, independent of individual and neighborhood characteristics. Drawing from Shaw and McKay's (1942) social disorganization theory, van Wilsem et al. argued that victimization likely occurred not only in disadvantaged neighborhoods but also in neighborhoods in which improvements have taken place. These neighborhoods were expected to suffer more from social instability caused by the strong influx of new residents and from social heterogeneity caused by the simultaneous presence of high-income and low-income groups. The study findings suggested that social disorganization is dependent not only on the socioeconomic composition of neighborhoods but also on socioeconomic dynamics. Changes in neighborhood status resulted primarily from the selective in- and out-migration of income groups.

D. Offender Mobility

A relatively new direction in geographical criminology is studies of offenders' mobility and spatial range (Tittle and Paternoster 1988). Three things are conceptually important in this research (Rengert 2004). It is necessary to assess a geographical point of departure of the offender(s), the distance to be traveled, and the activities carried out while the offender is at that location. These are related to and are influenced by the attractiveness of the target and the costs the offender incurs to commit the crime.

The home address of the offender is mostly taken as the point of departure. This choice is a practical one because almost all mobility research is based on police files of apprehended offenders (Rengert 2004). Personal interviews with (a random selection of) offenders about their journeys to commit crimes have not been carried out. Police files seldom contain information on the location from which the offender left to commit the crime. The home address, however, is always present in the file (except for homeless offenders). This choice, however, has two consequences. First, the researcher is forced to ignore that other departure points might be as important. The school, pub, bar, or restaurant in which dealers sell their drugs or where an offender works may all be as relevant as the home (Elffers and van Koppen 2003). Second, the group of apprehended offenders is a selection of all offenders because local people have a greater chance of being caught by the police than others do[11] (Bruinsma 2000a; Rengert 2004). These selection effects may lead to systematic biases in outcomes. Both international and Dutch geographical research face this problem.

The distance between the departure location and the crime place can vary from none to worldwide depending on the type of crime (Bruinsma 2000a). For crimes such as tax evasion, computer crimes, or spouse battering, the offender need not travel. Other crimes such as (transnational) trade in drugs or arms cover longer distances. Mobility research demonstrates clearly that most people tend to commit crimes close to where they live, travel, or work. Fiselier (1972) and Bruinsma (1999a), for instance, made clear that varying proportions of adult of-

---

[11] Strictly speaking, one must know the addresses of all offenders in a city to justify this argument.

fenders committing crimes in cities lived in the surrounding areas. These figures resembled findings from research elsewhere in the world (Bottoms and Wiles 1992, 2002). In the 1960s, about 25 percent of all apprehended Nijmegen offenders did not live in the city (Fiselier 1972). In Enschede in the 1990s, about 11.9 percent of suspects were outsiders; in Almelo, 23.7 percent; and in Hengelo, 28.4 percent (Bruinsma 1999*a*). In the villages in the region of Twente, the number of known offenders living elsewhere was close to zero. In other cities such as Arnhem, this percentage was about 50 percent and in Amsterdam around 60 percent (Bruinsma 2000*b*). These differences can largely be explained by variation in the number of people from elsewhere visiting cities for shopping, recreation, or business. For juvenile offenders, these percentages were in general much lower and confirmed other research findings that young offenders have a narrower geographical range than older offenders do.

For offenders who lived where the crime took place, most traveled to the center and committed many of their crimes there. Fiselier (1968) was the first criminologist in the Netherlands who showed that crime places and living areas of perpetrators differ. His data demonstrated that most offenders of crime in the center lived in the surrounding neighborhoods. Fewer offenders committing crimes in the city center lived in neighborhoods further away. Hesseling (1992) elaborated the mobility research by specifying distances in kilometers and types of crime. Using the shortest distance between the home address and the crime location for several types of crime, he showed that the average distance for violent crimes was 1.5 km; for vandalism, 1.6 km; for bicycle and car theft, 1.9 km; and for residential burglary, 1.7 km. For all other property crimes Hesseling found a radius of 1.8 km. Of all violent crimes, 44 percent were committed within 1 km from the home of the offender.

A number of characteristics of the offender, but not all, affected the distance of the journey to crime. Juvenile offenders tended to stay closer to their home or school when committing offenses whereas adult offenders had larger ranges (Elffers 2004). Rovers (1996) demonstrated that juvenile Moroccan and Surinamese offenders were more mobile than other juvenile offenders. Drug users and recidivists seemed to cover greater distances for their crimes (Hesseling 1992), but other research indicated on the contrary that drug users and other recidivists limited their criminal activities to a small territory in the city with which they are familiar (Grapendaal, Leuw, and Nelen 1995). Adult burglars from ethnic minorities traveled greater distances for their crimes than others did. There was no relationship between the sex of the offender and the distance of the crime journey (Hesseling 1992; Kleemans 1996).

The type of crime is also relevant to distance. Residential burglaries (Kleemans 1996; Bruinsma 1999a; Bernasco and Luykx 2002), vandalism (Rover 1997), and intimate violence (Lünneman and Bruinsma 2005; Smeenk and Malsch 2005) were committed more frequently in offenders' own neighborhoods or nearby. Robberies (van Wijngaarden and Boerman 1997; van Wijk and Ferweda 1998), stranger violence, shoplifting, or theft (Hesseling 1992), and breaking and entering cars (Hesseling 1987; Bruinsma 1999a) were more often committed in city centers by offenders living in proximity to the center. For bank and other kinds of robberies, offenders traveled longer distances (van den Eshof and van der Heijden 1990).

The consistency in research findings suggested a kind of law of offender mobility: the distance decay hypothesis (van Koppen and de Keijser 1997). This law, however, is not without debate in criminology (van Koppen and de Keijser 1997; Rengert, Piquero, and Jones 1999; Bruinsma 2000a; Elffers 2004). It could result from the selectivity of the police data used in mobility research. Moreover, it is based on studies of traditional street crimes (especially residential burglary) without considering other types of crimes such as organizational crime or white-collar crime.

To explain the mobility of offenders, routine activity theory is popular in Dutch studies, mostly in combination with mental mapping and rational choice theory (Brantingham and Brantingham 1991; Kleemans 1996; Bottoms and Wiles 2002; Elffers 2004). The underlying assumption is that offenders do not differ much from other people. Their daily routines make them more familiar with certain physical locations and geographical areas. Through these routine activities people acquire an awareness of the space in which they live and move. By living in a neighborhood, going to school, work, or friends, or traveling to shopping malls, people build up spatial geographical knowledge with which they can observe opportunities to commit crimes. Whether they commit a crime depends on a weighing of possible profits and costs.

Kleemans (1996) studied the mobility of burglars from this perspective. On the basis of rational choice and routine activity theories, he constructed a two-step explanation of a macro phenomenon as urban crime patterns. Using data on 6,266 residential burglaries from 1987 to 1992, he observed in Enschede great similarities to the concentric zone theory of the Chicago school but also differences. Burglars, mostly men, did not restrict themselves to one specific form of collaboration: sometimes they acted as solo offenders, sometimes they burglarized with one co-offender, and sometimes more than two co-offenders were involved. Most burglaries were committed by citizens of Enschede who lived in the neighborhood in which the burglary took place or in the surrounding areas (Kleemans 1996, p. 244). Both Kleemans and Bernasco and Luykx (2003) explained the preference of burglars for areas near their own in terms of short distances and familiarity (space awareness).

But proximity is not the only criterion in target selection. De Poot et al. (2005) observed in adjoining neighborhoods in The Hague that social barriers prevented offenders from looking for targets in other areas. If neighborhoods differed from each other socially, the likelihood that offenders committed crimes in older neighborhoods was lower when neighborhoods did not resemble each other closely in social respects. The researchers selected a number of neighborhoods on the basis of characteristics such as average income, number of ethnic minorities, and lifestyle indicators. To determine social borders of neighborhoods they asked other practitioners to assist them.

Elffers (2004) extended the investigation of the journey to crime by specifying the decision processes of offenders. Most earlier studies assumed a decision process on plausible arguments but did not test it. According to Elffers, a better way to understand the spatial distribution of crime is to distinguish among motivated offenders, wandering criminals, and haphazard offenders. The decision-making processes of these types of offenders differ and are likely to generate different journey to crime distributions. The motivated offender makes an inventory of possible targets, evaluates their expected costs and benefits, and chooses the one that provides the best-expected outcome. The wandering offender follows a sequential decision-making scheme: after having decided that there is a target with an intrinsic value, he evaluates whether it will be good enough or not. The haphazard offender has no plans to commit a crime: on his way to a certain location, he observes an attractive target that he cannot resist. Elffers stresses that routine activity theory sounds convincing but lacks solid empirical tests. We simply do not know very much about people's routine activities and their associated spatial behavior (p. 194).

New studies suggest methodological improvements in geographical research. Bernasco and Nieuwbeerta (2005) developed a new analytical model for selection of crime targets. This model integrated offender-based and location-based approaches to explain target selections in neighborhoods. They introduced a discrete spatial choice approach to the study of criminal location choice based on a microeconomic framework for assessing traveling demands in urban settings. The assumption is that offenders are faced with choices among discrete spatial alternatives. The offender is expected to evaluate the utility for each alternative. This discrete spatial choice model then can take the form of a statistical, conditional logit model. The approach was used to assess whether residential burglars were attracted by affluent, accessible, and poorly guarded target areas. The importance of these criteria was postulated to vary across burglars. The model was tested using data on 548 residential burglaries and 290 burglars (age, ethnicity) in The Hague. The likelihood of a neighborhood being selected for burglary is positively influenced by its expected lack of guardianship, its physical accessibility, and the number of potential targets in the neighborhood. No independent effects were observed for affluence and residential mobility. Potentially, the model can be extended to encompass other variables such as characteristics of adjacent neighborhoods and daily or weekly variations in burglary opportunities. Proper tests of routine activity theory will become possible.

In a reversed form, this analytic model can also be used for geographic offender profiling to assist police investigations (Bernasco 2004). This profiling model, called Herman,[12] is based on a generalization of the distance decay hypothesis and can support predictions on the probable departure locations of serial offenders (Bernasco 2004, forthcoming). A computer simulation compared three alternative geographic offender profiling tools. The first tool assumes that potential targets are uniformly distributed in space and that all potential targets are equally attractive. The second assumes that all targets are identical but are not uniformly distributed in space. The last assumes neither. The simulation showed the last tool to be the most effective for predicting the home address of the offender. According to Bernasco, the

---

[12] "Herman" is an abbreviation of the Dutch description of the model, which can be translated as "the reversed random utility maximization model."

reversed spatial target selection model can be elaborated and expanded in the future. The target selection may be based on multiple criteria of attractiveness instead of a monotonic distance decay function. Non-monotonic distance effects can also be modeled and the sequence order of the crimes can be included. Bernasco concluded that further empirical research will be needed to assess all the tools for geographical offender profiling, but that the outcomes of the simulation were promising.

III. Looking Back, Looking Forward

Dutch research reveals significant differences in crime rates that are not consistent with urbanization theory in criminology. Consistent with the theories of Clinard (1942) and Wirth (1964), size, density, heterogeneity, and impersonal relations correlate with higher crime rates (property and violent) in Dutch urban settings. Although seldom cited explicitly, the theory of Durkheim was influential in past studies in presenting and examining data. Recent research indicates that residents in rural areas are less confronted with crime because of higher levels of social cohesion and informal social control and lower offender rates in well-ordered physical surroundings. Criminals including chronic offenders live more frequently in cities.

Crime places in the Netherlands are concentrated in city centers and their surroundings. Shopping districts, theaters, cinemas, bars, restaurants, discotheques, and railway and bus stations are concentrated in these central areas, attracting great numbers of tourists, daily visitors, travelers, and offenders. Studies of specific types of crimes, especially residential burglary, demonstrate a zone pattern in Dutch cities similar to those described by Burgess (1967) in Chicago. The greater the distance to the city center, the less crime occurred. In a few peripheral suburban neighborhoods in large cities, crime places have emerged in recent years. Past and recent research points at persistent crime places and persistent high-offender neighborhoods (delinquent areas). These neighborhoods do not necessarily contain high numbers of ethnic minorities. Like findings on residential mobility, findings on the impact of the ethnic compositions of neighborhoods are not conclusive. Overall, studies demonstrate that other social disorganization indicators including low economic status, unemployment rates, number of singles, bad housing, low levels of social cohesion and informal social control, and demographic composition (age, type of households) correlate with high crime and victimization rates in neighborhoods. The opportunity structures of neighborhoods and the presence of high numbers of resident criminals are also relevant.

Environmental research was guided by original ideas of the Chicago school, sometimes extended by recent theoretical developments on the concept of disorganization as advocated by Wikström and Sampson (2003). Studies that combine individual characteristics with structural neighborhood factors in multilevel models show mixed results, sometimes indicating that the effects of neighborhood characteristics on crime are low and sometimes showing that these aggregate properties have significant independent effects. Informal social control and social cohesion of neighborhoods seem to mediate the influences of other neighborhood characteristics. Studies on neighborhoods with economic and housing improvements showed that social dynamics is an additional factor in causing higher crime rates.

The distance decay hypothesis of offender mobility was observed in most Dutch research, especially for residential burglars. Burglars chose their targets close to their own homes. Proximity and attractiveness of targets were important factors in the decision-making processes of offenders. Guardianship and social barriers, however, were obstacles to committing crimes in other areas. New methodologies will in the future allow more complex models to be tested including target characteristics and offender properties.

Some general critical observations can be offered about geographical and environmental research in Dutch criminology.

1. Almost all research uses only existing official data. Police data and data from the Politiemonitor Bevolking were combined with statistical characteristics of neighborhoods as local governments collected them. In one rare occasion, special data on residents' social networks in neighborhoods were collected. There is little fundamentally wrong with this practice, but it forces criminologists to accept definitions and classifications of governmental agencies of structural characteristics of neighborhoods and administrative boundaries. These boundaries and classifications might not be suitable as measurement tools for testing theoretical concepts.

2. The theoretical concepts used in disorganization research are seldom elaborated empirically by Dutch researchers. Concepts were borrowed from American environmental research without consid-

ering whether these concepts are applicable in the same empirical sense in Dutch cities (Bruinsma et al. 2004).

3. Because of a lack of own independent theory-driven data collection in some research, causal mechanisms are assumed without proper and solid tests. For instance, the presence of ethnic minorities is sometimes assumed to be synonymous with less informal social control in neighborhoods.

4. Most Dutch geographical and environmental research is cross-sectional. Strictly speaking, cross-sectional data do not allow proper causal inferences because the time ordering of variables remains unknown. But what really matters is that urbanization theory is essentially about long-term processes in society affecting crime rates. In order to study the effects of these changes on crime, longitudinal (preferably historical) data are more appropriate.

5. Most Dutch environmental research is descriptive (correlating descriptive factors). Theory tests are of recent date.

6. No (systematic) intercity research exists. In so densely populated a country, it is remarkable that no attention has been paid to differences in crime rates across cities and on the causes of these differences.

7. Except for one study (Elffers and van Koppen 2003), the roles of laws, rules, and law enforcement practices on the geographical distributions of crime or on offenders' mobility have not been taken into account. Policing approaches must affect these distributions.

8. A lot of *other* criminological research is carried out in Dutch cities. Studies of juvenile delinquency, families, developmental issues, criminal careers, and self-reports are undertaken without referring to ecological contexts. This is a missed chance to assess the influence of the surroundings. Progress can be made when Dutch criminologists become more aware of the effects neighborhood context or physical characteristics have on their research. The theoretical models will undoubtedly become more complicated and the empirical research more expensive and time-consuming (Wikström 2005).

9. Police use of GIS and other crime-mapping activities presents opportunities and challenges for geographical criminology. One problem is that the categories used by crime analysts increasingly

differ from criminologically relevant classifications. This practice of "inventing" new categories prevents criminologists from presenting the original figures of each crime according to criminological relevant classifications. For instance, the category "car crimes" is a new popular police category in some regions and includes car thefts, breaking and entering cars, and intentional damage to cars. In the long run this practice can disturb geographical research in which specific and detailed information about the crime is vital. Another problem is that all these data are published for police regions, not for each city separately and for areas or administrative entities that sometimes change from year to year (for internal organizational reasons). An intercity comparison of crime rates and a subsequent test of possible explanations such as Sampson (1986) undertook for these reasons is almost impossible.

Ambitious suggestions for a future research agenda can be offered. One important task for Dutch criminology is the establishment of a nationwide systematic research program on urbanization and crime. With the exception of the NSCR and the SCP (research institute of the Ministry of Welfare, Health, and Sports), only scattered attention is paid to the causes of unequal geographical distributions in crime, victimization, and feelings of insecurity. With such a program, fundamental scientific knowledge on urbanization can be built up in a more systematic way by answering a series of sequential research questions on the basis of reliable data.

Attention should be paid to special topics such as the causes of the differences in crime rates between rural areas (including smaller municipalities) and cities and across cities to newly troubled suburban areas of larger cities. The effects of law enforcement, especially policing, can no longer be neglected. When the strengths of different universities and research institutes are joined in such a program, a theory-driven database can be established containing longitudinal data over longer periods and at several levels of aggregation. With these data, it will be possible to compare the effects of changes in our society and in our cities on crime rates with those in other European countries. Good examples are the research programs of criminologists in Sheffield and Chicago who systematically and over a long period of time collected data to test traditional and new hypotheses on processes of social disorganization affecting crime rates across neighborhoods.

This data set must contain not only statistical aggregates for areas or neighborhoods but also data specially collected for geographical and environmental research. Dutch criminology needs essential valid data on concepts such as social cohesion and informal control. We need to know more in depth about how and why residents live with each other and how they organize social cohesion and social control. In this program, systematic data should be included on how and why offenders observe and evaluate crime targets and what stimulates or prevents them from traveling to targets. Interviewing offenders is a high priority. Interviewing larger numbers of criminals in certain neighborhoods will enable us to gain more insight into the processes of how they influence each other in committing crimes or in establishing criminal infrastructures while others organize social control. In this respect, Shaw and McKay's (1942) concept of cultural transmission of values and Sutherland's (1947) concept of differential association can be inspiring and helpful (Bruinsma 1999*b*, 2000*a*). New research can also critically assess and improve the applicability to the Netherlands of theoretical models developed in the United States, the United Kingdom, and elsewhere.

REFERENCES

Baldwin, J., and A. E. Bottoms. 1976. *The Urban Criminal*. London: Tavistock.
Bernasco, W. 2004. "Een kennismaking met Herman: Geografische daderprofilering en ruimtelijke gelegenheidsstructuur." *Tijdschrift voor Criminologie* 46:2–17.
———. Forthcoming. "The Usefulness of Measuring Spatial Opportunity Structures for Tracking Down Offenders: A Theoretical Analysis of Geographic Offender Profiling Using Simulation Studies." *Psychology, Crime and Law*.
Bernasco, W., G. J. N. Bruinsma, and W. Huisman. 2004. "Ruimtelijke strategieën van misdadigers: Sociale relaties voor criminele infrastructuur." *Stedenbouw en Ruimtelijke Ordening* 85(3):34–37.
Bernasco, W., and Floor Luykx. 2002. "De ruimtelijke spreiding van woninginbraak: Een analyze van Haagse buurten." *Tijdschrift voor Criminologie* 44(3):231–46.
———. 2003. "Effects of Attractiveness, Opportunity and Accessibility to Burglars on Residential Burglary Rates of Urban Neighborhoods." *Criminology* 41:981–1001.
Bernasco, W., and P. Nieuwbeerta. 2005. "How Do Residential Burglars Select

Target Areas? A New Approach to the Analysis of Criminal Location Choice." *British Journal of Criminology* 45:296–315.

Bervoets, Eric, and Wouter Stol. 2002. "Marokkanen en Nederlanders over hun wijk—een analyze van Haagse buurten." *Tijdschrift voor Criminologie* 44(3):247–61.

Blickman, T., D. J. Korf, D. Siegel, and D. Zaitch. 2003. *Synthetic Drug Trafficking in Amsterdam*. Amsterdam: Transnational Institute.

Bottoms, A., and P. Wiles. 1992. "Explanations of Crime and Place." In *Crime, Policing and Place: Essays in Environmental Criminology*, edited by D. J. Evans, N. R. Fyfe, and D. T. Herbert. London: Routledge.

———. 2002. "Environmental Criminology and Crime." In *The Oxford Handbook of Criminology*, 3rd ed., edited by M. Maguire, R. Morgan, and R. Reiner. Oxford: Oxford University Press.

Bovenkerk, F., and W. I. M. Hogewind. 2003. *Hennepteelt in Nederland: Het probleem van de criminaliteit en haar bestrijding*. Zeist: Kerckebosch.

Brantingham, P. L., and P. J. Brantingham, eds. 1991. *Environmental Criminology*. Prospect Heights, IL: Waveland.

———. 1999. "A Theoretical Model of Crime Hot Spot Generation." *Studies on Crime and Crime Prevention* 8(1):7–26.

Bruinsma, G. J. N. 1997. *De achtergronden van de crossrellen in Enschede*. Enschede: IPIT Instituut voor Maatschappelijke Veiligheidsvraagstukken.

———. 1999a. *Criminaliteitsbeeld van Twente in 1995, 1996 en 1997*. Enschede: Instituut voor Maatschappelijke Veiligheidsvraagstukken.

———. 1999b. "Stedelijke criminaliteit, sociale netwerken en differentiële-associatietheorie." *Tijdschrift voor Criminologie* 41:138–40.

———. 2000a. "Geografische mobiliteit en misdaad." Inaugural lecture. Leiden: Universiteit Leiden.

———. 2000b. "Spreiding van geregistreerde criminaliteit." In *Criminaliteitsanalyze in Nederland*, edited by H. Moerland and B. Rovers. The Hague: Elsevier.

Bruinsma, G. J. N., et al. 2004. *De stad en sociale onveiligheid: Een state-of-the-art van wetenschappelijke kennis in Nederland*. The Hague: Kluwer.

Bruinsma, G. J. N., and F. Bovenkerk. 1996. *De georganizeerde criminaliteit in Nederland: De branches*. Parlementaire Enquête Commissie Opsporingsmethoden, deel IX. The Hague: SDU.

Bruinsma, G. J. N., and F. Luykx. 2003. "De vuurwerkramp en de gevolgen daarvan op de criminaliteit in Enschede." *Tijdschrift voor Veiligheid and Veiligheidszorg* 2(1):3–14.

Bruinsma, G. J. N., and H. G. van de Bunt. 1996. *De georganizeerde criminaliteit in Nederland: Een analyze van de situatie in Enschede, Nijmegen en Arnhem*. Parlementaire Enquête Commissie Opsporingsmethoden, deel XI. The Hague: SDU.

Brunt, L. 1996. *Stad*. Amsterdam/Meppel: Boom.

Burgess, Ernest W. 1967. "The Growth of the City: An Introduction to a Research Project." In *The City: Suggestions for the Investigation of Human*

Behavior in the Urban Environment, edited by Robert E. Park and Ernest W. Burgess. Chicago: University of Chicago Press. (Originally published 1925.)

Bursik, R. J., and H. G. Grasmick. 1993. *Neighborhoods and Crime.* New York: Lexington.

Buruma, Ybo. In this volume. "Dutch Tolerance: On Drugs, Prostitution, and Euthanasia."

Clinard, Marshall B. 1942. "The Process of Urbanization and Criminal Behavior." *American Journal of Sociology* 48(2):202–13.

Cohen, Lawrence, and Marcus Felson. 1979. "Social Change and Crime Rate Trends: A Routine Activity Approach." *American Sociological Review* 44: 588–608.

De Poot, Christianne, Floor Luykx, Henk Elffers, and Chantal Dudink. 2005. "Hier wonen en daar plegen? Sociale grenzen en locatiekeuze." *Tijdschrift voor Criminologie* 47:255–68.

Duchateau, I., H. B. Ferweda, and P. H. M. Versteegh. 2003. *Jongerencriminaliteit in de regio Haaglanden III: Een analyze (2000–2001) naar de omvang, aard en achtergronden.* Arnhem/The Hague: Advies en Onderzoeksgroep Beke/Politie Haaglanden.

Durkheim, E. 1964. *The Division of Labor in Society.* New York: Free Press. (Originally published 1893.)

Eck, J. E. 1993. "The Threat of Crime Displacement." *Criminal Justice Abstracts* 25:527–46.

Eck, J. E., and D. Weisburd, eds. 1995. *Crime and Place.* New York: Criminal Justice Press.

Eggen, A. Th. J., and W. van der Heide. 2005. *Criminaliteit en rechtshandhaving 2004: Ontwikkelingen en samenhangen.* The Hague: Research and Documentation Center, Netherlands Ministry of Justice/Boom Juridische uitgevers.

Eisner, M. 2003. "Long-Term Historical Trends in Violent Crime." In *Crime and Justice: A Review of Research*, vol. 30, edited by Michael Tonry. Chicago: University of Chicago Press.

Elffers, H. 2002. *Haagse jaarwisseling: Diefstal in plaats van rellen?* Leiden: Netherlands Institute for the Study of Crime and Law Enforcement.

———. 2004. "Decision Models Underlying the Journey to Crime." In *Punishment, Places and Perpetrators: Developments in Criminology and Criminal Justice Research*, edited by G. J. N. Bruinsma, H. Elffers, and J. W. de Keijser. Cullompton, Devon, UK: Willan.

Elffers, H., W. Bernasco, and G. J. N. Bruinsma. 2005. *Ruimtelijke effecten van plaatsgebonden maatregelen tegen misdaad: Een overzicht van de stand van zaken.* Leiden: Netherlands Institute for the Study of Crime and Law Enforcement.

———. 2006. "De methodologie van onderzoek naar ruimtelijke neveneffecten van plaatsgebonden maatregelen tegen criminaliteit." *Panopticon* 26(1):31–45.

Elffers, H., and P. J. van Koppen. 2003. *De Aanpak van Straatroof in Rotterdam.* Rapport NSCR-2003-2. Leiden: Netherlands Institute for the Study of Crime and Law Enforcement.

Elffers, H., and M. Visscher. 2002. *Bijeffecten van grootschalig politieoptreden: Zien boeven hun kans schoon als de politie de handen elders volheeft?* Leiden: Netherlands Institute for the Study of Crime and Law Enforcement.

Elias, N. 1976. *Über den Prozess der Zivilisation: Soziogenetische und psychogenetische Untersuchungen.* Frankfurt: Surhkamp Verlag.

Fijnaut, C., and F. Bovenkerk. 1996. *De georganizeerde criminaliteit in Nederland: Een analyze van de situatie in Amsterdam.* Parlementaire Enquête Commissie Opsporingsmethoden, deel XI. The Hague: SDU.

Fijnaut, C., F. Bovenkerk, G. J. N. Bruinsma, and H. G. van de Bunt. 1998. *Organized Crime in the Netherlands.* The Hague: Kluwer Law International.

Fiselier, J. P. S. 1968. *Kriminaliteit van Nijmegen.* Nijmegen: Universiteit Nijmegen, Criminologisch Instituut.

———.1972. "Kriminaliteit en buurt." *Nederlands Tijdschrift voor Criminologie* 14:93–105.

Fletcher, J. 1848. "Moral and Educational Statistics of England and Wales." *Journal of the Statistical Society of London* 11:344–66.

———. 1849. "Moral and Educational Statistics of England and Wales." *Journal of the Statistical Society of London* 12:151–335.

Glaeser, Edward L., and Bruce Sacerdote. 1999. "Why Is There More Crime in Cities?" *Journal of Political Economy* 107:S225–S256.

Goeminne, B., E. Enhus, and P. Ponsaers. 2003. *Criminaliteit in de publieke ruimte: Een inleiding in de hot spot analyze.* Brussels: Politeia.

Grapendaal, M., E. Leuw, and H. Nelen. 1995. *A World of Opportunities.* Albany: State University of New York Press.

Grapendaal, M., and W. van Tilburg. 2002. "Veelplegers in Nederland." *Tijdschrift voor Criminologie* 44(3):214–30.

Groen, K. 1962. *Misdaad in de hoofdstad.* The Hague: Bert Bakker.

Guerry, A.-M. 1833. *Essai sur la statistique morale de la France.* Paris: Crochard.

Haller, M. H. 1971. "Organized Crime in Urban Society: Chicago in the Twentieth Century." *Journal of Social History* 5(2):210–34.

Hauber, A. 1977. *Gedrag van mensen in beweging.* Krommenie: Rotatie Boekendnrk.

Hesseling, R. 1987. *Kleine criminaliteit in Utrecht: Een case studie.* The Hague: Research and Documentation Center, Netherlands Ministry of Justice.

———. 1992. "Dadermobiliteit, een eerste verkenning." *Tijdschrift voor Criminologie* 34(2):98–114.

Huisman, W., M. Huikeshoven, and H. G. van de Bunt. 2003. *Marktplaats Amsterdam: Op zoek naar de zwakste schakel in transnationale criminele processen aan de hand van Amsterdamse rechercheonderzoeken.* The Hague: Boom Juridische uitgevers.

Johnson, Eric A. 1992. "Cities Don't Cause Crime: Urban-Rural Differences in Late Nineteenth and Early Twentieth Century German Criminality." *Social Science History* 16(1):129–76.

Kaal, H., and D. Korf. 2003. "Overlast door drugsverslaafden: Een analyze van dijkverboden in Amsterdam." *Tijdschrift voor Criminologie* 45:153–65.

Kempe, G. Th., and J. Vermaat. 1938. *Criminaliteit in Drenthe.* Utrecht: Dekker and van der Vegt.

Kleemans, E. R. 1996. *Strategische misdaadanalyze en stedelijke criminaliteit: Een toepassing van de rationele keuzebenadering op stedelijke criminaliteitspatronen en het gedrag van daders, toegespitst op het delict woninginbraak.* Enschede: Instituut voor Maatschappelijke Veiligheidsvraagstukken.

———. In this volume. "Organized Crime, Transit Crime, and Racketeering."

Kleemans, E. R., M. E. I. Brienen, and H. G. van de Bunt. 2002. *Georganizeerde criminaliteit in Nederland: Tweede rapport op basis van de WODC-monitor.* The Hague: Research and Documentation Center, Netherlands Ministry of Justice.

Klerks, P. P. H. M., and N. Kop. 2004. *De analyze van criminele infrastructuren.* Apeldoorn: Politie and Wetenschap.

Kubrin, Charis, and Ronald Weitzer. 2003. "New Directions in Social Disorganization Theory." *Journal of Research in Crime and Delinquency* 40: 374–402.

Lünneman, K. D., and M. Y. Bruinsma. 2005. *Geweld binnen en buiten: Aard, omvang en daders van huiselijk en publiek geweld in Nederland.* The Hague: Boom Juridische uitgevers.

Mayhew, Henry. 1950. "London's Underworld." In *London Labor and the London Poor,* vol. 4, *Being Selections from Those That Will Not Work,* edited by Peter Quennell. London: Spring. (Originally published 1851.)

Meloen, J. D., R. Landman, H. de Miranda, J. van Eekelen, S. van Soest, m.m.v. P. C. van Duyne, and W. van Tilburg. 2003. *Buit en besteding: Een empirisch onderzoek naar de omvang, de kenmerken en de besteding van misdaadgeld.* Zoetermeer: Dienst Nationale Recherche Informatie.

Ministerie van BZK. 2004. *Jaarrapportage Veiligheid.* The Hague: Ministerie van Binnenlandse Zaken en Koninkrijksrelaties.

Moerland, H., and B. Rovers, eds. 2000. *Criminaliteitsanalyze in Nederland.* The Hague: Elsevier.

Morenoff, J. D., R. J. Sampson, and S. W. Raudenbush. 2001. "Neighborhood Inequality, Collective Efficacy, and the Spatial Dynamics of Urban Violence." *Criminology* 39:517–60.

Musterd, S., W. Oostendorf, and R. Deurloo. 2004. "Stedelijke context en onveiligheid: Gelegenheid en criminaliteit." *B en M* 31(3):163–72.

Nagel, W. 1949. *De criminaliteit van Oss.* The Hague: Daamen.

Nationaal Rapporteur Mensenhandel. 2002. *Mensenhandel—eerste rapportage van de Nationaal Rapporteur.* The Hague: Bureau Nationaal Rapporteur Mensenhandel.

Nieuwbeerta, P., and I. Deerenberg. 2005. "Geografische verschillen in de kans om door moord of doodslag te overlijden." *Bevolkingstrends* 53(4):62–69.

Park, Robert E. 1967. "The City: Suggestions for the Investigation of Human Behavior in the Urban Environment." In *The City: Suggestions for the Investigation of Human Behavior in the Urban Environment,* edited by Robert E. Park and Ernest W. Burgess. Chicago: University of Chicago Press. (Originally published 1925.)

Park, Robert E., and Ernest W. Burgess. 1967. *The City: Suggestions for the*

Investigation of Human Behavior in the Urban Environment. Chicago: University of Chicago University Press. (Originally published 1925.)

Peeples, F., and R. Loeber. 1994. "Do Individual Factors and Neighborhood Context Explain Ethnic Differences in Juvenile Delinquency?" *Journal of Quantitative Criminology* 10:141–57.

Pennings, L., G. J. N. Bruinsma, and F. Weerman. 2006. "Jeugd en georganizeerde misdaad: Een empirische verkenning naar de doorstroming van jongeren in de georganizeerde misdaad." *Tijdschrift voor Criminologie* 48(1): 51–66.

Quetelet, M. 1847. "Statistique morale de l'influence du libre arbiter de l'homme sur les faits sociaux, et particulièrement sur le nombre des marriages." *Bulletin de la Commission Centrale de Statistique* 3:135–55.

Reiss, A. J. 1986. "Why Are Communities Important in Understanding Crime?" In *Communities and Crime*, edited by A. J. Reiss and M. Tonry. Vol. 8 of *Crime and Justice: A Review of Research*, edited by Michael Tonry and Norval Morris. Chicago: University of Chicago Press.

Reiss, A. J., and M. Tonry, eds. 1986. *Communities and Crime*. Vol. 8 of *Crime and Justice: A Review of Research*, edited by Michael Tonry and Norval Morris. Chicago: University of Chicago Press.

Rengert, G. F. 1991. "Burglary in Philadelphia: A Critique of an Opportunity Structure Model." In *Environmental Criminology*, edited by P. L. Brantingham and P. J. Brantingham. Prospect Heights, IL: Waveland.

———. 2004. "The Journey to Crime." In *Punishment, Places and Perpetrators: Developments in Criminology and Criminal Justice Research*, edited by G. J. N. Bruinsma, H. Elffers, and J. W. de Keijser. Cullompton, Devon, UK: Willan.

Rengert, G. F., A. R. Piquero, and P. R. Jones. 1999. "Distance Decay Reexamined." *Criminology* 37:427–30.

Rephann, Terance J. 1999. "Links between Rural Development and Crime." *Papers in Regional Science* 78:365–86.

Rood-Pijpers, E., B. Rovers, F. van Gemert, and C. Fijnaut. 1995. *Preventie van jeugdcriminaliteit in een grote stad*. Rotterdam: Sanders Instituut.

Rovers, B. 1996. *Criminografie van Rotterdam: Jeugdigen en veel voorkomende criminaliteit in de periode 1990–1994*. Rotterdam: Sanders Instituut.

———. 1997. *De buurt een broeinest? Een onderzoek naar de invloed van woonomgeving op jeugdcriminaliteit*. Nijmegen: Ars Aequi Libri.

Sampson, Robert J. 1986. "Crime in Cities: The Effects of Formal and Informal Social Control." In *Communities and Crime*, edited by A. J. Reiss and M. Tonry. Vol. 8 of *Crime and Justice: A Review of Research*, edited by Michael Tonry and Norval Morris. Chicago: University of Chicago Press.

Sampson, Robert J., and W. B. Groves. 1989. "Community Structure and Crime: Testing Social Disorganization Theory." *American Journal of Sociology* 94:774–802.

Sampson, Robert J., and S. W. Raudenbush. 1999. "Systematic Social Observation of Public Spaces: A New Look at Disorder in Urban Neighborhoods." *American Journal of Sociology* 105:603–51.

Sampson, Robert J., S. Raudenbush, and F. Earls. 1997. "Neighborhoods and

Violent Crime: A Multilevel Study of Collective Efficacy." *Science* 277: 918–24.

SCP. 2004. *De sociale staat van Nederland.* The Hague: Sociaal en Cultureel Planbureau.

———. 2006. *Thuis op het platteland: De leefsituatie van platteland en stad vergeleken.* The Hague: Sociaal en Cultureel Planbureau.

Shaw, C. R. 1929. *Delinquent Areas: A Study of the Geographical Distribution of School Truants, Juvenile Delinquents, and Adult Offenders in Chicago.* With F. M. Zorbaugh, H. D. McKay, and L. Cotrell. Chicago: University of Chicago Press.

Shaw, C., and H. McKay. 1942. *Juvenile Delinquency and Urban Areas.* Chicago: University of Chicago Press.

Smeenk, W., and M. Malsch, eds. 2005. *Family Violence and Police Response.* Aldershot, UK: Ashgate.

Spierenburg, P. 1996. "Long-Term Trends in Homicide: Theoretical Reflections and Dutch Evidence, Fifteenth to Twentieth Centuries." In *The Civilization of Crime: Violence in Town and Country since the Middle Ages,* edited by E. A. Johnson and E. H. Monkkonen. Urbana: University of Illinois Press.

Stachhouwer, J. 1950. *Criminaliteit, prostitutie en zelfmoord in Amsterdam.* Utrecht: Dekker and van der Vegt.

Stark, R. 1987. "Deviant Places: A Theory of the Ecology of Crime." *Criminology* 25:893–909.

Sutherland, E. H. 1947. *Principles of Criminology.* Philadelphia: Lippincott.

Tittle, C. R., and R. Paternoster. 1988. "Geographic Mobility and Criminal Behavior." *Journal of Research in Crime and Delinquency* 25(3):301–43.

van Beckhoven, E., and R. van Kempen. 2002. *Het belang van de buurt.* Utrecht: DGVH/Nether Partnership.

van den Eshof, P., and A. W. M. van der Heijden. 1990. "Tienduizend overvallen: Beschrijving van de overvallen sinds 1990." *Tijdschrift voor Criminologie* 32(2):56–66.

van der Laan, Bouma-Doff. 2004. "Restricted Contact: Residential Segregation of Ethnic Minorities and Their Interaction with Indigenous People." *Mens en Maatschappij* 79(4):348–66.

van der Leun, J., E. Snel, and G. Engbersen. 1998. "Ongelijkheid in veiligheid." *Tijdschrift voor Criminologie* 40:370–84.

van der Poel, Agnes, Cas Barendregt, Marjolijn Schouten, and Dike van de Mheen. 2003. *De leefsituatie van gebruikers in de Rotterdamse harddrugscene (resultaten van de survey 2003).* Rotterdam: Instituut voor Onderzoek naar Leefwijzen and Verslaving.

Vanderveen, G. 2006. *Interpreting Fear, Crime, Risk and Unsafety.* The Hague: Boom Legal Publishers.

van der Voordt, D. J. M., and H. B. R. van Wegen. 1991. *Sociale veiligheid en gebouwde omgeving: Theorie, empirie en instrumentontwikkeling.* Delft: Publicatiebureau Faculteit der Bouwkunde.

van Dijk, J. J. M. 1991. *Criminaliteit als keerzijde: Een theoretische en empirische verkenning van de relaties tussen welvaart en criminaliteit.* Arnhem: Gouda Quint.

van Dijk, Tom. 2005. "Victimization in the Neighborhood: A Sociological Explanation for Differences in Criminal Victimization across Local Communities." MA thesis, University of Utrecht, Department of Sociology.

van Koppen, P. J., and J. W. de Keijser. 1997. "Desisting Distance Decay: On the Aggregation of Individual Crime Trips." *Criminology* 35:505–15.

van Rooy, H. 1949. *Criminaliteit van stad en platteland: Nijmegen en omgeving.* Utrecht: Dekker and van der Vegt.

van Tilburg, W., F. Boerman, and L. Prins. 2002. *Landelijke Criminaliteitskaart 2002.* Zoetermeer: Dutch National Police.

———. 2004. *Landelijke Criminaliteitskaart 2004.* Zoetermeer: Dutch National Police.

van Wijk, A., and H. Ferweda. 1998. "Twee gezichten van straatroof in kaart gebracht." *Tijdschrift voor Criminologie* 40(4):404–16.

van Wijngaarden, J. J., and F. A Boerman. 1997. *Criminaliteit in Nijmegen: Een beschrijving van aard, omvang en spreiding van criminaliteit, met speciale aandacht voor berovingen.* Amsterdam: Vrije Universiteit.

van Wilsem, J. A. 2003. *Crime and Context: The Impact of Individual, Neighborhood, City and Country Characteristics on Victimization.* Nijmegen: Radboud University Nijmegen.

van Wilsem, J. A., K. Wittebrood, and N. D. de Graaf. 2003. "Buurtdynamiek en slachtofferschap van criminaliteit: Een studie naar de effecten van sociaaleconomische stijging, daling en stabiliteit in Nederlandse buurten." *Mens en Maatschappij* 78(1):4–28.

Wikström, P.-O. 1991. *Urban Crime, Criminals, and Victims: The Swedish Experience in an Anglo-American Comparative Perspective.* New York: Springer Verlag.

———. 2005. "The Social Origins of Pathways in Crime: Towards a Developmental Ecological Action Theory of Crime Involvement and Its Changes." In *Integrated Developmental and Life Course Theories of Offending,* edited by D. P. Farrington. New Brunswick, NJ: Transaction.

Wikström, P.-O., and L. Dolmén. 2001. "Urbanization, Neighborhood Social Integration, Informal Social Control, Minor Disorder, Victimization and Fear of Crime." *International Review of Victimology* 8:121–40.

Wikström, P.-O., and R. Loeber. 2000. "Do Disadvantaged Neighborhoods Cause Well-Adjusted Children to Become Adolescent Delinquents?" *Criminology* 38:1109–42.

Wikström, P.-O., and R. J. Sampson. 2003. "Social Mechanisms of Community: Influences on Crime and Pathways in Criminality." In *Causes of Conduct Disorder and Juvenile Delinquency,* edited by B. B. Lahey, T. E. Moffit, and A. Caspi. New York: Guilford.

Wirth, L. 1964. "Urbanism as a Way of Life." In *Louis Wirth on Cities and Social Life: Selected Papers,* edited by Albert J. Reiss Jr. Chicago: University of Chicago Press. (Originally published 1938.)

Wittebrood, K. 2000. "Buurten en geweldscriminaliteit: Een multilevel-analyze." *Mens en Maatschappij* 75(2):92–109.

Zaitch, D. 2001. *Traquetos: Colombians Involved in the Cocaine Business in the Netherlands.* Amsterdam: Universiteit van Amsterdam.

———. 2002. "From Cali to Rotterdam: Perceptions of Colombian Cocaine Traffickers on the Dutch Port." *Crime, Law and Social Change* 38:239–66.

Rolf Loeber and Wim Slot

Serious and Violent Juvenile Delinquency: An Update

ABSTRACT

This essay updates findings set out in *Ernstige en gewelddadige jeugddelin-quentie: Omvang, oorzaken en interventies* [Serious and Violent Juvenile De-linquency: Prevalence, Causes, and Interventions] (2001), edited by Rolf Loeber, N. Wim Slot, and Joseph A. Sergeant. Recent secular changes in the prevalence of antisocial behavior and serious delinquency are either unknown or inclusive. Developmental aspects of sexually delinquent be-haviors remain poorly undertood. Similar risk factors explaining delin-quency apply to different ethnic groups. The severity of delinquency is positively associated with the presence of mental health disorders, but not all studies agree. Increasing population diversity requires use of measure-ment instruments that are culturally sensitive and reliable. Similar rela-tionships between family factors and antisocial behavior hold for different ethnic groups. Progress has been made with the construction of screening devices for the identification of high-risk groups of youths. Advances have been made in implementing and evaluating preventive programs for differ-ent age groups, but evaluations of interventions in juvenile institutions and in the justice system remain a high priority.

The Netherlands occupies a special place in criminology—a smallish country that until recent years traditionally has been characterized by low levels of crime and few of the risk factors associated with high crime levels in the United States, such as high concentrations of pov-erty, urban gangs, and widespread gun ownership.

In 2001, with the help of thirty-four colleagues, we published a book

We are very grateful to the following collaborators for updating their earlier contri-butions to Loeber, Slot, and Sergeant (2001): Arnold A. J. Bartels, Bram Orobio de Castro, Maja Deković, Andrea G. Donker, Theo A. H. Doreleijers, Marijke Hofstra, Jan M. A. M. Janssens, Marianne Junger, Josine Junger-Tas, Wim Meeus, Evert M. Scholte, Robert Vermeiren, Frank C. Verhulst. Nicole M. C. van As, Peter van der Laan, and Anton Ph. van Wijk.

on serious and violent juvenile crime in the Netherlands, *Ernstige en gewelddadige jeugddelinquentie: Omvang, oorzaken en interventies* (Loeber, Slot, and Sergeant 2001). The purpose of this extended essay is to provide an update of that volume. Most of the key authors of chapters in the earlier book were ready to provide updates on their areas of expertise.

Before letting the authors speak, we reiterate the aims of the 2001 volume because they apply to this essay. We wanted to present current empirical knowledge of the development of serious and violent criminal behavior by juveniles, associated risk factors, and the best interventions to prevent and reduce crime. A second objective was to place Dutch findings in an international context. This is important because research opportunities in the Netherlands to generate more insights into juvenile crime have been and continue to be limited. Another objective was to link information to preventive and remedial interventions so that policy and practice could focus on evidence-based interventions.

These objectives remain important and are reflected in this essay, which covers the following topics (with collaborators shown in parentheses): crime trends (Meeus), sex offenders (van Wijk), ethnic aspects of juvenile crime (Orobio de Castro and Junger), co-occurring problems (Doreleijers, Scholte, and Vermeiren), development of antisocial behavior (Verhulst, Donker, and Hofstra), and family aspects of juvenile delinquency (Deković, Janssens, and van As). A separate section deals with justice policy and applications, including screening (Scholte and Doreleijers), prevention (Junger-Tas), interventions in institutions (Bartels), and interventions by the police and the courts (van der Laan). Each section very briefly summarizes past work and presents important findings since 2001. Major changes are taking place in the Netherlands that are relevant for reducing and preventing serious juvenile delinquency. We conclude the essay with comments on several key issues and their policy implications.

I. Serious, Violent, and Persistent Youth Delinquency[1]

In this section we focus on trends in serious, violent, and persistent juvenile delinquency between 1950 and 2004 and some key features of the association between serious, violent, and persistent forms of delin-

---

[1] Wim Meeus provided the material on which this section is based.

quency. Serious offenders are defined as those youngsters who committed at least one of the following offenses during the last year: fencing, arson, burglary, theft from a car, carjacking, and pickpocketing. Violent offenders are those who committed at least one of these offenses during the last year: homicide, maltreatment, robbery, rape, assault, threats, fighting, public violence, and injury by weapon. Persistent offenders are those who committed five or more offenses during the last year. These definitions of serious and violent delinquency differ in two respects from the definitions by Loeber, Farrington, and Waschbusch (1998): violent offenses were not necessarily a subcategory of serious offenses, and less severe indicators of serious and violent delinquency were used.

A. Review of Earlier Findings

Two types of data are available: police statistics (CBS 1996) and national self-report surveys (Junger-Tas and Kruissink 1987, 1990; Junger-Tas, Kruissink, and van der Laan 1992; Junger-Tas and van der Laan 1995; van der Laan et al. 1998).

1. *Serious Delinquency (1985–96).*   Police data, covering the period 1985–96, showed an increase in burglary after 1991 and a decrease in fencing. Self-report data showed no systematic trend for arson. In sum, no evidence was found for a systematic increase or decrease in serious youth delinquency during this period. No other trend data on serious delinquency were available.

2. *Violent Delinquency (1952–96).*   Police statistics contain information on homicide and child maltreatment for the period 1952–96. Between 1952 and 1970, almost no cases of murder were reported (a rate of less than one adolescent per 100,000 per year). The homicide rate increased to nine adolescents per 100,000 a year by the end of the 1980s and to thirty per 100,000 during 1990–96. For maltreatment a similar pattern was found: a relatively stable figure of forty to fifty per 100,000 in the period 1952–72, an increase to about 130 between 1972 and 1990, and a steeper increase to more than 340 between 1990 and 1996. Self-report data on maltreatment showed an increase between 1988 and 1990 and stabilization between 1990 and 1996.

Police statistics were available for robbery, rape, and assault for the period 1978–96. Robbery increased regularly from about thirty youngsters per 100,000 at the end of the 1970s to almost 180 per 100,000 in 1996. Rape did not show a regular trend: in the 1980s a small increase was reported; in 1987 there was a sudden decrease, followed by a strong increase between 1987 and 1996. The number of offenders in the period 1994–96 was clearly higher than in prior years. The figures for assault fluctuated in the 1980s but increased strongly from 1991 on. From 1992 onward the prevalence of violence was consistently higher than in the preceding years. The self-report surveys showed a linear increase in threats and fighting between 1988 and 1996.

Several conclusions can be drawn from these results. First, the prevalence of all types of violent delinquency was higher in 1996 than in 1952 or 1978 and increased strongly from 1988 onward. Second, the observed trends were not consistent: the figures on murder and maltreatment showed hardly any change between 1952 and 1970, whereas the same was observed for the data on rape and assault in the 1980s. We concluded that violent delinquency rose in the observed time period. However, there were two caveats: our conclusion was valid only if we assumed that the definitions of the various categories of offenses did not change over time and no changes in recording practices were operating during the observed period. The observed increase in violence could be attributed to an increased readiness by Dutch police to record violent offenses and to improved registration methods due to automation (Wittebrood and Junger 1999). Contrary to this interpretation, the self-report surveys also showed an increase in violent offenses in the period 1988–96, indicating that changes in recording methods by the police could not be the sole cause of the increasing figures.

3. *Co-occurrence of Serious, Violent, and Persistent Youth Delinquency.* To demonstrate co-occurrence between serious, violent, and persistent youth delinquency, we used data from the 1991 wave of the Utrecht Study of Adolescent Development (USAD), 1991–97 (Meeus and 't Hart 1993). The 1991 wave includes data on 3,392 youngsters aged twelve to twenty-four. 'T Hart (1992) compared the 1991 sample of the USAD with other samples and found it to be representative of the indigenous Dutch adolescent population in 1991.

Of the 3,392 youngsters, 849 (25 percent) were classified as serious, violent, or persistent offenders. Of this group, 251 were classified as serious offenders (7.4 percent of the total sample), 279 as violent offenders (8.2 percent of the total sample), and 659 as persistent offenders (19.4 percent of the total sample). Figure 1 shows the co-occurrence of serious, violent, and persistent delinquency and shows that 29 per-

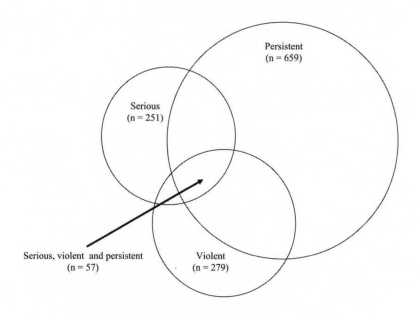

FIG. 1.—Co-occurrence of serious, violent, and persistent delinquency, 1991

cent of the serious offenders ($N = 73$) were also violent offenders, 63 percent of the serious offenders ($N = 158$) were also persistent offenders, 59 percent of the violent offenders ($N = 166$) were also persistent offenders, and 6.7 percent of the total group of offenders ($N = 57$) were serious, violent, and persistent offenders (1.6 percent of the total sample). We concluded that the co-occurrence of serious and persistent delinquency and the co-occurrence of violent and persistent delinquency were substantially bigger than the co-occurrence of serious and violent delinquency.

4. *Age and Age of Onset.*   Serious, violent, and persistent delinquency all showed a curvilinear relation with age: an increase from early ages (twelve to fourteen) to middle adolescence (fifteen to seventeen), a decrease from middle to late adolescence (eighteen to twenty), and a further decrease from late to postadolescence (twenty-one to twenty-three). So, for serious, violent, and persistent delinquency, the same age-crime curve (Farrington 1986) was found as for youth delinquency in general. In middle adolescence, the prevalence of serious, violent, and persistent delinquency in boys rose to 15, 18,

TABLE 1

Backgrounds of Serious, Violent, and Persistent Delinquency

	Serious Delinquency	Violent Delinquency	Persistent Delinquency
Mean age of onset	14.77	14.47	10.22
	Alone or Together?		
Always alone	43.9%	12.3%	21.8%
Sometimes alone, sometimes together	6.6%	5.6%	45.6%
Always together	49.6%	82.1%	32.6%
	Contribution of Persistent Offenders to Total Volume of Delinquency		
Persistent offenders (19 percent of total sample)	67%	62%	. . .
Serious, violent, and persistent offenders (1.6 percent of total sample)	27%	21%	. . .

and 40 percent respectively and for girls to 5, 5, and 15 percent respectively.

Table 1 shows mean ages of onset of serious, violent, and persistent delinquency. Mean age of onset was found to be substantially lower for persistent delinquency than for serious and violent delinquency: 10.22, 14.77, and 14.47, respectively. At age ten, 55.8 percent of the persistent offenders have already committed delinquent acts, whereas the groups of serious and violent offenders reach this percentage only at the age of fifteen.

5. *Co-offending.* Table 1 shows to which extent youngsters committed serious, violent, and persistent delinquency alone or together with peers. More than 80 percent of violent offenses were committed together with other peers, whereas only 43.9 percent of serious offenses were. Violent delinquency mostly took place collectively with peers, whereas serious delinquency had a more individual profile. Persistent delinquency did not show a clear profile with respect to the dimension alone or together.

6. *Contribution of Persistent Offenders to Total Delinquency.* Table 1 shows that the persistent offenders, 19 percent of the total sample, were responsible for 67 percent of the serious and 62 percent of the

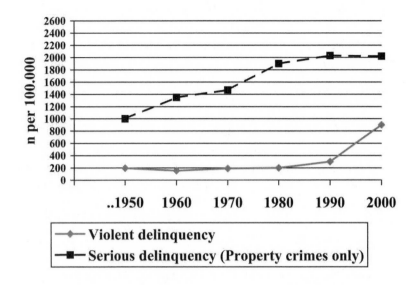

FIG. 2.—Police statistics of serious and violent delinquency, 1950–2000

violent offenses, respectively. The serious, violent, and persistent offenders, 1.6 percent of the total sample, were responsible for 27 percent
of serious offenses and 21 percent of the violent offenses, respectively.
These findings supported the classical findings of Wolfgang, Figlio,
and Sellin (1972) that persistent offenders constitute a smaller portion
of all offenders but are responsible for a disproportionately huge share
of all offenses.

B. Recent Findings

Did the level of juvenile delinquency change between 1996 and 2004
(the most recent available data)? Regular repeated self-report surveys
(Wittebrood 2003; Zeijl 2003; Kruissink and Essers 2004; Blom, van
der Laan, and Huijbregts 2005) and updates of police statistics (Wittebrood 2003; Blom, van der Laan, and Huijbregts 2005) make it possible to present additional trend data on serious and violent delinquency. Figure 2 shows police statistics on serious (property offenses
only) and violent offenses between 1950 and 2004 and shows that serious delinquency systematically rose between 1950 and 1985. The figure also confirms our earlier observation that between 1985 and 1996
serious delinquency did not increase. However, between 1996 and

2004, a substantial increase in serious delinquency was observed. Self-report data on serious delinquency from 1990 to 2004 (Kruissink and Essers 2004; Blom, van der Laan, and Huijbregts 2005) substantiate that serious delinquency did not rise between 1990 and 1996, but failed to find support for the increase between 1996 and 2004. Taken together, these data show that serious delinquency rose between 1950 and 1985 and stabilized between 1985 and 2000, but the findings for the period 1996–2004 are inconclusive.

Data on violent delinquency (fig. 1) confirm our earlier observation of a particularly strong increase from the 1980s on. This increase continued between 1990 and 2004. However, self-report data on violent delinquency from 1990 to 2004 (Kruissink and Essers 2004, p. 11; Blom, van der Laan, and Huijbregts 2005, p. 44) suggest that violent delinquency peaked in 1996 and stabilized thereafter. In sum, these findings show that violent delinquency did not change much between 1950 and 1980 and increased from 1980 on. Findings are inconclusive as to whether the increase continued between 1996 and 2004.

One possible reason for the increase in youth delinquency could be that young people start committing offenses earlier. Recently, Kruissink and Essers (2004) published findings of age of onset for various offenses for the period 1990–2001; they did not find any systematic change. Thus decrease of age of onset did not seem to offer a valid explanation for recent increases in juvenile delinquency. However, Blom, van der Laan, and Huijbregts (2005) found a slight increase in age of onset between 2002 and 2004.

Two recent nationwide surveys (Zeijl 2003; Kruissink and Essers 2004) reported on various backgrounds and predictors of youth delinquency. Both studies showed the well-known and often-reported risk factors to be predictive of youth delinquency: poor parent-adolescent relations, poor peer relations, poor school performance, substance use, and internalizing problems. So, no new risk factor of delinquency was found, and the same risk factors as before seemed to be predictive of youth delinquency.

Under Dutch juvenile criminal law, most young offenders are sentenced to alternative sanctions or to community service. Data show a strong increase in the use of alternative sanctions between 1990 and 2000 (Wittebrood 2003). In 1990, about six per 1,000 twelve- to seventeen-year-olds were sanctioned, whereas in 2000, twenty out of 1,000 were. Statistics Netherlands data show the same picture for sentences to community service: in 1990 about 2,000 young offenders were convicted to these duties, whereas in 2000, the number rose to about 12,000 (Wittebrood 2003). These findings are not inconsistent with an increase in serious and violent delinquency we reported earlier and also indicate that Dutch justice personnel probably apply sanctions to delinquent acts at a higher rate than before.

C. Conclusions

Serious delinquency rose between 1950 and 1985 and remained stable between 1985 and 2000; findings for the period 1996–2004 are inconclusive. Violent delinquency did not change much between 1950 and 1980 and increased from 1980 on; findings are inconclusive as to whether the increase continued between 1996 and 2004.

The co-occurrence of serious and persistent delinquency, and the co-occurrence of violent and persistent delinquency, were found to be substantially larger than the co-occurrence of serious and violent delinquency.

Serious, violent, and persistent delinquency all showed a curvilinear relation with age. A decrease in the age of onset (and an associated higher prevalence of early-onset cases) does not seem to offer a valid explanation for recent increases in youth delinquency.

The mean age of onset was substantially lower for persistent delinquency than for serious and violent delinquency: 10.22, 14.77, and 14.47, respectively.

Most violent offenses were committed together with other peers, whereas less than half of serious offenses were.

Although persistent offenders constitute a small portion of all offenders, they are responsible for a disproportionately large share of all offenses.

Recent nationwide studies show the same risk factors to be predictive of youth delinquency as in earlier studies.

Dutch justice personnel probably apply sanctions to delinquent acts at a higher rate than before.

D. Implications

Knowledge about criminal careers in the Netherlands for a long time has been hampered by the absence of large-scale longitudinal studies. This led Dutch researchers to design new longitudinal studies (beyond the traditional three-wave design) that focus on how risk and protective factors influence developmental trajectories of juvenile delinquency. Recent examples include the Research on Adolescent Development and Relationships study (known as RADAR) by Meeus and Koot and the Tracking Adolescents' Individual Lives Survey (known as TRAILS) by Ormel and Verhulst. The planned number of waves of these studies ranges between eight and twenty. Combining these new designs with new statistical tools, especially Latent Growth Modeling, makes it possible to document different developmental trajectories of juvenile delinquency. For instance, Bongers et al. (2004) found four trajectories of status violations in four- to eighteen-year-olds: extremely high persisters, high persisters, low decreasers, and a near-zero group.

It is clear that longitudinal studies should focus on developmental transitions. Because of these transitions, life arrangements change and risk factors can have effects completely different from those in earlier periods. For instance, the early adolescent transition from primary to secondary education may change parental monitoring and affect frequency and number of offenses.

Longitudinal studies should include measures of various levels of individual functioning: neurobiological measures, measures of basic behavioral tendencies such as inhibition and activation, personality tests, and sociocognitions such as empathy and perspective taking. Longitudinal studies should focus on relationship dynamics, for instance, on how parents influence friendship and intimate partner choices of their children and—through this influence—affect the relational contexts in which their children operate and that affect childrens' development. Selection and influence in friendships are other important issues: does initial similarity in delinquency between friends become stronger or weaker over time, and is it possible to disentangle processes of selection and influence in the friendship dyad?

The new longitudinal studies will be able to detect mechanisms that are crucial for the designing of individual, family, and peer-oriented programs to prevent juvenile delinquency.

II. Juvenile Sex Offenders[2]

The study of sexual violence as a specific form of violent juvenile delinquency has been going on in the United States for decades, but it accelerated in the Netherlands only from the mid-1990s onward (van

---

[2] Anton Ph. van Wijk provided the material on which this section is based.

Wijk et al. 2001). A few studies have focused on the type of offense and the characteristics of the victim (Bruinsma 1996; Boelrijk 1997; van Wijk 1999), whereas other studies have been based on the ways in which sexual offenses are committed (Hendriks and Bijleveld 1999) or the nature of the criminal career (van Wijk and Ferwerda 2000). Results vary much because of different sampling strategies, use of different measurement instruments, and different scientific disciplinary approaches. Nevertheless, results show that juvenile sex offenders tend to have their first contact with the justice system around age fifteen when they often are referred for rape of peers. There is a small number of studies that consider the social relationships of juvenile sex offenders, their sexual development, drug use, and psychopathology. Cognitive treatment of juvenile sex offenders has been the method of choice in most English-speaking countries and has focused on improving communication, empathy, and taking on responsibility for one's own behavior.

A. Review of Earlier Findings

We used Barbaree, Marshall, and McCormick's (1998) integrated model of sexual offenders, which explained the origin and development of juvenile sexual delinquent behavior, and proposed that the family in which the youngster grows up is an important etiological element. If there is a lack of care (neglect or abuse, e.g.), the youngster may find it difficult to bond with others. If the youngster has been the victim of sexual violence and is impulsive by nature, this could lead to the syndrome of social disability, consisting of an inability to form social relationships, low self-esteem, and antisocial and delinquent behavior. These factors, when co-occurring with a developing sexually deviant excitement pattern, can eventually result in sexual offenses.

The question is whether this model applies to all sexual delinquents. Studies on juvenile sex offenders present different classification schemes and show that juvenile sexual offenders constitute a heterogeneous group of offenders. Aside from clinical distinctions and the distinction between hands-on and hands-off sexual offenses, the literature distinguishes between child molesters and rapists. In addition, some studies focus on the two kinds of characteristics of the offense (such as male or female gender of the victim, use of violence or not). In each instance, the two types have in common that offenders often

TABLE 2

Prevalence of Sexual Offenses (per 10,000 Juveniles 12–17 Years Old)

	Exhibitionism	Rape	Sexual Assault	Other	Total
1991	.59	.79	1.09	.74	3.21
1993	.32	1.03	1.71	1.01	4.07
1995	.42	1.31	2.94	1.07	5.74
1997	.43	1.61	3.09	2.61	7.74
1999	.62	1.64	4.65	1.81	8.72
2001	.63	1.80	3.65	1.76	7.84
2003	.54	1.78	4.21	1.69	8.22

SOURCE.—WODC/CBS.

come from problematic families with few attachments between the child and parents.

Recidivism rates of nonsexual offenses tend to be higher than for sexual offenses. Whether differences in the recidivism rate vary depending on ethnicity of the parents of the sexual offenders is not clear because of methodological differences among the studies. Child molesters appear to have problems in peer relationships and are often described as loners with internalizing problems. Compared to rapists, child molesters have often been sexually maltreated in their youth. In contrast, rapists often are more oriented toward group offending and are characterized by externalizing problem behaviors. Studies do not show a consensus about the use of alcohol and drugs or the cognitive functioning of juvenile sex offenders.

B. Recent Findings

Since the earlier review (van Wijk et al. 2001), several studies have shed light on the behavior and risk factors of juvenile sex offenders.

1. *An Increase in Sexual Offenses?*   Data from Statistics Netherlands show that the number of underage youngsters (twelve to eighteen years old) who come into contact with the police as a result of a sexual crime increased between 1990 and 2003 (385 youngsters in 1990 compared to 973 in 2003). However, the increase is not evident for all types of sex crimes. The prevalence of exhibitionism remained fairly stable during that period, but the prevalence of indecent assaults increased substantially, as did the prevalence of rape and other sex offenses (e.g., child molestation), though to a lesser degree (see table 2). An explanation for the increase is that sex offenses are reported by victims more

often than before. Further, victims and authorities such as the police and justice personnel may be more inclined to consider certain excessive sexual behavior as punishable (e.g., Bullens 1999).

2. *Male Group Rapists.*   During the juvenile years, the majority of delinquent acts are committed in the company of peers (e.g., Warr 2002). To what extent does this apply to sex offenses? On the basis of data from prosecution cases, Looije et al. (2004) reported that one-third of sex crimes committed by juveniles typically take place in a group. A case study of ninety-one group offenders and accomplices who underwent a pretrial psychological assessment showed that groups on average consist of four individuals and were ethnically homogeneous. Ethnic minorities, especially Antilleans, were overrepresented. In the majority of cases, the crime consists of vaginal rape and threats to their victims, even after the offense. According to the psychologist who assessed the juveniles, the offenders were characterized by having an inadequately developed conscience and scored average on many personality characteristics, such as impulsivity and extroversion. They tended to have low intelligence and were easily influenced by others, although the number on this last item is low. There is little evidence of preconceived collective planning of the sex offense. One-third of the groups had a leader who orchestrated the crime. Group members were close to each other and perceived group rape as a form of entertainment. The authors suggest that a group offense is a means to attain status within the group.

A Belgian study sheds further light on group sexual assault and rape (de Wree 2004). Based on file information on about 100 group offenders, the study identified offenders from different ethnic backgrounds: Moroccans and people from the former Congo. In contrast to the Moroccan groups, the juveniles from the Congo are described as "gangs." An explanation for the involvement of ethnic groups in group (sex) offenses can be found in the weak social-economic position of ethnic minorities, inadequate schooling, cultural elements, and the focus on deviant groups of friends. In summary, the Dutch and Belgian studies showed that male group rapists were often from ethnic minorities. Group dynamic processes underlay the perpetration of sex offenses.

3. *Child Molesters and Peer Abusers.*   Studies often make a distinction between juvenile child molesters and peer abusers (e.g., van Wijk 1999; Hunter, Hazelwood, and Slesinger 2000; Hunter et al. 2003). Hendriks

and Bijleveld (2004) compared fifty-eight child molesters with fifty-four peer abusers who underwent a pretrial psychological assessment. Child molesters more often came from a Dutch background than from ethnic minorities and were more neurotic and more introverted according to psychological tests. Child molesters, compared with peer abusers, had more often been bullied and had less self-esteem. The victims of child molesters almost always were familiar to the offender. In contrast to the victims of child molesters, the victims of peer abusers often were fellow students or strangers against whom physical violence was used. The majority (63 percent) of peer abusers came from an ethnic minority background and seem to have had fewer personality problems than the child molesters.

4. *Sex-Only and Sex-Plus Offenders.*   Offending by some youths is restricted to sexual offenses only ("sex-only offenders"), whereas others commit various kinds of nonsexual offenses as well ("sex-plus offenders"). Van Wijk et al. (2006), using police information from 1996 to 2002 on 4,391 juvenile sex offenders, found that 44 percent of the offenders were sex-only offenders, and the remainder were sex-plus offenders. Compared with the sex-only offenders, the sex-plus offenders tended to begin their criminal careers at a younger age, continued to offend over a longer period of time and at a higher rate, and belonged more to ethnic minorities. For them, the sexual offense constituted a minor proportion of the total number of crimes, which mostly involved property crimes. These juvenile offenders rarely repeated another sexual offense.

5. *Are Sexual Juvenile Offenders Different from Nonsexual Juvenile Offenders?*   Three Dutch studies shed light on this important question. A first study compared thirty imprisoned juvenile sexual offenders and 368 nonsexual offenders and showed that the two groups were in many respects similar (van Wijk, Vreugdenhil, and Bullens 2004). However, sexual offenders seemed to be more inhibited than nonsexual offenders and used drugs less often. A higher proportion of sexual offenders compared to the nonsexual offenders were ordered to undergo compulsory treatment.

In a second study, van Wijk et al. (2003) compared 229 juvenile sexual offenders with 139 nonsexual offenders, all of whom had undergone a pretrial physiological assessment. Compared with nonsexual offenders, sexual offenders tended to be younger and were often of Dutch origin. Sexual offenders usually lived with their families and attended special education because of learning or behavioral problems. The juvenile sex offenders were less impulsive and less extroverted but more neurotic than the nonsexual offenders and were less likely to drop out of school. The two groups were very similar for IQ and self-esteem.

A third study, largely based on the same database, compared fifty-seven peer abusers, fifty-five child molesters with eighty-five violent offenders, and eighty property offenders (van Wijk, van Horn, et al. 2005). Most (76 percent) child molesters had a Dutch rather than a minority background. Compared with the other groups, the child molesters scored higher on neuroticism, had more problems with their peers, and were less likely to have repeated a grade. In contrast, the violent offenders, compared with the other offender groups, had higher scores on impulsivity, extroverted behavior, and an underdeveloped conscience. Violent offenders were the most problematic of the various groups.

These studies found distinctions among child molesters, rapists, violent offenders, and property offenders, which underline that juvenile (sex) offenders constitute a heterogeneous group of offenders. Neglecting this heterogeneity can camouflage possible differences between subtypes of offenders.

6. *Girl Sexual Offenders.* Among arrested juvenile sexual offenders, only a small number are female (2–3 percent) (van Wijk et al. 2006), about whom little research has been done. Hendriks (2003), in an exploratory study ($N = 10$), summarized the backgrounds and characteristics of young female sexual offenders referred for a psychological assessment as a result of a sexual offense. Half were under age thirteen. Seven had committed the offenses (rape or sexual assault) in the company of others. In almost all cases, the offender and victim knew each other. The girls used much violence during the sexual crime (beating, kicking, and threatening). The young female sexual offenders tended to come from problem families (alcohol abuse, divorce, neglect). They often had a negative self-image, were neurotic, and were easily influenced. According to the forensic psychologist, it was probable that the girls' consciences were underdeveloped. In summary, girls who committed sexual offenses, compared to male juvenile sex offenders, tend to come from problem families and showed poor psychological functioning (Hendriks 2003).

7. *Recidivism.* Hendriks and Bijleveld (2004) examined the recidi-

vism rate of 114 juvenile sexual offenders (who had received treatment in an enclosed institution) over a median follow-up period of six and a half years. The authors distinguished between opportunistic sex offenders (peer abusers) and obsessive sex offenders (most child abusers). About 60 percent of the total group relapsed to any delinquent offense. Sexual recidivism was found only in the group of obsessive sex offenders (10 percent). Opportunistic offenders relapsed more often to a non-sex offense, including violent offenses, than child molesters. Sexual recidivism was related to a preference for young children, especially girls from outside the family. Child molesters appeared to be a group at risk of sexual recidivism, whereas opportunistic sex offenders displayed a more diverse criminal profile.

8. *Care and Treatment.* A survey among psychologists working in youth detention and treatment centers shows that institutionalized juvenile sex offenders tend to be placed among other nonsexual delinquents (Timmer, Workel, and van Dijck 2001). This study showed that line staff tends to be inadequately specialized in dealing with juvenile sex offenders. One problem is the lack of background information on the juvenile sex offenders at the institution. There are long waiting lists before juvenile sex offenders can be admitted to a treatment institution. The treatment institutions often have separate programs in which attention is paid to sexual problems. Besides individual therapy, the institutions offered cognitive behavior therapy in the form of group sessions. A major problem is the reintegration of juveniles into the community. There is confusion as to which authority is responsible for follow-up care.

C. Conclusions

Juvenile sex offenders are a heterogeneous group. The typical juvenile sex offender does not exist, as recent studies have confirmed. We reviewed different subtypes such as girls, group offenders, child molesters, peer abusers, sex-only offenders, and sex-plus offenders. An important question raised is which categorization is the most valuable for judicial and clinical purposes. Empirically based differences in types of offenders need to be linked to the practice in the courts and clinics.

Some recent publications stress that ethnicity in relation to sex offenses should be better studied. That juveniles from ethnic minorities are more often involved in violent sex offenses and less often involved in child molestation requires explanation (van Wijk et al. 2006). It is unclear whether sex offenses by minority youths stem from cultural misconceptions about Western morals regarding sexuality, result from an antisocial lifestyle, or reflect an aberration in sexual preference.

Because of the scarcity of longitudinal studies in the Netherlands, the development of sexually delinquent behavior is still poorly understood. Barbaree, Marshall, and McCormick's (1998) model could be a good starting point for the testing of developmental trajectories in sexual offending. In a U.S. population longitudinal study, the Pittsburgh Youth Study (van Wijk, Loeber, et al. 2005), it proved possible to examine the development of rapists and compare them to nonsexual offenders. The results show that the two groups do not differ on demographic, family, individual, or peer risk factors, but it is not clear to what extent sexual offending in Pittsburgh is comparable to that in the Netherlands. There is clearly a need to study developmental pathways of juvenile (sexual) delinquency in the Netherlands. An important question is how sexual offenses affect the total development of juveniles. The identification of predictive factors is likely to help in the early detection of sexual offenders and may have a positive effect on interventions.

The important question remains whether it is useful or even necessary to have specific treatment programs for juvenile sex offenders. Aside from differences between sex and nonsex offenders, some juvenile sex offenders are generalist offenders for whom sex offenses are part of a broader criminal career. It is possible that for these youngsters, general interventions aimed at reducing criminal offenses of any type are sufficient, but evidence for this hypothesis is certainly needed. Along this line of reasoning, specific treatment programs for sexual crimes (particularly child molestation and, possibly, rapists and exhibitionists) should be reserved for juvenile sex offenders who have committed a sexual crime because of deviant sexual preference and fantasy.

According to police records, some juvenile sex offenders appear as a sexual first offender. This is interesting because the assumption within developmental criminology is that serious delinquent behavior typically occurs after less serious offenses. A possible explanation is that this information comes from police records and that not all crimes are reported to the police. Sexual offenses often are hidden crimes. Victims do not report sexual attacks for various reasons, including fear of reprisals by the offender, guilt, and feelings of shame. It is also known that a youngster could have committed a sexual offense previously but that it was never reported to the police (e.g., Ryan 1997). Further investigation is necessary into the dark number concerning sex crimes by juveniles.

That some juvenile sex offenders stop after a first sex offense raises the question whether sufficient sanctions were imposed after the offense or whether the youngster stopped of his own accord. One aspect that must certainly be addressed in future studies concerns the connection between imposed sanctions and the course of the criminal (sexual) career. It is possible that an effective sanction is imposed but that it does not stop nonsexual criminal behavior. Some sex offenders might be termed experimenters, such as youngsters whose behavior crosses the boundary of sexually acceptable behavior, not because of a deviant sexual preference or an antisocial lifestyle but as a result of "experimentation" in the course of trial-and-error learning. Future studies should focus on the connection between forms of interventions, subtypes of juvenile sex offenders, and general and sexual recidivism.

In the light of this, the development of screening and risk-assessment instruments should be revised. The main question is to which care category the juvenile delinquent belongs, especially youngsters who need further special intervention because of their disturbed psychosexual development and their high risk of recidivism. Although this group seems relatively small in number, it is important for them and for society that they receive proper care. Valid and reliable assessment instruments can be of great use here (Bullens et al. 2004; van Wijk, 't Hart, et al. 2005). Besides this, professional care and supervision are important elements that deserve further attention.

III. Ethnicity and Juvenile Delinquency[3]

Perspectives on relations between ethnicity, immigration, and juvenile delinquency appear to be changing dramatically in the Netherlands, provoking intense discussion in societal debate (e.g., Scheffer 2000). In this debate four hypotheses concerning relations between ethnicity, immigration, and the development of juvenile delinquency may be discerned, with increasing emphasis on culture as a determining factor: (i) juvenile delinquency is not related to ethnicity or immigration; (ii) there is a relation between ethnicity, migration, and juvenile delin-

[3] Bram de Orobio de Castro and Marianne Junger provided the material on which this section is based.

quency, because essentially the same criminogenic factors operate for native Dutch and migrant youths but occur more often for immigrants (e.g., low socioeconomic status [SES]); (iii) migration itself invokes additional determinants (e.g., less binding with institutions); and (iv) for certain ethnic groups, additional factors specific to their cultural background operate (e.g., revenge for insults to the family). Unfortunately, societal debate tends to polarize on the first and last hypotheses and rarely seems informed by scientific evidence.

A. Review of Earlier Findings

Non-Western immigrant youths and their parents in the Netherlands have predominantly migrated from Morocco, Turkey, Surinam, and the Netherlands Antilles (CBS 2004). Approximately half of these youths born in the Netherlands have parents who immigrated in the 1960–70s as guest workers. Until the 1990s, a strong belief existed that ethnic groups did not differ with respect to criminal behavior (de Haan and Bovenkerk 1993). Once this belief was questioned, research focused almost exclusively on the question whether prevalence of crime was higher in ethnic groups than in native Dutch youths.[4] Junger, Wittebrood, and Timman (2001) summarized prevalence information from different sources. Compared with native Dutch youths, prevalence of serious delinquency was found to be higher in specific ethnic groups, for specific types of crimes. Prevalence of violent crime was markedly higher among Moroccan youths and Antillean girls than among other groups, whereas prevalence of self-reported drug-related crime was particularly high among Antilleans. For other kinds of crime and other ethnic groups, differences in prevalence were smaller. Although these group differences have been misinterpreted in many ways (see the paragraph on current trends below), they raise the question how they have come about.

One explanation might be that the same determining factors operate for native Dutch youths and ethnic groups but are more prevalent in the concerning ethnic groups. To test this hypothesis, prospective longitudinal research should regress several indices of delinquency later in life on risk factors at early ages. Unfortunately, no such data existed in the Netherlands. In the absence of longitudinal data, we analyzed a large cross-sectional data set (Junger 1990) concerning aggregated po-

---

[4] For brevity, we use the term "native Dutch youths" for all youths born in the Netherlands from parents who were also born in the Netherlands.

lice and self-report data on serious and violent delinquency in youths of native Dutch, Moroccan, Turkish, and Surinamese descent. Delinquency was regressed on established risk factors, including SES, urban/rural place of residence, behavior problems at school, school performance, free time spent outdoors, attitudes toward education and crime, family conflict and communication, and parental monitoring. Overall, these factors were related similarly to delinquency in native Dutch youths and the ethnic groups alike.

To test whether migration and cultural factors were related to delinquency over and above the general factors mentioned above, length of stay in the Netherlands, country of birth, urban/rural descent, traditionalism, Islamic religiousness, and general religiousness were next included in the regression equation. Only religiousness was weakly *negatively* related with delinquency, particularly for Moroccan youths. Interestingly, the same factors related similarly to delinquency in all ethnic groups. Total explained variance was, however, modest (19 percent), suggesting that additional variance might be explained by inclusion of other factors, not necessarily with the same importance for each ethnic group.

We concluded that the limited available data suggest that delinquency in immigrant youths may best be explained by higher prevalence of the same risk factors known from the international literature. Prospective longitudinal studies are needed, including assessment of potential risk factors for the general population, migration factors, and cultural practice factors.

B. Recent Findings

Since 2001 the debate concerning ethnicity and crime appears to have polarized further following ethnic incidents that revealed sharp divisions of opinion between populist native Dutch and immigrant spokesmen. Prevalence findings continue to suggest higher prevalence of specific crimes among specific ethnic groups. Recent prevalence estimates based on offense reports are particularly high for Antillean youths (10.6 percent) and Moroccan youths (4.6 percent) in comparison with native Dutch youths (2.3 percent) (Ministry of Justice 2004). The extremely high prevalence among Antillean youths is primarily due to drug-related (violent) crime.

Interpretation of prevalence findings has been hindered by three misconceptions. First, only a minority of youths in the groups with the highest prevalence commit such crimes. Therefore, prevalence figures are not appropriate to describe behavior of ethnic groups as a whole. Second, the descriptive findings on group differences have mistakenly been considered indicative of culture-specific causes. Differences in prevalence may, however, result from any of the factors discussed in this essay, whether they be universal, due to migration, or due to culture. Third, each ethnic group has mistakenly been considered to represent a relatively homogeneous group in terms of culture and behavior. However, cultural and behavioral differences within ethnic groups are considerable and appear to be increasing to such an extent that it may be more sensible to study (sub)cultural or individual differences within ethnic groups than to compare between groups (Pels and de Haan 2004). Because of these limitations, further contributions of comparative prevalence studies to our understanding of juvenile delinquency may be limited.

Concerning risk factors for delinquency in relation to ethnicity, considerable progress has been made. Even though no single study prospectively compared the development of delinquency in different cultural groups in the Netherlands, a consistent picture emerges when one compares the above cross-sectional study, other cross-sectional studies of externalizing behavior problems in Moroccan and Turkish youths, and international longitudinal studies of delinquency in different ethnic groups. Stevens (2004) (also see Stevens et al. 2003) conducted a cross-sectional study of externalizing behavior problems in Moroccan, predominantly low-SES, youths. Information concerning child factors, parenting, parental psychopathology, family functioning, and migration factors was obtained. Externalizing behavior problems were related with roughly the same child, parenting, and family factors generally found in Western countries. Child and parental Muslim orientation was weakly related with less externalizing behavior. Self- and parent-perceived discrimination was related with externalizing behavior problems according to parents and self-reports, but not according to teachers. In contrast with the findings on Moroccan youths, a cross-sectional self-report study of Turkish immigrant boys reported less delinquent behavior than among native Dutch boys (Murad et al. 2003). Self-reported externalizing behavior by these children was explained by low parental education and SES. Because of the exclusive reliance on self-reports, it remains unclear whether behavior problems and their determinants are in effect different for Turkish immigrant youths than for native Dutch and Moroccan youths or whether an informant effect may explain the different findings.

The inclusion of discrimination-related variables in the study of Moroccan boys reflects a growing interest in possible iatrogenic effects of actual or perceived discrimination. It has been suggested that frequent experiences of discrimination may limit opportunities in education and employment and may contribute to hostile attribution tendencies and ultimately to the formation of delinquent peer groups (Vollebergh 2002). Systematic research on these issues has unfortunately not been conducted yet. The findings on self- and parent-perceived discrimination in Moroccan youths discussed above and recent evidence concerning considerable discrimination in job selection[5] (Kruisbergen and Veld 2002) suggest that this is an increasingly important issue.

Internationally, Loeber and Farrington (2004) compared risk factors for delinquency between ethnic groups and majority population youths in Pittsburgh (United States) and London (United Kingdom). Similar risk factors were found to predict delinquency for Caucasians and African Americans alike. Higher delinquency in African American boys was explained in part by higher incidence of these risk factors. Overall, findings on risk factors for serious delinquency were found to be remarkably similar across countries and ethnic groups, suggesting that the same proximal factors may have roles in the development of delinquency in different ethnic groups.

Much of the recent debate in the Netherlands has concerned culture-specific factors purportedly contributing to juvenile delinquency. Hypotheses have been formulated concerning distrust as a characteristic of Moroccan culture (van Gemert 1998) and attitudes favoring violence in Antillean mothers (van San 1998). Some of these have been presented as established facts in the Dutch education system (CITO 2001) and government reports (Ministry of Justice 2002). However, virtually no sound research has been conducted on the culture-specificity hypotheses. Only anecdotal findings have been obtained with nonrepresentative immigrant samples (van Gemert 1998; van San 1998). Observations in line with the hypotheses under study were then attributed to the ethnic backgrounds of delinquent participants, even

---

[5] Eight percent of Dutch small-business employers report not being willing to hire immigrant applicants, even if they cannot find any native Dutch applicants; 16 percent indicate they prefer native Dutch over immigrant applicants with the same qualifications.

though no comparison was made with other ethnic groups or native Dutch youths. Thus hostility and violence-favoring attitudes were attributed to ethnicity, ignoring a large body of research demonstrating that these factors are related to delinquency regardless of ethnicity or migration history (e.g., Huesmann and Guerra 1997; Orobio de Castro et al. 2002).

In the absence of adequate tests of culture-specific hypotheses concerning the development of juvenile delinquency, we discuss recent studies bearing indirectly on this issue. In the cross-sectional studies discussed above, religiousness as a characteristic of Moroccan culture was related to less rather than more behavior problems. Allegedly deviant moral views in ethnic groups were recently examined by Oosterwegel and Vollebergh (2003). Endorsements of a wide range of moral values assessed with questionnaires were studied in relation to self-reported delinquency in several ethnic groups. Ethnic groups did not differ from native Dutch youths in their endorsement of moral values. In sum, the very limited evidence so far provides no support for culture-specific risk factors for delinquency in ethnic groups.

C. Conclusions

Despite far-reaching claims concerning causal effects of immigrant cultures on delinquency, little scientific study of these relations has been conducted. Prevalence of violent crimes is higher among Moroccan youths, and prevalence of drug-related crime is higher among Antillean youths than among other ethnic groups and native Dutch youths, but it remains to a large extent unclear why this is so. Even though much research has focused on prevalence comparisons between ethnic groups, their value seems increasingly limited, since within-group differences in migration history, cultural practices, and social circumstances are large and may increase as individuals from the large migrant groups adapt differently to life in the Netherlands over the prolonged period since their migration in the 1960s (Pels and de Haan 2004).

The limited available evidence suggests that the higher prevalence of the same risk factors found in international research may explain delinquency in immigrant youths from different ethnic groups. There is some evidence for additional factors related to migration, such as rural descent and (experienced) discrimination. Possible contributions of specific cultural factors have scarcely been studied. The few findings on this issue may best be considered indicative for promising avenues of further research rather than established facts.

Societal debate has concerned relatively vague hypotheses concerning "culture," "integration," or "attitude" and a broad notion of "deviant behavior." Testing such vague hypotheses would tell us little about the causal processes involved, providing few clues for prevention, intervention, or policy making. To better understand the development of delinquent behavior, it may be more fruitful to study individual differences in specific cultural practices by individuals and their relation to delinquency. A positive consequence of this approach would be the need to explain and operationalize the factors presumed to mediate hypothesized relations between ethnicity, migration, and delinquency.

The findings on prevalence demonstrate that the relation between prevalence and ethnicity depends on the kind of behavior examined. Similarly, relations with migration or culture depend on the aspect of migration or culture studied. In this regard "ethnicity" per se may not be a very relevant independent variable. Individual-difference constructs concerning ethnicity and migration with a clear theoretical rationale may be more useful. These may concern migration history (such as age of migration, migration motives, urban/rural descent, and binding with Dutch society at large) and cultural practices variables (such as religious fervor, family hierarchy, and adherence to codes of honor). More explicit hypotheses concerning specific cultural or migration factors, specific delinquent behavior, and the proposed processes linking these are prerequisites for advancement in this field.

IV. Co-occurrence of Serious and Violent Delinquency with Other Problems[6]

Policy makers and treatment staff members of institutions have become more aware of mental health needs of detained boys and girls. This is relevant for forensic diagnostic assessment, the development of specific treatment programs, and decision making by judicial authorities when these juveniles enter the juvenile justice system.

---

[6] Theo A. H. Doreleijers, Robert Vermeiren, and Evert M. Scholte provided the material on which this section is based.

A. Review of Earlier Findings

We speak of co-occurrence (in medical jargon, comorbidity) of disorders (or problems) when two or more distinct disorders occur at the same time at an observed rate that is higher than can be expected by chance alone. Serious and violent delinquents often have co-occurring problems, such as school dysfunction, substance abuse, attention deficit hyperactivity disorder (ADHD), and internalizing problems (Huizinga and Jacob-Chien 1998; Vermeiren, Jespers, and Moffitt 2006). Knowledge is needed to answer key questions about the etiology and developmental patterns of delinquent behavior and co-occurring problems for early identification and for targeted treatment. The co-occurrence of delinquent behavior with mental health problems poses major questions about legal culpability and how justice officials should deal with nonlegal but often severely impairing problems that delinquent juveniles present. The association between delinquency and co-occurring problems does not have to be causal, in that one condition may cause one or more other conditions.

The chronology of the various problems is of importance but is often hard to disentangle. For example, it was thought for a long time that drug users needed their delinquent behavior to finance their drugs and that drug use preceded delinquent behavior. However, studies have also shown the reverse, that delinquency often precedes drug abuse (see, e.g., Robins and McEvoy 1990). Such findings are of great relevance for prevention programs for drug users (Hawkins, Catalano, and Miller 1992).

Angold, Costello, and Erkanli (1999) suggested that comorbidity constitutes an "instrument" to better understand the etiology and pathogenesis of complex disorders. Co-occurrence between delinquency and other problem behaviors may have different causes, some of which are artifacts. On the basis of a meta-analysis of large population-based studies, Angold, Costello, and Erkanli explained the condition of *epiphenomenal comorbidity*, when some forms of comorbidity constitute an artifact. For example, they found that depression and anxiety disorder often co-occur, as well as depression and conduct disorder, and anxiety disorder and conduct disorder. However, the latter association is an artifact because anxiety disorder is more likely to be found in an antisocial person who is also suffering from depression.

Some Dutch research on co-occurring problems in delinquent minors has been based on population samples. For example, Ferwerda,

Bottenberg, and Beke (1999*a*, 1999*b*) found that serious delinquents, compared to less serious delinquents, attended school less often and were more often unemployed. Also, they found that more serious delinquents attended lower-level schools than less serious delinquents. Most of the Dutch research on co-occurring problems, however, has focused on studies of specific groups of delinquents, such as juveniles with contacts with the police, juveniles in custody, and juveniles in detention. In Doreleijers et al.'s (2000) study of youths brought before the juvenile court, 48 percent of participants self-reported school problems, whereas their parents reported behavioral problems at school in 23–32 percent of the cases.

Studies on the co-occurrence of delinquency and substance use are hampered. There is no clear understanding among Dutch scholars of what constitutes harmful drug or alcohol use. This has to do with the cultural, moral, and penal opinions about the use of these substances, which have changed much over the past twenty years. Kuipers, Mensink, and de Zwart's 's (1993) study of school children aged ten and over showed a significant association between cannabis use and criminality. In 1996, the Dutch National Institute for Budget Information study among school children (SCP 1996) reported that as many as 63 percent of juveniles who used soft drugs had committed a delinquent offense, compared to 23 percent of nonusers. Schreuders, Korf, and Poort (1994) investigated the idea that delinquency and cannabis use reciprocally reinforce each other, which can particularly be found among socially deprived groups. Interestingly, gender and nightlife behavior proved to be better predictors of criminality than soft drug use; likewise, nightlife behavior accounted to a greater extent for soft drug use, although criminality also played a role.

Ferwerda, Bottenberg, and Beke (1999*a*, 1999*b*), in a population-based study, reported that nearly 60 percent of serious delinquents had ever used drugs versus 3 percent of nondelinquents. The former were more frequent users and more often users of magic mushrooms and smart drugs. Eighty-five percent of serious delinquents consumed alcohol versus more than 50 percent of nondelinquent youths. The former group more often used throughout the whole week, whereas the latter group consumed alcohol predominantly at parties or on the weekend. The seriously delinquent group had a much higher alcohol use: fifteen glasses per night out compared to five and a half glasses for the nondelinquent group. Likewise, the serious delinquents consumed more "cocktails" of different combinations of alcohol and drugs.

The studies discussed so far did not report on ADHD or other externalizing behavior. Doreleijers et al. (2000), depending on the instrument used, reported large differences in the measurement of ADHD in delinquents brought before court. For example, the Youth Self-Report (YSR) yielded attention and hyperactivity problems in 6 percent of the group of adjudicated youths, whereas interviews (of juveniles and their parents) identified 28–30 percent of youths with ADHD. When DSM III-R criteria were used, 14 percent of the juveniles were diagnosed with ADHD. A Belgian study largely replicated these results (18 percent ADHD; Vermeiren, de Clippele, and Deboutte 2000). Subsequent analyses of Dutch data collected by Doreleijers showed that when the group of criminal minors was split into younger (twelve to fourteen) and older (fifteen to seventeen) subgroups, a diagnosis of ADHD could be made three times more often in the younger than in the older subgroup (Moser and Doreleijers 1996). Moreover, the "total" rate of comorbidity—in addition to ADHD itself—turned out to be greater in the juveniles with ADHD than in those without.

In the same group, Doreleijers et al. (2000) found that about 30 percent showed internalizing problems (on the basis of interviews with the juveniles, the YSR, and interviews with their parents and the Child Behavior Checklist). In addition, a strikingly large number of physical complaints and sleep problems were found. A DSM III-R diagnosis of depression/dysthymia could be made in 11 percent of the juveniles. In the earlier-mentioned Belgian study (Vermeiren, de Clippele, and Deboutte 2000), 15 percent were diagnosed with depression and 14 percent with posttraumatic stress disorder (a classification that could not be made in the Dutch study because no suitable instrument was used). In Doreleijers' Dutch sample, an association was reported between the degree of comorbidity, the level of functioning, and the total amount of stress experienced. However, although comorbidity may be considered to relate to both delinquent behavior and help-seeking behavior, there was no association between the degree of comorbidity and the level of functioning or the severity of the delinquent behavior.

B. Recent Findings

Two Dutch studies using systematic assessments in juvenile justice institutions in the Netherlands have provided new insights into the co-occurrence of delinquency and mental health problems. The first study investigated a representative sample of twelve- to eighteen-year-old adjudicated delinquent boys ($N = 208$) detained in juvenile justice institutions (Vreugdenhil, Doreleijers, et al. 2004) who were incarcerated either without special treatment ($N = 114$; called the detention group) or with compulsory treatment ($N = 90$); 62 percent and 86 percent of the detention group and the treatment group, respectively, had been referred because of a violent index offense. The child version of the diagnostic interview for children was used (Diagnostic Interview Schedule for Children [DISC-C]; Shaffer et al. 2000) to determine the prevalence of psychiatric disorders. Ninety percent of all participants met criteria for any psychiatric disorder, 75 percent for any disruptive behavior disorder, and 67 percent for at least two disorders. These high comorbidity rates indicate the need for professional mental health services for these youths. All boys showed serious functional impairment (Children's Global Assessment Scale score below 61). However, Dutch juvenile justice institutions were also shown to lack mental health resources to address delinquents' mental health problems.

The second study focused on 218 twelve- to eighteen-year old detained girls, of whom 92 percent had a civil court order of child protection (mainly because of status offenses); only 8 percent were placed under penal sanctions, although a majority had committed delinquent behavior (Hamerlynck et al. 2005). Assessments using the Kiddie Schedule for Affective Disorders—Present and Lifetime version (Kaufman et al. 1997) found that a large proportion of girls had one or more externalizing disorders or substance use disorders, whereas self-report instruments showed high levels of internalizing problems, specifically, depression and posttraumatic stress. From the aggression items from the conduct disorder (CD) diagnosis (violent theft, use of a weapon, battery, sexual violence, and maltreatment of animals) as a criterion, 59 percent of the girls showed at least one of these behaviors, whereas almost 20 percent displayed two or more. Interestingly, the study also reported an association between severity of the aggressive behavior and the prevalence of externalizing and internalizing disorders.

With regard to substance use disorders (SUD), Vreugdenhil, van den Brink, et al. (2003) found a six-month prevalence of any SUD of 55 percent and a lifetime prevalence for polysubstance use of 83 percent (defined as the use of at least two different substances, except tobacco). The presence of an SUD was associated with a significantly higher probability of the presence of another SUD. No relationship between use of alcohol and drugs and violence and aggression was found, however, presumably because the detained population represents an extremely disordered group, which hampers the likelihood of differentiating according to this factor. Hamerlynck et al. (2005) reported drug abuse and dependence in 52 percent and 30 percent of the girls, respectively. Hard drug abuse was positively related to levels of aggression, with highest rates in the most aggressive group.

Vreugdenhil, Doreleijers, et al. (2004) found ADHD in 8 percent of the boys, which may be an underestimate because external (parent, teacher) information was not available. In contrast, 21 percent of the girls in the Hamerlynck et al. (2005) study qualified for ADHD. The results for girls and boys may not be comparable because the instruments used in the two studies were different: diagnoses for the boys were made with a fully structured psychiatric interview, whereas a semistructured interview was used in the girls' study (where professionals are allowed to consider their own observations as well). Overall, the issue of ADHD in delinquents needs further consideration since evidence-based treatments for these disorders are available at present.

With regard to internalizing disorders, Vreugdenhil, van den Brink, et al. (2003) found an anxiety disorder in 9 percent of the boys and a depressive disorder in 6 percent. Thirty-four percent reported one or more psychotic symptoms, although it is unclear what the meaning of this finding is. Because paranoid thinking was the most prevalent symptom, the presence of a personality disorder rather than a psychotic disorder may be present in these youths. Alternatively, such symptoms may be the result of substance use or a history of trauma.

Hamerlynck et al. (2005) found (on the basis of self-report questionnaires) a clinical indication for depression in 33 percent of the girls; 22 percent were suspected to have a posttraumatic stress disorder and 6 percent a dissociative disorder. Forty-seven percent reported suicidal symptomatology. On average, the lives of the girls had been marked by almost five traumatic experiences, and again, an association was found between the number of experienced traumas and the severity of aggression.

C. Conclusions

Recent Dutch studies on detained young delinquents confirm and extend the results of the prevalence studies carried out over the last decades. Findings suggest that the severity of delinquency in young offenders is positively associated with the presence of mental health disorders, although findings are not consistent at this point.

Several key research questions remain unanswered that are relevant for our understanding of the nature and clinical implications of co-occurring problems, their assessment, and interventions. One question concerns the direction of the relationship between crime and co-occurring problems such as substance abuse and school problems. Such knowledge may be important for the design of prevention programs aimed at avoiding later delinquency.

Furthermore, there are no known studies—and this is a serious shortcoming—on vulnerability, in the sense of a mental handicap, psychiatric disorders, or traumatizing factors, and substance abuse and delinquency, from either a sociological/criminological or a behavioral scientific/medical point of view. Which co-occurring problems are etiologically significant in the development of delinquency or play a mediating role (see also Loeber 2004)?

Well-designed population-based and clinical follow-up studies are needed in order to gain better insight into the developmental psychopathology of delinquent behavior in relation to other impairing problems. Outcome and efficacy studies should provide insight into the need for services, which are currently poorly provided in Dutch correctional facilities. The core task of these facilities is still to keep society safe and to apply judicial sanctions, thereby largely neglecting the long-term perspective, namely intervening so that future harm can be avoided.

Better care is needed to reduce mental health problems found at high rates in forensic populations. Because such care should not be a focus of justice authorities, this task needs to be transferred to mental health agencies. Fortunately, this view is gaining ground in the Netherlands: a second youth forensic residential clinic opened last year, as well as several youth forensic day treatment facilities. Ambulatory settings are now using functional family therapy and multisystemic therapy, and these interventions are being evaluated for their effectiveness. However, better forensic care is still needed in the youth detention centers since the majority of detainees do not receive adequate treatment for their mental health needs.

V. Prevalence and Development of Antisocial Behavior[7]

Because of the high individual, familial, and societal burden associated with antisocial behaviors in young people, it is important to obtain information on the occurrence and development of these behaviors and on factors influencing their prevalence. Cultures may differ in various ways from each other. Cross-cultural variations in the occurrence and development of antisocial behaviors in youngsters may aid in understanding which factors are involved in the etiology of these behaviors.

It is also important to study antisocial behaviors within a developmental context, because these behaviors do not arise anew but are assumed to be the result of the development of such behaviors in some ordered fashion. The development of antisocial behaviors is influenced by genetic factors or social learning or is the culmination of neurological, psychological, or social damage to the child. Understanding the course of such development can provide better insight into factors that are responsible for the emergence of violent and serious forms of delinquency in general, and this may aid in developing effective prevention or intervention strategies. Large-scale, prospective, longitudinal studies of general population samples are especially useful types of study for untangling the roots and consequences of antisocial behaviors across the life span (Rutter, Giller, and Hagell 1998).

A. Review of Earlier Findings

A number of important studies shed light on the prevalence and development of antisocial behavior.

1. *Population Prevalence of DSM Antisocial Disorders.*   We used the DISC (Shaffer et al. 1993) to assess DSM-III-R diagnoses of the most common psychiatric conditions among Dutch adolescents aged thirteen to eighteen (Verhulst, van der Ende, et al. 1997). The prevalence of conduct disorder (5.6 percent), oppositional defiant disorder (0.7 percent), ADHD (1.3 percent), and SUD (3.3 percent) were in the same range as is found for other Western societies (e.g., Earls and

---

[7] Frank C. Verhulst, Andrea G. Donker, and Marijke Hofstra provided the material on which this section is based.

Mezzacappa 2002). Higher prevalence of antisocial disorders in males than females is a ubiquitous finding.

2. *Development of Antisocial Behaviors: The Zuid-Holland Prospective Longitudinal Study.*   Few Dutch studies have investigated the longitudinal course of antisocial behaviors from childhood into adulthood. To determine the development of psychopathology from childhood or adolescence into adulthood, we conducted a fourteen-year prospective longitudinal study in four- to sixteen-year-olds from the general population. The sample was assessed at two-year intervals over an eight-year period, and again six years later, fourteen years after the first assessment (Hofstra, van der Ende, and Verhulst 2000, 2001, 2002*a*, 2002*b*). We are currently conducting a twenty-three-year follow-up of this sample, including the offspring of the original participants. Problem behavior was assessed with the Child Behavior Checklist (CBCL; Achenbach 1991*a*) and related instruments for assessing psychopathology in adulthood. At the last assessment, subjects were interviewed using a standardized psychiatric interview generating DSM-IV diagnoses. Results showed considerable continuity of antisocial behaviors across the fourteen-year time span from ages four through sixteen to eighteen through thirty. For example, between 37 and 52 percent of the individuals who could initially be regarded as deviant could still be regarded as deviant fourteen years later. A remarkable finding was that the continuity of antisocial behaviors *was no less* for females than for males. A somewhat different picture emerged when we looked at the prediction of DSM-IV-defined antisocial personality disorder in young adulthood from CBCL scores obtained in childhood or adolescence. The CBCL scales predicted later antisocial personality disorder in males but not in females, perhaps because the prevalence of DSM-IV antisocial personality disorder in females was very low. However, the diagnostic criteria for antisocial personality disorder reflect antisocial behavior that is more typical for males than for females. If the criteria for antisocial personality disorder had been more representative of female antisocial behavior, then the prevalence, and possibly also the prediction of antisocial behavior in adult women from earlier problems, would have been different.

The findings of the Zuid-Holland study corresponded with those reviewed by Loeber and Farrington (1998). Antisocial behavior in childhood or adolescence is a predictor of antisocial behavior in adulthood, even across the long follow-up interval of fourteen years as in our study. The combination of covert antisocial behavior and affective problems in childhood/adolescence was found to be an especially potent predictor of adult antisocial behavior.

We also reported unexpected findings. Despite its stability over time, overt aggressive behavior was only weakly associated with later antisocial behaviors after correction for the influence of other problems. The same was true for attention problems, which did not independently predict later antisocial behaviors.

B. Recent Findings

Research on these subjects has expanded. Analyses increasingly take account of cross-cultural comparisons and findings from other countries.

1. *Cross-Cultural Comparisons of Self-Reported Problems.*   To test the cross-cultural generalizability of antisocial behaviors in a more rigorous way than we did earlier, we compared YSRs (Achenbach 1991*b*) for 7,137 adolescents aged eleven through eighteen from the Netherlands with general population samples from Australia, China, Israel, Jamaica, Turkey, and the United States (Verhulst et al. 2003). The YSR, which is the self-report version of the CBCL, yields scores for the two broadband scales designated as internalizing and externalizing and for eight specific syndrome scales.

Deviations from the overall mean score across the seven cultures for the externalizing scale were smaller than deviations from the overall mean for the internalizing scale. All effects of culture for the eight YSR syndrome scales, including the scales designated as attention problems, delinquent behavior, and aggressive behavior, were small according to Cohen's (1988) criteria, ranging from 3 percent to 5 percent. The effect size of culture yielded the smallest cross-cultural variation for the aggressive behavior scale. For the externalizing and delinquent behavior scales, boys scored higher than girls across the various cultures.

On the basis of these analyses, we concluded that adolescents from different cultures responded in fairly similar ways to the problem items of the YSR, despite large variations in language, customs, religion, socioeconomic circumstances, and health care facilities. This was even more the case for antisocial behaviors than for internalizing behaviors, for which slightly greater cross-cultural variation was found. Because cultural differences associated with ethnic, linguistic, religious, and regional variations within countries may pose challenges for evaluating problem behaviors in youths living in multiethnic urban societies, cross-cultural comparisons of problem behaviors may be important for determining which youths need professional help and which do not.

2. *Developmental Trajectories of Antisocial Behaviors.* To test major developmental pathways models as described by Loeber et al. (1993) and Moffitt (1993), group-based developmental trajectories of CBCL problem scores were computed using a semiparametric mixture model-fitting procedure as proposed by Nagin (1999) (Bongers et al. 2004). Analyses were performed on the four measurements with two-year intervals across an eight-year period in the Zuid-Holland longitudinal sample. Trajectories covered developmental changes from ages four to eighteen. Associations were computed between developmental trajectories and psychiatric or criminal outcomes assessed at fourteen years from the initial assessment. To organize the CBCL externalizing items, the following four clusters of behaviors as proposed by Frick et al. (1993) were used: aggression, opposition, property violations, and status violations. The trajectories for the scales designated as aggression, opposition, and property violations showed an overall decrease in severity from childhood to adolescence, whereas status violations showed a developmental increase from childhood to adolescence. Within each of the four behavioral problem clusters, three to six different group-based developmental pathways could be determined, and most of these different trajectories followed the shape of the average trajectories at various levels of severity. Within each cluster the largest group of individuals followed a developmental trajectory at a low level, indicating that most individuals showed very few externalizing problems during their development from four to eighteen years as reported by their parents.

Because much less is known about the development of antisocial behaviors in girls than in boys, it was important to find that more boys than girls could be assigned to the higher (more problematic) trajectories, even though the shapes of the trajectories did not differ for boys versus girls.

The high-level trajectories indicated that the most troublesome children tended to be the most troublesome adolescents. Individuals who persistently showed high levels of antisocial behaviors from childhood into young adulthood followed a developmental pattern that was designated as life course persistent by Moffitt (1993). However, we could not identify a developmental pattern of antisocial behaviors that is called adolescence-limited by Moffitt. Within the clusters opposition and status violations we identified a group with increasingly high levels in adolescence, but the severity of these problems did not level off until the upper limit of eighteen years in this study.

Contrary to studies indicating that oppositional behaviors become less common after the transition from childhood to adolescence, we found that behaviors represented by the opposition cluster remained more common than those represented by the other clusters. Of course, it should be stressed that this study used parental information, and it may well be that parents were largely unaware of externalizing behaviors exhibited by their adolescent sons or daughters.

Individuals in the most problematic trajectories run the highest risks for a variety of psychiatric disorders, including antisocial personality disorder and mood disorders. However, it was a surprise to find that, despite the recent emphasis on physically aggressive behavior as a precursor of later violent delinquency, deviant trajectories of physically aggressive behaviors were the least problematic. Only in combination with deviant trajectories of opposition or status violations did they show adverse outcomes.

C. Conclusions

Recent developments showed a move toward more culture-sensitive evaluation of problem behavior in youths. This is important in contemporary societies, such as the Netherlands, containing many immigrants and refugees. When evaluating children of different cultures, mental health professionals must determine whether problems merely reflect cultural differences or whether they reflect needs for professional help. To help these children, we need cross-culturally robust instruments for identifying variations in behavioral and emotional problems that can be applied by diverse professionals under diverse conditions. A number of studies have contributed to the development of such robust instruments (Ivanova et al. nd; Rescorla et al. nd; Stevens 2004). However, much more work needs to be done.

Another topic in need of cross-cultural comparison is the documentation of secular changes in antisocial behavior over time. An earlier study on the ten-year secular change in problems in children and adolescents from the Dutch general population, using similar methodologies to assess problems, failed to show a dramatic increase in problems from 1983 to 1993 (Verhulst, van der Ende, and Rietbergen 1997). We are analyzing the data from a new population survey that will enable us to look at twenty-year secular changes in problems as reported by parents, teachers, and youths themselves and at secular changes in the use of mental health services and factors associated with mental health and with the use of mental health services. The first results showed that there was a slight increase in problems between 1983 and 2003, but that this increase could be attributed mostly to an increase in internalizing problems rather than externalizing problems. An exception was a slight increase (accounting for less than 1 percent of the variance) in parent- and teacher-reported oppositional behaviors. Though these types of studies are limited by their nonexperimental designs, which hamper any causal explanations of possible effects, they provide clues about possible effects of economical, political, social, or familial changes over time, especially if such studies can be replicated cross-culturally.

Progress has also been made in the methodology of identifying individuals who show developmental trajectories that deviate from pathways followed by normally developing children. Longitudinal screening, that is, the identification of individuals who are at risk for showing long-lasting problem behaviors based on multiple measurements, may be a more accurate approach than the identification of at-risk children through cross-sectional screening. It is important to gain more experience in the identification of children who are most at risk for serious deviant development.

To understand better the complex interplay between nature and nurture in the development of antisocial behaviors, future studies should consider well-measured risk environments in genetic-sensitive designs. Future studies should also consider both age differences in causal processes and gender differences in effects. Such an approach calls for research in which (molecular) genetic and psychosocial research is well integrated in prospective epidemiological strategies. A few years ago a unique study was launched in the city of Rotterdam in which 10,000 pregnant women and their newborn babies were followed over time. In 2005, the last pregnant woman was included. This multidisciplinary study with a heavy behavioral component will enable us to study the interplay between various biological risk factors, including genetic risk, and environmental factors in the development and course of problem behaviors (Hofman et al. 2004). A related study among a cohort of initially ten-year-olds, TRAILS, is being carried out in the northern provinces in the Netherlands. This study is more exclusively focused on the development of problem behaviors, including substance use and antisocial behaviors (De Winter et al. 2005). It will be possible to investigate mechanisms responsible for the development of antisocial behaviors, especially aimed at identifying risk factors, either biological risks or risks in the environment.

VI. Family Factors[8]

In the last few decades, juvenile violence in the Netherlands has increased. In company with this trend, significant research has gone into identifying the factors responsible for the development and maintenance of youths' violent antisocial behavior. There is general agreement that the development of violent antisocial behavior should be conceived as a result of a complex interplay of multiple factors. These factors include individual characteristics, such as impaired social-cognitive functioning (Orobio de Castro et al. 2002), neurobiological factors, co-occurrence of psychiatric disorders, and early aggressive behavior. Individual factors, however, interact with and are to a great degree influenced by the social environment in which an individual functions. Understanding the impact of the social environment is a critical step needed to fortify prevention and intervention efforts aimed at reducing adolescent violent behavior. Although the social environment encompasses many different contexts (such as neighborhood, school, or larger microsystems: political factors, media, poverty, and discrimination), empirical research consistently shows that social factors most directly linked to an individual's risk for violence are close interpersonal relationships: youth peer group factors (Loeber et al. 2001, chaps. 8, 9) and families.

A. Review of Earlier Findings

In our initial review of the literature on relationships between family factors and adolescent antisocial behavior, we reported on the results of two Dutch studies. Their aims were to specify more precisely how family factors relate to adolescent antisocial behavior by defining different levels of family functioning, by using a comprehensive, multi-

[8] Maja Deković, Jan M. A. M. Janssens, and Nicole M. C. van As provided the material on which this section is based.

agent assessment of these factors, and by examining their combined and unique predictive power. Both studies included large community samples of both boys and girls between twelve and twenty-one years old and their families. Family factors examined in these studies were ordered according to the level of proximity to the child's everyday experience into *proximal* (parental child-rearing behaviors: responsiveness, involvement, punishment, monitoring, consistency, and the quality of the parent-adolescent relationship: attachment, rejection, conflict, and communication), *distal* (dispositional characteristics of parents: depression and parental feelings of competence regarding child rearing), *contextual* (the quality of other relations within the family: marital satisfaction and family cohesion), and *global* factors (e.g., family SES and parental educational level). Four major findings emerged.

First, most of the assessed parental child-rearing behaviors (proximal factors) differentiate between violent and nonviolent youths. The way in which parents exert control seems especially to differ across the two groups. Second, the negative quality of the parent-adolescent relationship (another proximal factor) emerged as a strong risk factor for involvement in violence. Both mothers' and fathers' relationships with adolescents in the violent group seem to be characterized by a lack of closeness, intimacy, acceptance, and understanding. Third, significant differences emerged also regarding distal factors (parental characteristics). Both mothers and fathers of violent adolescents report more depressive feelings and less confidence in their own competence regarding child rearing than parents of nonviolent adolescents. Fourth, in comparison with proximal factors and distal factors, contextual factors (family characteristics) and global factors (SES and education) appear to differentiate less well between the two groups. Consistent with the social interactional perspective, the more distant the factor is to the adolescent's everyday interaction, the less important it seems to be.

Consistently with findings from many other studies (e.g., Reese et al. 2000), we found that family factors associated with risk for violence include harsh discipline, poor communication, lack of supervision and monitoring, lack of paternal support, parental pathology, and incompetence. These findings highlight the importance of family factors, especially those related to the parent-adolescent interaction, as an explanation of adolescent involvement in violent antisocial behavior. Moreover, it appears that families also affect the peer-related risk factors. Involvement with deviant peers, one of the most important risk factors for antisocial behavior, is closely related to problematic family functioning (Hill 2002).

B. Recent Findings

There are several noticeable trends in Dutch studies on the role of the family in the development of problem behavior (many of the cited studies did not focus specifically on violent behaviors, but use terms such as delinquency, antisocial behavior, or externalizing problems). First, recognition of the limitation of cross-sectional studies led to an increase in the number of longitudinal studies that test mutual influences of family functioning and antisocial behavior over time (see, e.g., Delsing 2004; Reitz 2004). Moreover, availability of more than two measurement points and the use of sophisticated analytic techniques (such as latent curve analyses) made it possible to examine factors that predict not only the occurrence but also the course of development of problem behavior (Deković, Buist, and Reitz 2004).

Second, in recent years, there has been increasing attention to ethnic diversity in the community, and studies are forthcoming that examine families belonging to different ethnic minority groups. The most important question in these studies is whether the same model of families' influences is applicable to different ethnic groups. Results to date support cross-ethnic generalizability of findings but also suggest some ethnic differences. In both Moroccan (Stevens 2004) and Turkish (Murad et al. 2003) groups, the same family factors predicted adolescent externalizing problems as in Dutch samples. But the strength of associations between family factors and antisocial behavior was stronger and the percentage of explained variance in antisocial behavior was larger in the Dutch sample than in the ethnic minority samples (Deković, Wissink, and Meijer 2004). In other words, models of family influences on adolescent antisocial behavior fit most adequately the data of Dutch adolescents. This is not entirely surprising given that this model was developed and tested in samples with similar characteristics: white, Western adolescents from a dominant culture.

Third, there is increasing recognition that family is a complex and multifaceted phenomenon and that if we are to gain a better understanding of the family as a context of development, we need to conceptualize it in a more complex fashion than has been common practice. Although there has been much progress recently (Delsing 2004;

Deković and Buist 2005), there is still a remarkable lack of integration regarding the links of different levels of family functioning with child outcomes.

Finally, the field seems to be moving beyond identifying the list of risk factors, to the search for mediating mechanisms that can explain the links between risk factors and negative outcomes. For example, Deković, Janssens, and van As (2003) showed that the global impact of contextual and distal factors on antisocial behavior is accounted for by the ways in which these factors shape the more proximal experience.

1. *Family-Based Intervention.*   In our summary of research to 2001 (Deković, Janssens, and van As 2001), we showed that there is no shortage of family-based interventions in the Netherlands, although many were developed with the general aim of supporting parents (mostly parents of younger children) and preventing child problem behavior rather than reducing adolescent violent behavior. One conclusion was that there is a clear need, in addition to early intervention programs, for theory-based, "developmentally sensitive" interventions that are designed specially for troubled adolescents and their families. A second, more important and worrisome conclusion was that little information is available about the effectiveness of existing interventions in the Netherlands.

Unfortunately, the situation has not been changed. In 2003 Verdurmen et al. published an overview of Dutch studies that examined the effectiveness of interventions. Although they also found an abundance of different interventions, they were able to identify only twelve evaluations that examined interventions aimed at reducing youth delinquency. Moreover, because of serious methodological shortcomings, most of the studies do not allow for reliable and valid conclusions. Surprisingly, despite a body of evidence that social environment clearly has an impact on adolescent delinquent behavior, the majority of evaluated interventions focused only on target adolescents, and only two interventions were designed to affect social context (school environment). None of the interventions included a family component, despite general conclusions from several reviews (Reese et al. 2000; Perkins-Dock 2001) and recent meta-analytic studies (Dowden and Andrews 2003; Farrington and Welsh 2003) that family-based interventions are effective in reducing persistent and violent antisocial adolescent behavior and preventing recidivism. These reviews showed that effective family programs focus on two aspects of family functioning that, in our studies also, appeared to be the most important predictors of adolescent violent behaviors: parental behavior (enhancing parental monitoring through behavioral parent training) and the quality of the parent-adolescent relationship (improving communication within the family through family therapy).

Veerman, Janssens, and Delicat (2004) analyzed ninety-two Dutch family preservation programs aimed at preventing or diminishing children's behavioral problems. Only seventeen of these programs have been evaluated by research designs with valid and reliable psychometric pre- and posttests. None of the programs was compared to a control group. The designs used were pre-experimental. On the basis of pre- and posttest scores, Veerman et al. found positive effect sizes of 0.52 on children's externalizing behavior and 0.55 on parental stress. They argued that more internally valid designs are necessary to assess effects of Dutch prevention and intervention programs aimed at preventing youth delinquency and juvenile recidivism.

In the last two years, however, there have been some positive developments. The need to work in an evidence-based manner has been increasingly emphasized by state health and criminal justice agencies (Ministry of Justice 2003). In 2005 a best-practices initiative, focusing on identifying the most promising approaches to prevention of youth delinquency and violence, was launched. In addition, several new family-based intervention programs have been implemented, such as multisystemic therapy and functional family therapy. Both interventions have been evaluated in randomized controlled trials and show promising results in reducing adolescent antisocial behavior and preventing recidivism (Alexander et al. 1998; Curtis, Ronan, and Borduin 2004). These interventions, however, have been developed and tested in the United States. Owing to the differences between the two countries in social and political climate, organization of mental health services, availability of different treatments, and types of clients, Dutch studies are needed to examine whether the same favorable results will be obtained here (Deković, Prins, and Laan 2004).

C. Conclusions

Recent findings confirmed the importance of family factors, especially those related to the parent-adolescent interaction, for development of violent antisocial behavior, both concurrently and longitudinally. Moreover, these findings seem to hold for different ethnic groups. Studies on families have a potential to inform us about important conceptual, applied, and policy issues regarding youth violence. Even if the family is not the only contributor to the development of antisocial behavior, it is certainly the central vehicle by which change can be made to turn development in a more positive direction.

Research in the Netherlands is steadily moving toward more complex comprehensive assessments of different levels of family, better designs, and more attention to diversity. But there is still much to be done. More research is needed with families who are most at risk (those living in poverty and in bad neighborhoods, with multiple risks present, with children who show aggressive behavior at an early age). Moreover, these families should be followed longitudinally over a long period. This is an extremely difficult kind of research: such families do not normally become subjects in large surveys because they are hard to recruit and hard to keep. In spite of these difficulties, such studies have been conducted (see, e.g., Thornberry and Krohn 2003). Given the degree of problems and the negative consequences for both individuals and society, such studies should be given the highest priority, and more effort (and money) should be put into such investigations.

Intervention research in the Netherlands is lagging behind. Nonevaluated parent education and family support programs continue to dominate the field. In the absence of any form of accountability or quality control to ensure that evidence-based family interventions are promoted, a diverse range of untested, perhaps even harmful, interventions are offered to the public. There is a great need for methodologically sound evaluation studies. Such studies provide not only valuable information for the clinical practice but also ways to test models devised from fundamental research in a full social context. The experimental nature of interventions yields opportunities for causal inference not available in correlational field investigations. But in order to fulfill this role, evaluation studies should be conducted rigorously, including a sound treatment rationale, clear problem specification, appropriate controls, adequate sample size and power, randomization of groups, checks for treatment integrity, multiple outcome measures, and follow-up assessments (Farrington 2003). In addition, more efforts should be put into revealing the "black box" of the intervention: the processes through which the intervention influences ultimate outcomes.

VII. Screening of Serious and Violent Juvenile Offenders[9]
Increases in violent offending behavior among youngsters in the Netherlands have given impetus to the idea of early identification and intervention. If serious and violent offenders can be identified at an early stage, corrective measures could be taken to prevent the further development of serious and violent offending behavior in juveniles. These early interventions, when successfully applied, would make society safer. They also would limit the need to build expensive corrective institutions for juvenile offenders. The individual youngsters would also benefit because successful intervention would prevent their exclusion from society.

However, identification of (potential) serious and violent offenders is not an easy task. The topic is surrounded by many questions. For example, can screening indeed identify potential serious and violent juvenile offenders? What factors must be included? Where must screening take place and by whom? What devices must be used?

A. Review of Earlier Findings

Our initial review (Scholte and Doreleijers 2001) focused on development of screening devices and screening strategies to identify youths at risk for serious and violent offending. Violent offenses constitute a subgroup of serious offenses, but serious offenses also include nonviolent offenses, such as theft, car theft, burglary, extortion, arson, and drug trading. However, because of different penal laws, definitions vary considerably between countries (Le Blanc 1998). Differences also exist in definitions used by different researchers. Some Dutch researchers have proposed limiting the definition of serious offending behavior only to index offenses that cause physical harm to others (Philipse et al. 2000). We used the Loeber et al. definition, which also includes property-related serious index offenses such as burglary, extortion, and drug trading one or more times (Loeber, Farrington, and Waschbusch 1998; Loeber, Slot, and Sergeant 2001).

Screening can further serve different purposes. Policy makers can aim to screen for serious and violent offending behavior to learn whether offending in the nonreferred population has increased or improved. In this case, the screening device is straightforward and simply requires using a clear definition and counting the number of cases that

[9] Evert Scholte and Theo A. H. Doreleijers provided the material on which this section is based.

fit the definition. However, with prevention in mind, policy makers and mental health professionals need to be able to identify youngsters "at risk" for future serious and violent offending behavior. This complicates matters considerably since the screening must take place before the offending behavior has occurred. This calls for a predictive screening device.

In the past, predictive screening devices were often based on behavioral or psychological classifications of offenders. Most current screening devices rely on a risk assessment of the multiple behavioral, psychological, and social risk factors associated with the development of serious and violent offending behavior. Over recent decades, risk- and needs-assessment instruments have been developed for dismissal, detention, probation, parole, and placement decisions. Although these instruments often display a sound face validity, their reliability and empirical validity are often controversial (Wiebush et al. 1995). Screening devices to identify (potential) serious and violent juvenile offenders must, however, be accurate and correctly identify youngsters at risk, since intervening in cases not really at risk directs resources to the wrong individuals and implies an unjustifiable stigmatization of youngsters.

Good screening instruments need to be both reliable and valid (Corcoran and Fisher 2000). Reliability refers to the consistency with which an instrument measures the same construct every time it is administered across persons, situations, and time. Validity pertains to whether an instrument accurately assesses the phenomenon it was designed to assess. Predictive validity is particularly important for instruments that screen for potential serious and violent juvenile offenders, since these instruments must be able to accurately predict the target offending behavior in the future. Predictive validity is, however, often hard to achieve, since longitudinal empirical research is needed to establish this type of validity. In the case of serious and violent offending behavior, predictive validity is even more difficult to establish, since the development of this type of problem behavior is often moderated by the interventions of the police, the justice system, and the welfare system.

The Committee of Test Affairs assesses whether the psychometric conditions of reliability and validity are sufficiently met (Evers, van Vliet-Mulder, and Groot 2000). Norms must be provided to identify the extent to which assessed individual juveniles diverge from the normal Dutch youth population. These requirements correspond with the quality standards set in the United States for screening devices assessing risks and needs (American Educational Research Association, American Psychological Association, and National Council on Measurement in Education 1999; Myers and Winters 2002).

Screening for potential serious and violent juvenile offenders at the level of general youth populations is not feasible for statistical and practical reasons. The low estimated base rate of about 4 percent of youngsters at risk for serious and violent offending in the general Dutch youth population (Eggen et al. 2005) would result in too many false identifications. Screening general populations of millions of youngsters would also result in unmanageable costs. Screening with regard to prevention can best be done at places in which children and families come into contact with officials monitoring the (mal)adaptive development of children, for example, at general health centers, at schools, and during leisure time projects. Screening with regard to correction can be done at places in which youngsters come into contact with juvenile justice authorities, at the boards for the protection of children, and in organizations for the execution of court orders, juvenile detention institutions, and resettlement organizations.

In the distant past the various mental health and juvenile justice organizations used screening procedures of their own. These instruments often displayed sound face validity but were not psychometrically underpinned. However, in the last decade a few new screening devices have been developed and empirically validated. These instruments are based on the premise that serious and violent offending is usually not caused by one determining factor, but results from complex processes in which biological and psychological vulnerabilities in children and juveniles interact with multiple factors in the daily living environment provided by parents, teachers, friends, caretakers, and other educators (Loeber, Farrington, and Waschbusch 1998; Zuckerman 2002). In these interactions, protective factors (e.g., appropriate medication, stable self-esteem, firm but sensitive parenting, supportive teaching, and prosocial peers) can support the adaptive development of children, whereas risk factors (e.g., drug abuse, psychopathic traits, child abuse and neglect, being a school dropout, and deviant peers) increase the chance that the development will take a maladaptive course. To offer youngsters appropriate help, justice and mental health professionals use these instruments to identify the risk and protected factors involved, so that interventions can be appropriately targeted.

An extensive risk-assessment questionnaire was developed for professionals working in the Dutch organizations that execute court orders (Scholte 1998). Predictive validity was established with regard to serious behavioral and emotional problems (Scholte 2000). Longitudinal research found that the use of this screening device makes service delivery more efficient and that assessed children and juveniles display an improved behavioral and emotional development compared with the nonassessed youngsters (Scholte and van der Ploeg 2003).

Doreleijers et al. (1999) developed a questionnaire and protocol for needs assessment in juvenile justice cases that standardizes the assessment procedure with regard to youngsters with penal law problems, called the BARO. It is based on the Problem Oriented Screening Instrument for Teenagers (Dembo 1994). Eight relevant fields are assessed: offending behavior, psychosocial development, physical development, behavioral problems, emotional problems, and problems with regard to the family, school, and peer group. The instrument produces a standard report that feeds the police, the public prosecutor, and the juvenile judge with background information. The BARO also produces an indexed indication whether individual youngsters are in need of further psychiatric assessment and mental health treatment. Research showed that the internal consistency of the BARO index is satisfactory when information is retrieved from both youngsters and their parents. The BARO is used by all officials working in the offices of the board for the protection of children with regard to juvenile penal law cases; it is appreciated for having led to a better systematization of relevant information (Bailey, Doreleijers, and Tarbuck 2006).

These instruments target underlying psychosocial or psychiatric needs of youngsters but are not designed to assess the risk for potential serious and violent juvenile offending. For that reason, we suggested the development of a device based on the Cambridge Screening Device (Blumstein, Farrington, and Moitra 1985; Le Blanc 1998). This proposal has not been pursued by Dutch researchers and policy makers.

B. Recent Findings

Although juvenile delinquency has generally been stable during the last decade, some remarkable changes have taken place. Census findings have suggested not only that serious offending has risen among children and youngsters, but that the onset of violent behavior has shifted toward lower ages (Ferwerda and Versteegh 1999; Kruissink and Essers 2003; Eggen et al. 2005). These developments have paved the way for comprehensive new governmental measures to correct this undesirable trend.

Preventive measures pertain to increasing the opportunities for youngsters to participate in society, for example, by guaranteeing safe homes, schools, and leisure time activities and by offering an easily accessible and well-organized infrastructure of health and day care for children and of educational, sport, and recreational facilities. Secondary preventive and curative measures aim at detecting juveniles at risk of dropping out of society at an early stage and correcting the maladaptive development of these children as soon as it is observed, for example by offering children and families appropriate material, psychological, and social help. Parallel to this, the maintenance of law and order has been tightened. Policies for first and light offenders is directed toward stopping the further development of criminal behavior, whereas juveniles who have committed multiple or serious and violent offenses are incarcerated in closed institutions, to receive a treatment directed at reeducation and resocialization (Justice Department 2003).

The screening of risks and needs has a central position in the execution of these new measures. To decide what must be done with regard to first and light offenders, police and justice officials need to identify the likelihood that serious and violent offending behavior will develop. To decide whether the treatment of already serious and violent offenders is successful or whether violent youngsters can be safely released, justice officials need to assess the likelihood that the serious and violent offending behavior will not be repeated. To decide whether children and families are in need of support, mental health professionals must be able to appropriately assess risks and needs. And finally, to decide whether the interventions initiated by these policy measures indeed meet their objectives, devices are needed to determine outcome effects. As a result, development of devices and procedures that reliably and validly screen risks and needs has moved higher on researchers' and practitioners' agendas in years.

To standardize the multiple risk assessments with regard to children at risk across mental health, child welfare, and child protection organizations and to make the assessments less time-consuming, proposals have been put forward to develop and implement less extensive screening devices. Proposals pertained first to the Strength and Difficulties Questionnaire, a brief behavioral screening questionnaire that can be completed in five minutes by parents or teachers of children aged four to sixteen. This device claims to detect behavioral and emotional problems in children as well as the well-known but more extensive CBCL (Goodman and Scott 1999).

However, developmental improvements in the youngster or in his environment due to the interventions cannot be assessed by this device. With this in mind, Dutch researchers have proposed a new short screening device, the standard taxation of the severity of problems (STEP). This new device is administered by social workers in about ten minutes. Risks with regard to the personal development of the youngster, and with regard to the socialization environment, are assessed on five-point scales. Twelve global leading questions (such as "Is there a chance that the youngster (still) will have problems with regard to his personal functioning?") are used and are clarified by extensive definitions and instructions. The instrument can be characterized as a guided risk schedule.

Preliminary research has suggested that social workers find this device useful (van Yperen, van der Berg, and Eijgenraam 2003). However, to rule out subjective bias, the reliability and predictive validity must be satisfactorily established in future research, since many earlier guided assessment schedules had difficulties with interrater reliability (Quay 1979). If the psychometric quality of the STEP turns out to be good, it will be suitable for assessing risk and needs in children at risk in a quick and standardized way, and it will be suitable for assessing the efficiency of the interventions taken to address the risks found (Slot et al. 2004).

With regard to the assessment of the psychiatric treatment needs of sexual juvenile offenders, a special module was developed for the BARO to estimate the risk of repetition of offending behavior by young sex offenders. Preliminary research suggested that the practitioners highly appreciated the extra information with regard to sexual offending that was added to the files of the youngsters by using this module. However, the implementation of the new module did not result in an increase in the predictive power of the original BARO (van Wijk, 't Hart, et al. 2005).

In the realm of assessment of delinquency-related social-emotional problems in youngsters, Scholte and van der Ploeg (2005) developed a seventy-two-item questionnaire for children aged four to eighteen to be filled in by parents and teachers. The screening device measures

DSM-IV-related symptoms of ADHD, oppositional-defiant disorder (ODD), CD, major anxiety and mood disorders, and autism. An additional module was developed to measure social and emotional detachment (or psychopathic personality traits) in youngsters. Reliability and validity were established in large samples of the general Dutch youth population. The instrument is of particular interest with regard to serious and violent juvenile offending because of its ability to screen for comorbid disorders in youngsters that have proven to be predictive of antisocial personality disorder at young adulthood, for example, ADHD, ODD/CD, and emotional detachment (Loeber, Burke, and Lahey 2002).

These instruments screen delinquency-related psychiatric and mental health problems in youngsters. They do not, however, directly target (potential) serious and violent offending behavior. This screening issue was taken on by researchers working in the area of juvenile forensic psychology and psychiatry, who introduced instruments to assess and control the risk for serious and violent offending behavior in youngsters.

With regard to young children, the Early Assessment Risk List for Boys (EARL 20B; Augimeri et al. 2001) has been translated into Dutch. This twenty-item questionnaire is designed to bring down the risk for violent behavior in boys till the age of twelve by assessing and controlling risk factors in the family (e.g., family problems, lack of support, family stress, bad parenting, and deviant norms), in the child (e.g., behavioral problems, trauma, and impulsivity), and around the child (school problems, deviant friends, and police contacts). However, the validity of this device is yet unknown since research is still under way (Lodewijks et al. 2001).

With regard to adolescents, a translation into Dutch was made of the Structured Assessment of Violence in Youth screening device (SAVRY; Lodewijks et al. 2001; Borum, Bartel, and Forth 2002). The SAVRY is composed of twenty-four risk items drawn from existing research and professional literature on adolescent development and violence and aggression in youths. The risk items cover three domains: historical (e.g., previous violent and nonviolent offending, age of onset, history of child abuse, dropping out of treatment in the past, parental criminality, and poor school performance in the past), contextual (e.g., antisocial peers, poor parenting, and living in bad neighborhoods), and individual (e.g., attentional problems, impulsive behavior, drug abuse, psychopathic traits, avoidance of treatment, and detachment from school/work). The device also includes a set of items measuring protective factors (e.g., prosocial life orientation, social support, and positive attitudes toward work). Predictive validity was investigated in various retrospective and cross-sectional samples of incarcerated juveniles and in one twelve-month longitudinal sample in forensic institutions (Borum, Bartel, and Forth 2005). Receiver Operator Curve analysis showed areas under curve (AUC $=s$) of about 0.66 for general offending and of 0.74 for violent offending, suggesting that the screening device predicts the reoccurrence of violent offending behavior slightly better than chance. These findings suggest that the instrument is potentially useful but that more research is needed. This pertains not only to the reliability of the risk assessments but also to the predictive validity. Moreover, longitudinal controlled studies are needed to establish that the interventions directed at the risks targeted by the SAVRY indeed control the (further) development of serious and violent offending behavior in youngsters. Regarding these issues, research is planned in Australia, Sweden, the United Kingdom, the United States, Canada, and the Netherlands in which its usefulness and the psychometric properties will be investigated in various institutions for incarcerated juveniles (Lodewijks, de Ruiter, and Doreleijers 2003).

C. Conclusions

Since the mid-1990s, serious and violent offending among children and youngsters increased in the Netherlands. Preventive measures were proposed to strengthen the bonds of youngsters and families to society and to enable early detection and correction of juveniles at risk. Corrective measures pertain to stopping and correcting the offending behavior.

To execute measures efficiently, juvenile justice and mental health practitioners need valid and reliable screening instruments, first to screen the risk of (potential) serious and violent offending behavior in youngsters and second to screen the underlying material, psychological, psychiatric, and social needs of youngsters and their families.

In the distant past, most Dutch professionals working with delinquent juveniles used their own screening devices, usually information sheets. Although these instruments often had a sound face validity, their reliability was often controversial. New risks and needs screening devices have been developed, or imported from other countries, that were based on empirical research revealing multiple relevant factors associated with the development of serious and violent delinquent behavior.

Instruments cover not only the offending problem behavior but also multiple risk factors (biological, psychological, and environmental—e.g., family, school, and peer group factors). Recent instruments also screen for the precursors of antipersonality disorder in children, for example, ADHD, ODD/CD, and psychopathic personality traits.

Although most instruments display good psychometric properties, according to practitioners the administration of the instruments often takes too much time and effort. There is a call for screening devices that can be administered in a shorter amount of time.

Assessment devices have been introduced to ascertain the risk for juvenile serious and violent offending behavior. To assess risk in young children, the EARL 20B has been translated into Dutch. To assess this risk in adolescents, the SAVRY screening device has been implemented in various institutions for incarcerated juveniles in Holland.

More research is needed to establish the reliability and validity of the various screening instruments. More research is also needed to establish that interventions directed at the risk targets pointed by identified various risk-assessment instruments indeed reduce the (further) development of serious and violent offending behavior. To establish this, longitudinal case control studies are needed.

VIII. Prevention[10]

The Netherlands is passing through a difficult period of instability and transition related to important social and economic change, a period that started some fifteen to twenty years ago. Some obvious changes include the shift from a social welfare state into a more market-oriented state, economic recession, and problems with immigrants. Although two political murders within hardly a year worsened the situation, these changes are not limited to the Netherlands, since they are clearly to be seen in many European countries. One consequence is an increase in insecurity and fear: fear for one's job or one's income, fear for what the future might bring, and fear of crime, all leading to demands for more security, more police, more repressive policies, and longer sentences.

[10] Josine Junger-Tas provided the material on which this section is based.

One question is to what extent these trends have affected juvenile justice and prevention policies. From 1985 through the 1990s the Ministry of Justice was associated with, and initiated, a program of national and local prevention policies. This has now changed. Extensive budget cuts and public opinion pressures for harsher punishments made it difficult to meet all challenges simultaneously. The present minister of justice believes that prevention is not an essential task of the Ministry of Justice, although it collaborates with the Ministry of Public Health and Welfare in a number of projects. However, the main responsibility for youth policies in general and prevention policies in particular is in local and provincial authorities.

A. Review of Findings

Originally the objective of most prevention programs was not to prevent serious and violent criminality. Their main goal was to improve the lives of mothers and their young children in deprived neighborhoods by addressing the health and educational skills of the mother and the cognitive development of the child. Examples are programs developed and evaluated by Olds and his colleagues (1986, 1988). Only when longitudinal research showed the stability of early antisocial and aggressive behavior (Olweus 1979; Huesmann et al. 1984; Farrington and West 1990; Loeber 1991) did the importance of the prevention of later criminal behavior become evident. In the Netherlands there was a similar development. Programs such as early education and parent training have developed from concerns about children's permanent lags in education, young people's lack of labor force participation, and intergenerational poverty.

1. *Early Intervention.*   The focus on prevention has shifted from the Ministry of Justice to the Ministry of Public Health and Welfare. Great sums of money are invested by the funding agency Zorg Onderzoek Nederland (Research on Welfare and Care in the Netherlands), instituted by the Ministry of Public Health and Welfare, in different kinds of prevention research programs, such as an extensive test of the Olds program, including parent training. The program has been adapted to Dutch culture and will be evaluated by an experienced research unit of the Sophia Children's Hospital (Erasmus University Rotterdam). More generally, research on the development of young children is encouraged, and ways are looked for to improve screening methods of (very) young children and their mothers so as to detect eventual psy-

chosocial family or child problems. The local health authorities, administered by the local authorities, play an increasingly important role.

Local health care is organized in so-called consultation offices in which babies up to age two are regularly examined—free of charge—and small children aged two to four remain under medical control. This is a universal program reaching about 95 percent of all families. The consultation offices follow a recently established basic health care program that is increasingly standardized, making sure that it is uniformly applied. Considerably more focus is placed on screening for early psychosocial family problems and antisocial child behavior. In addition, many of the existing parent training programs, focusing on transfer of educational skills to assist parents, have been developed and are administered by these offices.

One problem with the original training programs was their voluntary character. Families that ideally should be reached from a perspective of crime prevention, that is, multiproblem families or families under a civil supervision order, were not reached, as appeared from reviews of participating parents (Bakker et al. 1997). However, parent training may now selectively be imposed on parents whose children are persistent truants or in the case of families under a supervision order. In addition, the minister of justice, considering that parents have considerable responsibility for the actions of their children, is examining the possibility (taking the United Kingdom as a model) of imposing parent training as a measure on parents when their children have committed an offense.

There has been undeniable progress since the late 1990s in terms of prevention programs for families and young children. At the same time, parent training is increasingly used by the child care and juvenile justice system as a sort of parent disciplining measure.

2. School Programs.   With respect to early education, a number of tested programs are available. For example, a Dutch version of the Perry Pre-school Project (Schweinhart 1987; Schweinhart et al. 1993) and Slavin's "Success for All" (Slavin et al. 1990, 1993) have been carefully tested and found effective (Lesemann et al. 1998, 1999). They have been introduced in Dutch schools under the names of *Kaleidoscoop* and *Piramide*. In addition, there are three other original Dutch programs (*Kea, Opstap,* and *Overstap)* focused on the improvement of cognitive development of primary school pupils, which have also been found effective (Kook 1996; Wolfgram 1999; van Tuijl 2002). Two

American social competence programs, the Good Behavior Game (Kellam et al. 1998), a program for primary school pupils, and Skills for Life for secondary school students, have been adapted to Dutch culture and have been extensively tested and found effective (van Lier 2002; Gravesteijn 2003).

In the late 1990s the Ministry of Education made a start with introducing tested early education programs in all schools situated in deprived areas. For budgetary reasons it was a gradual approach, and at the end of the last century one-third of all target schools had been reached. However, since then, decentralization policies made local authorities responsible for primary education, and we do not know what has been left of these policies. This is all the more uncertain since the ministry considerably reduced school budgets for extra educational assistance to deprived children.

a. Education Programs.   Several programs have been set up to get persistent truants and dropouts back to school or into an apprenticeship. These young people are referred to the program by the education authorities. Most have considerable problems with parents, such as neglect and abuse, alcohol abuse, and incest, and at school, such as conflicts with teachers and pupils, alcohol and drug abuse, gambling, delinquency, and a lack of social skills and self-confidence. Careful screening is the basis of a treatment plan, combining instruction with monitoring and assistance. Most stay six to twelve months; the majority take up school again or join the labor market. The program is followed by several months of aftercare and monitoring. These programs are supported by the local community, the police, child care agencies, and labor organizations. Although they have not been scientifically evaluated, they seem quite successful in helping troubled youths to resume their education or to get a job.

Finally, communities continue to create so-called *Large Schools* in deprived neighborhoods (so called because they combine educational and social services under one roof). Their objective is to improve the effectiveness of the education process; to enlarge the school's functions; to relate home, school, and leisure; and to reinforce pupils' social competence. To achieve this, communities have reintroduced social work in the school, lengthened the school day with recreational activities, involved neighborhood residents, and included offers of parent training and social competence programs for pupils. Although most of the

Large Schools are primary schools, some secondary, technical schools have also adopted the model.

b. Community Programs. In 1999 both the Ministry of Justice and the Ministry of Public Health and Welfare funded the implementation and evaluation of the American program Communities That Care (CTC; Hawkins, Catalano, and Associates 1992; Catalano and Hawkins 1996), a very structured and rational prevention model. The program is based on research-based risk and protective factors in relation to behaviors such as delinquency, drug abuse, violence, being a school dropout, and teen pregnancy. Priorities for preventive action are based on careful analysis of risks and protections in the community and are followed by the input of effective intervention programs addressed to the selected risk factors.

The CTC was piloted in four sites, two of which were deprived neighborhoods in Amsterdam and Rotterdam. Since the funded experimental period was no more than four years and since the introduction of such an elaborate program was not without considerable practical difficulties, the accompanying research had to be limited to an implementation evaluation. The interim results of the process evaluation (DSP Research Group 2004) refer mainly to output data, that is, to information on the possibility of directing, administering, and controlling the operation of relevant organizations and service providers. Several conclusions can be drawn concerning the number of different organizations involved in CTC, the share of social service providers, the extent of mutual collaboration, and the degree of support by community leaders. It appeared to be considerably more difficult to involve residents and young people in the CTC process. So far the Dutch outcomes do not differ greatly from what has been found in the United States: increase of the quality of planning and decision making; greater collaboration among service providers; more coordination in the input in programming of preventive interventions; greater focus of preventive interventions on risk and protective factors; greater use of demonstrated effective and promising approaches; and more involvement of young people and other citizens in preventive interventions. The Verwey-Jonker Institute in Utrecht has been commissioned to conduct a process and outcomes evaluation of three new pilots (The Hague, Leeuwarden, and Almere) and a restricted outcome evaluation of the four first pilots (since that study was limited to a process evaluation). This study has only recently started so that nothing can be said about the program's possible effects. Amsterdam, however, wants to spread CTC to other parts of the city, and Rotterdam wants to introduce it in the whole city. One of the Netherlands' thirteen provinces (South Holland) has adopted CTC as a provincial program to be introduced on a large scale.

C. Conclusions

In a review of the main developments in the last five years, the question is to what extent there have been changes and to what extent one could—cautiously—identify new trends. We have three observations. First, the principles of evidence-based interventions have gained considerable ground, as is testified by numerous examples. In research, the main progress is undoubtedly to be found in the public health field: it is there that research standards are highest, the best outcome evaluations are to be found, and the first longitudinal studies have started. However, progress may also be noted in criminology. For example, the Dutch Ministry of Justice is following the British model, introducing an Accreditation Commission for treatment programs. Also prompted by budget cuts, the ministry realized that it was impossible to continue funding all kinds of projects and interventions, most of which had no demonstrated effects. The ministry is determined to put together a pool of effective, or at least promising, programs (to be evaluated as soon as possible), so as to know what interventions to use and to have better control over spending. Another example is a survey done by the Nationaal Instituut voor Zorg en Welzijn (National Institute of Care and Welfare [NIZW]) on behalf of the CTC experiments of all effective and promising prevention programs in the Netherlands (Ince et al. 2004). The same institute is setting up a database of all effective Dutch interventions in the field of (psychosocial) health and justice. Finally, although this has taken some time, practitioners increasingly realize that for their programs to be accepted, good-quality research has to demonstrate its effectiveness.

Second, there is some difference in focus between the United States and the Netherlands as far as prevention is concerned. The U.S. literature focuses mainly on programs for specific risk situations and addressed to individual children or youths; the trend in the Netherlands is to think in terms of broad national or local policies. This is illustrated, for example, by the consultation offices, which produce national rates of infant and young children's health, which are among the best in the world. It is also demonstrated by initiatives introducing early-education programs in all schools in deprived neighborhoods or in the Large Schools, initiatives that may assist numerous children to succeed in their school careers. Whether this will be the case should of course be measured in terms of truancy and dropout rates, but the focus in these cases is more on policies of local authorities than on effective prevention programs. Another example is the initiatives of schools for technical and vocational training to modify their curricula (promoting job training) and to connect with the business community around the schools so as to allow pupils to get jobs. Again, practitioners should be trained to put registration systems in place so as to have some control over what they try to achieve, but it is the difference in focus that we find of interest here.

This brings me to my third point, a nagging problem for which no satisfying solution has been found. We refer to the dissemination of effective interventions into standing practice. For example, a social competence program for primary schools, the Good Behavior Game, has been implemented in the Netherlands with great care and evaluated in an excellent study. Now what will happen if a great number of schools would wish to adopt this program? Although there is an implementation manual for practitioners, taking into account the way teachers usually maintain order and discipline, it is clear that they would need careful training in how to apply the game. This is true for many programs if one wishes to guarantee program fidelity and treatment integrity, but unfortunately in practice this is not always possible, if only for reasons of cost-effectiveness.

This problem has been considered in the United States and Canada, and on the basis of Lipsey's work, Howell discusses it from the standpoint of local juvenile justice interventions (Howell 2003, pp. 216–623). Lipsey conducted a meta-analysis of practical juvenile justice programs that had a rehabilitative orientation but were *not* research demonstration projects (Lipsey 1999; cited by Howell), finding that nearly half of them reduced recidivism by 10–24 percent, whereas some of the best reduced recidivism by 20–25 percent. In this respect the following characteristics were important: the provision of services, a sufficient amount of services, relation of these services to the relevant target group, and a distinct role for the juvenile justice system. The more of these characteristics an intervention realized, the greater the reduction in recidivism. Howell pleads (p. 221) for a pragmatic approach by which program principles and guidelines for effective interventions resulting from previous evaluations are taken up by communities and used in practical program development. This might then lead to evidence-based practices or "best" practices. Although this problem has not yet really been dealt with in the Netherlands, given the Dutch tendency to look for pragmatic solutions in policy terms, it seems to me that more reflection is needed if we want to improve prevention policies.

IX. Interventions[11]

Effectiveness studies have not been published in the Netherlands since 2001, but several have been started. Although an interest remains in outcome studies, official policy has been noncommittal and sometimes reluctant. Implementation of findings from outcome studies has been noncommittal and unrigorous.

A national recidivism study, however, showed alarmingly high serious recidivism by juveniles discharged from justice institutions, which made it increasingly clear that the practice of juvenile justice care needed a better theoretical and empirical basis and improved day-to-day practices in working with juvenile delinquents. The Ministry of Justice has now adopted a policy of establishing such bases.

A. Review of Earlier Findings

When we initially reviewed the Dutch intervention studies on delinquency (Bartels, Schuursma, and Slot 2001), we presented the results of four meta-analyses of interventions with juvenile delinquents: Lipsey and Wilson's (1998) meta-analysis of 200 intervention effect studies; Hollin's (1994) meta-analysis of meta-analyses, covering more than 500 effect studies; and the meta-analyses by Kazdin (1997*a*, 1997*b*) and Breston and Eyberg (1998) for youth in noninstitutional settings. An essential element of effect research is the use of an experimental design, a random clinical trial (or in some cases a strictly controlled quasi-experimental design) with one or more intervention groups, and at least one control group of no intervention or a different intervention. Random assignment of individuals to experimental and control groups is methodologically the most sound, but nonrandom assignment with checks on comparability is often used in quasi-experimental designs.

---

[11] Arnold A. J. Bartels provided the material on which this section is based.

For noninstitutional interventions with delinquents, Lipsey and Wilson (1998) found consistent positive results for individual counseling, training of interpersonal skills, and behavioral interventions, with positive but less consistent effects for multiple services and probation and parole. The best interventions in institutional programs were based on interpersonal skills training and teaching-family homes. Lipsey and Wilson reported positive but less consistent findings for behavioral programs, community residential programs, and multiple services. Hollin's (1994) meta-analysis provided insight into the characteristics of effective programs, such as the presence of a clear structure (such as behavioral programs and social and interpersonal skills training), cognitive components (covering modification of cognitive processes that accompany or cause antisocial behavior or a set of behaviors that leads to antisocial behavior), and a focus on change of attitudes, core beliefs, behavioral standards, and values. The best programs were carried out in the social networks of juveniles or program components concentrated on influencing these networks.

Kazdin's (1997b) qualitative review made explicit criteria for promising interventions that are not yet fully supported by effect research. They include the following: the intervention is conceptually sound, on the basis of at least some fundamental research regarding the core concepts; there are clear signs of intervention effectiveness; and a specified relationship between the interventions as a source of change contributes to the results. Kazdin recommended four intervention types: training cognitive interpersonal solution skills, parent management training (PMT), functional family therapy (FFT), and multisystemic therapy (MST). On the basis of their analysis of eight-two effect studies over a period of twenty-nine years (covering 5,272 youths), Breston and Eyberg (1998) also concluded that PMT and FFT were effective.

Van Gageldonk and Bartels (1991) undertook a meta-analysis of interventions in child and youth psychiatry, psychology, psychotherapy, and psychosocial help programs in the Netherlands from 1974 to 1990 (fifty-four evaluation studies). Positive treatment effects were associated with interventions with a clear structure teaching juveniles and families daily life skills for crucial life transitions. Examples were behavioral programs improving social competence and interpersonal and social skills training. In contrast, nondirective interventions did not show positive results, and the effectiveness of "therapeutic camping" was inconsistent or negative. Juveniles who dropped out from programs showed little or no improvement.

Meta-analyses (van Gageldonk and Bartels 1991; Lipsey and Wilson 1998) suggest a possible relationship between the degree of criminality and the degree of positive results. If the dropout rate can be kept low, the worst cases tend to demonstrate the most progress (they have the most to "win"). According to van Gageldonk and Bartels, there is also an indication of a relation between degree of criminality and duration or intensity of the intervention. A short duration tends to result in slight to moderate improvements, and a moderate duration or intensity is associated with moderate to high improvement. A longer duration or a large intervention investment gives less positive results. The duration and intensity of interventions often are a sign that the juvenile problems are intransient.

Not all interventions are beneficial. The Cambridge-Somerville study (started in 1937; interventions ended in 1945, and follow-ups continued until 1990) for a long time was thought to have had no treatment effects because of its nondirective approach to child and family problems. However, a reexamination of the original data showed that the intervention was followed by a worsening of delinquency and that a strong negative factor associated with this worsening was juveniles' attendance at summer camps (Dishion, McCord, and Poulin 1999; the summer camps were for "normal" youth, not for juvenile delinquents). The authors concluded that peer group processes probably contributed to the negative results.

There is, however, a plethora of effective interventions. Documentation about the best intervention (and prevention) programs can be found at the Web site http://www.Colorado.edu/cspv/blueprints, which is a collection of programs with proven effectiveness, screened by scientists, and replicated at more than one site. The reader is referred to this source for details.

B. Recent Findings

Interventions routinely undertaken with delinquents in the Netherlands often are characterized by the following features (based on Boendermaker and Verwers [1996], Le Sage [2004], and the author's knowledge from contacts with board members, directors and workers in institutions, and from annual reports of institutions). Service personnel usually make their own selection of what they think to be the core of effective treatment components without making use of known effective interventions. Target categories are defined, treatment rationales formulated, and treatment strategies stated. Nine of the eighteen juvenile justice institutions have chosen to use the social competence model (Le Sage 2004), which is based on operant, cognitive, interpersonal, and social skills training including the teaching-family home approach, a combination that was proven to be effective (Bartels 1986; Slot 1988; van Gageldonk and Bartels 1991; Kazdin 1997*a*, 1997*b*; Lipsey and Wilson 1998). However, treatment integrity usually has not been systematically evaluated, and compliance with program implementation is rarely carried through. In addition, methodologically sound evaluation studies including comparisons between appropriate control and intervention groups (randomized controls and experimental subjects) have not been carried out.

Recidivism rates remain of high concern because they are alarming. Juvenile recidivism rates after discharge from juvenile justice treatment institutions remain high. A recent recidivism study by the Ministry of Justice (Wartna, el Harbachi, and van der Laan 2005) covers 7,978 youngsters, of whom 6,160 were placed in institutions because of delinquency and the others for nondelinquent problematic behaviors (88 percent for boys). Age groups were fifteen years and younger, sixteen to seventeen, and eighteen years and older. The youths left juvenile justice institutions in the period 1997–2000. There were no differences between age cohorts: general recidivism, serious recidivism (potential detention punishment at least four years), and very serious recidivism (eight years) after one year were 40 percent, 36 percent, and 12 percent, respectively; after four years, 70 percent, 62 percent, and 29 percent; and after seven years, 78 percent, 69 percent, and 36 percent. Differences in the recidivism levels between institutions, although not reported, are likely because they included detention centers, other institutions set up for diagnostic purposes, and treatment institutions.

In the past, intervention in Dutch justice institutions focused on personality assessment, crisis intervention, and treatment. However, much of this focus shifted in 2004 when the Ministry of Justice with its new policy, To the New Juvenile Institution (Naar de Nieuwe Inrichting), gave the highest priority to the reduction of recidivism, the implementation of sanctions, and expansion of the number of juveniles and cost reduction per youth (Geerdink 2004, 2005). As part of this reorientation, programs now stress prison characteristics while keeping in mind that the detainees are adolescents and are in a crucial developmental phase of their life. "Old" managers who had been youth-oriented received retraining on how to focus on sanctions and management. Plans were made for placing two youngsters in one room, and in some institutions this has been implemented.

Treatment in facilities supervised by the Ministry of Justice appears (for some time in 2003, 2004, and the beginning of 2005, although less at the moment) to have turned to interventions based on old psychodynamic ideas of Aichorn (1930) and Redl and Wineman (1950) with no known documented effectiveness in reducing recidivism. In its present incarnation, the interventions have been combined with a very strict individual and group regime (resembling friendly military training of recruits) in a clear hierarchy between group leaders and juveniles; thus the opposite of a "soft and naive friendly" approach.[12] Jonker (2004) has reported a 9 percent recidivism rate after one year, but there are no appropriate controls (only estimated comparable recidivism figures of 38 percent). And it is not clear whether the 9 percent pertains to all the youngsters who left the institution or those who completed the program fully (dropout out rates are not reported.

A recent meta-analysis of the Ministry of Justice (Baas 2005) came to the same conclusions as Lipsey and Wilson (1998), which is not surprising because the analysis was to a large extent based on Lipsey and Wilson's findings. Generally the conclusion was that no effect or a negative effect was found for Scared Straight programs (visiting prisons as means of prevention, e.g.), group counseling in homogeneous groups, boot camps, noninstitutional vocational guidance, and regular probation. Positive effects were found for parent training, FFT, MST, therapeutic foster care, behavioral training (institutional and noninstitutional: social skills training in heterogeneous groups or anger management), and educational programs.

Currently, an outcome study on FFT is being carried out (Breuk et al. 2005). The Glen Mills approach (applying group dynamics and hierarchy in the context of an operant and modeling approach) also is the subject of research (van den Bogaart, Mesman Schultz, and van Muijen 2003). MST, PMT, and multidimensional family therapy (Rowe et al. 2002) are applied in some outpatient juvenile justice settings as

---

[12] A series of seven thirty-minute television programs on Friday nights in March and April 2005 on Evangelische Omroep (Evangelic Broadcasting) discussed this issue.

well, but outcome studies based on these interventions have not yet been carried out.

The importance of stimulating moral development by presenting youths with moral dilemmas and discussing them (the Equip program: Gibbs, Potter, and Goldstein 1998) has shown a positive effect on moral development in a random clinical trial (Nas 2005). However, it remains unclear whether the program reduces recidivism.

On September 7, 2005, the Ministry of Justice put into operation a committee to authorize behavioral interventions in the field (Erkenningscommissie Gedragsinterventies Justitie) and give permission for certain programs to be implemented. The committee adopted as guiding principles the Canadian What Works? approach (Andrews 1995; Lipsey 1995; van der Laan and Slotboom 2002; de Ruiter and Veen 2004), which is comparable to the intervention principles formulated by Kazdin (1997b).

C. Conclusions

Our past summary of recommendations (Bartels, Schuursma, and Slot 2001) still stands and can be supplemented by the following observations.

Outcome research data.   Outcome research has very recently started to become a standard for juvenile justice care. Programs should in principle be evidence-based.

Treatment.   An important component of interventions is the use of effective skills training aimed at preparing juveniles and families for daily life tasks and for critical periods in their lives. Interventions need to teach juveniles and members of their family alternative lifestyles that give fewer opportunities for antisocial behavior and delinquency. Intervention programs therefore should routinely teach youths and families to recognize the first signs of a behavioral chain (scenario) leading to antisocial behavior, and what to do instead. There is an implicit assumption, however: once juveniles have learned these new skills, they have to experience success in using them in society. The interventions should focus not only on behaviors, skills, and scenarios of antisocial behavior but also on emotions and cognitions (core beliefs and implicit life rules). Personality development and family and systems interventions are recommended as well as multimodal interventions.

Differentiations should be made among target groups.   No one approach works for all. Differentiated applications are required. More research is necessary on deviant developmental pathways, particularly taking into account conflicting cultural, behavioral, and religious standards and values among minorities. Interventions may have to be differentiated according to gender, age, intelligence, social status, psychiatric disorders, familial and social network configurations, and cultural, ethnic, and religious characteristics, and also neurobiological and personality features. Although the concept of psychopathy is widely used in forensic psychiatric settings for adults (Hildebrand et al. 2002; Hildebrand 2004), it is used much less for juveniles.

Potential negative effects of treatment.   Group treatment can potentially be harmful and should be structured to overcome potential negative effects (Dishion, McCord, and Poulin 1999). Experimental evaluation of the handling of group dynamics is essential.

Program evaluation.   Program integrity, the mutual influence between program and organization, requires continuous monitoring. The initiator of the intervention program has a crucial role in program integrity (van Gageldonk and Bartels 1991; Hollin 1994). The longer he or she is working on the program, the better. The initiator should also be responsible for program renewal and for organizational embeddedness of the program. In a chaotic organization, even the most sound program is likely to fail.

Methodologically sound evaluations and treatment effects research remain highly necessary. We have a very limited understanding about what works for whom and under what circumstances. An important requirement is periodically to repeat effect evaluations.

For effect research *the difference between internal and external validity* should be kept in mind. An intervention program with a proven effectiveness for noninstitutionalized adolescents between, for example, ages fourteen and eighteen (with sound internal validity) may very well be not effective for the same target group in another country or in different circumstances. The extent to which program effectiveness generalizes to other populations is a matter of external validity and often does not receive the attention that it deserves.

Screening for risk.   Risk assessment and prognostic instruments have to be developed and refined (but see Sec. VII of this essay). Yet in the Netherlands there is not a sound validated and standardized risk-assessment or prognostic instrument for juvenile offenders. Such an instrument is also necessary for risk management and ascertaining improvement rates (improvement in criteria that can reflect change). The

Psychopathy Checklist Revised (Hare et al. 2001) has a youth version that is being validated in the Juvenile Justice Treatment Institution, Harreveld, in the Netherlands. In addition, the SAVRY (Lodewijks, de Ruiter, and Doreleijers 2003), which is based on a comparable instrument for adults (Historic, Clinical, and Risk, twenty items; Philipse et al. 2000; Webster, Müller-Isberner, and Fransson 2002), is being validated. An outstanding and cross-validated Dutch risk-assessment instrument for juvenile delinquents (Brinkman and Kars 1974; Mesman Schultz 1977; Bartels 1986) was not used because of the social climate in the 1970s: professionals did not want to judge persons by figures. Risk-assessment instruments can teach us a great deal about important causal factors that we now know only in very broad terms.

X. Police and Justice Interventions[13]

Some tens of thousands of young people between ages twelve and seventeen come into contact with the police in the Netherlands every year because they have committed a criminal act (65,100 in 2004).[14] The number of serious and violent delinquents among these youths has increased.[15] All are confronted with an official response from the police, and often from the public prosecutor and a juvenile judge. This section focuses on these responses and, as far as this has been studied, their impact on the delinquent behavior of the youths involved.

This overview is subject to a number of limitations. First, the focus is on juvenile offenders aged twelve to seventeen, the boundaries of juvenile criminal justice in the Netherlands. Second, many interventions are not oriented toward particular categories of offenders or offenses, but toward a phase in the proceedings or toward a particular traditional intervention with a view to replacing it. One can seldom speak of an exclusive focus on serious and violent delinquents. It may be assumed, however, that nearly all youths who have to account for their actions in court will fall under the definition of serious and violent delinquents (Loeber, Farrington, and Waschbusch 1998). The same applies for youths involved in projects designed as a substitute for unconditional detention. A third limitation is that many interventions are

---

[13] Peter van der Laan provided the material on which this section is based.

[14] At the end of the 1990s, this figure was stable at around 47,000. At the start of this century, the number increased sharply to 65,100 in 2004 (Eggen and van der Heide 2005).

[15] The share of youths suspected of a violent crime against a person was 9 percent in 1990. By 2004, that share had doubled to 21 percent.

not subject to evaluation and are certainly not regularly evaluated. Moreover, many evaluations are directed toward a process or implementation rather than toward outcomes. Finally, many of the evaluations are mediocre.

A. Review of Earlier Findings

The Dutch juvenile justice system rests on two pillars: a civil law pillar and a criminal justice pillar. A criminal justice response is possible if a youth is aged twelve or over. A civil justice response is also possible, in the form of a child protection order. This may be issued in respect of children under age twelve but also in respect of children aged twelve and over. The latter applies particularly if the criminal act is seen as a symptom of serious psychosocial problems, meaning that support should be offered to the youth, and possibly to the family. No records are kept of how often this happens.

Three levels can be identified in the criminal justice approach to juvenile crime: the police, the public prosecution service, and the courts. In the event of an arrest, the police decide whether to charge the individual with an offense and refer the case to the office of the public prosecutor. The public prosecutor decides whether to prosecute. Many cases are dismissed or settled, often on condition that the juvenile completes an alternative sanction. This is not the outcome for other young people; they are indicted by the prosecutor and have to appear in court. The court generally deals with individuals only six to twelve months after they were first arrested.

1. *Police.*   The precise number of cases handled by the police is not known because charges are not always issued. Given a trivial offense or problems of a psychosocial nature, cases will be handled informally with a reprimand or diverted to a support agency. In the 1980s, it was estimated that a third of all juvenile contacts with the police were handled in this way (van der Hoeven 1985). Another important way that the police may deal with cases is by referring them to "Halt." The Halt option is designed for youths who have been found guilty of vandalism or shoplifting. The youths carry out damage compensation activities or cleaning tasks (for up to a maximum of twenty hours), and if the tasks are successfully completed, the charges against them are dropped. The police sent over 23,000 youths to Halt in 2003. In other, more serious cases, the police issue charges and refer the cases for further

processing by the public prosecutor. In 2004, the number of such cases was almost 34,000.

2. *Public Prosecutor.*   The public prosecution service has been dealing with juvenile cases in ever growing numbers. The number of cases registered in 1998 was 26,000. By 2004, this had increased to over 33,800. Public prosecutors deal with 63 percent of these cases themselves, settling the cases or dismissing them. Often this settlement or dismissal is arranged under the condition that an alternative sanction is carried out or compensation paid. The public prosecution service imposed 11,500 alternative sanctions in 2004. In contrast to previous years, the share of settlements and, particularly, dismissals has decreased markedly. More cases end up with an indictment: 11,900 cases were presented to court in 2004.

3. *Court.*   In the 1980s and 1990s, the number of cases handled by the court fluctuated around 6,300. That number has increased since the mid-1990s to nearly 11,900. The court imposed 17,500 sanctions in these cases. The majority (44 percent) were alternative sanctions. Most involved periods of community service (70 percent), though educational punishments (social skills training, courses, etc) were also imposed frequently. Alternative sanctions replaced many fines, which are being imposed less and less often (700 in 2004). In 2004, 6,100 conditional and unconditional detentions were imposed; this was 86 percent more than in 1997. The share of these detentions in all sanctions imposed did not change, however (35 percent). Many conditional detentions are imposed in combination with an alternative sanction. The number of unconditional detentions doubled to almost 2,000. The average duration of the unconditional detention was eighty-seven days, which is, on average, forty-three days shorter than in 1998.[16] In 2004, a further 2,270 youths were obliged to pay damage compensation. And 9,200 youths were required to undergo probationary supervision as a condition in a conditional sentence. Again, this number is much higher (95 percent) than at the end of the 1990s. The most severe sanction in Dutch juvenile criminal law is the "placement in a juvenile institution" measure. This measure, which may be imposed for a maximum of six years, was imposed on 250 youths in 2004.

4. *Youths in Contact with Police and the Judiciary.*   The points made above illustrate the filter-like working of the different levels of the

---

[16] Youth detention can last up to one year for twelve- to fifteen-year-olds inclusive and up to two years for sixteen- and seventeen-year-olds.

TABLE 3

Flow Chart of the Dutch Juvenile Justice System

Juvenile population of the Netherlands (12–17 years old inclusive)	1,100,000
Youths who commit offenses[a]	400,000
Unrecorded police contacts	Unknown
Recorded police contacts	65,100
Referred to support or child protection agencies	Unknown
Referred to Halt (2003)	23,000
Charges issued	34,000
Cases registered with the public prosecutor	31,000
Dismissal	3,700
Settlement	13,500
Indictment	11,900
Other (joined cases, transfers)	4,000
Alternative sanction	11,500
Cases handled by the court	11,900
Guilty with no punishment imposed	Unknown
Fine	700
Conditional youth detention	4,100
Unconditional youth detention	2,000
Placement in a juvenile institution	250
Alternative sanction	9,700
Other responses:	
Preventive custody (estimate)	2,900
Youth probation	9,200

[a] Extrapolation from outcomes from national self-report research (van der Laan et al. 1998).

judicial system. The approach to tackling juvenile delinquents may therefore be typified as a system of "minimal intervention." Restraint is the aim at every level: not every police contact is recorded, not every offense charged is sent to the public prosecutor, not every charge leads to an indictment, and not every indictment results in a detention. Table 3 quantifies this approach in approximate terms for the year 2004. On a cautionary note, the table can provide only a broad indication, since different measurement units are represented.

5. *Effectiveness of Interventions at the Police Level.* Police actions against young people have rarely been the subject of research. Junger-Tas and colleagues (Junger-Tas 1983; Junger-Tas, Junger, and Bar-endse-Hoornweg 1985) conducted research into the effects of recorded contacts with the police and the judiciary. They found that 56 percent of the 300 youths who had been in contact with the police did not come into contact with the police or the judiciary again. Since the

nature of the police decision was not incorporated in the research, we can learn little about the specific effects of an informal reprimand, referral to Halt, or issuance of charges.

Many support projects were set up in the Netherlands in the 1980s and 1990s designed for young people who had become known to the police. By participating in such a project, a young person could avoid further contact with the judiciary. Various projects were evaluated, but the research designs were far from ideal. Control groups either did not exist at all or did not match the experimental or intervention group on all relevant criteria. Effects were established on the basis of exclusively self-report data or exclusively police data, or during a limited period of time. It was not always clear what support was offered. In some cases, the cautious conclusion was drawn that offering support to young people who had been in contact with the police may reduce delinquent behavior and renewed police contacts (Scholte 1988; Boendermaker and Schneider 1991; Terlouw and Susanne 1991; Duipmans 1993; Terpstra 1997). The longer-term effects (one year and longer) are not known.

Five separate research studies have investigated the effect of Halt. Korf (2003) recently examined this collection of studies. He concludes that the hypothesis that Halt leads to lower recidivism rates is not based on a sound foundation. Only two of the studies used a control group, which in both cases deviated from the Halt group in essential characteristics. This leaves us unable to portray interventions at the police level in any comprehensive way. A particular oversight was the lack of research attention to or comparison with cases dismissed by the police (minimum intervention).

6. *Effectiveness of Interventions at the Level of the Public Prosecution Service.*   Junger-Tas, Junger, and Barendse-Hoornweg (1985) also reviewed the effects of contact with the public prosecution service. Of the 150 youths who were involved with the public prosecutor, 60 percent had no further contacts in the subsequent two years. The nature of the prosecutor's decision (dismissal, indictment, etc.) was not incorporated in the analyses, so no statements can be made about the consequences of such decisions. As far as is known, research studies have not been conducted in the past two decades at the level of the public prosecutor that would support statements on the *impact* of prosecution service decisions. Studies have, however, focused on alternative sanctions. Only one study (van der Laan 1991) examines the role that al-

ternative sanctions imposed by the public prosecutor may play in preventing recidivism. Of 300 youths who were sentenced to an alternative sanction by the public prosecutor in 1984 and 1985, 51 percent reoffended during a period of three and a half to five and a half years. By way of comparison, of the 700 youths who were sentenced to an alternative sanction by the juvenile judge, 76 percent reoffended. These percentages are not, however, directly comparable since the public prosecutor cases were less serious than the cases handled by the juvenile judge.

7. *Effectiveness of Interventions at the Court Level.*   The situation is most favorable for interventions at the level of the court. Various sanction types have been evaluated once or repeatedly (van der Laan and Essers 1990, 1993; Spaans and Doornhein 1991; van der Laan 1991; Drogt 1992; Vreeman 1992; Spaans 1993; Spaans and Reurslag 1994; Essers, van der Laan, and Veer 1995; Blees and Brouwers 1996; Duipmans 1996; van der Genugten, Timmerman, and Nijboer 1996; van der Steeg and Niemeijer 1996; Eggermont 1997; Baerveldt, Derksen, and Bijlsma 1997; Groen 1997; Horjus 1997; Kleiman and Terlouw 1997; Boendermaker 1999). It may be said of alternative sanctions, including the intensive educational punishments, youth probation, and "hard-core" projects designed for serious and multiple offenders, that they produce a better result than traditional sanctions. The proportion of reoffenders is somewhat lower; and if reoffending does take place, it is later, less frequent, and less serious. This applies particularly to interventions comparable with unconditional detention, that is, interventions imposed on juveniles who have committed serious offenses or have repeatedly been in contact with the police and the judiciary. But here too, as with the interventions at police and public prosecutor levels, many evaluations have been confronted with methodological problems. The research designs were often far from ideal, which has limited the persuasiveness of the results.

B. Recent Findings

The number of youths who come into contact with the police and the judiciary in recent years has increased (van der Laan 2005). The marked increase in the first years of this century is not easy to explain. For instance, the number of young people arrested by the police in 2002 increased by as much as 17 percent in relation to the preceding year and by a further 7 percent in 2003. Such major increases are almost certainly the result of changes in the system, priorities, and recording, and only in part related to changes in the behavior of young people. An increase in the number of police and judicial responses has been observed for a longer period. More young people are receiving a sanction rather than having their case dismissed. In particular, the numbers of alternative sanctions and detentions have increased. This increase can be only partly explained by the increase in serious and violent offenses. It should therefore be attributed to societal attitudes that have prompted a more repressive response (van der Laan 2005).

Three recent studies within the framework of the "recidivism monitor" project, initiated by the Research and Documentation Center of the Dutch Ministry of Justice, have shed some light on young people's recidivism after judicial interventions. Of all youths placed in a judicial juvenile institution, 70 percent came into contact with the judiciary again within four years of leaving (Wartna, el Harbachi, and van der Laan 2005). The most important predictor of recidivism is a history of contact with the judiciary. Research into recidivism among minors who appeared before a judge in 1997 shows that 59 percent of sentenced youths came into contact with the judiciary again within seven years (Wartna, Tollenaar, and Blom 2005). Recidivism is highest after an unconditional detention (84 percent). Of all youths who received a community service punishment in 1997, 58 percent reoffended within seven years. When the punishment took an educational form, the rate of reoffending was 64 percent. The recidivism rate after a fine was 53 percent. The third study explores recidivism after probationary supervision (van der Laan, van der Knaap, and Wartna 2005). A third of youths reoffended while under the supervision of the youth probation service, and two-thirds reoffended in the subsequent four years. Whether and how these interventions contribute to behavioral change is not shown by these studies. Targeted research into relevant offender, offense, and intervention characteristics is needed to explore these questions.

Recent years have seen an increased amount of research into judicial juvenile institutions. New treatment methods have been introduced and evaluation studies have started at the same time. The evaluations to date are limited to reporting the implementation process, changes in (prosocial) attitudes held by youths, general recidivism disconnected from the nature and content of treatment, and studies that lead to cautious estimations of effectiveness (Nas 2005; van Dam 2005; van Heerwaarden, Hilhorst, and Slabèrtje 2005).

Two residential programs for juvenile delinquents have attracted a great deal of media attention in recent years: the Glen Mills School and the judicial juvenile institution Den Engh. Considerable social and political support for their approach is evident, but controversy is also attached to the group-oriented approach and the programs' similarity to American "boot camps." The institutions have presented their own findings, which at first appeared very positive (van den Boogaart, Mesman Schultz, and van Muijen 2003; Jonker 2004) but on further consideration were characterized as unreliable (van der Laan, Spaans, and Verhagen 2004). Two program evaluations have concluded that various aspects of the approach are questionable, tempering expectations that these interventions will prove effective (Hilhorst and Klooster 2004; van Heerwaarden, Hilhorst, and Slabèrtje 2005).

C. Conclusions

Little is known about the effectiveness of many of the interventions imposed by the police and judiciary as a criminal justice response. The recidivism studies carried out by the Research and Documentation Center of the Dutch Ministry of Justice have given more insight into recidivism in general, but whether and how different types of interventions contribute to behavioral change is mostly unknown. The methodological and other drawbacks associated with much of the Dutch evaluation research constitute an important reason for this lack of knowledge. These drawbacks undermine the validity of the research outcomes. In summary, the failings are as follows: the lack of control or comparison groups; problems matching control groups; young people dropping out of intervention programs before they end; young people dropping out of research groups at the time of follow-up contacts; small numbers of youths involved in interventions or evaluation; different definitions and operational understandings of effects and recidivism that hamper comparison; recidivism studies carried out over a short period of time; gaps in knowledge of the nature and content of the intervention; inconsistency of the content and method of the intervention; and outdated research data. Having considered these failings, we offer several suggestions for future research. Some relate to the object of the research, whereas others concern the nature and quality of the research. First, there is a need for greater transparency in police and judiciary responses to reveal who ends up in the system and what decisions are made about them. Although more information is available now than five or so years ago, unreliable data and assumptions still leave too many gaps.[17] A second challenge lies in obtaining better insight into the content and effects of *all* police and judicial interventions. The current situation is typified by selective and incidental evaluations. Third, the quality of evaluation research must be improved. Designs should achieve a minimum score of four or five on the Scientific Methods Scale (Farrington 2003). This means that the research should follow at least quasi-experimental designs, though ideally studies would follow randomized controlled designs. The research should meet a number of basic conditions, such as the standardization of recidivism measures and periods (see Wartna 1999). The nature, content, and method of interventions should be properly described. It should be established how an intervention was implemented and whether its execution went according to plan. This implies the need for good process evaluations in addition to sound research into effects. Such research clarifies to what extent interventions are directed by theoretical considerations. This is important because a clear, well-conceived, and elaborated theory will considerably increase the chances that an intervention will be effective. Many interventions in the Netherlands do not have such a theoretical basis. For the same reason, problems experienced by young people must be assessed, and the risk of repeat offending estimated, so that the right intervention can be applied "to measure." This assumes availability of valid and reliable *risk-assessment* instruments. In this way, a real step forward can be made toward evidence-based practice.

XI. Next Steps

The preceding sections illustrate many of the strengths of efforts to understand the course and risk factors of serious delinquency and ways to deal with, prevent, and reduce serious offending by juveniles. In our earlier volume (Loeber, Slot, and Sergeant 2001), we articulated many conclusions. We see the following as the most urgent to be addressed in research and policy.

First, official national records of juvenile delinquency are still made

---

[17] Reliable national data on sanctions and measures imposed have been available only for a couple of years.

available only after three to four years (e.g., Sec. I could report on data only through 2000, whereas we are now writing six years later). No well-formulated crime policy relevant to the present and reaching toward the future can be built on such out-of-date information.

Second, efforts to improve the early identification of youth at risk of escalating from age-normative problem behaviors to serious antisocial and delinquent acts remain at a very early stage of development and as yet do not appear to be instituted on a regional or broader basis to serve whole segments of the population.

Third, the evaluation of interventions, although slightly improving, remains of the highest urgency. Whereas evaluations of medications for health-endangering and communicable illnesses for their effectiveness are commonplace (an activity that is supervised by the government), it is extraordinary that intervention methods to improve the safety of people and the welfare of the present and future generations of youths do not receive similar scrutiny. No one is served by offering parents, teachers, and community workers programs that have uncertain outcomes. Offering intervention methods of unknown effectiveness on a large scale inevitably results in massive wastage.

Fourth, cost-benefit analyses of successful interventions are needed to document the costs in euros of implementing programs and the euros saved in terms of reduced delinquency, and other positive outcomes such as employment, better adjustment, and so forth.

Fifth, initiatives to move toward "evidence-based interventions" have been made, but there are no large-scale interventions yet.

Sixth, the implementation and dissemination of proven interventions is hampered by the absence of a structure of training programs, documentation, intervention protocols, and other supports needed to disseminate and reach those willing to change practices. There is no national central Web site to which individuals can turn for the best sources of information. The implementation of such a site has the highest urgency.

Seventh, structural problems in the administration of effective interventions remain in at least two key areas: mental health needs for juveniles in institutions and needs of schools to deal with juvenile problem behaviors that disrupt the academic functions of schools and the safety of students and school personnel. In the past, attempts have been made to involve institutional personnel and school personnel in organizing and maintaining programs. It is debatable whether this strategy is optimal because of time restraints, training and background deficits, and cultures that rightly aim to focus on other tasks (security in institutions and academic tasks in schools). Serious consideration should be given to alternative provisions for programs, such as the assignment of mental health services in institutions to alternative and better-equipped organizations supervised by a government mental health agency, and programs to prevent and reduce misbehavior and delinquency in schools to specialized agencies skilled at such tasks. In England, for example, mental health services in prisons have been transferred to the National Health Service, whose personnel are much better equipped than prison guards to deal with pressing mental health needs of inmates.

Eighth, progress has been made in the Netherlands to start a single longitudinal cohort study on developmental aspects of juvenile delinquency. Such research, however, can be best done with multiple age cohorts instead of a single age cohort, partly because research findings with the aid of an accelerated longitudinal design can be produced in a shorter time than is possible with a single cohort. Another major reason why multicohort studies are needed is to inform about changes in delinquency levels from one age cohort to other age cohorts and how such differences in levels are related to patterns of risk and protective factors. This is essential knowledge for an eventual better understanding of secular crime waves in communities, which after all are composed of the accumulation of offending levels of different age cohorts.

Ninth, increasingly, Dutch policy is concerned about the safety of its population (Boutellier 2002; special issue of *Justitiële Verkenningen*, July 2004; Wittebrood and van Beem 2004). While it is laudable to attempt to improve the sense of safety of whole populations, the bottom line is the reduction of violence in communities. The litmus test is whether government actions, combined with actions of others involved, can reduce violence to a significantly lower level.

REFERENCES

Achenbach, T. M. 1991*a*. *Manual for the Child Behavior Checklist/4–18 and 1991 Profile*. Burlington: University of Vermont, Department of Psychiatry.

————. 1991*b*. *Manual for the Youth Self-Report and 1991 Profile*. Burlington: University of Vermont, Department of Psychiatry.

Aichorn, A. 1930. *Wayward Youth*. New York: Viking.

Alexander, James, et al. 1998. *Blueprints for Violence Prevention: Functional Family Therapy*. Boulder: University of Colorado.

American Educational Research Association, American Psychological Association, and National Council on Measurement in Education. 1999. *Standards for Educational and Psychological Testing*. Washington, DC: American Educational Research Association.

Andrews, D. 1995. "The Psychology of Criminal Conduct and Effective Treatment." In *Whatever Works—Reducing Offending*, edited by J. McGuire. Chichester, UK: Wiley.

Angold, A., E. J. Costello, and A. Erkanli. 1999. "Comorbidity." *Journal of Child Psychology and Child Psychiatry* 40:57–87.

Augimeri, L. K., C. D. Webster, C. J. Koegl, and K. S. Levene. 2001. *Early Assessment Risk List for Boys: EARL-20b*. Toronto: Earlscourt Child and Family Centre.

Baas, N. J. 2005. *Wegen naar het rechte pad: Strafrechtelijke interventies voor delinquente jongeren right path*. The Hague: Scientific and Documentation Center.

Baerveldt, C., M. Derksen, and J. W. Bijlsma. 1997. "De effecten van opleiding en werk op recidive van gedetineerde jongeren." In *Jeugd en cel: Over justitiële inrichtingen, jongeren en jongvolwassenen*, edited by C. Baerveldt and H. Bunkers. Utrecht: De Tijdstroom.

Bailey, S., Th. Doreleijers, and P. Tarbuck. 2006. "Recent Developments in Mental Health Screening and Assessment in Juvenile Justice Systems." *Child and Adolescent Psychiatric Clinics of North America* 15:391–406.

Bakker, I., K. Bakker, A. van Dijke, and L. Terpstra. 1997. O + O = O²— *Naar een samenhangend beleid en aanbod van Opvoedings-ondersteuning en Ontwikkelingsstimulering voor kinderen en ouders in risicosituaties*. Utrecht: NIZW.

Barbaree, H. E., W. L. Marshall, and J. McCormick. 1998. "The Development of Deviant Sexual Behaviour among Adolescents and Its Implications for Prevention and Treatment." *Irish Journal of Psychology* 19:1–31.

Bartels, A. A. J. 1986. *Sociale vaardigheidstraining voor probleemjongeren*. Lisse: Swets and Zeitlinger.

Bartels, A. A. J., M. S. Schuursma, and N. W. Slot. 2001. "Interventies." In *Ernstige en gewelddadige jeugddelinquentie*, edited by R. Loeber, J. A. Sergeant, and N. W. Slot. Houten: Bohn Stafleu van Loghum.

Blees, L. W., and M. Brouwers. 1996. *Taakstraffen voor minderjarigen*. Arnhem: Gouda Quint.

Blom, Martine, André van der Laan, and Ger Huijbregts. 2005. *Monitor Jeugd terecht 2005*. The Hague: Ministry of Justice, WODC.

Blumstein, A., D. P. Farrington, and S. D. Moitra. 1985. "Delinquency Careers: Innocents, Desisters and Persisters." In *Crime and Justice: A Review of Research*, vol. 6, edited by Michael Tonry and Norval Morris. Chicago: University of Chicago Press.

Boelrijk, M. 1997. *Minderjarige zedendelinquenten en het strafrecht: De strafrecht-elijke aanpak van minderjarige plegers van seksuele delicten*. Amsterdam: VU Uitgeverij.

Boendermaker, L. 1999. *Justitiële behandelinrichtingen voor jongeren*. Leuven/Apeldoorn: Garant.

Boendermaker, L., and S. M. Schneider. 1991. *Prejop: Een preventieproject voor jongeren*. Arnhem: Gouda Quint.

Boendermaker, L., and C. Verwers. 1996. *Een veld in beeld: Een beschrijving van het werk in justitiële behandelinrichtingen*. Arnhem: Gouda Quint.

Bongers, I. L., H. M. Koot, J. van der Ende, and F. C. Verhulst. 2004. "Developmental Trajectories of Externalizing Behaviors in Childhood and Adolescence." *Child Development* 75:1523–37.

Borum, R., P. Bartel, and A. E. Forth. 2002. *Manual for the Structured Assessment of Violent Risk in Youth (SAVRY)*. Consultation ed., version I. Tampa: University of South Florida.

———. 2005. *SAVRY-Research*. http://www.fmhi.usf.edu/mhlp/savry/SAVRY Research.htm.

Boutellier, H. 2002. *De veiligheidsutopie hedendaags onbehagen en verlangen rond misdaad en straf*. The Hague: Boom Juridische Uitgevers.

Breston, E. V., and S. M. Eyberg. 1998. "Effective Psychosocial Treatment of Conduct Disordered Children and Adolescents." *Journal of Clinical Child Psychology* 27(2):180–89.

Breuk, R., A. van Dam, C. M. Disse, and T. A. H. Doreleijers. 2005. "Functionele gezinstherapie in de behandeling van jeugdige forensisch-psychiatrische patiënten." In *Behandelingsstrategieën bij forensisch-psychiatrische patiënten*, edited by C. de Ruiter and M. Hildebrand. Houten: Bohn Stafleu van Loghum.

Brinkman, W., and H. Kars. 1974. *Aanpassing en predictie van aanpassing*. The Hague: Staatsuitgeverij.

Bruinsma, F. 1996. *De jeugdige zedendelinquent*. Utrecht: SWP.

Bullens, R. A. R. 1999. "Nemen zedendelicten door jongeren inderdaad toe?" *Perspectief* 5:15.

Bullens, R. A. R., J. E. van Horn, A. van Eck, and J. Das. 2004. *J-SOAP: De Nederlandes vertaling en bewerking van de J-SOAP II (Juvenile Sex Offender Protocol II)*. Handleidung. Utrecht: Forum Educatief.

Catalano, R. F., and J. D. Hawkins. 1996. "The Social Development Model: A Theory of Antisocial Behavior." In *Delinquency and Crime: Current Theories*, edited by J. D. Hawkins. Cambridge: Cambridge University Press.

CBS (Central Bureau of Statistics). 1996. *Jaaroverzicht politie*. Voorburg: Central Bureau of Statistics.

———. 2004. *Statline*. http://www.statline.cbs.nl.

CITO. 2001. *Eindexamen Nederlands tekstverklaren VWO*.

Cohen, J. 1988. *Statistical Power Analysis for the Behavioral Sciences*. 2nd ed. Hillsdale, NJ: Lawrence Erlbaum.

Corcoran, K., and J. Fisher. 2000. *Measures for Clinical Practice: A Sourcebook*. New York: Free Press.

Curtis, Nicola, Kevin R. Ronan, and Charles M. Borduin. 2004. "Multisystemic Treatment: A Meta-Analysis of Outcome Studies." *Journal of Family Psychology* 18:411–19.

de Haan, W., and F. Bovenkerk. 1993. "Moedwil en misverstand: Overschatting en onderschatting van allochtone criminaliteit in Nederland." *Tijdschrift voor Criminologie* 35:277–300.

Deković, Maja, and Kirsten L. Buist. 2005. "Multiple Perspectives within the Family: Family Relationship Patterns." *Journal of Family Issues* 24:467–90.

Deković, Maja, Kirsten L. Buist, and Ellen Reitz. 2004. "Stability and Changes in Problem Behavior during Adolescence: Latent Growth Analysis." *Journal of Youth and Adolescence* 33:1–13.

Deković, Maja, Jan A. M. A. Janssens, and Nicole M. C. van As. 2001. "Ge-zinsfactoren en het gebruik van ernstig geweld." In *Ernstige en gewelddadige jeugddelinquentie: Omvang, oorzaken en interventies*, edited by Rolf Loeber, Wim Slot, and Joseph Sergeant. Houten: Bohn Stafleu van Loghum.

———. 2003. "Family Predictors of Antisocial Behavior in Adolescence." *Family Process* 42:223–35.

Deković, Maja, Pier Prins, and Peter van der Laan. 2004. *Multisystemic Therapy with Violent Antisocial Adolescents and Their Families: Effectiveness, Mechanisms of Change and Differential Response*. Grant application 473-04-408, Dutch Or-ganization for Scientific Research. Utrecht: University of Utrecht.

Deković, Maja, Inge B. Wissink, and Anna Maire Meijer. 2004. "The Role of Family and Peer Relations in Adolescent Antisocial Behavior: Comparison of Four Ethnic Groups." *Journal of Adolescence* 27:497–514.

Delsing, Marc. 2004. *Family Justice and Trust*. Nijmegen: Triprint.

Dembo, R. 1994. *Use of the Problem Oriented Screening Instrument for Teenagers (POSIT) in the Juvenile Justice System*. Tampa: University of South Florida.

de Ruiter, C., and V. Veen. 2004. *Terugdringen van recidive bij drie typen gewelds-delinquenten: Werkzame interventies bij relationeel, seksueel en algemeen geweld*. Utrecht: Trimbos Instituut.

De Winter, A. F., A. J. Oldehinkel, R. Veenstra, J. A. Brunnekreef, F. C. Ver-hulst, and J. Ormel. 2005. "Evaluation of Non-response Bias in Mental Health Determinants and Outcomes in a Large Sample of Pre-adolescents." *European Journal of Epidemiology* 20:173–81.

De Wree, E. 2004. *Daders van groepsverkrachting: Een daderprofiel in maatschap-pelijke context*. Antwerp/Apeldoorn: Maklu.

Dishion, T. J., J. McCord, and F. Poulin. 1999. "When Intervention Harms: Peer Groups and Problem Behavior." *American Psychologist* 54:755–64.

Doreleijers, T. A. H., B. Bijl, M. C. van der Veldt, and E. Loosbroek. 1999. *BARO, Standaardisatie en protocollering basisonderzoek strafzaken Raad voor de Kinderbescherming*. Amsterdam/Utrecht: Vrije Universiteit/NIZW.

Doreleijers, T. A. H., F. Moser, P. Thijs, H. van Engeland, and F. H. L. Bey-aert. 2000. "Forensic Assessment of Juvenile Delinquents: Prevalence of Psy-chopathology and Decision-Making at Court in the Netherlands." *Journal of Adolescence* 23(3):263–75.

Dowden, Craig, and D. A. Andrews. 2003. "Does Family Intervention Work for Delinquents? Results of a Meta-Analysis." *Canadian Journal of Criminology* 45:327–42.

Drogt, A. 1992. *Seksuele vorming als alternatieve sanctie*. Delft: Eburon.

DSP Research Group. 2004. *Eindrapportage vier pilotprojecten CtC*. Amsterdam: DSP.

Duipmans, D. 1993. *Preventie of pretentie? De effecten op recidive van een preventieproject in de provincie Groningen*. Amsterdam: Thesis Publishers.

———. 1996. *In beeld gebracht: Gebruik, beeld en effecten van de cursus Slachtoffer in Beeld als taakstraf voor minderjarigen*. Drachten: Bureau Duipmans.

Earls, F., and E. Mezzacappa. 2002. "Conduct and Oppositional Disorders." In *Child and Adolescent Psychiatry*, edited by M. Rutter and E. Taylor. Oxford: Blackwell.

Eggen, A. Th. J. N., M. Krussink, P. van Panhuis, and M. Blom. 2005. *Criminality and Maintenance of Law and Order*. The Hague: Ministry of Justice, Research and Documentation Center.

Eggen, A. Th. J. N., and W. van der Heide. 2005. *Criminaliteit en rechtshandhaving in cijfers 2004*. The Hague: CBS, WODC.

Eggermont, M. 1997. *Beter dan zitten . . . Jongeren over taakstraffen*. Alphen aan den Rijn: Samsom H. D. Tjeenk Willink.

Essers, A. A. M., P. H. van der Laan, and P. N. Veer. 1995. *Cashba: Een intensief dagprogramma voor jeugdige en jongvolwassen delinquenten*. Arnhem: Gouda Quint.

Evers, A., J. C. van Vliet-Mulder, and C. J. Groot. 2000. *Documentation of Tests and Test Research in the Netherlands*. Assen/Amsterdam: van Gorcum/NIP.

Farrington, David P. 1986. "Age and Crime." In *Crime and Justice: An Annual Review of Research*, vol. 7, edited by Michael Tonry and Norval Morris. Chicago: University of Chicago Press.

———. 2003. "Methodological Quality Standards for Evaluation Research." *Annals of the American Academy of Political and Social Science* 587:49–68.

Farrington, David P., and Brandon C. Welsh. 2003. "Family-Based Prevention of Offending: A Meta-Analysis." *Australian and New Zealand Journal of Criminology* 36:127–51.

Farrington, David P., and Donald West. 1990. "The Cambridge Study in Delinquent Development: A Long-Term Follow-up of 411 Males." In *Criminality: Personality, Behaviour, Life-History*, edited by G. Kaiser and H. J. Kerner. Berlin: Springer-Verlag.

Ferwerda, H. B., M. Bottenberg, and B. M. W. A. Beke. 1999a. *Jeugdcriminaliteit in de politieregio Zaanstreek-Waterland: Een onderzoek naar omvang, aard, spreiding en achtergronden*. Arnhem/Middelburg: Advies- en Onderzoeksgroep Beke.

———. 1999b. *Jeugdcriminaliteit in Zeeland: Een onderzoek naar de omvang, aard, spreiding en achtergronden*. Arnhem/Middelburg: Advies- en Onderzoeksgroep Beke.

Ferwerda, H. B., and P. Versteegh. 1999. *Juvenile Crime in the Region of The Hague: A Trend-Analysis (1988–1997)*. Arnhem: Beke Consultancy Group.

Frick, P. J., B. B. Lahey, R. Loeber, L. Tannenbaum, Y. van Horn, M. A. G.

Christ, E. L. Hart, and K. Hanson. 1993. "Oppositional Defiant Disorder and Conduct Disorder: A Meta-Analytic Review of Factor Analyses and Cross-Validation in a Clinic Sample." *Clinical Psychology Review* 13:319–40.

Geerdink, B. 2004, 2005. *De nieuwe inrichting betekent een fundamentele verandering werkwijze JJI's: visiedocument.* Amsterdam: Ministry of Justice. http://www.justitie.nl.

Gibbs, J. C., G. B Potter, and A. P. Goldstein. 1998. *The EQUIP Program. Teaching Youth to Think and Act Responsibly through a Peer-Helping Approach.* Champaign/Urbana, IL: Research Press.

Goodman, R., and S. Scott. 1999. "Comparing the Strengths and Difficulties Questionnaire and the Child Behavior Checklist: Is Small Beautiful?" *Journal of Abnormal Child Psychology* 27:17–24.

Gravesteijn, C. 2003. *Effecten van Levensvaardigheden: Een sociaal-emotioneel vaardigheidsprogramma voor adolescenten.* Rotterdam: GGD.

Groen, H. 1997. *Preventie jeugdcriminaliteit: Eindanalyse van het interventieproject Hellend Pad in Haarlem.* Amsterdam: Bureau Toegepast Jeugdonderzoek.

Hamerlynck, S., Th. A. H. Doreleijers, R. Vermeiren, L. M. C. Nauta-Jansen, and P. Cohen-Kettenis. 2005. *Psychopathologie en agressie bij meisjes die gesloten opgenomen zijn in de Nederlandse justitiele jeugdinrichtingen.* Amsterdam: VUmc.

Hare, R. D., H. Vertommen, W. van den Brink, and C. de Ruiter. 2001. *De Psychopathie Checklist Revised: Handleiding.* Lisse: Swets and Zeitlinger.

Hawkins, J. D., R. F. Catalano, and Associates. 1992. *Communities That Care.* San Francisco: Jossey-Bass.

Hawkins, J. D., R. F. Catalano, and J. Y. Miller. 1992. "Risk and Protective Factors for Alcohol and Other Drug Problems in Adolescence and Early Adulthood: Implications for Substance Abuse Prevention." *Psychological Bulletin* 112:64–105.

Hendriks, J. 2003. "Meisjes als zedendelinquent—een exploratieve studie." *Tijdschrift voor Criminologie* 4:401–12.

Hendriks, J., and C. C. J. H. Bijleveld. 1999. "Jeugdige zedendelinquenten: Verschillen tussen groeps-en alleenplegers." *Delikt and Delinkwent* 29:722–36.

———. 2004. *Recidive van jeugdige zedendelinquenten: Een onderzoek naar de algemeen-, zeden- en geweldsrecidive van in JJI Harreveld behandelde jeugdige zedendelinquenten.* Leiden: NSCR.

Hildebrand, H. 2004. *Psychopathy in the Treatment of Forensic Psychiatric Patients.* Amsterdam: Dutch University Press.

Hildebrand, H., C. de Ruiter, V. de Vogel, and P vander Wolf. 2002. "Reliability and Factor Structure of the Dutch Language Version of Hare's Psychopathe Checklist—Revised." *International Journal of Forensic Mental Health* 1:139–54.

Hilhorst, N., and E. van Klooster. 2004. *Programma-evaluatie van de Glen Mills School.* Amsterdam: DSP Research Group.

Hill, Jonathan. 2002. "Biological, Psychological and Social Processes in the Conduct Disorders." *Journal of Child Psychology and Psychiatry* 43:133–64.

Hofman, A., V. W. Jaddoe, J. P. Mackenbach, H. A. Moll, R. F. Snijders, E. A. Steegers, F. C. Verhulst, J. C. Witteman, and H. A. Buller. 2004. "Growth, Development and Health from Early Fetal Life until Young Adulthood: The Generation R Study." *Pediatric Perinatal Epidemiology* 18:61–72.

Hofstra, Marijke B., Jan van der Ende, and Frank C. Verhulst. 2000. "Continuity and Change of Psychopathology from Childhood into Adulthood: A 14-Year Follow-up Study." *Journal of the American Academy of Child and Adolescent Psychiatry* 39(7):850–58.

———. 2001. "Adolescents' Self-Reported Problems as Predictors of Psychopathology in Adulthood: 10-Year Follow-up Study." *British Journal of Psychiatry* 179:203–9.

———. 2002a. "Child and Adolescent Problems Predict DSM-IV Disorders in Adulthood: A 14-Year Follow-up of a Dutch Epidemiological Sample." *Journal of the American Academy of Child and Adolescent Psychiatry* 41(2): 182–89.

———. 2002b. "Pathways of Self-Reported Problem Behaviors from Adolescence into Adulthood." *American Journal of Psychiatry* 159:401–7.

Hollin, Clive R. 1994. "Designing Effective Rehabilitation Programmes for Young Offenders." *Psychology, Crime and Law* 1:193–209.

Horjus, B. 1997. "De kunst van het effectieve bloemschikken: Bejegening van jongens in justitiële inrichtingen." In *Jeugd en cel: Over justitiële inrichtingen, jongeren en jongvolwassenen*, edited by C. Baeveldt and H. Bunkers. Utrecht: de Tijdstroom.

Howell, J. C. 2003. *Preventing and Reducing Juvenile Delinquency*. Thousand Oaks, CA: Sage.

Huesmann, L. R., L. D. Eron, M. M. Lefkowitz, and L. O. Walder. 1984. "Stability of Aggression over Time and Generations." *Developmental Psychology* 20(6):1120–34.

Huesmann, L. R., and N. G. Guerra. 1997. "Children's Normative Beliefs about Aggression and Aggressive Behavior." *Journal of Personality and Social Psychology* 72:408–19.

Huizinga, D., and C. Jacob-Chien. 1998. "Serious and Violent Delinquency and Co-occurring Problems." In *Serious and Violent Juvenile Offenders: Risk Factors and Successful Interventions*, edited by R. Loeber and D. P. Farrington. Thousand Oaks, CA: Sage.

Hunter, J. A., A. J. Figueredo, N. M. Malamuth, and J. V. Becker. 2003. "Juvenile Sex Offenders: Toward the Development of a Typology." *Sexual Abuse: A Journal of Research and Treatment* 1:27–48.

Hunter, J. A., R. R. Hazelwood, and D. Slesinger. 2000. "Juvenile-Perpetrated Sex Crimes: Patterns of Offending and Predictors of Violence." *Journal of Family Violence* 15:81–93.

Ince, D., M. Beumer, H. Jonkman, and M. Vergeer. 2004. *Veelbelovend en effectief, overzicht van preventieprojecten en—programma's in de domeinen gezin, school, kinderen en jongeren, wijk*. Utrecht: NIZW.

Ivanova, M. Y., et al. nd. "Multicultural Invariance of the Child Behavior

Checklist Syndromes in 29 Cultures." Unpublished paper. Burlington: University of Vermont, Center for Children, Youth, and Families.

Jonker, A. 2004. *Niet opsluiten, maar opvoeden.* Utrecht: Agiel.

Junger, M. 1990. *Delinquency and Ethnicity: An Investigation on Social Factors Relating to Delinquency among Moroccan, Turkish, Surinamese and Dutch Boys.* Boston: Kluwer.

Junger, M., K. Wittebrood, and R. Timman. 2001. "Etniciteit en ernstig en gewelddadig crimineel gedrag." In *Ernstige en gewelddadige jeugddelinquentie: Omvang, oorzaken en interventies,* edited by R. Loeber, N. W. Slot, and J. Sergeant. Houten: Bohn Stafleu van Loghum.

Junger-Tas, J. 1983. *Jeugddelinquentie: Achtergronden en justitiële reactie.* The Hague: Staatsuitgeverij.

Junger-Tas, J., M. Junger, and E. Barendse-Hoornweg. 1985. *Jeugddelinquentie II: De invloed van justitieel ingrijpen.* The Hague: Staatsuitgeverij.

Junger-Tas, J., and M. Kruissink. 1987. *Ontwikkeling van de jeugdcriminaliteit.* The Hague: Ministry of Justice/Staatsuitgeverij, WODC.

———. 1990. *Ontwikkeling van de jeugdcriminaliteit: Periode 1980–1988.* The Hague: Ministry of Justice/Staatsuitgeverij, WODC.

Junger-Tas, J., M. Kruissink, and P. H. van der Laan. 1992. *Jeugdcriminaliteit 1980–1990.* The Hague: Ministry of Justice/Staatsuitgeverij, WODC.

Junger-Tas, J., and P. H. van der Laan. 1995. *Jeugdcriminaliteit 1980–1992.* The Hague: Ministry of Justice/Staatsuitgeverij, WODC.

Justice Department. 2003. *Jeugd Terecht: Programma aanpak jeugdcriminaliteit 2003–2006.* The Hague: Justice Department.

Kaufman, J. P., et al. 1997. "Schedule for Affective Disorders and Schizofrenia for School-Age Children—Present and Lifetime Version (K-Sads-PL): Initial Reliability and Validity Data." *Journal of the American Academy of Child and Adolescent Psychiatry* 36:980–88.

Kazdin, A. E. 1997a. "Parent Management Training." *Journal of the American Academy of Child and Adolescent Psychiatry* 36(10):1349–56.

———. 1997b. "Practitioner Review: Psychosocial Treatments for Conduct Disorders in Children." *Journal of Child Psychology and Psychiatry* 62:161–82.

Kellam, S. G., X. Ling, R. Merisca, C. H. Brown, and N. Ialongo. 1998. "The Effect of the Level of Aggression in the First Grade Classroom on the Course and Malleability of Aggressive Behavior into Middle School." *Development and Psychopathology* 10(2):165–85.

Kleiman, W. M., and G. J. Terlouw. 1997. *Kiezen voor een kans: Evaluatie van harde-kernprojecten.* The Hague: Ministry of Justice, WODC.

Kook, H. 1996. *Effectevaluatie van Overstap: Een interventieprogramma voor leesbevordering.* Amsterdam: University of Amsterdam, Instituut voor Taalonderzoek en Taalonderwijs voor Anderstaligen.

Korf, D. J. 2003. "Hoe successvol is Halt?" *Tijdschrift voor Criminologie* 45(1): 17–34.

Kruisbergen, E. W., and T. Veld. 2002. *Een gekleurd beeld: Over beoordeling en selectie van jonge allochtone werknemers.* Assen: Koninklijke van Gorcum.

Kruissink, M., and A. A. M. Essers. 2003. *De ontwikkeling van de jeugdcrimi-*

naliteit 1990–2001. The Hague: Ministry of Justice, Research and Documentation Center.

———. 2004. *Zelfgerapporteerde jeugd-criminaliteit in de periode 1990–2001*. The Hague: WODC.

Kuipers, S. B. M., C. Mensink, and de Zwart, W. M. 1993. *Jeugd en riskant gedrag: Roken, drinken, druggebruik en gokken onder scholieren vanaf 10 jaar*. Utrecht: NIAD.

Le Blanc, M. 1998. "Screening of Serious and Violent Juvenile Offenders: Identification, Classification and Prediction." In *Serious and Violent Juvenile Offenders*, edited by R. Loeber and D. P. Farrington. Thousand Oaks, CA: Sage.

Le Sage, L. 2004. *De gebrekkige gewetensontwikkeling in het jeugdstrafrecht*. Amsterdam: SWP.

Lesemann, P., M. Fahrenfort, W. Oud., J. Schoufour, R. Betrand, and A. Klaver. 1998. *Experimenten Opvoedingsondersteuning*. Amsterdam: SCO Kohnstamm Instituut.

Lesemann, P., A. Veen, B. Triesscheijn, and M. Otter. 1999. *Evaluatie van Kaleidoscoop en Piramide—verslag van de tussentijdse resultaten*. Amsterdam: SCO Kohnstamm Instituut.

Lipsey, M. W. 1995. "What Do We Learn from 400 Research Studies on Effectiveness of Treatment with Juvenile Delinquents?" In *What Works: Reducing Reoffending—Guidelines from Research and Practice*, edited by J. McGuire. Chichester, UK: Wiley.

———. 1999. "Can Rehabilitation Programs Reduce the Recidivism of Juvenile Offenders?" *Virginia Journal of Social Policy and the Law* 6:611–41.

Lipsey, M. W., and D. B. Wilson. 1998. "Effective Intervention for Serious Juvenile Offenders." In *Serious and Violent Juvenile Offenders: Risk Factors and Successful Interventions*, edited by R. Loeber and D. P. Farrington. Thousand Oaks, CA: Sage.

Lodewijks, H. P. B., C. de Ruiter, and T. Doreleijers. 2003. "Risicotaxatie en risicohantering van gewelddadig gedrag bij adolescenten." *Directieve Therapie* 23(1):25–42.

Lodewijks, H. P. B., T. Doreleijers, C. de Ruiter, and. H. de Wit-Grouls. 2001. *Gestructureerde taxatie van geweldsrisico bij jongeren (geautoriseerde vertaling en onderzoeksversie van de SAVRY)*. Eefde: Rentray.

Loeber, R., 1991. "Anti-social Behavior: More Enduring than Changeable?" *American Academy of Child and Adolescent Psychiatry* 30(3):393–97.

———. 2004. *Delinquency Prevention in a Mental Health Context*. Utrecht: Trimbos Instituut.

Loeber, R., J. D. Burke, and B. B. Lahey. 2002. "What Are Adolescent Antecedents to Antisocial Personality Disorder?" *Criminal Behaviour and Mental Health* 12:24–36.

Loeber, R., and D. P. Farrington. 1998. *Serious and Violent Juvenile Offenders: Risk Factors and Successful Interventions*. Thousand Oaks, CA: Sage.

———. 2004. "Are Between-Race and Between-Country Causes of Delinquency the Same? Longitudinal Analyses of Young Males in Pittsburgh and London." *Tijdschrift voor Criminologie* 35:277–300.

Loeber, R., D. P. Farrington, and D. Waschbusch. 1998. "Serious and Violent Juvenile Offenders." In *Serious and Violent Juvenile Offenders*, edited by R. Loeber and D. P. Farrington. Thousand Oaks, CA: Sage.

Loeber, Rolf, Wim Slot, and Joseph Sergeant, eds. 2001. *Ernstige en gewelddadige jeugddelinquentie: Omvang, oorzaken en interventies.* Houten: Bohn Stafleu van Loghum.

Loeber R., P. Wung, K. Keenan, B. Giroux, M. Stouthamer-Loeber, W. B. van Kammen, and B. Maughan. 1993. "Developmental Pathways in Antisocial Child Behavior." *Development and Psychopathology* 5:101–32.

Looije, D., C. Bijleveld, F. Weerman, and J. Hendricks. 2004. "Gedwongen seks als groepsactiviteit: Een dossierstudie naar groepszedendelicten." *Tijdschrift voor Seksuologie* 28:183–96.

Meeus, W., and H. 't Hart, eds. 1993. *Jongeren in Nederland.* Amersfoort: Academische Uitgeverij.

Mesman Schultz, K. 1977. *Aanpassing en predictie van aanpassing 2.* The Hague: Staatsuitgeverij.

Ministry of Justice. 2002. *Jeugd terecht: Actieprogramma aanpak jeugdcriminaliteit 2003–2006.* The Hague: Ministry of Justice.

———. 2003. *Jeugd terecht: Actieprogramma aanpak jeugdcriminaliteit.* The Hague: Ministry of Justice.

———. 2004. *Notitie Antilliaanse risicojongeren.* The Hague: Ministry of Justice.

Moffitt T. E. 1993. "Adolescence Limited and Life-Course-Persistent Antisocial Behavior: A Developmental Taxonomy." *Psychological Review* 4: 674–701.

Moser, F., and Th. A. H. Doreleijers. 1996. "Juvenile Delinquents with ADHD: The Importance of Early Diagnostic Assessment." *European Journal on Crime Policy and Research* 5(2):267–81.

Murad, Sarwa D., Inez M. Joung, Frank J. van Lenthe, Leyla Bengi-Arslan, and Alfons A. M. Crijnen. 2003. "Predictors of Self-Reported Problem Behaviours in Turkish Immigrant and Dutch Adolescents in the Netherlands." *Journal of Child Psychology and Psychiatry* 44:412–23.

Myers, K. M., and N. C. Winters. 2002. "Ten-Year Review of Rating Scales. I: Overview of Scale Functioning, Psychometric Properties and Selection." *Journal of the American Academy of Child and Adolescent Psychiatry* 41:114–22.

Nagin D. S. 1999. "Analyzing Developmental Trajectories: A Semiparametric, Group Based Approach." *Psychological Methods* 4:139–57.

Nas, C. 2005. "'EQUIPping' Delinquent Male Adolescents to Think Prosocially." PhD dissertation, University of Utrecht.

Olds, D. L., C. C. R. Henderson, R. Chamberlin, and R. Tatelbaum. 1986. "Preventing Child Abuse and Neglect: A Randomized Trial of Nurse Home Visitation." *Pediatrics* 78:65–78.

Olds, D. L., C. C. R. Henderson, R. Tatelbaum, and R. Chamberlin. 1988. "Improving the Life Course Development of Socially Disadvantaged Mothers: A Randomized Trial of Nurse Home Visitation." *American Journal of Public Health* 78:1436–45.

Olweus, D. 1979. "Stability of Aggressive Reaction Patterns in Males: A Review." *Psychological Bulletin* 86(4):852–75.

Oosterwegel, A., and W. Vollebergh. 2003. "Jongeren in Nederland en hun waarden: Een onderzoek onder adolescenten van Nederlandse, Turkse, of Marokkaanse herkomst." *Migrantenstudies* 19(4):214–27.

Orobio de Castro, Bram, Jan W. Veerman, Willem Koops, Joop D. Bosch, and Heidi J. Monshouwer. 2002. "Hostile Attribution of Intent and Aggressive Behavior: A Meta-Analysis." *Child Development* 73:915–34.

Pels, T., and M. de Haan. 2004. *Continuity and Change in Moroccan Socialization: A Review of the Literature on Socialization in Morocco and among Moroccan Families in the Netherlands*. Utrecht: Verwey-Jonker Instituut.

Perkins-Dock, Robin E. 2001. "Family Interventions with Incarcerated Youth: A Review of the Literature." *International Journal of Offender Therapy and Comparative Criminology* 45:606–25.

Philipse, M., C. de Ruiter, M. Hildebrand, and Y. Bouman. 2000. *HCR-20: Beoordeling van het risico van gewelddadig gedrag, versie 2*. Nijmegen/Utrecht: Pompestichting/van der Hoeven Stichting.

Quay, H. C. 1979. "Classification." In *Psychopathological Disorders of Childhood*, edited by H. C. Quay and J. S. Werry. New York: Wiley.

Redl, P., and D. Winemann. 1950. *Children Who Hate*. Glencoe, IL: Free Press.

Reese, Le'Roy E., Vera M. Elizabeth, Thomas R. Simon, and Robin M. Ikeda. 2000. "The Role of Families and Care Givers as Risk and Protective Factors in Preventing Youth Violence." *Clinical Child and Family Psychology Review* 3: 61–77.

Reitz, Ellen. 2004. *Problem Behavior during Early Adolescence and Child, Parent, and Friend Effects: A Longitudinal Study*. Amsterdam: Thela Thesis.

Rescorla, L., et al. nd. "Problems Reported by Parents of Children Ages 6 to 16 in 30 Cultures." Unpublished paper. Burlington: University of Vermont, Center for Children, Youth, and Families.

Robins, L. N., and L. McEvoy. 1990. "Conduct Problems as Predictors of Substance Abuse." In *Straight and Devious Pathways from Childhood into Adulthood*, edited by L. Robins and M. Rutter. Cambridge: Cambridge University Press.

Rowe, C. L., H. A. Liddle, K. McClintic, and T. Quille. 2002. "Integrative Treatment Development: Multidimensional Family Therapy for Adolescent Substance Abuse." In *Comprehensive Handbook of Psychotherapy*, edited by F. W. Kaslow and J. Lebow. New York: Wiley.

Rutter, M., H. Giller, and A. Hagell. 1998. *Antisocial Behavior by Young People*. Cambridge: Cambridge University Press.

Ryan, G. 1997. "Incidence and Prevalence of Sexual Offenses Committed by Juveniles." In *Juvenile Sexual Offending: Causes, Consequences and Corrections*, edited by G. Ryan and S. Lane. San Francisco: Jossey-Bass.

Scheffer, P. 2000. "Het multiculturele drama." *NRC Handelsblad*. http://www.nrchandelsblad.nl.

Scholte, E. M. 1988. *Jeugd, politie en hulpverlening: Een onderzoek naar preventieve hulpverlening aan jongeren met psychosociale problemen.* Leuven/Amersfoort: Acco.

———. 1998. "Psychological Risk Characteristics of Children in Welfare Programs in Holland: The Role of Risk-Factor Analysis in the Planning of Welfare Services for Children." *Childhood: A Global Journal of Child Research* 5:185–205.

———. 2000. *De Vragenlijst en Sociale en Pedagogische Situatie (VSPS), versie 4.2.* Delft: Eburon.

Scholte, E. M., and Th. Doreleijers. 2001. "Screening van ernstige en gewelddadige delinquentie." In *Ernstige en gewelddadige jeugddelinquentie Omvang, oorzaken en interventie,* edited by R. Loeber, N. W. Slot, and J. A. Sergeant. Houten: Bohn Stafleu van Loghum.

Scholte, E. M., and J. D. van der Ploeg. 2003. *Effectieve hulpverlening aan jeugdigen met meervoudige psychosociale problemen. Deel II: Effecten van de hulp en werkbare bestanddelen in de hulpverlening.* Amsterdam: Nippo.

———. 2005. *Sociaal Emotionele Vragenlijst.* Houten: Bohn Stafleu van Loghum.

Schreuders, M., D. J. Korf, and E. Poort. 1994. "Cannabisgebruik en criminaliteit: Een kwestie van leefstijl?" *Tijdschrift voor Criminologie* 36(3):252–63.

Schweinhart, L. J. 1987. "Can Preschool Programs Help Prevent Delinquency?" In *From Children to Citizens.* Vol. 3, *Families, Schools, and Delinquency Prevention,* edited by J. Q. Wilson and G. C. Loury. New York: Springer-Verlag.

Schweinhart, L. J., S. McNair, H. Barnes, and M. Larner. 1993. "Observing Young Children in Action to Assess Their Development: The High/Scope Child Observation Record Study." *Educational and Psychological Measurement* 53(2):445–55.

SCP (Sociaal en Cultureel Planbureau). 1996. *Sociaal en Cultureel Rapport 1996.* Rijswijk/The Hague: SCP/VUGA.

Shaffer, D., K. Restifo, C. P. Lucas, M. K Dulcan, and M. E. Schwab-Stone. 2000. "NIMH Diagnostic Interview Schedule for Children Version IV: Description, Differences from Previous Versions, and Reliability of Some Common Diagnoses." *Journal of the American Academy of Child and Adolescent Psychiatry* 39(1):28–38.

Shaffer, D., M. Schwab-Stone, P. Fisher, P. Cohen, J. Piarenti, M. Davies, K. Conners, and D. Regier. 1993. "The Diagnostic Interview Schedule for Children—Revised Version (DISC-R). I." *Journal of the American Academy of Child and Adolescent Psychiatry* 32:643–50.

Slavin, R. E., N. A. Madden, L. J. Dolan, B. A. Wasik, S. M. Ross, and L. J. Smith. 1993. "'Whenever and Wherever We Choose'—the Replication of 'Success for All.'" *Phi Delta Kappan* 75(8):639–47.

Slavin, R. E., N. A. Madden, N. L. Karweit, B. J. Livermin, and L. Dolan. 1990. "Success for All: First-Year Outcomes of a Comprehensive Plan for Reforming Urban Education." *American Educational Research Journal* 27(2): 255–78.

Slot, N. W. 1988. *Residentiële hulp voor jongeren met antisociaal gedrag*. Lisse: Swets and Zeitlinger.

Slot, N. W., M. C. A. E. van der Velt, and L. G. M. Beemker. 2004. *Effectief beschermd: Een onderzoek naar de haalbaarheid van een instrument voor het meten van de effectiviteit van de uitvoering van kinderbeschermingsmaatregelen*. Amsterdam: PI-Research.

Spaans, E. C. 1993. *Jeugdreclassering in Rijksinrichting 't Nieuwe Lloyd: Een inventarisatie van anderhalf jaar vrijwillige begeleiding*. The Hague: Ministry of Justice, WODC.

Spaans, E. C., and L. Doornhein. 1991. *Evaluatie-onderzoek jeugdreclassering: De effectmeting*. Arnhem: Gouda Quint.

Spaans, E. C., and K. Reurslag. 1994. *Sailing as an Alternative Disposition*. The Hague: Ministry of Justice, WODC.

Stevens, G. W. J. M. 2004. *Mental Health in Moroccan Youth in the Netherlands*. Rotterdam: Optima.

Stevens, G. W. J. M., T. Pels, L. Bengi-Arslan, F. C. Verhulst, W. A. M. Vollebergh, and A. A. M. Crijnen. 2003. "Parent, Teacher and Self-Reported Problem Behavior in the Netherlands—Comparing Moroccan Immigrant with Dutch and with Turkish Immigrant Children and Adolescents." *Social Psychiatry and Psychiatric Epidemiology* 28:576–85.

Terlouw, G. J., and G. Susanne. 1991. *Criminaliteitspreventie onder allochtonen*. Arnhem: Gouda Quint.

Terpstra, J. 1997. *Preventie voor jongeren met politiecontacten*. The Hague: Ministry of Justice.

't Hart, H. 1992. *Overwegingen bij de herweging van de WIL-steekproef*. Utrecht: Vakgroep Jeugd, Gezin en Lievensloop.

Thornberry, Terence, and Marvin D. Krohn. 2003. *Taking Stock of Delinquency: An Overview of Findings from Contemporary Longitudinal Studies*. New York: Kluwer Academic/Plenum.

Timmer, S., M. Workel, and H. M van Dijck. 2001. *Opvang en behandeling van jeugdige zedendelinquenten in Nederland: Een verkennend onderzoek*. The Hague: Ministry of Justice.

van Dam, C. 2005. *Juvenile Criminal Recidivism*. Nijmegen: Trioprint.

van den Bogaart, P. H. M., K. Mesman Schultz, and H. van Muijen. 2003. *De Glen Mills School*. Groningen: E and M Syntax.

van der Genugten, M. D., H. Timmerman, and J. A. Nijboer. 1996. *Sociale vaardigheidstraining als taakstraf*. Groningen: Rijksuniversiteit Groningen, Vakgroep Strafrecht en Criminologie.

van der Hoeven, E. 1985. *Allochtone jongeren bij de jeugdpolitie: Verschillen in aantal, aard en afdoening van politiecontacten*. The Hague: CWOK.

van der Laan, A. M., L. M. van der Knaap, and B. S. J. Wartna. 2005. *Recidivemeting onder jeugdreclasseringscliënten*. The Hague: Ministry of Justice, WODC.

van der Laan, P. H. 1991. *Experimenteren met alternatieve sancties voor jeugdigen*. Arnhem: Gouda Quint.

————. 2005. "Jeugd, criminaliteit, politie en justitie." *Delikt en Delinkwent* 35: 986–1013.

van der Laan, P. H., and A. A. M. Essers. 1990. *De Kwartaalkursus en recidive.* Arnhem: Gouda Quint.

————. 1993. "Helpt DTC? Over recidive en andere effecten." In *Vast of zeker: Een kansrijke aanpak buiten de gevangenis: Het Dagtrainingscentrum Eindhoven.* Utrecht: SWP.

van der Laan, P. H., A. A. M. Essers, G. L. A. M. Huijbregts, and E. C. Spaans. 1998. *Ontwikkeling van de jeugdcriminaliteit: Periode 1980–1996.* The Hague: Ministry of Justice, WODC.

van der Laan, P. H., and A. Slotboom. 2002. "Wat werkt?" In *Het recht van binnen: Psychologie van het recht*, edited by P. J. van Koppen, D. J. Hessing, H. L. G. J. Merckelbach, and H. F. M. Cromborg. Deventer: Kluwer.

van der Laan, P. H., E. C. Spaans, and J. L. M. Verhagen. 2004. "De Glen Mills School onderzocht." *Delikt en Delinkwent* 62:809–25.

van der Steeg, M., and E. Niemeijer. 1996. *Leren (en) werken als straf.* Amsterdam: Vrije Universiteit, Vakgroep Criminologie.

van Gageldonk, A., and A. A. J. Bartels. 1991. "Evaluatieonderzoek in de jeugd-dhulpverlening." *Kind en Adolescent* 2(1):1–18.

van Gemert, Frank.1998. *Ieder voor zich: Kansen, cultuur en criminaliteit van Marokkaanse jongens.* Amsterdam: Spinhuis.

van Heerwaarden, Y., N. Hilhorst, and A. Slabbèrtje. 2005. *Programma-evaluatie van Den Engh.* Amsterdam: DSP Research Group.

van Lier, P. A. C. 2002. *Preventing Disruptive Behavior in Early Elementary Schoolchildren.* Rotterdam: Erasmus University.

van San, M. 1998. *Stelen en steken: Delinquent gedrag van Curacaose jongens in Nederlan.* Amsterdam: Spinhuis.

van Tuijl, C. 2002. *Effecten van Opstap Opnieuw bij follow-up: Effecten van Opstap Opnieuw bij Turkse en Marokkaanse leerlingen op middellange termijn.* Alkmaar: Extern Print.

van Wijk, A. Ph. 1999. *Een verkennend onderzoek naar jeugdige zedendelinquenten.* Arnhem: Advies- en Onderzoeksgroep Beke.

van Wijk, A. Ph., Th. A. H. Doreleijers, R. A. R. Bullens, and H. B. Ferwerda. 2001. "Kenmerken en achtergronden van jeugdige zedendelinquenten." In *Ernstig gewelddadige jongeren*, edited by R. Loeber and N. W. Slot. Houten: Bohn Stafleu van Loghum.

van Wijk, A. Ph., and H. B. Ferwerda. 2000. "Criminaliteitsprofielen van zedendelinquenten: Een analyse van politiegegevens." *Maandblad Geestelijke Volksgezondheid* 12:1131–45.

van Wijk, A. Ph., R. Loeber, R. Vermeiren, D. Pardini, R. Bullins, and Th. A. H. Doreleijers. 2005. "Violent Juvenile Sex Offenders Compared with Non–Sex Offenders: Explorative Findings from the Pittsburgh Youth Study." *Sexual Abuse: Journal of Research and Treatment* 17(3):333–52.

van Wijk, A. Ph., S. R. F. Mali, R. A. R. Bullens, L. Prins, and P. P. H. M. Klerks. 2006. *Zedencriminaliteit in Nederland: Delicten en delinquenten nader in beeld gebracht.* Zeist: Uitgeverij Kerckebosch.

van Wijk, A. Ph., L. 't Hart, Th. A. H. Doreleijers, and R. A. R. Bullens. 2005. *Ontwikkeling screeningsinstrument voor jeugdige zedendelinquenten: Verslag van het onderzoeksproject.* Amsterdam:VUmc/VU.

van Wijk, A. Ph., J. van Horn, R. A. R. Bullens, C. Bijleveld, and Th. A. H. Doreleijers. 2005. "Juvenile Sex Offenders: A Group on Its Own?" *International Journal of Offender Therapy and Comparative Criminology* 49(1):25–36.

van Wijk, A. Ph., J. van Horn, R. A. R. Bullens, and J. Hendricks. 2003. "Jeugdige zedendelinquenten, een aparte groep?" *Tijdschrift voor Criminologie* 4:391–400.

van Wijk, A. Ph., C. Vreugdenhil, and R. A. R. Bullens. 2004. "Zijn jeugdige zedendelinquenten anders dan niet-zedendelinquenten?" *Proces* 5:205–8.

van Yperen, T., G. van der Berg, and K. Eijgenraam. 2003. *Standaard Taxatie Ernst Problematiek (STEP).* Utrecht: NIZW-jeugd.

Veerman, J. W., J. M. A. M. Janssens, and J. W. Delicat. 2004. *Opvoeden in onmacht, of . . . ?* Nijmegen: Praktikon.

Verdurmen, Jacqueline, Maureen van Oort, Jolanda Meeuwissen, Toine Ketelaars, Ireen de Graaf, Pim Cuijpers, Corine de Ruiter, and Wilma Vollebergh. 2003. *Effectiviteit van preventieve interventies gericht op jeugdigen: De stand van zaken.* Utrecht: Trimbos Instituut.

Verhulst, F. C., T. M. Achenbach, J. van der Ende, N. Erol, M. C. Lambert, P. W. L. Leung, M. A. Silva, N. Zilber, and S. R. Zubrick. 2003. "Comparisons of Problems Reported by Youth." *American Journal of Psychiatry* 160(8): 1479–85.

Verhulst, F. C., J. van der Ende, R. F. Ferdinand, and M. C. Kasius. 1997. "The Prevalence of DSM-III-R Diagnoses in a National Sample of Dutch Adolescents." *Archives of General Psychiatry* 54:329–36.

Verhulst, F. C., J. van der Ende, and A. Rietbergen. 1997. "Ten-Year Time Trends of Psychopathology in Dutch Children and Adolescents: No Evidence for Strong Trends." *Acta Psychiatrica Scandinavica* 96:7–13.

Vermeiren, R., A. de Clippele, and D. Deboutte. 2000. "A Descriptive Survey of Flemish Delinquent Adolescents." *Journal of Adolescence* 23(3):277–85.

Vermeiren, R., I. Jespers, and T. E. Moffitt. 2006. "Mental Health Problems in Juvenile Justice Populations." *Child and Adolescent Psychiatry Clinics of North America* 15(2):335–51.

Vollebergh, W. 2002. *Gemiste kansen: Culturele diversiteit en de jeugdzorg.* Nijmegen: Oratie, Katholieke Universiteit Nijmegen.

Vreeman, M. J. 1992. *Leerprojecten orthopedagogisch gewikt en gewogen.* Groningen: Stichting Kinderstudies.

Vreugdenhil, C., Th. A. H. Doreleijers, R. Vermeiren, L. F. J. M. Wouters, and W. van den Brink. 2004. "Psychiatric Disorders in a Representative Sample of Incarcerated Boys in the Netherlands." *Journal of the American Academy of Child and Adolescent Psychiatry* 43(1):97–104.

Vreugdenhil, C., W. van den Brink, C. F. J. M. Wouters, and Th. A. H. Doreleijers. 2003. "Substance Use, Substance Use Disorders, and Comorbidity Patterns in a Representative Sample of Incarcerated Male Dutch Adolescents." *Journal of Nervous and Mental Diseases* 191:372–78.

Warr, M. 2002. *Companions in Crime: The Social Aspects of Criminal Conduct.* Cambridge: Cambridge University Press.

Wartna, B. S. J. 1999. "Recidive-onderzoek in Nederland." *Tijdschrift voor Criminologie* 41(1):40–56.

Wartna, B. S. J., S. el Harbachi, and A. van der Laan. 2005. *Jong Vast.* The Hague: Boom Juridische Uitgevers/WODC.

Wartna, B. S. J., N. Tollenaar, and M. Blom. 2005. *Recidive 1997.* The Hague: Boom Juridische Uitgevers/WODC.

Webster, C. D., R. Müller-Isberner, and G. Fransson. 2002. "Violence Risk Assessment: Using Structured Clinical Guides Professionally." *International Journal of Forensic Mental Health* 1(2):185–93.

Wiebush, R. G., C. Baird, B. Krisberg, and D. Onek. 1995. "Risk Assessment and Classification for Serious, Violent and Chronic Offenders." In *Sourcebook on Serious, Violent and Chronic Juvenile Offenders*, edited by J. C. Howell, B. Krisberg, J. D. Hawkins, and J. J. Wilson. Chicago: University of Chicago Press.

Wittebrood, K. 2003. "Preventieve en strafrechtelijke interventies ter voorkoming van jeugdcriminaliteit." In *SCP, Rapportage jeugd 2002.* The Hague: SCP.

Wittebrood, K., and M. Junger. 1999. "Trends in geweldscriminaliteit." *Tijdschrift voor Criminologie* 41:250–67.

Wittebrood, K., and M. van Beem. 2004. *Sociale veiligheid vergroten door gelegenheidsbeperking: Wat werkt en wat niet?* The Hague: Raad van Maatschappelijke Ontwikkeling.

Wolfgang, M., R. Figlio, and T. Sellin. 1972. *Delinquency in a Birth Cohort.* Chicago: University of Chicago Press.

Wolfgram, P. 1999. *KEA schooljaar 1998–1999—de resultaten op een rijtje.* Rotterdam: Centrum Educatieve Dienstverlening.

Zeijl, E. 2003. "Indicatoren voor ontwikkelingsstaat." In *Rapportage Jeugd 2002*, edited by E. Zeijl. The Hague: SCP.

Zuckerman, M. 2002. *Vulnerability to Psychopathology: A Biosocial Model.* Washington, DC: American Psychological Association.

Index

9/11, 107, 468

Aalders, Marius, 243
abolitionists, 135, 136
abortion, licensing of certain hospitals and clinics to perform, 100
academic researchers, allowed access to police files on offenders, 225
active euthanasia, 105
Act on Special Investigative Police Powers (BOB Act), 194–97
Act on the Termination of Life on Request and Assisted Suicide (Act on Euthanasia 2001), 99, 104
actuarialism, and new penology, 60–61
Addicts Supervision Section (VBA), 62
administrative approach: in Amsterdam, 199; fines, 239, 240; to organized crime, 169–70; sanctions, 243
administrative regulation, due process character of, 253
Afghanistan, asylum migrants from, 399
Agnew, Robert, 292
Ahold, accounting fraud at, 227, 244
Akers, Ronald L., 292
Aletrino, Arnold, 120–21
alien detention, 424–25
Aliens Act 2000, 391, 391n1, 399, 422-23, 424

aliens police, 391, 412
Almelo, 476, 486
Almere, 467n7, 470
Althoff, M., 426, 427
Ambonese (Indonesian) boys: more often registered as crime suspects than Dutch boys, 412
ambulatory treatment, for sex offenders, 349
American Bloods, 284
American Crips, 284
amphetamines, 91, 177
amplification of deviance, 221
Amsterdam, 7, 407, 469, 476; full-service drug-trafficking market, 183; infrastructure for distribution of illegal goods, 472; worldwide reputation in 1960s as a crucible of tolerance and cultural experimentation, 36
Amsterdam red-light district, 45, 96, 166, 174, 199, 474
Amsterdam-Schiphol Airport, 8, 64, 93, 173, 174, 175, 186, 424
Amsterdam Securities Exchange, securities fraud, 244
Amsterdam Stock Exchange, 246
Amsterdam-Utrecht IRT, dismantled because of the use of unacceptable investigation methods, 165
Androcur, 350
Angola, 399, 417
anomie, 409